PEOPLE OF THE UNDERGROUND RAILROAD

A Biographical Dictionary

Tom Calarco

GREENWOOD PRESS
Westport, Connecticut • London

Library of Congress Cataloging-in-Publication Data

Calarco, Tom, 1947-
People of the Underground Railroad : a biographical dictionary / Tom Calarco.
p. cm.
Includes bibliographical references and index.
ISBN 978–0–313–33924–0 (alk. paper)
1. Underground Railroad—Dictionaries. 2. Abolitionists—United States—Biography—Dictionaries. 3. African American abolitionists—Biography—Dictionaries. 4. Fugitive slaves—United States—Biography—Dictionaries. 5. Antislavery movements—United States—History—19th century—Dictionaries. 6. United States—History—1783-1865--Biography—Dictionaries. 7. United States—Biography—Dictionaries. I. Title.
E450.C38 2008
973.7'115—dc22 2008019934

British Library Cataloguing in Publication Data is available.

Library of Congress Catalog Card Number: 2008019934
ISBN: 978–0–313–33924–0

First published in 2008

Greenwood Press, 88 Post Road West, Westport, CT 06881
An imprint of Greenwood Publishing Group, Inc.
www.greenwood.com

Printed in the United States of America

The paper used in this book complies with the Permanent Paper Standard issued by the National Information Standards Organization (Z39.48–1984).

10 9 8 7 6 5 4 3 2 1

Contents

Alphabetical List of Entries

List of Entries by State or Country

List of Entries by Roles or Profession

List of Sidebars

Preface

This biographical dictionary provides a representative geographic sample of 100 key people involved in the Underground Railroad. It narrates the stories of their lives and their contributions. Its goal is to provide a broad picture of the secret and sometimes not-so-secret network.

Entries were prepared using both contemporary and original sources, and the two were often compared to ensure accuracy. Most people included were major figures in the Underground Railroad, but a number of minor characters have been included to add scope and bring attention to some whose names have been neglected in the history books. In recent years attention has been focused on including equitable representation by race and gender, and this was taken into account. The breakdown by race is 61 white and 39 black individuals. It is true that blacks were more likely to assist fugitive slaves; however, in 1860 there were about seventy times as many whites as there were free blacks in the United States. Ten women are included, and the small number is a reflection of the primarily domestic role of women in the antebellum period. However, some women—such as Catharine Coffin and Jean Rankin, the wives of the prominent conductors, Levi Coffin and John Rankin—were very much a part of the Underground Railroad operations, in preparing meals and providing accommodations. On at least one occasion, Catharine Coffin even forwarded a fugitive slave to another location in the city of Cincinnati. The husbands of two of the women included, Lucretia Mott and Hannah Cox, were equal collaborators in their Underground Railroad activities.

Available information was also a factor in making the selections. Research in Underground Railroad history has increased exponentially since the National Park Service directive of 1995 called for greater attention to be paid to the history of the Underground Railroad. Important figures as yet little-known may come to light. This biographical dictionary has tapped into the latest information available within the limits of time and space. Especially provocative efforts were made south of the Mason-Dixon Line. Details of the escapes of a representative number of fugitive slaves, and the efforts of the more well-known slave rescuers, those who entered the South to aid slaves to freedom, are included among the entries. All of those profiled in the entries shared a common hatred of slavery, and a deep and abiding compassion for those oppressed by it.

This biographical dictionary supports the belief that the most accurate depiction is provided by the people who were present at the creation. The charge of exaggeration and falsehoods attributed to memoirs told years later is overstated. Certainly, some individuals have rearranged events or details for personal gain. However, this has happened throughout the recounting of history, and the depiction of events is relative to the observations and prejudices of those describing them. Among those whose claims have been called into question is the slave rescuer Alexander Milton Ross. Although much of his story has not been corroborated, the evidence against it is still not strong enough to dismiss it. Numerous accounts related to the Underground Railroad that had been thought to be unreliable were later confirmed by independent sources.

Memories of events may fade over the years, but as people age, they are more likely to forget what happened yesterday rather than thirty years earlier. When it concerns significant events, they are likely to remain clear and vivid throughout their lives. This is why I consider the thousands of letters written by Underground Railroad conductors and their family members, recounting actual events, now stored in the Wilbur H. Siebert archives at the Ohio Historical Society and at Harvard University, to be the most significant resources at our disposal.

Readers should pay close attention to the number of associations among the entries and the persons mentioned in the various sidebars. **Bolded** cross-references throughout the text direct readers to other entries of interest. These provide evidence of the networking and organization that occurred in the Underground Railroad. These heroic individuals whose guiding principle was the Golden Rule are perhaps the nation's greatest role model for future generations. They were early combatants of the racial prejudice that justified slavery and that continues to plague our nation.

It is because of this that I have been sensitive about terminology related to race. I have chosen to use the term black rather than African American to describe people of color. This is because the term black is both more objective and universal than the latter and later term, which has political connotations.

Front matter lists, arranged alphabetically, geographically, and by role in the Underground Railroad, allow the reader to find entries of interest quickly. A timeline of significant events in the Underground Railroad is found in the front matter. A selected bibliography of recent and historical sources further helps the student and researcher to dig deeper into the scholarship.

People of the Underground Railroad taps into the latest research and provides a good overview of the Underground Railroad nationwide. Its entries overall offer in-depth portraits of the most significant individuals involved, as well as detailed depictions of some of the Railroad's most dramatic episodes. Citations of original sources also provide researchers with a useful tool in their further exploration of one of the most interesting, exciting, and important epochs in our history.

The Underground Railroad is a shining example of how black and white people worked together for the common good. Its continued study, I think, will contribute to a better future for all.

Acknowledgments

I would like to thank my contributors, who gave freely of their wisdom, not only for their contributions but for other matters related to this encyclopedia. Others who offered their words of wisdom were Bryan Prince, Owen Muelder, Diane Coon, Judith Wellman, and, last but not least, Fergus Bordewich.

Tom Calarco
Cincinnati, Ohio
2008

INTRODUCTION

The Underground Railroad is the term for the informal system and network of individuals who aided slaves fleeing from slavery, offering them shelter, food, money, transportation, and protection along their way to the Northern states and Canada. It operated between 1800 and 1860, and its activities were generally kept secret because such activities were illegal. Estimates of how many fleeing slaves it assisted range between 50,000 and 100,000.

The Underground Railroad covered a lot of territory. It reached from Maine to Kansas, developed below the Mason-Dixon line in the District of Columbia, which became an active though perilous location, and extended even into the Deep South along the Mississippi River.[1] It had multiple manifestations: isolated Good Samaritans helping those in need; daring "slave stealers" defying death to invade the South; steadfast conductors working carefully with comrades to protect their passengers; well-knit organizations whose connections reached hundreds of miles. The Underground Railroad was all of this and more. A metaphor for hope, freedom, and goodwill. The living expression of the Golden Rule.

Slaves were seldom submissive. They had been escaping bondage since the founding of the American colonies. Herbert Aptheker's groundbreaking work, *American Negro Slave Revolts* (1939), documented the ceaseless efforts of slaves to resist. Another study, Lathan Windley's *Runaway Slave Advertisements* (1983), collected 7,286 such advertisements from 1732 to 1790.

The evil of slavery had long been recognized in America. As early as 1688 the Germantown Friends Meeting in northern Philadelphia made the first public condemnation of slavery, citing the Bible: "Thou shalt not deliver unto his master the servant which is escaped from his master unto thee. He shall dwell with thee, even among you, in that place in which he shall choose in one of thy gates, where it liketh him best; thou shalt not oppress him" (Deut. 23: 15–16).

This early assault on slavery by Quakers put them in a leadership role that continued until Abraham Lincoln's Emancipation Proclamation. In Philadelphia around the time of the American Revolution, Quakers formed first organization to help fugitive slaves. One of its leaders was Benjamin Franklin. The organization was mentioned in a letter by George Washington when one of his slaves had received its assistance.

"And if the practice of this Society . . . is not discountenanced," Washington wrote, "none of those whose misfortune it is to have slaves as attendants, will visit the city if they can possibly avoid it . . ."[2]

The problem became serious enough for Congress to pass the Fugitive Slave Law of 1793, which criminalized the acts of the Good Samaritans. Philadelphia, with its large and relatively prosperous free black population and its strong Quaker roots, was the perfect location to launch the Underground Railroad. A Philadelphia Abolition Society member, Isaac T. Hopper, used the court system and his connection to the city's black community to create a system that became a model for future Underground Railroad organizations. The courts became an important tool of the Underground Railroad, spawning one Supreme Court chief justice, Salmon Chase, called the "attorney general for the fugitive slave," and two future presidents, Chester A. Arthur and Rutherford B. Hayes.

Among the earliest established Underground Railroad stops was Wrightsville, Pennsylvania, along the Susquehanna River not far from the Maryland border, near where the mother-in-law of noted Underground Railroad conductor William Whipper was the first reported escaped slave in that region in 1804.[3] Along the Ohio River Valley, fugitive slaves began coming with increasing regularity after the battles of the War of 1812 made slaves aware of freedom north of the Mason-Dixon Line.[4] On ships bound for New England and New York City, docked in the harbors of the Carolinas and Virginia, slaves began stowing away, often with the complicity of seaman, many of whom were black and sympathetic.[5]

In the South, some of the earliest manifestations occurred, as in Guilford County (North Carolina) and the New Garden Quaker meeting of Levi Coffin's youth, where slaves were being assisted before 1820.[6] In the South, too, the first call for immediate emancipation came from Charles Osborn, a Quaker and native of North Carolina, when he formed the Tennessee Manumission Society in December 1814.[7]

In the years before noted abolitionist William Lloyd Garrison launched *The Liberator* in Boston in 1831, the bulk of anti-slavery agitation occurred in the South.[8] However, that changed with a series of developments that included the invention of the cotton gin in 1793, the outlawing of international slave trading in 1808, and the aborted slave revolts of Gabriel Prosser in 1800 and Denmark Vesey in 1822. The gin resulted in greater reliance on slave labor, the end of international slave trading shifted emphasis to the domestic trade, and the revolts stiffened laws with regard to the freedom of slaves. In sum, these developments caused an increase in slavery and a more repressive system that resulted in greater numbers of slaves fleeing.

By the 1820s slaves were regularly fleeing across the Ohio River and up from Maryland through Delaware into southeastern Pennsylvania. The slave trade also had stimulated a market for kidnappers of free blacks who operated along the borders between the North and the South. One kidnapping ring included more than 30 members working between Virginia and Philadelphia.[9] Kidnappings of free blacks along the Ohio River Valley also were common during this period and were an extremely serious problem in southern Illinois.[10] The inability of whites in America to accept free blacks as their equals led to continuing conflict, culminating in the Cincinnati riot of 1829. This led citizens in the area to seek a haven in Canada and form the first expatriate black American colony, Wilberforce, the forerunner of many to follow that became the asylums of thousands of fugitive slaves during the period of 1835 to 1860, the most active years of the Underground Railroad.

In the South, increased tensions reached a climax following the Nat Turner insurrection in Virginia in 1831 that resulted in the brutal murder of more than fifty whites. It shocked southern whites and prompted a brutal response, especially in Virginia and Maryland, where white vigilantes went on a rampage, assaulting and lynching innocent blacks, including some who were free. As a result, still harsher laws and restrictions governing slaves and free blacks were instituted.

With the formation of the American Anti-Slavery Society in 1833 and hundreds more auxiliary branches formed mainly through the outreach efforts of Theodore Weld and his band of seventy from 1835 to 1837, the networks of the Underground Railroad were established. The New York Committee of Vigilance, founded in 1835, brought the Underground Railroad to a new level of organization and led to similar committees in Philadelphia and Boston. Committees also formed in smaller communities, as in upstate New York, where the state society called for their establishment based on the New York model in 1838.[11] An inexorable march of events had set the stage for laying down the tracks of the Underground Railroad by the end of the decade.

Waterways served as important thoroughfares for fugitive slaves during the Underground Railroad's early years. The Ohio, Susquehanna, Hudson, and Connecticut rivers all served as major thoroughfares, along with the widespread auxiliary canal system that began to develop during the 1820s. The prevalence of black boatman, especially in the South, played an important role in the flight of numerous fugitive slaves.[12] By the late 1830s the steamers and schooners plying the waters of Lake Erie and Lake Ontario were carrying hundreds to freedom in Canada West (today Ontario).

Three major arteries developed, from which branched a multitude of tributaries:

- The eastern route served fugitive slaves who traveled up through Virginia, Maryland, and Delaware to Lancaster and Chester counties in Pennsylvania, where they were sent up through eastern or central Pennsylvania and farther north, or to Philadelphia and then to New York City. Sometimes they went by ship directly to New York City or the New England seaports. From New York City they were sent up the Hudson River; in New England, a primary destination was New Bedford, Massachusetts. In 1842 Charles Torrey organized an Underground Railroad network in the District of Columbia that continued to function until the Civil War.
- A central route had major crossing points along the Ohio River at Evansville, New Albany, and Madison, Indiana; and at Cincinnati, Ripley, and Marietta, Ohio. These led up to the lake ports along Lake Erie that included Sandusky and Cleveland, and sometimes to Detroit. Both Indiana and Ohio had hundreds of Underground stations, most of them conducted by Quakers, Baptists, New School Presbyterians, and free blacks.
- A route coming from the western end of the Underground Railroad developed during the early 1840s. The route led mainly from Quincy, Illinois, through Galesburg, Princeton, Chicago, and southern Michigan, ending in Detroit. This route extended across Iowa by 1854 and had some traffic coming through St. Louis and Alton, Illinois.

The hundreds of tributaries branching off were dependent on many variables, including the period, as locations and conductors changed over time.[13]

Among the foremost conductors along the eastern route were Thomas Garrett of Wilmington, Delaware; William Still of Philadelphia, Pennsylvania; Stephen Myers of Albany, New York; and Jermaine Loguen of Syracuse, New York. Along the central route: John Rankin of Ripley, Ohio; Levi Coffin of Newport, Indiana, and Cincinnati, Ohio;

Elijah Anderson of Madison and Lawrenceburg, Indiana; George DeBaptiste of Madison, Indiana, and Detroit, Michigan; and William Lambert of Detroit, Michigan. Along the western route: John Cross of various localities in Illinois; Owen Lovejoy of Princeton, Illinois; and Erastus Hussey of Battlecreek, Michigan.

These conductors were generally individuals who organized a community of agents to support and forward fugitive slaves. Some, such as Coffin, Rankin, and Garrett, had an unwritten rule to avoid entering the South and enticing slaves to freedom. A few, such as Elijah Anderson, did both. But this work fell primarily to those daring individuals who might be called slave rescuers. Among the most notable were Harriet Tubman, John Fairfield, Charles Torrey, John Parker, Calvin Fairbank, Delia Webster, William L. Chaplin, and Alexander Milton Ross. An organization that was effective in carrying out the Underground Railroad on both sides of the border was the Anti-Slavery League, described by William M. Cockrum. Some slave rescuers were not always as ethical as abolitionists, especially those who resided in the South, where their activities were extremely dangerous. Those individuals usually worked for a fee. A few just as easily would become a slavecatcher for the right price, as was attributed to Patrick Doyle, who led a slave insurrection in central Kentucky in 1848.[14]

The Underground Railroad was inspired by the evangelical movements of the day and the devout Quaker beliefs in freedom, equality, and human dignity. Many Underground Railroad conductors, such as John Brown and Gerrit Smith, could recite Biblical passages verbatim from memory. It included individuals from all walks of life, and all races and genders. Sometimes whole families participated, including the children, such as Mordecai Benedict in Marengo, Ohio, who began forwarding fugitive slaves when he was only six years old.

It also had varying degrees of organization dependent on time and place, but its actors had one common unifying purpose: "to help the oppressed go free." Those who made up its unofficial membership were among the most honorable, courageous, and compassionate individuals in our nation's history.

NOTES

1. See Thomas C. Buchanan, "Rascals on the Antebellum Mississippi: African American Steamboat Workers and the St. Louis Hanging of 1841," *Journal of Social History*, Vol. 34, No. 4, 2001: 797; Stanley Harrold, *Subversives: Antislavery Community in Washington, D.C.*, Baton Rouge: Louisiana State University Press, 2003; M. H. Peters, "An Abolitionist: A True Story of Life in Ante-bellum Days," *Home and Country*, July 1893 (from Wilbur Siebert Collection, Box 61, Vol. 14, No. 76).

2. Paul Boller, "Washington, the Quakers, and Slavery," *Journal of Negro History*, April 1961: 83–88.

3. Robert C. Smedley, *History of the Underground Railroad in Chester and Neighboring Counties of Pennsylvania*, Lancaster, PA, 1883: 27–28.

4. See Wilbur H. Siebert, "Beginnings of the Underground Railroad in Ohio," *Ohio History*, January 1947: 70–93.

5. See Wilbur H. Siebert, *The Underground Railroad in Massachusetts*, Worcester, MA: American Antiquarian Society, 1936; Horatio Strother, *The Underground Railroad in Connecticut*, Middletown, CT: Wesleyan University Press, 1962.

6. See Levi Coffin, *Reminiscences*, Cincinnati, OH: Robert Clarke & Co, 1880.

7. William M. Boyd, "Charles Osborn: Pioneer American Abolitionist," *Phylon*, Vol. 8, No. 2, 1947: 133–137.

8. Alice Dana Adams, *The Neglected Period of Anti-Slavery in America 1808–1831*, Cambridge, MA: Radcliffe College, 1908.

9. Carol Wilson, *Freedom at Risk: The Kidnapping of Free Blacks in America—1780–1865*, Lexington: University Press of Kentucky, 1994: 25.

10. Jon Musgrave, *Slaves, Salt, Sex & Mr. Crenshaw*, http://www.IllinoisHistory.com, 2005.

11. "Vigilance Committees," *Friend of Man*, April 18, 1838: 170.

12. David Cecelski, "The Shores of Freedom: The Maritime Underground Railroad in North Carolina, 1800–1861," *North Carolina Historical Review*, Vol. 1, No. 2, April 1994: 174–205.

13. For an examination of the various routes, see the works of Wilbur Siebert and numerous others, including Blockson, Calarco, Cockrum, Coon, Griffler, Grover, Kashatus, Muelder, Sernett, Smedley, Still, Strother, and Switala.

14. James M. Prichard, "This Priceless Jewel—Liberty: The Doyle Conspiracy of 1848," paper delivered at the 14th Annual Ohio Valley History Conference, October 23, 1998.

Timeline of the Underground Railroad

1775	Founding of the Society for the Relief of Free Negroes Unlawfully Held in Bondage, later called the Pennsylvania Abolition Society, first organization to aid fugitive slaves.
1780	Gradual emancipation law in Pennsylvania, first of its kind in the United States, sets the stage for the development of the Underground Railroad in Philadelphia.
1793	Passage of first Fugitive Slave Law, making it illegal to aid slaves fleeing from slavery.
1796	Isaac Hopper, noted Quaker abolitionist, joins the Philadelphia Abolition Society.
1803	Judicial decision by Chief Justice of Lower Canada, William Osgoode, declares slavery inconsistent with British law, setting a precedent that leads to the end of slavery in Canada.
1808	Outlawing of International Slave Trade puts more emphasis on America's domestic slave trade, which becomes major cause of slaves seeking freedom.
1814	Charles Osborn, a Presbyterian minister from Tennessee, makes first public declaration in favor of immediate emancipation of slaves.
1816	Founding of American Colonization Society, which seeks to send American blacks to Africa because they believe blacks cannot coexist in the United States on equal terms with whites.
1817	Meeting of blacks in Philadelphia to protest colonization. They insist as Americans that they should have the same rights and opportunities as whites.
1822	John Rankin, Presbyterian minister, moves from Kentucky to Ripley, Ohio, and enlarges the Underground Railroad already in existence there.
1822	Thomas Garrett, Quaker businessman, moves to Wilmington, Delaware, and puts his abolitionist principles into action by aiding fugitive slaves.
1826	Levi Coffin, a Quaker from North Carolina, moves to Newport, Indiana, and begins operating his legendary station on the Underground Railroad.
1827	*Freedom's Journal*, the first black newspaper, begins publication; it opposes colonization and calls for immediate emancipation.
1829	David Walker, black used clothes dealer from Boston, publishes his *Appeal* and calls on slaves to revolt.

1829	Cincinnati race riot causes some black citizens to flee and form the Wilberforce Colony, the first colony of expatriate American blacks in Canada.
1831	The *Liberator* begins publication in Boston and calls for immediate emancipation.
1831	Nat Turner Revolt massacres more than fifty whites in Southampton, Virginia, in an attempt to bring about the end of slavery; it terrorizes the South, and harshly repressive measures are instituted to control the future behavior of not only slaves but also free blacks in the South.
1832	Rankin's "Letters on Slavery," which illustrate the moral shortcomings of slavery, are serialized in *The Liberator.*
1833	England outlaws slavery in the British Commonwealth, ending the last vestiges of slavery in Canada.
1833	American Anti-Slavery Society forms in Philadelphia.
1834	Lane Debates at Lane Seminary in Cincinnati led by abolitionist Theodore Weld galvanize the attention of the nation on the issue of immediate emancipation of slaves.
1835	Ohio Anti-Slavery Society forms, strengthening the connections of that state's Underground Railroad.
1835	New York Committee of Vigilance forms, the first well-organized Underground Railroad organization upon which later similar groups will base their model.
1835	Charles C. Burleigh abolitionizes Chester County, Pennsylvania, an area from which spring more Underground Railroad agents per capita than anywhere in the United States.
1835	Gerrit Smith, Peterboro, New York, multimillionaire, converts from his support of colonization to the cause of immediate emancipation, and begins his one-man war on slavery, which includes numerous activities in support of the Underground Railroad.
1835–1837	Theodore Weld and his band of seventy abolitionize the North and recruit thousands who become part of the Underground Railroad.
1837	Elijah Lovejoy, religious editor, is murdered in Alton, Illinois, after refusing to abandon discussion of slavery in his newspaper, converting thousands to support immediate emancipation and the Underground Railroad.
1838	William L. Chaplin, secretary of the New York State Anti-Slavery Society, calls for the organization of the Underground Railroad in upstate New York.
1838	"Eliza," real-life model for Eliza Harris in *Uncle Tom's Cabin*, escapes to freedom, aided by John Rankin and Levi Coffin.
1838	Frederick Douglass escapes from slavery, which soon leads to the beginning of his career as the nation's leading black civil rights advocate in America.
1841	Founding of the British and American Institute, industrial school for fugitive slaves, in Dawn, Ontario, by Hiram Wilson.
1842	*Prigg* decision by the Supreme Court, ruling that states have no jurisdiction in fugitive slave cases, causes some fugitive slaves in the North to flee to Canada and also results in passage of laws by northern states to undermine it.
1842	Charles Torrey, radical abolitionist minister living in Albany, New York, organizes the Underground Railroad in Washington, D.C. He dies in prison four years later, after being convicted of aiding fugitive slaves.

1843 Henry Highland Garnet calls for slaves to revolt in his "Address to the Slaves" at National Negro Convention in Buffalo, New York.

1843 John Cross, Congregational minister in Illinois, organizes the western Underground Railroad leading from Quincy, Illinois, to Detroit, Michigan. The route expands across Iowa by 1854.

1843 Calvin Fairbank and Delia Webster, former Oberlin students, rescue Kentucky slave Lewis Hayden and his family but are captured and sent to prison.

1845 Captain Jonathan Walker, seaman, is arrested for aiding fugitive slaves, and his hand is branded with the initials *SS* for *slave stealer*. John Greenleaf Whittier writes a poem commemorating the incident.

1846 Race riots in Madison, Indiana, remove black abolitionist George DeBaptiste to Detroit, where he joins with William Lambert and William Munroe in organizing the Detroit Vigilance Committee.

1846 Militant abolitionist Gerrit Smith and peripatetic evangelical abolitionist John Brown meet in Peterboro, New York.

1847 Levi Coffin moves to Cincinnati to open Free Produce store and reorganizes the city's Underground Railroad.

1847 Frederick Douglass begins publication of the *North Star*, becomes a leading spokesman for black America, and joins the Underground Railroad in Rochester, New York.

1848 Thomas Garrett is found guilty of aiding fugitive slaves in Delaware and pays large fine, but he vows to continue aiding fugitive slaves.

1848 Seventy-seven fugitive slaves attempt to flee in a schooner named the *Pearl* from the harbor of Washington, D.C.

1848 Slaves William and Ellen Craft escape from Georgia to freedom in the North. They eventually are forced to flee to England because of attempts to enforce the Fugitive Slave of 1850.

1849 Slave Henry "Box" Brown escapes to freedom. Like the Crafts, he is forced to flee to England because of pressures exerted by the Fugitive Slave Law of 1850.

1849 Slave Harriet Tubman escapes to freedom from Maryland.

1849 Founding of the Elgin Association by Rev. William King in Buxton, Ontario, a settlement seeking to advance the moral and educational improvement of blacks in Canada.

1850 Chance meeting of long-lost brothers, former slave Peter Friedman and abolitionist William Still, prompts the latter to begin keeping records of fugitive slaves aided during his work for the Philadelphia Vigilance Committee.

1850 Second Fugitive Slave Law is passed, effectively turning all American citizens into slavecatchers.

1850 Harriet Tubman conducts first rescue mission.

1851 *National Era* begins serialization of novel *Uncle Tom's Cabin* by Harriet Beecher Stowe.

1851 Henry Bibb begins publication of the *Voice of the Fugitive* in Toronto.

1851 Christiana Riot led by former fugitive slave William Parker prevents slavecatchers from apprehending their slaves and results in the death of Maryland slaveholder Edward Gorsuch.

1851	Jerry Rescue led by Syracuse citizens prevents federal authorities from returning Jerry Henry to slavery.
1851	Fugitive slave Shadrach Minkins rescued from federal authorities in Boston by Lewis Hayden and unofficial black members of the Boston Vigilance Committee.
1852	Philadelphia Vigilance Committee reorganizes under the leadership of William Still.
1852	Anti-Slavery League, as reported by Indiana abolitionist William Cockrum, organizes in the Ohio River Valley to bring slaves out of the South.
1853	Mary Shadd and Samuel Ringgold Ward begin publication of the *Provincial Freeman* in Windsor, Canada.
1854	Federal authorities successfully apprehend fugitive slave Anthony Burns despite rescue efforts of the Boston Vigilance Committee under the leadership of Lewis Hayden and Thomas Wentworth Higginson.
1854	Kansas-Nebraska Act nullifies the Missouri Compromise and makes all future states north of Missouri subject to slavery to be determined by state referendum.
1855–1856	Detroit Vigilance Committee reports aiding upwards of 1,600 fugitive slaves in each of these years.
1856	John Brown goes to Kansas and becomes nationally known exponent of using force to end slavery.
1858	Oberlin-Wellington Rescue by Oberlin, Ohio, citizens and students prevents authorities from returning fugitive slave John Price of Oberlin to slavery.
1859	John Brown, captured at Harpers Ferry, Virginia, and hanged at Charlestown, Virginia, galvanizes the attention of the Union.
1860	Harriet Tubman leads rescue of fugitive slave Charles Nalle from federal authorities in Troy, New York.
1872	William Still publishes *The Underground Railroad: A Record* . . . based on records he made as chairman of the acting committee of the Philadelphia Vigilance Committee.
1875	Levi Coffin publishes his *Reminiscences.*
1883	Robert C. Smedley publishes *The Underground Railroad in Chester County, Pennsylvania*, providing the most thorough description to date of the Underground Railroad in a selected locality.
1898	Wilbur Siebert publishes *The Underground Railroad: From Slavery to Freedom*, to date, the most comprehensive consideration of the Underground Railroad.

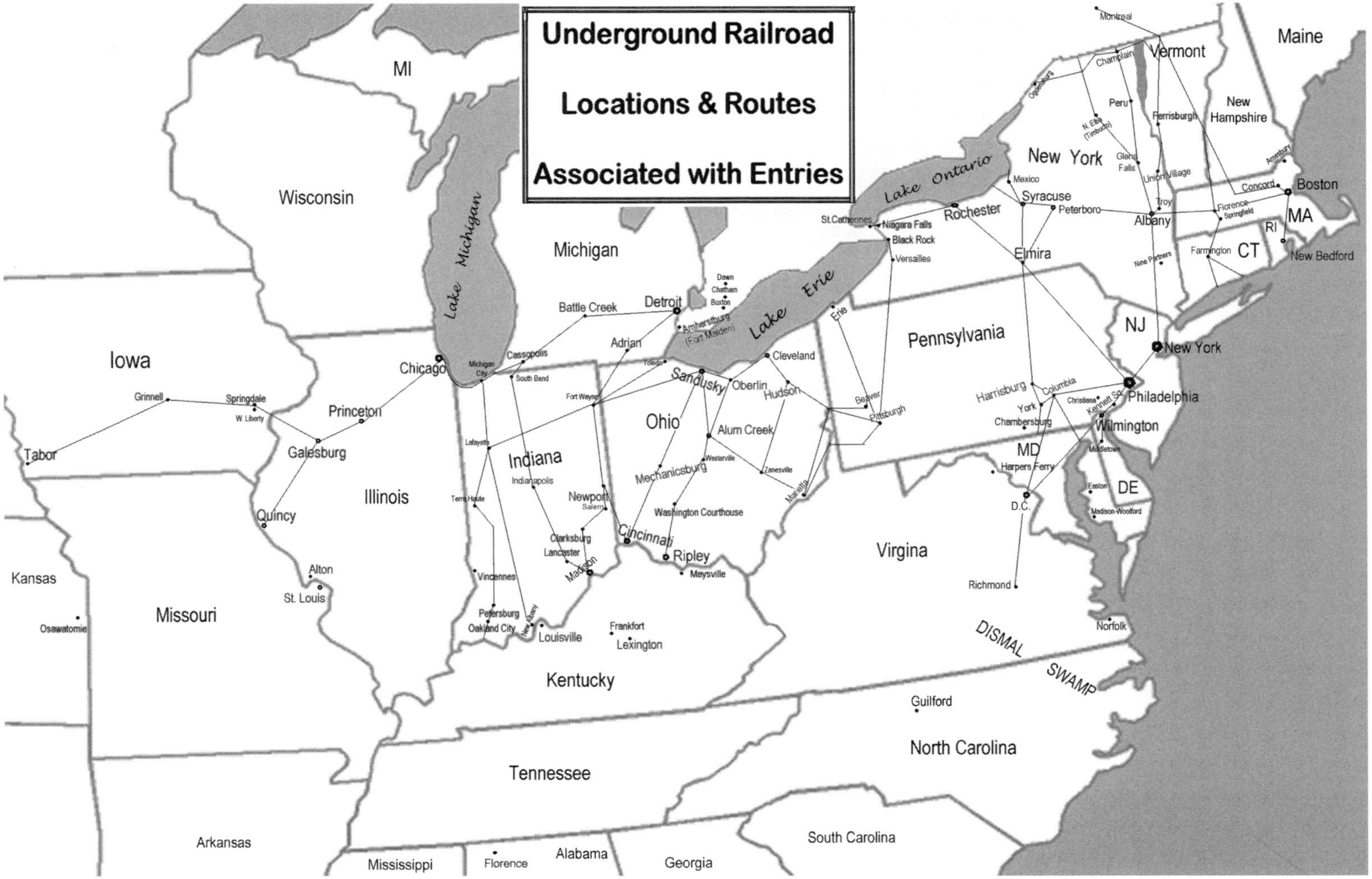
Underground Railroad
Locations & Routes
Associated with Entries
Maine
Vermont
New Hampshire
Boston
MA
RI
CT
New Bedford
Concord
Amesbury
Florence
Springfield
Farmington
Montreal
Champlain
Ogdensburg
Peru
Ferrisburgh
N. Elba (Timbucto)
Glens Falls
Union Village
Troy
Albany
New York
Mexico
Syracuse
Peterboro
Nine Partners
Lake Ontario
Rochester
St.Catherines
Niagara Falls
Black Rock
Versailles
Elmira
NJ
New York
Pennsylvania
Erie
Beaver
Pittsburgh
Harrisburg
Columbia
York
Chambersburg
Christiana
Kennett Sq.
Philadelphia
Wilmington
Middletown
MD
Harpers Ferry
D.C.
Easton
DE
Madison-Woolford
Richmond
Norfolk
Virgina
DISMAL SWAMP
Guilford
North Carolina
South Carolina
Georgia
Alabama
Florence
Mississippi
Tennessee
Kentucky
Frankfort
Lexington
Louisville
Maysville
Ripley
Cincinnati
Washington Courthouse
Mechanicsburg
Westerville
Alum Creek
Zanesville
Marietta
Ohio
Hudson
Oberlin
Cleveland
Sandusky
Toledo
Lake Erie
Amherstburg (Fort Malden)
Dawn
Chatham
Buxton
Detroit
Michigan
Adrian
Battle Creek
Cassopolis
South Bend
Fort Wayne
Indiana
Indianapolis
Newport
Salem
Clarksburg
Lancaster
Madison
New Albany
Petersburg
Oakland City
Vincennes
Terre Haute
Lafayette
Michigan City
Lake Michigan
MI
Wisconsin
Chicago
Illinois
Princeton
Galesburg
Quincy
Alton
St. Louis
Missouri
Iowa
Springdale
W. Liberty
Grinnell
Tabor
Kansas
Osawatomie
Arkansas

A

Allen, Richard (1760–1831). Born a slave, Richard Allen was the founder and first bishop of the African Methodist Episcopal Church, the first fully independent black denomination in America.

Allen described his owner, Benjamin Chew, as a "good master." But because of financial difficulties, Chew was forced to sell three of Allen's siblings and his mother. Nevertheless, he encouraged Allen and his two brothers, who remained with him, to attend religious services, saying, "If I am not good myself, I like to see you striving yourselves to be good." Allen persuaded Chew to allow preachers to come to their house, and one of them, a black preacher named Garrison, convinced Chew that it was wrong to own slaves. Chew agreed to let Allen and his brothers purchase their freedom, allowing them to pay him with the earnings of their own free labor.

On leaving his master, Allen wrote, "I may truly say it was like leaving our father's house; for he was a kind, affectionate, and tender-hearted master, and told us to make his house our home when we were out of a place or sick." Allen worked as a woodcutter and a bricklayer, and also hauled salt for the American army during the Revolution. A deeply religious young man, he also became an itinerant Methodist preacher. He attracted the notice of several important clergy, including Francis Asbury, the first American bishop of the Methodist Church, who in 1786 appointed him as an assistant minister in Philadelphia at the racially mixed congregation of St. George's Methodist Church.

Allen's ministry quickly found its focus in the social needs of Philadelphia's black community. On April 12, 1787, he and Absalom Jones founded the Free African Society of Philadelphia, a mutual aid organization that cared for the sick, buried the dead, and helped support widows and orphans. However, the society was drawn to other denominations because of Methodism's poor treatment of blacks, including its refusal to allow African Americans to be buried in the congregation's cemetery, and the segregation of blacks in a newly built gallery at St. George's Methodist Church. The society asked Allen to be the pastor of a new church that they had built, the African Episcopal Church, but Allen rejected the offer. He could not leave his faith despite its prejudices.

Instead, in 1793, he formed his own black Methodist "Bethel" congregation that met in a blacksmith shop. That year a yellow fever epidemic erupted. Few consented to attend the sick, but Allen and Jones were "unremitting in their labors for the relief of the sick, and in burying the dead." When the epidemic abated, the city's mayor praised them for their "diligence, attention, and decency of deportment."

By then Allen had a growing family and had become quite prosperous. In addition to his work as a preacher, he also opened a shoe repair shop and a chimney-cleaning business. Allen's Bethel Church prospered as well. In 1795 its congregation numbered 121, and in 1813 it reached 1,272. A new edifice had been built in 1805, and in that building's basement the congregation began harboring fugitive slaves.

After the passage of the Fugitive Slave Act of 1793, Allen's Free African Society began petitioning state and national governments to end slavery and the slave trade, and to repeal the Fugitive Slave Act of 1793, which prevented blacks from testifying on their own behalf and gave license to the practice of kidnapping free blacks into slavery. In 1800 the society sent a petition to the U.S. Congress, asking the federal government to address the issue of kidnapping: "Can any Commerce, Trade or transaction so detestably shock the feelings of Man, or degrade the dignity of his nature equal to this?" In the petition, they provided a detailed description of actual kidnappings. Though an impassioned debate over the petition occurred in the U.S. House of Representatives, no action was taken.

Allen's activities opposing the rendition of fugitive slaves led to suspicions that he was aiding them, which in fact was occurring at his church. On one occasion, two slaveowners searching for fugitive slaves forced their way into his home while he was away. When Allen's wife told him of the incident, he went to the local authorities and had the men arrested. Allen asked only that they "ask my pardon, promise not to repeat the offensive conduct, and pay the [court] cost; or, if they prefer to pay to the overseers of the poor in the ward where they live, ten pounds each."

On another occasion, in 1806, a Maryland plantation owner and his two sons came to Philadelphia searching for a slave who had fled four years earlier. One of the sons mistook Allen for the slave, and they had a warrant served for his arrest. Upon seeing that the captured man was Allen, who had been living in Philadelphia for twenty years, the judge immediately released him. Seeking compensation for this indignity, Allen summoned **Isaac Hopper**, the noted abolitionist, who won a judgment for $800. Unable to pay, the father was sent to a debtor's prison, where he remained for three months until Allen interceded, saying he believed the man had "suffered enough."

Allen was a man with high moral principles. He was in complete agreement with the Methodist Church's strict sanctions against drinking, gambling, and infidelity, which helped bring order to the lives of black Americans. Allen also believed in justice, even going so far as to publish an advertisement in Poulson's *American Daily Advertiser*, offering ten dollars for the rendition of Robert Rich, a runaway servant who owed services to a Captain Rich.

Nevertheless, Allen grew increasingly dissatisfied with the Methodist Church's refusals to oppose slavery and give equal treatment to blacks. In 1816 he obtained recognition of Mother Bethel as an independent church and met there with representatives from four other black Methodist congregations. They organized the first fully independent black denomination in America, the African Methodist Episcopal Church, and chose Allen as its first bishop.

While free blacks were making progress in one direction, another development set back their hopes of equality in America. This came in the guise of a benevolent organization, the American Colonization Society. Founded in 1817 by a distinguished group of Southern slaveholders, the society proposed the creation of a settlement in Africa as the best solution for American blacks seeking a better life. Allen called for an open meeting of blacks at Mother Bethel to discuss this solution. More than 3,000 attended, some coming from hundreds of miles away. Allen, who at first had looked favorably upon the scheme, quickly found that his brethren overwhelmingly condemned it. Among the resolutions passed was one that stated, "Whereas our ancestors (not of choice) were the first successful cultivators of the wilds of America, we their descendants feel ourselves entitled to participate in the blessings of her luxuriant soil."

Nevertheless, Allen considered emigration to be a legitimate choice for many African Americans and sought alternatives to the African plan. In 1824 he supported the Haitian Emigration Society, but when this venture failed, he reconciled himself to the reality that blacks should instead strive to carve a place for themselves in America. "This land which we have watered with our tears and our blood is now our mother country," he wrote in *Freedom's Journal*, the nation's first black newspaper. After a race riot in Cincinnati in 1829 drove out 1,000 free blacks, the first National Negro Convention was called in Philadelphia to address the situation. Allen was called to the chair. While continuing to condemn the American Colonization Society, the convention recommended Canada as the destination for blacks forced to flee their homes. A committee was appointed to support the establishment of a black colony in Canada West, which black citizens of Cincinnati had started, named Wilberforce after the noted British abolitionist.

Allen died the followed year. His tomb was placed in the basement of the Mother Bethel Church, and remains today beneath the present Mother Bethel Church built in 1889 on the original site.

SUGGESTED READING: Richard Allen, *The Life, Experience, and Gospel Labours of the Right Rev. Richard Allen*, Philadelphia: Martin & Boden, Printers, 1833; James Henrietta, "Richard Allen and African-American Identity: A Black Ex-Slave in Early America's White Society Preserves His Cultural Identity by Creating Separate Institutions," *Early America Review*, Spring 1997; Daniel Meaders, "Kidnapping Blacks in Philadelphia: Isaac Hopper's Tales of Oppression," *The Journal of Negro History*, Vol. 80, No. 2, Spring, 1995; Nilgun Okur, "Underground Railroad in Philadelphia, 1830–1860," *Journal of Black Studies*, Vol. 25, No. 5, May 1995, 537–557.

Allen, William G. (1820–unknown). William G. Allen was among the first men of color in the United States to become a college professor. The son of a white father and a free mulatto mother, Allen was born in Urbana, Virginia, near Norfolk. He attended a school for black children and was a precocious student, but the school closed after the **Nat Turner** Rebellion in 1831. Allen's parents died shortly after, and he was adopted by a free black family. When the family moved to Fort Monroe, they were unable to find a school for Allen, but an army officer befriended and educated him. Then in 1838 Allen enrolled in a school started by a minister from New York. He impressed the minister, and was referred by him to **Gerrit Smith**, who sponsored him at Beriah Green's interracial Oneida Institute, near Utica, New York.

A hotbed of abolitionist ferment, the Oneida Institute brought Allen in contact with black abolitionists such as **Henry Highland Garnet**. Allen also went to Canada and worked with Hiram Wilson, teaching newly settled fugitive slaves. After graduating from Oneida in 1843, Allen moved to Troy, New York, and worked with Garnet in editing the *National Watchman*. By 1847 Allen was in Boston, clerking for Judge Ellis Gray Loring, a founding member of the American Anti-Slavery Society and an active member of the Boston Vigilance Committee. (Gray was among those who sheltered the fugitive slave Ellen Craft.) Allen also began speaking publicly about immediate emancipation, racial equality, and amalgamation, which became a significant theme for him. Allen believed that American blacks were in reality a mixed race, rather than pure Negroes. At the same time, he became well known for his lectures on African culture and history, an interest that Allen may have developed from his association with Garnet, who was also an Afrophile.

Hiram Wilson: The Fugitive Slave Missionary

Hiram Wilson, one of the Lane Rebels, became the most noted missionary serving the fugitive slave community in Canada. In 1837 he was sent to Canada by the American Anti-Slavery Society to investigate the condition of former fugitive slaves. He estimated that 10,000 had settled there, and described them as "loyal, well behaved, and law-abiding." In 1841 he conceived the plan of establishing the British and American Institute, an industrial school, to train former fugitive slaves.

He began the school with fourteen students, and managed the school for seven years. By the mid-1850s, there were about sixty students attending the school, and about 500 blacks had settled in the surrounding communities of Dawn and Dresden, which prior to the establishment of the school were mostly wilderness.

Despite Wilson's struggles—his wife died in 1847, and he lived in poverty—he maintained his optimism. In 1848 he moved to St. Catharine's, where he continued to minister to the needs of former fugitive slaves, remaining in Canada until after the Civil War. As one observer wrote of him, "he managed to keep himself free from the care of riches, by giving to the needy, as fast as he earned it."

In 1849 Allen was appointed a professor of Greek Language and Literature at McGrawville College in Cortland, New York, which offered interracial, mixed-gender education. The school was founded by Free Mission Baptists and received substantial financial support from Gerrit Smith. Allen developed a close friendship with one of his students, Mary E. King, the daughter of Rev. Lyndon King, a white abolitionist minister of the Wesleyan Methodist Church in Fulton, New York, an active stop on the Underground Railroad.

Allen had met Mary King when she was his student. In the beginning, his relations with her family were cordial and approved by her father. However, when the couple announced their engagement, the disapproval of Rev. King's wife (the stepmother of his children) and sons changed Rev. King's mind. Allen was informed that he was no longer welcome at the King home to court their daughter.

The couple decided to meet at the home of a friend. But they were discovered while there, and an anti-amalgamation mob of 500 "gentlemen of property and standing," armed with a pole, buckets of tar and feathers, and a large, empty barrel spiked with nails, surrounded the house. They ordered Allen to come out. In fear of his life, Allen remained inside until some abolitionist friends arrived and escorted him to safety.

In the intervening weeks, Mary wrote to Allen, breaking their engagement. She had been forced to do so, having been made a virtual prisoner in her own house. Through mutual friends Allen learned the truth, and with their help, Mary was able to join him secretly. They eloped to New York City, where they were married, and fled to England.

The American Prejudice Against Color, which Allen wrote in England, describes this experience and the horrible effects of racism. The irony of the affair is not only that a devoutly abolitionist community exhibited this racial hatred, but that this community was actively involved in the Underground Railroad. Allen also went on the lecture circuit in England, as had other renowned American blacks before him, including **Frederick Douglass**, **Henry Garnet**, **William Wells Brown**, and **Henry "Box" Brown**. However, Allen did not experience the success they had. In 1856 the Allens moved to Ireland, where they lived for three years. Allen earned a living mainly as a private tutor, and Mary gave birth to three children.

Moving back to England, Allen wrote to Gerrit Smith, asking him for money with which to purchase a home to use for his tutoring services. Smith, embroiled in the events surrounding **John Brown** and Harpers Ferry, failed to respond.

A couple of years later, Allen became involved with the committee that won the release of **John Anderson**, the fugitive slave who had been held in Canada for extradition for a murder he had committed while escaping from slavery in Missouri. In 1863, through the influence of the Anderson committee's president, Harper Twelvetrees, Allen was made principal of a new school devoted to educating poor children in London. Throughout Allen's five-year tenure, the school was confronted with financial problems until finally it was forced to close. After this failure, Mary opened a school of her own for girls. It is not known how long this school existed, but by 1874 the Allens had moved again. In 1878 they were living in a boarding house in West London, the last known record of their lives.

Allen concluded *The American Prejudice Against Color* in true Christian spirit: "I judge not mortal man or woman, but leave Mrs. King, and all those who thought it no harm because of my complexion, to abuse the most sacred feelings of my heart, to their conscience and their God."

SUGGESTED READING: William G. Allen, *The American Prejudice Against Color,* London: W & F. G. Cash, 1853; R. J. M. Blackett, "William G. Allen: The Forgotten Professor," *Civil War History,* March 1980.

Anderson, Elijah (1808–1861). Blacksmith Elijah Anderson was one of most active conductors along the Underground Railroad corridor from Madison, Indiana, to Sandusky, Ohio. Freeborn in Virginia, Anderson moved to Madison in 1837, where he prospered and had a two-story brick home built at 626 Walnut Street. But earning a livelihood was merely a sideline to Anderson's business of helping slaves escape to freedom.

The light-skinned Anderson traveled freely between the North and South, and had no fear of going into Kentucky to aid fugitive slaves. A key crossover point for his operations was at Carrollton, Kentucky, twelve miles east of Madison. It is believed that he went as far south as Frankfort on his slave-rescuing expeditions. In the latter years of his Underground activities, he often took fugitive slaves by train, posing as their master.

John Henry Tibbetts, one of many abolitionists at the Underground Railroad terminal in Lancaster, Indiana, seven miles northwest of Madison, described Anderson in his memoirs. He related an incident in which Anderson accompanied two fugitive slaves on a train to Indianapolis, another in which he and Anderson forwarded fugitive slaves from Madison at night, and a third in which an elaborate plan was hatched to rescue a slave from a family visiting Madison.

Following an attack on black abolitionists in Madison by a mob of 100 proslavery whites, during which homes were ransacked and one man was nearly lynched, Anderson was involved in the beating of a prominent black Madison citizen, John Simmons. Anderson had learned that Simmons was luring fugitive slaves to his home and turning them over to slavecatchers to collect a reward. In 1847 Simmons brought suit against Anderson and won a judgment of $700.

Anderson needed to borrow the money to pay off the fine, and this incident, coupled with the recent attacks, induced him to leave town. He moved downriver to Lawrenceburg, Indiana, about twenty miles west of Cincinnati. Home to a fairly large black population and some white abolitionists, Lawrenceburg was a good place for Anderson to relocate his Underground Railroad operations.

About this time, Anderson began to regularly escort fugitive slaves on the train to the Lake Erie port of Sandusky, from which Canada was a short boat ride. Prominent Sandusky conductor Rush Sloane wrote that Anderson told him during a visit in 1855 that he had aided more than 1,000 fugitive slaves—more than 800 after the passage of the Fugitive Slave Law of 1850.

However, Anderson's boldness proved his undoing. Even though Kentucky slave-owners offered a reward for his capture, he continued his aggressive slave-rescuing missions. After a mission escorting fugitive slaves to Cleveland, he was betrayed by a fellow black for the reward money. Louisville police officers arrested Anderson aboard an Ohio River steamboat in December 1856. Incriminating papers were found on Anderson, proving his involvement in rescuing slaves in the vicinity of Carrollton, Kentucky. The papers also implicated some "distinguished northerners."

A black abolitionist from Madison, **William J. Anderson**—whom some claim was Elijah's brother, despite William's denials—was also arrested in the same vicinity a few days before Elijah's arrest. Some suspect that he was the one who betrayed Elijah, although this has never been proven.

In June 1857 Elijah Anderson was convicted of "enticing slaves to run away" and sentenced to an eight-year term in the Kentucky Penitentiary. Scheduled for an early release on March 4, 1861, he was found dead in his cell on that very day. The cause of his death was never determined.

SUGGESTED READING: Diane Perrine Coon, "Southeastern Indiana's Underground Railroad Routes and Operations. A Project of the State of Indiana, Dept. of Natural Resources, Division of Historic Preservation and Archaeology and the U.S. Dept. of the Interior," 2001; Keith P. Griffler, *Front Line of Freedom: African Americans and the Forging of the Underground Railroad in the Ohio Valley*, Lexington: University Press of Kentucky, 2004; J. Blaine Hudson, *Fugitive Slaves and the Underground Railroad in the Kentucky Borderlands*, Jefferson, NY: McFarland and Company, 2001; James M. Prichard, "Into the Fiery Furnace: Anti-Slavery Prisoners in the Kentucky State Penitentiary 1844–1870," http://www.ket.org/underground/research/prichard.htm; Rush R. Sloane, "The Underground Railroad of the Firelands," *The Firelands Pioneer*, Norwalk, Ohio: The Historical Society, 1888.

Anderson, John (1830–unknown). John Anderson was a fugitive slave who killed a man while escaping from slavery, and later faced extradition from Canada in a case of international concern.

Born on a farm near Fayette, Howard County, Missouri, Anderson lost both of his parents at an early age. His father, a servant on Mississippi steamboats, escaped from slavery when Anderson was an infant, and his mother, the property of Moses Burton, was sold to a slave trader after a fight with her mistress when Anderson was seven years old.

Anderson, who was then known as Jack Burton, became a favorite of his mistress. In later years he spoke of her with affection, and as a child even called her mother. He was raised in his mistress's house and used to care for her daughters. As a result, he had a happy childhood and was given positions of increasing responsibility. He became expert in the cultivation of tobacco, wheat, corn, and the various kinds of fruit that grew on the farm. By the time he was fifteen, he was made overseer and said he used "to knock other slaves about" to keep them in line.

Anderson's mistress died when he was nineteen. To her he owed his eminent position among the slaves on the farm. By then he had grown into a powerfully built young man with broad shoulders, about 5'6", who had the respect of his master. When he was twenty, he married Maria Tomlin, a slave on a neighboring farm. She had been a widow only six months when they met, and she had two children of her own. Her father was a barber in Fayette who had purchased both his own and her mother's freedom. About two years after Anderson and Tomlin were married, they had a child of their own.

Anderson's problems with Moses Burton began, however, because of his marriage. Burton had given Anderson permission to visit his wife on Saturday nights and stay over

Fugitive slave John Anderson. Used with permission of *Documenting the American South*, the University of North Carolina at Chapel Hill libraries.

on Sunday, so long as he was ready to work on Monday morning. Anderson was unhappy with this arrangement. His wife lived only two miles away, and he began seeing her almost every night. One night when he snuck off, Burton was waiting for him when he returned. He demanded to know where Anderson had been, and when Anderson evaded the question, Burton came at him with a piece of rawhide. Anderson warded off the blows, but then Burton got a rope and threw it over the branch of a tree. He ordered Anderson to strip, but Anderson refused. Then Burton went to get his gun, only the pleas of Burton's daughter stopped him from using it.

A second confrontation convinced Burton to sell Anderson. In the meantime he hired Anderson out to another farmer. At this time, Anderson's prospective owner came to look him over, and agreed to purchase him. However, Burton wanted to keep him until his tobacco was harvested, about three months later, but did not reveal that to Anderson. Finally, on the day before his new master was to take him, Burton told him.

Anderson's new owner, Reuben McDaniel, lived about thirty miles away on the other side of the Missouri River, which it made very difficult for Anderson to see his family. When McDaniel asked Anderson if he would promise to stay with him. Anderson said he could not. Nevertheless, McDaniel offered him a very desirable position, that of being his coachman. But Anderson also refused that. He was only concerned about seeing his family, and if he were the coachman, he would not have Sundays off so he could see them. He was already contemplating running away, and he carefully observed the route they took to McDaniel's farm so that he could return or escape when the need arose.

After six weeks with McDaniel, Anderson asked for permission to see his wife. McDaniel told him that he should never see her again and that he would not permit Anderson to cross to the other side of the Missouri River. McDaniel suggested that instead Anderson should take one of the slaves on the plantation for his wife.

The next Sunday presented a favorable opportunity for Anderson to escape. McDaniel had to attend a church meeting to investigate a claim that one of the church members had whipped a slave to death. Anderson borrowed one of his master's mules, took some rope in case he needed to construct a raft, and two hours before daybreak headed toward the Missouri River.

When he arrived at the river, the ferryman refused to take him across without a pass. Anderson had to wait until night before he found a boat to use. Once across, he went to see his father-in-law, who agreed with Anderson's decision to flee to Canada and even offered him a gun to use for protection. However, Anderson said the knife he carried was all he needed. He then went to see his wife to bid her farewell.

While resuming his journey to freedom, Anderson passed a field belonging to Seneca T. P. Digges, who was supervising his slaves in the drying of tobacco. Digges demanded to know who Anderson was and whether he had a pass, as Missouri state law stated that any slave more than twenty miles from his owner's property without a pass was liable to arrest. Anderson admitted he didn't have a pass but said he was on a legitimate errand. Digges offered him dinner, but when Anderson refused, he accused him of being a fugitive. At once Anderson fled. Digges heaved an ax at him, but missed and called his slaves to pursue him.

For nearly four hours Digges's slaves chased Anderson. The slaves finally had him surrounded and were closing in. Digges had joined them, and he confronted Anderson face to face. Digges wielded a club and Anderson his knife. But Digges was an elderly, slight man and no match for the strong, young Anderson. Despite Digges's cries for help to his slaves who were nearby, Anderson was able to stab him twice, the second a fatal blow to Digges's left side. Anderson then made his getaway, and Digges's slaves gave up the chase after only a short distance.

Anderson returned to see his wife and child one last time. He told her of the confrontation, and bade her farewell again. It was the last time he would ever see them.

Anderson began his long journey to Canada, traveling by night and resting during the day. He ate whatever he could find, sometimes pilfering food from the kitchens of homes along the way, and he had several narrow escapes from capture. After he crossed the Mississippi into the free state of Illinois, he encountered a white settler who gave him lodging and food. Another white settler who also welcomed him into his home and fed him tried to entrap him. Fortunately, Anderson realized this before it was too late.

Two days later Anderson reached the Illinois River and shortly after came to a railroad line. He followed the tracks until he reached Bloomington. There he took the train to Rock Island, where he received assistance from the Underground Railroad. He remained there a couple of days, working for a barber and becoming acquainted with the local abolitionists, who paid his railway fare to Chicago. He stayed in Chicago with another barber for three more weeks before moving on to Detroit, where he was taken across the river to Windsor, Canada.

In Windsor, he changed his name to William Anderson and found work laying ties for the Great Western Railway of Canada. After finishing his work with the railway, he entered Henry Bibb's Refugee Home Society, and wrote two letters to Missouri, one to his wife, care of his father-in-law, and another to a black shoemaker friend. One of his teachers was **Laura Haviland**; she informed him of a surprising letter that had come for him. It claimed that his family had arrived in Detroit and was waiting to see him.

Henry Bibb: The Voice of the Fugitive

Henry Bibb escaped from slavery in Kentucky in 1837. Only twenty-two, he left a wife and daughter, but not for long. Six months later he snuck back in disguise and made arrangements for them to join him in Cincinnati. Instead, he was captured and returned to slavery, and he and his family were sold into the Deep South. It was the beginning of an incredible odyssey of hardship, during which he and his family escaped, fought off wolves in a swamp, were recaptured, and were then separated through sale. Bibb passed through a series of masters before being purchased by a Cherokee Indian. On the night of the death of the old Indian, Bibb made his final escape.

Bibb became involved in the abolition movement and gained a reputation as a lecturer. He was a spellbinding speaker. He would contrast the horror of his being nearly whipped to death with the pathos of being separated from his first wife and child, whom he never saw again. He made audiences cheer, laugh, and weep.

In 1848 Bibb remarried, and after the publication of his narrative in 1850, he went to Canada and began to publish the *Voice of the Fugitive*. It soon became the main source of information for and about fugitive slaves, and was especially helpful to those seeking family and work.

Bibb also was one of the founders of the Refugee Home Society, an organization that offered land and education to fugitive slaves. It was fairly successful its first two years. But in 1853 the *Provincial Freeman*, another black publication started by Samuel R. Ward and Mary Shadd, exposed misappropriation of its funds by Bibb and others. Following a fire that destroyed the *Voice of the Fugitive's* press, Bibb died in 1854 at the age of thirty-nine.

Experienced with the operations of slavecatchers, she advised him to write back and say that his whereabouts could be learned by contacting Haviland at her home in Adrian, Michigan. She also suggested that he move from Windsor to Chatham, where the Refugee Home Society supplied him with a contact, and change his name. He now became known as William Jones.

As Haviland had suspected, a Southern man showed up at her residence some days later, claiming to represent Anderson's family. At first she wasn't sure whether he was lying and divulged to him that Anderson was in Chatham. She quickly realized her mistake, and after the slavecatcher left, she telegraphed a message to **George DeBaptiste** in Detroit, asking him to warn Anderson to leave Chatham at once. DeBaptiste, who coordinated the Underground Railroad in those parts, sent messages to his contacts in the black communities in Canada to protect Anderson, who had left Chatham two days before the arrival of slavecatchers and changed his name again to James Hamilton. Their trail was now cold. Anderson had eluded them for the time being.

Anderson settled in Caledonia, a village south of Hamilton, Canada West, buying a house and working as a mason. It would be more than five years before he would have to confront the slavecatchers again.

In 1860 after a quarrel a man named Wynne, whom Anderson considered to be his friend, revealed Anderson's past to a local magistrate, William Mathews. He had Anderson arrested and put in jail for several weeks. In the meantime, Mathews contacted private detectives in Detroit, who investigated the charges against Anderson. Though Anderson finally was released, he was incarcerated again three days later when a police official from Detroit came and testified that Anderson had indeed committed a murder in Missouri. Again Anderson's lawyers were able to obtain his release after a few weeks.

Five months later in September of 1860, Anderson was arrested a third time. A hearing was held during which evidence of his guilt was presented by witnesses from Missouri, including family members and a slave of Seneca Digges. Diplomatic efforts also had begun for Anderson's extradition.

Under the Webster-Ashburton Treaty of 1843, the United States and Great Britain had mutually agreed to deliver criminals charged with murder, assault with intent to commit murder, piracy, arson, robbery, or forgery. However, their crimes needed to be judged as such by the country where the alleged criminal was lodged. Anderson had obviously killed Digges. The catch was that the prosecutors failed to reveal to the British authorities that Anderson was a fugitive slave fighting to obtain his freedom when the death of Digges occurred. Great Britain did not recognize slavery, and if an attempt to enslave someone occurred in British territories, the intended victim had every right to defend himself.

On November 24, 1860, Anderson was brought before the Court of Queen's Bench, consisting of Chief Justice Robinson and Justices Burns and McLean. S. B. Freeman represented Anderson. Freeman claimed that Anderson's act was justifiable homicide and that his extradition would be tantamount to Canada's recognition of the slave laws of the United States. Nevertheless, the court ruled in favor of extradition by a vote of 2 to 1. Later, Chief Justice Robinson claimed that his decision was based on the stipulations of the Ashburton Treaty.

As soon as the decision of the Court of Queen's Bench was given, Toronto's abolitionists decided to carry the case to England and secured an order from the Court at Westminster to bring the Anderson case there.

On December 19, the prominent British abolitionist John Scoble reported at a public meeting in Toronto the opinions of Lord Ashburton and Lord Aberdeen regarding the extradition treaty between the United States and Great Britain. In their opinion, Scoble said, special care needed to be taken so that the treaty wasn't misused by slaveholders to claim fugitive slaves on false charges. Because of this, they said the treaty was not to be applied in the cases of fugitive slaves.

On January 15, the prominent U.S. abolitionist **Gerrit Smith**, noting Scoble's comments in Toronto, added his influence in favor of Anderson, arguing that at worst Anderson was guilty of manslaughter. But even that was a moot point because the Ashburton Treaty did not recognize the surrender of fugitive slaves. Anderson's extradition could be decided only by Great Britain.

In the meantime the case was carried to a higher court in Canada, the Court of Common Pleas in Toronto. On February 16, 1861, Chief Justice Draper acquitted Anderson. "In the first place," his decision stated, "the magistrate's warrant was defective inasmuch as the words used in the warrant did not imply the charge of murder, though perhaps expressing more than manslaughter; secondly, the warrant of commitment was also defective in not adhering to the words of the treaty."

The case was closed.

In June 1861 Anderson arrived in England as a special guest of celebrations in his honor. He spoke before numerous audiences and was applauded for his bravery and determination in gaining his freedom. After eighteen months in England, he left for the African nation of Liberia, where he had been provided with free passage and a tract of land, and where he hoped to make a fresh start.

SUGGESTED READING: Patrick Brode, *The Odyssey of John Anderson,* Toronto: Toronto University Press, 1989; Harper Twelvetrees, ed., *Story of the Life of John Anderson, The Fugitive Slave,* London: William Tweedie, 1863.

Anderson, William (1801?–1867). William Anderson was born free in Hanover County, Virginia. His father, a slave who had served in the Revolutionary War, died when Anderson was a boy. As a result, Anderson's mother bound him over to a slave owner, which made his life indistinguishable from that of a slave. It also subjected him to the master's beatings and whippings. To make matters worse, Anderson was sold into slavery and sent from Richmond, Virginia, to Nashville, Tennessee in a coffle gang, a march on foot of more than 500 miles that took two months. In Anderson's autobiography, he described the horrors he experienced in slavery:

> I have been sold, or changed hands about eight or nine times; I have been in jail about sixty times; I had on irons or handcuffs fifty times; I have been whipped about three or four hundred times. I lived at a place where I could see . . . wives taken from husbands and husbands from wives, never to see each other again—small and large children separated from their parents. . . . I have seen them and heard them howl like dogs or wolves, when being under the painful obligation of parting to meet no more.

Anderson's life was one of continual suffering until he finally escaped from his eighth master in 1836, following several failed attempts. His success was as much the result of luck as a good plan. Writing himself a pass—he had taught himself to read and write as a boy by observing scraps of paper with writing—he boarded a boat bound for Louisville. The crewman who examined his pass was skeptical but allowed him on nonetheless. Fortunately for Anderson, a gang of slaves was being transported on the boat, and the captain mistook him for one of them. It was only after the slaves disembarked that the captain realized his mistake. By this time, they were nearing Louisville, and the captain told Anderson that he would turn him over to the authorities when they reached Louisville. This was when Anderson's guile and cunning came into play.

"It grew late," Anderson wrote of this defining moment. "The cocks began to crow . . . Indiana was on one side and Kentucky on the other . . . I would have to make another bold strike. . . . I could not swim, neither could I fly, nor walk on the water. . . . A thousand thoughts would flash across my mind in a moment, for my time was now getting very short."

Just before daybreak, the opportunity came when one of the watchmen came to check on him. Anderson feigned sleep, snoring loudly. When the watchman moved on to another part of the boat, Anderson jumped into a lifeboat, cut the rope that secured it, and let it drop into the river. The steamboat continued on its way, and unobserved, Anderson rowed the boat to the Indiana shore.

On July 15, 1836, Anderson arrived in Madison, Indiana and found work as a laborer. He also joined the Methodist Episcopal Church. The next year, he married. He improved his reading, bought and sold land, and was promoted in his church, becoming a licensed exhorter and finally a preacher, taking charge of the small congregation. Having only a log cabin in which to worship, Anderson directed the building of a small frame building on Walnut Street that functioned as both parsonage and house of worship. His life prospered.

He also helped the needy and the hungry, including fugitive slaves, as he explained in his autobiography:

> In the good book we are commanded to feed the hungry and clothe the naked, and no mention is made of color or condition. Besides, I had learned by sad experience how the poor hound-driven slave pants for freedom from such inhuman bondage—how the heart is made to leap with joy when a friend indeed offers the protection sought. . . .
>
> My two wagons, and carriage, and five horses were always at the command of the liberty-seeking fugitive. Many times have my teams conveyed loads of fugitive slaves away while the hunters were close upon their track. I have carried them away in broad daylight, and in the grim shades of night.

In 1849 Anderson left his church and joined the African Methodist Episcopal Church, which was more active in antislavery matters. Although he severed his spiritual ties with his former church, he maintained his connection to it and directed the construction of a brick church for the congregation. He was always engaged in some business in addition to his ministerial duties, such as farming, selling groceries, or selling books.

In 1856 Anderson was arrested for stealing slaves in Kentucky. In his autobiography, which he wrote the following year, he admitted to helping as many as one hundred fugitive slaves but denied ever going South to entice them. His arrest may have been the result of authorities mistaking him for Elijah Anderson, another black conductor from southern Indiana, who for a time lived in Madison and who crossed into Kentucky on numerous occasions to entice slaves to freedom. Some believe that William, sometimes mistaken for Elijah's brother, may have provided authorities with information that led to the arrest and conviction of Elijah, which sent him to the Kentucky State Penitentiary. William denied this, but this belief is understandable considering that Elijah was arrested the same day that William was released after five days in custody.

Not long after this incident, William moved to Indianapolis. The arrest and resulting legal entanglements had set him back financially, and he was forced to sell properties in Madison to cover the costs. As a result, according to public records he was not permanently moved until 1859, but in his autobiography he dated the move to 1857. Nevertheless, he died in Madison, which indicates that he never completely severed his ties with that city.

Anderson's autobiography may contain some inaccuracies. For example, based on his claim to have been a slave for twenty-four years, he would have been an infant of one year old when he was sold into slavery and became part of the coffle gang that marched from Virginia to Tennessee for two months in 1812. It is more likely that he was closer to ten years of age at this time.

SUGGESTED READING: William Anderson, *Life and Narrative of William J. Anderson, Twenty-Four Years A Slave; Sold Eight Times! In Jail Sixty Times!! Whipped Three Hundred Times!!! Or The Dark Deeds of American Slavery Revealed*, Chicago: Daily Tribune Book and Job Printing Office, 1857; "The Story of the Georgetown District in Madison, Indiana," Underground Railroad Network to Freedom, Indiana Division of Historic Preservation and Archaeology.

B

Bailey, Gamaliel (1807–1859). Gamaliel Bailey, editor of *The Philanthropist* in Cincinnati, Ohio, and the *National Era* in Washington, D.C., was among the most influential abolitionists of the antebellum period. If it hadn't been for Bailey's foresight and courage, **Harriet Beecher Stowe** would never have written *Uncle Tom's Cabin.* Bailey's ability to mediate his position and compromise on issues helped forge alliances in the abolitionist movement that led to the Republican Party. It also enabled him to survive as an editor in hostile, proslavery locations such as Cincinnati and Washington, D.C., where he sometimes assisted those in the Underground Railroad.

Born in Mount Holly, New Jersey, Bailey was a short, slightly built man with an agreeable nature, but he had health problems throughout his life. His father was a devout Methodist Episcopal minister for sixty years, and Bailey's spiritual roots were a source of fortification throughout his life. After earning his medical degree in Philadelphia, Bailey signed on as a sailor on a voyage to China, as he had come from a family of mariners. When an outbreak of cholera occurred among the crew, he was appointed to be the ship's physician.

Returning to the United States, Bailey took his first editorial position at *The Methodist Protestant* in Baltimore, where he became a member of the American Colonization Society. In 1832 he signed on for an expedition to Oregon, but when it was cancelled, he moved to Cincinnati where his parents had relocated. When a cholera epidemic scourged Cincinnati, Bailey was appointed a physician at the Hospital for Strangers. The next year he married Margaret Shands, a well-educated young woman from a family of Virginia slaveholders.

The turning point in Bailey's life came in 1834 when he attended the Lane Seminary debates. The debates were instrumental in converting him to abolitionism, and he maintained a close association with many of the Lane rebels, several of whom later worked for his abolitionist publications.

Bailey was secretary of the Ohio Anti-Slavery Society in 1836, when it established a relationship with *The Philanthropist,* the abolitionist newspaper of **James Birney**, which began publishing that year. Despite its press being destroyed by a mob, the newspaper continued publishing with support from the Ohio State Anti-Slavery Society, and Birney hired Bailey as his assistant editor. The following year, Birney moved to New York to assume a more national role in the abolition movement, and Bailey took over as the editor.

The first great crisis of Bailey's professional career occurred in 1841, when his press was destroyed during a race riot that lasted several days. The riot was a reaction to the state legislature's passage of a law that automatically emancipated any slaves brought into Ohio voluntarily by their owners. The mob was armed and at times numbered as many as 1,500. It also targeted Bailey's home, but fortunately he and his family were absent.

Bailey's subsequent reaction to the crisis was characteristic of his ability to disarm his enemies and survive in a hostile environment. In order "to allay unnecessary excitement, and place ourselves in a proper position before the community," Bailey placated the proslavery element by denying that abolitionists were amalgamationists (those who believed in interracial marriage) or that they encouraged the flight of slaves—at least those abolitionists who published *The Philanthropist.* Although he did blame the racial conflict on the black laws, Bailey also said that the realization of the objectives of the abolitionists would decrease the northward migration of blacks. It was typical of his ability to play to both sides of the issue.

Bailey's ability to survive in hostile pro-slavery Cincinnati considerably enhanced his position in the Ohio Anti-Slavery Society, and enabled him to remove any control it had over his newspaper. This freedom allowed Bailey to seek a broader audience and to include coverage of other reform movements and the publication of literary works. He also expanded advertising and initiated pay-in-advance subscriptions.

While Bailey, the businessman, was solidifying the position of his newspaper, he was also working to advance the cause of abolition. In 1842 he defiantly published a list of abolitionists in the city to inform Southerners so that they could avoid carrying on trade with them: They included Bailey, Rev. William Brisbane, George Fry, Samuel Lewis, Thomas Morris, Salmon Chase, and Nicholas Longworth, among others. Notable among the list was Longworth, a prominent businessman, who had been opposed to *The Philanthropist* when it began publishing.

Bailey also opened his home at Sixth and College streets as a refuge for fugitive slaves, as his Christian beliefs would not allow him to turn away those who were homeless or hungry. And he worked behind the scenes to gain support for the Liberty Party, which he believed could be a forerunner of a more mainstream party that would gain a large enough following to eventually legislate the end of slavery.

Bailey's editorial skills gained him praise. Both Joshua Leavitt and Theodore Weld complimented him for his high journalistic standards and thoughtful editorials. Some suggested he was the best abolitionist writer of his time, and much more palatable than the often mean-spirited William Lloyd Garrison, editor of *The Liberator*.

In 1847 Lewis Tappan searched for an editor for a proposed newspaper in Washington, D.C., later named the *National Era*, to bring the issue of abolition to the doorsteps of the federal government, which many abolitionists believed was the source of the political power of the South. Bailey's success in hostile Cincinnati, coupled with his editorial abilities, made him the clear choice.

Bailey's prime motive when he began publication of the *National Era,* as the organ of the Liberty Party, was political influence. He sent his first issue to every member of Congress, and he announced that his "leading object" would be "to throw further light upon the questions of slavery." He also indicated that he would not attempt to force the Southern states to abolish slavery, but would support "their efforts by the moral influence of" his party. His stated belief was that if slavery were not eliminated through lawful means, a race war would eventually occur in the South when the slave population became too large to control.

Before long Bailey maneuvered his way into sole proprietorship of the *Era*, just as he had done with *The Philanthropist.* No longer affiliated with the Liberty Party, which had lost its national following, or with Lewis Tappan, Bailey shouldered full responsibility for the paper's operation. As a result, in 1848 he found himself in a position similar to the one he faced in Cincinnati in 1841.

An attempt to commandeer the escape of seventy-seven slaves from the port of Washington in a ship named the *Pearl* was discovered shortly after the ship left the harbor in April of 1848. Because the *National Era* was the most visible representative of the abolitionists, the newspaper took some of the blame. The night after the story broke, a mob went to the *National Era* building and pelted it with stones until drenching rain and police dispersed them.

On the following night, however, a demonstration was planned, and as many as 3,000 gathered outside the *Era* building. Several local leaders asked the crowd to disperse but they were shouted down. One persuaded the mob to allow him and some others to go to Bailey's home and try to persuade him to shut down his newspaper. When the group arrived at his door, Bailey greeted them politely. But when they demanded that he close down the newspaper, he was firm in his answer: "You are demanding from me the surrender of a great constitutional right—a right which I have used, but not abused." Bailey added that he would rather die than abandon the newspaper and be "a party to my own degradation."

After receiving this message, the mob marched on the *Era.* Stones and bricks were hurled through windows and against the door, and friends of the Baileys rushed the entire family to safety. The efforts of police and citizens to admonish the mob finally subdued it. The following evening President James K. Polk appealed to government clerks to aid the enforcement of law and order. The clerks assisted nearly 100 police officers in preventing a recurrence of the previous night. Also helping to deflate the crisis was a handbill written by Bailey and published in the city daily, the *National Daily Intelligencer,*

Fleeing from the Capital of Freedom: The *Pearl* Incident

On the night of April 15, 1848, seventy-seven fugitive slaves and three white men slipped down the Potomac River out of Washington, D.C., on a small schooner named the *Pearl.*

After traveling half a mile, the *Pearl* met the incoming tide and anchored. Near dawn the occupants resumed their voyage toward freedom. At the mouth of the river, strong northerly winds prevented the boat from sailing up Chesapeake Bay, and so it was anchored. By noon the steamboat *Salem,* with more than thirty armed men commissioned by slaveholders, was in pursuit. During the wee hours of April 17, the men boarded the *Pearl* while its occupants slept. Having no weapons, the fugitive slaves did not resist.

The three white men, Edward Sayres (the *Pearl*'s owner), Daniel Drayton, and Chester English were charged with stealing slaves, while most of the fugitive slaves were sent to be sold to new owners in the Deep South. In fact, the threat of sale had been the cause of the slaves' attempt to escape. Drayton was found guilty of stealing slaves, but Sayres was acquitted, and the charges against English were dropped. The mastermind of the daring rescue was William L. Chaplin, who led a campaign to purchase many of the captured slaves.

The escape attempt brought national attention to the ongoing clash between abolitionists and slaveholders over the existence of slavery in the nation's capital, and the widespread activities of the slave trade there. As **Frederick Douglass** so cleverly described it in the *North Star:* "Slaves escaping from the Capital of the 'model Republic.' What an idea!—running from the Temple of Liberty to be free!"

whose proprietor was the city's mayor and a neighbor of Bailey, in which Bailey denied any foreknowledge of or complicity in the *Pearl* affair.

The survival of this second professional crisis also led to further success. Adding substantial appeal to the *Era* newspaper was the regular appearance of essays and poems by John Greenleaf Whittier, who was the paper's literary editor. Bailey also attracted a number of other fine writers. But by far his most significant discovery was **Harriet Beecher Stowe**.

Bailey was well acquainted with the Beecher family who lived in Cincinnati during the entire period he lived there. He solicited some stories from Stowe, and then encouraged her to send him a story about which she had queried him:

> I am at present occupied upon a story which will be a much longer one than any I have ever written, embracing a series of sketches which give the lights and shadows of the "patriarchal institution" written either from observation, incidents which have occurred in the sphere of my personal knowledge, or in the knowledge of my friends . . .
>
> Up to this year I have always felt that I had no particular call to meddle with this subject. . . . But I feel now that the time is come when even a woman or a child who can speak a word for freedom and humanity is bound to speak.

Stowe had no idea how long the piece would be, but she said that once she began, the book imposed itself upon her. The story began as a serial, "Life Among the Lowly," and the first installment was published on June 5, 1851. It continued for nine months. During that period, a publisher was contracted. The book came out on March 20, 1852, and was an overnight sensation, becoming the most commercially successful book of the nineteenth century. Although Bailey had relinquished all royalties to Stowe, he did profit immensely as a result of the huge increase in the *Era's* circulation.

Bailey's success compelled him to expand his offerings and publish the *National Era* as a daily in 1854. However, competition from the *New York Tribune, Evening Post,* and *Times* during the next couple of years cut into his subscription list. The losses hurt Bailey financially, and he struggled to keep the newspaper afloat. Nevertheless, he maintained the *National Era*'s quality and continued to be "the pioneer press of Liberty on Slave Soil," as he described it. Among Bailey's achievements were the publication of material from twenty-one books that first appeared in the *Era,* and the continual offering of fresh voices such as that of Jon Henri Kagi, who reported on the war in Kansas and eventually died with **John Brown** at Harpers Ferry.

On June 5, 1859, while returning from a trip to Europe to restore his health, Bailey died at sea. The *Era* closed within the year. Bailey had tried to bring together those for freedom and those for slavery peacefully, always speaking out against slavery and its grave moral defects, always offering his Southern audience the opportunity to mend its ways, and never advocating the use of force to change them.

SUGGESTED READING: Stanley Harrold, *Gamaliel Bailey and Antislavery Union*, Kent, OH: Kent State University Press, 1986; Mary Kay Ricks, *Escape on the Pearl,* New York: William Morrow, 2007.

Beard, William (1787–1873). William Beard was a Quaker farmer and minister who lived in Union County, Indiana. He was born in Guilford, North Carolina, and his family was part of the large Quaker emigration from North Carolina to the Midwest because of their opposition to slavery. Beard worked with prominent abolitionists **Luther Donnell, Laura Haviland**, and **Levi Coffin**. It was said that the majority of those slaves passed to

Coffin's station in Indiana were forwarded by Beard, who lived on a farm near Salem, Indiana, which was near the state's border with Ohio. This is corroborated by Coffin's statement that Beard lived about thirty miles south of Coffin's Newport, Indiana, home.

In 1844 Beard came to Coffin and asked if he would like to accompany him on a mission to Canada to check on fugitive slaves they had sent there. Coffin readily accepted. After receiving the support of their Quaker Meetings, they set out on horseback on September 9. Along the way they visited black settlements in Ohio and Michigan, and on September 25 arrived in Detroit, where a Dr. Porter brought them to black schools and to families of fugitive slaves. The following day they crossed over to Windsor, Canada, and in that community and nearby Sandwich, they visited families whom they had aided.

From Sandwich they traveled to Amherstburg and stopped at the mission of Rev. Isaac Rice, where they made their headquarters. A Presbyterian minister, Rice operated a school for black children and a temporary shelter for fugitive slaves. He had been pastor of a church in Ohio before undertaking this mission six years earlier. Beard and Coffin visited all of the major fugitive slave communities. Only one, the Wilberforce Colony, had no residents whom they had aided.

Beard continued to work with Coffin following the latter's move to Cincinnati in 1847. Beard was a principal agent used by the Cincinnati Underground Railroad to forward slaves north. His general mode of operation was to bring a covered wagon loaded with produce to the city for sale and return with a wagonload of fugitive slaves. On one occasion it was reported that he hauled a load of fourteen fugitive slaves from Lane Seminary. The same source claimed that Beard transported hundreds from Cincinnati.

Beard was the conductor who received the fugitive slave Caroline and her four children in the Luther Donnell prosecution. Other notable passengers on Beard's freedom wagon included a slave girl named Jane from Covington, Kentucky, who along with her infant daughter was rescued by the black Cincinnati slave rescuer William Casey. They had been taken to Levi Coffin, who forwarded them to Beard. The latter took them to Randolph County, Indiana, where Jane entered the Union Literary Institute. After some months, she was forwarded to Canada for fear that her whereabouts might be discovered.

On another occasion while visiting Cincinnati, Beard received from Levi Coffin a slave girl who was under close surveillance. Coffin's wife Katy had created a disguise for her, dressing her in a nurse's uniform and giving her a rag doll to carry. Katy then dressed herself up in fashionable clothes and had the girl follow her to make it look as though she was the Coffins' nursemaid. They walked to the house of another local conductor, William Fuller, where Beard came for her.

Beard's Underground Railroad activities extended over a wide geographic area that included southwestern Ohio and southeastern Indiana. In Henry County to the northwest, a female antislavery society sent clothing to supply the numerous fugitive slaves Beard assisted, which likely numbered more than a thousand.

SUGGESTED READING: Levi Coffin, *Reminiscences of Levi Coffin,* Cincinnati: Robert Clarke & Co., 1880; Hurley C. Goodall, compiler, "The Invisible Road to Freedom through Indiana," as recorded by the Works Progress Administration Writers Project, Muncie, IN: H. C. Goodall, 2000.

Bearse, Austin (1808–1881). Born in the seafaring village of Barnstable, Massachusetts, the Boston Vigilance Committee's resident mariner Austin Bearse was going to sea by the age of eight. He worked on merchant vessels that not only traded with the South, but also transported rice, cotton, and slaves from the plantations for sale to the Southern ports. It gave him a firsthand view of the horrors of slavery. He recounted that as many as seventy or eighty slaves might be shipped at a time. What he recalled with particular anguish was the separation of families that sometimes resulted in slaves committing suicide.

These experiences during Bearse's youth turned him into an implacable foe of slavery. He became an abolitionist and a member of the Boston Vigilance Committee. His first notable mission was in 1847, when he sailed up the Hudson River to Albany, New York, in his yacht *Moby Dick* to rescue a fugitive slave in danger of being captured. Lydia and Abigail Mott had been harboring George Lewis, who had escaped from Virginia, finding him work and a place to live. But his true identity was learned, and a warrant had been put out for his arrest. Lewis had hoped to get to Boston to be with his daughter Lizzie, whose whereabouts he had learned from Boston minister and vigilance committee member Leonard Grimes on a visit by the minister to Albany.

The mission was successful, and Lewis was reunited with his daughter. He found work as a carpenter at a Boston shipyard during the next three years. Also, through the fundraising efforts of Rev. Grimes, Lewis's wife and five other daughters were purchased from slavery and joined Lewis in Boston. However, when the second Fugitive Slave Law was passed, they opted to move to Nova Scotia.

Bearse became the Vigilance Committee's all-purpose agent. In addition to transporting fugitive slaves, he was the official doorkeeper at meetings, posted broadsides, distributed handbills, collected donations, and delivered payments for expenses agents incurred while harboring fugitive slaves. Several opportunities also arose for him to put his skills as a seaman to work for the Committee, rescuing stowaways from ships arriving from the South. In 1853 the Committee learned that a fugitive was aboard the brig *Florence*, which had come from Wilmington, North Carolina, and was anchored just outside Boston harbor. On the morning of July 15, the Committee sent members Henry Kemp, John W. Browne, and **William I. Bowditch**, along with two black seamen under the command of Bearse.

When they pulled alongside, Bearse asked to see the captain. The sailor said the captain wasn't aboard but that he was the first mate. Acting as a government official, Bearse issued the following demand:

"Well, I want that nigger damned quick!"

The sailor obeyed without a question and brought them the runaway. The other members of the Committee shared a laugh at the charade Bearse pulled off. They dressed the slave, Sandy Swain, in a fishing outfit, and then took him to Brookline that night. From there he was taken to Framingham, then to Worcester, and on to Canada.

In the autumn of 1854 Bearse was sent after a fugitive slave on the schooner *Sally Ann*, also out of Wilmington, North Carolina, where the Committee had an informant. Again, Bearse demanded that the slave be brought to him, but this time instead of the expected obedience he was threatened with violence. He sailed off and devised a plan. He nailed a dozen coats and hats to the railing of his boat, waited until dusk, and returned to the *Sally Ann*. In the dim light, it appeared to the schooner's captain that Bearse now was accompanied by twelve men. The ruse worked, and the slave was quickly handed over.

Not long after this, the Committee learned that a fugitive slave from Jacksonville, Florida, was aboard the brig *Cameo* in dock at Boston harbor. Several agents were sent to look for the ship. When they found it, they obtained a search warrant. But instead of finding the fugitive slave on the *Cameo*, they found him on another nearby ship, the

William, the sister ship of the *Cameo*. The fugitive slave was then brought to the home of Lewis Hayden, where he stayed for two weeks, after which he was transferred to the home of Judge Nathan Brooks in Concord.

About this time, Bearse devised a scheme to operate as a pirate off the Virginia coast, harassing Southern ships patrolling for fugitive slaves. The scheme was taken so seriously that a special ship, the *Wild Pigeon*, was built for him just for this purpose. Bearse never did undertake his mission as a pirate in the *Wild Pigeon*, but he did use it for at least one mission to rescue fugitive slave John Allen in 1855.

Austin Bearse served the Committee until the end of its existence in 1861. His memoir, "Fugitive Slave Days in Boston," which told how he became an abolitionist and included the story of his involvement in the Boston Vigilance Committee was published in 1880, one year before his death.

SUGGESTED READING: Austin Bearse, *Reminiscences of Fugitive Slave Days in Boston*, Boston: Warren Richardson, 1880; Wilbur H. Siebert, *The Underground Railroad in Massachusetts*, Worcester, MA: American Antiquarian Society, 1936; Harold Parker Williams, "Brookline in the Anti-Slavery Movement," Brookline, MA: Brookline Historical Publication Society, Publication No. 18, 1899.

Benedict, Aaron Lancaster (1804–1867). Aaron Lancaster Benedict was a member of the Benedict clan, who were among the most active conductors of the Underground Railroad in central Ohio. The clan originated with his grandfather Aaron Benedict, who was born in Dutchess County, New York. Aaron Lancaster's father, whose name also was Aaron, moved to the Alum Creek Quaker settlement in Marengo, Ohio, founded in 1811 by his uncle Cyrus. Their settlement was directly in line with the Underground route that started in Ripley, Ohio. Stories about the Benedicts' involvement in the Underground Railroad began during the 1830s. Nevertheless, their participation could have begun earlier, as Ripley began aiding fugitive slaves as early as 1815. Among those most active in conducting slaves to Alum Creek were William Cratty, fifteen miles to the southeast in Delaware, Ohio, and **Udney Hyde**, forty-five miles also to the southeast in Mechanicsburg, Ohio.

Hundreds of fugitive slaves were aided by the Benedicts; the first recorded incident occurred in 1835. Four slaves, a mother and her children, were rescued from a slaveowner on the way to Missouri while he was camped on the banks of the Scioto River outside Columbus. They were hidden in Columbus, and then transported to Ozem Gardner's farm and on to the Alum Creek residence of Daniel Benedict, the brother of Aaron L., where they remained several days. With the help of two slavecatchers, the slaveowner traced them to the Benedict residence and spotted two of the children in the yard of Daniel, who was attending a church meeting. They attempted to abduct the children, but before they got very far, Daniel and others were able to stop them at the settlement gate. Justice of the Peace Barton Whipple was summoned, and he charged the slavecatchers with kidnapping and told them they were liable to a heavy fine. Daniel, however, suggested dropping the charges if the men agreed to leave, and the matter was concluded.

An 1839 incident in which the Benedicts played a major role involved a fugitive slave known as "Black Bill," alias Mitchell, alias Anderson, from the Kanawha Salt Works in Virginia. He came to Marion County in the fall of 1838 and worked as a butcher, barber, and laborer. "Black Bill" also was a talented fiddle and banjo player, and became popular at dances in Marion. Someone recognized him and informed his

Alum Creek Underground Railroad conductor Aaron L. Benedict. Courtesy of the Ohio Historical Society.

former master. In July 1839 eight representatives of the Kanawha Court House arrived to claim Bill as the fugitive slave of Adnah Van Bibber, and he was arrested and jailed as a fugitive from slavery according to Ohio state law.

Shortly before Bill's trial was to begin, his wife asked the assistance of the Quakers at Alum Creek. Among the nine men who went to Marion were Aaron L. Benedict and William Cratty. Learning that Bill's owner had brought witnesses and possessed evidence testifying to his ownership of Bill, it was decided that the only alternative was to plan an escape.

With the help of a black friend to accompany Bill, the Quakers planned to surround the two immediately following the judge's decision and block the path of the authorities while the two made their getaway through a nearby field, where two horses would be waiting. However, when the hearing concluded, the judge adjourned for his decision.

The next day the courtroom overflowed, the horses were in place, and the Quakers were prepared to resist. To their surprise, the judge ruled in favor of Bill, stating that the testimony only showed him to have been owned by John Lewis, a cousin of Van Bibber.

Outraged, the Virginians, armed with pistols and bowie knives, seized Bill and ordered the crowd to stand back. They took Bill from the courthouse and dragged him through the streets, while dodging stones and objects thrown by the citizenry. They took shelter in the office of a local judge. While the crowd attempted to break down the door, the sheriff intervened. He served a warrant issued by another judge, and with the help of the crowd broke into the building.

Bill managed to escape, running to the edge of a field where Aaron L. Benedict waited with horses. On the way, they were met by Aaron's brother Martin, after which they went to the home of their uncle, Reuben Benedict. With the Virginians locked up in jail, he was safe for the time being. After Bill had rested for several days, Aaron L. Benedict and his brother-in-law Griffith Levering took him to the Owl Creek Friends settlement, and then to Greenwich, before depositing him in Oberlin. From there, he was sent to Canada.

The summer of 1844 was a particularly active one. Daniel Osborn, one of the Alum Creek conductors not in the Benedict family, recorded aiding forty-five fugitive slaves himself during a five-month period from April 14 to September 10, 1844. All but two came from Kentucky; the two were from Virginia. Among them was a black man who had gone from Ohio to Kentucky and returned with his wife, child, and sister-in-law. Another was a woman who had come from Canada to Kentucky and brought back four of her children and one grandchild.

A much publicized incident in 1849 involved another member of the Alum Creek settlement, **Richard Dillingham**, who went to Nashville, Tennessee, and attempted to aid in the escape of a slave family suffering from the tyranny of a cruel master. However, they were caught en route, and Dillingham was sent to prison where he died. Aaron Lancaster wrote the *Memoir of Richard Dillingham,* which was published in 1852 and preserved Dillingham's story.

The passage of the Fugitive Slave Law of 1850 ushered in another period of high activity at Alum Creek. A particularly busy period occurred during the years of 1854 and 1855. This high activity corresponds to periods of high activity in others areas, such as Detroit, Michigan, and upstate New York. For example, one month during that period Aaron L. Benedict aided sixty fugitive slaves, and on one occasion entertained twenty for dinner. By 1857 Aaron L. had built a large brick house, where he hid fugitive slaves in a cellar under his kitchen. His notoriety had put a $1,000 price on his head.

SUGGESTED READING: E. Delorus Preston, Jr., "The Underground Railroad in Northwest Ohio," *The Journal Of Negro History*, Vol. 17, No. 4., October 1932; Wilbur H. Siebert, "A Quaker Section of the Underground Railroad in Northern Ohio," *Ohio History,* Vol. 39, No. 3, July 1930; Ralph M. Watts, "History of the Underground Railroad in Mechanicsburg," *Ohio History,* Vol. 43, No. 3, July 1934.

Benedict, Mordecai (1845–1927). Mordecai Benedict was the son of Daniel Bendict of Alum Creek and a member of the Benedict clan that founded the Alum Creek settlement in Marengo, Ohio, and may have been the youngest Underground Railroad conductor in history. He was only six in 1851 when he began driving fugitive slaves by the wagonload to the home of conductor Joseph Morris at the Shaw Creek Quaker settlement, a distance of nine miles. Mordecai's older cousin, Livius, the son of Aaron Lancaster Benedict, also drove wagons carrying fugitive slaves.

Mordecai was eighty-one when interviewed in 1926; he corroborated the reminiscences of his father's cousin Aaron Benedict, a younger cousin of Aaron L., and those of others that had been published in 1897. He lived in the same house then where he grew up, and he recalled the floors of the house crowded with sleeping fugitive slaves, and the names of conductors both to the North and to the South. They included Jason Bull in Columbus; Ozem Gardner in Worthington; Joseph Easton and Gardner Bennett, both near Alum Creek; and Joseph Mosher in Mt. Gilead.

One incident involving Mordecai dealt with a man who rescued his wife and two children from slavery in Kentucky. Elisha Young, a fugitive slave, came to the Alum Creek in 1857 and changed his name to John Green. He had left his wife and children, whom he hoped to rescue. Aaron Benedict gave him a job and also promised to help him rescue his family. During early autumn, Benedict and Green set out in the evening in a two-horse carriage and drove to Ripley. They met with John Rankin, and one of the Rankin family took Green across the river in a rowboat. Green was told that he should return to that spot and light a signal when he was ready to return. Naturally, all travel was to be done during the night, and Green set out on a sixty-mile journey into Kentucky.

Two weeks later, Green returned with his family. One of the Rankins retrieved the Green family, and on the following night they were returned to Alum Creek. About six weeks later, while Green was away hunting, several men arrived in a wagon late at night, entered his cabin, and abducted his wife and children. Someone spotted the wagon pulling away and blew the horn, warning the settlement of trouble. Green and Mordecai chased them on horseback to Delaware, Ohio, and attempted to get a warrant to stop them but couldn't find the sheriff. Finally they found a police official near Bellepoint on the Scioto River, just south of Delaware, but the official refused to serve the warrant. Green and Mordecai followed the kidnappers as far as West Jefferson, but there was nothing they could do to stop them.

When it was no longer safe for Green to remain in Alum Creek, he was sent along the Underground Railroad to Canada. After the Civil War he returned to the United States and went to Kentucky, where he located his daughter; he brought her and her husband back to Ohio, where they settled in Van Wert County.

SUGGESTED READING: E. Delorus Preston, Jr., "The Underground Railroad in Northwest Ohio," *The Journal Of Negro History*, Vol. 17, No. 4., Oct. 1932; Wilbur H. Siebert, "A Quaker Section of the Underground Railroad in Northern Ohio," *Ohio History*, Vol. 39, No. 3, July 1930; Ralph M. Watts, "History of the Underground Railroad in Mechanicsburg," *Ohio History*, Vol. 43, No. 3, July 1934.

Birney, James Gillespie (1792–1857). James G. Birney was among the abolitionist movement's greatest leaders. Although he wasn't directly involved in the Underground Railroad, he was personally connected to some of its leading figures, among them **Gerrit Smith**.

Born in Danville, Kentucky, to a wealthy slaveholder, Birney was educated by private tutors and graduated from Princeton in 1810. He studied law in Philadelphia, and at age twenty-three he returned to Danville and opened a law practice. After marrying the niece of a Kentucky governor, Birney won election to the state legislature. Having political aspirations, he saw greater opportunity in Alabama and moved his family and their handful of slaves to Huntsville, Alabama. His law practice flourished, and he became mayor of Huntsville.

It was in Huntsville in 1832 that Birney met the charismatic abolitionist Theodore Weld, who was on a trip sponsored by the Tappan brothers of New York to gather information for establishing a national manual labor college. Many have claimed that this meeting persuaded Birney to espouse the abolitionist cause, but he already was opposed to slavery, and Weld had yet to enter his abolitionist period. What the meeting did was set the stage for their important contributions that began two years later.

After Weld's visit, Birney sold his plantation in Alabama and moved back to Danville. He also was recruited to be an agent for the Colonization Society. He accepted with some hesitation. On his mission through the South, Birney found only mild support for the idea, because few wanted to give up their slaves. Following his mission, he wrote a series of articles in 1833, circulated in a number of important Southern publications, in which he advocated not only for colonization but also for a program of gradual emancipation. Slavery could be abolished, he believed, only through the political process. His suggestion was to abolish slavery first in Maryland, Virginia, and Kentucky. This would set the stage for a political solution to the problem of slavery. This idea, however, was not favorably received.

Abolitionist leader James G. Birney. Library of Congress, from a Currier and Ives print based on a Chilton daguerreotype.

In 1834 Birney visited Lane Seminary following the great debates on slavery. He was in the process of resigning his position with the Colonization Society and had composed a lengthy "Letter on Colonization" to explain his reasons. With the help of the Lane students, Birney had the letter published and distributed. He also renewed his acquaintance with Weld, which blossomed into a lifelong friendship. That year also saw him finally emancipate his six slaves.

By 1835 Birney was fully converted to the cause of immediate emancipation and, at the suggestion of Weld, committed himself to publishing an abolitionist newspaper in Kentucky. He made this known to various circles while attempting to organize abolitionists in the state. In April, Birney attended the organizational meeting of the Ohio State Anti-Slavery Society. After the convention, he embarked on an eastern lecture tour for three months, making known his desire to organize abolition in Kentucky. His opinions were highly respected, considering that he was a former slaveowner and past vice president of the American Colonization Society.

However, on his return to Kentucky, Birney found that opposition to his proposed newspaper had marshaled throughout the state. At first he ignored the warnings he received

Theodore Weld: The Abolitionist Orator

If any man deserved to be called the abolitionist orator, it was Theodore Weld. Although not involved in the Underground Railroad himself, he persuaded many others to take part.

To say that Weld was eccentric is an understatement. His appearance was unkempt, and he had little concern for shaving or even combing his hair. He couldn't remember people's names or faces, and would lose track of the day of week, sometimes even the season of the year. He was too abstracted in his thoughts. But once he gave power to them in speech, he became transformed. His voice was melodious, and the beauty of his powerful intellect would come to the surface. Once, after a visit from Weld, John Greenleaf Whittier, literary editor of the *National Era*, said that it was "as if an archangel had visited our home."

Weld's mesmerizing powers were first used in the cause of abolition in 1834 during the famed Lane Debates. The public discussion of slavery was held for eighteen evenings in Cincinnati. They drew nationwide attention, and led Weld to organize a team of seventy abolitionist preachers to travel throughout the North and organize antislavery societies calling for the end of slavery. By the end of the decade, there were about 2,000 antislavery societies with 100,000 members.

In 1839 Weld published *Slavery As It Is*, one of the most influential and bestselling books of the antebellum period. Worn out from incessant lecturing, which at times caused him to lose his voice, he retired to New Jersey with his wife, Angelina Grimke, one of the first female anti-slavery lecturers.

against publication. These warnings escalated to threats on his life, and he could not find a printer for his newspaper. Birney's family was harassed, and his friends began to avoid him. He realized that his home was no longer a hospitable place for him, and he moved his wife and children from Danville to Cincinnati.

Birney's intentions were to publish his newspaper in Cincinnati, but perceiving the pro-slavery sentiment of the city and receiving a warning from its mayor, Samuel Davies, he decided to locate his offices in New Richmond, Ohio. A small Ohio River town twenty miles east of Cincinnati, New Richmond was the home of Thomas Donaldson, a Welsh-born businessman who offered to financially support the paper if Birney published it there. The citizens of New Richmond also formed a vigilance committee to patrol the streets to protect the newspaper from disgruntled Kentuckians. The first issue of *The Philanthropist* came out on January 1, 1836.

The paper was anything but inflammatory. It simply made the argument that slavery and freedom could not coexist, and that unless slavery was abolished, an uprising by the rapidly increasing black population would eventually occur. However, the Cincinnati newspapers made false and provocative claims that stirred up the citizenry. A public meeting was called to discuss its effect on the community. Birney, who was living in Cincinnati, attended with his teenage son.

After listening to scurrilous charges against him and the paper, Birney boldly rose and asked to be recognized. For forty-five minutes, he made a rational and cogent argument for free speech that calmed the audience and disarmed their violent impulses. It appeared for a time that the hysteria had blown over, and it was enough to give Birney the confidence to move his offices to Cincinnati.

The Philanthropist's printer, Achilles Pugh, a devout Quaker abolitionist, supported the move, but Pugh's partners refused. Pugh contracted to print it alone. Unable to rent a building in which to locate the press, he erected one in the rear of his residence on Walnut Street. He undertook the printing as a matter of business. "If slavery cannot stand discussion," he said, "then slavery is wrong. Therefore, as a printer, it is in the line of my business to print this paper." By April the paper was made the official organ of the Ohio Anti-Slavery Society, and it had relocated.

Prospects were improving: the paper's circulation had doubled; Northern abolitionists expressed their approval, some finding its presentation preferable to that of *The Liberator*; on the surface the anger directed toward it had evaporated. Birney did not realize that there was a cauldron boiling underneath. Without warning at midnight on July 12, a band of men broke into his office, destroyed the week's issue, and carried away parts of the press. Nevertheless, Pugh purchased a new press and the next day was printing the weekly issue. Threats were made against Birney's life, but he persisted. On the night of July 29, a second mob broke into the office, tossed the press into the street, and were about to set the building on fire when Mayor Davies advised against it because of the danger to adjacent property. They then hauled the press by rope and cast it into the Ohio River.

Next, the mob went to Birney's home, preparing to tar and feather him. His seventeen-year-old son William answered the door, telling them Birney was out of town presenting a lecture. Going back inside, William stationed himself on the stairway leading to the door with a rifle ready to shoot the first man who tried to enter. Frustrated, the mob went into the black community and for four hours wreaked havoc on the neighborhood's homes.

Hearing of the riot, Birney waited a couple of days before riding into town on horseback during the wee hours of the morning. Nevertheless, his abolitionist friends advised that it wouldn't be safe for him to remain in Cincinnati until the situation cooled.

Birney was not about to be scared off, however. He moved the paper temporarily to Springboro, Ohio, about forty miles north, and his steadfastness and courage brought increased support and converts. Before long he moved back to Cincinnati. In October **Gamaliel Bailey**, who had been appointed by the Ohio Anti-slavery Society in April to help Birney, was made assistant editor. This gave Birney more time to spend on organizing and outreach, which were his greatest talents.

In 1837 Birney was drawn into the surreptitious world of the Underground Railroad, which he later confessed was mainly the work of black agents during the time he lived in Cincinnati. It involved his housekeeper, a young woman named Matilda. She had been a slave in Virginia when her master moved to Missouri. Traveling by steamboat, Matilda and her owners arrived at Cincinnati, and while the boat was docked, they went ashore. Matilda, who easily passed for white, slipped away and found refuge with local blacks. Shortly after, she found employment with the Birneys, who had presumed that she was free. Though the owner continued to Missouri without Matilda, he asked authorities to be on the lookout for her. She was discovered one day at the Birneys' home and was seized. Salmon P. Chase, whose abolitionist views had been formed during the Lane Debates, was hired as counsel, his first in a series of cases defending fugitive slaves. He argued that when a slaveowner voluntarily brought a slave into a free state, the slave automatically became free, an argument that Birney had developed in some of his earlier writings on slavery. However, the judge ruled against him, and Matilda was returned to her master.

Proceedings were brought against Birney for harboring a fugitive slave. The case was heard before the same judge, with Chase appearing as counsel. Birney was found guilty and fined. Chase appealed the case before the Ohio Supreme Court, and argued that as Matilda was not a slave, Birney could not possibly have harbored a slave. But the court upheld the lower court's decision. Reflecting back on the case, Birney would write Chase that he believed few things contributed more to keep the abolitionist spirit alive than did rescuing slaves.

At the end of 1837, Birney was called to a national stage and asked to become the secretary of the American Anti-Slavery Society, which was undergoing a rift among its leadership. It was hoped that Birney might be the man to help heal it.

Birney was a strong exponent of adding political agitation to the abolitionist crusade. "[A congressman] has almost daily occasion for agitation," he argued, "and he speaks to the whole people. We can reach the South through no other means. The slaveholders gain their advantages in national politics and legislation, and should be met in every move they make." Birney withdrew the national society's agents from organizational work and sent them to influence state and local elections, confident that this would increase the membership of local societies.

But Birney's advocacy of political action only increased the rift between the evangelical abolitionists led by the Tappans, who believed in political action, and the anticlerical Garrisonians, who opposed political action because they believed the constitution was a pro-slavery document. In 1840 a major split occurred in the American Anti-Slavery Society that spawned the first abolitionist political organization, the Liberty Party. Birney accepted the party's nomination as its presidential candidate in the upcoming election.

Gamaliel Bailey put the influence of *The Philanthropist* behind Birney and his running mate, Thomas Earle of Michigan, by calling a third-party convention in Ohio. Abolitionist leaders in the states of Illinois, Indiana, and Michigan came out in support. But it made little impression on voters, as the state abolition societies in those states refused to endorse the new party. With few third-party candidates running for state and local offices, few voted the Liberty Party line. Birney drew only 7,069 votes, running strongest in Massachusetts, Michigan, Vermont, and New York. Most abolitionists were Whigs, and with Burney having no chance to be elected, they cast their votes for the Whig candidate, William Henry Harrison, who won the election.

But the Liberty Party's organization gained momentum after that first election. It presented full slates of candidates on the ballots in the following years, and in the 1844 election Birney drew 62,300 votes. That election resulted in the defeat of Henry Clay. With the Liberty Party vote in New York State being larger than the plurality of his opponent James K. Polk in that state, it was New York with the largest number of electoral votes that tipped the scales of victory against Clay. It was a bitter defeat for the slaveholder Clay, who had been Birney's political idol during his early years in Kentucky politics, but whom Birney later viewed as a self-serving hypocrite.

In 1846 Birney was paralyzed by a stroke. After the death of his first wife in 1839, he had married the sister-in-law of Gerrit Smith, and had moved to Michigan. Thereafter, he retired from public life, living out his last eleven years as an invalid. His ultimate legacy resided in the development of political action to combat slavery. His leadership among abolitionists to pursue political action led to the development of the Free Soil and Republican parties, whose more mainstream ideas gained larger support for the eventual goal of abolishing slavery. This important development brought on the Civil War and resulted in the end of slavery.

SUGGESTED READING: William Birney, *James G. Birney and His Times*, New York: D. Appleton and Company, 1890; Betty Fladeland, *James Gillespie Birney: Slaveholder to Abolitionist*, Ithaca, NY: Cornell University Press, 1955.

Bowditch, Henry I. (1808–1892). Henry Bowditch was the son of the famed mathematician and scientist Nathaniel Bowditch, and a dedicated member of the Boston Vigilance Committee and the Underground Railroad.

Henry Bowditch wrote that his involvement in the abolition movement began as a result of his indignation at the near-lynching in Boston of William Lloyd Garrison in 1835. Bowditch's first important contribution to the cause came in 1842 after the attempted rendition of the fugitive slave couple, **George and Rebecca Latimer**, who had escaped from Virginia but who were recognized on their arrival by a Southerner. The latter sent word to Latimer's owner, who, within three days, arrived in Boston and had Latimer arrested.

Up to then no fugitive slave had been brought back to slavery from Boston. Bowditch joined with William F. Channing and Frederick Cabot to publish *The Latimer Journal* in order to rally public opinion against this. A week after the first edition, Bowditch provided Timothy Gilbert and **Rev. Nathaniel Colver** of the Tremont Temple with the $400 necessary to purchase Latimer's freedom. With the master of Latimer's wife declining to pursue her, the couple was now free. Nevertheless, publication of the weekly continued as Bowditch, Channing, and Cabot lobbied for a state law that would make the federal Fugitive Slave Law unenforceable in Massachusetts. With the help of the newspaper, they collected 65,000 signatures on a petition requesting the state legislature to prevent the rendition of fugitive slaves in Massachusetts. On March 24, 1843, the legislators passed a law that forbade the use of state authorities or facilities in the prosecution of the federal government's Fugitive Slave Law, severely hindering its enforcement in the state. Having accomplished its mission, *The Latimer Journal* suspended publication on May 16.

However, three years later, when a fugitive slave, who had stowed away aboard a ship in Boston, was captured and returned to slavery, the third incarnation of the Boston Vigilance Committee was formed. Forty members, including Henry's brother **William Bowditch** met at Henry's house "to secure the protection of the laws to all persons" attempting to flee slavery and who were in danger of being captured. It was shortly after this first meeting that Henry also participated in making the funeral arrangements for the slave rescuer **Charles Torrey**, who died in a Maryland prison after spending two years of his sentence for aiding fugitive slaves.

With the passage of the second Fugitive Slave Law, Boston's very visible profile in the abolition movement, and the ascent of Boston's very own Daniel Webster into the office of Secretary of State, the federal government focused its attention on making an example of the city in enforcing the new law. Three of the most famous of all fugitive slaves were then living in Boston: William and Ellen Craft, and **Henry "Box" Brown**.

When an attempt was made to kidnap Brown while he was in Providence, Brown opted to leave the country for England, where he could continue to present his panoramas on slavery and tell about his famous escape in a box. However, the Crafts had settled in Boston and did not want to leave. When representatives of their masters came to Boston, Ellen was put in hiding in Brookline, Massachusetts, for a time with William Bowditch. Meanwhile William Craft armed himself and openly vowed that he would shoot anyone who attempted to arrest him. He moved in with **Lewis Hayden**, who rigged his home with explosives in case an attempt was made to take Craft. Since it was public knowledge that Craft and a host of others were ready to resort to violence, the warrant for Craft's arrest went unserved. In addition, a campaign of harassment forced the slavecatchers to leave town.

Nevertheless, the Crafts no longer felt safe in Boston, and Henry Bowditch brought William to rendezvous with his wife. Having never been officially married as free persons, the Crafts then had Theodore Parker officiate at their wedding. In a dramatic gesture, Parker used a Bible and a sword during the ceremony and had William vow to use the sword, if necessary, to prevent him and his wife from being returned to slavery. Shortly after, Parker sent them on their way along the Underground Railroad to Nova Scotia, where they took a boat to England.

SUGGESTED READING: Austin Bearse, *Reminiscences of Fugitive Slave Days in Boston,* Boston: Warren Richardson, 1880; Vincent Y. Bowditch, *Life and Correspondence of Henry Ingersoll Bowditch,* Boston: Houghton, Mifflin & Company, 1902; Wilbur H. Siebert, *The Underground Railroad in Massachusetts,* Worcester, MA: American Antiquarian Society, 1936; Harold Parker Williams, "Brookline in the Anti-Slavery Movement," Brookline, MA: Brookline Historical Publication Society, Publication No. 18, 1899.

Bowditch, William I. (1819–1909). Attorney William Bowditch was as passionate about the cause of antislavery as his brother Henry and, like him, was a member of the Boston Vigilance Committee. William's house, still standing today in Brookline, Massachusetts, was often used to harbor fugitive slaves.

"Generally, I passed [fugitives] on to **William Jackson** of Newton," Bowditch wrote in an 1893 letter to historian Wilbur Siebert. "He could easily forward them, his house being on the Worcester Railroad." In addition to harboring Ellen Craft, Bowditch also provided a safe haven for John Brown, Jr., after his escape following the tragic events at Harpers Ferry. Bowditch also participated with **Austin Bearse** in at least one successful rescue of a fugitive slave, Sandy Swain, aboard a ship offshore from Boston harbor; Swain stayed with Bowditch until being forwarded the next day to Framingham. On another occasion, Bowditch transported a fugitive slave by wagon to Concord. He also boarded **Henry "Box" Brown**, following Brown's arrival in the Boston area, and employed **Lewis Hayden** in his law offices.

In 1854, following the rendition of Anthony Burns, which the Bowditch brothers had agonized over together during the emergency vigilance committee meetings that proved fruitless, they formed the Anti-Manhunting League to combat any further attempts by slavecatchers to apprehend fugitive slaves from

Ellen and William Craft and the Cross-Dressing Caper

Georgia slaves William and Ellen Craft had fallen in love but knew they needed to escape slavery or live with the constant fear of separation. As a result, they pulled off one of the most unlikely flights to freedom in all of Underground Railroad lore.

Because Ellen could pass for white, and because slave mistresses seldom traveled alone with a male slave, she and William decided that she would pose as a white man and he as her slave. However, Ellen couldn't read or write, and she didn't feel she could disguise her voice to sound like that of a man. To prevent this, they put a bandage around her jaw and her arm in a sling. It looked rather preposterous.

Nevertheless, the couple began their journey, with Ellen, having cut her hair and wearing spectacles, dressed in a top hat and man's suit. They had to travel nearly 1,000 miles, going by train to Savannah; by steamer to Charleston, South Carolina, and Wilmington, North Carolina; and by train to Philadelphia. For much of the journey, William had to remain in separate quarters reserved for black patrons. On one occasion, Ellen actually was engaged in conversation by a slavecatcher who wanted to purchase William.

After five days, on Christmas day in 1848, the train speeding the Crafts to freedom pulled into Philadelphia. In his narrative of their escape, *Running 1000 Miles to Freedom,* William wrote:

> On leaving the station, my master—or rather my wife, as I may now say—who had from the commencement of the journey borne up in a manner that much surprised us both, grasped me by the hand, and said, "Thank God, William, we are safe!" then burst into tears, leant upon me, and wept like a child.

Boston. William was made president, but apparently it was Henry who had come up with the idea for the league. In his unpublished manuscript, *Thirty Years of War with Slavery*, Henry described the conception of the league as follows: "I gladly accepted the thought of a secret league in Boston with affiliated leagues in various towns of the State to entrap and 'kidnap' . . . the slaveholder."

However, the plan was that, prior to a kidnapping, league members would locate the slavecatcher's place of lodging and send a large number of members there. They would then enter into a discussion with the slavecatcher to try to reason with him either to end his mission and return home or, if he were the owner of the slave in question, to sell him or her for a fair price. Naturally this discussion would be conducted with league members far outnumbering the slavecatcher. But if he would not agree to the league's terms, then the league members would abduct the slavecatcher and conduct him randomly from place to place, the uncertainty of the destination and the purpose striking terror into him and dissuading him from ever pursuing any slave in New England again. It was thought to be a good plan, but it was one to which they never had to resort.

SUGGESTED READING: Austin Bearse, *Reminiscences of Fugitive Slave Days in Boston*, Boston: Warren Richardson, 1880; Vincent Y. Bowditch, *Life and Correspondence of Henry Ingersoll Bowditch*, Boston: Houghton, Mifflin & Company, 1902; Wilbur H. Siebert, *The Underground Railroad in Massachusetts*, Worcester, MA: American Antiquarian Society, 1936; Harold Parker Williams, "Brookline in the Anti-Slavery Movement," Brookline, MA: Brookline Historical Publication Society, Publication No. 18, 1899.

Boyd, Samuel Gregory (1843–1931). In 1927 Samuel Gregory Boyd, an eighty-four-year-old resident of Glens Falls, New York, wrote about a tale from childhood that most everyone had forgotten and that had accumulated its share of skeptics over the years.

[Before the Civil War], he wrote, "the fugitive slave law was in force, compelling anyone called on by an officer to aid in capturing a fugitive slave." Related to this, he recalled an incident that accidentally touched his life.

One morning in 1851 when he was eight years old and he and his friend Add Stoddard were roller-skating on the sidewalk, a stranger approached them. The man had just gotten off a stagecoach and asked them if they knew where he could find John Van Pelt, a local black barber.

Naively, Boyd answered in the affirmative, but as he began to inform the stranger, Add interrupted. "He don't know, but I will show you," he said. However, instead of pointing the stranger in Van Pelt's direction, Add sent the man to the home of another black family. It turned out that Add had heard the talk about Van Pelt's wife being a fugitive slave and that her master was looking for her. The boys immediately went home to warn their fathers, both of whom were agents on the Underground Railroad. Van Pelt immediately took his family to safety by carriage. He returned to Glens Falls, sold his shop, and then joined his family in Prescott, Canada.

As the years passed, Boyd's story came to be questioned. It was the exaggeration of an old man, some historians concluded. But the story of Samuel Boyd was confirmed seventy years later by a local historian who unearthed several accounts from 1851. One was in the September 17 issue of the *Glens Falls Free Press*; another was in the *New York Herald Tribune* in which Van Pelt was interviewed by a *Tribune* correspondent. Van Pelt explained that his wife Lucretia was from Georgia and had escaped during a trip north in 1846. Her master had come to Glens Falls asking for payment for her freedom because he said he was being pressured by other Georgians. The newspaper added that the Van Pelts had moved to Canada.

On September 18 *The Pennsylvania Freeman* also ran the story and editorialized that "the woman is no more a fugitive slave than is the wife of Millard Fillmore, and she has an equal right, legally, to protection as a free citizen of New York. Is the sacrifice of women legally free also required as a compromise for the safety of the Union?"

SUGGESTED READING: Samuel G. Boyd, *In the Days of Old Glens Falls—As I Remember It.* Glens Falls, 1927; "Another Fugitive Slave Case," *Glens Falls Free Press*, September 17, 1851; "Slave-Hunting Excitement in Saratoga," *The Pennsylvania Freeman*, September 18, 1851.

Brown, Abel (1810–1844). The classic example of the evangelical Christian minister, Abel Brown grew up during the fevered ministries of the Second Great Awakening that scorched upstate New York and western New England during the early nineteenth century.

Born in Springfield, Massachusetts, in 1810 to a devoutly religious family, Brown was eleven when they moved to Madison County, New York. At age nineteen he moved to Fredonia in Chautauqua County, in the southwest corner of New York State, during a period of intense revivalism in that region. A year later he entered Hamilton College in Madison County to study Theology. Following graduation, he became a Baptist minister and took up the temperance cause.

Brown boldly confronted people about their sins and demanded their repentance. For example, during his early years as a minister, he went to the village of Auburn, openly avowing his temperance views and his intention to convert the people there. After spending a few days making observations, he called a public meeting to present his conclusions about the problems being caused by alcohol consumption. He also had made a list of the wrongdoers that he later said he meant to keep private. Somehow, it was taken from him and read publicly.

The village erupted. A mob of about 500 gathered while Brown was whipped at a local grocery. His journal described what followed: "I was . . . at last was forced to . . . submit to the fury of a mob, headed by a number of grocery keepers. . . . My 'crime' *was* that of visiting about one hundred Drunkards' families, and telling to the community their wretchedness."

Brown separated himself from the mob and fled into the woods, hiding out until late into the night, when the mob called off its search. It was not the last time his life was to be threatened for his boldness.

In 1837 Brown moved to western Pennsylvania. By this time he had become an abolitionist "in the full sense of the word," and he became a lecturer for the American Anti-Slavery Society. The next seven years of his life cast him into an incessant and obsessive drive to combat slavery. Mobbings, beatings, prosecutions, and death threats became part of his everyday existence.

One of Brown's causes within the overall cause was to rid the Baptist Church of its association with slavery. He sent a series of letters to abolitionist newspapers and made protests at Baptist conventions, attacking Baptist ministers in the South who owned slaves and demanding that the Baptist denomination cease fellowship with any Baptist who owned slaves.

Brown also became active in the Underground Railroad. His home in Beaver, Pennsylvania, near the Ohio River, became a frequent stop. He also began to travel into the South to rescue slaves. In one case he went to Baltimore and aided the escape of a

Virginia woman, crossing Mason–Dixon line near York, Pennsylvania. After forwarding the woman to another conductor, Brown was arrested and brought before the court. However, when sufficient evidence could not be found, the charges were dropped. In another case, he aided the escape of a fugitive slave from Louisville to Cincinnati.

In 1839 Brown moved east and took a pastorate in Northampton, Massachusetts. He joined the Massachusetts Abolition Society, which advocated that abolitionists become involved in the political process in opposition to Garrison, and Brown became associated with one of its leaders, the radical abolitionist **Charles Torrey**. In 1841 both Brown and Torrey moved to Albany, New York, and were active in the organization of the Liberty Party and the starting of a militant abolitionist newspaper, the *Tocsin of Liberty*. Brown was also involved in organizing the Eastern New York Anti-Slavery Society. His most productive efforts in the Underground Railroad began here.

Torrey and Brown were cut from the same cloth so far as their bold and uncompromising manner was concerned. With Torrey as a correspondent spending time in Washington, D.C., the two organized a gateway to freedom from the nation's capital to Albany. The *Tocsin* brazenly reported their activities on the Underground Railroad and published open letters to the fugitive slaves' masters proclaiming the slaves' successful escapes to Canada.

Among Brown's efforts here were those in behalf of a newly freed slave who needed an additional $200 to purchase his wife and six children from slavery. Brown wrote in the *Tocsin:*

> There arrived in this city from Washington D. C. during the last week, a man by the name of FREEMEN, a carpenter by trade. . . . He has formerly been a slave of the Hon. Mr. B., late Sec'y of the U. S. Navy, from whom he purchased himself for the sum of $800. The said Sec'y now holds in bondage his wife and six children; and utterly refuses to give them up unless the husband and father will pay him the sum of $1,800, and has promised to retain them nine months, to give the father an opportunity of purchasing them at the expiration of that time: otherwise they are to be sold, and perhaps separated, never more to meet on earth. Mr. Freemen wishes to obtain in this and adjoining places, the sum of $200, which with what he has now in his possession, will enable him to obtain from that *Honored American Robber,* that which now justly belongs to him. He is willing to work for a term of years, for any person who will furnish him means to thus bless his family.

With the organization of the Eastern New York Anti-Slavery Society (ENYAS), Brown developed a network of conductors from New York City to the lower Adirondack region. Assisting him was the New York Committee of Vigilance, some of whose members also sat on the executive committee of the ENYAS, which coordinated its Underground Railroad efforts. The level of their activity in the Underground Railroad is reflected in the following, taken from the June 20, 1842, issue of the *Tocsin of Liberty* and signed Forwarding Merchants, Albany, New York:

> The vigilance committee are up to their elbows in work, and are desirous to have you inform a few of those men who have lately lost property consisting of articles of merchandize (falsely so called) in the shape, and having the minds and sympathies of human beings, that we are always on hand, and ready to ship cargoes on the shortest notice, and ensure a safe passage over the "Great Ontario."

Among the members of the ENYAS was Troy minister **Rev. Henry Highland Garnet**, who was closely associated with the New York Committee of Vigilance. In a letter from that time concerning a fugitive slave, Garnet wrote: "The bearer is travelling northward, in quest of his wife (who obtained her freedom by operation of natural assumption), and he is also endeavoring to secure to himself the same advantage. I am under the impression that she did not go to Troy, but was directed to Mr. Abel Brown, of Albany, to whom I have directed some forty or fifty, within a short time."

In addition to his Underground Railroad participation, Brown continued doing outreach and lecturing. By this time his antislavery efforts had fully consumed his life so that he had no time left for a pastorate; he therefore resigned from his final position in Sand Lake, New York, in April 1842.

Brown's experience certainly refutes the claims by some revisionist historians that secrecy was unnecessary in upstate New York because slaveholders were unlikely to follow slaves to those sections. Unlawful searches, seizures, and assaults at the home of free colored persons in Albany were frequent occurrences. As Brown's biographer wrote, "The Vigilance Committee of Albany often found themselves in personal contest with slaveholders and their abettors, on account of the infringement on the rights of colored citizens." In addition, Southern slaveholders offered Albany law enforcement officials a reward for the apprehension of Brown, Torrey, and their associate and editor of the *Tocsin,* Edwin Goodwin.

The tumult of Brown's life was aggravated in 1842 by the death of his first wife, Mary Ann, a strong supporter of his activities, only five weeks after the birth of their second child. Brown placed his children in his parents' care in Fredonia and pledged to work with yet greater earnest for the cause of the slave. That fall he made a trip to Dawn, Canada West, to visit fugitive slaves he had assisted, and his lectures now often featured "interesting and intelligent fugitive slaves," who would relate their experiences to the audiences. One of them, Lewis Washington, was appointed as an agent of the Eastern New York Anti-Slavery Society and became Brown's regular traveling companion.

In May of 1843, Rev. **Charles Ray** of the New York Committee of Vigilance married Brown and Catherine Swan in New York City. Swan worked closely with Brown in his abolition efforts, often accompanying him to lectures and singing abolition songs. The summer of their marriage, they went on an abolition speaking tour that took them to Cleveland, Chicago, Milwaukee, and Detroit, meeting with some of the leading abolitionists of the region, including **Owen Lovejoy**, Zebina Eastman, James H. Collins, and Guy Beckley.

About this experience, Brown wrote, "The abolitionism was none of the half-way sort—there are no fence men here; but the friends feel deeply and think more deeply than many Eastern abolitionists."

During 1844 Brown continued his frenetic pace, touring the Adirondacks on two occasions. He moved to Troy that year, and his home continued to be a constant refuge for fugitive slaves. A serious riot occurred there when Brown was attempting to rally support for the Liberty Party. He was assaulted on the street but fortunately escaped serious injury. The pace of his life and the continued assaults were taking a toll on his health, however.

In November of 1844 Brown undertook a journey to central New York along with black lecturer James Baker, a fugitive slave. The men were caught in a storm during the night without a place to stay, and Brown became ill. Finally reaching the home of a friend and fellow abolitionist, Brown was taken in and given care. But it was too late; he contracted a case of meningitis and died on November 8, 1844, the day before his thirty-fourth birthday.

The *American Freeman,* an abolitionist paper in Prairieville, Wisconsin Territory, where Brown lectured on his western tour and where his mother had moved, wrote a lengthy obituary, an excerpt of which follows:

> He sustained for the last four years past, the relation of Agent to the Eastern New York Anti-Slavery Society. In every department of the Anti-Slavery enterprise, he exhibited a spirit that could not rest while so much was at stake and so much required to be done. In circulating anti-slavery publications, in urging religious denominations to practice the principles they avowed, and . . . in assisting, as a member of the vigilance committee, trembling Americans, to the number of not less than one thousand.

SUGGESTED READING: Tom Calarco, *The Underground Railroad in the Adirondack Region,* Jefferson, NC: McFarland, 2004; Tom Calarco, ed., *Abel Brown Abolitionist,* Jefferson, NC: McFarland, 2006 (reprint of Catherine S. Brown, *Memoir of Rev. Abel Brown,* Worcester, MA: C. S. Brown, 1849; Stanley Harrold, *Subversives: Antislavery Community in Washington, D.C.,* Baton Rouge: Louisiana State University Press, 2003; *The Tocsin of Liberty/The Albany Patriot,* Albany, NY: Abel Brown, 1841–1848.

Brown, Henry "Box" (1815–?). The celebrated fugitive slave Henry "Box" Brown was born at the Hermitage, a tobacco plantation of a benevolent slaveowner, John Barret, in Louisa County, Virginia, about forty-five miles northwest of Richmond. Brown worked primarily in the main house, waiting on his master's family, and was one of about forty slaves who included his mother, three brothers, and four sisters. Brown was a favorite of his master, and when he became an adult, it was said that his master raised him.

Brown admitted that he had it easy as a slave. For instance, he was never whipped. He was always nicely dressed and well fed, and his family was kept together when he was a boy. He also was allowed to pass freely among the neighboring farms and plantations. Brown lived his youth with the hope that his master's promise to set them free someday would come true. However, from his earliest childhood, Brown's mother warned him not to expect this.

As fate dictated, Brown's master died before emancipating his slaves. Brown was fifteen, and when their master's holdings were passed on, Brown's family was divided among his master's four sons. Along with his mother and two of his sisters, Brown became the property of William Barret, who lived in Richmond and operated a tobacco factory. While his mother and sisters remained at the Barret plantation, Brown was brought to live in a Richmond rooming house and work at the factory, which employed 120 slaves and thirty free blacks.

Brown's life actually improved when he moved to Richmond. Living in an apartment, away from the master, gave him more freedom. He also received a salary and was able to work overtime to increase his earnings. As a result, Brown took a wife, though with some reservations, because he realized that either of them could be sold and sent away at any time. Despite this, he attempted to persuade his wife's owner to promise not to sell her; as part of the bargain, Brown paid her owner for her services rendered as his wife. This promise was broken, and Brown's wife was sold several times. To their good fortune, she went to masters in Richmond. During this period, they had three children, and Brown joined the African Baptist Church of Richmond and became a devoted member of its choir. He struck up a close friendship with a leading choir member, a free black businessman and sometime dentist, James Caesar Anthony Smith.

One day at work Brown learned that his wife and children were to be sold to a minister and sent away. At once he went to his master and begged him to purchase his

The resurrection of Henry "Box" Brown. Library of Congress.

wife and children. But his master refused. Frantic to see his wife and children, Brown started over to the jail where they were being held until their removal, but he was stopped by a friend who warned him not to go. "They'll put you in jail and sell you too," the friend said, apparently because his wife's former owner had told some lies about Brown to his master, which had persuaded Brown's master to request the jailer to imprison him also if he went to the jail. So Brown sent a friend in his place. He learned that his wife and children were to be sent to North Carolina in a coffle gang.

The next day Brown stationed himself along the street where they were to pass: "Soon [I] had the melancholy satisfaction of witnessing the approach of a gang of slaves, amounting to three hundred and fifty in number," he wrote in his autobiography.

> I stood in the midst of many who, like myself, were mourning the loss of friends and relations . . . [They] were marched with ropes about their necks, and staples on their arms, and . . . this train of beings was accompanied by a number of wagons loaded with little children of many different families, which as they appeared rent the air with their shrieks and cries and vain endeavors to resist the separation . . . but what should I now see in the very foremost wagon but a little child looking towards me and pitifully calling, Father! Father! . . . My eldest child . . . My wife . . . jumped aside; I seized hold of her hand while my mind felt unutterable things, and my tongue was only able to say, we shall meet in heaven! I went with her for about four miles hand in hand, but both our hearts were so overpowered with feeling that we could say nothing.

For the first time in his life, Brown contemplated running away. Brown also left his church because he couldn't follow a religion whose ministers believed in slavery and did not care if they broke up a man's family and separated children from their mothers and fathers. About this time an account of four slaves from Brown's area who had escaped to freedom was published. Such accounts surely made Brown aware that the Underground Railroad was operating in Richmond.

Brown was likely introduced to one of these Underground men by J. C. A. Smith, who himself may have been involved in the Underground Railroad. Samuel Alexander Smith (unrelated to J. C. A. Smith) was a white shoe store dealer about four feet nine inches tall, who also was involved in a gambling operation, which may have been a front for his Underground activities.

Samuel advised Brown that a plan was needed, so Brown went home and came up with an idea:

> I felt my soul called out to heaven to breathe a prayer to Almighty God. I prayed fervently that he who seeth in secret and knew the inmost desires of my heart, would lend me his aid in bursting my fetters asunder, and in restoring me to the possession of those rights, of which men had robbed me; when the idea suddenly flashed across my mind of shutting myself up in a box, and getting myself conveyed as dry goods to a free state.

Brown agreed to pay Smith $88, half of his life savings (about $2,000 today), to assist him. Smith went to Philadelphia and met with members of the Philadelphia Vigilance Committee at the Pennsylvania Anti-Slavery Society Office. He told them of Brown's scheme and asked if Brown could be mailed to their office in a box. They were reluctant, warning that Brown could die, but Smith told them there was no way to change Brown's mind, and that he was determined to get his freedom, even if he had to die trying.

Brown had to manufacture an excuse to get out of work; he did this by intentionally injuring his finger. This injury, however, was not good enough for his overseer to excuse him, so Brown caused further damage by dipping his finger in acid. One look at his finger and the overseer excused him.

On March 23, 1849, at about 4 a.m., Brown met his accomplices, James and Samuel Smith, probably in Samuel's shop or office. There they shut him up in the box. Brown later wrote

> The box which I had procured was three feet one inch wide, two feet six inches high, and two feet wide . . . I went into the box—having previously bored three gimlet holes opposite my face, for air, and provided myself with a bladder of water, both for the purpose of quenching my thirst and for wetting my face, should I feel getting faint. I took the gimlet also with me, in order that I might bore more holes if I found I had not sufficient air. Being thus equipped for the battle of liberty, my friends nailed down the lid and had me conveyed to the Express Office.

On arriving at the shipping office to begin his journey, Brown wrote: "I had no sooner arrived at the office than I was turned heels up, while some person nailed something on the end of the box. I was then put upon a wagon and driven off to the depot with my head down . . . I had no sooner arrived at the depot, than the man who drove the wagon tumbled me roughly into the baggage car," so that he became upright again.

The first leg of Brown's journey, from Richmond to the outlet of the Potomac River was approximately seventy-five miles. At the river, he was put aboard a steamboat and the box was put on its end so that he was turned on his head again. "In this dreadful position," he wrote, "I remained the space of an hour and a half . . . when I began to feel . . . that my eyes were almost swollen out of their sockets, and the veins on my temple seemed ready to burst. I made no noise however, determining to obtain victory or death." Brown endured this for more than another hour when he began to pray. His prayers were answered when a workman in the baggage car moved his box so that he was no longer upside down.

The forty-mile steamboat ride took Brown to Washington. Here his box was thrown from a wagon, which caused a severe blow to his neck. Then, after the handlers debated whether to put him on the train to resume his journey because of the lack of room in the baggage car, they decided in his favor. Again he was placed on his head, but not for long, and thereafter he remained on his side for the next 135 miles from Washington to Philadelphia.

Meanwhile, Samuel Smith sent a telegram to Philadelphia, notifying the vigilance committee of Brown's forthcoming arrival. When he arrived, Brown waited in his box until a courier sent by the vigilance committee came for him. He was placed on a wagon and taken to the committee's office.

Inside the office, Brown heard the gathering around him, but kept quiet. **J. Miller McKim**, the society's director and a member of the vigilance committee, rapped on the box and said, "Is all right within?" to which Brown replied, "all right." After they detached the lid, Brown arose, feeling so weak that he fainted. After he came to, he broke out into a song he had vowed to sing if he were successful, from Psalm 40, "I waited patiently for the Lord."

William Still, one of the four men present—who also included McKim; Lewis Thompson, printer of the *Pennsylvania Freeman,* who lived in the building; and Charles Dexter Cleveland, a teacher at a nearby girls' school—wrote that "The witnesses will never forget the moment. Saw and hatchet quickly had the five hickory hoops cut and the lid off, and the marvelous resurrection of Brown ensued. Rising up in his box, he reached out his hand, saying, 'How do you do, gentlemen?' . . . He was about as wet as if he had come up out of the Delaware."

After cleaning up at the home of McKim, Brown was taken to a reception at the home of **Lucretia and James Mott**. The next two nights he stayed with Still. Thereafter, he was forwarded to New York City, where he stayed briefly before being sent to New Bedford, Massachusetts. This movement of Brown from Philadelphia to New York to New Bedford shows the Underground Railroad in operation.

Brown was immediately given laborer jobs. In May he attended his first abolition meeting in Boston, the annual convention of the New England Anti-Slavery Society. Brown was not the only fugitive slave to make his appearance at this convention that began on May 29, 1843. **Frederick Douglass** was there; so were **William Wells Brown** and William and Ellen Craft. Here on stage together were five of the most famous of all fugitive slaves in the history of the Underground Railroad.

Meanwhile, Samuel Smith was helping two more fugitive slaves who were attempting to follow the example of Box Brown and have themselves shipped to Philadelphia and freedom. On May 8, 1849, Smith had the boxes taken to the Adams Express shipping location. A worker became suspicious when he heard a grunt come from one of the boxes while moving it. The boxes were opened, and the fugitive slaves implicated Smith, who eventually was sent to prison for six and a half years.

It wasn't long afterward that Brown moved to Boston and was put on the abolitionist lecture circuit to tell his amazing story. In addition, Brown published the story of his life and escape, with the help of the New England printer Charles Stearns, who did the writing, as Brown was not very literate at this time, and who joined him on his lecture tours.

Brown was fairly successful in selling his book. Not only did he tell his story but he also performed as a singer. His success gave him the confidence to try a new form of entertainment called the Panorama, which functioned like a movie today. In the panorama, rolls of painted canvases of scenes were used to tell a story onstage while a narrator lectured or performers sang. The producer of the panorama would hire artists to paint the scenes, which usually were copies of various published paintings or illustrations.

Brown, in his panorama, decided to tell the story of slavery, and called it "The Mirror of Slavery." His panorama had forty-four scenes; some scenes included musical performances by him. In this endeavor, Brown was joined by his friend from the choir in Richmond, the free black man James Caesar Anthony Smith, who had helped put Brown in the box. Smith had been arrested for suspicion of involvement in the Underground Railroad but was released. He immediately fled to the North and located Brown in Boston, where they shared an apartment on Southac Street, the same street where **Lewis Hayden** lived.

In 1850, after the passage of the second Fugitive Slave Law, Brown was walking down the streets of Providence, Rhode Island, when he was suddenly attacked by two men who were attempting to kidnap him back into slavery. He was able to fight them off, but he decided that his notoriety had made it unsafe for him to remain in America. So he decided to go to England, where other American fugitive slaves had gone and been quite successful on the lecture circuit.

By the time Brown went to England, he had entered a partnership with James Caesar Smith, now being called Boxer because of his help in shipping Brown. While in England, they published a revised version of Brown's narrative and presented his panorama, which had been shipped to England along with his celebrated box. Having sung together for years in the church choir, they now performed together on stage during the presentation of the panorama.

However, something went wrong with the partnership. Apparently Brown and Smith had a falling out, because Brown had taken a liking to the nightlife and was doing a little drinking and partying, which conflicted with the temperance principles of Smith. Perhaps even more discomforting to Brown was Smith's nagging him about using his earnings to pay for the freedom of Brown's wife and children in America. To obtain donations, the pair sometimes used the ploy that Brown needed money to free his family. In any case, their partnership ended less than nine months after they arrived in England.

Brown became more and more of a showman after his parting with Smith. On one occasion he staged a reenactment of his escape to freedom. Enclosed in his box, he was paraded in a wagon down the main street of Leeds, England, to the theater where he was showing his panorama at the opening of a run of performances.

Brown continued to show his panorama in England throughout the 1850s. By 1859, at the age of forty-four, he remarried, and he and his new wife, an actress, began showing a second panorama about the English warfare then occurring in India. By the 1860s Brown had enlarged his talents to include mesmerism, or hypnotism, which had become a fad.

Once the fascination with mesmerism subsided, Brown became a magician. His persona also had taken on the titles of African prince and professor. He now had a daughter who had grown up as part of his act. After the publication of William Still's book in 1872 brought Brown back into the public eye, he and his family brought their magic act to America. From 1875 to 1878 they toured the theaters. In 1878, Brown was sixty-three, and that is the last that is known of him.

SUGGESTED READING: Henry Brown, *Narrative of Henry Box Brown, Who Escaped from Slavery Enclosed in a Box Three Feet Long, Two Wide, and Two and a Half High*, Boston: Brown & Stearns, 1849 (available electronically through Chapel Hill Library at the University of North Carolina); Henry Brown, *Narrative of the Life of Henry Box Brown*, Manchester, England: Lee and Glynn, 1851 (available electronically through Chapel Hill Library at the University of North Carolina); Jeffrey Ruggles, *The Unboxing of Henry Brown*, Richmond, VA: Library of Virginia, 2003; William Still, *The Underground Railroad*, Philadelphia: Porter & Coates, 1872, (rev. 1886), reprinted, New York: Arno Press, 1968; "New England Anti-Slavery Convention," *The Liberator*, June 8, 1849; "Attempt to Kidnap a Colored Woman," *The Liberator*, September 6, 1850.

Brown, John (1800–1859). Abolitionist John Brown was the quintessential example of a legend in his own time. Today, more than 150 years after his death, he remains the subject of controversy. Believing himself to be the chosen agent of God to deliver America's slaves from bondage, Brown was driven by an all-consuming passion that no one has fully explained. The mesmerizing effect he had on those he met and the power of his persona lit the conflagration of the Civil War that brought an end to slavery in America.

Brown was born in Torrington, Connecticut, to a strict, religious, and patriotic family. Both of his grandfathers had fought in the Revolutionary War, one of them giving his life. When Brown was five, his family moved to Hudson, Ohio, which was still a wilderness populated mainly by Native Americans. When Brown was eight, his mother died, which saddened him throughout his youth. He had little schooling as a boy and was mostly self-taught, reading books about great men and the Bible, much of which he committed to memory. Headstrong from his earliest days, Brown listened to no one but his conscience and the word of God.

Brown's father, Owen, taught him the tanner's trade and the art of raising livestock, both of which he used later in life as a means of livelihood. Owen provided beef to the army during the War of 1812, and he sent John on cattle drives as long as 100 miles when John was only twelve years old. As an adult, John learned another trade, surveying, which he later used to disguise his abolitionist intentions.

Brown inherited his hatred of slavery from his father, who was an abolitionist from his earliest days. However, he had his own personal experience that reinforced his father's strong abhorrence of slavery. During one of his cattle drives, Brown stayed with one of his father's business acquaintances, who owned a slave about Brown's age. The misery of the slave, who was poorly clothed, insufficiently fed, without a mother or father, and beaten with a shovel, was the real beginning of Brown's "eternal war on slavery."

At the age of sixteen, Brown joined the Congregational Church at Hudson and considered studying for the ministry, entering a preparatory school in Connecticut. However, he found it difficult to concentrate, and returned home and married Diantha Luske, his first wife. They had seven children, two of whom died in infancy. Among the earliest recollections of Brown's first son, John Brown, Jr., was of his father aiding fugitive slaves:

> When I was four or five years old, and probably no later than 1825, there came one night a fugitive slave and his wife to father's door,—sent, perhaps, by some townsman who knew John Brown's compassion for such wayfarers. . . . Mother gave the poor creatures some supper; but they thought themselves pursued, and were uneasy.
>
> Presently father heard the trampling of horses . . . so he took his guests out the back door . . . giving them arms to defend themselves. . . . It proved a false alarm: the horsemen were people of the neighborhood going to Hudson village. Father . . . brought them into the house again, sheltered them awhile, and sent them on their way.

John Brown, circa 1850. Courtesy of the Massachusetts Historical Society.

In 1826 Brown moved to Richmond, Pennsylvania, a rural village ten miles east of present day Meadville, where he lived for ten years. Here he established a tannery, served as postmaster, and was active in organizing a Congregational society. Brown hid fugitive slaves in the haymow of his barn, where he constructed a hidden room that could be entered by a trap-door.

It was in Richmond that Diantha died during childbirth. Brown married Mary Ann Day, a girl of sixteen who did sewing for the Brown family. A large, strong woman, she bore thirteen children in a span of twenty-one years, seven who died in childhood and two at Harpers Ferry.

In 1835 financial difficulties caused Brown to become a partner in a tanning business in Kent, Ohio. It led to further financial problems when he made some unwise speculations. Brown declared bankruptcy but continued trying to make his fortune by breeding race horses, driving cattle, and finally breeding sheep.

Despite being consumed by his business affairs, Brown maintained his fervent interest in the antislavery movement. He was a subscriber to *The Liberator* and *The Philanthropist*, and, in later years, the *North Star* and the *National Era.* When abolitionist editor Elijah Lovejoy was murdered in 1837, Brown and his father attended a memorial service. Before it ended, Brown raised his hand, requesting to speak. "Here, before God, in the presence of these witnesses, from this time," he proclaimed, "I consecrate my life to the destruction of slavery!"

Shortly after, Brown united his family in a formal consecration of his mission. His son John Jr. later recalled the incident:

> Father, mother, Jason, Owen and I were . . . seated around the fire in the open fire-place of the kitchen . . . and there he first informed us of his determination to make war on slavery . . . He said that he had long entertained such a purpose—that he believed it his duty to devote his life, if need be, to this object. . . . After prayer he asked us to raise our right hands, and he then administered to us an oath, the exact terms of which I cannot recall, but in substance it bound us to secrecy and devotion to the purpose of fighting slavery by force and arms to the extent of our ability.

Brown moved from Kent to Richfield, Ohio, where he supervised the sheep of Captain Heman Oviatt. Although it was a period of financial stability, as Brown was absolved of bankruptcy, it was also one of great personal tragedy. In 1843 during a plague of dysentery, four of Brown's children died within less than two weeks, three of them buried the same day.

Two years later Brown moved the family to Springfield, Ohio, representing Simon Perkins, a wealthy businessman with whom he had formed a partnership. Brown's job was to help wool growers evaluate and price their goods, and to sell Midwestern wool. It was in Springfield in 1847 that Brown first met **Frederick Douglass**, who described the meeting in his 1881 autobiography:

> [Brown] was a respectable [wool] merchant . . . and our first place of meeting was at his store. This was a substantial brick building, on a prominent, busy street. A glance at the interior, as well as at the massive walls without, gave me the impression that the owner must be a man of considerable wealth.

Douglass learned the truth, however, when he was brought to Brown's home.

> I was, however, a little disappointed with the appearance of the house and with its location. . . . In fact, the house was neither commodious nor elegant, nor its situation desirable. . . . Plain as was the outside . . . the inside was plainer. . . . My first meal [was] . . . beef soup, cabbage, and potatoes; a meal such as a man might relish after following the plow all day . . . the table announced itself unmistakably of pine and of the plainest workmanship. There was no hired help visible. The mother, daughters, and sons did the serving and did it well. . . . In [this house] there were no disguises, no illusions, no make believes. Everything implied stern truth, solid purpose, and rigid economy. I was not long in company with the master of this house before I discovered that he was indeed the master of it, and was likely to become mine too if I stayed long enough. . . . His wife believed in him, and his children observed him with reverence. Whenever he spoke, his words commanded earnest attention. . . . Certainly I never felt myself in the presence of a stronger religious influence than while in this man's house.
>
> In person he was lean, strong, and sinewy, of the best New England mould, built for times of trouble, fitted to grapple with the flintiest hardships. Clad in plain American woolen, shod in boots of cowhide leather, and wearing a cravat of the same substantial material, under six feet high, less than 150 pounds in weight, aged about fifty, he presented

> a figure, straight and symmetrical as a mountain pine. . . . His head was not large, but compact and high. His hair was coarse, strong, slightly gray and closely trimmed, and grew low on his forehead. His face was smoothly shaved, and revealed a strong square mouth, supported by a broad and prominent chin. His eyes were bluish gray, and in conversation they were full of light and fire. When on the street, he moved with a long, springing racehorse step, absorbed by his own reflections.

That evening Brown described his dream of leading a large-scale slave revolt in the South. His idea was to organize a guerilla army that would undertake missions from somewhere in the Allegheny Mountains and entice slaves to liberate themselves and join them.

> God has given the strength of the hills to freedom. They were placed here for the emancipation of the Negro race; they are full of natural forts, where one man for defense will be equal to a hundred for attack; they are full also of good hiding-places, where large numbers of brave men could be concealed, and baffle and elude pursuit for a long time.

Brown added that he would send those who did not join him North by the Underground Railroad. Brown made a strong impression on Douglass, who said that his own antislavery militancy originated from this meeting.

That same year Brown met another black man with whom he became close friends. The free son of a white Southerner and a black woman, Willis Augustus Hodges had been a farmer in Virginia and was one of the foremost supporters of black agriculture in the North. He and Brown became friends after Hodges began publishing the black newspaper *The Ram's Horn* in 1847. Hodges subsequently published "Sambo's Mistakes," a satirical essay by Brown, in which he posed as a black author criticizing other blacks for their submissiveness to racism. It was Hodges who told Brown about black farming colonies in upstate New York that had formed with land given by **Gerrit Smith**.

Brown decided to see for himself. When he first gazed upon the snow-capped peaks of the Adirondacks, he said he felt the presence of God. It was 1848, and he found the black farmers huddled together in crude dilapidated wooden shacks with stovepipes for smokestacks. They had named their colony Timbucto, which was in the town of North Elba, just south of present-day Lake Placid. After his visit, Brown wrote Smith, offering his services to move there and help.

> I am something of a pioneer. I grew up among the woods and wild Indians of Ohio, and am used to the climate and the way of life that your colony finds so trying. I will take one of your farms myself, clear it up and plant it, and show my colored neighbors how much work should be done; will give them work as I have occasion, look after them in all needful ways, and be a kind of father to them.

In April 1848 Brown showed up at Smith's mansion after riding on horseback for several days from Springfield, a distance of about 150 miles. Brown was dressed in a ragged homespun shirt, holey boots, and a shabby Sunday dress jacket soiled with mud and blood. He also was packing a revolver. Nevertheless, Brown's farming knowledge and passion impressed Smith, who agreed to sell Brown land in the area for a small sum.

In the meantime Brown's friend Hodges emigrated to the northern New York wilderness. With funds from the sale of *The Ram's Horn*, he purchased a 200-acre plot overlooking Loon Lake. On May 12, 1848, Hodges, his family, and eight others arrived in Franklin County, where they formed a colony called Blacksville about twenty miles from the Smith lands in North Elba.

A year later Brown moved his family from Springfield to North Elba. He first rented a small house, a two-story dwelling, although the second story was unfinished and little more than an attic.

Nevertheless, Brown was still trying to make a go of his wool business. In an attempt to open an export trade to England, Brown shipped wool there. In September of 1849 he undertook a voyage to England to promote its sale. It turned into another financial setback, as he was forced to sell the wool at a loss. Brown also used the time to visit European fortifications and battle sites, an indication that he was already planning his military assault on slavery.

Brown returned to North Elba, and he and his sons bought the farm that would be his eventual resting place. The land was poorly suited for crops, but he managed to sustain a living. He is said to have participated in the Underground Railroad and to have collaborated with others, including Hodges, whose sons claimed that their home was an Underground Railroad station. Lyman Epps, a free black who was five at the time, remembered Brown assisting fugitive slaves there. "After John Brown come, they got him to help 'em into Canada," Epps said, adding that Brown transported his passengers in an oxcart.

Although Brown raised prizewinning Devon cattle, which he showed at the County Agricultural Fair in 1850, this triumph was followed by the second Fugitive Slave Law. Brown seemed to welcome the law, seeing it as an opportunity for action. "It now seems the fugitive slave law was to be the means of making more abolitionists than all the lectures we have had for years," he wrote to his wife Mary from Springfield. Attending to his wool business there, Brown contacted black friends who had been fugitives and organized a militant band of forty-four black men and women, whom he called the Gileadites in reference to the biblical passage: "Whosoever is fearful or afraid, let him return and depart early from Mount Gilead." In a manual he wrote for his followers, he urged them to arm themselves, defy the Fugitive Slave Law, and refuse to be taken alive.

When he returned to North Elba, Brown gave similar instructions to his family and the black farmers there. However, obligations to his business partner Perkins forced Brown to move back to Akron, Ohio. He also was faced with a series of lawsuits brought on by financial losses suffered by wool customers, suits that could have severely damaged the fortune of Perkins.

For two years Brown dealt with one case after another, and was fortunate to win several. When the final case was closed, Brown was penniless. Meanwhile, he terminated his partnership with Perkins, which ended on friendly terms despite the losses. Brown was determined now to return to North Elba, but in order to raise the necessary funds, he had to work three farms, which he rented the next year.

On May 30, 1854, an event occurred that marked a turning point in Brown's life: the passage of the Kansas-Nebraska Act. It allowed territories north of Missouri the right to choose whether or not to allow slavery, nullifying the Missouri Compromise. It signaled the start of a contest between antislavery and proslavery groups over the fate of the future state of Kansas.

Brown wrote an angry letter to *Frederick Douglass's Paper* opposing the act. His sons also were upset, and his five oldest sons, John Jr., Jason, Owen, Frederick, and Salmon, all residents of Ohio, agreed to move to Kansas and support the side of freedom. In August 1854 John Jr. wrote his father, urging him to join them. Brown encouraged them to go but said he had other plans.

As it turned out, after Brown moved his wife and Mary and their children back to North Elba, he changed his mind. In letters from Kansas, John Jr. had explained the difficulties and the discrimination he and his brothers, as Northerners, faced in certain areas from Southern settlers. A battle was brewing, and John Jr. said the Southerners were well armed. He asked his father to bring guns.

In the summer of 1855, at a convention organizing the Radical Abolitionist party in Syracuse, Brown offered his services to fight for freedom in Kansas and asked for contributions. The president of the convention was longtime New York Committee of Vigilance member James McCune Smith; other leading members were Gerrit Smith, Frederick Douglass, Samuel May, Arthur Tappan, William Goodell, and **Jermaine Loguen**. Gerrit Smith read aloud the letters of Brown's sons, which stated that large armed groups of proslavery vigilantes were coming into Kansas from Missouri to intimidate the settlers and that Free-Staters needed more support. Douglass and some others endorsed Brown, but the convention did not give full endorsement. Rather, the hat was passed, and $60 was raised, though Gerrit Smith and others contributed additionally behind the scenes, with Smith providing Brown both money and guns.

Brown brought his son Oliver and son-in-law Henry Thompson with him to Kansas. In Iowa Brown bought a horse and covered wagon, concealing Sharps rifles that he had purchased. On the way, Brown disinterred the body of his four-year-old grandson Austin, the son of Jason, who had died during a cholera epidemic on the trip earlier that year. On October 7, 1855, Brown arrived to find his family living in tents and in poor condition.

With a proslavery and a Free State government opposing each other, a battle loomed in Lawrence, Kansas two months after Brown's arrival. Brown and three of his sons were among 500 Free-Staters ready to defend the town against 2,000 proslavery men. Fortunately, the intercession of the Territory's governor, Wilson Shannon, averted hostilities in a confrontation that came to be known as the Wakarusa War.

There is no doubt, however, that Brown's primary motive in going to Kansas, where he now was referred to as Captain Brown, was to begin his personal war on slavery. An interview he had with journalist William A. Phillips on July 2, 1856, testified to this. Philips wrote:

> I soon discovered that his tastes ran in a military rather than a commercial channel. He had visited many of the fortifications in Europe, and criticized them sharply, holding that the modern system of warfare did away with them, and that a well armed, brave soldier was the best fortification. He criticized all the arms then in use, and showed me a fine specimen of repeating-rifle which had long-range sights, and, he said, would carry eight hundred yards; but, he added, the way to fight was to press to close quarters.

The interview was a month after Brown's celebrated victory at the Battle of Black Jack, which has been called the first battle of the Civil War, a battle in which Brown's band of about fifteen men overcame a force of fifty proslavery men led by H. C. Pate. It was precipitated by two earlier events: the sacking of Lawrence and the infamous Pottawatomie massacre. In the first, the presses and offices of two Free State newspapers in Lawrence were destroyed, the town was vandalized and looted, and the Free State Hotel and the home of Free State party founder Charles Robinson were burned to the ground. Three days later, the massacre of five proslavery settlers at Pottawatomie was carried out by Brown and his sons, perhaps the most notorious and misunderstood event in Brown's life.

Historians have cited some of Brown's motivations: the sacking of Lawrence, and Brown's anger at the passive response of his Free State brethren, who did nothing to stop the mayhem. They also have noted the caning of Charles Sumner in the Senate, which was widely publicized and known to have upset Brown. But in recent years it has also been brought out by revisionist historians that the proslavery men slain by the Browns were not as peaceful as they had been portrayed. In fact, they had burned homesteads in the Osawatomie area and, according to Brown, were planning to kill him and his family. He had learned this firsthand when he posed as a surveyor and entered one of the proslavery camps.

It was also a calculated move. Brown aimed to inflict a savage blow that would strike fear into the forces of slavery and rally his abolitionist brethren. After going off alone to pray to God for direction, Brown led his sons to the home of three proslavery families who lived along the Pottawatomie Creek. Armed with broadswords, Brown's sons Frederick, Owen, and Salmon, along with his son-in-law Henry Thompson and their neighbor Theodore Weine, brutally hacked five men to death, cutting off the hand of one and the arms of another. Among those killed were James P. Doyle, a violent and outspoken racist, and two of his sons, Brown sparing the youngest Doyle son at the plea of his mother.

Later in Missouri Doyle's wife testified before a hearing that served a warrant for Brown's arrest and described Brown as a demon. But the Battle of Black Jack that occurred only a week later served to make Brown a hero, and his later defense of his settlement at Osawatomie with thirty men against an army of 250, as well as his escape after he had been reported killed, served to feed the legend of "Osawatomie Brown."

At Black Jack, Pate's company had set out to avenge Pottawatomie. They swooped down upon the camps of Brown's sons John and Jason, and took them captive. As soon as Brown learned of this, he gathered his band of Free State men and tracked Pate's company down to their camp at a point called Black Jack, where a three-hour battle took place. Brown's victory owed much to the use of tactics in which Brown employed a cross fire on the camp that intimidated his foes and caused some to take flight and the remainder to surrender.

Nevertheless, only the intercession of federal troops quelled the bloodshed as the pro-slavery forces, given the name Border Ruffians, had initiated a rampage of terror following Pottawatomie that culminated in the burning of the settlement at Osawatomie and the death of Brown's son Frederick. As Brown fled his Osawatomie homestead, watching his home being engulfed by smoke and flames, he said to his son Jason, tears streaming down his face, "God sees it. I have only a short time to live—only one death to die, and I will die fighting for this cause. There will be no more peace in this land until slavery is done for. I will give them something else to do than to extend slave territory."

From this point forward, Brown would be a fugitive from justice, something that would follow him the rest of his life. Injured in the battle at Osawatomie, Brown headed north with his son Owen and a band of other followers. Warrants had been served on him for the Pottawatomie murders, and federal troops were pursuing him. Slowly, Brown and his followers made their way to the Nebraska border with a fugitive slave hidden in one of their wagons. They continued on to Iowa and the fervently religious and abolitionist community of Tabor, Iowa, which had developed a fairly busy Underground Railroad terminal under the direction of Rev. **John Todd**, and where Brown had earlier sought care for his injured men after the Battle of Black Jack. When Brown regained his strength, he headed back east. The rest of his life was now spent recruiting his army for his war to end slavery and raising money to support it.

After meeting with Douglass and Gerrit Smith, Brown went to Boston where, for the first time, he met Franklin Sanborn, who introduced him to Thomas Wentworth Higginson, Samuel Gridley Howe, and Theodore Parker. He also met George Stearns. These influential and wealthy New Englanders, along with Smith, became known as "the Secret Six," conspiring together to supply funds and other support for Brown's military campaign. All were of high distinction: Sanborn, an accomplished writer; Higginson, a minister, a reformer, a soldier in the Civil War, and, later, an editor of poet Emily Dickinson's works; Howe, a soldier who fought with Garibaldi in the European wars of revolution, the husband of composer Julia Ward Howe, and pioneer in the care of the blind; Parker, a radical minister and writer, who was an early advocate for using force to end slavery; Stearns, a highly successful businessman who was involved in the Underground Railroad; and last, but not least, Smith, America's greatest philanthropist and among the nation's most outspoken foes of slavery.

Brown also met Thoreau and Emerson in Concord, both of whom became avid admirers. Thoreau described him as a "volcano with an ordinary chimney-flue," and Emerson wrote that "everyone who has heard him speak has been impressed alike by his simple, artless goodness joined with his sublime courage."

John Brown sensed his destiny and prepared himself to face it. In April of 1857 he went to Torrington, Connecticut, to retrieve the tombstone of his grandfather, whom he had long venerated for his service in the American Revolution. He wanted the tombstone placed at his own grave. Steamboat operator James Allen of Westport, New York, remembered transporting the stone when it arrived at his wharf on Lake Champlain. Brown took it to a stonecutter and had the name of his son Frederick inscribed on the reverse. He then took it with him to North Elba, his first trip home since leaving for Kansas in 1855. He placed it on his porch when he left again two weeks later.

Brown resumed his fundraising and recruiting. This took him through the Midwest, and by August he was back in Tabor, Iowa. During his travels he had met an English aristocrat and self-styled military expert, Colonel Hugh Forbes, who had fought with Garibaldi and who impressed Brown with his talk of revolution and knowledge of military exercises. Brown enlisted him to be his second in command and to be in charge of training his army. Forbes met Brown in Tabor for that purpose shortly after Brown's arrival.

Earlier that spring Brown had a shipment of 200 rifles and thousands of rounds of ammunition, along with other supplies, sent by the Kansas Committee to the home of Rev. Todd for use ostensibly in the Kansas War. But it was apparent that Brown also was looking ahead for their use to his guerilla war in Virginia. It was quiet on the Kansas battlefront. With no men to train and some disagreements, Brown and Forbes parted company in November. Forbes headed east, and Brown went to Kansas, where he began a serious effort to recruit his army.

Within two weeks Brown had collected a band of ten, including his son Owen, six of whom would go with him to Harpers Ferry. On December 4 they began a long trek in harsh weather from Tabor across Iowa. Slowly, with some of the men on foot, they made their way with two wagons filled with the rifles and ammunition that had been stored in Tabor. It took them a little over three weeks to go the 250 miles to Springdale, Iowa, where they stopped and rested for two weeks. During this time Brown revealed his plan to attack Harpers Ferry. "God had created him to be the deliverer of slaves the same as Moses had delivered the children of Israel," he declared to his men.

On January 15, 1858, Brown continued east, stopping in Ohio before heading to the home of Douglass. From January 28 until February 17, Brown stayed with Douglass and wrote his "Provisional Constitution and Ordinances for the People of the United States," which he would present at a convention of his supporters in May in Chatham, Canada West. Once finished, he went to New York and stayed with Gerrit Smith for a week in Peterboro to discuss Brown's plan for guerilla war in Virginia, the first time he would reveal it to Smith. Brown had requested that the other five members of the Secret Six attend, but only Sanborn was able to make the trip. With some reluctance, Smith and Sanborn approved the plan and agreed to provide Brown with the support he requested.

Brown resumed his fundraising activities during the next two months, stopping in North Elba for one week at the end of March. His travels took him to Boston, Central New York, Canada West, Chicago, and Iowa to pick up his recruits, and then back through Chicago and Detroit before ending up in Chatham, Canada West, for the convention that met on May 8 and 9. Forty-seven delegates attended, including Brown and his son Owen; of the participants, thirty-four were black, and there were no women. Several veterans of the Underground Railroad were delegates, including **William Lambert**, Abraham Shadd, Martin Delany, **George Reynolds**, and William Munroe, who was the convention's president. The preamble of Brown's constitution, which was the basis for his provisional government, made no distinction of race or sex, and read as follows:

> Whereas, slavery throughout its entire existence in the United States, is none other than a most barbarous, unprovoked, and unjustifiable war of one portion of its citizens upon another portion, the only conditions of which are perpetual imprisonment and hopeless servitude or absolute extermination; in utter disregard and violation of those eternal and self-evident truths set forth in our Declaration of Independence: Therefore We, citizens of the United States, and the Oppressed People, who, by a recent decision of the Supreme Court are declared to have no rights which the White Man is bound to respect; together with all other people degraded by the laws thereof, Do, for the time being ordain and establish ourselves, the following PROVISIONAL CONSTITUTION and ORDINANCES, the better to protect our Persons, Property, Lives, and Liberties; and to govern our actions.

A number of the convention delegates promised to join Brown in Virginia, but only one not already a member of his band actually kept his promise: Osborne Perry Anderson. Five other delegates, all of them white, participated in the raid at Harpers Ferry.

At the time, Brown's intention was to prepare for the Harpers Ferry attack that summer. However, his plans were delayed when it was learned that Forbes had notified several persons, including two Northern U.S. Senators, of the plans. A meeting of the Secret Six was called in Boston, and they notified Brown of the decision. A week later he went there to discuss his options. It was decided that he should go to Kansas and undertake a raid of Missouri and rescue some slaves.

Money was supplied for this purpose, and after a brief visit to North Elba, Brown headed back to Kansas. He arrived with his men on June 26. He now took the alias of Shubel Morgan. This was one of a number of aliases that Brown had begun using since the Pottawatomie incident. He also had assumed the image of the John Brown of Harpers Ferry, the Old Testament patriarch with the full white beard.

About a month before Brown's arrival, a major atrocity occurred when Charles Hamilton, a proslavery settler living near West Point, Missouri, crossed the border and abducted eleven antislavery men, and then brought them before a firing squad. Only five of them died, thanks to Eli Snyder, a blacksmith who lived nearby and went for help.

James Montgomery, a Free-State vigilante, who lived near the border, attempted to apprehend Hamilton, but he was unsuccessful. Because of the lawless nature of the region during this period, Hamilton was never prosecuted. This worked to the advantage of Brown, whose warrants continued to follow him. Brown visited Montgomery and gave him his support. Brown set up headquarters near the home of Snyder. He would alternate staying there and at the home of Augustus Wattles, near the present village of Mound City, for the next six months.

During much of this period, Brown was sick with ague, a malaria-like illness characterized by chills and fever. It became so severe that in August he was taken to Osawatomie and the cabin of family member Samuel Adair, a Congregational minister and the husband of Brown's half-sister, Florella. Brown remained bedridden there for four weeks.

In addition to his illness, Brown was also stymied by difficulties in obtaining funds. By November, despite his alias and low public profile, word of his presence began to circulate. This led to an increase in hostilities because of attempts to capture him. Kansas was no longer an ideal location for Brown. Fortunately, an opportunity presented itself by which he could accomplish his purpose there. Jim Daniels, a Missouri slave, approached one of Brown's recruits, asking for help for his family to escape from slavery. Their need was urgent because their owner was preparing to sell them, which meant possible separation.

On the night of December 19, Brown began his raid of Missouri. His band split into two companies. Brown's company liberated the family of Daniels at one plantation and five persons at another. Aaron Stevens, who led the other company, shot and killed a slaveholder, David Cruse, while freeing one of his slaves. The two companies then came together and retreated to Kansas. In addition to bringing out eleven slaves, they confiscated horses, oxen, saddles, harnesses, a wagon, and numerous provisions. Local newspapers characterized the raid as the work of horse thieves and robbers. The fugitive slaves were taken first to the home of August Wattles and then on Christmas Eve to the Adair homestead. The day after Christmas the fugitives were hidden in an abandoned cabin south of Osawatomie. The fugitive slaves quickly fashioned a hearth and chimney for their needs, and friendly neighbors gave them food. They were to remain there for nearly a month, as Brown prepared to take them out of Kansas along the Underground Railroad.

The raid was not well received in Kansas. Nevertheless, reports indicating that some Missouri slaveholders had moved their slaves farther south vindicated Brown and gave him confidence that his plan to raid Virginia also would push the boundaries of slavery farther south until it eventually no longer existed.

On January 20 Brown began his long journey east, setting out with one large covered wagon transporting the fugitive slaves, pulled by the oxen confiscated during the raid. The fugitives' number had increased to twelve with the birth of a baby boy who was named after Brown. Of Brown's men, only George Gill was by Brown's side. Aaron Stevens, Jon Henri Kagi, and Charles Tidd had gone ahead to arrange for provisions. The group's progress was slow as they confronted snowstorms and frigid weather. They also would have to deal with attempts by law enforcement to stop them. The governor of Missouri had offered a $3,000 reward for their capture, and, incredibly, Brown had sent a letter to the *New York Tribune* that month boldly defending his actions.

At Lawrence, Stevens took Gill's place, and on January 28 they reached Holton, Kansas, eighty miles from their starting point. A little north of Holton, a posse of eighty men led by Marshal A. P. Wood was intent on apprehending them. Gill, Kagi, and Tidd arrived from Topeka with a posse of seventeen men in sympathy with Brown. The marshal and his men had stationed themselves on the opposite side of a location called Muddy Creek and prepared for battle. Brown arranged his men in two columns and told them to march directly toward their adversaries. As they closed in, Wood's men began to fall back and suddenly, without firing a shot, turned and fled, some failing to mount their horses properly in their haste. The cowardly flight of Wood and his men resulted in the derisive nickname "the Battle of the Spurs" and demonstrated the fear that Brown's reputation now instilled. Taking several prisoners, Brown took possession of their horses and forced them to walk about twenty miles before letting them go, walking with them part of the way and lecturing to them about the evils of slavery.

Brown's company moved through Kansas and into Nebraska, with another posse in pursuit. Their next destination was the friendly community of Tabor, the notable Underground Railroad terminal, where Brown had stayed the year before. As expected, the town welcomed the fugitive slaves. Although no one was about to report Brown to the authorities, he was no longer warmly received. The next day at Sabbath, Rev. Todd's congregation refused to bless Brown's journey. It turned out that the townspeople were upset because of the murder of Cruse, and also because they opposed enticing slaves to flee and taking slaveholders' property.

Nevertheless, Brown's company needed rest, and they spent four days in Tabor before moving on. They headed east through Toole's, Lewis, Grove City, Dalmanutha, Aurora, and then the home of State Senator James Jordan, just east of Des Moines. All of these were stops on an established line of the Underground Railroad. Passing through Des Moines, Brown was worried about possible trouble, and secretly sought the help of John Teesdale, the editor of the *Iowa Citizen* to get a ferry across the Des Moines River. After a couple more stops, Brown's group reached Grinnell, the home of Josiah Grinnell, the state's foremost abolitionist.

Brown went directly to Grinnell's home and introduced himself as a friend of Grinnell's father-in-law, who lived in Massachusetts. As soon as Brown identified himself, Grinnell welcomed him enthusiastically. He also showed Brown an article in the *New York Tribune* that reported Brown's raid into Missouri and his abduction of slaves. It stated that Brown was fleeing with them through Iowa in an effort to reach Canada, and that a reward was being offered for their capture. Grinnell also showed him a note that he had received from the marshal in Iowa City, who was his friend, advising him to tell Brown not to stay long because the marshal would have to send a posse to arrest him. Despite this, Grinnell was happy to give Brown as much support as he could.

That night the local Congregational Church became the site of the first of two meetings at which both Brown and Kagi spoke amid the cheers of admirers. When they left Grinnell, the group was provided with food and clothing, as well as cash. That same day Grinnell left for Chicago to try to arrange passage for the Brown party on the Rock Island Railroad, whose managers were sympathetic to helping fugitive slaves.

The next leg of the journey headed straight through Iowa City. The group quickly passed through and stopped in Springdale, where Brown's men had stayed earlier that year and where Brown had many supporters—including the Coppick brothers, who would join him at Harpers Ferry. However, Brown needed to see William Penn Clarke in Iowa City for additional help in arranging the rail passage. This led to a hair-raising escape from a mob when Brown was recognized at an Iowa City restaurant. Nevertheless, he contacted Clarke, and through the efforts of both Clarke and Grinnell, a railroad freight car was made available for the Brown party at West Liberty, just south of Springdale. On March 10 Brown and his men and the fugitive slaves boarded the freight car and loaded their entire cargo in it; the car was then attached to a train that came from Iowa City. They had one last hurdle to overcome, a stop in Davenport, Iowa, on the state line. There the train was searched by Marshal Laurel Summers who, fortunately, neglected to check the freight car where they were hidden.

Brown's group arrived in Chicago the next day. Here they were taken under the wing of the famed detective Allen Pinkerton, who also participated in the city's Underground Railroad. Brown was taken to the home of the prominent black Chicago businessman, John Jones, and the others to Pinkerton's home. Not only were arrangements made by Pinkerton to forward the party to Detroit on the Michigan Central Railroad, but also a large sum of money was raised to assist Brown, who was sent ahead of the fugitive slaves on an earlier train.

In Detroit Brown met with Frederick Douglass, who happened to be visiting, and **George DeBaptiste**, as well as other radical black abolitionists. A meeting was convened, during which Brown's plan to invade Virginia was discussed. Brown also had the satisfaction of seeing off the twelve fugitive slaves, whom he had guided 900 miles, on their ferryboat to freedom. Brown had completed possibly the longest overland and best-publicized rescue of fugitive slaves in the history of the Underground Railroad. This gave him and his supporters confidence that he could succeed in his greater mission.

Nevertheless, Brown knew the odds were against him, and during his last visit to North Elba in the middle of June, he etched his initials on the tombstone of his grandfather, where the name of his son Frederick had already been inscribed. When Brown said good-bye, he told his family to place the stone near a huge boulder behind which the snowcapped peak of Mt. Marcy towered in the distance.

In July 1859, under the name of Isaac Smith, Brown rented a farm in Maryland about five miles from Harpers Ferry. Here his band of men waited for the moment to strike. Joining them from North Elba were his sixteen-year-old daughter Annie and his daughter-in-law Martha, Oliver's wife, to minister to their domestic needs. In late August Brown had a much-recounted meeting with Douglass at a deserted quarry outside Chambersburg, Pennsylvania, about forty miles north of the Kennedy farm.

Douglass brought a fugitive slave, Shields Green, who had settled in Rochester and was friendly with Brown. They found Brown disguised as a fisherman, looking as if the weight of the world was pressing in on him. While Henri Kagi stood guard, Brown appealed to Douglass to join in the Harpers Ferry raid. Instead Douglass tried to persuade Brown to abandon the plan. At last, when Brown realized his logic could not sway Douglass, he put his arm around Douglass and said: "Come with me, Douglass, I will defend you with my life. I want you for a special purpose. When I strike the bees will begin to swarm, and I shall want you to help hive them."

As Douglass turned to leave, Green decided differently: "I b'leve I'll go wid de oleman." It was the last time Brown and Douglass would meet.

In all, Brown had twenty-one men at his command for the assault at Harpers Ferry, including three of his sons, Owen, Oliver, and Watson. Brown's daughter and daughter-in-law were sent back to North Elba on October 1. He had planned on making the assault on October 24, but when suspicions about the group's purpose started to surface among locals, Brown decided to move up the date. This may have hindered his chances, because area slaves, who had been informed of the raid and who were expected to mobilize, thought it was coming at a later time.

The day of the raid was described as very solemn and passed with readings from Scripture and a review of the group's assignments. One of Brown's last instructions before setting out on the night of October 16, 1859, was to spare life if at all possible:

> And now, gentlemen, he said, let me impress this one thing upon your minds. You all know how dear life is to you, and how dear your life is to your friends. And in remembering that, consider that the lives of others are as dear to them as yours are to you. Do not, therefore, take the life of anyone, if you can possibly avoid it; but if it is necessary to take life in order to save your own, then make sure work of it.

Brown entered Harpers Ferry, a distance of about five miles, with eighteen men, determined to begin the grandest scheme in the history of the Underground Railroad: not merely to set a few slaves free, but to end slavery itself. Three of his men, including his son Owen, had been left at the Kennedy Farm in charge of their store of weapons and supplies. Taking control of Harpers Ferry was relatively easy while its citizens slept. Only two watchmen were on guard, and cutting the telegraph lines effectively prevented communication with outside authorities. As a result, Brown had the town and the armory under his complete control for about twelve hours. He had taken more than thirty hostages, including Colonel Lewis Washington, a relative of President George Washington, and could easily have commandeered a load of weapons and left the scene with a great victory.

However, despite pleas from his second-in-command Henri Kagi to leave, Brown stalled. A small number of local slaves had left the plantations and were ready to assist him, but the number was not as large as Brown had hoped, and it is possible he was waiting for a greater number to gather and join him. Brown's excuse that he was concerned about the welfare of his prisoners does not seem to make sense.

At about noon on October 17, the local militia from Charles Town entered Harpers Ferry, securing the bridge across the Potomac to Maryland and blocking the way to the Kennedy Farm and Brown's best chance to escape. From that point on, with the killing of Dangerfield Newby, who was trying to guard the bridge—the first of Brown's men to die—the situation for Brown progressively worsened.

More local militia arrived, and hundreds of locals began peppering the engine house where Brown and the last of his men who had not escaped were confined. The militia members were fortified by both alcohol and the news that federal troops under the command of then Colonel Robert E. Lee had been dispatched, and it became a game of shooting practice for them. Brown tried to negotiate by offering the release of his hostages in return for his release, but his humane treatment of his prisoners, and his refusal to even threaten their harm, made them useless as bargaining chips.

Finally, federal troops arrived. After Brown refused an offer to surrender, the troops stormed the engine house and captured Brown and the remainder of his men still alive, several of them only clinging to life, including Brown's son Watson. Although Oliver had already succumbed, Owen at the Kennedy farm was able to escape. In all, ten of Brown's men were killed, seven were executed, and five escaped Harpers Ferry, two of those dying in battle during the Civil War. Owen Brown was the last surviving member of the group, dying in California in 1891.

Brown's failure was not only due to his delay in leaving Harpers Ferry but also to some tactical errors. Among those were permitting a train, which had been stalled for a number of hours, to pass through. The train personnel quickly alerted the authorities of the raid. Although the local militia had killed a number of Brown's men and had surrounded the engine house where Brown was confined, the militia was disorganized, and many of its members were impaired by alcohol. Had the train not been permitted to pass, given the impairment of the militia, Brown might have had an opportunity to escape. However, because the authorities had been alerted, the arrival of federal troops under Robert E. Lee sealed his doom.

An ironic turn of events also affected the outcome. Shephard Hayward, a free black porter on the train that had been stalled, was killed despite being unarmed. Hayward was an associate of the town mayor and the railroad agent there, Beckham Fontaine. When Hayward was shot, Fontaine left his office to see what was happening, and one of Brown's men shot and killed him as well, under the erroneous impression that Fontaine was preparing an assault on Brown's group. The irony of killing a free, unarmed black man was exacerbated by the killing of Fontaine, who sympathized with the plight of slaves and had recently begun proceedings to purchase the freedom of a slave family. Killing Fontaine, a beloved and respected citizen of Harpers Ferry, only increased the wrath of the militia and made them more determined.

Some of Brown's supporters, such as Douglass, Howe, and Stearns, whose letters to Brown were found in a bag at Harpers Ferry, disassociated themselves from him or fled to Canada for fear of prosecution. Gerrit Smith had a nervous breakdown and went into a mental hospital. To the end, Smith would disavow knowledge of the raid at Harpers Ferry.

Though the raid was a failure, Brown later turned it into a great moral victory for those fighting slavery. Severely injured during the storming of the engine house, Brown was still recovering when he stood trial. It was in this spotlight, in another ironic turn, that he altered the course of history. Brought to the courtroom on a cot, Brown managed to rise up and deliver several brilliant monologues that were widely publicized. Among the most often quoted was his extemporaneous speech delivered prior to his sentencing:

> Had I so interfered in behalf of the rich, the powerful, the intelligent, the so-called great, or in behalf of any of their friends . . . or any of that class, and suffered and sacrificed what I have in this interference, it would have been all right. . . . I believe that to have interfered as I have done, as I always have freely admitted I have done, in behalf of [the almighty Father's] despised poor, I did not wrong, but right. Now, if it is deemed necessary that I should forfeit my life for the furtherance of the ends of justice, and mingle my blood further with the blood of my children, and with the blood of millions in this slave country whose rights are disregarded by wicked, cruel and unjust enactments . . . Let it be done.

While in captivity awaiting his execution, Brown was barraged by visitors and interviewers. When talk of a mission to rescue him surfaced, he discouraged it and said he was resigned to his fate. He stated, "I am worth inconceivably more to hang than for any other purpose." Provided with a platform to speak, Brown now used his words to destroy the moral legitimacy of slavery.

The night before Brown's execution, his wife, Mary, was allowed to spend a few hours with him. After she left, he gave the jailer whom he had befriended a note that prophesied: "I, John Brown, am now quite certain that the crimes of this guilty land will never be purged away but with Blood."

Brown also refused the offer to see clergy before his execution. "There are no ministers of Christ here," he said. "These ministers who profess to be Christian, and hold slaves or advocate slavery. . . . My knees will not bend in prayer with them, while their hands are stained with the blood of souls."

The next morning as they led him to his execution, Brown stopped to kiss the baby of his jailer. He rode to his death seated on his empty coffin in a wagon, his hands bound. Quietly he remarked to the driver about the beauty of the surrounding countryside, regretting that he had not noticed it before.

Around the scaffold, 1,500 armed soldiers were stationed, with another 1,500 guarding the roads leading there, fearing the much-talked-about attempt to rescue Brown. The noose was placed around his neck, and a hood was draped over his head. As the snare drums rolled, Brown was forced to wait twelve endless minutes for the troops to march into place, but he showed no fear or movement. Then the trap door sprung, and Brown was hanged in the gentle, sunny breeze.

At the hour of Brown's death, church bells tolled and cannons saluted him throughout the North. Public prayer meetings and speeches praising him were held in all of the centers of abolitionism and Republicanism. Brown's body was delivered to his wife by an army escort. It had been Brown's intention to be buried in the Adirondacks, overlooking the range's highest peak, Mt. Marcy. His grandfather's headstone awaited him in North Elba. From Virginia the body was taken by train to Philadelphia. A large crowd had gathered at the train station, and fearing that the body might be stolen, authorities used an empty coffin to draw them away, and then secretly loaded the coffin with Brown's body onto a boat for New York City. There his body was transferred into another coffin, and Mary Brown and her escorts, among whom was the noted Boston abolitionist Wendell Phillips, began the procession northward.

The farther north they proceeded, the greater a hero John Brown became. The long last leg of the trip to North Elba was up steep mountain roads in sleet and rain. On December 8, a cold, bleak, damp day, Brown was laid to rest. In his eulogy, Phillips said that Brown "has loosened the roots of the slave system; it only breathes—it does not live—hereafter."

SUGGESTED READING: Evan Carton, *Patriotic Treason: John Brown and the Soul of America*, New York: Simon and Schuster, 2006; Louis A. DeCaro, *Fire from the Midst of You: A Religious Life of John Brown*, New York: NYU Press, 2002; Josiah Bushnell Grinnell, *Men and Events of Forty Years: Autobiographical Reminiscences of an Active Career From 1850 to 1890*, Boston: D. Lothrop Company, 1891; Stephen B. Oates, *To Purge This Land With Blood: A Biography of John Brown*, New York: Harper & Row, 1970; Edward J. Renehan, *The Secret Six: The True Tale of the Men Who Conspired with John Brown*, New York: Crown Publishers, 1995; David S. Reynolds, *John Brown, Abolitionist: The Man Who Killed Slavery, Sparked the Civil War*, New York: Random House, 2005; F.B. Sanborn, *The Life and Letters of John Brown; Liberator of Kansas, And Martyr of Virginia*, Concord, MA: F. B Sanborn, 1885; Charles Edward Smith, *The Underground Railroad In Iowa*, Master's Thesis, Northeast Missouri State College, Kirksville, MO, August 1971; Barrie Stavis, *John Brown: The Sword And The Word*, New York: A. S. Barnes And Company, 1970; Oswald Garrison Villard, *John Brown, 1800–1859: A Biography Fifty Years*, Boston and New York: Houghton Mifflin Company, 1910.

Brown, William Wells (1814–1884). William Wells Brown was, after **Frederick Douglass**, the foremost black writer of the antebellum period. Although a tireless advocate of abolition, he was most interested in the elevation of people of color, for he realized that the end of slavery was not the solution to the race problem in America. As a young man Brown was involved in the Underground Railroad, but after his position as a literary figure was established, he confined his efforts to writing and lecturing.

Born in Lexington, Kentucky, Brown was the slave of John Young, who also owned Brown's mother, Elizabeth. Brown's father was George W. Higgins, a relative of his master, but it is not clear who fathered Brown's three brothers and his sister. While Brown was still an infant, Young moved to Missouri, taking with him the entire family. Here Brown, whose name was changed from William to Sandford, on the orders of his master, spent the first nineteen years of his life. He worked in a number of positions, including as a medical assistant for Young, as an assistant in the newspaper office of abolitionist martyr Elijah Lovejoy, whom he called the best master he ever had, and as a handyman for a slave trader. The horrible atrocities Brown witnessed during this last experience burned a resolve in him to gain his freedom.

By 1833 Young had sold Brown's sister and three brothers, leaving only Elizabeth and William. When Brown's sister was sold, she pleaded with William to take their mother and escape to freedom. The family fled through Alton, Illinois, and had gone about 150 miles when slavecatchers finally caught up with them. They were taken back, and Brown's mother was sold to a slave trader to be taken to a cotton plantation in the Deep South. William also was sold, but to a local man because of a promise his owner had made to William's father never to sell him South. Through his resourcefulness, however, Brown managed to see his mother one last time, aboard the ship on which she was sent away.

After a time Brown's new owner sold him to a wealthy merchant, Captain Enoch Price. Mrs. Price urged Brown to take a wife, and after failing to join him with one of her slaves, she purchased a new slave, whom she learned that Brown fancied. However, Brown was resolved not to marry as a slave. He could not bear to endure another tragic breakup of family. It was freedom that consumed him now. When Brown was informed of a trip his master was about to take to Cincinnati, he realized he had his opportunity. He went to a fortune-teller just before the journey, and indeed the seer foretold that he would have his freedom.

On December 31, 1833, Price's steamboat, the *Chester*, arrived in Cincinnati. The next day, after bringing a trunk ashore, Brown set out through the city until he reached a wooded area, where he hid until dark. Then he set out, following the North Star, walking about twenty-five miles, he guessed, before resting.

It was winter, and though Brown had brought enough food to last four days, he was soon suffering from exposure. Nevertheless, he pushed on and came upon a barn with some corn that he was able to roast. He also dined on raw turnips he was able to dig up. On the sixth day, he ran into freezing rain that chilled him to the bone, and he took refuge in an abandoned barn. Brown wrote later that the barn saved him from freezing to death. He persisted for two more days, but he realized that he would need help if he was to survive.

The next morning Brown hid along the highway, resolved to request help from the first person that he deemed approachable. When an old man in a broad-brimmed hat and long coat came along, walking a white horse, Brown's intuition told him he was the one.

Brown told the man that he was sick and asked if he could help. The man first asked if he was a fugitive slave. Reluctantly, Brown said he was. The man said that he was in a pro-slavery neighborhood, and that Brown should wait there, out of sight, until the man could return with his wagon to bring Brown to his house.

Brown had little choice but to trust the man. His intuition proved correct; the man, whose name was Wells Brown, was a Quaker and opposed to slavery. The Friend returned after about an hour and a half in a two-horse covered wagon.

The Friend and his wife were quite hospitable, and told Brown that he could stay with them as long as it took for him to recover his health. Brown was at first apprehensive, but after a day or two he began to feel comfortable with the Quakers, who treated him as if he were a family member. Also, being in a free state made Brown feel totally different.

"The fact that I was a freeman—could walk, talk, eat and sleep as a man," he later wrote "and no one to stand over me with the blood-clotted cowhide—all this made me feel that I was not myself."

Brown stayed with the Quakers for about two weeks. Now that Brown was free, Wells Brown suggested that the former slave take a new name. As Brown had always called himself William, he kept that as his first name, but at the suggestion of the Quakers, he adopted their name, and from that day forward, he was known as William Wells Brown. Brown provided little specific information about his Quaker helpers, aside from their last name and the fact that they lived about fifty miles from Dayton and more than 100 miles from Cleveland. It is possible, though, that Wells Brown may have been Nathan Wells Brown, who died in Norwalk, Ohio, in 1853. In any case, Brown was forever grateful to them, and dedicated his *Narrative of William Wells Brown*, his first important writing, to his Quaker benefactor.

Brown left his namesake and took with him new clothes, new shoes, some food, and money. His destination was Cleveland, where he hoped to take a boat to Canada, but after four days he had traveled only half of the 100 or so miles and had run out of food and money. While stopping at an inn, Brown heard talk of fugitive slaves in the vicinity, and he became alarmed, worried that he might be discovered, so he spent another night in the woods.

The next day Brown took another chance and stopped at a farmhouse to ask for something to eat. At first, the man of the house turned him away, but the man's wife interceded and agreed to feed him. As Brown wrote, "I was never before so glad to see a woman push a man aside! Ever since that act, I have been in favor of woman's rights!"

When Brown arrived in Cleveland, he found Lake Erie frozen and no boats running. He would either have to wait until the spring thaw or journey to Detroit or Buffalo to get to Canada. He decided to stay in Cleveland and look for work. He also began educating himself and reading antislavery newspapers.

The following summer, Brown got a job on a Lake Erie steamboat and married his first wife, Betsey Schooner. Their first child died a few months after birth, but they had a second child, a girl, in 1836, and a third, another daughter, in 1839. Because Buffalo was a terminal port on Lake Erie, and living there allowed Brown more time at home, he moved his family there in 1836. Another possible reason was because he was a fugitive slave and subject to arrest at any time, and Buffalo provided much easier access to Canada.

By the time of his move, Brown had been helping to transport fugitive slaves on his boat to Canada. In one case, a fugitive slave had been traced to the home of a Cleveland abolitionist, whose house was being watched by slavecatchers. Brown accompanied the man, who was dressed as a woman and whose complexion was lightened with makeup, to his boat and then took him to freedom.

Shortly after moving to Buffalo, Brown participated in a dramatic incident involving fugitive slaves. The Stanford family had escaped from Tennessee and was living in St. Catharine's. A slavecatcher from Nashville, Bacon Tate, had come to New York to see if he could bring the Stanford family and some twenty other fugitive slaves back. Tate learned that the Stanfords were living in St. Catharine's, and so he enlisted the aid of a free black woman in Buffalo to go there as a spy to learn where they lived, and to get information about their daily routine. The woman found them, and after staying with them briefly as a boarder, she returned to New York with the necessary information.

Tate enlisted four men to kidnap the Stanfords. After plans were made, the men hired a carriage and took the ferry to Canada. They drove to St. Catharine's and broke into the Stanford house in the middle of the night. They tied up Stanford and gagged him and his wife, but gave her enough freedom to attend to their infant child. Then, with the kidnapped Stanfords, the men returned by way of the ferry and began their journey south.

In the morning, a neighbor discovered what had happened and sounded the alarm. One man in the neighborhood picked up the trail to the ferry and went to Buffalo and aroused the black community. Brown was among those who responded. Because there were two likely roads that the kidnappers could have taken, the responders split into two posses. Brown's posse was the one that tracked the men to a tavern in Hamburg. The kidnappers quickly locked themselves in a room when they saw the posse outside. But the tavern-keeper was sympathetic to the blacks, and he gave them permission to break into the room. The rescuers retrieved the Stanford family, but one of the kidnappers managed to get word back to Tate, who called upon local law enforcement officials to back up his claim.

The rescuers were informed that the local sheriff was on his way with his own posse to stop them. They resolved to die before they surrendered the Stanfords. Shortly before they reached the Black Rock ferry, the group encountered the sheriff. A great melee took place, but the rescuers stood their ground. During the melee, a lawyer by the name of Pepper came on the scene and challenged the legality of the Sheriff's actions, saying he needed a warrant to obstruct these people. That gave the rescuers enough leverage to get to the ferry and send the Stanfords back to Canada as free citizens again.

About forty of the rescuers gave themselves up to the sheriff and were put in jail for a night. Whether or not Brown was one of those is not known. Of those, twenty-five were eventually charged with a minor offense and fined from five to fifty dollars. Only one man suffered serious injuries in the melee, and he died three months later. Brown called it "one of the most fearful fights for human freedom that I ever witnessed."

In another incident, Brown and other local abolitionists retained future U.S. President Millard Fillmore to represent a fugitive slave in court. Fillmore, the man who signed the second Fugitive Slave Law, served without a fee. It is not known how many fugitive slaves Brown helped during his nine years in Cleveland and Western New York, but in one seven-month period in 1842, he claimed to have conducted sixty-nine to freedom.

In addition to his Underground Railroad work, Brown was a strong temperance advocate and organized the first temperance society in Western New York. But more significant was his involvement in the abolitionist movement. This led to his appointment as an agent for the Western New York Anti-Slavery Society in the fall of 1843. It was the beginning of a prolific career for him as a lecturer and writer, which in the coming years became his sole occupation. In Western New York, where Brown gave numerous lectures, he gained the experience that would develop him into one of the abolition movement's most effective speakers. He also participated in the Negro Convention movement, including the famed 1843 convention when **Henry Highland Garnet** gave his "Address to the Slaves," and made an appeal for revolt. In 1845 Brown moved to Farmington, New York, south of Rochester, where he continued his work with the Western New York Anti-Slavery Society.

Two years later, Brown moved to Boston, which he would call home the remainder of his life. It was 1847, the year of the publication of his *Narrative of William W. Brown,*

A Fugitive Slave. Becoming associated with William Lloyd Garrison, Brown was appointed as an agent of the Massachusetts Anti-Slavery Society. He now moved away from his involvement in the Underground Railroad and devoted his time solely to lecturing and writing. His presentations elicited such responses as "It is enough to say that he held the large audience in almost breathless silence for nearly two hours," or at another, "None could fail to be impressed with the eloquence, wit and pathos with which friend Brown addressed us, and his dignified, gentlemanly deportment won all hearts."

But Brown was not always well received. In Harwich, Massachusetts, on August 27, 1848, while speaking with Parker Pillsbury and Stephen Foster, the husband of Abbey Kelly Foster, Brown was thrown off the platform and beaten.

In 1849 Brown went to England, where he remained for five years. He was one of a number of black abolitionists—including Frederick Douglass, Henry Garnet, **Henry "Box" Brown**, and others—who toured England during this period and enlightened audiences about American slavery. By the end of 1849, Brown's autobiography had gone through four editions in America and one in England. He also had a written a monograph of antislavery songs and poems, *The Anti-Slavery Harp.*

This period in England marked the beginning of Brown's literary career and the death of his first wife, Betsy, in 1851. He began writing sketches about American slavery for English publications, including such newspapers as *The Daily News, The Morning Chronicle,* and *The Leader.* Among notable related pieces were eulogies of Henry Clay and Daniel Webster. In 1852 his book *Three Years in Europe; Or, Places I Have Seen and People I Have Met* was published, and the following year, his book *Clotel* was the first novel to be published by a black American. It later went through several editions and revisions.

Brown also began to polish his speaking ability, and provided audiences in England with a clear, firsthand picture of slavery in America. During his five years there, he made more than 1,000 speeches and became well known. He continually pointed out that he was still legally a slave and that in the United States he was liable at any time to be sent back to slavery. This led a group of English philanthropists to purchase his freedom before his return to the United States in September 1854.

Back in the United States Brown continued his lectures and writing. He was a Garrisonian in principle and did not advocate violence. "We do not ask you to take up arms," he told his audiences, "we do not ask you to do any act, or utter any language, unbecoming Christians; but we ask you to learn the facts and the truth of this matter, and honestly to speak out upon it." He also repeatedly conveyed the message that to destroy slavery required a commitment to end racism. By the spring of 1856 Brown wrote a three-act play entitled *Experience; Or, How to Give a Northern Man a Backbone,* which satirized the proslavery polemic, "A South Side View of Slavery," by Rev. Nehemiah Adams. This was followed by another play based on his own experience in slavery, *The Escape; Or, Leap for Freedom,* A Drama in Five Acts. These were perhaps the first plays written by a black American. These plays were often modified by Brown during his lectures so that he could give one-man performances of them. Brown was joined in the literary field by his daughter Josephine, who wrote a biography of her father, *A Biography of an American Bondman,* that was published in 1856.

As the Civil War approached, Brown talked less of the atrocities of slavery, and said that the time for those stories had passed and what was needed was action. During the war he helped to recruit black soldiers and continued his support of temperance. After the war, he dabbled in the clothing and publishing business, and even practiced as a physician. In these activities, Brown was assisted by his second wife, Annie E. Gray Brown, a native of Cambridge, Massachusetts, whom he married in 1860.

Brown's later published works included *The Black Man, His Antecedents, His Genius, and His Achievements*, published in 1863; *The Negro in the American Rebellion: His Heroism and His Fidelity*, in 1867, a pioneering study of black military history; *The Rising Son; or, The Antecedents and Advancements of the Colored Race*, in 1874; and *My Southern Home; or, The South and Its People in 1880*, a response to apologists of slavery.

Brown died in Chelsea, a suburb of Boston, on November 6, 1884, and was buried three days later in the Cambridge, Massachusetts, cemetery. His grave remained unmarked until the year 2001, when a bronze plaque was placed on it.

"The love of liberty cannot be extinguished by municipal laws or tyrannical mandates," he once said to an English audience. "This love of liberty, fellow-citizens, is universal, and the African possesses his share equally with the Anglo–Saxon. But the American people consider it a crime in the black man to aspire to be free, and upon terms of equality with the whites, and the white American thinks it his duty to strike at the colored man wherever he sees him."

SUGGESTED READING: William Wells Brown, *Narrative of William W. Brown, An American Slave*, London: Charles Gilpin,1849; Edward M. Coleman, "William Wells Brown as an Historian," *Journal of Negro History*, January 1946; W. Edward Farrison, "William Wells Brown," *Phylon*, Vol. 9, No. 1, 1948; W. Edward Farrison, "A Flight Across Ohio: The Escape Of William Wells Brown From Slavery," *Ohio History*, Vol. 61, No. 3, July 1952; W. Edward Farrison, "William Wells Brown in Buffalo," *The Journal of Negro History*, Vol. 39, No. 4, October 1954; Richard W. Leeman, ed., *African-American Orators: A Bio-Critical Sourcebook*, Westport, CT: Greenwood Press, 1996.

Burns, Anthony (1834–1862). Anthony Burns lived a short but eventful life, and was the subject of perhaps the best-known slave rendition of the antebellum era. Born in Stafford County, Virginia, Burns was the property of John Suttle, and was the youngest of his mother's thirteen children. His father, who was her third husband, was Suttle's overseer. Both Suttle and Burns's father died when Burns was very young, and his mother was hired out, during which time he didn't see her for two years.

In Virginia it was common for slaves to be hired out, and when Burns turned seven, his new master, Charles Suttle, the son of John, began the practice of hiring Burns out. Two of Burns's early, temporary masters operated schools for children, and he began to learn the rudiments of reading and writing in spite of the law prohibiting it. Already he was hearing about a land in the north where all men were free.

When Burns was thirteen, while working as a steam engine attendant, he injured his hand, which caused permanent damage. Later he worked for a tavern owner, a merchant, and a druggist. He grew increasingly independent and found consolation in the Baptist Church into which he was baptized in Falmouth, Virginia. So strong was Burns's faith that he was made a preacher and at a very young age began officiating the marriages and funeral services of slaves.

A fortunate circumstance occurred when Burns's master turned over the management of his slaves to one of Burns's former temporary masters, William Brent, who allowed Burns to find his own work situation. With an eye to freedom, Burns located himself in Richmond with a druggist, who allowed him to work on his own, pay the druggist a fixed amount, and keep what was left over. Burns's plan was to save what he could to purchase his freedom, or perhaps stow away on a ship leaving Richmond. He was forced to follow the latter plan when the druggist decided to change the terms of their working arrangement.

One morning before sunrise, wearing four sets of clothing, his work clothes on the outside, Burns walked down to the docks and boarded a ship, where a seaman had arranged a hiding place for him. It was the beginning of a three-week journey during which Burns was shut up in a dark hole and forced to lie in one position with nothing but bread and water—which he received only every three or four days, when the sailor could manage it without being seen.

Burns's hardships grew even worse because it was winter, and as they moved farther north, the temperatures grew more frigid. By end of the voyage, his feet were frozen in his boots. Somehow, he limped into a boardinghouse, where he stayed in bed a week to recover.

Burns found a job as a baker, but didn't last long because he couldn't make his bread rise. His next job, at a clothing store, suited him better. Everything seemed to be going well, and he had written his brother in Virginia, being careful to send the letter by way of Canada. However, he inadvertently had datelined it Boston, and Suttle, also his brother's master, opened it.

On May 24, 1854, after Burns left at the close of business, he was surprised by federal marshals who literally picked him up and carried him to the courthouse. He was immediately confronted by his master, who had come to Massachusetts, along with his business associate Brent, for the rendition. Burns feigned responsibility for his flight, saying he had fallen asleep aboard the ship and was out to sea by the time he had awakened. His mistake was admitting in front of his captors that Suttle was his master, because this was later used in court to convict him.

Burns was locked up in one of the jury rooms for the night, as state law prevented the use of state facilities in Fugitive Slave Law prosecutions. The next morning Richard Dana, a member of the Boston Vigilance Committee, learned of the arrest as he walked past the courthouse on his way to work. He went inside and found the court proceedings about to begin. He approached Burns, who was in a state of shock, and offered his services. But Burns was unreceptive. He assumed it was futile. Minutes later, four more vigilance committee lawyers, to whom Dana had sent word, entered the courtroom, as did the federal commissioner, Judge Edward Loring.

The hearing continued until finally, after several protests by a vigilance committee lawyer, Theodore Parker, Burns was coaxed into accepting representation. Once this was agreed upon, Dana asked for a two-day postponement to prepare the case.

A meeting was held by the vigilance committee. Two sides formed: one wanted to break into the courthouse and rescue Burns; the other called for peaceful efforts and legal means. In the meantime, leaflets were distributed throughout Boston, informing the public of the situation, and a decision was made to call a public meeting at Fanueil Hall the following night to rally the public. This was to be used as a cover for an assault on the courthouse, which was near the Hall, to take place after the audience had been sufficiently roused. Following the Sims rendition three years earlier, public opinion in Boston had shifted to the side of the abolitionists, and it was the hoped that the speakers would be able to incite the public to assist in the rescue.

More than 2,000 supporters attended the meeting. Wendell Phillips and Theodore Parker were the featured speakers. Phillips assured the audience that the city was opposed to the removal of Burns but that the public's support was needed to help them oppose the power of the federal government. He urged a strong showing at the courthouse the next morning when the hearing was to begin. Parker spewed out vitriol against the authorities in Virginia demanding the return of Burns. But before he concluded, he was interrupted by a planted messenger who notified the meeting that an attempt was being made to break into the courthouse.

The crowd rushed out, as anticipated, and on signal the assault on the courthouse began. The rescuers were led by Thomas Wentworth Higginson, **Lewis Hayden**, and Syracuse resident Martin Stowell, a veteran of the Jerry Rescue who had to come to assist them. Following them were about twenty-five men, both black and white.

The men were armed with guns, axes, and butcher knives, and about ten of them were using a battering ram in an attempt to break down the door on the west side. The crowd closed in, some throwing stones at windows, and a few rescuers forced open the door. Suddenly, there was a series of shots, and one of the police guards was injured. The rescuers halted and then retreated. The wounded guard was a truckman named Batchelder who had been sworn in by the federal marshal for temporary duty. He was carried to a room, but an artery had been severed, and he bled to death on the spot.

Police soon restored order and arrested thirteen of the attackers, including Stowell. Higginson, one of the rescuers who went inside, was cut in the chin by a cutlass, but managed to escape. No one was charged in the death of Batchelder because it was believed he had been accidentally shot by one of his fellow guards. Forty years later, however, Higginson revealed that Batchelder had been the victim of a bullet from a pistol fired by Martin Stowell.

The rescue attempt had failed, and now the committee members needed to put all their energies into the legal effort. Meanwhile, the death of Batchelder and the angry demonstrations had terrified Suttle. A group of local ruffians had been enlisted to put him under constant surveillance, which unnerved him further. He began to think that it might be better to offer Burns for sale and end the rendition. On Saturday morning at the hearing, Suttle made it known that he was willing to sell Burns for $1200, but only after the surrender of Burns was legally completed. Rev. Leonard Grimes, pastor of the Church of the Fugitive Slave, where Burns was a member, was present and asked if he could speak privately with Suttle. While conferring with Suttle, Grimes persuaded him to remove that condition, and it was agreed that if Grimes could raise the funds, Suttle would give up Burns. As a result, Judge Loring granted another delay in the proceedings.

Grimes promised to meet Suttle back in the courthouse at ten o' clock that evening with the money. He spent the rest of the day in a frantic effort to raise the funds. It was not until well into the evening that he succeeded, and he arrived at the appointed hour to meet with Suttle and his lawyer. They agreed to meet in the chambers of Commissioner Loring to legally authorize the transaction. It was at this juncture that federal attorney Benjamin Hallett objected. Orders had come down to Hallett from the White House that Burns be sent back to slavery at all costs. The federal government wanted to show that violations of the Fugitive Slave Law would not be tolerated.

However, Hallett was overruled by Loring. Unfortunately, as Suttle was about to sign over Burns, Hallet pointed out that it was after midnight, and state law prohibited any business transacted on the Sabbath. Loring halted the proceeding until Monday morning.

On Monday, however, Suttle had changed his mind—probably due to pressure from Hallett—and the hearing resumed. On Tuesday and Wednesday, the committee's lawyers did their part, eliciting false testimony from the prosecution that buoyed their hopes of a favorable decision. There were hopes that perhaps Loring would rule in Burns's favor.

On Thursday, the night before the decision, Federal Marshal Asa Butman, who had arrested Burns, presented him with an expensive new suit. The Marshal had taken up a collection among the jailers. Whether out of sympathy for Burns or not, their motives have never been made clear. But the next day, on June 2, Burns went to the courthouse to learn his fate dressed in that suit.

In his decision Judge Loring stated that the Virginia courts had already proven that Burns owed service to Colonel Suttle and that he had escaped from that service. It was only left for the judge to determine that the man being held for those charges was the same Anthony Burns. Based on statements he made when he first confronted Suttle in the courthouse, Loring said he had determined that the man being accused was the Anthony Burns to whom Suttle had legal title.

That afternoon, people crowded State Street in Boston several rows deep. More than 50,000 people, it was estimated, watched along a route that began in Court Square, and then led down State Street less than a half mile to the wharf. The federal government was not taking any chances and had made funds available to bring as many military and law enforcement personnel as might be needed. First in line was a company of men on horseback, brandishing lancers, and a battery of U.S. artillery, followed by a platoon of Marines. They were followed by the U.S. marshal and Burns accompanied by an officer on each side, with arms interlocked, and surrounded by 124 deputies. Two more platoons of Marines followed with a symbolic cannon, and another platoon of Marines brought up the rear. All of the troops were prepared for action, being supplied with eleven rounds of ammunition and fixed bayonets, with orders to use their weapons if necessary. Behind the procession walked Attorney Dana and Rev. Grimes.

It was Friday, but all businesses were closed downtown, and some had draped their offices in black. At the corner of Washington and State Street, a coffin was suspended from a window covered with a banner reading "The Funeral of Liberty." Cries of "Shame!" and hisses drew the ire of the soldiers, one of whom hacked the hand of a spectator. A sudden right turn off State Street in front of the Custom House had caused unwary spectators at the front to be pushed into the street. Some of the cavalry thought an attack was beginning, and they instinctively charged at unsuspecting spectators, waving their lancers and wounding the heads of several, as well as knocking many off their feet. The edgy soldiers caused serious injuries to several people that day.

The show of force and authority by the federal government was costly, equal to the value of many slaves. Among the costs was $14,000 merely to bring in federal troops. Adding on the legal costs, the cost of deputy marshals, damages to the courthouse, the transport of Burns to the South, and other financial considerations, it was estimated to be more than $100,000. While the federal government had won their case, it certainly was nothing more than a pyrrhic victory, for it did much to polarize the North and the South.

Burns was placed aboard the steamer *John Taylor*, waiting at the Long Wharf. It transported him to the U.S. revenue cutter *Morris*, which President Pierce himself had ordered to return Burns to slavery. Suttle and his associate Brent were already aboard. They had skipped going to court earlier that day, so sure were they of the verdict.

Burns was escorted aboard the cutter by Marshal Butman and five deputies. They would stay with him until he reached Virginia. Suttle offered Burns his freedom if he would reveal the name of the captain whose ship had brought him to Boston. Burns refused, and in any case did not know his name. Sailing near the port of New York, the *Morris* was met by a steamer in which Suttle and Brent departed. They'd had enough of seafaring, preferring to take the rest of their journey overland.

Upon reaching Norfolk, Virginia, Burns was placed in the city jail for two days until his journey to Richmond resumed. There he spent ten more days in its jail until he was transferred to the slave pen of the notorious slavecatcher, Robert Lumpkin. The slave pen was where slaves about to be sold or moved to another owner were kept. A large brick structure, three stories in height, it was located on the outskirts of Richmond and surrounded by a high fence, at the top of which were iron spikes.

Burns suffered miserably in Lumpkin's slave pen for four months. His cell was a six-by-eight-foot room, with only a hard bench to sleep upon. There was no ventilation, and he was kept in handcuffs and fetters the whole time. The shackles wore the flesh from his wrists and left scars for the remainder of his life. These manacles also prevented him from removing his clothing. His food consisted of corn bread and bacon, which he was given once a day and which he had to eat with his hands. Once a week, a pail of water was supplied to meet his needs.

In the first weeks of Burns's stay, curiosity-seekers regularly came for a look, and he was paraded outside. This was his only human contact in the beginning. But later, both Lumpkin's wife and his mistress, both of whom were women of color, took pity on Burns and began to talk with him. Though he was prohibited from interacting with other slaves there, Burns found ways to communicate through the walls. Through his ingenuity, he also was able to have some letters mailed, one of which reached Suttle with complaints about the conditions at the pen.

Finally a slave fair in Richmond offered an opportunity to sell Burns. His presence raised the ire of the crowd, and there was at first a reluctance to purchase him. In the end he was purchased by David McDaniel, a North Carolina farmer, for $905, considerably less than what Suttle could have gotten had he sold Burns in Boston, to say nothing of the fees Suttle had to pay to lodge him in the slave pen.

McDaniel was a planter, slave trader, and horse dealer. His plantation was extensive and devoted to cotton. The cotton culture, however, was merely a complement to his primary occupation of slave trader. McDaniel was a hard master but a fair one. Burns was at first defiant, but instead of provoking his new master, Burns's defiance brought his respect. Sensing this, Burns promised never to run away so long as he was well treated. Given his education and experience, he was placed in a position of considerable responsibility and supplied with the privileges that went with it.

Burns's job was that of coachman and stable keeper. McDaniel kept a large herd of horses, but Burns's duties were confined to grooming and serving the carriage horses and McDaniel's filly. He was also required to chauffeur McDaniel's wife on visits to friends or for other necessities, and also to take her to church. An apartment was supplied that he shared with McDaniel's overseer, and Burns took his meals in McDaniel's residence. He also had access to goods at a store owned by McDaniel. Because of the respect in which Burns was held, McDaniel even allowed him to preach on occasion to the slaves, though Burns was careful to do it out of his master's sight. For a time, it seemed that he had been forgotten by his friends in the North, and being a man of his word, he was content to attend to his duties without any thought of running away.

However, by chance, a woman visiting from the North learned of Burns's whereabouts and revealed this to a clergyman, Rev. G. S. Stockwell, who sent a letter to McDaniel asking him at what price he would sell Burns. McDaniel wrote back that $1300 would be sufficient. The clergyman then contacted Rev. Leonard Grimes. At once, Grimes contacted McDaniel, accepting the terms, and then set out to raise the funds. It was no easy task, and he had to take out a loan from a bank to furnish the full amount.

Without delay, Grimes set out for Baltimore, where he was to meet McDaniel and Burns to complete the transaction.

The trip for McDaniel and Burns was no small matter. It had to be kept secret, for Southerners were still angry about the matter. Their trip took them aboard a train and then a steamer, on which McDaniel was forced to confront an angry mob when someone revealed Burns's identity. McDaniel had to hold them off at gunpoint for more than an hour. Another group offered to purchase Burns and offered McDaniel more than Grimes. But McDaniel refused, saying that he had made an agreement and was going to stick by it.

Finally, the meeting was consummated at the P. T. Barnum Hotel. If it weren't for the famed Barnum, the transaction might not have taken place, for he not only cashed Grimes's check when McDaniel demanded cash, but also underwrote a bond for Grimes so that Burns could be a passenger on the train returning north.

After completing a speaking tour, Burns set out to fulfill his avocation as a minister. Supplied with a scholarship by a Boston woman, he entered Oberlin College in 1855. He also spent a year at the Fairmont Theological Seminary in Cincinnati before returning to Oberlin and graduating. From 1858 to 1859, he was the pastor of a congregation in Indianapolis, but he was forced out by Indiana black laws that prevented out-of-state blacks from remaining as residents. Around 1860 he took over the congregation of the Zion Baptist Church in St. Catharines, Canada West. He helped the church become solvent and was well respected in the community. However, on July 27, 1862, he died at the age of 28 while still in that post.

SUGGESTED READING: Virginia Hamilton, *Anthony Burns: The Defeat and Triumph of a Fugitive Slave*, New York: Random House, 1988; Daniel Hill, *The Freedom Seekers*, Toronto: Stoddardt Publishing, 1981; Samuel Shapiro, "The Rendition of Anthony Burns," *Journal of Negro History.* January 1959; Charles Emery Stevens, *Anthony Burns: A History,* Boston: John P. Jewett & Company, 1856.

C

Cockrum, William M. (1837–1924). William M. Cockrum grew up on his father's farm in Gibson County near Oakland City, Indiana, amid a flurry of Underground Railroad activity. His father, James W. Cockrum, was a community leader in Gibson County, and was elected to the state legislature in 1848 and 1852. James Cockrum belonged to the General Baptist Church and staunchly opposed slavery. He aided numerous fugitive slaves, often hiding them in a cellar in his barn. William Cockrum later wrote a narrative account of the Underground Railroad, *History of the Underground Railroad: as it was Conducted by the Anti-Slavery League.* Due to some of the dramatic stories in this narrative, as well as the use of aliases by some members, certain historians have been reluctant to accept Cockrum's narrative history. Cockrum described the Anti-Slavery League (ASL) as a complex organization formed after the second Fugitive Slave Law by abolitionists in the East. Its purpose was to send role-playing agents into the South to aid slaves escape to freedom. Its agents included well-educated, young and middle-aged men, who posed as fishermen, teachers, map-makers, mineralogists, clock tinkers, and book peddlers.

These men were well organized and well supplied. Agents used procedures that assisted in successful escapes. For example, fish shacks were located along the rivers, where ASL agents, posing as fishermen, were especially active at nighttime when fugitive slaves would attempt to escape. One of these shacks was across the river from Owensboro, Kentucky, on the Indiana side, just south of a thicket of vegetation that had grown up as a result of deforestation from a hurricane. It provided good cover for fugitive slaves during the beginning of their journey. Turpentine balls were used to signal boatman along the river to make a pickup of fugitive slaves. Also, as bloodhounds were typically used by slavecatchers in tracking fugitive slaves, capsicum (red pepper) was spread along the paths to disrupt the dogs. ASL agents sometimes carried Sharps rifles, hidden under long coats slung over their arms, and sometimes they blackened their faces, if they were white, to disguise their identities.

The group's work involving Cockrum included a route that typically began with a stop at Ira Caswell's farm, which was about fifteen miles north of the Ohio River in Warrick County. The route then proceeded to the home of George Hill, another five miles north. Next fugitives moved another ten miles north to Cockrum's farm in Gibson County. The next leg of the journey headed to **John Posey**'s coal bank near Petersburg in Pike County. These men were all members of the executive committee of the Anti-Slavery

League. Another individual was Isaac Street, a Quaker who operated a country store in Dongola near the Patoka River. This was the scene of a dramatic confrontation with a posse of slave catchers described in detail in Cockrum's book.

Slavecatchers were common in southwest Indiana, not only in search of fugitive slaves but also to abduct free blacks. Cockrum described a number of kidnapping incidents. He stated that it was a common practice of local judges to dismiss charges of kidnapping against those indicted. Recent studies have shown that kidnapping of free blacks during the antebellum period was common in southern Illinois and southwest Indiana.

Some of the most interesting stories Cockrum told involved the use of force and deception by the ASL to discourage slavecatchers. Two such incidents were related in detail by him. In the chapter, "Kidnappers Kidnapped," spies circulated information that a meeting of about a dozen free blacks was to be held at the home of a black man named Booker, who lived four miles south of Oakland City. As an inducement, the spies claimed that an offer of $1,000 per man was being offered for the sale of slaves in Kentucky. Finally, ten men agreed to be part of the raid. Preparations made at the home of Booker included a wide plank seat that faced a hanging sheet, which partitioned the large room where the alleged meeting was to take place. The room was dimly lit to help hide the identities of the participants.

The slavecatchers were led by two ASL spies, who escorted them into the house. When the slavecatchers entered, they sat down on the seat, and the door was locked. Then the sheet was pulled aside, revealing twelve men—those who were white in black face—pointing rifles at them. The slavecatchers were handcuffed, and then forced to read an oath swearing never again apprehend a black man, whether free or slave. Thereafter, the slavecatchers were led into another room. The two spies were taken first. A loud ruckus occurred, with screaming by the spies, whose murder was faked. To heighten the intimidation, the spies reclined under a table, letting their feet stick out, so they were sure to be seen by the slavecatchers when they were brought in.

The slavecatchers followed, two at a time. They were told that it had been decided not to kill them as they had done to the first two (the spies), but that as a remembrance of their visit, they would be branded with a cross on their chest and shoulders. Their coats and vests were then burned. In addition, several others, who were known to be vain, had their long whiskers burned off, and still others, who were known as gamblers, had the balls of their thumbs and forefingers singed so they could not shuffle cards. Young Cockrum was among the participants, as were Ira Caswell and George Hill, the latter functioning as their leader. The slavecatchers were so humiliated by it that they never revealed what had happened, and so the incident was kept secret.

Not all slave escapes facilitated by the group were so dramatic. The Cockrums hid fugitive slaves in a cellar under their barn in which they stored produce. Another common hideaway for fugitive slaves was John Posey's coal bank. Cockrum's narrative accounted for assistance to about 150 fugitive slaves, but according to him the group assisted well over a thousand, attributing more than a thousand to John Posey alone.

Cockrum says the group was also aided by agents who were slaves, such as Jeff Lewis. Lewis faked mental illness so that he could meet with ASL members to arrange escapes. Other blacks who worked with the group included George Sturges, Sam Lynn, John Bunday, and Ben Swain. In an attempt to help others escape to freedom, Swain lost his life. Other interesting characters were Job Turner, an ASL operative who posed as an itinerant peddler, and John Dole, a powerful logger from Maine, who was an ASL spy and role-playing agent.

Cockrum, who served in the Union Army during the Civil War, was wounded twice during the war, the second wound causing a permanent disability. However, he continued as a leading citizen in Oakland City, and was one of the founders of Oakland City University. Cockrum was a man of strong character and principles, and was widely respected. In addition to his Underground Railroad book, he wrote a *Pioneer History of Indiana*, published in 1907.

Cockrum also contributed lengthy sections to Gil R. Stormont's, *History of Gibson County.* In Stormont's history, Cockrum covered both the Underground Railroad and the history of regional transportation. Gil Stormont owned several newspapers in his lifetime, studied at Indiana University, and served in Indiana's 58th Regiment during the Civil War, which was raised by ASL leader, Andrew Lewis. In addition, Stormont's father, William, and two uncles were known agents of the Underground in Gibson County. His publication of Cockrum's accounts serves as further corroboration of their accuracy.

Henry Roberts: The Slave Smuggler

Henry Roberts was a young blacksmith from Cortsville, Ohio, four miles southeast of Springfield. Sometime around 1852 he left his home and found a job as an overseer on a Louisiana plantation not far from the Mississippi River. His purpose was to engage in assisting slaves to freedom.

Roberts was conspiring with Northern abolitionists who owned boats and businesses that were active along the Mississippi River. Boats, such as the *Gladenel*, which he rode on one mission, often stopped in the middle of the night to pick up wood for their engines. The boats also would pick up fugitive slaves. Their destination was Cincinnati, traveling there by way of the Ohio River. In Cincinnati, Roberts forwarded the slaves to Underground Railroad agents. On occasion, however, he accompanied them farther north, sometimes to Canada. One of his collaborators was a Mr. Paul from Cleveland.

On his last mission, Roberts assisted the escape of eighteen slaves from the plantation where he was working. It was around this time that he met an orphan, Matt Peters, who was twelve years old. Roberts brought him home to Cortsville to be raised by his mother. Roberts died shortly after, at age twenty-five, following a trip to Canada.

SUGGESTED READING: William M. Cockrum, *History of Indiana, Including Stories, Incidents and Customs of the Early Settlers*, Oakland City, Indiana: Press of Oakland City Journal, 1907; William M. Cockrum, *History of the Underground Railroad: as It Was Conducted by the Anti-Slavery League*, Oakland City, IN: J. M. Cockrum Press, 1915; Gil R. Stormont, *History of Gibson County*, Indianapolis: B. F. Bowen, 1914.

Coffin, Levi (1798–1877). There have been many individuals who have been called the president of the Underground Railroad, but no one better deserves that title than Levi Coffin. A shrewd manager of men and a masterful leader, he assisted an estimated 3,300 fugitive slaves at his homes in Newport (now Fountain City), Indiana, and Cincinnati, Ohio, from 1826 up through the Civil War.

Born on a farm in Guilford County, North Carolina, near present-day Greensboro, Coffin was a descendent of Quakers who settled Nantucket Island in Massachusetts. His father, also named Levi, grew mainly corn and wheat, and raised hogs for the market. It was one of many small Quaker farms in the area where slaves were not needed. The Quaker injunction against owning slaves that was circulated during the Revolutionary War in America and England had, for the most part, put an end to slavery among the Friends. In 1780 the New Garden Meeting of Coffin's family had followed that example by disowning those who continued to own slaves.

Portrait of Levi Coffin, circa 1845, by Marion Blair. Courtesy of Levi Coffin House.

The Cofin farm was near a route through which coffle gangs passed on their way south. Coffin recalled the first time, at the age of seven, he witnessed a coffle. He had seen slaves working on neighboring farms before, but never had seen them chained together. Coffin's father, who was chopping wood, asked them, "Well, boys, why do they chain you?"

"They have taken us away from our wives and children, and they chain us lest we should make our escape and go back to them," one slave said sadly.

Coffin asked his father why they were being treated like this, and his father explained their status as slaves. Coffin remembered thinking how terrible he would feel if his father was taken away from him.

Some years later Coffin noticed a group of wagons pass, and not long after he saw a lone black man carrying a large bundle trailing after the wagons. The man stopped and asked Coffin how far ahead the wagons were, and then hurried off in pursuit. The next time Coffin saw the man was at a blacksmith's shop, where a chain had been latched to his neck. Coffin discovered that the man was a slave who had been running after his family, who had been sold, and that the man had been arrested. Coffin then witnessed the arrival of the slave's master in his buggy.

"Now you shall know what slavery is," the master said. "Just wait till I get you back home!"

The master grabbed the chain latched to the slave's neck and attached it to the axle of his buggy. Setting off in his buggy, he had his horse trot so swiftly that the slave had to race after to prevent himself from being dragged onto the ground. With horror Coffin watched as the slave and buggy disappeared into the distance but not out of his memory.

Such incidents of cruelty commonly triggered the deeply felt abomination that motivated many of the Underground Railroad's most dedicated workers.

During Coffin's youth, North Carolina Quakers continued their efforts to eliminate slavery in their state. The New Garden Meeting formed a manumission society, which purchased slaves in an effort to help them become emancipated, and of which Coffin became a member. However, state laws discouraged manumission, and public opinion supported the newly formed Colonization society. The North Carolina Manumission Society especially frustrated Coffin when it made expatriation to Africa a condition of freedom for those the society emancipated. It drove the Quakers, along with the many slaves they had emancipated, to the Northwest Territories, where slavery was prohibited.

Vestal Coffin, Levi's older cousin, led him into the work of aiding fugitive slaves. It began around 1818 when a free black man, Benjamin Benson, was kidnapped by a slave trader, John Thompson, and brought to the New Garden area. A local slave named Saul learned of this and told Vestal, who contacted authorities in Delaware. They issued a warrant for Thompson's arrest. Before the warrant could be served, Thompson sent Benson to Georgia and denied he knew any such person. Without Benson, there was no evidence to charge him with a crime. Before long, proof of Benson's existence was established, and the courts ordered Thompson to bring Benson back.

During this affair, there was an attempt in New Garden to kidnap John Dimery, a newly emancipated slave. The man's daughter went for help to Vestal, who with another Quaker was able to catch the kidnappers and force them to release him. Dimery was then sent to live in Richmond, Indiana, where a settlement of North Carolina Quakers had been established.

Vestal continued to aid slaves seeking their freedom, and enlisted Levi's help. In 1821 Jack Barnes, a slave who had been given his freedom in the will of his master, fled to New Garden after the heirs had claimed him as their slave. When advertisements for his capture began appearing in the newspapers, Barnes asked for help in moving to a free state, and it was arranged to send him to Indiana with Bethuel Coffin, one of Levi's cousins. At the same time, another slave named Sam was hiding on the grounds of Levi's father's farm, fleeing from a cruel master named Osborne, who lived not far from the Coffins. Hearing that a black man had left for Indiana with Bethuel Coffin, Osborne left in pursuit of them, thinking the black man might be Sam. Fearing that Osborne would recognize Barnes from the advertisements, Levi was sent on the family's fastest horse to warn his cousin.

Coffin met Osborne along the way. He explained to Osborne that he was on his way to a relative's home. Glad to find company on the lonely road, Osborne asked Coffin to join him and possibly help him catch up with his slave. Coffin agreed to help. This was the first time in Coffin's life that he would need to use his powers of deception, a skill he would use many more times in his future Underground Railroad work, and he ably acted the part of Osborne's friend. Having traveled along this route in the past, Coffin was acquainted with a local tavern owner and judge, whom he knew was sympathetic to slaves, and he suggested that they stop there. He confided his predicament to the tavern owner, and when Osborne asked to hire a posse of men to help with the rendition of Sam, the tavern owner saw to it that the posse would only consist of men who would prevent Osborne from trying to take Jack Barnes, if he recognized him. In the end, this was unnecessary as Osborne failed to recognize Barnes.

When Coffin returned to New Garden, his next objective was to move Sam to safety. While continuing to help Osborne with his search for Sam, Coffin and his cousin arranged to send Sam with another Quaker, David Grose, who was moving west. The plan was to supply Sam with papers testifying to his freedom and have him travel on foot at night behind Grose. Each morning, he would join Grose for breakfast and obtain other provisions he might need. Unfortunately, one night, because of a problem with wolves, Sam lost track of Grose somewhere in Virginia. He ended up at the cabin of a poor white family. They pretended to be his friends, but instead sent for the Sheriff, thinking they could collect a reward for his rendition. To make matters worse, Sam's freedom papers had been left with Grose. An advertisement was placed in various newspapers, and Osborne came across one and found Sam in the Wythe Court jail. Osborne took possession of Sam, and he never was seen again. Osborne claimed to have sold him, but many believed that he had murdered Sam somewhere in the Virginia mountains. Osborne also sought to arrest Jesse and Abel Stanley, cousins of the Coffins, for "negro stealing," because he had received reports that Sam had been seen with them. Jesse fled immediately to Philadelphia, and Abel, who had already made arrangements for the sale of his farm, moved soon after.

The increasing hostility to those who showed sympathy to slaves, and noxious laws like one that required all emancipated slaves to leave the state, pushed Quakers out of North Carolina. During these years Levi taught school, including a school for slaves on Sundays, and aided his cousin Vestal in helping slaves gain their freedom. The slave Saul, who had informed them about Benson, became their close associate. It was his job to watch the coffle gangs and inquire among the slaves if any were kidnap victims. According to Addison Coffin, the son of Vestal, Levi and Vestal would conceal those they were aiding in a thicket where they would meet at night and plan their method of escape. Among their obstacles were slave patrols that had been formed to hunt fugitive slaves. Of this time Levi wrote that "My sack of corn generally contained supplies of bacon and corn bread for the slaves, and many a time I sat in the thickets with them as they devoured my bounty, and listened to the stories they told of hard masters and cruel treatment."

By 1822 Coffin decided that his future did not reside in Carolina, and he took a trip west with Benjamin White, who was moving his family there. It took them five weeks to get to Richmond, Indiana, just west of the border with Ohio and about fifty miles north of the Ohio River. They spent several weeks traveling among the Quaker settlements visiting relatives. Coffin settled down for the winter in Honey Creek, about thirty miles from Richmond, teaching school at several locations. In the spring his cousin, Allen Hiatt, asked Coffin to join him on a trip to western Illinois. Coffin went as far west as Springfield, but when his cousin wanted to push farther west with a family they had met along the way, Coffin decided he had gone far enough and turned back. He returned to Honey Creek, where he resumed teaching, and then in the fall returned to North Carolina.

The next year he married Catharine White, the sister of Benjamin, and took teaching positions at several schools. However, when his parents left for Indiana in 1825, leaving him as the last member of his family in North Carolina, he and Catharine decided to move to Indiana. In 1826 they purchased property in Newport (today called Fountain City), about eight miles north of Richmond, where a number of Quakers from his meeting had settled and had established a meeting which they also called New Garden. Coffin opened a general store, purchasing his goods in Cincinnati, which was sixty-five miles south.

That year Vestal died unexpectedly at the age of thirty-four. For the next forty years, Coffin, then twenty-nine, would put into practice all that he had learned from Vestal as a conductor of the Underground Railroad. He soon found that there was a great need for someone like him in Newport as it was on a direct line of the Underground Railroad, primarily because of a black settlement in Cabin Creek, fifteen miles north of Newport. Coffin made it known to his neighbors that his home welcomed fugitive slaves. He aided his first emigrants from slavery during the winter of 1826, and encouraged other Quakers to join him.

Coffin's home became well known to other conductors in the region, and became an important terminal for those being conducted north from New Albany, Jeffersonville, and Madison, Indiana, and from Cincinnati. Many came through Union County and were assisted by conductor **William Beard**, another Guilford County native who had moved to Salem, Indiana, thirty miles south of Newport. "Seldom a week passed without our receiving passengers by this mysterious road," Coffin wrote.

Fellow Quakers, who had formerly avoided participation, began to contribute clothing and to forward fugitive slaves along their way, but most still were reluctant to harbor them. Because of this, the Coffins were prepared to accommodate them day or night. Generally it was at night, and often after he and his wife had gone to bed. A gentle rap at the door was the signal. He would lead them in quietly and keep the house dark until everyone was safely inside. Then the shades would be drawn, the candles lit, and the fireplace stoked, and his wife Katy would begin preparing food. Coffin also tried to keep a team of horses ready in case the fugitive slaves needed to be moved quickly, and if more than one wagon was needed, he could call on his neighbors. For small groups that he transported, he used a false-bottomed wagon to hide them. At other times he would dress up men as Quaker women, a commonly used subterfuge.

"The care of so many necessitated much work and anxiety on our part, but we assumed the burden of our own will and bore it cheerfully," Coffin wrote. "It was never too cold or stormy, or the hour of night too late for my wife to rise from sleep, and provide food and comfortable lodging for the fugitives. Her sympathy for those in distress never tired, and her efforts in their behalf never abated."

The Coffins lived in Newport for twenty years, aiding on average about 100 fugitive slaves a year. Not only were they required to provide food, shelter, and transportation, but also they supplied clothing and many shoes. A sewing society of local women met at the Coffin house to make clothing. Also, frequently some fugitives required medical assistance, and the Coffins called on their good friend Dr. Henry H. Way. On some occasions, fugitive slaves stayed and worked before moving on. Those who had left their masters for weeks or months were thought to be relatively safe to do this because after such a lengthy period, slavecatchers likely were no longer looking for them.

Not surprisingly, Coffin was frequently visited by slavecatchers. "They knew me well, and knew that I harbored slaves and aided them to escape," he wrote, "but they never ventured to search my premises, or molest me in any way." This was, in part, because of the aggressive manner in which he dealt with them, saying that he would have them arrested for trespassing or kidnapping if they did not have proper legal papers to enter his house and the proper proof that they were the owners of the slaves they sought. In addition, Coffin was well respected in his community, not only as a successful business man but also as director of the Richmond branch of the Indiana State Bank, so he had the support to back up his words.

Among the many fugitive slaves he aided, Coffin singled out some whose stories were especially compelling and related them in his *Reminiscences.* A separate entry has been devoted to one of them, **Aunt Rachel**, and a summary of several more is included here.

John Moore (called Jim by Coffin), a slave in Kentucky, made a successful escape through Madison, Indiana, and, with the help of **George DeBaptiste** and William Beard, was forwarded to Coffin and on to Canada. He remained in Canada for several months, but was not happy because he had left his wife and children behind in slavery. He wanted to bring them out. He hatched a plan, one that few would dare to undertake. He would go back to his master, tell him he was sick of freedom, and beg his forgiveness; then when the moment was right, he would flee with his family.

On his return, Moore meekly and remorsefully approached his master: "I thought I wanted to be free, master," he said, "so I run away and went to Canada. But I had a hard time there and soon got tired of taking care of myself. I thought I would rather live with master again and be a good servant. I found that Canada was . . . too cold, and . . . those people called abolitionists . . . are a mean set of rascals."

Moore's convincing performance charmed his master, who readily accepted his explanation. In the next months, Moore was as faithful a servant as any master could want. At the same time, he was making arrangements for a second flight to freedom, this time with his wife and children. In the spring, the appointed day arrived, and Moore took not only his family but also other slaves, his party numbering fourteen in all. His familiarity with the route to freedom prevented them from being apprehended despite the fact that a posse of slavecatchers had been dispatched in pursuit of them. Coffin hid them for several days in Newport. He then sent them along an alternate route by way of Spartansburg, Greenville, and Mercer County, Ohio, and finally to Sandusky, where they took a boat to Fort Malden (Amhersburg), Canada.

Coffin had a reunion with Moore on one of his visits to Canada. Moore said he hoped God would forgive him for lying to his master, but that he was happy now that he would never have to return to his master's plantation in Kentucky.

A large network was developed by Coffin, and his name became legendary in the Midwest. Not surprisingly he collaborated with **John Rankin**. One of the most famous of all fugitive slaves was aided by both men. The story of Eliza Harris was related by Coffin with a detail not provided in the stories by the Rankin family: that two of her own children already had died. When Eliza returned to the Rankins three years later, the reason for her visit was to get her grown daughter and grandchildren out of slavery, something which is not mentioned in the Coffin account. On her first trip, Eliza stayed several days with Coffin, who forwarded her along the Greenville branch of the Underground Railroad to Sandusky, where she took a boat to Canada. In 1854, while on a visit to Chatham, Canada, Levi and Katy had a reunion with her.

Another collaboration between Coffin and Rankin involved a black man, Robert Burrel. Coffin had hired him at the recommendation of Burrel's former employer who was not able to retain him during the winter months. Burrel was usually quiet and seemed to have serious matters on his mind, Coffin wrote. After some months trust had developed between them. Burrel confessed that he was a fugitive slave who had left his free wife and children behind in Tennessee, and had come north in an effort to save money to purchase his freedom after which he would resume life with his family.

Coffin advised Burrel to seek another resolution to his problem. Buying one's freedom was fraught with difficulties. Instead, Coffin contacted Rankin, a native of Tennessee, to see if he might be able to contact Burrel's wife and, through the Underground Railroad, bring her to Newport. Coincidentally, relatives of Rankin were visiting that area of Tennessee, so Coffin sent money to cover the costs of transport. However, when the Rankin relatives contacted Burrel's wife, she didn't trust them, thinking it was a trick. After two years of trying to convince her of Rankin's reliability, they finally persuaded her, and she and her children were brought to Ripley. Rankin forwarded them to Newport, and the Burrel family was reunited. Burrel continued to work for Coffin, and bought a house in Newport. When the second Fugitive Slave Law was passed, the Burrels moved to Canada.

The correspondence between Coffin and Rankin is an example of how the Underground Railroad could work quietly behind the scenes without inciting slaveholders. It is worth pointing out that it was a rule of Coffin, Rankin, and **Thomas Garrett**, probably the three most prolific Underground Railroad conductors, never to entice slaves to use the Underground Railroad. They felt it would jeopardize their roles as conductors, but they did support those who crossed the borderline and rescued slaves.

Interestingly, Coffin claimed that the origin of the Underground Railroad lay in the South, where its operation was significantly different. While most Northerners involved in the Railroad operated out of principle and selfless concern for humanity, Coffin said that in the South the motivation was more likely economic. "For the sake of money, people in the South would help the slaves escape and convey them across the Line," he wrote. "Free colored people who had relatives in slavery were willing to contribute . . . to aid in getting their loved ones out of bondage."

This was how seventeen fugitive slaves, the largest party received by Coffin, were able to make their way from Kentucky to Newport. They had organized their own escape and hired a white man to ferry them across the river near Madison, Indiana. The slaves stayed with Coffin for two days, though not without anxiety as slavecatchers were close behind. Coffin had to split them up and move them to various homes in Cabin Creek until they could be forwarded to Canada.

In 1844 Coffin made his first trip to Canada, with his Underground Railroad collaborator, William Beard, to check on the welfare of fugitive slaves. That same year he began to meditate more deeply on the matter of the use of goods produced by slave labor. "I read the testimony of John Woolman and other writers, and became convinced that it was wrong to use the product of slave labor. I felt that it was inconsistent to condemn slaveholders for withholding from their fellow-men their just, natural and God-given rights, and then, by purchasing the fruits of the labor of their slaves, give them the strongest motive for continuing their wickedness and oppression."

What troubled Coffin was that not only was he using these products, but also he was selling them at his store, and there was no remedy because free labor products were hard to get. But this wasn't going to stop Coffin. He took a trip east and discovered that Friends in Philadelphia had built their own cotton factory, and were getting their raw cotton from Quaker farms in North Carolina. He also visited New York City, and found free labor goods being imported from the West Indies. He purchased goods from merchants in both cities for his store. The only problem was that the purchased goods were much more expensive, and he could not make much of a profit selling them.

In 1846 a free labor produce convention was held at the Friends Meeting in Salem, Indiana. Prominent abolitionists from Ohio and Indiana attended, including Cincinnati residents Rev. William Brisbane, entrepreneur Edward Harwood, and attorney John Joliffe. They were among the leaders of a resolution to open and subsidize a free produce store and distribution center in their city. When a vote was held to select someone to operate the store, Coffin was chosen by acclimation. But he refused the offer. Neither he nor his wife wanted to leave Newport. Only seven years earlier the Coffins had built their house, where they planned to live out their lives.

After some months and with encouragement from many individuals, however, Coffin accepted when the Free Produce Committee put in a second call for his services. In April 1847 he moved to Cincinnati, selling his business in Newport and renting out his house for five years. Little did he realize that Cincinnati would remain his home for the rest of his life.

When Coffin moved, he expected that his twenty-year service in the Underground Railroad would come to an end. In Newport, he left behind a close-knit group of co-workers who included Dr. Way, William Hough, Benjamin Thomas, Billy Bush, Harvey Davis, Robert Green, Samuel Clark, Harmon Clark, William R. Williams, and Robert Bailey.

"My wife and I. . . . hoped to find in Cincinnati enough active workers to relieve us from further service, but we soon found that we would have more to do than ever." Cincinnati was the constant refuge of fugitive slaves because its large black population had many relatives still in slavery. Also, because the city was located directly across the river from Kentucky, it was a major port of trade with the South. Among Coffin's closest co-workers in the Underground Railroad in Cincinnati were the leaders in the free produce movement that brought him there, such as Rev. Brisbane of the First Baptist Church and Harwood. He also could call on John Hatfield and William Casey of the Zion Baptist Church, black entrepreneur Henry Boyd, confectioners Cornelius and Thomas Burnett, attorney and educator Samuel Lewis, philanthropist Nicholas Longworth, local pork producer George Davis, the Doram family, Rev. Jonathan Hall, and William Fuller, among others. He also had a number of reliable co-workers in the College Hill area, including Rev. Jonathan Cable and the Wilson family.

Coffin said that one of the reasons he was needed by the Underground Railroad in Cincinnati was its lack of management there. This was a skill that Coffin had in abundance. An example of this was the funeral procession arranged to pass twenty-eight fugitive slaves conducted by John Fairfield through the city. Another was his use of the city's judicial system, as related by Rutherford B. Hayes, the future U.S. President, who was an assistant district attorney in Cincinnati during this time. "There was a period there when I never went to bed without expecting to be called out by Levi Coffin," he said. "I should say that there came to my knowledge forty cases (regarding fugitive slaves); but of this number only three or four cases came to the ears of the public."

Hayes said that a number of local justice officials were sympathetic to fugitive slaves, including Justice of the Peace David Fisher, County Prosecuting Attorney Joseph Cox, and Prosecuting Attorney of the Police Court William Dickson. Also at Coffin's disposal were the prominent abolitionist attorneys Joliffe and Salmon Chase, the latter called "the attorney of the fugitive slaves."

Like the sewing society that the Coffins had established in Newport to provide clothing for fugitive slaves, they organized a similar society in Cincinnati. They began to meet at the Coffins' home weekly. Another responsibility the Coffins accepted was the operation of the Colored Orphan Asylum, whose services were in need of rehabilitation.

Coffin was a master in dealing with people. In the continuing search to find cheaper and more accessible free labor products, he and others in Cincinnati formed the Western

Free Produce Manufacturing Company. They eventually came up with an arrangement to get cotton from Mississippi and have it refined for production with a cotton gin that the company purchased for the planter. In search of other farms that didn't use slave labor, Coffin took a trip into the Deep South where he socialized with many slaveholders. Despite his obviously antagonistic views, he was not shy about revealing them. Instead, he would calmly and logically explain why he believed slavery was wrong. Considering the animosity held in the South for abolitionists, it is quite remarkable that Coffin was not only able to maintain a congenial relationship with the slaveholders, but in some cases convert them. "I believe that our traveling through the cotton-growing States and buying free-labor cotton, encouraging paid labor and discouraging unpaid labor, were the means of preaching abolitionism in the slave States," he wrote, "and was really pleading the cause of the poor slave."

During their early years in Cincinnati, the Coffins had as a frequent house guest **Laura Haviland**, who not only ministered to the needs of the black community, but also undertook several missions into the South to bring out fugitive slaves. The latter was against the Coffins' advice but with their full support.

A number of important court cases involved Cincinnati incidents during the 1850s in which Joliffe, Hayes, and Chase defended fugitive slaves. The unsuccessful outcome in 1858 of the case involving news reporter John Connelly may have been avoided had Coffin not been out of town and thus not able to assist in the passage of the two fugitive slaves whom Connelly had hidden until his return. The tragic consequences of Margaret Garner in 1856 may also have been avoided had Coffin's help been enlisted earlier. But by the time his advice was sought, the authorities had been alerted to her whereabouts.

However, a court case in 1853 involving a fugitive slave named Louis owed its successful conclusion in part to the management skills of Coffin. Louis had escaped from Kentucky and settled in Columbus. After several years, in 1853 his master learned of his whereabouts and had him arrested under the jurisdiction of the Fugitive Slave Law. While the marshal of Columbus was enroute to Cincinnati by railroad with Louis in custody, on the way to Kentucky, a message for help was telegraphed to John Joliffe. He immediately went to see Coffin and they obtained a warrant to arrest the marshal for kidnapping. When the marshal and Louis got off the train, the marshal was arrested by the sheriff of Cincinnati, and Louis was placed in custody to await the disposition of the case. Meanwhile, the slaveholder was allowed to return to Kentucky to obtain evidence that Louis was indeed his legal property.

The trial lasted several days, and after its completion, Commissioner S. S. Carpenter deferred his ruling until the next day. In the center of the courtroom was a long table, which was extremely crowded. On one end were the judge and lawyers, behind whom was a crowd of blacks supportive of Lewis; on the other end were the slaveholder and the defense attorney, behind whom was a crowd of whites, many also supportive of Louis, including Coffin himself. The hearing was tedious and the judge labored over his words. He spoke in a low tone and was difficult to understand, which caused everyone to carefully focus attention on him. After the failure of Joliffe to win the freedom of another fugitive slave, Wash McQuerry, earlier that year, the worst was expected.

Louis felt the crowd moving in on him, and moved his chair back slightly to get more room. No one seemed to notice, so he moved it back farther. With no one yet taking notice, he slowly rose from his seat. Coffin, who was standing close behind him, wrote later that an abolitionist nudged him with his foot to move him even farther back. Then another abolitionist put a hat on his head, and others pushed him behind

> **Margaret Garner**
>
> What could ever possess a mother to murder her-two year-old daughter? This is a question that is at the heart of the story of Margaret Garner.
>
> A Kentucky slave, Garner had four children, three of whom it was believed were those of her master, and whom some historians believe were the result of her being raped. She was twenty-two years old when, on a bitterly cold night in January of 1856, she and her slave husband Robert, his parents, and her four children crowded into a sleigh for a twenty-mile trip to the Ohio River and Cincinnati. Their destination was the home of Elijah Kite, a cousin of Garner.
>
> They arrived about 3 a.m., and it was so cold that they were able to walk across the frozen river. It took them awhile to locate Kite's residence, and this may have led to their discovery. Fearing this, Kite went to see **Levi Coffin** following breakfast. "Kite felt alarmed for the safety of the party that had arrived at his house," Coffin wrote in his *Reminiscences*. "I told him that they were in a very unsafe place and must be removed at once."
>
> But when Kite returned home, it was already too late, as the slavecatchers surrounded his house just after he had re-entered. Robert Garner attempted to hold them off in a gun battle. However, he was outnumbered. When the slavecatchers battered down the door, Margaret grabbed a butcher knife and slit the throat of her daughter Mary, and then began to go after her other children but was stopped by the slavecatchers.
>
> She was tried for murder, which resulted in her conviction. Her sentence was to be returned to slavery, and she was sold to a trader who sent her into the Deep South. While en route on a steamboat, she jumped off with another daughter, who drowned. Garner died two years later of tuberculosis.

the crowd. Somehow, without the notice of his master or the marshal, Louis was out of the courtroom and racing through the streets of Cincinnati. It happened so fast that the authorities had no time to apprehend him.

A vigorous search was begun for Louis, who was hiding in the outskirts of the city. Coffin and his vigilance committee met and agreed that he needed to be moved, and they had him disguised as a woman and brought to a house in the city where he remained for about a week. In the meantime, Coffin arranged for Louis to be moved a local church where he was hidden in the basement. He remained there several more weeks, while Coffin conspired to create disinformation about his whereabouts. A telegram was sent to Cincinnati from Columbus, and published in the *Cincinnati Gazette,* claiming that Louis had passed there on the train bound for Cleveland. Another telegram was sent from Cleveland, saying he had arrived there and had taken the boat for Detroit. However, Louis had never moved from the church. Three weeks had passed when a Presbyterian minister and his wife, who were visiting Cincinnati, offered to convey Louis out of the city in their personal carriage. Arrangements were made, and they drove to the back door of the church one morning and picked up Louis disguised as a woman with a veil over his face. They took him to an Underground Railroad conductor, located thirty miles outside the city, who conveyed him to Sandusky where he took a boat to Canada. In the end, Louis's master sued the marshal from Columbus for his failure to deliver Louis to Kentucky, and the marshal agreed to pay him $800.

In 1856 Coffin sold his store and leased a large building with more than thirty rooms in what was then the northern part of the city. In addition to making it his residence, he also used it as a boarding house for local educators and clergy, as well as a meeting place for personal friends and Quakers who came to Cincinnati on business. As would be expected, it also functioned as "a very suitable depot of the Underground Railroad." During this time, Coffin had a wagon made specifically for the purpose of transporting fugitive slaves. It had a passenger compartment with curtains and seats for six passengers. Friends called it "the Underground Railroad car," and Coffin's horse, "the locomotive."

Among the shipment of fugitive slaves Coffin assisted during this time was a party of fourteen who had crossed a frozen Ohio River from Covington on foot.

By the time of the Civil War Coffin had retired from business, "with very limited means," as he described it. This humanitarian, who had been eminently successful in his business, apparently had spent most of his money helping others. But he did not retire from his personal obligations. He helped to organize the Western Freedmen's Aid Commission, which sent aid to freedmen in Mississippi and Arkansas, and in 1864 he went to England where he helped to organize the English Freedmen's Aid Society, which raised hundreds of thousands of dollars to help newly emancipated slaves.

Following the adoption of the Fifteenth Amendment, which gave black men the right to vote, a celebration was held in Cincinnati to celebrate the occasion. Coffin, of course, was invited and asked to speak. He closed with the following often quoted words:

> I have held the position of President of the Underground Railroad for more than thirty years. The title was given to me by slave-hunters who could not find their fugitive slaves after they got into my hands. I accepted the office thus conferred upon me, and endeavored to perform my duty faithfully. Government has now taken the work of providing for the slaves out of our hands. The stock of the Underground Railroad has gone down in the market, the business is spoiled, the road is of no further use. . . . I now resign my office and declare the operations of the Underground Railroad at an end.

SUGGESTED READING: Fergus Bordewich, *Bound for Canaan,* New York: HarperCollins, 2005; Levi Coffin, *Reminiscences of Levi Coffin, the Reputed President of the Underground Railroad; Being a Brief History of the Labors of a Lifetime in Behalf of the Slave, with the Stories of Numerous Fugitives, Who Gained Their Freedom Through His Instrumentality, and Many Other Incidents,* Cincinnati: Robert Clarke & Co., 1880; Charles Theodore Greve, *Centennial History of Cincinnati and Representative Citizens,* Chicago: Biographical Publishing Co., 1904; Bryan Prince, *I Came as a Stranger,* Toronto: Tundra Books, 2004; Wilbur Siebert, *The Mysteries of Ohio's Underground Railroads,* Columbus, OH: Long's College Book Company, 1951.

Colver, Nathaniel (1794–1870). A simple farm boy who had learned the shoemaker's trade, Nathaniel Colver was called to the ministry by the evangelical movements of his day, following in the footsteps of his Baptist minister father. It was a path that led him to national prominence, though he sometimes drew the ire of abolitionists such as William Lloyd Garrison for refusing to adopt the policy of "no union with slaveholders" by maintaining close personal ties with Baptist colleagues in the South who owned slaves.

At the age of twenty-five, Colver accepted his first pastorate in Clarendon, Vermont, in 1819. From the start his natural gifts as a preacher were evident. An account of a sermon he gave as a circuit rider in 1825 at Lebanon Springs, New York, is illustrative: "The preacher seemed to speak almost as one inspired," wrote William Kendall. "One thing is certain, he held his audience in rapt attention for nearly an hour and a half . . . let me say that no sermon I ever heard, and I have heard a great variety, made such a lasting impression on my mind."

Such comments about the preaching ability of Colver were commonplace throughout his life. He was a tall, powerfully built man whose presence and voice commanded respect. Ministers called him the best preacher they'd ever heard. People were known to be brought to tears at his sermons, or to have their "blood run cold," as another expressed it. His sermons even brought praise from slaveholders who sat in his church and were the object of his nerve-rattling rhetoric and razor-sharp logic.

After seven years in Franklin County, Colver moved to Fort Ann in 1828, and from there to the Bottskill Baptist Church of Union Village, Washington County, New York. It was in 1834, just before accepting the position in Union Village, while passing through Washington, D.C., en route to Richmond for a pastorate interview that the direction of his life changed.

> I saw an old man, with gray hair and tottering limbs, going down Pennsylvania avenue, hobbling upon his crutches as fast as he could, weeping and lamenting, trying to catch a glimpse of his lost child, sold to the soul-drivers, and now bound for the rice-swamps of the South, and saying, 'They promised me he should never be taken from me, but they've sold him, and I shall never see him again!'—I could stand it no longer.

Needless to say, Colver turned down the Southern pastorate and embraced abolition. Though he was effective in converting others to abolition, his efforts met with great difficulty during his early years there. The Bottskill Church had to deal with mobs who threw rocks and other "missiles" at the church during services, and Colver often was heckled during his sermons. In one instance he was required to exercise "muscular Christianity" in removing one particularly obnoxious heckler.

Colver also became a lecturer for the state antislavery society during his pastorate at the Bottskill church. In 1836 he revisited his former congregations in Franklin County and helped to organize that county's first antislavery society.

In 1837 Colver made an abolition tour through western Massachusetts, giving eighteen lectures in twelve days. One newspaper account stated that he spoke "thoughts that breathe and words that burn." At another lecture, a mob fired a cannon into one of his meetings and blew off the hand of a young man in the audience.

He also organized antislavery societies in Essex County, New York, and that year, a curious letter from an anonymous minister from Union Village was published in the *Emancipator*. The author was undoubtedly Nathaniel Colver.

> Not 36 hours since, the writer of this note was called on by a colored man who had with him testimonials of the highest character, from several clergymen, and gentlemen known to the writer, showing him to have recently been a slave in ________, and now on his way to Canada, a land of freedom.

In 1838 Colver decided to resign from the Bottskill Church. By this time the church had added 600 members and was offering a monthly abolition service in concert with the Free Church, an abolitionist church, whose house of worship had not yet been built. Colver's decision to leave the Bottskill Church was agonizing because of his great success. "It was a hard struggle," Colver wrote, "but the blood of Lovejoy turned the scale." Influenced by the murder of abolitionist newspaper editor Elijah Lovejoy, Colver appears to have felt that he could do more for the cause of abolition in higher-profile Boston than in the remote town of Union Village. The church trustees responded that, "In dissolving this relationship . . . we know it is not the result of any dissatisfaction on either side. . . . No man could be more pleasantly situated . . . and no church could be more cordially satisfied."

Colver left Union Village for Boston in 1839, with regrets from both parties (as was usually the case during his ministry), to take over as pastor of the then-nascent Tremont Street Church. His power as a preacher quickly gained a following, and he turned the church into the most important venue for debate on the question of slavery in a city that was the intellectual leader of abolitionism. He also became a member of the Boston's famed vigilance committee.

Little information is available about his role in the committee, but one case involving the fugitive slave **George Latimer** and his wife was resolved with the help of Colver when he became involved in the agreement to pay $400 to their owner in return for their freedom. When the Fugitive Slave Law of 1850 was passed, he publicly attacked it in his sermons. "I do not say that resistance to every unrighteous law is a duty," he said in regard to the law. "Laws may make very unrighteous and oppressive exactions upon us, and it may be our duty to submit. . . . It is only when the law commands the subject to do that which the law of God forbids, or to fail to do that which the law of God commands, that he is bound to resist it."

In 1852, after thirteen years at Tremont Temple, he decided to take a respite from its pressing duties and he took a one-year pastorate in a village twenty-one miles southeast of Boston. Coincidentally, just before he left, a fire destroyed the Tremont, and a black man who had been living in the attic fortunately got out alive. It is believed that this may have been a hiding place that Colver reserved for fugitive slaves.

The Temple had become an institution in Boston, so plans to rebuild were immediately put in place, and within a year a new edifice was completed. In 1853 Colver became pastor of the First Baptist Church in Detroit, and then in 1856 the First Baptist Church in Cincinnati. Both were major terminals on the Underground Railroad, but whether or not he was working behind the scenes is not known. However, he had now reached the height of his powers as a preacher, his legend preceding him, and he made his views on slavery well known.

In Cincinnati he announced a series of Sunday evening lectures on "Slavery as a Sin." It drew overflowing crowds. On one occasion, when Colver declared that the Fugitive Slave Law was a "flagrant outrage on the laws of God" that should not be obeyed, a man in the audience cried out, "That is nothing but rank treason." Colver paused, stood tall, and looked the man in the eye. "Treason to the devil," he said, "is loyalty to God."

After **John Brown** was arrested at Harpers Ferry, Colver wrote a series of letters to Virginia Governor Wise. In one he said, "That day that sees John Brown on the scaffold sees your horizon obscured by a cloud that no sun shall ever chase from your skies . . . that day the grappling iron of your doom will have fastened upon your own soul. . . . Thence John Brown with calm, honest, loving, serene, sorrowing face is to be your companion. . . . And in that last, lone hour to which we are all hastening, when the summons shall come which calls you to your last account, the voice of John Brown will strangely mingle with that summons."

Colver moved to a farm near Chicago in 1861. But he had one last project to complete his devotion to the cause of the oppressed. He coordinated a project in Richmond, Virginia, for the American Baptist Home Mission Society, which wanted to establish a theological institute to train freedmen. Ironically, the property Colver chose to house this educational institution included the notorious slave pen of Robert Lumpkin. It had been known as The Devil's Half Acre, and had come into the possession of a former slave, who leased the property to the society. Today that training center is Virginia Union University.

Colver died in Chicago in 1870, a man who left behind many accomplishments, and who was one of the most powerful spokesmen in the battle against slavery.

SUGGESTED READING: Rev. J. A. Smith, *Memoir of Nathaniel Colver, D.D.*, Boston: Durkee and Foxcroft, Publishers, 1873.

Concklin, Seth (1802–1851). Seth Concklin performed one of the most heroic and selfless deeds in the history of the Underground Railroad. Born at Sandy Hill (now Hudson Falls), New York, he came from humble beginnings which he maintained throughout his life. His mother had been a teacher in Vermont before she married his father, who regularly went into the South for his work as a mechanic. His father died prematurely in Georgia, leaving Seth, at the age of fifteen and the oldest of five children, to be the family's sole means of support.

This circumstance established a pattern that continued throughout Concklin's life: one of self-sacrifice. Shortly afterward his mother moved to Canada, and Seth joined the army. However, while he was in the service, his mother died, and he was given a discharge to look after his sisters and brothers. He found a home for them at the Shaker community in Watervliet, New York, where he also lived for three years.

After leaving the Shakers, Concklin drifted from place to place and job to job. About this time, in 1830, he became an abolitionist. This is known because of a letter he wrote his sister condemning Colonization and praising the abolitionists. He also is listed as a financial contributor in early issues of the *Emancipator.*

Concklin was fiercely independent and fearless in defense of his moral principles, despite his small stature and slight frame. On occasions in Syracuse and Rochester, he defended black men against mobs. During the latter occasion, he attacked a man who had put a noose around the neck of a black man, and then had to run for his life. On another occasion, Concklin publicly exposed a black man who was fraudulently collecting donations for the Wilberforce Colony in Canada.

Concklin also lived in Springfield, Illinois, for a time and aided fugitive slaves. However, as was his custom, he acted alone. William Furness' profile in *The Kidnapped and the Ransomed* also suggests that Concklin ventured into the slave states at this time to assist the slaves, probably in St. Louis, which he is known to have visited.

In 1838 Concklin became excited about the outbreak of the Patriot War in which a fringe group of Americans was attempting to annex Canada to the United States. Wanting to preserve Canada as a refuge for fugitive slaves, he joined the side of the so-called Patriots with the intention of obtaining intelligence for the Canadians. He ended up being imprisoned, but was finally released when the Canadians took possession of the stockade where he was held.

That didn't stop him from heading down to Florida a few months later and joining the American army in the second Seminole War. He joined, he said, not to fight Indians but to see firsthand what it was about. What he found were lies being told about the Indians, and a war that was totally unjust.

For the next decade Concklin resided principally in Troy, New York. Despite his abolitionist beliefs, there is no record of his membership in any abolition society or the Liberty Party, which was quite active in that area. However, when William L. Chaplin was arrested and imprisoned in Maryland in 1850, Concklin hatched a plan for his rescue. Chaplin was released before it could be enacted, but Concklin found another heroic mission in the pages of the *Pennsylvania Freeman,* the rescue from slavery of the family of **Peter Still**. **William Still** later wrote that Concklin's mission was known only to the Still family and to **J. Miller McKim**, the Anti-Slavery Society's executive director. They were skeptical of its success and thought it much too dangerous. But with the likelihood that purchasing Peter's family would be far too expensive, the Still family and McKim decided to take their chances with Concklin, who agreed to undertake the mission for expenses only.

Peter, who had purchased his own freedom, but kept it secret from his former masters in Alabama, had gone to Alabama posing as a slave, and revealed to his wife Vina that a rescue plan was being hatched. He took a gingham cape from Vina to give to Concklin, by which she could identify him. When Peter returned to Philadelphia, he provided Concklin with as much information as possible about the geography of Tuscambia and the McKiernan plantation where Vina lived. Peter told Concklin to contact the slave minister, William Handy, who lived on the plantation and would assist in the escape.

Concklin departed for Cincinnati unarmed, with only a few items of clothing and the $100 supplied by the Stills. Despite the danger of his mission, he never bore arms, he said, for fear that he would have to use them. In Cincinnati he met with **Levi Coffin**, the acknowledged leader of the Underground Railroad in the west. Concklin's first idea was to take the family by steamboat to Cincinnati, the plantation being only a few miles from the Tennessee River and the city of Florence, where there was steamboat service to the Ohio River. However, on the trip down to Alabama by steamboat, he realized that the irregularity of the steamboat schedules ruled out an escape by this means.

Concklin arrived in Alabama on January 28, 1851 on a reconnaissance mission, disguised as an unemployed miller. He set out to the McKiernan plantation and the cabin of William Handy, who arranged a secret meeting with Vina. At that time, Concklin showed her the gingham cape and explained the escape plan. They would take a rowboat by way of the Tennessee River to the Ohio River, and then go up the Ohio River to the Wabash River, which they would follow to central Indiana where they would connect with the Underground Railroad. The next day he met with her sons, Peter and Levin, young men of twenty-two and twenty, who would accompany their mother on the trip.

In a letter from Eastport, Mississippi dated February 3, during his return to the north, Concklin expressed some of the difficulties he was experiencing:

> Our friends in Cincinnati have failed finding anybody to assist me on my return. Searching the country opposite Paducah, I find that the whole country fifty miles round is inhabited only by Christian wolves. It is customary, when a strange Negro is seen, for any white man to seize the Negro and convey such Negro through and out of the state of Illinois to Paducah, Ky., and lodge such stranger in Paducah jail, and there claim such reward as may be offered by the master.

On his return, Concklin traveled through Illinois and Indiana. He realized now that that the most hazardous part of his journey would be near the Ohio River borderline between the free states of Illinois and Indiana and the slave state of Kentucky, where many slavecatchers kept a close watch. In Indiana, he found the assistance of David Stormont in Princeton. His plan was to take Peter Still's family to Stormont, who had boasted he had never lost a fugitive slave, and leave them with him to supervise the rest of their journey to Canada.

Returning to Cincinnati, Concklin procured a six-oared barge, essentially a large, flat bottomed rowboat, and had it shipped to South Florence before he made his departure by steamboat. The plan was to depart on March 1, but the escape had to be delayed until the night of March 16. The slated time of departure was 3 a.m., but again they were delayed and didn't start on their arduous journey down the Tennessee River until daybreak.

Fortunately, Peter and Levin were able oarsmen, and the group arrived at the junction with the Ohio River 250 miles downstream in only fifty-one hours. Their journey, however, had been all downstream. Now the sons had to row upstream on the Ohio and cope with colder temperatures, aggravated by heavy rain. The group also faced the most dangerous part of their journey, as slavecatchers lurked everywhere. The plan was to travel solely at night, but they found this difficult because of the extreme cold.

After rowing seventy-five miles up the Ohio and forty-four miles up the Wabash River, the group disembarked at New Harmony, Indiana, on March 23, the seventh day of their journey. They had traveled about 369 miles and only had two threatening situations, one in Mississippi when men along the shore hailed them with gun shots, but which they ignored, and the other near Paducah, Kentucky, when a boat with armed men approached. However, seeing a white man aboard, they did not scrutinize further.

From New Harmony, the group hiked thirteen miles before they received their first assistance from the Underground Railroad at the home of a black man, Charles Grier. He provided them with a change of clothes: jeans and black cloth coats for Peter and Levin, plaid shawls for Vina and her daughter, and the more formal dress of a prosperous Midwest farmer for Concklin. Because the family didn't have passes, the story they were using was that Concklin, their former master, had emancipated them and was bringing them to his brother's farm for work.

The group continued to the home of Stormont. Why Concklin remained with them thereafter and did not let Stormont take over as previously planned is unknown. In any case, they continued up through Vincennes, probably along a route later described by **William Cockrum**: following the Wabash through Terre Haute toward a point on Lake Michigan in Lake Porter or LaPorte counties where fugitive slaves were smuggled aboard a so-called lumber bark built especially for this purpose.

Some time along their journey through Indiana, the group also met with Rev. N. R. Johnston, a Cincinnati minister and cohort of Levi Coffin, who later reported on their progress in letters to William Still.

But twenty-three miles north of Vincennes, their journey to freedom was aborted when they were apprehended by a group of white men led by John Emison. A private citizen who apparently was in the business of slavecatching, Emison questioned Concklin about his companions' identity and destination. Concklin became flustered, and after first claiming that the slaves were his property, changed his story, saying they were his brother's. This was enough to arouse Emison's suspicions. Despite acting without any legal authority, he had them tied up and placed in a wagon to be brought back to Vincennes. Concklin protested vehemently, and Emison realized the illegality of his actions, and so released him. Nevertheless, Concklin secretly followed the group. When the slavecatchers stopped for the night, he went into the wagon and attempted to untie the fugitive slaves, but was discovered by one of the slavecatchers, who pulled a gun and ordered him to leave.

In Vincennes, Vina and her family were lodged in the city jail, while telegraphic inquiries were made Southward about missing slaves who might fit their description. Meanwhile, Concklin, who identified himself as J. H. Miller, visited them every day despite Vina's pleas for him to leave and save himself. Instead, he hired a lawyer and attempted to get them released on a writ of habeas corpus, claiming that the fugitive slaves were his property. However, the writ was denied by Judge Bishop, and they were returned to jail until the following day, based merely on the suspicion that evidence would arrive by then.

Later that day, a message came to Vincennes that Bernard McKiernan was offering a reward of $400 for four fugitive slaves and $600 for the capture and return of the person responsible to Florence, Alabama. The federal marshal from Evansville, John Gavitt, said he would come to Vincennes with the necessary documents to detain Miller (Concklin) and the fugitive slaves, but only if he could share in the reward with Emison. He arrived six hours later, and a court order was obtained to detain them.

Concklin's lawyer came to release him, but Concklin feared for his safety as a result of mobs that had gathered, and his request to remain was granted by the judge. When McKiernan arrived, the Still family finally admitted that they were his property, and it became obvious that Concklin was guilty of assisting them. So he was arrested and held with the slaves.

Gavitt brought the group to Evansville, Indiana, to await the arrival of a boat to Alabama. While there, they were kept at the home of one of Gavitt's relatives, a law enforcement officer named Sherwood. The residence was also the home of Gavitt's mother. An interview was conducted with her shortly after. She said she had tried to convince Concklin to provide information about his accomplices to save himself. But he said no one was to be blamed but himself, and that he was not at all sorry: He had done his Christian duty and had a clear conscience.

Gavitt delivered the defendants to the boat, *Paul Anderson*, and placed them in the custody of McKiernan and Emison. Concklin was heavily shackled to prevent his escape. When the boat docked in Smithland, Kentucky, a barge passed. It was reported that Concklin tried to jump into the barge, but failed and fell into the river where he drowned. Later his body was recovered still in chains with his head bashed in. Levi Coffin, for one, expressed the belief that he was murdered. Considering that McKiernan told Gavitt that he would be willing to pay $1,500 to see Concklin hung, it is possible that Emison, who had split the initial $1,000 reward with Gavitt, may have committed the murder for the additional $500.

Concklin was buried in his chains in Smithland. A headboard was placed at his grave with the inscription, "Nigre thief."

SUGGESTED READING: Kenneth R. Johnson, "Peter Still, the Colbert County, Alabama, Slave Who Bought His Freedom: A Slave Family's Struggle for Freedom," *The Journal of Muscle Shoals History*, vol. 6, 1978, reprinted with permission of the Tennessee Valley Historical Society; Kate E. R. Pickard, *The Kidnapped and the Ransomed: Being the Personal Recollections of Peter Still and his Wife "Vina," after Forty Years of Slavery*, Syracuse: William T. Hamilton, also New York and Auburn: Miller, Orton and Mulligan, 1856; William Still, *The Underground Railroad*, Philadelphia: Porter and Coates, 1872.

Corliss, Hiram (1793–1877). A born leader and renowned surgeon, Hiram Corliss grew up in the farming community of Easton in Washington County, New York, coincidentally the same year the first Fugitive Slave Law was passed in 1793. As fate would have it, his life would turn him into an implacable foe of those whom that law sought to protect.

Corliss settled in nearby Union Village and his reputation as a surgeon had already been firmly established when he took up the cause of abolition in 1833. The following year he was elected president of the Washington County Anti-Slavery Society, and the year after that led a defection from his Dutch Reformed Church because of their tolerance of slavery. Two years later he led the formation of his own church based on principles of temperance and antislavery, the Orthodox Congregational Church, known as the "Free Church."

Described by his contemporaries as a commanding figure, Corliss spearheaded the formation of eight antislavery societies in the county by 1837, and that year he chaired the annual meeting of the New York State Anti-Slavery Society. Reports of fugitive slaves arriving in Union Village also were being published that year. In 1839 a major antislavery convention that he chaired was held at the newly constructed Free Church that sat across the street from his home and medical office. Among the speakers were **Gerrit Smith**, Joshua Leavitt, William L. Chaplin, and Luther Lee. All of them would make their mark as important figures in the Underground Railroad.

When the Liberty Party formed in 1840, Corliss was quick to support it. The following year, when Rev. **Abel Brown** organized the Eastern New York Anti-Slavery Society (ENYAS), which pledged its allegiance to the Liberty Party, it elected Corliss as its president. The society encompassed every county that touched the banks of the Hudson River from New York City to the Adirondacks. By this time the Hudson had become the primary thoroughfare for fugitive slaves heading north out of New York City, and the ENYAS became notorious for its forwarding of fugitive slaves, regularly announcing their comings and goings in its newspaper, the *Tocsin of Liberty,* which later changed its name to the *Albany Patriot.* Several members of the New York Committee of Vigilance were also members of the ENYAS, including Schenectady barber Richard P. G. Wright, father of the Committee's president **Theodore Wright**.

Corliss was not reticent about harboring fugitive slaves. An illustration of Corliss's devotion to antislavery is provided in a letter dated March 21, 1843, that he wrote to the *Albany Patriot.*

> We have districted our town on the plan of pledging days to labor for the slave from house to house conversing on the subject, obtaining signatures to the Liberty roll, distributing tracts and obtaining signatures to the petition for the abolition of some part of the slave system. I pledged four days, and my place of labor was in a distant part of the town, eleven miles from my residence. . . . We continued laboring from house to house until nearly 9 o'clock in the evening. We then left for home after having obtained 65 names, to the petition, 35 to the Liberty Association, 12 of whom were voters, and now pledged to vote for liberty.

In 1850 Corliss moved from Main Street around the block into an opulent Victorian mansion on Bridge Street, where he built a secret windowless room to hide fugitive slaves and which, legend claims, had a hidden passageway leading to the Battenkill River behind it. From that location the river meandered unobstructed, but for one series of rapids, to the Vermont border, a distance of twenty miles, where many sympathetic abolitionists awaited. But how many fugitive slaves came to Union Village is unknown, and it is likely that after 1850 there were few. A report that year, however, of a meeting protesting the second Fugitive Slave Law proclaimed that there were fugitive slaves living in the village at that time. One of those was a Maryland native, John Salter, who it is believed was urged by Corliss to settle there and who was the object of a rendition by slavecatchers who came to Washington County in 1858.

It was in 1851 that the Saratoga District Anti-Slavery Society was organized and installed Corliss as its president. Its guest speaker at its first annual meeting was William Lloyd Garrison, and two years later **Frederick Douglass** made a lecture tour of the county. During this time, Easton Quaker Oren B. Wilbur's memoirs testify to Corliss's participation in aiding fugitive slaves.

Corliss's influence reached all the way to Kentucky, and he contributed money for Rev. John Fee's antislavery church in Bracken County, which eventually was burned down in 1857. Among Corliss's close associates in the abolition movement was **Gerrit Smith**.

About a month prior to Harpers Ferry, he was Smith's guest at Peterboro. Considering their association as officers in the New York Anti-Slavery Society and Smith's visit to Union Village in 1839, this was a long, ongoing relationship. Such relationships among abolitionist leaders suggest some manner of organization of the Underground Railroad in upstate New York.

Corliss, whose sons George and William became internationally renowned inventors (George, being the inventor of the huge Corliss steam engine), continued his practice as a surgeon until he was eighty. He died in 1877.

SUGGESTED READING: Mary Corliss, *Corliss-Sheldon Families: Genealogical, Biographical*, Hartford: States Historical Society, 1932; *Manual of the Congregational Church in Union Village, Washington County, N.Y.*, Albany: Munsell & Rowland, 1860; Grant J. Teftt, *The Story of Union Village*, Greenwich, N.Y.: *Greenwich Journal*, 1942.

Cox, Hannah (1797–1876). Hannah Cox and her husband John were among the leading abolitionists in Kennett Square, Pennsylvania, a major terminal on the Underground Railroad, whose agents worked closely with **Thomas Garrett**. They also were founding members of the Longwood Meeting in Kennett Square, a radical group of Quakers whose members included Garrett, **Lucretia Mott**, and **Robert Purvis**.

Hannah was born in Kennett Square in the house known as Longwood, where she eventually settled and lived out her life with her husband John. He was born in nearby East Goshen, only fifteen miles away. Both were widowed when they met, John having two sons. They had two daughters and two sons. In 1829 they moved into Longwood.

Their interest in abolition stemmed from their reading *The Liberator* and attending antislavery lectures, and in particular to the inspiring lectures of the noted antislavery lecturer Charles Burleigh, who came to Kennett Square in 1835. At the time, Burleigh was twenty-five years old and unknown. Burleigh was known for his unkempt appearance, much like Theodore Weld, and showed up unannounced at a meeting on phrenology, walking all the way from Philadelphia, a distance of about thirty miles. After asking permission to speak, he captivated his listeners, and afterward, when he asked if he could present a lecture on slavery the following evening, there was enthusiastic approval. At that meeting, Burleigh's words inspired the agitation and ferment for abolition and the Underground Railroad for which Kennett Square would become famous. Shortly after, the Kennett Anti-Slavery Society was founded, installing John Cox as president. In 1838 the society resolved that whoever "aids in the restoration of the fugitive to his master . . . is guilty of a crime against humanity and religion." That same year the Coxes met William Lloyd Garrison on May 17, 1838, the infamous day when Pennsylvania Hall was burned down by an anti-abolitionist mob, and thereafter they maintained a lifelong friendship. It was Garrison who in 1873 celebrated the service of the Coxes in the Underground Railroad with the following testimonial:

> What a refuge your sweet quiet home has been to the poor hunted fugitives from southern cruelty and oppression! What perils (you) cheerfully encountered in their behalf! How broad and liberal has been your charity to the weary and foot-sore traveler, to the poor and needy, to the wretched and suffering, of every degree! How many have hospitably fed at your tables, and kindly accommodated "to help the cause along"—the cause of mercy and freedom, of progress and reform! Perhaps in some instances you may have "entertained angels unawares"; but, if not, one thing is certain—they to whom you have given friendly shelter have received angelic treatment.

Along a major thoroughfare, Longwood became a regular stop for fugitive slaves coming from Delaware, being only three miles from the border and ten miles from the home of Thomas Garrett. Fugitive slaves often were brought to the Cox house by a black man named Jackson from Wilmington. If they were women and children, they were brought in a dearborn (a four-wheeled carriage with curtains); if they were men only, they would be brought on horseback or on foot. Jackson would signal with three raps on their fence and call out "Friends." He would then dispatch the fugitive slaves and leave immediately. The Coxes had an unfinished attic in which they hid the fugitive slaves. The number they fed, clothed, and sheltered was estimated to be in the hundreds.

As many as eighteen fugitive slaves came to the house at one time. This occurred in 1857 after a tragic confrontation along the way that led to the death of one of those who had confronted them.

The Coxes also may have been among those in Kennett Square who provided **Charles Torrey** with the wagon and horses that he used in his ill-fated rescue attempt when he was caught and sent to prison. They later assisted another famed slave rescuer, **Alexander Milton Ross**, in obtaining a wagon and horse in a successful rescue during which slave-catchers chased him to the Delaware border. After being shot at, Ross returned their fire and shot the horse pulling their carriage.

Ross was introduced to the Coxes by **Gerrit Smith**. This occurred during Ross's trip with Smith when he was introduced to Underground Railroad agents in New York, Pennsylvania, Ohio, and Indiana, from whom he could expect assistance during his mission to the South. He later stayed with the Coxes on several occasions. In Ross's memoirs, he gave much praise to Hannah Cox:

> The house of this noble woman had for years been one of the depots of the Underground Railroad, where many poor fugitives have come with bleeding feet and tattered garments relying upon the humanity of this noble woman, who shielded the outcasts from their pursuers. She possessed great sweetness of disposition, combined with energy, courage . . . a highly cultivated mind and the ease and grace of a queen. . . . There never lived a more noble woman than Hannah Cox.

During the years when the abolition movement began, a conflict arose among many Quaker meetings about whether to take an active role, and not only participate in abolition meetings but also aid fugitive slaves. Kennett was no different. Both John and Hannah and their daughter were suspended from their meeting. On May 22, 1853, they were among a large group of Quakers who met at the Old Kennett Meetinghouse to "consider the propriety" of organizing a new society to speed the general social progress of man. It was later called the Longwood Meeting, and its meeting house was constructed on property formerly owned by the Coxes, and completed in 1855.

The Longwood Meeting became the site of not only antislavery meetings but also progressive movements and discussion of all kinds, including women's rights, phrenology, vegetarianism, free produce, spiritualism, and bloomerism. It adopted **Lucretia Mott's** slogan, "Truth for Authority, not Authority for Truth," as its guiding principle. The meeting hosted many social events and, contrary to the traditional Quaker faith, allowed music at its services. Among its founders who were notable Underground Railroad conductors, in addition to the Coxes, were Thomas Garrett, Dinah and Isaac Mendenhall, Simon and Eusebius Barnard, **Robert and Harriet Purvis**, **Bartholomew Fussell**, and Elijah Pennypacker.

SUGGESTED READING: Christopher Densmore, "Truth for Authority, Not Authority for Truth": address presented at the 150th anniversary celebration of the Longwood Progressive Friends Meetinghouse, Kennett Square, Pennsylvania, May 22, 2005; Roy Joseph Ingraffia, Jr., "Longwood: A Building Investigation and Intervention Proposal for the Cox House, Kennett Square, Pennsylvania," A Master of Science Thesis In Historic Preservation, University of Pennsylvania, Kennett Square, 2004; R. C. Smedley, *History of the Underground Railroad in Chester and Neighboring Counties of Pennsylvania*, Lancaster PA: Office of the Journal, 1883.

Cross, John (1797–unknown). Rev. John Cross established the westernmost route of the Underground Railroad through Illinois and into Michigan. Born in Massachusetts, he moved with his family as a child to upstate New York, where he lived until 1839 when he moved to Illinois. There is little information about him during his early years, aside from his marriage to Lucinda Hurlburt of Pittsfield, Massachusetts, in 1818 and his union with the Congregational Church as a minister in 1833. The details of Cross's Underground Railroad work are also sparse, but his name surfaces in a number of obscure reminiscences and tales that suggest his activities were widespread. All of them attribute to him a significant role in laying down the tracks of the Underground Railroad from Western and Central Illinois to Southern Michigan.

Cross was one of Theodore Weld's legendary seventy antislavery lecturers. These young men were personally chosen and trained by Weld as agents for the American Anti-Slavery Society, and sent on an evangelical mission to abolitionize the North in 1836. Cross was sent to northern New York, where a June 1837 report in *Friend of Man* tells of his lecturing in Jefferson County and being burned in effigy at the village of Smithville. He attended the organizational meeting of the Pennsylvania Anti-Slavery Society in Harrisburg earlier that year.

Cross moved to the town of Elba in Knox County, Illinois, in 1839. His blatantly defiant views on slavery are revealed in an anecdote from local history there. After finishing his sermon one Sunday, he was walking home when a member of his congregation, Jacob Kightlinger, approached in his wagon with his family. He asked Cross if he'd like a ride. Once Cross got in, he proceeded to begin another sermon, this one on the injustice of the laws in Illinois regarding the treatment of black folks. He vowed not to obey them and said he "would harbor, feed, and convey off Negroes" in defiance of those laws. However, Cross was unaware that Kightlinger, a local justice of the peace, was not sympathetic to abolitionists. He responded that if he caught Cross breaking the law, he would be obliged to arrest him, and Cross retorted, "That sir, is just what I want."

Cross was a ubiquitous Underground Railroad organizer during the early 1840s. Often he took fugitive slaves along the routes himself in his own wagon. W. B. Williams of LaPorte, Indiana, which is just east of Chicago, said that Cross wrote letters to him and others asking them to be part of the Underground Railroad in a line that led out of Chicago, and to be "ready to receive visitors at any hour of the night." Cross visited the home of the noted Battle Creek, Michigan, conductor **Erastus Hussey**, but when he found him absent, sent him a similar letter, asking him to be an agent. Hussey accepted, as did Nathan Thomas of Schoolcraft, Michigan, who also received a letter from Cross, and the two of them became probably their state's most active Underground Railroad conductors. In an 1885 interview Hussey said that he eventually met Cross in 1848 at the Free Soil Party Convention in Buffalo.

Contemporary accounts portray Cross as a fearless individual. About 1843 he moved to the town of La Moille in Bureau County, Illinois, sixty miles north of Elba. Despite their illegality, Cross had handbills and posters circulated throughout the county advertising his

Underground work. These ads displayed a bobtail horse in a dearborn wagon with the driver leaning forward and applying the whip, while the heads of two fugitive slaves peered out from under the seat. It was shortly after his move to Bureau County that he had to face charges in Knox County for aiding fugitive slaves. It stemmed from his involvement in the case dealing with Susan Richardson (Aunt Sukey) and her family during their attempted escape in the fall of 1842.

While the Richardson family was being transported in a wagon to Cross's home by Eli Wilson and his son, it passed the residence of Kightlinger who happened to see it. He suspected the blacks were fugitive slaves and were being brought to Cross. When the wagon returned without the blacks, Kightlinger stopped Wilson and his son. He asked where they had taken the blacks, but they refused to answer. Kightlinger and his posse then went to Cross's house and found Richardson and her family resting in Cross's cornfield. Cross was away, apparently "down south after some Negroes," and his wife was cooking corn and potatoes for her guests. Kightlinger took custody of the fugitive slaves and brought them to the Knox County jail.

On his return late that night, Cross was confronted by Kightlinger and his posse, brandishing rifles. Two versions of this encounter exist: one told by Cross after his indictment, and the other by Kightlinger nearly forty years later.

According to Cross, he was with Wilson and they were approached by Kightlinger and his posse, demanding to know if either of them were Cross. Kightlinger's shouting startled Cross's horses, which took off at full speed. Kightlinger and his men gave chase; down the road Cross and Wilson encountered more men, who used rails to bash the heads of their horses and effectively stop them in their path. Kightlinger then searched Cross's wagon but found nothing.

In Kightlinger's version, both Cross and Wilson were driving wagons. But Cross transferred his cargo into Wilson's wagon, or so Kightlinger surmised. Cross then led Kightlinger's posse on a chase while Wilson escaped with the fugitive slaves in the opposite direction. It is likely that Kightlinger's version was the more accurate because Cross was not going to admit to helping fugitive slaves when being accused of it in court. More likely a rendezvous between Cross and Wilson was taking place to transfer the fugitive slaves, especially since Cross's house was being watched by Kightlinger.

When the time for the trial arrived, a deputy sheriff named John Long was sent to bring Cross into court. The anecdote that describes his trip to Knox County to face the charges reveals the mischievous and defiant nature of Cross. Cross and Long left LaMoille on Saturday and stayed overnight in Osceola. Coincidentally, Cross was slated to preach there the next day, and he asked permission to fulfill his engagement. At first Long refused, but when members of the congregation pressured him, he acquiesced. Rumors circulated that the townspeople were going to give Long trouble.

The following day when they set out for Galesburg, a posse of Cross's friends was following them. Long expressed his anxieties to Cross, who began to toy with the deputy. He insisted that he had nothing to do with his friends' actions, but warned that they were angry because of his arrest, and that he had no control over what they might do. In case there might be trouble, he suggested that the deputy hide under a blanket in the back of the wagon. Cross promised to do his best to outrun his friends if they attempted to approach them.

Cross's suggestion was made with the knowledge that they were coming upon a section of corduroy road, which was made with logs, and which caused an extremely rocky ride. Once the deputy was under the covers, Cross cracked the whip and raced the horses over the rough road, jostling and banging the head and limbs of the deputy as he went along. Every so often along the way, he called out to individuals to make the deputy believe his friends were still close behind. Finally, when the corduroy road ended, he told the anxious deputy he could come out of hiding as his friends had turned back.

In Galesburg Cross found that his attorney was delayed but instead of posting bail which had been provided by friends, he said he would act as his own attorney. The prosecutor, unprepared to offer any witnesses to support the charges, was surprised by this move, and dismissed the charges.

The "Aunt Sukey" incident led Cross to write an account of his experiences for the July 18, 1844, issue of the *Western Citizen,* a Chicago abolitionist newspaper, which was accompanied by the caricature he created that has become far more widely known than its creator. It was entitled "LIBERTY LINE" and depicted a train heading into a tunnel through the center of a mountain. It stated that "the improved and splendid Locomotives, Clarkson and Lundy [after the noted British abolitionist and the noted American Quaker abolitionist] with their trains fitted up in the best style of accommodation for passengers, will run their regular trips during the present season, between the borders of the Patriarchal Dominion and Libertyville, Upper Canada. Gentlemen and Ladies, who may wish to improve their health or circumstances, by a northern tour, are respectfully invited to give us their patronage." It was signed J. Cross, proprietor.

Sometime around 1846 Cross organized an antislavery society in Lee County. The 1850 census shows that he had moved again to the town of China in Lee County, about fifteen miles or so from LaMoille, and local legend claims that his house in Temperance Hill was an Underground Railroad station.

How active or how much organization Cross was involved in during the next decade is unknown. He was likely to be in contact with conductors in Michigan, as referred to by Erastus Hussey, regarding their 1848 meeting. And multiple legends claim that Cross was coordinating lines between Quincy and Alton to Chicago.

The Quincy, Illinois, Abolitionists

In 1835 Rev. David Nelson heard a lecture by Theodore Weld in Pittsburgh that inspired him to pledge himself to abolition. Nelson was president of Marion College near Palmyra, Missouri, a stronghold of slavery, where the people were passionate about their right to hold slaves.

Nevertheless, Nelson began preaching abolition at his church and promoting it at his school. Several incidents occurred. The final one resulted in a scuffle between a supporter of Nelson and a slaveholder that nearly caused the latter's death. The riot that followed caused the people of Palmyra to insist that Nelson leave the state.

In Quincy, Illinois, across the Missouri River, less than twenty miles away, Nelson was welcomed by a community already abolitionized and aiding fugitive slaves, the first station at what was then the westernmost point of the Underground Railroad. With the support of Richard Eells and Rev. Asa Turner, Nelson founded the Mission Institute, an evangelical school quite similar to Marion College except for its abolitionist principles.

Students were introduced to the Underground Railroad managed by Nelson and Eells, as a former student explained in an 1891 letter to Wilbur Siebert. In 1841 students James Burr and George Thompson, and Alanson Work, a resident of Quincy living at the Institute, arranged to conduct two slaves to freedom, but were betrayed by them, surrounded by a mob, and tried and convicted for slave stealing. They were sentenced to twelve years in prison, though all were pardoned within five years.

Their case created a national furor, and two years later, a mob from Missouri came and burned down the college. It recovered for a few years, but by 1855 had closed its doors. However, Quincy continued to be a destination for fugitive slaves.

In 1855 Cross joined with a group of ministers from Galesburg in an effort to establish a theological college on the model of Oberlin College in Page County, Iowa. The location was only three miles from the border of Missouri, from which fugitive slaves had begun escaping with increasing frequency since the controversy in Kansas began in 1854. They called the settlement Amity, and in 1857 Cross moved there. Local legends indicate that Amity was a stop on the Underground Railroad, and Rev. William W. Merritt, a conductor in Montgomery County just to the north, said he received fugitive slaves from a Congregational minister in Amity, quite possibly Cross.

Converting to the Wesleyan Methodist Church during the Civil War, Cross continued to lead congregations until 1875 when his wife, Lucinda, died. According to the 1880 census, he was living in Amity, Iowa, with his son-in-law, a widower, as Cross's daughter Sarah had died two years earlier. He was described as man of great accomplishments in the 1880 Page County Iowa History, one who exercised "strenuous" efforts in the antislavery cause and "aided many fugitive slaves."

SUGGESTED READING: Charles Chapman, *History of Knox County, Illinois,* 1878; "First Annual Meeting of the Jefferson County Anti-Slavery Society," *Friend of Man,* Feb. 22, 1837; *History of Page County, Iowa,* 1880; Owen Muelder, *The Underground Railroad in Western Illinois,* Jefferson, NC: McFarland and Company, Inc., 2007; Carol Pirtle, *Escape Betwixt Two Suns: A True Tale of the Underground Railroad in Illinois,* Carbondale, IL: Southern Illinois University Press, 2000; "Rev. John Cross," *Friend of Man,* July 12, 1837; Wilbur Siebert, "The Underground Railroad, *New England Magazine,* 1903; Siebert Collection, 48–01–05, from interview with Erastus Hussey written by Charles E. Barnes and published in *Michigan Pioneer and Historical,* 1885; Siebert Collection, 41–01–29, from Roderick B. Frary to Wilbert Siebert, LaMoille, Illinois, August, 3, 1896; *United States Federal Census,* 1850, 1880.

Culver, Erastus D. (1803–1889). One of the nation's most successful anti-slavery politicians, Erastus Culver was a congressman, a leader in the organization of the Republican Party, and finally the ambassador to Venezuela during Abraham Lincoln's presidency. The magnitude of his stature is illustrated at the occasion of the 1855 anniversary meeting of the New York Anti-Slavery Society, when he was the featured speaker, though he shared the podium with William Lloyd Garrison. Whether he participated in the illegal operations of the Underground Railroad is open to speculation, but his actions as an attorney, legislator, and judge showed that he did all in his power to help the oppressed go free.

Born in Champlain, New York in 1803, and a nephew of Rev. **Nathaniel Colver**, Culver graduated from the University of Vermont College in 1826. While teaching school, he set up a law practice in Fort Ann, Washington County, New York. There he became justice of the peace and town clerk. One of the founders of the Washington County Anti-Slavery Society in 1834, he moved to Union Village in 1836. Elected to the state legislature two years later, he introduced a bill to enforce sanctions against mobbing, which was prevalent at antislavery meetings during this time. He also was a devout Baptist and a leader at the Washington Union Baptist Association convention of 1838 that strongly condemned slavery. The association comprised twenty-six churches in Washington and neighboring Warren County, and played a role in the radical abolitionist character of the region.

Though as ardent an abolitionist as many Liberty Party members, Culver maintained a careful distance from them. It was a shrewd political move because his mainstream Whig Party affiliation enabled him not only to win a seat in Congress in 1844, but also to maintain strong support in the county because of his abolitionist views. In

December 1845 he presented a petition on behalf of his constituency to abolish slavery in Washington, D.C., and on January 30, 1846, he made a major address on the House of Representatives floor arguing against the extension of slavery in Texas and Oregon.

Culver pointed to the abhorrence many of the Founding Fathers felt toward slavery. He stressed that they believed that slavery eventually would be abolished because it violated the cherished principles of life and liberty. Pointing out that slaveholders were a minority and that their views did not reflect the majority of the nation, he argued that to allow slavery in Texas and Oregon would allow the minority to overrule the wishes of the majority.

At a meeting that supported the Fugitive Slave Law of 1850, Culver bitterly denounced the law and President Fillmore, and advocated resistance. In January 1851 Culver moved his law practice to Brooklyn, New York, where he came to national prominence as a judge and attorney who defended the rights of free blacks and fugitive slaves. His first major case involved eight blacks who were the slaves of Jonathan Lemmon.

In 1852 Lemmon, a Virginia slaveholder, was traveling by sea with his eight slaves. The boat docked in New York harbor, and Lemmon sent the slaves to a boarding house in the city. According to an 1841 state law, slaveholders were prohibited from bringing their slaves into the state, and once they did, the slaves had the right to declare their freedom. Louis Napoleon, a free black man who worked closely with **Sidney Howard Gay**, learned that the slaves had been brought into the city and petitioned the court for their freedom. Culver, along with junior partner and future president Chester Arthur, who had grown up in Union Village, successfully defended the slaves.

Culver was elected to the position of Judge of the City Court of Brooklyn in 1854. This put him in a position of authority in which he could rule on cases similar to that of the Lemmon slaves; such cases were not uncommon in the New York City area.

A case that brought Culver national attention that year occurred when the brother and the nephews of Rev. James Pennington, a prominent New York City minister, were apprehended. The three men, who were fugitive slaves, had been taken into custody in Manhattan, which was not in Culver's jurisdiction. Two days later, Culver was scheduled to be a speaker during services at Rev. Pennington's church. Pennington told Culver that his family members were being denied counsel by the court authorities, who claimed the men did not desire counsel and freely admitted that they were the fugitive slaves who had escaped from Virginia. With the help of Mrs. Pennington, Culver managed to locate the prisoners in lockup. Contrary to what the court had said, the men did desire counsel and a trial. But before Culver could obtain a writ of habeas corpus, the fugitive slaves were taken away. It made him so angry, Culver said, that he felt like tearing down the city courthouse.

Culver also had a role in the case of Jane Johnson involving **William Still** and Passmore Williamson, who helped Johnson and her family to freedom. Following a court ruling in Philadelphia that convicted Williamson of enticing Johnson and her children to freedom in violation of the Fugitive Slave Law, she and her children were spirited away to New York. Judge Culver gave her a hearing at his court during which she made a statement, publicized in the New York papers, exonerating Williamson of the charge of enticing her to freedom.

It is quite possible that Culver was sending fugitive slaves to Washington County and other destinations North. A case brought before Culver in 1857 is suggestive of this. A fugitive slave by the name of Jeems had taken passage aboard a steamer headed to New York City. Police in New York had been notified that a fugitive slave was aboard, and

Writ of Habeas Corpus

The writ of habeas corpus was used in numerous cases to release fugitive slaves who were claimed by slaveholders and slavecatchers. The purpose of the writ was to challenge the claimants' legal right to the slaves and permit them to be released in the custody of their legal representatives. The writ allows the judicial authority to reflect on the merits of a case after thoughtful consideration of the evidence, which the defendant's counsel and the claimant are both given the opportunity to present. Sometimes slavecatchers had nothing but their word as proof, and even slaveholders did not always bring sufficient evidence to support their claim, which gave judges no alternative but to release the fugitive slave(s).

when the ship entered the harbor, the police apprehended him. They were preparing to send him South and claim a large cash reward when this was brought to the attention of Judge Culver, who immediately issued a writ of habeas corpus. The authorities took custody of Jeems and brought him to Culver's house at ten o'clock that evening, and the Judge summarily released Jeems at once so that the latter could continue on his voyage to freedom.

Two versions of what happened at the judge's court the next day exist, and both may be true. One says that the police, who had taken Jeems off the boat and confined him, came to respond to the writ. But instead of listening to their claims, Culver charged them with two separate counts of conspiracy and kidnapping. Another says that the slaveowner's attorney came to claim possession of Jeems. The attorney challenged the legality of the writ and several other actions taken by Culver, all of which the judge dismissed. Frustrated, the attorney asked that Jeems be presented to the courtroom, apparently so that he could question Jeems. But Culver said that was impossible because he had discharged Jeems the night before.

Culver became a prominent speaker at organizational meetings of the Republican Party, and campaigned vigorously for both General John C. Fremont and Abraham Lincoln.

In 1862 he was rewarded by President Lincoln with an ambassadorship to Venezuela. He later returned to Greenwich, where, in semi-retirement, he was made president of the Greenwich National Bank. He died in 1889 at age eighty-six. His obituary in the *Whitehall Chronicle* described him as "a most witty and effective story-teller, all of his stories being spiced with the most amusing of anecdotes. He was a man conscious of strength, and, like all strong men, he loved to exercise his strength. He loved to be in the midst of the world's life, and to take a hand in shaping its destinies."

SUGGESTED READING: Frederic Lathrop Colver, *Colver-Culver Genealogy*; Samuel May, *The Fugitive Slave Law and Its Victims*, New York: American Anti-Slavery Society, 1861.

D

DeBaptiste, George (1818–1875). George DeBaptiste was one of the Underground Railroad's most prolific conductors, operating first along the Ohio River in Madison, Indiana, and later becoming a leader in the Underground Railroad's most active gateway to Canada at Detroit, Michigan.

DeBaptiste was born in Fredericksburg, Virginia of free black parents, who were members of the Baptist Church. In his early youth he went to Richmond, where he was apprenticed to learn the barber trade with Lomax Smith. At the age of eighteen, he traveled throughout the Southern states as Smith's body servant. After Smith's death, DeBaptiste returned to Virginia and married Lucinda Lee, of Fredericksburg. About the year 1837 they moved to Madison, Indiana, where he worked as a merchant trading with Cincinnati, occasionally traveling between the two places by steamboat.

By chance DeBaptiste met General William Henry Harrison, whose home was in North Bend, an Ohio River port near the Ohio border with Indiana. DeBaptiste became Harrison's servant, traveling with him during his political campaign of 1840. Upon the inauguration of Gen. Harrison as President of the United States, DeBaptiste was appointed steward of the White House. He became close with the President, and was one of his caretakers during the illness that took his life one month after his inauguration.

Shortly afterward DeBaptiste returned to Madison, Indiana, where he opened a barber shop, and became involved in the Underground Railroad. He sometimes went into Kentucky, and secretly arranged plans with slaves to cross the river. At other times he met with slaves in Madison, who were trusted by their masters to cross into Indiana. After making arrangements, he waited at night along the banks of the Ohio, listening for the sound of oars from an expected boat.

Among those with whom DeBaptiste collaborated were members of the Neil's Creek Anti-Slavery Society, who lived ten miles northwest of Madison in the vicinity of Lancaster, Indiana. DeBaptiste sometimes led the fugitive slaves to Lancaster on foot, which was a steep uphill journey of about seven miles, and he would need to return before morning to open his barber shop. Other times DeBaptiste would use horses that he would borrow from the Madison livery stable of notorious slavecatcher, Wright Ray, a very risky procedure. On still other occasions he would conceal fugitive slaves aboard a steamer bound for Cincinnati, where agents would be notified by telegraph to receive them.

However, suspicions of DeBaptiste's Underground Railroad activities had become so well known that his customers, some of whom were Kentucky slaveholders, often chided him at his barbershop. He would respond by saying that he "wished he was smart enough to steal the niggers, [because then] he would steal all there were in old Kentuck."

Because of these suspicions, there were a number of attempts to entrap him. One of DeBaptiste's customers, a slaveholder who lived a short distance across the river in Kentucky, sent one of his slaves to DeBaptiste's house one Saturday night, asking to be shown the way to Canada. Suspecting that he had been sent, DeBaptiste told him he knew nothing about this. A few days afterwards the Kentuckian confessed that the slave belonged to him, and then remarked that nothing could tempt "the boy" to run away. DeBaptiste responded by betting a new hat that he could steal the slave within a month. The bet was accepted. Shortly afterward he met with the slave and persuaded him to run away, personally conducting him to the first stop along the Underground Railroad. When the Kentuckian next came to the shop, DeBaptiste claimed his new hat and the Kentuckian honored his bet.

Finally, a reward was offered for DeBaptiste's capture while "stealing" slaves. Following a riot in Madison that occurred in 1846 because of opposition to the Underground Railroad, DeBaptiste decided to move to Detroit. In all, DeBaptiste claimed to have personally assisted 108 fugitive slaves while living in Madison. But this was only the beginning of his Underground activities.

In Detroit, DeBaptiste joined **William Lambert** on the Detroit Vigilance Committee, becoming its president. After the passage of the Fugitive Slave Law in 1850, Detroit, which was separated from Canada only by the Detroit River, became the most active crossover point in the nation for fugitive slaves. During an eight-month period between May 1855 and January 1856, DeBaptiste reported that his committee had assisted 1,043 fugitive slaves.

DeBaptiste was involved in a number of business ventures in Detroit. When he arrived there, he purchased an interest in a barber shop though he did not work there. At the same time he found employment in a wholesale clothing store. In 1850, when that business closed, DeBaptiste purchased a bakery, and after selling it, he went into the transportation business, operating the steamboat *T. Whitney* between Detroit and Sandusky. Under the law, blacks could not get a license to run a steamboat, so DeBaptiste employed a Captain Atwood to manage the boat. While DeBaptiste's steamboat was ostensibly hauling freight, it was suspected that the real business of his boat was the hauling of fugitive slaves from Sandusky, which was one of two major terminals of the Underground Railroad on Lake Erie.

Some concrete evidence of DeBaptiste's work can be found in a court case involving a slaveholder who attempted to take back a family of five named Crossthwaite, who had settled in Marshall, Michigan, just east of Battlecreek. The family's former owner had come with a group of slavecatchers and kidnapped the family members, but they were rescued by local citizens led by Charles Gorham, a prominent Marshall attorney. The family members were sent on to DeBaptiste in Detroit, and he had them safely transported to Canada. The slaveholder brought a suit against Gorham and recovered a judgment of $5,000, which was paid with a fund started by the state's abolitionists, among whom DeBaptiste was among the leading contributors.

An indication of DeBaptiste's influence was his association with **Gerrit Smith**, possibly the nation's richest and most powerful abolitionist, who lived in central New York. Smith visited DeBaptiste in Detroit on several occasions to consult with him about the

Militant Underground Railroad conductor George DeBaptiste. Courtesy of Burton Historical Collection, Detroit Public Library.

Underground Railroad, and contributed liberally to the funds of DeBaptiste's vigilance committee. DeBaptiste's militancy was second to none. At a meeting in Detroit of black abolitionists with John Brown, after Brown's Missouri rescue, DeBaptiste took the most radical position, advising even stronger measures than Brown had planned and suggesting that he blow up churches.

During the Civil War DeBaptiste helped recruit a black regiment from the state of Michigan. After the regiment was sent to South Carolina, he and J. D. Richards were sent to coordinate their provisions. After the war, DeBaptiste returned to the business of catering. When the Fifteenth Amendment was passed, he organized a grand celebration and said it was the happiest day of his life. DeBaptiste afterwards established restaurants and ice cream parlors, and accumulated considerable property, much of which he donated to charity. He was married twice, outliving his first wife who bore him ten children, eight of whom he outlived.

SUGGESTED READING: Fergus Bordewich, *Bound for Canaan*, New York: HarperCollins, 2005; Diane Perrine Coon, *Southeastern Indiana's Underground Railroad Routes and Operations*. A Project of the State of Indiana, Dept. of Natural Resources, Division of Historic Preservation and Archaeology and the U.S. Dept. of the Interior, NPS, April 2001; "Death of George DeBaptiste," *Detroit Daily Post*, February 23, 1875; "George DeBaptiste," *Detroit Advertiser and Tribune*, February 23, 1875; John Henry Tibbets, "Reminiscences of Slavery Times," Unpublished memoir, 1888.

Dillingham, Richard (1823–1850). Richard Dillingham gave up his life in an unsuccessful attempt to help those in slavery become free.

Brought up in a pious Quaker family in Morrow County, not far from the Alum Creek settlement, one of Ohio's most active Underground Railroad stations, Dillingham was a teacher and a dedicated abolitionist. In 1847 he was among a group of Quaker abolitionists who helped forty-five black settlers in Michigan move from Cass County to Battlecreek after the infamous Kentucky Raid. The following year, while teaching black children in Cincinnati, he was asked to go to Nashville, Tennessee, and bring out a slave family suffering under a cruel master.

He arrived in Nashville in April 1849. Hiring a free black man to drive the carriage to transport the three slaves, he rode alongside on horseback. When they reached the bridge to cross the Cumberland River and stopped to pay the toll, they were surprised by a law enforcement officer, who had been informed by a black man in whom Dillingham had confided. "You are just the man we wanted. We will make an example of you," said Constable M. D. Maddox, who arrested Dillingham and the others and, with the help of the bridge-keeper, took them into custody.

From the outset, Dillingham readily admitted his guilt and prepared himself to face the consequences. "I have no hopes of getting clear of being convicted and sentenced to the Penitentiary; but do not think that I am without comfort in my afflictions," he wrote in a letter from the jail where he spent four months before being brought to trial. "I have a clear conscience before my God, which is my greatest comfort and support through all my troubles and afflictions. The greatest affliction I have is the reflection of the sorrow and anxiety my friends will have to endure on my account."

Dillingham's demeanor and honesty impressed all who met him, and the charges might have been dropped if he had implicated those who had helped him arrange the escape. But Dillingham said in his letters that he knew that those he might implicate would likely face worse consequences than he would, and he didn't want others to suffer on his account.

Dillingham had other opportunities to free himself. A man came and offered to pay his bail, which was set at $7,000, too much for family or friends to cover. However, when Dillingham learned that the funds were obtained through illegal means, he declined the offer. He also was offered saws and files with which to make a jail break, but these too he refused. "Thou need not fear that I shall ever stoop to dishonourable means to avoid my severe impending fate," he wrote in another letter.

His mother and her brother attended the trial, which took place 750 miles from Morrow County; they sat by his side. Dillingham pleaded guilty to the charges but made a plea for mercy to the jury before they decided on a verdict. "I have violated your laws," he said. "I now stand before you, to my sorrow and regret, as a criminal. But I was prompted to it by feelings of humanity. It has been suspected, as I was informed, that I am leagued with a fraternity who are combined for the purpose of committing such offences as the one with which I am charged. But gentlemen, the impression is false. I alone am guilty—I alone committed the offence—and I alone must suffer the penalty."

Dillingham then begged forgiveness and leniency, considering the age and poor health of his parents and the likelihood that his imprisonment would severely harm them. At the conclusion of his plea, it is said that most of those in the jury actually were weeping. They retired and quickly reached their verdict: three years in the penitentiary, the shortest allowable sentence.

The warden of the penitentiary, John McIntosh, thought the sentence too light, and at first felt prejudiced against Dillingham. However, the latter's integrity and unimpeachable character soon changed the warden's opinion, and he actually became one of McIntosh's favorite prisoners. As a result, after nine months spent in hard labor, McIntosh moved Dillingham to the prison hospital, where his duties as a steward were much less taxing. He was in that position for less than three months, however, when a cholera epidemic broke out at the prison, forcing Dillingham to work round the clock to attend the sick and dying.

Dillingham had been engaged to be married when he was arrested, and although he had released his fiancée from her vows when he entered prison, she promised to wait for him. In his last letter from prison, addressed to her, he wrote: "What must that system be which makes it necessary to imprison with convicted felons a man like this, because he loves his brother man, not wisely but too well?"

On a Sunday morning, the symptoms of cholera became evident in Dillingham, and he died that afternoon and was buried shortly afterwards in an unmarked grave. McIntosh and another prison official were moved to write sincere letters of regret and sympathy to Dillingham's family for his loss. But it merely underscored the immorality and injustice perpetuated by the system of slavery.

SUGGESTED READING: A. L. Benedict, *Memoir of Richard Dillingham*, Philadelphia: Merrihew & Thompson, 1852; Levi Coffin, *Reminiscences of Levi Coffin*, Cincinnati: Robert Clarke & Co., 1880; Harriet Beecher Stowe, *The Key to Uncle Tom's Cabin*, London: Clarke, Beeton, and Co., 1853.

Donnell, Luther A. (1809–1868). Luther Donnell of Decatur County, Indiana, was among southern Indiana's leading Underground Railroad conductors. He was the product of a family of Scotch-Irish Presbyterians who settled in northern Kentucky after the American Revolution, and grew to hate slavery as a child. The Donnells joined with two other clans, the McCoys and the Hamiltons, in organizing the Kentucky Abolition Society in 1807, and initiated what became a long relationship with famed abolitionist and Underground Railroad conductor **John Rankin** when he became the minister of their church in Concord in 1817. However, slavery was too entrenched in Kentucky, and Rankin moved to Ripley, Ohio, in 1821. The abolitionist clans left Kentucky for Indiana soon thereafter, settling in Decatur County.

Luther Donnell was fourteen when his family moved to Indiana. He became a strong temperance man and, along with his five brothers and the Hamilton and McCoy families, helped to organize the Decatur Anti-Slavery Society in 1836. Two years later he was a representative at the organizational meeting of the Indiana State Abolition Society.

By the late 1840s a closely knit Underground Railroad organization was in place. It involved the Donnell, Hamilton, and McCoy families, along with a number of free blacks, most of whom lived in the settlement of Greenbrier, also called Little Africa, not far from Clarksburg. Many of them were former slaves who had escaped slavery, been freed, or purchased their freedom. The operation of the region's Underground Railroad was illustrated in a landmark court case that convicted Donnell for his participation in aiding a slave mother and her four children in 1847.

Court records are sketchy because the defendants were careful not to reveal the workings of the Underground Railroad, but several other accounts of this incident exist. The one given most credence was written some years afterward by William Hamilton, one of the participants. According to Hamilton, Caroline, the slave and mistress of George Ray, brother of the slavecatcher Wright Ray, crossed over the Ohio River with her children—Francis, age twelve; Amanda, age eight; John, age four; and Henry, age two—and was met by George Waggoner waiting with his double-bed wagon. This was known to have occurred on October 31, 1847. However, other accounts claim that the family was taken up through Eagle Hollow to Rykers Ridge and the home of John Carr, who moved them north to the Hicklin settlement in San Jacinto, about fifteen miles north and slightly west. It was at one of these locations that the family rendezvoused with George Waggoner, who then took them about twenty miles to meet George McCoy, arriving between 2 and 3 a.m.

McCoy took the family on horseback in an attempt to get to Little Africa before daybreak, and on the way William Hamilton joined them. The group was unable to get to its destination in time, so the fugitive slaves were left at the home of George Pernell, who was uneasy about it. Hamilton sought the advice of Donnell, who agreed to go to Little Africa and ask one of its residents to pick up the fugitive slaves. As Hamilton and Donnell went their separate ways, Hamilton met Pernell with the fugitive slaves. The latter was bringing them to the home of Jane Speed, where they were deposited in an old barn on her property and covered up with hay. The barn was near the home of Woodsen Clark, a friend of George Ray, the master of the fugitive slaves, who had gathered a posse and was approaching Clarksburg.

The next day Clark noticed one of Speed's children taking food to the barn. He went inside and found the fugitive slaves. He told them that it was dangerous for them to be there, and deceived them into believing that he would help them. He brought them to a fodder house on his son's property and locked them in. When the party of several men from Little Africa came to retrieve the fugitive slaves, they were alarmed to find that the slaves were gone. They suspected Clark had something to do with it, and Donnell and Cyrus Hamilton, William's father, went at once to Greenburg to obtain a writ of habeas corpus from Judge John Hopkins, an in-law of Donnell's.

A party of about twenty men from Little Africa were left to keep watch on Clark's house, but when the Donnell returned with the sheriff to serve the writ, they, of course, did not find the fugitive slaves. It was decided that the search be extended to the properties of Clark's sons.

Realizing she had been betrayed, Caroline broke out of the fodder house, leaving her children, and went searching for Little Africa, but became lost. Fortunately, some residents of Little Africa found her. After retrieving the children, the men from Little Africa hid Caroline and her children in a ravine while Donnell and Hamilton decided how they would forward the fugitives without being detected by the slavecatchers.

Hamilton wrote: "Now there was a colored man and his wife who had recently moved from Union County and they were in the habit of traveling to and fro with their two children in a horse and buggy. They boldly exchanged Francis and John, Caroline's children, for two of their own, and took these two in broad daylight to Quaker **William Beard**'s in Salem, Union County."

As for Caroline and her other two children, the plan was to dress Caroline up as a man and ride in the middle of several black men through Clarksburg. The children were then to be taken on a different route by Donnell and Hamilton, and all of them were to meet at a point west of Clarksburg. This was accomplished, and the fugitive slaves were then taken to the house of Luther's brother, Thomas Donnell, in Springhill until the next night. Luther's brother, John Donnell, offered his enclosed carriage with curtains for use; it was escorted by Robert Stout, Nathaniel Thompson, John, Luther, and Lowry Donnell—a nephew—to Beard's station to reunite Caroline and her two children with the rest of the family.

The family eventually arrived safely in Canada, and in later years Caroline changed her name to Rachel Beach. She told **Laura Haviland** that when she was separated from her children during the rescue, she wondered if she would ever see them again, and when she finally was reunited with them at Beard's station, she sank to the ground, sobbing and hugging them. Then she thanked God for bringing them all back together. She also wrote to Luther Donnell after arriving in Canada, thanking him.

George Ray, the slaveowner, sued Donnell for violating the Indiana Fugitive Slave Law of 1824. The trial that took place about a year after the rescue turned in favor of Ray when Richard Clark, in whose fodder house his father had placed the fugitive slaves, testified he saw Donnell and Hamilton take the children. A judgment totaling $125 in fines was brought against Donnell, which he promptly paid. Ray then brought a civil suit to the U.S. court in Indianapolis and won a judgment of $3,000. It is said that Donnell received help from abolitionists in both Indiana and Ohio to help pay the latter fee. However, in 1852 the Indiana State Supreme Court overturned that decision, and it is unclear whether Donnell paid that fine.

It is interesting that, after the passage of the Fugitive Slave Law of 1850, most of the blacks in Little Africa moved to Canada or Cass County, Michigan, and no trace of that community remains today. Nevertheless, the determination of the abolitionists of Decatur County to operate the Underground Railroad was stronger than ever, as expressed by Rev. Benjamin Nyce, the minister of Sand Creek Presbyterian, Kingston, to whose congregation most of them belonged:

> It is well known to you that the fugitive slave bill has become law. To a law framed of such iniquity, I owe no allegiance. Humanity, Christianity, and manhood revolt against it. For myself—I say it solemnly—I will shelter, I will help, I will defend the fugitive with all my humble means and power, I will act with any body of decent and serious men, on the head or foot, or hand in any mode not involving the use of deadly weapons to nullify and defeat the operation of this law.

SUGGESTED READING: Diane Perrine Coon, *Southeastern Indiana's Underground Railroad Routes and Operations.* A Project of the State of Indiana, Dept. of Natural Resources, Division of Historic Preservation and Archaeology and the U.S. Dept. of the Interior, NPS, April 2001; Camilla and Emma A. Donnell, *The Donnell Family: A History and Genealogy of the Descendents of Thomas Donnell of Scotland*, Greenfield, IN: William Mitchell, 1912; A. Lewis Harding, *History of Decatur County*, Indianapolis: B. F. Browne Co., 1915; Laura Haviland, *A Woman's Life-Work: Labors and Experiences of Laura S. Haviland*, Cincinnati: Walden & Stowe, 1882; Mary Elizabeth Donnell Mitchell, "Luther Donnell—Decatur County, Indiana's Great Enemy of Slavery," *Black History News and Notes*, vol. 97, August 2004.

Douglass, Frederick (1818–1895). Frederick Douglass, the great abolitionist and former slave, was the most significant black American of the nineteenth century. He escaped from slavery in 1838, and with the help of the Underground Railroad settled in New Bedford, Massachusetts. There he met William Lloyd Garrison and began his career as an abolitionist speaker. Douglass later became America's foremost black orator and writer, editing his newspapers, *The North Star* and *Frederick Douglass' Paper,* and writing three memorable autobiographies that remain today as outstanding works of literature. Not only did he give his support to all who were involved in the Underground Railroad, but he also opened his home in Rochester, New York, as a refuge for those fleeing slavery.

Douglass was born Frederick Bailey, the slave of Aaron Anthony, on the Holmes Hill plantation near Easton on Maryland's eastern shore. His mother, Harriet Bailey, worked in the corn fields, and some believe Douglass's father was her master. During early childhood Douglass lived with his grandparents, Betsey and Isaac Bailey, in a cabin about twelve miles from the Holmes Hill Farm. He rarely saw his mother, who died not long after he reached the age of seven.

When Douglass was six, his grandmother took him to live on the plantation with his older brother and sisters. Douglass remembers it as a horrible period when he was fed cornmeal mush and had to sleep on the floor without blankets at night, huddled close to his siblings. An early experience that revealed to him the brutality of slavery was one night when he was awakened by his aunt's screaming; he was able to peer through a crack in the wall and see her being beaten by his master.

At the age of nine Douglass was sent to live in Baltimore with Hugh Auld, the brother-in-law of Anthony's daughter, Lucretia. It was much preferable to living on the plantation, as his only duties were to run errands and look after the Aulds' infant son. Auld's wife Sophia often read the Bible to him and began to teach him how to read. Douglass was a fast learner. However, when her husband learned of this, the lessons stopped. Nevertheless, Douglass persisted, and with the help of white children he met on errands, he continued to improve his reading skills. With money he had earned from his errands, he bought a book, *The Columbian Orator*, a collection of speeches and essays dealing with liberty, democracy, and courage. His first yearnings to become free developed from reading this book.

When Douglass was about thirteen, Aaron Anthony died, and he became the property of Lucretia Auld, who sent him back to Baltimore. A year after Douglass's return to Baltimore, Lucretia Auld died, and Thomas Auld demanded that he be returned. Now fifteen, Douglass was sent to live at Thomas Auld's new farm near the town of Saint Michaels, and was put to work as a field hand. It was a difficult time for Douglass because, in addition to the backbreaking work, Thomas Auld did not feed his slaves well and frequently beat them. Douglass became rebellious, and in an effort to control him, Auld sent him to work for Edward Covey, known to be a slave-breaker.

Although Covey fed his slaves much better, he also worked them harder and beat them more frequently. After a beating during which Covey had battered him senseless, Douglass fled to the Auld plantation and begged to remain there. Despite Douglass's bruised and bloodied appearance, Auld refused. With great trepidation Douglass returned, but the fury that Covey displayed when he saw Douglass made it obvious that another beating was to follow, and so Douglass fled into the woods. He encountered another slave named Sandy, who was married to a free woman. Sandy brought Douglass home with him, giving him a few days to recuperate. Douglass was now faced with the alternatives of either taking flight or returning to Covey. At Sandy's urging, he returned on a Sunday because Covey was devoutly religious.

This time when Covey saw Douglass approach, he acted totally different, almost as if he had completely forgotten his anger. The next day he called Douglass for work a little earlier than usual, and as Douglass was tending to his chores, Covey snuck up behind him and tried to slip a rope under his feet. Douglass was able to elude it, but both fell to the ground and began to grapple. As Douglass later wrote, "Whence came the daring spirit . . . I do not know; at any rate, I was resolved to fight." For two hours they fought, until exhausted and bleeding, Covey called an end to their battle. It may have been no more than a draw but for Douglass it was a great victory: "I was a changed being after that fight. I was nothing before; I was a man now. It recalled to life my crushed self-respect and my self-confidence, and inspired me with a renewed determination to be a free man."

After a year with Covey, Douglass was sent to work for a farmer named William Freeland, a much kinder master. But all Douglass cared about now was his freedom. He began to meet secretly on Sundays with five other slaves to plan an escape. However, their plot was exposed, and when they set out just before the Easter holiday in 1836, they were captured and put in jail. Douglass expected to be sold to the Deep South, but to his surprise Thomas Auld came and released him, sending him back to Hugh Auld in Baltimore.

Auld, who worked in a shipyard, apprenticed him to a boat builder who taught him the caulker's trade. After Douglass got into a confrontation and was beaten by some white apprentices, Auld brought him to work with him. Douglass became proficient as a caulker and earned good wages, which he had to turn over to Auld, who occasionally let him keep a little.

During this time, Douglass joined the East Baltimore Mental Improvement Society. At one of the meetings, he met his future wife, a free black woman named Anna Murray, who worked as a servant. They fell in love, but Douglass had no desire to marry as a slave, knowing the hardships that could occur. Rather, he became even more determined to obtain his freedom. He knew that escaping would be difficult because of the slave patrols, and he realized that he would need money to carry out his plan. With this in mind, he persuaded Auld to hire him out and let him live on his own, paying his own room and board, and giving a predetermined amount to Auld. What was left over, he would be allowed to keep.

Everything was working well until one Sunday when Douglass attended a camp meeting and was late in returning. This caused him to be a day late in paying his weekly dues. It angered Auld, who immediately put an end to the arrangement.

The time had come for Douglass to make his escape. After at first refusing to go to work, Douglass returned and pretended to accept Auld's decision. However, he began making plans to leave within three weeks. Escaping would not be easy. Blacks traveling by train or steamboat had to carry official papers listing their name, age, height, skin color, and other distinguishing features. He was unable to acquire free papers, but he was able to obtain a sailor's ID from a free black seaman he had met at the shipyard.

On September 3, 1838, using money from Anna to purchase a ticket, and dressed in sailor's dress of red shirt and black cravat, he snuck aboard a train to Philadelphia with the help of a friend who worked for the railroad. Bypassing the ticket office was important because he had determined that the IDs of blacks who paid for their tickets aboard a train were not examined as carefully. This was crucial because the seaman did not look like him. Douglass described what followed as he waited for the conductor to examine his papers:

> He was somewhat harsh in tone, and peremptory in manner until he reached me, when, strangely enough, and to my surprise and relief, his whole manner changed. Seeing that I

> did not readily produce my free papers, as the other colored persons in the car had done, he said to me in a friendly contrast with that observed towards the others.
>
> "I suppose you have your free papers?"
>
> To which I answered: "No, sir; I never carry my free papers to sea with me."
>
> "But you have something to show that you are a free man, have you not?"
>
> "Yes, sir," I answered; "I have a paper with the American eagle on it, and that will carry me round the world."
>
> With this I drew from my deep sailor's pocket my seaman's protection, as before described. The merest glance at the paper satisfied him, and he took my fare and went on about his business. . . . This moment of time was one of the most anxious I ever experienced.

Douglass successfully completed the first train ride. The next obstacle was a ferryboat ride across the Susquehanna River. During this short trip, he encountered several black acquaintances he feared might unintentionally betray him. He evaded this, but when he got off the boat, he saw a white man for whom he once had worked. Luckily, the man didn't notice him. Yet another threat materialized on the train to Wilmington and the Delaware border, when another white man he knew saw him. Again fate smiled kindly, for the man paid no attention. The last leg of his flight was a steamboat ride from Wilmington to Philadelphia. All went without a hitch, and from Philadelphia, he took another train to New York. Douglass now found himself overwhelmed by the experience of freedom:

> In less than a week after leaving Baltimore, I was walking amid the hurrying throng, and gazing upon the dazzling wonders of Broadway. A free state around me, and a free earth under my feet. . . . A whole year was pressed into a single day. A new world burst upon my agitated vision. . . . It was a moment of joyous excitement . . . sensations too intense and rapid for words. Anguish and grief, like darkness and rain, may be described, but joy and gladness, like the rainbow of promise, defy alike the pen and pencil.

Soon, however, Douglass began to feel the loneliness and insecurity of being in a new and strange place. To his surprise, he saw a fugitive slave that he knew. Jake warned him about the numerous slavecatchers in the city, and that he had to be careful even among black people because some of them were hired to find fugitive slaves. Douglass said he sensed that Jake thought that perhaps he was hired to find him. Jake was little help, and Douglass received none until he met a sailor who took him home, and summoned **David Ruggles**, secretary of the New York Committee of Vigilance. Douglass wrote:

> I was hidden with Mr. Ruggles several days. In the meantime, my intended wife, Anna, came on from Baltimore—to whom I had written, informing her of my safe arrival at New York—and, in the presence of Mrs. Mitchell and Mr. Ruggles, we were married, by Rev. James W. C. Pennington.

Ruggles was the first member of the Underground Railroad whom Douglass had encountered. Discovering that Douglass knew the caulker's trade, Ruggles sent Douglass and his wife to New Bedford, Massachusetts. Their destination was the home of Nathan Johnson, an active Underground Railroad agent whose wife ran a local bakery. It was Johnson who suggested the name Douglass when Douglass, born Frederick Bailey, was trying to decide upon a new name that would conceal his slave origin. Life in New Bedford was full of surprises for Douglass. A community of Quaker mariners, it was per capita one of the wealthiest communities in America. Its black population, which was quite large, in part owing to the Quakers who were disposed to hiring black seamen, was the wealthiest of any other city. Both Douglass and his wife quickly found work.

One of the turning points in Douglass's life came when he purchased a subscription to *The Liberator*. He became an avid reader, and thereafter attended every antislavery meeting in New Bedford. When news came of William Lloyd Garrison coming to speak in New Bedford, Douglass relished the opportunity to hear him.

"His words were . . . full of holy fire, and straight to the point," Douglass later wrote. "Learning to love him, through his paper, I was prepared to be pleased with his presence. Something of a hero worshiper, by nature, here was one, on first sight, to excite my love and reverence."

In 1841 Douglass was surprised when an abolitionist named William Coffin, who had heard him talk at a local school, asked him if he'd like to speak about his experiences in slavery. He had never considered becoming an antislavery lecturer but agreed to participate at a convention in Nantucket. Douglass was extremely nervous and by his own account stumbled through his speech. To make matters worse, his speech was followed by a virtuoso performance by Garrison. Nevertheless, he had impressed Garrison and his associates enough that they asked him to join the abolition circuit for a three-month lecture assignment with the Garrison-led American Anti-Slavery Society. Douglass reluctantly agreed. It was the beginning of a four-year tour as an abolitionist lecturer in the United States.

The three-month tour of duty through Massachusetts was enough to make Douglass an accomplished speaker. "As a speaker, he has few equals," said the esteemed *Herald of Freedom* in Concord, New Hampshire, of one of his speeches during this tour. "He has wit, arguments, sarcasm, pathos . . . all that first rate men show in their master effort." Audiences also enjoyed his sarcastic description of his liberating fight with slavebreaker Edward Covey, as well as his mockery of Southern clergy, who warned slaves of their sins against God when they disobeyed their masters.

As his confidence grew, Douglass extended the range of his discussion beyond personal experience into the realm of ideas. In fact Garrison and others preferred that he stick to his personal story and let the more experienced speakers discuss ideas and strategies. But his abilities were unquestioned, and he had become one of the society's most valued speakers.

By 1843 he joined a group of lecturers that included Charles Remond on a 100-convention tour sponsored by the American Anti-Slavery Society. His assignment took him from Vermont through New York, including Albany, Syracuse, Rochester, and Buffalo. Then he moved on to Ohio, paired with Remond, and finally to Indiana. The latter state provided one of his most memorable experiences as a lecturer.

After being pelted with eggs in Richmond, Indiana, not far from the home of **Levi Coffin**, the tour moved on to Pendleton, Indiana, just east of Indianapolis. A platform was erected for an outdoor lecture, and a large audience assembled. As Douglass and William A. White, the nephew of Coffin, prepared to begin, a mob of about sixty ruffians armed with clubs appeared and ordered them to stop because the mob took offense at the appearance of a black speaker. When Douglass and White resisted, the mob began pummeling White, knocking out his two of his teeth. Douglass who attempted to defend White with a club was quickly subdued and beaten until unconscious; his right hand was broken, an injury that would cause permanent damage. He was lucky, however, to be alive. Nevertheless, after recuperating, Douglass completed the full tour.

As Douglass became increasingly erudite, many began to doubt that he ever was a slave. A report by *The Liberator* of one of his lectures in 1844 stated that many people were finding it incredible to believe that "a man, only six years out of bondage, and who had never gone to school could speak with such eloquence." In order to silence the doubters and to capitalize on his growing reputation, he wrote his first autobiography, *Narrative of the Life of Frederick Douglass*, published in 1845.

The autobiography became an instant bestseller, but its notoriety threatened his freedom. It was decided that Douglass should take a trip to England, not only for his own benefit, but also as a representative of the American Anti-Slavery Society to rally support for the abolitionist cause in the United States. He left behind his wife and four children in Lynn, Massachusetts, where they had moved in 1842.

Douglass spent nearly two years lecturing throughout the British Isles. Everywhere he went, he was welcomed. "One of the most pleasing features of my visit thus far has been a total absence of all manifestations of prejudice against me, on account of my color," he wrote Garrison. "I go on stage coaches, omnibuses, steamboats, into the first cabins, and in the first public houses, without seeing the slightest manifestation of the hateful and vulgar feeling against me. I find myself not treated as a color, but as a man."

After about a year, he was joined by Garrison and Henry C. Wright, a veteran anti-slavery lecturer. The three Americans went on an extensive abolitionist lecture tour, along with the noted British abolitionist and orator, George Thompson. But the man everyone wanted to hear was Douglass, who was popular with both aristocratic and working-class audiences. He had become so popular that some even suggested that he send for his family and settle there. He was, after all, still a slave in the United States. But that problem was solved when two English friends sent $750 to the Aulds in Tennessee. On December 5, 1846, Hugh Auld, to whom brother Thomas had transferred the title to Douglass, signed the emancipation papers that declared Douglass free.

When Douglass returned to the United States in April 1847, he had grown in confidence. He wanted to start his own newspaper. An English woman named Julia Griffiths was a member of a group that had provided him with a stipend of $2,175 to use as he wished, and which he had earmarked for the start of the newspaper. Garrison was opposed to it. He wanted Douglass to continue lecturing for the American Anti-Slavery Society. He also pointed out that Douglass would be competing with three black newspapers—the *Mystery* in Pittsburgh, the *National Watchman* in Troy, New York, and *The Ram's Horn* in New York. To assuage Douglass, Garrison offered him an additional job as a correspondent for *The Liberator's* sister publication, the *National Anti-Slavery Standard* in New York City.

Douglass agreed to defer to Garrison, and during the fall of 1847, they went on tour together through New York, Pennsylvania, and Ohio, which Douglass reported to the *Standard*. Thousands turned out to hear them at a three-day event in Oberlin, but in other places churches were closed to them, mobs harassed them, and Douglass was continually confronted by prejudice. It was a rigorous trip, and Garrison became seriously ill in Cleveland, forcing Douglass to continue to Western New York without him.

Apparently, a misunderstanding occurred between Douglass and Garrison, who had sent Douglass on to their remaining appointments. However, Garrison later became upset when he became gravely ill and Douglass did not return to be with him. Garrison was slow in recuperating, and during that interval, Douglass renewed his efforts to start his own newspaper, prompted by the closing of two of the competing black newspapers, and the possible merger of his intended publication with *The Ram's Horn*, for which he also had been writing. In fact, the announcement of Douglass's venture was first made in that newspaper.

Douglass decided to base his newspaper, which he called the *North Star*, in Rochester, and moved his family to a large three-story house on South Avenue, which would become well known to fugitive slaves. The Underground Railroad was well established there, and it was only a short distance from Douglass's new home to a steamboat ride to Canada. The first issue of the *North Star* was published on December 3, 1847, and the motto on its masthead read: "Right is of no sex—Truth is of no color—God is the Father of us all, and we are all Brethren." His assistant editor for the early issues was Martin Delany, the former editor of the *Mystery*, who was shortly thereafter replaced by William Nell, the young black protégé of Garrison. Douglass's correspondents included some of the most talented free black men in America: James McCune Smith, George Downing, Samuel Ringgold Ward, **William Wells Brown**, **Jermaine Loguen**, and **William G. Allen**.

The *North Star* drew praise, even from Garrison, and support from the abolitionist community. Among them was **Gerrit Smith**, who sent Douglass a deed for a plot of land in Adirondack region, one of the 3,000 parcels he was giving away to free, temperate black men. Douglass had never met Smith, but it would be the beginning of a close friendship that would have a great influence on him.

The deed came with a check for a two-year subscription to the *North Star* and a letter welcoming Douglass to New York State. Not sure how to respond, Douglass published the letter. It was the first of many letters they would share and that Douglass would publish, and the beginning of a relationship that would move Douglass further away from Garrison. Smith, afterall, was Garrison's ideological opposite in the abolitionist arena. While Garrison eschewed political action based on his belief that the constitution was a proslavery document, Smith was the leader of the Liberty Party, the first abolitionist political party, whose members split in 1840 from the American Anti-Slavery Society on account of this fundamental disagreement.

Despite encouragement from many circles, subscriptions grew slowly. Not only did Douglass have to go out on the lecture circuit to raise money, but he had to mortgage his house. Julia Griffiths, a friend from England, who had helped raise the stipend presented to him when he returned to America, came to manage his business affairs, including the finances of the newspaper and the scheduling of his lectures. Within a year, her efforts doubled the newspaper's circulation to 4,000, paid off Douglass's mortgage, and paid all his debts.

In 1848 Douglass showed his support for women's rights when he attended the first women's rights convention in Auburn. He also got his first taste of abolitionist politics when he attended a convention of the Free Soil Party in Buffalo. The following year he attended the anniversary meeting of the New York State Vigilance Committee, whose organization was "instituted expressly for the management of the underground railroad." Originally founded to deal with the Underground Railroad in New York City, it expanded in 1848 to include the entire state of New York. Its president in 1849 was Gerrit Smith.

On August 21 and 22, 1850, just prior to the passage of the second Fugitive Slave Law, Smith organized one of the most historic gatherings in abolitionist and Underground Railroad history at Cazenovia, New York. Called the "convention of the fugitive slaves," an estimated fifty fugitive slaves were in attendance, among 2,000 participants, to protest the impending passage of the second Fugitive Slave Law. It also was part of an effort to raise bail for central New York abolitionist, William L. Chaplin, who had been arrested on August 8 after trying to make a getaway in a carriage with two armed fugitive slaves from the District of Columbia. Douglass was appointed president of the convention, and Smith read a document, which was as monumental as **Garnet**'s "Address to the Slaves," seven years earlier. Called "A Letter to American Slaves from those who have fled from American Slavery," it actually was written by Smith, who consulted with Douglass before completing the final draft. Its rhetoric was extremely militant:

> For you are prisoners of war, in an enemy's country—of a war, too, that is unrivalled for its injustice, cruelty, meanness and therefore, by all the rules of war, you have the fullest liberty to plunder, burn, and kill, as you may have occasion to do to promote your escape.
>
> We regret to be obliged to say to you, that it is not every one of the Free States, which offers you an asylum. Even within the last year, fugitive slaves have been arrested in some of the Free States, and replunged into slavery. But, make your way to New York or New England, and you will be safe.

Naturally, the "Letter" invited criticism from the nonresistant Garrison who editorialized: "We have the sincerest sympathy for the fugitive slave, and for all slaves, but we do not believe an armed fight, on stolen horses (in reference to a comment in the Letter that slaves should steal their master's fleetest horses to make their escape) is the legitimate method of procedure." It was an obvious criticism of Douglass, as well as Smith. The next year, at the annual meeting of the American Anti-Slavery Society held in Syracuse, it was decided not to support any paper that viewed the Constitution as an antislavery document. Douglass responded by saying that after considerable reflection, he had come to that opinion and supported political involvement. It effectively ended his friendship with Garrison.

Smith now became a financial backer of Douglass's newspaper, as a result of a merger of the *North Star* with the *Liberty Party Paper*, which was placed under the direction of Douglass. It also resulted in a change of the newspaper's name to *Frederick Douglass' Paper*, which continued as a weekly until 1860, and three more years as a monthly. As Douglass wrote, it chronicled everything he said during that period and much of what he did.

On July 4, 1852, Douglass was asked to give an address in Rochester to commemorate the holiday. Douglass wrote many great speeches. In this one, considered his masterpiece, he incisively illustrated the contrast of what America claimed to be and what it actually was. A brief excerpt follows:

> What to the American slave is your Fourth of July? I answer, a day that reveals to him more than all other days of the year, the gross injustice and cruelty to which he is the constant victim. To him your celebration is a sham; your boasted liberty an unholy license; your national greatness, swelling vanity; your sounds of rejoicing are empty and heartless; your shouts of liberty and equality, hollow mock; your prayers and hymns, your sermons and thanksgivings, with all your religious parade and solemnity, are to him mere bombast, fraud, deception, impiety, and hypocrisy—a thin veil to cover up crimes which would disgrace a nation of savages. There is not a nation of the earth guilty of practices more shocking and bloody than are the people of these United States at this very hour.

During the mid-1850s Douglass used his increasing influence and notoriety to support the causes of blacks while completing his second revised autobiography, *My Bondage and My Freedom*, published in 1855. He also supported the political activities of Gerrit Smith and campaigned vigorously for his successful election to Congress. He joined with Smith in the organization of the Radical Abolitionist Party, which held its first meeting in September 1855, and included James McCune Smith as its president, and Jermaine Loguen and Lewis Tappan among other leading members. It was there that **John Brown** requested funding for the war to make Kansas a free state.

Douglass had known Brown since 1847, when he had dinner at Brown's house in Springfield, Massachusetts. Brown had a great influence on him. At their first meeting Brown confessed his belief that slavery could be abolished only through the use of force, and he detailed his plan to foment a revolution of the slaves to achieve their emancipation. Brown advanced the belief that slaveholders "had forfeited their right to live, and that slaves had the right to gain their liberty in any way they could." Douglass admitted that, "From this night spent with John Brown . . . I became all the same less hopeful of [slavery's] peaceful abolition. My utterances became more and more tinged by the color of this man's strong impressions."

That meeting was the beginning of a friendship with Brown that continued up through the debacle at Harpers Ferry, and Brown was often Douglass's guest in Rochester. "In his repeated visits to the East to obtain necessary arms and supplies," Douglass wrote, "he often did me the honor of spending hours and days with me at Rochester. On more than one occasion I got up meetings and solicited aid to be used by him for the cause, and I may say without boasting that my efforts in this respect were not entirely fruitless."

But Douglass's work was not all writing, speaking, and supporting the work of other abolitionists. He also became actively involved in the Underground Railroad. "My agency was all the more exciting and interesting, because . . . I could take no step in it without exposing myself to fine and imprisonment . . . . the thought that there was one less slave, and one more freeman—having myself been a slave, and a fugitive slave—brought to my heart unspeakable joy."

Douglass's house in Rochester was a couple hundred yards from his closest neighbor, Rev. Joseph Marsh, which made it easy for fugitive slaves to find. Even more convenient was that Marsh also was an Underground agent. Although Douglass was often away lecturing, Anna Douglass and their children were always ready and had plenty of room to accommodate fugitive slaves. From Douglass's house, it was only a short distance to a steamer on Lake Ontario and passage to Canada. As many as eleven fugitive slaves were hidden in his home at a time, and it was not uncommon for Douglass to arrive at his newspaper office in the morning and find fugitive slaves waiting at the front door.

Among his most active collaborators were black barber Jacob P. Morris, bookseller Samuel Porter, and Quakers Amy and Isaac Post. Other Rochester agents included Asa Anthony, William C. Bloss, William Hallowell, and Myron Holley. Amy Post, who on one occasion hid sixteen fugitive slaves at her house, said that an average of about 150 per year came through Rochester during the peak years of the Underground Railroad, likely referring to the period after the passage of the second Fugitive Slave Law. Of those, the number assisted by Douglass and his family probably was several hundred.

One historic incident involving fugitive slaves was described in detail by Douglass when **William Parker** and two other men implicated in the murder during the Christiana Riot in 1851 came to Douglass for assistance. Not only were they provided with shelter, but Douglass himself piloted them to the steamboat on which they took passage to Canada.

In his 1855 autobiography, Douglass criticized those in the Underground Railroad who publicized their efforts:

> "I have never approved of the very public manner, in which some of our western friends have conducted what they call the 'Under-ground Railroad'. . . . In publishing such accounts, the anti-slavery man addresses the slaveholder . . . , he stimulates [him] to greater watchfulness, and adds to his facilities for capturing his slave. We owe something to the slaves, south of Mason and Dixon's line . . . and . . . we should be careful to do nothing which would be likely to hinder [them], in making their escape from slavery."

From January 27 to February 17, 1858, while staying with Douglass, John Brown wrote his "Provisional Constitution and Ordinances for the People of the United States." Brown was planning to implement his plan to foment a slave insurrection and fight a guerilla war that summer. However, his plan was revealed to a couple of members of Congress and some journalists, and it was decided to delay its implementation. In March 1859, Douglass met Brown and **George DeBaptiste**, among other radical abolitionists, to discuss Brown's plan to invade Virginia. According to Douglass, however, Brown did not reveal that his objective was now to first raid the U.S. Arsenal at Harpers Ferry. It was only in late August 1859 during his meeting at an abandoned stone quarry near Chambersburg, Pennsylvania, when Brown asked Douglass to join him that he claimed he learned of this change in Brown's plan. Douglass, however, declined and used all of his powers of persuasion to deter Brown from a course that Douglass believed was doomed to fail.

On October 18, when the news broke of Brown's raid at Harpers Ferry, Douglass was in Philadelphia presenting the speech "Self-Made Men," which became his trademark speech in later years. He received thunderous applause when he praised Brown's effort. However, a sack with Brown's papers was confiscated, including a letter from Douglass, and Governor Henry Wise of Virginia was seeking to charge Douglass with conspiracy in the raid.

Douglass knew he stood no chance of avoiding conviction if caught and immediately fled to Canada. In November 1859 he sailed to England and began a lecture tour, which he had planned before Harpers Ferry. The news of his near arrest increased his popularity. But in May 1860 he cut short his trip when he learned his youngest child, Annie, had died. He immediately returned home. By then the government had dropped the charges against him.

The coming election was the matter at hand, and Douglass supported Lincoln, who was not a radical or reformer. When the Confederacy was formed, Lincoln did not retaliate but instead promised not to interfere with slavery and to continue to enforce the Fugitive Slave Law. When the war began in April 1861, Douglass urged Lincoln to free the slaves and allow them to fight for the Union. However, Lincoln feared that emancipation would cause the four slave border states of Missouri, Kentucky, Maryland, and Delaware, which had not joined the Confederacy, to secede.

Lincoln's primary objective was to save the Union, and he was willing to forego emancipation to do it. He considered a plan of mass immigration of blacks to Africa or Central America, which caused Douglass to call him "a genuine representative of American prejudice." Finally, in September of 1862, he signed the Emancipation Proclamation, freeing all of the slaves in the Confederacy, but not the border states, to be effective on January 1, 1863. Douglass was in Boston at a telegraph office on the night that the proclamation was made official; the proclamation also called for the enlistment of blacks into the Union Army, something not included in its earlier draft.

"I shall never forget that memorable night, when in a distant city I waited and watched at a public meeting, with three thousand others not less anxious than myself, for the word of deliverance," Douglass wrote, "Nor shall I ever forget the outburst of joy and thanksgiving that rent the air when the lightning brought to us the emancipation proclamation."

Douglass immediately joined in the recruitment of black soldiers, and his sons Lewis and Charles were among the first to enlist. In August of that year Lincoln asked Douglass to come to the White House. It was the first of three times that they would meet. When Douglass entered, he was ushered in ahead of others waiting to see Lincoln, who rose to greet him.

"Mr. Douglass, I know you; I have read about you. . . . Sit down, I am glad to see you," Lincoln said, and acknowledged that Douglass was correct in his criticisms of him, and apologized for his tardiness in addressing emancipation. Douglass was deeply moved. He was impressed by Lincoln's honesty and sincerity.

A year later, in August 1864, Lincoln called for Douglass again. He wanted him to organize black scouts "to go into the rebel states, beyond the lines of our armies, and carry the news of emancipation, and urge the slaves to come within our boundaries." It was a plan similar to that of John Brown. This increased Douglass's respect for Lincoln because, although it never became necessary, it showed him how far Lincoln was willing to go for the cause of freedom.

The men met a final time at Lincoln's second inauguration. Douglass said the atmosphere was very solemn and that the president's speech was like a sermon. Later they spoke alone in the East Room of the White House. "Here comes my friend," Lincoln said, taking Douglass's hand. "I am glad to see you. . . . There is no man in the country whose opinion I value more than yours."

After the assassination, Douglass wrote that from the view of an abolitionist, "Mr. Lincoln seemed tardy, cold, dull, and indifferent," but "measuring him by the sentiment of his country . . . he was swift, zealous, radical, and determined."

With the close of the Civil War, William Lloyd Garrison had called a meeting to disband the American Anti-Slavery Society. But Douglass opposed him, stating that "Slavery is not abolished until the black man has the ballot." The society came out in favor of Douglass. Many abolitionists left the movement after their long struggle, but Douglass realized the work had only just begun. Fortunately, a faction of Radical Republicans in Congress led by Thaddeus Stevens and Charles Sumner continued the fight for black suffrage. Douglass did his part by making speeches throughout the North to support it.

After another milestone had been passed with the ratification of the Thirteenth Amendment to the U.S. Constitution in December 1865, officially abolishing slavery throughout the United States, Douglass, with his son Lewis and three other black leaders, went to see President Andrew Johnson to urge the adoption of an amendment granting black men universal suffrage. Johnson, a Southerner, was not favorable to the proposal. In fact, Johnson was preparing a reconstruction plan that would return power to the leaders of the Confederacy and fail to grant any rights to former slaves.

The Radical Republicans in Congress overrode Johnson's veto and passed the Civil Rights Bill, which gave full citizenship to blacks. They also passed legislation to divide the South into military districts and implement measures to divest confederate leaders of their power. In an effort to recover his diminishing support, Johnson offered Douglass the position as director of the Freedman's Bureau, but Douglass declined, realizing that it was a political ploy. Eventually impeachment proceedings against Johnson took place and failed by only one vote.

Despite the ratification of the Fourteenth Amendment in 1868, guaranteeing blacks their rights under the Civil Rights Bill, full suffrage to black men was not guaranteed until 1870 when Ulysses S. Grant as President signed the Fifteenth Amendment, guaranteeing all male citizens twenty-one years and older the right to vote, regardless of their race. It was the fruition of all Douglass had worked for since his escape from slavery more than thirty years earlier.

The American Anti-Slavery Society disbanded, and although Douglass angered his colleagues in the women's rights movement by saying that women needed to wait until black men got the vote, he felt he had reached a kind of mountaintop. A year before the termination of the antislavery society, with the reality of the Fifteenth Amendment at hand, Douglass had said at its annual meeting, "We stand tonight amid the bleaching bones of dead issues. . . . I have nothing to kick against."

Douglass, however, was not ready to retire. He purchased the old abolitionist newspaper, *National Era,* in Washington, D.C., and turned it into the *New National Era*, giving him a forum from which to express his views. He also increased his activity

Frederick Douglass, circa 1855. Used with permission of *Documenting the American South,* the University of North Carolina at Chapel Hill Libraries.

on the lecture circuit. During this time, his home in Rochester was consumed by a fire. No one was hurt, but it convinced him to move to the District of Columbia. Although his new paper stopped publishing in 1874, Douglass was hopeful of a major political appointment. In the meantime he was put in charge of the failing Freedmen's Savings and Trust Company, a bank that had been founded to encourage blacks to invest and save their money. But it was too late for help. Even though Douglass had lost money in his efforts to save the bank, he was still financially comfortable as a result of his lecturing, and he continued to speak out in newspaper articles about problems facing blacks in America.

In 1877 his long-awaited political appointment came when Rutherford B. Hayes, a former abolitionist, was elected President and offered him the position of Marshal of the District of Columbia. The job involved overseeing the operation of the criminal justice system there, but it was more of that of a figurehead and required few demands on his time. Douglass was criticized for accepting this patrimony position because the Republican platform had agreed to the removal of federal troops from the South and an end to the Black Reconstruction there. A return of the discriminatory practices of old was feared, and these fears were realized with implementation of the Jim Crow period.

Nearing the age of sixty, Douglass stepped back from the battle that had consumed his life, and following his appointment, he purchased a new home in the Washington area. The fifteen-acre estate, christened Cedar Hill, included a twenty-room house that held a huge library and was decorated with portraits of Abraham Lincoln, William Lloyd Garrison, Susan B. Anthony, and other influential people. That same year he also traveled to Maryland and visited his former master, Thomas Auld, now considerably aged. Auld was apologetic and respectful, and quick to clear up a misconception that Douglass had about the final years of his grandmother's life. Douglass had written in his second autobiography that the Aulds had abandoned her and sent to her die alone in a hut in the woods. Auld assured him that she had been cared for.

The 1880 election of James Garfield as President led to Douglass's appointment as recorder of deeds for the District of Columbia. This involved managing the records of property sales. The following year, Douglass published his third and final autobiography, *Life and Times of Frederick Douglass*, but the book had disappointing sales. After the death of his wife Anna in 1882, Douglass remarried in 1884, shocking the world because his wife, Helen Pitts, was white and twenty years younger than him. He had known Pitts from the time she was a child, as her father had collaborated with him in the Underground Railroad.

A brief appointment as ambassador to the Republic of Haiti followed in 1888. Seven years later, after participating in a meeting of the National Council of Women, Douglass died of a heart attack at Cedar Hill.

SELECTED READING: "Convention of Slaves at Cazenovia," *The North Star*, September 5, 1850; Frederick Douglass, *My Bondage and My Freedom*, New York: Miller, Orton, & Mulligan, 1855; Frederick Douglass, *Life and Times of Frederick Douglass*, Hartford, CT: Park Publishing Co., 1881; Gerald Fulkerson, "Frederick Douglass," *African-American Orators: A Bio-Critical Sourcebook*, Richard W. Leeman, editor, Westport, CT: Greenwood Press, 1996; Patsy Brewington Perry, "Before The North Star: Frederick Douglass' Early Journalistic Career," *Phylon*, vol. 35, 1974; Benjamin Quarles, "The Breach Between Douglass and Garrison," *Journal of Negro History*, April 1938; John Stauffer, *The Black Hearts of Men*, Cambridge, MA: Harvard University Press, 2002; John Stauffer, "Across the Great Divide," *Time Magazine*, June 26, 2005; Sandra Thomas, "A Biography of the Life of Frederick Douglass," http://www.history.rochester.edu/class/douglass/HOME.html; Booker T. Washington, *Frederick Douglass*, London: Hodder and Stoughton, 1906.

F

Fairbank, Calvin (1816–1898). Calvin Fairbank was a devout and fearless abolitionist who did not hesitate to venture into the South to rescue slaves. However, after being caught in the act and spending five years in prison, he was caught aiding fugitive slaves a second time, less than three years after being released, and was forced to spend another twelve years in prison. His personal sacrifice for the cause of ending slavery is one of the most remarkable stories of the Underground Railroad.

Fairbank grew up in the town of Pike, Wyoming County, in Western New York. His family was devoutly Methodist, and Burned-Over District revivalism was a major part of his upbringing: "I very early felt the need of the new birth in Christ, and week after week, year after year, mourned over my alienation from God, and from time to time promised myself resignation to His will."

On one occasion, while attending a revival with his parents, they stayed in the home of two blacks who had escaped from slavery. One related a heartrending story of thirty years in slavery, and being sold and separated from husband and family. Fairbank dated his intense hatred of slavery from that experience: "My heart wept, my anger was kindled, and antagonism to slavery was fixed upon me."

By the time Fairbank was ordained as a minister in 1842, he had already been aiding fugitive slaves for five years. His first experience aiding fugitive slaves occurred while hauling lumber on a raft down the Ohio River and noticing a black man walking on the southern shore of the river. Fairbank called to him and learned that the man who was a slave was disconsolate because his wife and children had been sold away. He offered the man a ride to freedom, and so began his days as a conductor:

> I piloted them through the forests, mostly by night—girls, fair and white, dressed as ladies: men and boys, as gentlemen, or servants—men in women's clothes, and women in men's clothes; boys dressed as girls, and girls as boys; on foot or horseback, in buggies, carriages, common wagons, in and under loads of hay, stray, old furniture, boxes and bags, crossed the Jordan of the slave, swimming, or wading chip deep, or in boats or skiffs, on rafts and often on a pine log. And I never suffered one to be recaptured.

In 1844 Fairbank enrolled at Oberlin College. He had already aided forty-three fugitive slaves to freedom, by his count. An African Methodist Episcopal minister in Oberlin, Rev. John M. Brown, asked if Fairbank would go to Lexington, Kentucky, to rescue the wife and children of an Oberlin fugitive slave, Gilson Berry. This required a dangerous trip of sixty miles through slave territory. After visiting Lexington and meeting with his accomplice, **Delia Webster**, Fairbank decided that an attempt to rescue the Berry family would not be possible. However, another slave, **Lewis Hayden**, a waiter with a wife and child, was willing to make the attempt. In preparation Fairbank visited Ripley, Ohio, in an effort to enlist support from **John Rankin**, as he had been advised to do by Cincinnati abolitionist John Blanchard. However, while crossing the ferry to Ripley, Fairbank was seen talking to a man in a skiff who was a slave patroller, and suspicions arose that he might be a proslavery spy, so the Rankins dismissed him. Nevertheless, Fairbank did persuade Eli Collins to be of assistance during the rescue.

On September 28, 1844, Fairbank and Webster rendezvoused with the Hayden family in a two-horse carriage near the home of Southern abolitionist Cassius Clay. Despite a problem along the way with one of the horses, they safely moved the Hayden family to Ohio. But when they returned to Kentucky to deposit Webster, they were arrested.

Witnesses testified to seeing Fairbank and Webster with the Hayden family in a carriage heading toward Ohio. While they were in jail awaiting trial, Webster steadfastly maintained her innocence and did everything possible to create the impression that she was wrongly accused. Fairbank, on the other hand, slept on the floor of his cell and aided the escape attempt of an inmate who was facing execution.

Webster's trial came first, and though she was convicted and sentenced to two years at the Kentucky State Penitentiary in Frankfurt, the jury recommended that she be pardoned. Fairbank requested a change of venue that would delay his trial but give him a better chance of winning his case. However, when it also delayed Webster's potential pardon, he agreed to his detriment to hasten his trial. Not surprisingly, he too was convicted, but to fifteen years of hard labor.

Webster charmed Warden Newton Craig and ingratiated herself with his wife, Lucy. She also began teaching his children. Other evidence suggests that Craig began to fall in love with Webster. About a week after Fairbank's conviction and less than two months after entering the penitentiary, Webster received her pardon.

In prison Fairbank exhibited exemplary behavior and began preaching the gospel to fellow inmates. By 1848 his elderly father, Chester Fairbank, began distributing petitions for his pardon and corresponding with Craig and Kentucky Governor James Crittendon. In April of 1849 Chester Fairbank came to Frankfort to deliver the petition, while Lewis Hayden in Boston began efforts to raise the $650 needed to satisfy the terms under which his master would approve the pardon. By June the stage was set for Fairbank's release, but it was delayed by the governor, who wanted to wait until after the coming election in August because of a slavery-related referendum that was on the ballot. This delay proved fatal to Fairbank's father when a cholera epidemic swept through Kentucky and claimed his life on July 7, 1849. Two weeks after the election on August 24, Fairbank received his pardon.

Naturally, it was a bittersweet moment for Fairbank. In demand at abolitionist centers of the North, he made a tour that brought him first to Cincinnati, where he met **Laura Haviland**, who became a lifelong friend. He then went to Oberlin, Cleveland, Detroit, and Sandusky, where he assisted a Father Jennings in the successful flight of six fugitive slaves to Canada. Fairbank then headed home, stopping in Buffalo on the way, before reaching Little Genesee, where his mother had moved in with his brother.

Fairbank was not there long, as the abolitionist circuit beckoned; he moved on to Syracuse, where a major convention involving the Liberty Party and the American

Anti-Slavery Society was in session. Fairbank later wrote of the event—which included William Lloyd Garrison, **Gerrit Smith**, and **Frederick Douglass** among many other notables—that it was "the most instructive and exciting" convention of his life. From there Fairbank went to Boston, where he stayed with the Hayden family. He traveled to various localities in New England to relate his experiences and received mostly enthusiastic receptions, though there were occasions when he was heckled. It was during this period that he met his future wife, Maudana Tileston, a teacher in Williamsburg, Massachusetts.

When the Fugitive Slave Law of 1850 was passed, Fairbank was still in Boston and joined in the effort to speak out against the law and raise bail for the release of William L. Chaplin, who had been detained in prison for aiding fugitive slaves in Washington, D.C. He also witnessed firsthand the efforts of Lewis Hayden to aid in the protection of the fugitive slaves William and Ellen Craft.

In the spring of 1851 Fairbank returned to western New York and secured a church to begin a series of lectures attacking the Fugitive Slave Law. The lectures raised a great stir and much shouting among the debaters but fortunately no violence. Some, however, threatened to throw eggs at Fairbank for calling the President a thief for signing the new law. In September Fairbank was a delegate to the Liberty Party convention in Buffalo, after which he headed to Kentucky to undertake the difficult task of bringing his father's body back to New York.

When Fairbank arrived in Cincinnati, the weather was still too hot to transport a body, so he took a journey to Indiana to participate in the debate over a proposed law that would prohibit persons of African descent from settling in that state. It was then that Fairbank made the fateful decision that altered the course of the rest of his life. In Jeffersonville, Fairbank was asked to rescue a slave named Tamar, who was about to be sold at auction in Louisville, just to the west across the Ohio River. Though Fairbank was advised by friends not to risk it, he agreed to try.

Fairbank had no problems getting Tamar out of Louisville, but on the passage across the river, the boat began to leak. They made it ashore, however, and by 4 a.m. were in Jeffersonville, a couple of miles downriver from Louisville, where Fairbank procured a buggy. About thirty miles from their destination in Salem, Indiana, they had an accident and were forced to flag down a train to complete the journey. Fairbank then placed Tamar in the care of a black barber named Jackson and returned to Jeffersonville.

On November 9, a week after his rescue of Tamar, and the day before Fairbank's intended journey to Lexington to retrieve his father's body, Fairbank was kidnapped by a group of Kentuckians led by Tamar's owner.

Fairbank was in jail, and he realized that his situation was dire. He sent a letter, in care of **Levi Coffin**, to Laura Haviland, requesting aid; Coffin, however, advised Haviland against going to Louisville. Just two weeks earlier **Seth Concklin** had lost his life on the Ohio River in an attempt to rescue a slave family. Haviland ignored Coffin's pleas and risked her life to bring amenities such as bedding and clothing to Fairbank and to fulfill another request, to assist him in retaining legal counsel. Fairbank also attempted several schemes, including an aborted jailbreak, all to no avail. He was convicted once again and sentenced to fifteen more years at hard labor. He wrote Maudana Tileston, to whom he was engaged, and said that he would understand if she called it off, but she responded by saying the only man she would marry would be Fairbank.

Newton Craig was still warden of the penitentiary, and he was in no mood to be benevolent to Fairbank—mainly because Craig's affections for Delia Webster had been spurned—and so he took out his frustrations on Fairbank. Immediately, Fairbank was put to work in the hackling house, where the preparation of the hemp plants was done. (Hemp production accounted for the main income of the prison.) This was the most unhealthy and least desirable job in the prison; after a few months Fairbank became ill and had to be removed from that duty.

Fairbank also became the object of rawhide whippings that increased in their frequency when Craig's term as warden ended in 1854 with the election of Zebulon Ward. The latter made whipping a regular practice for prisoners who didn't meet their respective job quotas. Fairbank, for instance, said the quota for production on his job was so high that it was impossible for him to reach, and so he was continuously whipped. Ward's tenure ended in 1858.

In all, Fairbank counted 35,108 lashes during his second stay, and his normal weight of 180 pounds, on a frame of 5 feet 9 inches, sank to as low as 117 pounds.

Perhaps only the support of friends and loved ones helped Fairbank to survive. After making two visits to see him in 1853 and 1855, Tileston took a teaching position in Oxford, Ohio (about 100 miles north of Frankfort) in 1858, so that she could visit him regularly while he was in prison. She also sent him bedding, money, and boxes of provisions, and did everything within her power to make him more comfortable. Other friends—including Tamar, whose freedom Fairbank had procured at his own expense—also sent him supplies, books, underwear, food, and money.

Finally, on April 15, 1864, Fairbank was pardoned and released from the penitentiary, having been incarcerated for seventeen years and three months during a period of about twenty years. When he reached Ohio, he kissed the ground and threw his hands in the air, then shouted, "Out of the Mouth of Death! Out of the Jaws of Hell!"

Fairbank's ordeal took a great toll on him; he was lucky to have survived. When he went to Cincinnati after his release, Levi Coffin and others did not even recognize him. Within two days of his release, Fairbank spoke at the Baptist Church on Longworth Street. More than 3,000 people attended, the audience spilling out into the street. His freedom dress, as Fairbank described it, of short pants, vest, scarf, and tattered hat was so poor that it compelled people to give him donations for a new suit.

Fairbank's next stop was Oxford, thirty miles to the north, where he was at long last reunited with Maudana Tileston. On June 9, 1864, they were married, and four years later she gave birth to their son, Calvin C. Fairbank.

Following their marriage, the couple went on an extended tour that brought Fairbank to pulpits and podiums in Chicago, Oberlin, Toronto, Philadelphia, and Washington, D.C. In Washington he preached at the church of **Henry Highland Garnet**, and attending were President Lincoln, Secretary of State Seward, Secretary of the Treasury Stanton, and Senator Sumner, among many other notables. Fairbank also attended the inauguration of Lincoln.

Though he was out of prison, life was not kind to Fairbank. Despite holding jobs with missionary and benevolent societies, he struggled to make a living. When his wife died in 1876, his eight-year-old son was sent to live with relatives. Fairbank then married again, in 1879, to Adeline Winegar. His memoirs, *Rev. Calvin Fairbank During Slavery Times: How He Fought the Good Fight to Prepare the Way*, were published in 1890. But they earned him little money. Fairbank was a forgotten man, and he died eight years later in poverty in Angelica, New York, where he is buried. In all, he aided about fifty-three slaves in obtaining their freedom.

Slave rescuer Calvin Fairbank. Courtesy of the Ohio Historical Society.

His lament following the death of his first wife serves as a testimony to his life of self-sacrifice:

> I have suffered an imprisonment of seventeen years and three months. I have suffered from hunger, cold, sickness, insult, corporal punishment, and discontent. But all these sink away into thin air, into dim, distant nothingness—I count them all joy for righteousness' sake. . . . Soon the last of the liberty army will have dropped away, and these records will appear to future generations as a tale of the past; but 'we shall meet beyond the river' our friends and loved ones, whom we now mourn, in an eternal communion—an eternal congregation of the disembodied spirits—to joy and rejoice in their society, where there shall be no night, no winter, no poverty, no sickness and death; but our union shall be complete and eternal.

SUGGESTED READING: Levi Coffin, *Reminiscences*, Cincinnati: Robert Clarke & Co., 1880; Calvin Fairbank, *Rev. Calvin Fairbank During Slavery Times*, Chicago: Patriotic Publishing, Co.,

1890; Laura Haviland, *A woman's life-work: labors and experiences of Laura S. Haviland*, Cincinnati: Walden & Stowe, 1882; Randolph Paul Runyon, *Delia Webster and the Underground Railroad*, Lexington, KY: University Press of Kentucky, 1996.

Fairfield, John (1813?–1856?). John Fairfield was perhaps the most mysterious and daring individual in the lore of the Underground Railroad. Allegedly born in Camden, Virginia, to a wealthy slaveholder, and educated in New England, Fairfield—this is not likely his real name—grew to hate slavery as a boy.

Most of the knowledge about him comes from **Levi Coffin**, with whom Fairfield stayed on occasion during his trips between the South and Canada, but several other accounts describing him have survived.

When he reached adulthood, Fairfield decided to seek a new life in a land where there was no slavery, and he thought that perhaps the nearby free state of Ohio was a good choice. Money was no object because he had inherited a fortune from his mother, though it is not known when she died.

On this first trip Fairfield arranged to help one of his uncle's slaves escape. The slave, Bill, stole a horse from Fairfield's uncle for the getaway. But instead of merely depositing Bill in Ohio, Fairfield took him all the way to Canada.

When Levi Coffin heard this story, he asked Fairfield if he'd had any worries about breaking the laws of horse stealing and slave stealing, which were punishable by death. Fairfield answered with a firm no, that Bill had worked faithfully for many years, and one horse was not nearly enough to compensate. "I would steal all the slaves in Virginia if I could," he said.

Fairfield returned to Virginia thereafter, and learned that his uncle suspected him of helping Bill and planned to have him arrested. Fairfield quickly prepared his departure, but before leaving, he took more of his family's slaves and escorted them to Canada as well. There he decided to make his home—that is, when not rescuing slaves. Many former fugitive slaves in Canada came to him, offering to pay him to help their relatives escape. But Fairfield hated slavery so much that he sometimes rescued slaves without pay. He was ruthless, always armed, and "devoid of moral principle," according to Coffin. He would not hesitate to kill someone who got in his way.

So Fairfield became a slave rescuer for hire. Probably the most prolific ever, if no less a source than **Laura Haviland** is correct in saying that Fairfield aided "thousands" of fugitive slaves. However, it is likely that Haviland was only speculating, based on stories Fairfield himself told—and he was not one whose veracity could be trusted.

Fairfield used various aliases. In some cases, he posed as a proslavery Virginia businessman; when in the Deep South, he became a Texas plantation owner. In 1835, that was the cover he was using while living in Mobile, Alabama, where his boyhood friend John Ward had set up a foundry business. Ward had purchased a four-year-old boy named Curtis at the request of Curtis's mother, a slave whom they knew from their neighborhood in Virginia, and whom Ward had by chance spotted during a slave auction. Ward was raising Curtis as if he were his son. Fairfield, in fact, would lead the boy's mother to freedom in Canada, and when Curtis grew up, he moved there and was reunited with her.

Fairfield also used a variety of methods. Sometimes, he would remain in an area as long as a year, sizing up the situation and secretly meeting with slaves before leading them away. On one occasion he led a party of armed men south from Kentucky into Tennessee to throw off the slavecatchers. He often crossed the Ohio into Cincinnati, sometimes going by way of Maysville. In Cincinnati, he stayed with a Mrs. Layman. Whether this was the real name of the person he described is not known, but there actually was a Mrs. Anna Layman Conroy, who ran the Spread Eagle Tavern just north of Cincinnati; that tavern was a well-documented Underground Railroad stop.

An example of the methods of subterfuge Fairfield employed were the use of powder and wigs on three separate parties of fugitives in the Washington, D.C., and Harpers Ferry area, whom he had been contracted to aid by their family members in Detroit and Canada. Fairfield took them by train through Harrisburg, Pittsburgh, and Cleveland, and on to Detroit. Although the third party was discovered near Pittsburgh and was forced to flee the train, they found refuge with abolitionists and eventually arrived safely in Detroit.

At times Fairfield also would have one or more free blacks with him, who posed as his slaves, so that through them he could learn the whereabouts of the slaves whom he had been hired to "steal." He was ready to undergo any hardship or privation to achieve his goal. Not surprisingly, he was betrayed and arrested on several occasions but somehow managed to get himself released (it was said that this was because he was a Freemason). On one occasion, however, he spent time in the Bracken County jail, from which he somehow escaped. Suffering from an illness he had contracted in jail, he crossed the Ohio at Ripley, where he was nursed for some weeks at the home of one of the Ripley abolitionists. Shortly after this, in 1853, his most famous rescue ruse was concocted with the help of Levi Coffin.

Fairfield was somewhere in Kentucky, working as a poultry dealer and deceitfully proclaiming pro-slavery views. Finally he made arrangements to help a group of slaves, who were able to pay him. They numbered twenty-eight in all, including an infant. He led them to where the Ohio River met the mouth of the Miami River, about a dozen miles west of Cincinnati; there Fairfield had three skiffs ready for use. However, the skiffs were barely able to accommodate the entire party, and the one that carried Fairfield sprung a leak. When he jumped out and tried to pull the boat to shore, he got caught in quicksand and had to be helped out. The entire party ended up wading in the water and getting very muddy and wet. It was rainy and cold that night, as well, and suffering from exposure, they waited in the underbrush along the shore a few miles from Cincinnati while Fairfield went to arrange the next leg of the journey.

Fairfield's first contact was John Hatfield, a barber and steamboat steward, who was a deacon at the Zion Baptist Church. Hatfield contacted Levi Coffin, who assembled his black associates. A plan was hatched to obtain two coaches from a German livery stable, and also dispatch several men in buggies to pick up the fugitive slaves. They would join the coaches to form a mock funeral procession along the road leading to College Hill, where there were agents who would shelter them, and where abolitionist minister Jonathan Cable would coordinate further arrangements.

While the procession was being organized, the Hatfield family and other black women prepared food, coffee, and blankets for the fugitive slaves. A buggy with the provisions was sent ahead with Fairfield for the fugitive slaves. How long they had been waiting, or the time of day or night, is unknown. On the road, they moved along slowly, but tragedy struck on the way; the mock funeral procession became a real one when the infant died, apparently of exposure. The procession ended at Farmer's College in nearby College Hill. The fugitive slaves were gathered in the house of the college janitor, "scared and trembling, waiting for the wagons to take them across the Ohio boundary into the safer Quaker settlements in Indiana . . . . Some daring students . . . had with others made all the necessary arrangements . . . to see them off."

The route out of Cincinnati passed through Hamilton, West Elkton, Eaton, Paris, and Newport, and on up through Michigan. In Cambridge, Michigan, the fugitive slaves stayed at the house of Fitch Reed, who later wrote that they were then armed with fifty-two rounds of ammunition. They left Reed's house at sunset in four wagons and spent the next day resting at the home of a black man named Brother Ray. Another black man, John M. Coe, was sent ahead by train to Detroit, where a reception was organized.

A party met the fugitive slaves on the road and led them to a boarding house ten miles from Detroit. In the wee hours of the morning, 200 abolitionists met them for breakfast and then led them to the harbor and the awaiting boats. As they shoved off for the Promised Land, they began singing, "I am on my way to Canada, where colored men are free," and began firing their guns in celebration. When they arrived in Canada, many of them kneeled down and thanked God. Fairfield said, "This scene has doubly paid me for risking my life, my liberty, and my fortune for God's very poorest of the poor."

Alexander Milton Ross: The Birdwatcher Who Rescued Slaves

Canadian Alexander Milton Ross's story of his surreptitious journey into the South to entice slaves to freedom is one of the more remarkable narratives in Underground Railroad lore—so remarkable that some historians doubt its veracity.

Ross claimed to have been sent into the South on a mission funded by **Gerrit Smith** and Lewis Tappan. In 1856, posing at times as an ornithologist, Ross made the first of three hazardous journeys, which took him throughout the South. It was through Smith that Ross "obtained much valuable and interesting information as to the workings of the different organizations having for their object the liberation from bondage of the slaves of the South," while accompanying Smith on a journey during which Ross was introduced to conductors of the Underground Railroad from Massachusetts to Indiana.

Ross's procedure was to gather fugitive slaves in secret, inform them that he would direct them to locations on the Underground Railroad, and supply them with money, weapons, and as much food as they could carry. He used a number of aliases and wrote letters to associates in code. In all, Ross accounted for directly assisting thirty-five fugitive slaves in their escapes, sometimes escorting them all the way to Canada.

Ross also claimed to have developed a close friendship with John Brown and to have undertaken a spy mission during the Civil War at the request of President Lincoln. But no corroborative evidence has as yet surfaced to confirm these claims.

Fairfield telegraphed friends in Windsor, and a dinner reception was provided at one of the black churches. One woman, who was more than eighty years old, shook hands with the refugees and shouted, "I's young again. Glory! Glory! Jesus is our Master for evermore, honey. Glory to Jesus! I's sixteen," as she pranced around and clapped with joy.

On a later excursion, Fairfield went back to Virginia, posing as a Kentucky businessman. This time, he posed as a victim of treachery by slaves who had stolen his property—but whom he was actually helping to get away. To confound the authorities, he led the posse in pursuit of the slaves, knowing that the posse would arrive at the river crossing long after the fugitive slaves. When the posse arrived, as Fairfield had expected, they found the empty boats that the fugitive slaves had left behind. With the chase given up, Fairfield met the fugitives in Ohio and led them the rest of the way to Canada.

"I never saw such a man as Fairfield," said one fugitive slave:

> He told us he would take us out of slavery or die in the attempt, if we would do our part, which we promised to do. We all agreed to fight till we died rather than be captured. Fairfield

> said he wanted no cowards in the company; if we were attacked and one of us showed cowardice or started to run, he would shoot them down.

Another time Fairfield showed Coffin bullet wounds he had received during one skirmish with slaveholders, and said:

> Slaveholders are all devils, and it is no harm to kill the devil. I do not intend to hurt people if they keep out of the way, but if they step in between me and liberty, they must take the consequences. When I undertake to conduct slaves out of bondage I feel that it is my duty to defend them to the last drop of my blood.

Sometime during the 1850s, Fairfield ran a grocery in Randolph, Indiana, but he closed it after a couple of years and disappeared. Coffin surmises that Fairfield may have the been the white man identified as stirring up slave revolts at the iron factories in Kentucky and Tennessee in 1856, and that he may have met his death during that failed attempt.

There are actual reports of such insurrections that took place in the iron foundries of Kentucky and Tennessee, which employed several thousand slaves. In one such insurrection at Dover, on the Cumberland, in December of 1856, eleven slaves were hung, and a white man was taken to the woods and sentenced to receive 900 lashes, which brought on his death.

Some accounts claim Fairfield rescued as many as 3,000 slaves from every state south of the Mason-Dixon Line during a period lasting about twenty years. While this number is probably exaggerated, the known exploits of John Fairfield probably represent only a small portion of his labors to free the slaves.

SUGGESTED READING: Marven B. Butler, *My Story of the Civil War and the Underground Railroad,* Huntington, IN: United Brethren Publishing, 1914; Levi Coffin, *Reminiscences,* Cincinnati: Robert Clarke & Co., 1880; Charles B. Drew, "Black Ironworkers and the Slave Insurrection Panic of 1856," *Journal of Southern History,* August 1975; Laura Haviland, *A woman's life-work: labors and experiences of Laura S. Haviland,* Cincinnati: Walden & Stowe, 1882; Wilbur Siebert, *The Underground Railroad from Slavery to Freedom,* New York: Macmillan, 1898.

Fountain, Alfred (dates unknown). Captain Alfred Fountain was an active Underground Railroad conductor operating out of the ports of Norfolk and Richmond, Virginia, with his boat, the *City of Richmond*. He rendezvoused with **Thomas Garrett** at the Rocks in Wilmington, Delaware, and at the port of Philadelphia with the Philadelphia Vigilance Committee. William Still's description of him is quite vivid:

> Although he had been living a seafaring life for many years, and the marks of this calling were plainly enough visible in his manners and speech, he was, nevertheless, unlike the great mass of this class of men, not addicted to intemperance and profanity. On the contrary, he was a man of thought, and possessed, in a large measure, those humane traits of character which lead men to sympathize with suffering humanity wherever met with.
>
> It must be admitted, however, that the first impressions gathered from a hasty survey of his rough and rugged appearance, his large head, large mouth, large eyes, and heavy eye-brows, with a natural gift at keeping concealed the inner-workings of his mind and feelings, were not calculated to inspire the belief, that he was fitted to be entrusted with the lives of unprotected females, and helpless children; that he could take pleasure in risking his own life to rescue them from the hell of Slavery; that he could deliberately enter the enemy's domain, and with the faith of a martyr, face the dread slaveholder, with his Bowie knives and revolvers—slave hunters, and blood-hounds, lynchings, and penitentiaries, for

Captain Alfred Fountain assists the mayor of Richmond in searching his boat. Courtesy of the William Still Foundation, Inc.

> humanity's sake. But his deeds proved him to be a true friend of the slave; whilst his skill, bravery, and success stamped him as one of the most daring and heroic captains ever connected with the Underground Railroad cause.

A celebrated incident involving Captain Fountain occurred in November 1855. Reports of an escape by a large number of slaves had circulated in Norfolk. It was suspected that they were taking passage in a boat still docked in the harbor. The city's mayor summoned local police to make a search. Leading the way, the mayor stormed aboard Fountain's ship with officers bearing an ax and a spear. Fountain had twenty-one fugitive slaves hidden, but he welcomed the mayor and allowed him to search. A large shipment of wheat had been loaded, and there was particular interest in it, as one of the officers began poking through it with the spear. Failing to locate anyone, the mayor ordered that the ax be used to chop up the deck.

As they were proceeding, Captain Fountain decided to intervene before they chopped his boat to pieces. "Give me the axe," he commanded. "Point out the spot you want opened, and I will open it for you very quick."

Showing that he was someone to be reckoned with, Fountain raised the ax overhead, and with all the fury and power he could summon, he swung the ax down upon the deck, causing splinters to fly. This startled the mayor and the officers, and put them in fear of Fountain's wrath. Before they could react, Fountain swung the ax down again, this time even more ferociously. The mayor was stunned. Not knowing where to resume the search, he decided he had completed the exercise of his official duties. He thanked the captain, then levied the five-dollar fee required for such searches, and led the officers off the ship.

How many fugitive slaves Captain Fountain assisted is unknown. Still refers to forty-seven, whom he not only identifies but for whom he also provides biographical information. The captain, who was known to frequent the slave trading markets of Richmond, Norfolk, and Petersburg, Virginia, readily accepted payment for his services, so the number he assisted could have been much greater. It is also believed that he ventured into Albemarle Sound, where the inlets to the Great Dismal Swamp in North Carolina were located. Daniel Carr, one of the fugitive slaves identified by Still as having been transported by Fountain, told of hiding in a swamp surrounded by reptiles. An area near Albemarle Sound was known to be invested with alligators.

The last we know of Fountain is a letter from Thomas Garrett to William Still, reporting that Fountain's boat had been burned by the Confederates and that Fountain had joined the army of General McClellan.

SUGGESTED READINGS: David Cecelski, "The Shores of Freedom: The Maritime Underground Railroad in North Carolina, 1800–1861," *North Carolina Historical Review*, Vol. 1, No. 2, April 1994; James A. McGowan, *Station Master on the Underground Railroad: The Life and Letter of Thomas Garrett*, Jefferson, NC: McFarland, revised edition, 2004; William Still, *The Underground Railroad*, Philadelphia: Porter and Coates, 1872.

Fussell, Bartholomew (1794–1871). Dr. Bartholomew Fussell was among the most active Underground Railroad conductors in Chester County, Pennsylvania. Underground Railroad historian Robert Smedley estimated that Fussell may have assisted as many as 2,000 fugitive slaves.

Fussell was born to Quaker parents whose ancestors were with William Penn when he founded Philadelphia. As a young man Fussell moved to Maryland, where he taught school and studied medicine. During this time he came under the influence of the noted Quaker abolitionist Elisha Tyson, whose efforts in behalf of kidnapped free blacks antedated those of **Isaac Hopper** and were equally as prolific and courageous. In addition to Fussell's obligations as a teacher and student studying medicine in night school, he opened a Sunday School for slaves, which drew as many as 90 students at a time.

Following graduation from medical school, Fussell spoke before the medical society of Baltimore and attacked the institution of slavery, calling it "preposterous and cruel," and looked forward to the time "when slavery . . . should have no abiding place in the whole habitable earth." Of course, this created a stir in a place where slavery was the accepted norm.

Fussell returned to Pennsylvania, married Lydia Morris, and started his practice as a physician. Having established a friendship with **Thomas Garrett**, Fussell made his home near Kennett Square, known as "the Pines," one of that community's earliest refuges for fugitive slaves. His son Joshua recalled that a free black named Davy who peddled fish and fruit was the agent who brought fugitive slaves from Garrett to the Fussell household. Frequently among the fugitive slaves Fussell sheltered were students whom he had taught at his Sunday School in Maryland.

One fugitive slave who made a great impression on Fussell's son, Joshua, was George Harris, who escaped from Georgia and walked the entire distance to freedom, and was able to recall in detail the places he passed through along his escape route. Harris was hired at a farm in nearby Marlborough but died soon afterward.

Fussell took out a subscription to William Lloyd Garrison's *The Liberator* when the paper began publishing in 1831, and he continued to receive the abolitionist weekly until it ceased publication in 1865. He also was a founding member of the American Anti-Slavery Society in 1833.

During the late 1830s, the Fussells moved to a farm adjoining that of his older sister Esther Lewis and her daughters in West Vincent, Pennsylvania, about 20 miles north of Kennett Square. Like Fussell, they were dedicated abolitionists and Underground Railroad workers. The Lewises and Fussells would work with Garrett throughout the antebellum period and also allied themselves with John Vickers of Lionville, five miles to the south, and Elijah Pennypacker of Phoenixville, five miles to the east.

While in West Vincent, the Fussells hired a farmhand and house servant named Eliza. A fugitive slave, Eliza had ridden 40 miles on horseback and then walked another 30 miles in a span of 24 hours to make her escape. They also hired another fugitive slave named James Washington, and he and Eliza were eventually married at a wedding ceremony held at the Fussell farm. A tally of the fugitive slaves that Fussell assisted in 1841, as just one instance, totaled 34.

Elisha Tyson: Defender of the Oppressed

Baltimore Quaker and philanthropist Elisha Tyson was an early abolitionist who actively defended the rights of blacks both free and slave. He not only agitated at private meetings but in public through the press and the courts. A member of the Maryland Abolition Society (founded in 1789), he continued to work personally for abolition after its dissolution seven years later.

When learning of blacks whose freedom was in jeopardy, Tyson sometimes took it upon himself to personally confront slavecatchers. On occasion when learning that three free blacks had been abducted, he went to the suspected slave abductor's door and demanded their release. His demand provoked the slavecatcher to pull a gun on him.

"Shoot if thee dare," said Tyson, "but thee dare not, coward as thou art, for well does thee know, that the gallows would be thy portion."

Whether it was Tyson's audacity or his reputation, or perhaps a bit of both, the slavecatcher withdrew his gun. In the cellar, Tyson found a woman who was shackled and gagged with two small children. After Tyson removed the gag, she explained that she had been emancipated and was leaving her former master to move to a place where she could find employment, when she was taken to this house under false pretenses.

Tyson obtained a court order that released the woman and her children. In the end, the slave-trader who had abducted them was sentenced to a year in prison.

Such instances were not uncommon in the life of Tyson, who faced down the guns of many a slave abductor during his life.

Dr. Bartholomew Fussell, who came under Tyson's influence after moving to Maryland, may have become acquainted with him through family ties, as both had ancestors who were with William Penn when he founded Philadelphia.

Fussell greatly admired his sister Esther, who had been a teacher and was interested in medicine, only to have her aspirations stymied by the lack of a medical college for women. As a result, in 1840, Fussell began holding classes in medicine for women and originated the idea to start a medical college, which in 1850 led to the establishment of the Woman's Medical College in Philadelphia, the nation's first female medical college.

Fussell's first wife, Lydia, died in 1840, and he married Rebecca Hewes in 1841. They moved to York, Pennsylvania, while his brother William—and later his nephew Edwin, also a physician—took up residence on the farm adjoining the Lewises, continuing the Lewis-Fussell Underground Railroad collaboration in West Vincent. While in York during May of 1843, Fussell was visited by his nephew, Dr. Edwin Fussell, then living in Indiana. Edwin Fussell came with a group of Ohio abolitionists in a wagon built to transport fugitive slaves by Abram Allen of Oakland, Ohio, called "The Liberator." The wagon could accommodate eight persons and had curtains and a bell mechanism that would record the number of miles it traveled.

Fussell's efforts in the antislavery cause intensified as the traffic along the Underground Railroad increased with the passage of the second Fugitive Slave Law in 1850. In 1851, he was one of those who helped **William Parker**, Abe Johnson, and Alex Pinckney, three of the participants in the Christiana Riot, escape from Lancaster County, hiding them at the Lewis home in West Vincent on the night following the riot.

In the latter part of the 1850s, Fussell moved back to Chester County. He continued to be an active member of the Pennsylvania Anti-Slavery Society until the end of the Civil War and the prohibition of slavery. His later years were marked by his colorful retelling of his many experiences in the Underground Railroad and the abolitionist movement. He spent much of his later life with his son, Joshua, in Pendleton, Indiana, and died at the home of his son, Dr. Morris Fussell, in West Pikeland, Pennsylvania.

SUGGESTED READING: William C. Kashatus, *Just Over the Line*, West Chester, Pennsylvania: Chester County Historical Society, 2002; R.C. Smedley, *History of the Underground Railroad in Chester and Neighboring Counties of Pennsylvania*, Lancaster, PA, 1883; William Still, *The Underground Railroad*, Philadelphia: Porter and Coates, 1872.

G

Garnet, Henry Highland (1815–1882). Henry Highland Garnet is generally regarded as the most important American black leader of the antebellum period, after abolitionist **Frederick Douglass**. Born a slave in Maryland, Garnet escaped to freedom with his family when he was only nine years old. The family left their owner's plantation under the pretense of attending a relative's funeral. Along the way, they were given shelter at the home of famed conductor **Thomas Garrett**, but during the escape Garnet suffered an injury that caused permanent damage to one of his legs.

Garnet's family settled in New York City, but for a time were hounded by slavecatchers. At the age of fifteen, Garnet was indentured for two years to Epenetus Smith, a Long Island Quaker, to relieve some of this pressure. Garnet also spent time at sea as a cabin boy. He attended a number of schools and was provided with an excellent education that included the study of Latin and Greek. It was as a student that he met Rev. **Theodore Wright**, pastor of the Negro Presbyterian Church in New York City, who had a crucial impact on Garnet's life. During this time Garnet developed an interest in African culture that continued throughout his life.

In 1835 Garnet attended a college in Canaan, New Hampshire. The residents did not want a school in their community that educated blacks, and a mob attacked the home of the family with whom Garnet was boarding. During this incident Garnet was forced to use a shotgun to defend himself. He left New Hampshire and transferred to Beriah Green's Oneida Institute to complete his formal education. At the institute, Garnet developed a reputation as an orator. In 1840 he settled in Troy, New York, with the family of minister Nathan Sidney Beman, and opened a school for blacks. The following year, Garnet's injured leg had to be amputated below the knee, and thereafter he used a wooden peg to allow him to get around.

In 1842 Garnet was ordained as a minister and installed as the first pastor of the Liberty Street Negro Presbyterian Church of Troy. This began a period of great activity in his advocacy for the rights of black Americans, highlighted by his electrifying "Address to the Slaves" at the Convention of Colored Citizens in Buffalo in 1843: "Brethren, arise, arise! Strike for your lives and liberties. Now is the day and the hour. . . . Rather die free men than live to be slaves."

Such unvarnished rhetoric from a black American man had yet to be heard on a public platform. It was criticized by fellow blacks such as Frederick Douglass and white abolitionists such as William Lloyd Garrison, but fifteen years later both would

Black abolitionist leader Henry Highland Garnet. National Portrait Gallery, Smithsonian Institution.

support such action. Nevertheless, the daring speech brought Garnet great attention. Among those affected was **John Brown**, who had the text published at his own expense.

During the remainder of the decade, Garnet became a speaker in demand at abolition conventions. He also was active in the Underground Railroad, working with

Rev. Wright and **Charles Ray** of the New York Committee of Vigilance, and he claimed to have aided as many as 150 fugitive slaves in a single year.

Garnet continued as pastor at the Liberty Street Church in Troy until 1848. During the next couple of years, he led a peripatetic existence, spending part of the time in Peterboro with **Gerrit Smith**. When the second Fugitive Slave Law was passed in 1850, Garnet was one of the first individuals prosecuted, as it was publicly known that he had been a fugitive slave. However, his case was dismissed, and Garnet fled to England.

Garnet was out of the country for the next five years, also spending time in Jamaica, and when he returned in 1855, he took over as pastor at the Shiloh Church of his mentor, Rev. Wright, who had died in 1848. Following the draft riots of 1863 in New York, during which blacks were brutally attacked by whites, Garnet became a vocal advocate of the patriotism of blacks and encouraged their enlistment in the Union Army.

In 1864 Garnet accepted the pastorate of the Fifteenth Street Presbyterian Church in Washington, D.C. His sermons drew the attention of President Lincoln's advisers, and Garnet was chosen as a speaker for the anniversary of the Emancipation Proclamation at the House of Representatives on February 12, 1865. It marked the first official appearance by a black man at the House.

Garnet returned to the Shiloh church in 1866, remaining there until 1881. While in Washington, Garnet had expressed interest in immigrating to Liberia, and he later stated publicly, "If I can just reach the land of my forefathers and with my feet press her soil I shall be content to die." His wish was granted when he was chosen as ambassador to Liberia in 1881, and he died in February 1882, two months after his arrival.

SUGGESTED READING: A. H. Gordon, "Henry Highland Garnet," *Journal of Negro History*, January 1928; Martin B. Pasternak, *Rise now and fly to arms: the life of Henry Highland Garnet*, New York: Garland Publishers, 1995.

Garrett, Thomas (1789–1871). Thomas Garrett was the only major Underground Railroad conductor who lived south of the Mason Dixon Line. A fearless man who did not mince his words, Garrett never denied helping slaves to escape, even in the face of knives or pistols brandished by slavecatchers. Calmly, he would push their weapons aside and tell them that only cowards resorted to violence. A powerfully built man, Garrett would not allow anyone to prevent him from doing what he thought was right in the eyes of God, and his fierce resolution intimidated even the boldest slavecatchers.

An example of this resolution occurred when Garrett was visited one day by a slaveholder, who recently had lost a slave whom the man suspected had escaped with Garrett's help. "If we ever catch you in our part of the world," the slaveholder threatened, "we will tar and feather you."

Garrett promised to return the visit the next time he was in the slaveholder's neighborhood—and he kept his promise. "Thee said thee wanted to see me when I was in this part of the world," he said, "and here I am." The slaveholder was flabbergasted and told Garrett to move along and not worry about anyone harming him.

Nevertheless, Garrett never enticed a slave to use the Underground Railroad, a policy also followed by **Levi Coffin** and **John Rankin**, the two other great conductors of the Underground road. In a letter to a supporter, Garrett wrote, "I have heretofore kept clear of persuading, or even advising slaves to leave their masters till they had fully made up their minds to leave, knowing as I do there is great risk in so doing, and if betrayed once would be a serious injury to the cause hereafter."

Garrett was born to Quaker parents in Upper Darby, Pennsylvania. His father was a farmer and toolmaker, and taught him that trade. Garrett also became acquainted with the ordeals of fugitive slaves in his youth, as his family harbored them in their barn.

While still living with his parents, at about the age of twenty-four, Garrett returned after an absence to learn that a black woman named Nancy, who worked on their farm, had been kidnapped. At once he set out to recover her. He noticed unusual markings left by a wagon with a broken wheel. He followed it to the Navy Yard in Philadelphia, and through his own inquiries tracked the occupants to Kensington, which was across the Delaware River, about seven miles from Upper Darby. It can only be imagined how Garrett managed to wrest Nancy from her abductors. It was during this pursuit that he claimed to have had an epiphany, imagining a voice from God telling him that his life's work was to defend those who were persecuted.

Shortly after, Garrett married Mary Sharpless. In 1822 they moved to Wilmington, Delaware. Three of their five children had been born, and Garrett opened a hardware store. It is believed he began harboring fugitive slaves about this time. As early as 1818 Garrett had joined an abolition society, and he is known to have been an advocate for kidnapped blacks at least as early as 1823. He also joined a group that encouraged the production and use of free-labor goods in 1826, and was a delegate from that society to the national meeting of the American Convention for Promoting the Abolition of Slavery in 1827.

That year Mary died, and in 1830 Garrett married his second wife, Rachel Mendinhall, whose father also was a Quaker merchant and abolitionist. They were married thirty-eight years and had one child, Eli. The Garretts regularly aided fugitive slaves at their 227 Shipley Street home. They sheltered and fed the fugitive slaves, arranged and paid for their travel, and often covered expenses out of their own pocket.

In those early days of abolition, only a small number of persons in the community supported Garrett, and his house was regularly under surveillance. But he believed the Lord was on his side, and ignored those who disagreed with him. He also found ways to add to his income, opening a tobacco snuff-making mill in addition to his store, which helped to support his Underground Railroad activities.

Although slavery was permitted in the state of Delaware, the number of free blacks was far greater than the number of slaves, and the disparity continued to increase up until the Civil War. For example, there were nearly three times as many free blacks as slaves in the state in 1820, but more than six times as many by 1850, and more than ten times as many by the Civil War. This provided Garrett with a bit of a buffer from local slaveholders, as a large number of free blacks were inclined to assist him in his Underground Railroad activities.

Garrett, who actually kept track, claimed to have aided about 1,400 fugitive slaves without any serious problems, until 1848. That year, however, Garrett was brought to trial for helping seven slaves obtain their freedom. The story of what led to Garrett's prosecution is a good illustration of the Underground Railroad in action.

At dawn on December 5, 1845, outside the village of Middletown, Delaware, about 25 miles south of Wilmington, a Quaker named John Hunn spied a wagon, with several men walking alongside, approaching his home. The area had been hit overnight by a snowstorm that had left six inches of snow, and this contrasted with the black complexion of the man walking up to him. The man handed Hunn a letter. It was from Hunn's cousin, Ezekiel Jenkins, who lived twenty-seven miles to the south in Camden.

It revealed that those in the group were fugitive slaves, and the man giving Hunn the letter was their conductor, Samuel Burris. There were thirteen persons in all, one being a freeman named Sam Hawkins, who was taking his wife, Emeline, and six children to freedom. The other four were men who had joined Burris and the Hawkins family in Camden.

The group had traveled all night through a snowstorm. They were tired, frozen, and hungry. Hunn and his wife fed them breakfast, then sent the men and the teenage boys into the barn, and put up the woman and her four youngest children in his house. Hawkins had been trying to purchase the freedom of his family for a number of years without luck, but when it appeared that their alleged owner was preparing to sell them away from him, he arranged with Burris to come to Ingleside, Queen's County, Maryland, and help bring them out.

That afternoon, one of Hunn's neighbors pulled up in a sleigh. He said he had noticed the wagon stop at Hunn's house and had reported it to the authorities in Middletown. Less than an hour later, law enforcement officials and slavehunters arrived. They displayed an advertisement with a $1,000 reward for the recovery of three fugitive slaves. When they asked Hunn if they could search his premises, he refused, demanding a warrant. It was during their banter that Hawkins suddenly stepped out of the barn and ran into the woods. The constables gave chase. Hawkins circled back. Hunn found him armed with a butcher's knife. One of the constables drew his pistol. However, Hunn intervened and reasoned with both to give up their weapons. Hawkins then produced a certificate that showed him to be free.

The constables said they knew Hawkins was free, but that their report indicated that he was fleeing with his family who were slaves. They demanded that he go to Middletown to talk to a judge. There was no other option, and so Hawkins and the constables went to see William Street, who happened to be Hunn's friend. At Street's office, one of the constables became more congenial with Hawkins and was brought into a separate room, where they spoke privately. When they came out, they had come to a compromise agreement. Hawkins would give up his two oldest sons, who were fourteen and sixteen, so that the rest of his family could go free. Hunn advised Hawkins that he was being tricked, but Hawkins refused to listen, so Hunn gave a note to the constables for his wife, saying it was okay to release Hawkins's family.

When the family returned, the constables had Street prepare commitment charges against the entire party, including Hawkins, despite his proof that he was free. The family was then taken to the jail in New Castle, about eighteen miles north. It was 2 a.m. when the Sheriff Jacob Caulk examined the commitment documents, but he found that Street had failed to properly sign and seal them. He told the constables that they needed to return to Middleton to have the papers properly administered. Nevertheless, they persuaded the sheriff to agree to maintain custody of the Hawkins family until their return.

Sheriff Caulk was a friend of Thomas Garrett, and he had his daughter send word to the Garretts. The next morning Garrett and the Quaker Edith Pusey came to the jail. After talking to the Hawkinses and being shown a copy of a will that established the manumission of Emeline and her four youngest children, Garrett was convinced that they were entitled to their freedom. However, Hawkins admitted that his oldest sons were still slaves because they were owned by a different master, Charles Glanding, of Queen's County, Maryland.

Garrett hurried back to Wilmington and enlisted the legal services of his close personal friend John Wales, a Wilmington attorney and politician. They petitioned the

Wilmington, Delaware, Underground Railroad conductor Thomas Garrett. Chester County Historical Society, West Chester, Pennsylvania.

New Castle Court for the release of the Hawkins family, and presented the faulty commitment papers and the copy of the will to Delaware Chief Justice James Booth, who resided in New Castle. Booth examined the defective commitment papers and will, and decided that because there was no evidence to hold the prisoners, he would release the entire family, including the two older boys. As Garrett later wrote, "The business was conducted by Attorney Wales in such a manner that the judge was induced to discharge the whole family."

Garrett hired a wagon and had the family taken to Wilmington, where they rejoined Burris and the other men. Shortly after, the group was taken to Pennsylvania, where they received help in getting settled from **Robert Purvis**.

When the constables returned to the jail in New Castle, they were shocked to find that the Hawkinses had been released. There was nothing they could do but take legal action. Both Garrett and Hunn were charged in a civil suit by Charles Glanding, owner of the

Hawkins's two oldest sons, and Elizabeth N. Turner, the alleged owner of Hawkins's wife and other four children.

Garrett and Hunn received their summons on May 23, 1846, but the trials—of which there were four—did not begin until May 24, 1848. During this time Hunn said that the publicity surrounding the incident led many fugitive slaves to both his and Garrett's residences, though it is not clear why this also did not result in the appearance of more constables.

At the trial the presiding judge was Chief Justice Roger Taney, the same judge who later presided over the infamous Dred Scott Supreme Court Decision, ruling that blacks had no rights that whites should respect. His instructions to the jury stated that all that needed to be proven was that the individuals in question were slaves and that Garrett and Hunn had known this and still transported them. Both were found guilty, with Hunn assessed damages of $2,500 and Garrett $5,400, to be awarded to the plaintiffs. However, a compromise settlement lowered Garrett's obligation to $1,500, something that many historical accounts fail to mention.

After his conviction Garrett made a statement. He said he did not believe he had done anything illegal and that the matter had been cleared at the hearing with Judge Booth. Garrett then said in defiance of the court that he was an abolitionist and had been aiding fugitive slaves for twenty-five years and was not about to stop because of this conviction:

> Had I believed every one of them to be slaves, I should have done the same thing. I should have done violence to my convictions of duty, had I not made use of all the lawful means in my power to liberate those people, and assist them to become men and women, rather than leave them in the condition of chattels personal. . . . I now pledge myself, in the presence of this assembly, to use all lawful and honorable means to lessen the burdens of this oppressed people, and endeavor, according to ability furnished, to burst their chains asunder, and set them free; not relaxing my efforts on their behalf while blessed with health and a slave remains to tread the soil of the state of my adoption.

Garrett closed by saying that the publicity created by the decision would raise the spirit of inquiry about the evils of slavery and hasten the day when it would be abolished.

While the decision was costly to both men, Hunn was able to absorb the losses better because he came from a wealthy family. Some business losses also at that time put Garrett in a more precarious position, but friends loaned him money, and he was able to continue his livelihood. Rather than being discouraged from his Underground Railroad work, Garrett resumed it with an even stronger resolve, just as he boldly declared that day in the courtroom, and added a second story to his house to shelter more fugitive slaves. Records of some of his activities during this period were documented in letters preserved by **William Still**, with whom Garrett became closely associated after the passage of the second Fugitive Slave Law.

It is unclear why law enforcement officials did not continue to prosecute Garrett despite the resumption of his lawbreaking activities. This likely was related to the personal relationships he had developed in his community. As noted in relating the story of the Hawkins family, Garrett was a friend of Sheriff Caulk at New Castle, who was an abolitionist. And John Wales, Garrett's lawyer and an abolitionist, shortly after became a U.S. Senator. Garrett had friends in high places, and this apparently gave him a measure of protection. Furthermore, the election of an abolitionist to the U.S. Senate indicated how strong the support was for abolitionism in the state.

Although Garrett was operating in a slave state, where a significant number of citizens considered his activities undesirable, he was probably supported by just as many.

In Hunn's accounts of the incident, he claimed that it was the first time he had been involved in the Underground Railroad. However, there is evidence to suggest that he may have been involved earlier, and that Burris may have previously used his house as a stop along his escape route. Hunn claimed that Burris brought hundreds of fugitive slaves through his Middletown residence.

Garrett developed a large network of agents to assist him in his Underground Railroad labors. A large cadre of black men from Delaware conducted fugitive slaves to Garrett's home. This group of conductors included Severn Johnson, Joseph G. Walker, Evan Lewis, George Wilmer, Joseph Hamilton, Abraham Shadd, Harry Craige, William Brinkley, Jackson, Davey Moore, Comegys Munson, and Burris. Among Garrett's white associates were Isaac S. Flint, Benjamin Webb, Thomas Webb, William Webb, Daniel Gibbons, John Alston, Daniel Corbit, and Hunn.

Most of the fugitive slaves were sent to Garrett's Quaker associates and relatives in nearby Chester and Delaware County, Pennsylvania. Among the most active were Allen and Maria Agnew, the former sometimes conducting the fugitive slaves himself; **John and Hannah Cox**; Isaac and Dinah Mendenhall; **Bartholomew Fussell**; **Graceanna Lewis**; and Elijah Pennypacker. Garrett also could call on his family: his cousins Benjamin Price and Samuel Rhoads; his brother Isaac and half brother Samuel; and his in-laws, the Mendinhalls.

A number of ship captains also brought fugitive slaves to Garrett through the port of Wilmington. Fugitive slaves smuggled on boats to Wilmington were often put ashore at the Old Swedes Church, where Garrett would send one of his agents to meet them. The most prominent captain was **Alfred Fountain**. In the four-year period from 1855 to 1859, Garrett mentions six trips Captain Fountain made to Wilmington, bringing at least fifty passengers. This letter from 1857 describes three men brought to him by Fountain. The swamp Garrett refers to is the Great Dismal Swamp, located partly in both Virginia and North Carolina, where small fugitive slave communities had formed.

WILMIGTON, 11th Mo. 25th, 1857.

RESPECTED FRIEND, WILLIAM STILL:- I write to inform thee, that Captain Fountain has arrived this evening from the South with three men, one of which is nearly naked, and very lousy. He has been in the swamps of Carolina for eighteen months past. One of the others has been some time out. I would send them on tonight, but will have to provide two of them with some clothes before they can be sent by railroad. . . . As most likely all are more or less lousy [that is, were infected with lice], having been compelled to sleep together, I thought best to write thee so that thee may get a suitable place to take them to, and meet them at Broad and Prime streets on the arrival of the cars, about 11 o'clock tomorrow evening. I have engaged one of our men to take them to his house, and go to Philadelphia with them tomorrow evening. Johnson who will accompany them is a man in whom we can confide. . . .

THOMAS GARRETT

Garrett also received the twenty-one fugitive slaves conveyed by Fountain in a famous incident described by William Still when the mayor of Norfolk boarded Fountain's ship. Garrett divided the large group into two groups and sent them to Still.

But Garrett's most celebrated conductor was **Harriet Tubman**, who sought Garrett's assistance on at least eight occasions. The first mention Garrett makes of Tubman is in the following letter from 1854:

> WILMINGTON, 12 mo, 29th, 1854.
>
> ESTEEMED FRIEND, J. MILLER MCKIM:- We made arrangements last night, and sent away Harriet Tubman, with six men and one woman to Allen Agnews, to be forwarded across the country to the city. Harriet, and one of the men had worn their shoes off their feet, and I gave them two dollars to help fit them out, and directed a carriage to be hired at my expense. . . .
>
> THOMAS GARRETT

A second episode involving Tubman demonstrated Garrett's ingenuity. Tubman was trying to reach Garrett's home in Wilmington with a group of fugitive slaves from Maryland. They were stalled because the Market Street bridge was being watched by police. Garrett sent two wagons filled with black men acting the part of bricklayers on their way to work. The men sang and shouted as they crossed the bridge, acting as if it was a typical day on their way to work. At the end of the day, the group returned, singing and shouting as they had been in the morning. The police paid no attention to the so-called bricklayers; little did the police know that Tubman and her fugitive slaves were hidden in the bottom of the wagon.

Garret coordinated the passage of as many as twenty-eight fugitive slaves at a time. But conducting fugitive slaves required not only management skills but cleverness and guile. On one occasion when a large group arrived in Wilmington with a couple of two-horse carriages, Garrett had the horses put in a stable, and passed the word around that they were stolen. Meanwhile, he forwarded the fugitive slaves in wagons with fresh horses. When the slavehunters came, they were directed to the stable, where they found their horses. As a result, they spent several days in Wilmington searching for the fugitive slaves while the latter were moving farther into the labyrinth of the Underground Railroad.

Samuel Burris: Freed on the Auction Block

Samuel Burris, a free black man from Delaware, piloted hundreds of fugitive slaves out of slavery. He was the conductor in the successful escape of eleven fugitive slaves in 1845 that led to the prosecution of Thomas Garrett. Burris continued his activities, but his luck ran out in 1847. A slave Burris had assisted was captured, and this led to Burris's arrest. He was put in jail in Kent, Delaware, where he spent ten months awaiting his trial. He was finally found guilty for aiding fugitive slaves, fined $500, and sentenced to be sold into slavery for a term of seven years.

However, Burris had many friends in the antislavery movement. Some friends sent Isaac Flint, a Quaker abolitionist from Wilmington, to the auction where Burris was to be sold. Flint, unknown in Kent and to Burris, posed as a slaveholder looking to buy slaves. Prior to the sale, it was common practice for prospective buyers to examine the merchandise from head to toe. Flint watched the technique of his adversaries and followed their example.

The auctioneer began, and a Baltimore trader bid $500 for Burris. Flint took the buyer aside and paid him to withdraw. When the gavel hit the desk and the auctioneer cried, "Sold," it was Flint who had the winning bid. Burris was prepared to spend the next seven years of his life in slavery when Flint whispered in Burris's ear that he had been bought with abolition gold and was now free. The experience ended Burris's days as an Underground Railroad conductor, and a few years later he moved to San Francisco.

Another time, a fugitive slave was caught. At the runaway's insistence, Garrett had sent him along a route that Garrett knew was being watched, and as Garrett had warned him, the man was caught. Garrett went to the jail as soon as he received word of the capture. Addressing the fugitive slave by name, he acted as if he knew him well and that he was actually a free man. The act fooled everyone, and Garrett took the man away. The second time, Garrett sent the fugitive on the route Garrett had originally intended.

The renown of Harriet Tubman was largely the result of her contacts with Garrett, who was a great admirer of hers and who wrote to many others—including Tubman's first biographer, Sarah Bradford—about her remarkable abilities. "I have never met with any person, of any color, who had more confidence in the voice of God," he wrote Bradford.

Garrett explained that Tubman said she had no fear of being arrested because she trusted that God would always direct her to safety. On one occasion, according to Garrett, Tubman was with a group of fugitive slaves and suddenly said she had been told by God to leave the road. They proceeded through the woods and across several streams. Their way led them to the cabin of a free black family, who sheltered them. Later, it was discovered that the masters of the fugitive slaves had been waiting for them at a train station, and likely would have captured them if they hadn't suddenly taken that detour.

The fastest way from Wilmington to Philadelphia and William Still's Vigilance Committee office was the train, or "cars" as they were called. However, the trains were closely watched for fugitive slaves in Delaware, and railroad employees who knowingly permitted fugitive slaves aboard were subject to harsh penalties. So, if no slavecatchers were in close pursuit, Garrett sent fugitive slaves on foot with one of his agents to the train stations in Chester or Marcus Hook.

If an agent was not readily available, Garrett sometimes sent a single fugitive slave alone, posing as a worker, carrying a hoe or rake. When the fugitive slave had crossed the state border, he would leave the farm implement under a specified bridge and proceed along the road that led directly to Kennett Square, where he could call on a number of conductors.

Although a member of the Wilmington Meeting at Fourth and West Streets, Garrett joined with other abolitionists, many of whom were his associates in the Underground Railroad, to form the Longwood Meeting at Kennett Square, Pennsylvania, in 1853. This group of political radicals was known to be in the forefront of many of the progressive crusades of the day, including temperance, abolition, and women's rights, not to mention other more esoteric movements such as phrenology and spiritualism.

In June 1862 Garrett joined the Longwood Meeting group in a personal visit in Washington, D.C., with President Lincoln. The group said that they saw the evils of the war as "vials of Divine retribution which are now poured out upon the whole land, for its grievous and unrelenting oppression of a guiltless and inoffensive race," and urged Lincoln to abolish slavery without delay.

The president's response was not encouraging. "It's a relief that the deputation are not applicants for office, for my chief trouble comes from that class of persons," he said. "And the next most troublesome subject is slavery."

However, Lincoln added that, "I've sometimes thought that perhaps I might be an instrument in God's hands of accomplishing a great work, and I'm certainly not unwilling to be. . . . It is my earnest endeavor, seeking light from above, to do my duty in the place to which I have been called."

A month later Lincoln apparently saw the light and presented a draft of the Emancipation Proclamation to the full cabinet. On September 22, 1862, Lincoln signed it, and it became effective on January 1, 1863.

After the Fifteenth Amendment, granting universal suffrage to black men, was passed in 1870, Garrett was carried through the streets by black men in an open barouche, as part of a parade celebrating that momentous occasion, surrounded by other black men carrying banners with the inscription, "Our Moses."

Garrett's last appearance in any public capacity was as president of a women's suffrage meeting in the Wilmington City Hall a few months before his death on January 25. Garrett kept careful track of how many slaves he helped to freedom, yet numbers still vary. Most accounts claim about 2,700.

SUGGESTED READING: "Flight to Freedom: Emeline's Story," Division of Historical and Cultural Affairs, Delaware, http://history.delaware.gov/freedom/default.shtml; Kate Clifford Larson, *Bound for the Promised Land: Portrait of an American Hero*, New York: Ballantine Books, 2004; James A. McGowan, *Station Master on the Underground Railroad: The Life and Letter of Thomas Garrett*, Jefferson, NC: McFarland, revised edition, 2004; R. C. Smedley, *History of the Underground Railroad in Chester and Neighboring Counties of Pennsylvania*, Lancaster, PA, 1883; William Still, *The Underground Railroad*, Philadelphia: Porter and Coates, 1872.

Gay, Sydney Howard (1814–1888). Massachusetts native Sydney Howard Gay was an important abolitionist editor who coordinated the movement of hundreds of fugitive slaves through New York City during the 1850s.

Gay became a journalist after abandoning the idea of becoming a lawyer like his father. Legend has it that he refused to take the Lawyers Oath to support the U.S. constitution because it upheld slavery. There is more to the story. Gay was from a privileged and principled but psychologically troubled Puritan New England family. In his youth, to his parents' dismay, he was an apologist for slaveholders. After he borrowed money from his father and lost it in a failed business venture, Gay sank into a deep depression. The experience transformed him. He soon found his calling with William Lloyd Garrison's American Anti-Slavery Society (AAS). A firm believer in Garrison's motto, "No union with slaveholders," Gay served the AAS in many capacities. He was one of its 100 Convention lecturers in 1843, and later contributed to the work of the executive committee, first as its corresponding secretary and later as president. Appointed resident New York City editor of the society's newspaper, the *National Anti-Slavery Standard* in 1844, Gay held that position until 1857. During those thirteen years, he became a key figure in a network of black and white Underground agents.

Gay received fugitive slaves from the Philadelphia Vigilance Committee and forwarded them to Massachusetts or through New York to Canada via **Stephen Myers** in Albany and **Jermaine Loguen** in Syracuse. Freeborn porter Louis Napoleon conducted the fugitives out of New York City for Gay, who kept a record of donations received and transportation and food costs for Napoleon and the fugitives he escorted. Gay also recorded the stories of fugitive slaves who had fled North from Washington, D.C., Virginia, and Maryland. Many had been assisted by **Thomas Garrett** in Wilmington, Delaware. After **Henry "Box" Brown** was sent to New York City from Philadelphia, Gay forwarded him to New Bedford, Massachusetts. On one occasion Gay welcomed General **Harriet Tubman** and four fugitives from Maryland.

Sydney Howard Gay left the *Standard* to join the *New York Tribune*, and Horace Greeley appointed him managing editor. During the Civil War, Gay kept the *Tribune* a war paper. He was a member of "the Bohemian Brigade," a band of reporters who trusted in lead pencils and kept "their paper dry." After the war he became managing editor of the *Chicago Tribune*, and then joined the editorial staff of the *New York Evening Post*. In his later years, Gay wrote a four-volume history of the United States for William Cullen Bryant. He also wrote a biography of James Madison.

In 1845 Gay married Quaker and Philadelphia native Elizabeth Neall, who had an abolitionist pedigree. She was a descendant of one of America's earliest abolitionists, Warner Mifflin, and she had been a delegate for the Philadelphia Female Anti-Slavery Society at the 1840 World Anti-Slavery Society Convention in London, where **Lucretia Mott** was refused a seat because of her sex. The incident inspired Mott and Elizabeth Cady Stanton to join forces and organize a separate women's rights movement. Although Elizabeth Neall Gay devoted herself to child rearing, her suffragist friends kept her informed of their progress.

When Sydney Howard Gay died at his Staten Island home at the age of seventy-four, the *New York Times* recalled the many years he devoted to abolitionist journalism and hailed him as "A MAN WHO ONCE REFUSED TO SUPPORT THE CONSTITUTION."

SUGGESTED READING: "Anniversary of the New York Anti Slavery Society," *New York Times*, May 9, 1856; Raimund Erhard Goerler, "Family, Self, and Anti-Slavery: Sydney Howard Gay and the Abolitionist Commitment," unpublished dissertation, Case Western Reserve University, Cleveland, OH, 1875; Kathryn Grover, *The Fugitive's Gibraltar*, Amherst: University of Massachusetts Press, 2001; Elizabeth M'Clintock to Elizabeth Neall Gay, August 23, 1848; Lucretia Mott to Elizabeth Neall Gay, May 7, 1858; "Record of Fugitives 1855," unpublished journal, Sydney Howard Gay Collection, Special Collections, Columbia University Libraries, New York; "The Bohemian Brigade," http://www.bohemianbrigade.com/alfred4.html; "Veteran Journalist Dead," *New York Times*, June 27, 1888.

Don Papson

Gibbs, Leonard (1800–1863). An attorney from Washington County, New York, Gibbs became a devout abolitionist during the mid-1830s, and from the start took a leadership role in a county that was afire with the cause of abolition.

After serving a term in the state assembly, Gibbs moved to New York City to practice law sometime around 1840. Though we have little information about his activities there, we know that he was a member of the executive committee of the American and Foreign Anti-Slavery Society from 1841 to 1846. Given his devotion to antislavery and the history that is known about his Underground Railroad activities in Washington County, it would not be surprising if he continued this in New York City. His home during that time was not far from the meeting places of the New York Committee of Vigilance.

From 1844 to 1846, Gibbs traveled out of New York, according to one of his letters published in the *Albany Patriot*, but he does not say specifically where his travels took him. The main thrust of the letter was his advocacy for unlimited "Negro" suffrage, which was a topic of great concern among the state's abolitionists at that time.

In 1846 Gibbs moved back to Washington County, settling in Union Village. There he joined the radical abolitionist Free Church and became a popular figure, being elected the village president (equivalent to mayor). He was involved in every antislavery event or convention in the county from 1846 until the Civil War, and was among the leaders in the massive county protest of the Kansas-Nebraska Act. His home also became one of the village's stops on the Underground Railroad.

His daughters, Mary and Helen, never married and continued to live in the house until their deaths in 1918. They were members of the local Daughters of the American

Revolution organization, and kept the memory of these Underground Railroad activities alive with tales they told at chapter meetings. "To hear Miss Mary and Miss Helen tell of the escape of slaves, the assistance rendered to them here and by the Quakers of Easton, was to be brought in touch with the past in a way which no printed page can equal," said a Miss McMasters at a meeting of the Willard's Mountain Daughters of the American Revolution in 1922. Few of the specifics regarding these incidents have survived.

In 1851 Gibbs had a role in one of the antebellum period's most memorable incidents. He was attending an antislavery convention in Syracuse when a messenger interrupted the proceedings with news that a fugitive had been taken into custody. **William Henry**, a black carpenter who had been living in Syracuse for a number of years, known to all as "Jerry," had been seized by law enforcement officials and taken to the City Hall, where he was charged with theft under the jurisdiction of the Fugitive Slave Act of 1850. At once, convention officials designated Gibbs and **Gerrit Smith** as Jerry's defense attorneys.

During an adjournment, during which Jerry nearly escaped, Smith put control of the courtroom proceedings in Gibbs's hands, while he met privately with a group who devised a plan for Jerry's rescue.

When the courtroom proceedings resumed, police placed Jerry under guard in a back room, and Gibbs proceeded without Smith. As Gibbs raised the point that the claimant needed proof that Jerry was indeed a slave, the mob outside began to throw stones through the windows. The commissioner quickly adjourned. Moments later, the mob was at the door of Jerry's holding room with a battering ram. The guards fled, and Jerry was carried away by friends who took him into hiding, and eventually to Canada.

Gibbs was active in the organization of the Republican Party and led a local mobilization against slavecatchers who came to Washington County in 1858 to apprehend a fugitive slave named John Salter who was living there. Active in the Personal Liberty Law movement that sought to give legal rights to fugitive slaves who had settled in New York State, Gibbs also advocated that a mission be undertaken to rescue John Brown, following Brown's capture at Harpers Ferry.

Gibbs died on September 12, 1863. William Lloyd Garrison noted his passing in *The Liberator*, referring to a visit he made to Union Village to attend an antislavery convention in 1852:

> Although our personal acquaintance with him was not intimate, we have had the privilege of enjoying his hospitality under his own roof, and have long known him as among the early and most thoroughly conscientious advocates of the Anti-Slavery cause. No man ever impressed us more favorably in regard to all those traits which constitute completeness of character, as a gentleman and a Christian in the finest sense. His intellectual, moral, and affectional development was as symmetrical as it was rare.

SUGGESTED READING: Charles L. Bacon, *The Gibbses of Granville, New York*, Milford, NH: Cabinet Press, 1984; "Obituary," *People's Journal* (Greenwich, N.Y.), October 22, 1863.

Goodridge, William C. (1804–1873). William Goodridge was a prosperous black barber, who became one of most active conductors along the well-traveled Underground Railroad route that connected Maryland to southeastern Pennsylvania.

Goodridge's mother and grandmother were slaves owned by Founding Father Charles Carroll. His mother was sold to a Baltimore physician, who may have been Goodridge's father. Born in Baltimore, Goodridge was apprenticed at the age of six to work in the tannery of Rev. William Dunn, a York, Pennsylvania, minister. The arrangement was a kind of indentured servitude, as Goodridge was obligated to work for Dunn until he was twenty-one. However, Dunn released him from his obligations when he was sixteen.

In 1823 Goodridge returned to York with a Maryland wife and opened a barbershop. He prospered and proved to be an excellent businessman. By the 1840s he owned a confectionery, sold animal hides to tanneries, and started York's first newspaper distribution business. His business interests also included real estate, and he owned a dozen buildings, including a five-story variety store, Centre Hall, the tallest building in the city. In addition, he operated the Goodridge Reliance Line Railroad whose thirteen cars served twenty Pennsylvania communities.

But Goodridge was not only making money. He was deeply involved in the Underground Railroad. York was in a strategic position along a well-established route from Maryland to the terminal of Columbia, Pennsylvania, on the Susquehanna River. Goodridge's home, where he had a secret room in the back of the cellar, was frequently used as a stop for fugitive slaves. Although no links have been documented between Goodridge and **William Whipper**, who lived in nearby Columbia, where most fugitive slaves were routed from York, it stands to reason that they were collaborating, considering their extensive business associations, including a mutual involvement in railroads, both under and above ground.

Among the known operators that Goodridge worked with were Quaker Amos Griest, who met fugitive slaves along the Baltimore-to-York turnpike and shepherded them to York, and Cato Jourdon, who conducted cars over the bridge across the Susquehanna River to Columbia. Other important agents in the York area were Joel Fisher, Samuel Willis, Jonathan and Samuel Mifflin, and **William Wright**. Providing protection to their operations were York Constable William Yokum and a local dispatcher named McCauley, who were sympathetic to their cause.

Goodridge also provided railroad transport to three of the resisters in the Christiana Incident, and to Osborne Perry, one of John Brown's men at Harpers Ferry who managed to escape. Goodridge's abolitionist reputation had grown so much that during the Civil War Confederate soldiers attempted to kidnap him. This forced Goodridge to take his family to Minnesota, where he lived his remaining years.

SUGGESTED READING: <http://muweb.millersville.edu/~ugrr/yorkcountyugrr.htm>; R. C. Smedley, *History of the Underground Railroad in Chester and Neighboring Counties of Pennsylvania,* Lancaster, PA, 1883.

H

Hanby, Ben (1833–1867). Ben Hanby composed two antebellum songs that became nationally known and inspired others to bring an end to slavery. One of the songs originated from a story told by Hanby's father about a fugitive slave who died under his care.

The oldest son of Rev. **William Hanby**, a Bishop of the radical abolitionist United Brethren Church, Ben was born in Rushville, Ohio. Ben Hanby modeled his life after his father, especially in his devotion to serve and help others. But Hanby had a talent that his father never developed: the ability to sing and make music.

Hanby's start as a musician came at the age of fourteen, when he bought himself a flute with money he earned from doing odd jobs. The instrument became his constant companion, and when he entered Otterbein College, of which his father was a founder, in Westerville, Ohio, in 1849, he began learning to play the piano.

Hanby had a great affinity for children, and started his own infant school—for children ages three through twelve. It was an informal arrangement with no specific meeting place. The kids would gather around him, and he would tell stories, read poems, or play music for them. Already, he had begun writing songs, and it was to the children that Hanby introduced them. It was also at this time that he began to compose "Darling Nelly Gray," which told of the loss of a fugitive slave's lover after she was sold into the Deep South.

In 1856 Hanby's family moved to Westerville. During this time the Hanby family participated quite actively in the Underground Railroad. They lived next door to Otterbein College president Lewis Day, an associate of Bishop Hanby in the United Brethren Church, who had been a conductor since the college opened in 1847. A barn behind the Hanbys' house, which served as Bishop Hanby's saddle and harness shop, was where the family hid fugitive slaves. The Hanbys had a special signal to alert their collaborators that fugitive slaves were present. They would put a vase of roses in their front window, with the number of roses indicating the number of slaves. The slaves would have dinner with the Hanby family, and it was Hanby's job to cover the windows to prevent them from being seen. It was also his job to lead the slaves out of the barn during the night to the false-bottom wagon of toolmaker Thomas Alexander, who would usually take them to Mount Vernon, which was about thirty miles north.

In the spring of 1856, Hanby went to Lexington with his father, where he witnessed a slave auction in the city square. His sister Elizabeth wrote of how it affected him:

"When brother Ben left . . . he was a happy singing man. When he came back he was a sober and saddened man. What he had seen broke his heart. He couldn't get it out of his mind." It compelled him to finish "Darling Nelly Gray."

O my poor Nelly Gray, they have taken you away,
And I'll never see my darling any more;
I am sitting by the river and I'm weeping all the day,
For you've gone from the old Kentucky shore.

At a party in honor of his piano teacher, Cornelia Walker, Hanby introduced the completed song, arranged for a quartet that included his friend William Perkins and Lydia and Sarah Winter, the cousins of his future wife, Kate. Ms. Walker urged Hanby to seek publication, so he sent the song to the Oliver Ditsen Company in Boston.

When Hanby didn't receive a response, he assumed that they weren't interested. However, while visiting Columbus, his sister Anna was shocked to hear someone singing the song, and learned that it was on sale at a local music store.

After seeing it in print, Hanby revised it further and sent the revisions to the publisher. Still, months went by without a word from Ditsen. Finally, the publisher responded that they had lost his address. When Hanby wrote back again and asked about royalties, they responded with the following:

Dear Sir: Your favor received. Nelly Gray is sung on both sides of the Atlantic. We have made the money and you the fame—that balances the account.

The song had become an immediate success. It was published in many forms, and an arrangement for band music became popular. The Christy Minstrels used it as their featured song. It became a favorite in England. It even became popular in the Confederacy. General George Pickett loved it and had his band play it in Chambersburg on the way to the Battle of Gettysburg. The publisher of the song must have made a fortune. After several years, Hanby hired a lawyer to sue for his royalties, but all he managed to obtain was $100, with half of it going to the lawyer.

After his graduation from Otterbein in 1858, Hanby married Kate Winter, whom he had been courting for several years, in spite of her mother's objection. He took a job as an endowment agent for Otterbein, and followed that with a position as a principal at Seven Mile Academy in Hamilton, Ohio. The Civil War had begun, and there were reports of slaves fleeing into Union army camps in search of protection. These slaves came to be known as contraband. A report in the newspapers prompted Hanby to write a song about this situation. He called it "Ole Shady."

Oh, Mass' got scared and so did his lady,
Dis chile breaks for Ole Uncle Aby,
"Open de gates, out here's Ole Shady
A coming, coming."
Hail mighty day.

Despite his previous difficulties with Oliver Ditsen, Hanby sent the song to them, and they published it and sent him a check for $300. The song quickly became popular with Negro minstrels. An interesting story that illustrates this came from Union army general William T. Sherman, in an article published in 1888:

A great many negroes, slaves, had escaped within the Union lines. Some were employed as servants by the officers, who paid them regular wages, some were employed by the quartermaster, and the larger number went north, free, in the Government chartered steamboats.

Sherman had a fond memory of one of those slaves, who was known as "Old Shady." After dinner, Old Shady, whose real name was D. Blakely Durant, would assemble other blacks, and they would sing for the soldiers. The slaves' favorite song was called "Ole Shady." Sherman wrote at the time that he thought it was composed by Durant because it seemed to be the pure expression of a man's deliverance from bondage. It was not until Kate Hanby, upon reading his article, wrote Sherman and corrected him on his error that he learned the truth.

After graduation, Hanby was a principal at a school and the pastor of two churches. He continued to compose music, including songs for children. In 1864 he published his best-known song, the holiday classic "Up on the Housetop."

At age thirty-three, while working for a music publisher in Chicago, Hanby died of tuberculosis. His legacy was his music, which helped bring slavery to an end, and which continues to bring joy to children today.

SUGGESTED READING: Dacia Custer Shoemaker, *Choose You This Day: The Legacy of the Handbys,*. Westerville, OH: Westerville Historical Society, 1983; H. A. Thompson, *Our Bishops: A Sketch of the Origins and Growth of the Church of the United Brethren in Christ, as Shown in the Lives of Its Distinguished Leaders,* Chicago: Elder Publishing Co., 1889.

Hanby, William (1808–1880). William Hanby was an important Underground Railroad conductor in Central Ohio, whose son wrote one of the most poignant songs of the antebellum period based on the life of a fugitive slave that William aided.

William Hanby grew up poor in western Pennsylvania, with his father dying when he was very young. As a result, Hanby's mother was forced to contract him out as an indentured servant. He served two masters, one beginning when Hanby was nine, the second, when he was fifteen. The latter arrangement proved disastrous, as the man for whom Hanby worked was dishonest and cruel, forcing him to work sixteen-hour days, seven days a week. Hanby eventually felt compelled to escape his harsh conditions, and at midnight on March 24, 1828, he fled to nearby Ohio, where indentured service was illegal. He had just turned twenty.

From that day forward, Hanby vowed that if he ever encountered anyone in a similar situation, he would never hesitate to help.

Hanby's fate landed him in Rushville, Ohio. He had been fortunate to have been helped along his journey by those sympathetic to his plight, including the wife of a U.S. congressman. This is not surprising, considering that the Underground Railroad had already been in place in this region for about fifteen years. After a few weeks, he got a job in Rushville with a saddler, Samuel Miller, and they arranged an apprenticeship. This led Hanby to another life-altering relationship: he and Miller's daughter fell in love.

In October 1830, after joining the ministry of the United Brethren in Christ, Hanby married Ann Miller. They settled in Rushville, and Hanby accepted an appointment as a circuit rider for the Scioto Conference. In 1834, at the age of twenty-six, he was named presiding elder of his conference, which consisted of forty-three preachers. That year he traveled 4,000 miles meeting his obligations, while also attending to the saddle and harness business that would remain his main source of income throughout his life. By this time his home had become a regular stop on the Underground Railroad.

Bishop William Hanby. Courtesy of the Hanby House Museum, Westerville, Ohio.

In 1839 Hanby took over as the editor of The *Religious Telescope,* his denomination's newspaper, whose office was in Circleville, Ohio, thirty miles away. He decided to move his wife and children with him to Circleville, and left his mother, sister, and brother-in-law, who also were living with him, to oversee his saddle and harness business and take care of his house.

It was during this period, in 1842, that an incident occurred that would later be recorded for posterity.

A fugitive slave, Joseph Selby, came to Rushville and found his way to the Hanbys' house. Selby was deathly ill, and Hanby's family summoned both Hanby and Simon Hyde, a physician who regularly collaborated with Hanby. But there was little they could do for the man but make him comfortable. During his last hours, Selby revealed the story of his beloved Nelly Gray, who had been sold south the day before they were to be married. Selby had escaped in hopes of earning enough money to purchase her freedom.

It was this story that Hanby would later tell his children. His oldest son, Ben, would go on to immortalize Selby's story in song, one of several he wrote that became popular and helped put an end to slavery.

Hanby continued to do the work of the Underground Railroad up through the Civil War. But in 1870, three years after losing his son Ben to tuberculosis, Hanby lost his house because of debts incurred as a result of loans he had cosigned for others in need. He also would face persecution because of his outspoken views on temperance in the 1870s. He died penniless and crippled in 1880.

SUGGESTED READING: Dacia Custer Shoemaker, *Choose You This Day: The Legacy of the Handbys,* Westerville, OH: Westerville Historical Society, 1983; H. A. Thompson, *Our Bishops: A Sketch of the Origins and Growth of the Church of the United Brethren in Christ, as Shown in the Lives of Its Distinguished Leaders,* Chicago: Elder Publishing Co., 1889.

Hansen, John, a.k.a. John T. Hanover (dates unknown). A man of mystery identified in **William Cockrum's** narrative, *History of the Underground Railroad as it was Conducted by the Anti-Slavery League,* Hansen was the league's Indiana superintendent. The Anti-Slavery League (ASL) was a complex organization of agents and spies who reportedly worked along the length of the Ohio Valley. The group used role-playing agents in slave states to get in touch with slaves seeking their freedom and assisted them in their escapes. Undercover spies often assumed the character of pro-slavery sympathizers or slavecatchers. This allowed them to provide surveillance of the real slavecatchers and misdirect their attempts to capture fugitive slaves. Cockrum said the group was similar to the Secret Service used by the Union forces during the Civil War.

John Hansen, superintendent of the Anti-Slavery League. From Cockrum's *History of the Underground Railroad* (1915).

Hansen's true name remains a mystery. He was known as John

The Anti-Slavery League

The Anti-Slavery League was organized to bring slaves to freedom after the passing of the 1850 Fugitive Slave Law. William M. Cockrum, a witness and member of the group, described the league's activities in Indiana. Approximately 100 agents worked along the length of the Ohio River, according to Cockrum, and their activities are illustrated by him in southwest Indiana and the Green River valley of Kentucky.

State superintendents reportedly coordinated operations in Illinois, Indiana, Ohio, and Pennsylvania. In addition, ten spies worked in the Ohio Valley and became acquainted with slavecatchers. These agents were often vocally proslavery in their public interactions. Other agents working in the South used cover identities, such as a peddler, to connect with slaveowners and slaves. Several enslaved men also aided the group.

The undercover agents developed relationships with slaves. A trustworthy, intelligent slave was asked to identify other reliable slaves who wished to escape. This process took several weeks. Next a detailed plan was arranged that included a rendezvous spot and at least one pilot. An armed guard often accompanied the slaves to the Ohio River. On the north side, they were met by other pilots and guards. Some enslaved abettors, who took great risks to aid slave escapes, were sent to Canada when it was believed their activities were suspected.

Hansen (or Hanson) when he worked in Indiana. But in a letter he wrote to Cockrum in 1865, Hansen identified himself as John T. Hanover, an employee of the Freedmen's Bureau in Washington DC. However, it is possible this change of identity was a ruse to confuse persons who might have wanted to injure him.

John Hansen came to Indiana in 1852, and obtained the legal services of attorney Andrew L. Robinson of Evansville for the ASL. Hansen posed as an eastern real estate agent. Yet Hansen was actually a naturalist like Alexander Milton Ross. William Cockrum, who was fourteen in 1852, wrote that Hansen boarded at his father's home in Oakland City for two or three days every two weeks. Hansen took his mail in Princeton, Indiana, which was eleven miles from the Cockrum farm. In Princeton lived David Stormont, an active underground conductor who assisted **Seth Concklin** during his failed attempt to rescue members of the **Peter Still** family. Stormont, however, is not mentioned in Cockrum's book. This may be because the Stormonts are not thought to have been a part of the ASL.

Members of the ASL often visited Hansen at the Cockrum farm. Hansen also kept a diary written in code, which members knew.

> [The code, Cockrum wrote,] had [the ASL members'] numbers and all that was said or done about him was by number, which numbers were referred to as numbers of land, towns, ranges and sections and by acres when the numbers were above thirty-six. The routes these men were on were called by the names of timber, such as linden, oak, maple, hickory, walnut, dogwood, sassafras, beech and all the sorts of timber that were native of the country in which they worked.

Unfortunately, Hansen's diary, in Cockrum's custody in 1907 when Cockrum wrote his account, has been lost.

In the 1865 letter, signed as J. T. Hanover, to Cockrum, Hansen estimated that the ASL aided as many as 4,000 freedom seekers annually during the mid-1850s along the Ohio River border. While this number seems high, the Underground Railroad did become more militant and active in the 1850s. Other than Cockrum's narrative, Hansen's letter, letters from other well-respected men (including Judge A. L. Robinson) acknowledging his work in Indiana, and the fact that he worked for the Freedmen's Bureau, little else is known about Hansen.

SUGGESTED READING: William M. Cockrum, *History of Indiana, Including Stories, Incidents and Customs of the Early Settlers,* Oakland City, IN: Press of Oakland City Journal, 1907; William M. Cockrum, *History of the Underground Railroad, as It was Conducted by the Anti-Slavery League,* Oakland City, IN: J. M. Cockrum Press, 1915; Gil R. Stormont, *History of Gibson County,* Indianapolis: B. F. Bowen, 1914.

Harris, Chapman (1803–1890). Chapman Harris, one of the leaders of the Underground Railroad in Madison, Indiana, was a black man who was born free in Nelson County, Virginia.

A blacksmith by trade, Harris was of a very dark complexion, tall and powerfully built. He came to Madison in 1837 and married Patsy Ann, a former slave from Kentucky, in 1841. He organized the Second Baptist Church in Madison in 1849 and served as its minister, continuing as a preacher throughout the remainder of his life.

But the work for which Harris is best remembered is as a conductor on the Underground Railroad. It was a close friendship with one of Madison's earliest conductors, John Carr, who owned a grocery in Madison, that drew Harris into the service of the Underground Railroad in 1846. A proslavery mob had attacked and nearly killed several blacks who were involved in the Underground Railroad in Madison sometime around 1846, and it is likely that because some of these agents had left town, Harris was enlisted to do the work. His first mission took him to Lancaster, Indiana, home to the leaders of the Neil's Creek Anti-Slavery Society, with whom he established a regular association, according to Lancaster conductor **John Tibbetts**.

With Madison being watched by slavecatchers, Harris's cabin along the ravine known as Eagle Hollow, three miles east of the city where he had moved in 1846, was a better location to begin the journey to freedom. At the top of the ravine, at Rykers Ridge, a number of conductors were available to assist Harris in forwarding fugitive slaves.

Of one typical occasion, Tibbetts wrote,

> While I had my harness shop near Madison a man called and left a note. [It] stated that Chapman Harris wanted five mule halters (a part of the harness) by a certain time. I understood at once and made my arrangements to help five fugitives on their way to Canada.

Tibbetts said Harris was often assisted by a slave in Kentucky who came to Madison on business for his owner and would notify Harris ahead of time when slaves were going to make an escape attempt. Harris or his older sons, George and Charles, who didn't reach their teens until the mid-1850s, often brought the escapees across the river by ferry. Harris had a unique system of communicating to his co-workers that fugitive slaves had crossed. With a spiked hickory cane he hammered on an iron plate embedded in a gigantic, hollowed-out sycamore tree.

In 1847 Harris was involved in the beating of John Simmons, a black citizen of Madison who was informing slavecatchers about Underground Railroad operations there. During the confrontation, Simmons bit off a piece of Harris's ear, and this served as evidence to convict Harris in the trial, which resulted in a steep fine. In November, 1856 Harris was arrested by Madison slavecatcher Wright Ray on suspicion of aiding fugitive slaves while Harris was on a steamboat en route to Charleston, Indiana. The boat was forced to anchor at Louisville, Kentucky, and Harris was ordered to leave the state at once.

Harris was armed when arrested, and his custom of carrying weapons suggests that he later may have been involved in organizing a slave revolt in Kentucky in 1859. According to an 1891 account of a former slave named Freman Anderson, Harris and other Madison-area and Kentucky Underground Railroad operatives met **John Brown** at Harris's cabin that year. They told Brown of their plans to incite a slave insurrection in Trimble County, Kentucky, but Brown urged them to wait until the larger revolt that he planned was in motion.

Harris, who late in his life moved upriver to Rising Sun, Indiana, was buried in Madison's Springdale Cemetery.

SUGGESTED READING: Diane Perrine Coon, *Southeastern Indiana's Underground Railroad Routes and Operations,* A Project of the State of Indiana, Dept. of Natural Resources, Division of Historic Preservation and Archaeology and the U.S. Dept. of the Interior, NPS, April 2001; Gwendolyn Crenshaw, *Bury Me in a Free Land: The Abolitionist Movement in Indiana,* Indianapolis: Indiana Historical Bureau, 1993; Blaine K. Hudson, *Fugitive Slaves and the Underground Railroad in the Kentucky Borderlands,* Jefferson, NC: McFarland, 2001.

Haviland, Laura Smith (1808–1898). If anyone involved in the Underground Railroad could be a candidate for sainthood, it probably would be Laura Haviland, or "Aunt Laura," as she was known during her later years. This tiny woman gave her whole heart and soul not only to the fugitive slaves she encountered, but to every sick, needy, poor, and uneducated person she could help.

Born in the township of Kitley, Ontario, a rural area north of the St. Lawrence River, Haviland was seven when her family moved near Lockport, New York, just north of Niagara Falls. A Quaker by birth, she was brought up with a hatred of slavery and exposed at an early age to the horrors of the slave trade by the writings of Quaker abolitionist John Woolman. As a child, Haviland was a voracious reader who was extremely inquisitive. Her sympathies for people of color developed through her first observations of their lowly position in society. Her compassion was especially aroused when a black man who worked as a kitchen helper at a local inn was severely burned as a result of a prank by schoolboys. In her early teens, she attended an evangelical Methodist meeting that made a strong impression and fulfilled a spiritual need in her that she found lacking in the Quaker faith.

At the age of seventeen, Laura married Charles Haviland, also a Quaker. After the birth of their first two children, Haviland and her husband followed her parents to Lewanee County, Michigan, then a wilderness being settled by Quakers that developed into the village of Adrian. She was twenty-one and would have six more children. The role of mother and caretaker was one that suited her naturally compassionate nature, and she often nursed others outside her family when the need arose.

In the 1830s, Haviland came under the influence of Elizabeth Chandler, a young Quaker whose family had moved to Lewanee County. Chandler's antislavery poetry had appeared in Benjamin Lundy's *Genius of Universal Emancipation* and Garrison's *The Liberator.* She influenced the Havilands to help organize Michigan's first antislavery society. Though Chandler died in 1834 at the age of 27, her spirit was carried on by the Havilands, who were among the first pioneers in Michigan to open their house to fugitive slaves.

Haviland's desire to help her fellow man, especially her affinity for orphan children, led to the opening in 1836 of a manual labor school, which she called the Raisin Institute, her home being situated near the Raisin River. She described it in her autobiography, *A Woman's Life Work,* as a manual labor school for indigent children:

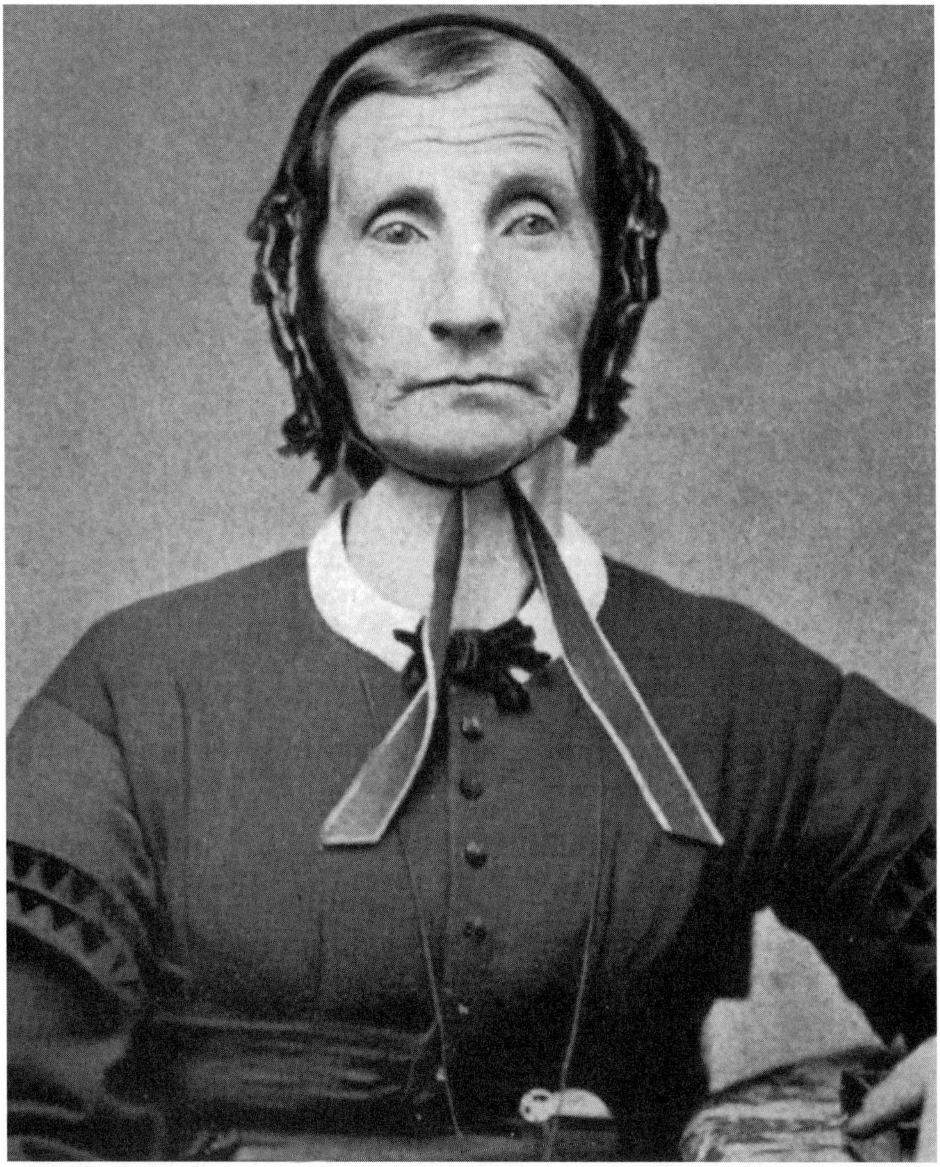

Adrian, Michigan, abolitionist Laura Haviland. Courtesy of the Massachusetts Historical Society.

With that object in view, we took nine children from our county house (Lenawee), and I taught them, with our four children of school age, four hours each day. The balance of the day was divided for work and play. The girls I taught house-work, sewing, and knitting. The boys were taken into the farm work by my husband and brother Harvey Smith. As our county superintendents of the poor gave us no aid, we found our means insufficient to continue our work on this plane. After one year of this work we secured homes for the nine children, except two invalids, who were returned to the county house. We then placed our school on a higher plane, on the Oberlin plan of opening the school for all of good moral character, regardless of sex or color.

Haviland's brother Harvey had attended Oberlin, and his experience helped in the design of the enterprise. The focus was shifted from indigent children to students with avocations to be teachers, and small cottages were built for students close to the school. The Havilands also hired principals with Oberlin roots, which led to making the Raisin Institute one of the best institutions of learning in Michigan, drawing students from as far as 100 miles away. Many of the students who came to the school with racial prejudice quickly learned to abandon it. Haviland's experiment to admit students regardless of race, sex, or creed was not only rewarding but successful, and the school also became known as a refuge for fugitive slaves around 1838, according to a letter she wrote to Underground Railroad historian Wilbur Siebert.

Looking back, Haviland wrote, "As the fleeing fugitive ever found a resting-place and cheer in our home, we richly earned the cognomen of 'nigger den,' yet Heaven smiled and blessed our work."

During this period, the Havilands were disowned by members of their Quaker meeting because of their proactive involvement in abolition work and the Underground Railroad. As a result, Haviland and her husband joined in the organization of Wolf Creek, the first Wesleyan Methodist church in Lenawee County. Then in 1845 tragedy struck: an epidemic of erysipelas, an infection that begins in the skin and enters into the blood. Within six weeks, it took the lives of Haviland's husband, her father, her mother, her sister, and her twenty-two-month-old baby.

Laura also contracted the disease but managed to recover, and in an age when women were not apt to shoulder such responsibilities, she nevertheless carried on, managing the business of both the farm and the school. The following year was happier, as the Haviland family celebrated the double wedding of Laura's oldest son, Harvey, and oldest daughter, Esther.

Haviland's greatest battles against slavery began at this time. The first involved the emancipated slave Willis Hamilton and his fugitive slave wife, Elsie, who had moved to the Haviland farm and worked as sharecroppers. They had formerly escaped to Canada when Elsie's owner, John Chester, threatened to sell her, but came to Adrian when there was a slowdown in the economy there. The Hamiltons had six children; however, they had left the oldest two behind in Tennessee and no longer knew their whereabouts. Willis sent a letter of inquiry to one of his former owners, Deacon Bayliss, who had helped the Hamiltons to escape, being careful to send a different return address, from which Bayliss's response would be forwarded. A suspicious letter came back, asking Willis for his exact address. The Hamiltons were eager to learn about their other children, so despite Haviland's advice not to reveal their true address, they went to one of the Raisin Institute's trustees, J. P. Dolbeare, who wrote back for them and gave detailed information about the Hamiltons. This turned out to be a serious error in judgment because, as Haviland and others had suspected, it was a ruse being played by Elsie's owner, Chester. Not long after, a letter came, saying that Bayliss was in a hotel in Toledo and seriously ill, and was requesting that the entire Hamilton family come to see him. This made everyone more suspicious, so Haviland, one of her sons, and James Martin, a black adult student at her school who posed as Willis, went to Toledo.

They met at a hotel where Chester, pretending to be a sick Bayliss on his deathbed, and his son Thomas tried to convince Haviland of his genuineness, but the ruse was obvious. A confrontation took place on the train back to Adrian, with the Chesters pulling out their guns and attempting to kidnap James Martin.

The Chesters posted a reward of $3,000 for the capture of Haviland dead or alive. Four years later, when the Fugitive Slave Law was passed, they hired a lawyer to have the Hamiltons arrested under the jurisdiction of the new law. But by then, the Hamiltons had left for Canada. The Chesters continued in their efforts to seek retribution against Haviland but were unsuccessful, and both met with untimely deaths some time before the Civil War.

Some months after that incident, a stranger visited the Haviland farm. He said he was an agent for the *National Era*, an abolitionist newspaper, and was soliciting subscriptions. He also was interested in the Underground Railroad and wanted to know how it worked in her area. Haviland was immediately suspicious and didn't reveal any details, but did offer the following description: "Let any slaveholder disturb an escaped slave, at any time of night or day," she said, "and the sound of a tin horn will be heard, with a dozen more answers in different locations, and men enough will gather around the fugitive for his rescue."

Haviland correctly suspected that the visitor was sent by slaveholders to obtain information about a Kentucky fugitive slave, John White, who had attended the Raisin Institute and was now working on a neighboring farm. While the visitor was touring the school, Haviland sent word ahead to White, who left for Canada the next day, foiling the attempts of the slavecatchers who, after learning the whereabouts of White, paid a visit to the farm where White had been living.

The slavecatchers, who included White's master, George Brazier, and the noted Madison, Indiana slavecatcher Wright Ray, caught up with Haviland in Toledo while she was on a mission of mercy to a sick neighbor. The slavecatchers were following Haviland because they suspected her involvement in the escape of other fugitive slaves, whose master was with Brazier and Ray. However, they were mistaken, and their surveillance of Haviland had allowed those fugitive slaves to make their escape through Cleveland. The slavecatchers swore they would eventually avenge their losses, and before returning to Kentucky, they submitted a warrant for the arrest of Haviland if White was not recovered within the year.

Haviland, however, was unfazed, and agreed to help White reunite with his wife, Jane, and their five children, who were enslaved by Jane's father, Benjamin Stevens, in Kentucky. Haviland traveled to Cincinnati to meet with **Levi Coffin**, and see if there was some way she could assist White's family.

Coffin called a meeting of his vigilance committee, and they proposed that Haviland go to Rising Sun, an Indiana town along the Ohio River, where she could arrange a meeting with Jane in Kentucky through the Edgerton and Barkshire families, prosperous black families in Rising Sun.

Haviland went with Joseph Edgerton's wife to the Stevens plantation in Boone County, not far from the river, posing as Jane's aunt. She was able to do this because Jane had no trace of color in her complexion, as had also been the case with her mother. Haviland informed Jane that her husband wished her to join him and that efforts would be made to assist her. However, two of Jane's children were away and would not be returning for two months. Haviland then returned to Michigan, where White informed her that a close friend of his, William Allen, would help rescue his wife and children.

Three months later, Haviland returned to Rising Sun and contacted Allen, who said he would get in touch with her within two weeks. However, because the river in that section was being watched for counterfeiters, Allen wasn't sure if it would be advisable to attempt a rescue at that time. While Haviland waited in Rising Sun, she learned of a slave named Caroline, in Trimble County, about thirty miles west, in need of assistance. The woman was the slave and mistress of George Ray, the brother of Wright Ray. She was the mother of five children, all fathered by Ray. Haviland, knowing the conductors along the line up through Jefferson County, Indiana, provided Caroline with the information necessary to organize an escape.

On October 31, 1847, Caroline and her four children crossed the river at Madison, Indiana, and made their way to freedom through the Underground Railroad. This case later became well known as a result of the successful prosecution of **Luther Donnell** of Clarksburg, Indiana, one of those who aided the family.

While still in Rising Sun, Haviland learned of the successful escape of Caroline; however, not long after, Haviland received tragic personal news—her oldest son Harvey had died. She at once left for Cincinnati, where she remained a few weeks longer because of a bout with pneumonia.

After returning to Michigan, Haviland advised John White that she was unable to arrange his family's rescue. He resolved to make the attempt himself, and went to Kentucky and obtained the aid of his friend William Allen, who was still enslaved, and Stevens's overseer, Solomon, who was also attempting to escape. During the night, the fugitive slaves slipped out and fled to the Ohio River. They took a skiff and attempted to row across to a point above Rising Sun, where a conductor was waiting with a wagon to receive them. But the water was high, and the current swift and strong, and they were pushed down river some distance below Rising Sun.

As daylight approached, the fugitives slaves hid in the thickets and remained there through the day. At night they ventured onto the road. A posse of men had been gathered and split up into two groups that searched the river. Before the fugitive slaves realized it, they were trapped, and six armed men confronted them. White and Allen managed to escape, but White's wife and children and the overseer were captured.

Allen apparently went back to his master's plantation to be with his wife and child, while White remained in the woods lamenting his failure. Though he managed to find the cabin of a free black man, White was captured there by Wright Ray, who took him to Madison, Indiana, and put him in jail. White realized that Ray didn't know that he was the slave of George Brazier, so he gave him the name of another fugitive slave, James Armstrong, whom he had met in Canada. When Ray contacted Armstrong's former owner, she refused to give him any money for the alleged Armstrong, so Ray suggested that White contact his friends in Michigan, where Armstrong had also lived after escaping. White wrote the sheriff in Michigan and asked him to forward the letter to an address where it would reach Laura Haviland. When she saw the letter, she concluded it was from White.

Haviland then set out for Cincinnati to seek Levi Coffin's assistance. She offered to go to Madison to purchase White, but Coffin suggested that it might be too dangerous, and he instead sent his nephew, M. C., who managed to negotiate a purchase arrangement. White was then sent on a packet boat to Cincinnati, where the transaction was completed. It was just in time, as George Brazier arrived in Cincinnati the next day. Coffin had Ray arrested for kidnapping, and Ray was lodged in the Madison jail for several days. But because White would've been required to testify against Ray to make the charges stick, the case was dropped.

Meanwhile, Benjamin Stevens sold his grandchildren for $1,000, though with the provision that they not be sold apart. Jane died soon after of cholera, and George Brazier, White's master and Haviland's adversary, died a few months later, also of cholera. Time passed, and White married a young woman in Canada. He also was reunited with his children, and after the Civil War, they settled in Ann Arbor, his oldest daughter marrying the overseer Solomon.

With the maturing of her children, and without the obligation to serve the needs of a husband, Haviland began to enlarge her mission in the Underground Railroad. Leaving her family to manage the farm, and with the school in the capable hands of its principal, John Patchin, Haviland moved to Cincinnati, boarding with the Coffins, where she was to live for most of the next four years. She aided a number of slaves while there, and one, who was clever and cunning, made a lasting impression.

His name was George, and he and another slave named James had escaped from Kentucky. They were sent north to a Quaker settlement from which James continued on to Canada. However, George had other ideas, and he remained at the settlement and worked as a farmhand. He had left his wife, Liz, behind in slavery, and this was part of his plan to arrange her escape. After a year of working to save money to give to his master, George went back to Kentucky and secretly visited Liz during the night. He explained his plan to her, that he would go back to his master, beg his forgiveness, and ask his master to take him back. At the same time he would openly disparage abolitionists and give his master the money he had saved. George's master was happy to take him and had no doubts about George's fidelity, especially after George explained that it was only because of a fight he had with his wife that he had left. In fact, he told his master, he no longer wanted to see her.

Another year passed with George playing the part of the devoted slave and disgruntled husband, and gaining the trust of not only his master, but the other slaveholders in the region. Finally, when the time was right, George and Liz fled separately and met at the mouth of the Licking River, where they crossed the Ohio River into freedom and ended up at the Negro Baptist Church in Cincinnati. It was then arranged for them to travel north with Haviland and five other slaves on a Miami and Erie Canal packet boat to Toledo. From there, Haviland arranged a boat ride to Canada.

The sight of Canada overcame the former slaves, and George and Liz began to cry. Haviland left them with only fifty cents to start their new life, and returned for a visit home to Michigan. The happiness of others always brought joy to Haviland, but her return home was not one of celebration. The school's original cabins were in need of repair or replacement, and the principal, John Patchin, was leaving. To make matters worse, two of its trustees, including the devoted J. P. Dolbeare, died within a few months of each other. Consequently, Haviland decided to suspend operations of the school.

Haviland returned to Cincinnati and took a position teaching young black girls at the Zion Baptist Church. Little did she realize that the Raisin Institute would not reopen until 1856. It was during this time that Haviland met **Calvin Fairbank** after his release from the Kentucky State Penitentiary in 1849. Their mutual passion to end slavery forged a bond that would last throughout their lives. Haviland also continued to offer her assistance to fugitive slaves, teach the uneducated, and nurse the sick. One day a letter came to Levi Coffin from a man in a Louisville jail, requesting assistance. It was signed using stars in place of letters, with six stars in the first name and eight in the second. Haviland realized it was from Calvin Fairbank, for he recently had stopped to visit and had mentioned a slave in Louisville whom he had been asked to help.

Haviland immediately went to Louisville by boat, with a trunk of bedclothes and underwear. From the ship's captain, she was able to obtain a letter of introduction to the city jailer, Colonel Buckner, and directions to the colonel's residence. There she asked the colonel for permission to see Fairbank. He said he couldn't allow it without the consent of the sheriff, who was away on business. Though a slaveholder, the colonel was very polite and said that Haviland could stay with him and his family until then, which Haviland accepted.

During her visit, Haviland and the colonel debated the merits of abolitionism and the ethics of slavery. Haviland also visited with the colonel's wife, who noted that their family had done their Christian best to help slaves, by purchasing some at the jail who were in desperate straits. Mrs. Buckner also revealed a new member of their household, an eight-month-old mixed-race baby, the daughter of one of their slaves (and apparently the colonel), and was excited about the price they would be able to get for the baby in the slave market.

Finally, Haviland got to see Fairbank. He was very grateful and later wrote about it in his memoir. He asked Haviland to go to Jeffersonville, Indiana, to see a lawyer named Thurston and request his services for Fairbank. Haviland complied with his wishes despite the danger it presented, as reports were being circulated in the newspapers that mistook her for the notorious slave stealer, **Delia Webster**. However, Haviland returned to Cincinnati unharmed.

Another slave whose life was changed by meeting Haviland was Mary French, who lived across the river from Cincinnati in Covington and who was hired out as a cleaning lady for the Zion Baptist Church. She had nine children, and her oldest daughter had fled to Canada with her baby because her master was going to sell her south. French was upset because her master was planning to sell another one of her children. French did have one thing in her favor, however: her master had complete trust in her and allowed her to go cross the river on a regular basis to sell his produce. Haviland advised French to use the wagon she took to market and hide her family under some hay and produce, and make her getaway to freedom. Haviland also pointed out three locations in Cincinnati where French would get her start on the Underground Railroad.

Some time later, after returning from a visit to Michigan during which Haviland heard that one of French's children had been sold, she heard a report that a market wagon had brought over nine or ten slaves who were in hiding and waiting to be routed along the Underground Railroad. Haviland asked the Coffins whether they knew anything about it, and Catharine said that there were two fugitive slaves being hidden in the attic. Haviland went up to take a look, and found French and her granddaughter.

Later the family was secreted out of the city and forwarded north on the Underground Railroad. A wagon with ten slave imposters also was sent out as a decoy. It was stopped by the authorities, which helped to delay the pursuit of the real fugitive slaves. Mary French and her family did succeed in reaching Canada, and she and Haviland were to see each other again in Windsor, when Haviland was visiting for an August first celebration there.

It was still several years before Haviland reopened the Raisin Institute, and she undertook two important missions: one to Toledo to operate a school for black children, and then a year in Windsor, Canada, to run a school for fugitive slaves.

Haviland was solicited for the Canada mission by the Refugee Home Society, whose committee members included Henry Bibb, Horace Hallack, and Rev. Charles C. Foote. The school was eight miles from Windsor. A frame schoolhouse had been erected near the settlement, where the refugees had built log houses and cleared from one to five acres each of their land. They raised corn, potatoes, other garden vegetables, and wheat. Haviland opened the school in the autumn of 1852. There was no age restriction, and she also offered a Sabbath school.

Haviland became more than just a teacher; she counseled the fugitive slaves in financial, legal, and religious matters, and often helped them write letters to family members still in slavery, which were sent to a trusted go-between, so the fugitive slaves' whereabouts would not be revealed. Among Haviland's students was the noted fugitive slave, **John Anderson**, who had fled from Missouri after killing a man who had tried to capture him during his escape from slavery. Anderson was going by the name of William at this time. Haviland became involved in Anderson's case after a letter was sent to him in Windsor that claimed to be from his family in Missouri. Anderson had written them and told them of his arrival in Windsor. The letter to Anderson said they had arrived in Detroit and were anxious to see him. Haviland was suspicious of it from the outset. She suggested that she should write a letter back to them, and inform them that they should contact her in Adrian, Michigan, where she was about to return. She would then inform them of how to contact Anderson. She also suggested that Anderson move to Chatham and change his name.

Some days later, a Southerner visited Haviland in Adrian. He claimed to be a representative of Anderson's family. Though Haviland was suspicious, she told him Anderson could be found in Chatham, Canada West, but after the man left, she realized her mistake and wired **George DeBaptiste** in Detroit, asking him to warn Anderson to leave Chatham. The slavecatchers arrived in Chatham two days later, but by then Anderson was gone. Anderson eluded authorities until 1860, when a decision was made to send Anderson back to the United States to be tried for murder, but the ruling was overturned by a higher court.

One of Haviland's most memorable incidents connected to the Underground Railroad occurred while teaching in Canada: the arrival of **John Fairfield**, with twenty-seven fugitive slaves he had successfully led from Kentucky.

After a year establishing the school at the Refugee Home Society, Haviland returned to Michigan to be with her family. There she made preparations to reopen the Raisin Institute, which took place in 1856. New construction also was begun. As in the past, Haviland hired Oberlin graduates to direct the school, and in the years up to the Civil War, enrollment rose above 200 students, most of them preparing to be teachers. There also were frequent arrivals of fugitive slaves, whose appearance Haviland said helped to remove any racial prejudices some students might have, and which was a source of great gratification for her.

Shortly before the Civil War, Haviland took one last daring trip into the South to assist a slave named Ann, the sister of a fugitive slave she had met at an antislavery convention. Ann lived in Little Rock, Arkansas, and Haviland thought that not only would she aid the escape of a slave, but also give herself the opportunity to witness slavery in the Deep South. Through correspondence with a black minister in Little Rock, arrangements were made; the Coffins also were made aware of the mission, as Cincinnati was where Haviland's journey began.

Haviland found lodging in the home of slaveowners who were passengers on the boat that took her to Little Rock. There she witnessed the cruel treatment of the slaves and heard horror stories about beatings and murders that had taken place. Though she was able to meet with Ann, Haviland was unable to convey the woman north because her presence had aroused suspicion.

With the start of the Civil War, enrollment at the Raisin Institute decreased as students and teachers enlisted in the Union army. The school was finally forced to close again in 1864. As a result, Haviland undertook a mission into the South to nurse wounded soldiers and care for refugees from slavery, getting official sponsorship from the governor of Michigan and one of its congressmen. Noting the cruelty and neglect shown by an officer in charge of a military hospital, Haviland succeeded in having the man removed. She also aided in the release of 3,000 Union soldiers imprisoned on islands in the Gulf of Mexico. Her mission of mercy expanded to Kansas, where she cared for freedmen there.

During a visit home, Haviland sold the Raisin Institute and ten acres of land to the State Freedmen's Aid Commission, for the establishment of a home for orphans. The institution was named the Haviland Home for Homeless and Destitute Children.

Following the war, Haviland visited Washington, interceding with President Andrew Johnson on behalf of a convict, and carried on rescue work in Virginia. Her work among freedmen was officially recognized in 1867 by the Wesleyan Methodist Michigan Annual Conference. Eventually Haviland rejoined the Quaker faith, and in her later years, she was always ready to aid the cause of the suffering and disenfranchised. In 1879, when blacks from the South began pouring into Kansas because of the rise of the Ku Klux Klan, Haviland went with Sojourner Truth to assist their needs. After a visit to Washington to raise funding for her mission, Haviland returned to Kansas in 1883 and directed a mission at Hell's Half Acre, which led to Haviland, Kansas, being named after her, though it's uncertain whether she ever visited that village.

In 1909, eleven years after Haviland's death, a life-size statue of her was erected in front of the city hall at Adrian. It remains today in front of a new city hall as a lasting tribute to this saintly woman.

The Haviland orphanage was moved to Coldwater, Michigan in 1874, and renamed the Coldwater Regional Mental Health Center. It went through numerous transformations over the years before becoming a psychiatric hospital, which closed in 1992.

SUGGESTED READING: Levi Coffin, *Reminiscences of Levi Coffin,* Cincinnati: Robert Clarke & Co., 1880; Mildred E. Danforth, *A Quaker Pioneer*, New York: Exposition Press, 1961; Calvin Fairbank, *Rev. Calvin Fairbank during Slavery Times,* Chicago: Patriotic Publishing, Co., 1890; Laura Haviland, *A Woman's Life-work: Labors and Experiences of Laura S. Haviland,* Walden & Stowe, 1882.

Hayden, Lewis (1811–1889). Born a slave in Lexington, Kentucky, Lewis Hayden became an important community leader and state senator in Massachusetts. His life was filled with excitement from the time of his escape from slavery to his daring acts of defiance against the Fugitive Slave Law in Boston. In his later years, he devoted himself to public service and promoting the elevation of people of color.

Hayden's mother was part Native American and white, and his father, black. He was owned by a Presbyterian minister, Rev. Adam Rankin, of Lexington, a distant relative of the celebrated conductor and abolitionist, **John Rankin**. In a short autobiography prepared for **Harriet Beecher Stowe's** *Key to Uncle Tom's Cabin*, he wrote,

> There may be ministers and professors of religion who think it is (more wrong to separate the families of slaves by sale than to separate any domestic animals) but I never met with them. . . . It may seem strange, but it is a fact. I had more sympathy and kind advice, in my efforts to get my freedom, from gamblers and such sort of men, than Christians.

Boston Underground Railroad conductor Lewis Hayden. Courtesy of the Ohio Historical Society.

Hayden was traded for two horses when he was ten years old. His new master sold clocks and traveled from town to town. This provided Hayden with an education of sorts as a result of his exposure to the discussions in the taverns of the day. Here he developed an interest in politics that continued throughout his life. He also learned that there were actually whites who hated slavery.

Sometime in the mid-1830s, Hayden married Esther Harvey and they had a son. However, she was purchased by Senator Henry Clay, who later sold both his wife and son to a slave trader, sending them where Hayden would never know of or see them again. In 1840 he was sold at auction. This master was not hesitant to use whippings as a means of controlling his slaves. But Hayden bore with it and taught himself to read by studying discarded newspapers and a Bible that he had acquired. In 1842 he married again. Now, more than ever, Hayden longed for his freedom. His growing self-confidence enabled him to convince two businessmen, Thomas Grant and Lewis Baxter, to purchase him and hire him out, allowing him to keep part of his wages so that he could save enough money to buy his freedom.

It was during this period that he met **Delia Webster** and **Calvin Fairbank**, two of the most notorious slave rescuers in the annals of the Underground Railroad. Fairbank had come from Oberlin to Kentucky after being solicited by Rev. John M. Brown, an African Methodist Episcopal minister, to rescue the family of fugitive slave Gilson Berry. However, when that attempt went awry, the opportunity to help Hayden presented itself.

On the night of Saturday, September 28, 1844, Fairbank and Webster rendezvoused with Hayden, his wife, Harriet, and his five-year-old stepson, Joseph, in a two-horse carriage driven by a slave and, coincidentally, near the residence of abolitionist Cassius Clay. The Haydens' identities were masked with flour and hoods that hid their faces, and Joseph was hidden under a seat inside the carriage. They ran into a minor problem when one of the horses became ill, but they were able to get a replacement. This delayed them about ninety minutes, and they crossed the Ohio River at Maysville, Kentucky without incident.

Fairbank first deposited Webster with Eli Collins in Ripley, Ohio before going to Red Oak, about five miles to the north, and the home of Gordon Hopkins, with whom he had arranged to leave the Haydens and start them along their Underground Railroad journey through Ohio. This leg of the journey was not without incident, as the Haydens were forced to alter their planned itinerary through Oberlin and go directly to Sandusky, where they took a boat to Canada.

A month later, a jubilant Hayden wrote a letter from Amherstburg, Canada West, to his former masters, which stated in part: "Sir, you have already discovered me absent. . . . I have concluded for the present to try freedom and how it will seem to be my own master." It is apparent from the letter and some of the references that Hayden, who still was learning the rudiments of writing, had help with it. Interestingly, he signed it Lewis Grant, the name by which he had been known as a slave, crossing out the name Hayden, which he had since adopted. Nonetheless, its bold declarations and confident air were characteristic of Hayden throughout the rest of his life.

Hayden was a man with great compassion, and was concerned about his rescuers, Fairbank and Webster, who had been sent to prison for helping him to freedom. It stimulated a desire to help others like himself who sought their freedom. Six months later, he decided to move his family to Detroit and to become part of the movement to free the slaves.

In Detroit he spoke out about his experience and raised funds for the organization of a school and an African Methodist Episcopal (AME) church. In 1845 he began an antislavery lecture tour with the same Rev. Brown who had solicited Calvin Fairbank to rescue the family of Gilson Berry. This tour, whose purpose was to raise money for the AME church in Detroit, brought him to Boston and the attention of the fervent abolitionist movement there. It inspired him with greater aspirations, and on May 25, 1846, he moved his family there. He immediately became a member of the newly formed Boston Vigilance Committee, and moved into the residence at 66 Southac Street that would become a notorious refuge for fugitive slaves. It wasn't long before he became its most trusted conductor. William Lloyd Garrison, though not an official member of committee, was often privy to their activities, and said of Hayden that he was "my staunchest ally." Hayden continued his lecturing, but interrupted it in 1847 to take a trip to Vermont, where it is believed he visited with Webster, who had been pardoned and released from prison, and whose equivocal public statements about slavery had been the subject of widespread criticism. But Hayden would never doubt Webster, and throughout his life, he expressed his gratitude to her.

In 1849 he opened a used-clothing store. Not only did it provide a source of income, but it was used by the vigilance committee to provide clothing to the fugitive slaves, who generally arrived with only the clothing that they were wearing. That year he also began efforts to aid his other rescuer, Calvin Fairbank, who sat in a Kentucky prison cell. A movement for his pardon had begun, and Hayden's owners stated that a sum of $650 would be sufficient for them to approve the pardon. At once Hayden set out to raise the sum, and within sixty days reached the total, with donations from 160 individuals. By the end of the year, Fairbank was out of prison and on the antislavery lecture circuit. It brought him to Boston, where he became a houseguest of Hayden.

At this time Fairbank was one of many abolitionists speaking out against the imminent passage of a new and stronger Fugitive Slave Law. Its inevitability had mobilized the Boston Vigilance Committee against anticipated attempts by slavecatchers to apprehend some of the more than 600 estimated fugitive slaves living in the city. It also brought the bold and courageous character of Hayden to the forefront. Among notable fugitive slaves living in Boston were **Henry "Box" Brown**, and William and Ellen Craft. An attempt was made to kidnap Brown, who was for a time a houseguest of Hayden. This compelled Brown to leave for England. The Crafts were determined to stay, but they had been targeted by the federal government to be apprehended under the jurisdiction of the new law.

When the slavecatchers appeared in Boston, however, the vigilance committee took action. Ellen was put in hiding in Brookline, and William was sent to Hayden's house. Hayden was ready. He had barricaded the windows and reinforced the locks on his door, and had organized a band of armed black mercenaries to guard the house. In the event that these measures failed, he had a keg of gunpowder in the basement ready for use. This was witnessed by Fairbank, whose visit lasted through this crisis. However, the need to resort to violence never came, as no local authorities were willing to serve the writ for the Crafts' arrest. Harassment from the vigilance committee and threats from Boston citizens who were unhappy with the law persuaded the slavecatchers to leave. Thereafter, the Crafts were able to make their getaway to Nova Scotia and, eventually, to the safe shores of England.

Four months later, Hayden was motivated to organize an even more daring exploit. **Shadrach Minkins**, a fugitive slave from Virginia, had been living in Boston for nine months and had found stable employment at the Cornhill Coffeehouse, just a few doors down from *The Liberator*'s office, which often was site of Boston Vigilance Committee meetings. Without warning, he was seized at the coffeehouse and brought to the federal courthouse. News of the arrest spread quickly to the black community, and six lawyers from the Boston Vigilance Committee were at the courthouse within an hour. A crowd of about 150 had pushed its way in, the majority of them black. The vigilance committee lawyers, among the best Boston had to offer, were able to obtain a three-day postponement to prepare their case.

However, the courthouse was still abuzz with hundreds of people still lingering inside and outside. Leading a band of about twenty blacks, Hayden charged into a private room where Minkins and his lawyers were discussing his case, overpowered the deputies there, picked up Minkins, and carried him out of the building.

They brought him to the attic apartment of a black woman who lived near Hayden while they arranged transportation out of Boston. Within days, Minkins was in Montreal, escaping as a passenger on the aboveground Fitchburg Railroad through Vermont.

Hayden was arrested and prosecuted, but the government lost the case when one member of the jury refused to convict Hayden. According to one account, this jury member had assisted in Minkins's escape.

Two months later, slavecatchers struck Boston again with even greater support from the federal government. In less than a week, they were able to apprehend and remove the fugitive slave **Thomas Sims**. When Hayden was asked by one of the vigilance committee's more radical members, Thomas Higginson, whether he would be able to attempt another rescue, he confessed privately that many of his brothers had left Boston for fear of being sent back to slavery.

"We do not wish any one to know how really weak we are. Practically, there are no colored men in Boston; the Shadrach prosecutions have scattered them all."

But the Sims rendition was costly to authorities, and had increased public opposition to the federal government and enforcement of the Fugitive Slave Law. The committee continued its efforts to aid fugitive slaves, and by 1854 had officially aided 230 fugitive slaves since the passage of the law in 1850, with a large number staying with Hayden. In fact, on one occasion in 1853 Harriet Beecher Stowe visited the Haydens and found thirteen fugitive slaves who were temporary guests.

In 1854 Hayden collaborated with Higginson in another daring rescue attempt. This one involved the fugitive slave, **Anthony Burns**, whose whereabouts had been discovered when he inadvertently wrote his address on a letter sent to his brother in Virginia that his brother's master opened. Their plan was a covert one not approved by the majority of the vigilance committee, though some of its leadership, including the noted radical abolitionist Theodore Parker, were privy to it. One night after a mass meeting of those who sympathized with Burns, they attempted to storm the federal courthouse where Burns was being held, using a battering ram to break open the doors. They were successful in doing so, but in the ensuing melee, one of the police guards was shots and killed, causing the attackers to retreat. Hayden had been one of the men trading gunshots with the police, but it was only many years later that it was learned who actually killed the guard, and it wasn't Hayden.

The following year, Hayden was involved in a different type of confrontation in the chambers of the state legislature. It was during a special hearing of a committee considering testimony about a pending personal liberty law to protect fugitives from slavery in the state. To the surprise of the committee, an Alabama slaveholder, John Githell, asked to speak. He argued that most slaves were well treated and contented, and that only the troublemakers ran away. He agreed that slavery should be abolished, but gradually. Hayden immediately rose in rebuttal. His words, though unprepared, demonstrate the eloquence that this formerly illiterate slave had acquired as a free man. In part, he said:

> The principal difference between us is that Mr. Githell was born in a free state surrounded by the sweet influences of free schools, free churches, and a free Bible; whereas I was born a slave upon a plantation, brought up under the humiliating influences of the slave driver's lash . . . .
>
> I have always said, Mr. Chairman, that you get here the poorest specimens of slaves. My brother Githell asserts it as a fact and thereby he and myself are agreed. Now, sir, you have all seen **Frederick Douglass**, Mr. Brown and other fugitive slaves, and if they are among the worst specimens, then you need no fear of letting loose those in bondage.

In 1858 Hayden's clothing store, which had been very successful, went out of business. The esteem with which he was held among the Boston elite, many of whom were vigilance committee members, became evident when he was hired by the state legislature as a special messenger to the secretary of state. It was the highest ranking public office a black man had ever held in Massachusetts up to that time, and it was a position he held until his death.

From 1857 to 1859, **John Brown** visited Boston at least seven times. During these visits he spent time with Hayden and enlisted his help in raising funds for his mission to end slavery. In October 1859, Hayden received a letter from Brown asking for funds. That very day he encountered Francis Merriam, the grandson of vigilance committee treasurer **Francis Jackson**, and Hayden inquired if Merriam might know where he could obtain some funds to send to Brown. Not only did Merriam agree to offer the money, but said he would deliver it in person. As a result, Merriam became Brown's last recruit in the assault on Harpers Ferry, and one of the few who escaped with his life.

During the Civil War, Hayden was instrumental in recruiting for Massachusetts' Fifty-fourth Colored Regiment, and his stepson Joseph lost his life while serving in the U.S. Navy. Following the war, Hayden continued his public service. He was active in the Free Masonry movement, and lobbied for women's suffrage and integrated schools, and in 1873, despite his reluctance to become a candidate for office, he was elected a senator in the Massachusetts State legislature.

His final effort to promote his race was a successful petition to erect a monument to Crispus Attucks, the Boston black man who was the first casualty of the American Revolution. This was especially significant to Hayden and other Boston blacks who participated in the Boston Vigilance Committee's efforts to prevent the renditions of Thomas Sims and Anthony Burns, both of whom were paraded past the very spot where Attucks had lost his life.

Following the unveiling of the monument in 1888, Hayden said, "I am happy and ready to die now." The following year he died of kidney failure, and his wife, Harriet, passed away five years later, leaving several thousand dollars in her estate to Harvard University to establish a scholarship fund for deserving black medical students.

SUGGESTED READING: Calvin Fairbank, *Rev. Calvin Fairbank During Slavery Times*, Chicago: Patriotic Publishing, Co., 1890; Kathryn Grover and Janine da Silva, *Historic Resource Study: Boston African American National Historic Site*, National Parks Service, 2002; Stanley J. Robby, and Anita W. Robby, "Lewis Hayden: From Fugitive Slave to Statesman," *The New England Quarterly*, December, 1973; Randolph Paul Runyon, *Delia Webster and the Underground Railroad*, Lexington: University Press of Kentucky, 1996.

Hayes, William (1795–1849). William Hayes was one of many unsung heroes common to the Underground Railroad. His life had been forgotten until recent scholarship uncovered letters passed down through his family. On the surface, he was a lawbreaker and a man who couldn't support his family and left them with his debts when he died. However, through the lens of history, his life has been rehabilitated and taken on a different meaning.

Hayes was born in Upstate New York in 1795. He was a deeply religious man and a member of the Reformed Presbyterian sect known as the Covenanters. In 1801 the Covenanters refused communion to slaveholders, one of the first denominations to do so. They opened their churches to abolitionist speakers and meetings, and some of their members participated in the Underground Railroad. They had no problem with breaking the Fugitive Slave Laws because their Christianity took precedence over any governmental authority.

Hayes moved to Illinois in search of opportunity. He only owned part of the land on which he lived in New York, and he had squabbles with his brother, who was the primary owner. He became interested in moving to Illinois after two friends from New York moved there and touted the fertility of the land and the opportunities it offered. He also had relatives living in Knox and Stark counties: his uncle, Silvanus Ferris, who helped found Knox College in Galesburg, and his brother, Harry, who had settled in Stark County.

In 1833 he left Galway, New York, with his wife, four children, two sisters-in-law, and a friend, Jonathan Edgecomb. The plan was to stop in Cleveland and leave the women with the sister of Hayes's wife, while Hayes and Edgecomb continued on to Illinois to survey the land there. One of his options was to settle on a military tract that had come down to him from a family member who was a veteran of the War of 1812. However, he finally chose a plot in what was then the tiny village of Peoria, a richly fertile patch of prairie situated along the Illinois River.

However, because of the precariousness of his wife's health and the danger of contracting malaria because of nearby swamps, Hayes decided to move again. This time he took his family to Columbus, in southern Illinois, where one of his friends from New York had moved. Though not as fertile as central Illinois, it was suitable for many crops and for dairy farming, which Hayes had done in New York. What Hayes didn't know was that his new home in Randolph County was a section where people favored slavery.

When Hayes became involved in the Underground Railroad is unknown. Being a Convenanter certainly predisposed him to it. Family letters begin to refer to it as early as 1840, but it was in 1842 that an incident occurred which would reveal his activities. Eight miles from his homestead was the farm of transplanted Southerner, Andrew Borders, who owned the services of two black woman, one of them **Susan Richardson**, and four children. While slavery was prohibited in Illinois, the state's Black Codes passed in 1819 permitted indentured servitude for women until the age of thirty-two, and for men until the age of thirty-five. This was virtually the same as slavery except for the age limitation.

On the night of August 31, 1842, Borders's servants, of which there were now five, owing to the flight of the other adult woman, fled to Hayes's home. Hayes took them in his wagon the next day to Chester Landing, then accompanied them on a steamboat to St. Louis, where they transferred to a packet boat on the Illinois River. On September 5, the servants arrived in Farmington, Illinois, on the border between Fulton and Knox County. However, they were apprehended in Knox County at the home of Rev. **John Cross**.

A legal battle ensued, and Hayes continued in his efforts to help his fellow abolitionists win the battle in court against Borders, trying to find documents that showed Borders did not possess legal claims to his former servants. During the process, Borders dropped his suits against the abolitionists Hayes was trying to help, and instead filed civil charges against Hayes, who was an easier target: a resident of Randolph County, where sentiment was strongly proslavery, and an individual without the financial means to wage a sustained legal battle. Borders's attorneys outmaneuvered those of Hayes at every turn, and one of Hayes's key supporting witnesses was turned into his foremost adversarial witness. Hayes never had a chance, and the case broke him financially.

Nevertheless, Hayes continued to operate as an Underground Railroad conductor. In 1846 he and Daniel Morrison were arrested for aiding a fugitive slave in Clinton County,

Illinois, north of his home. This time he faced a criminal charge. Again, he was convicted, and not only did he incur more financial burdens, but now he faced jail time. His lawyers prolonged the process with a series of appeals. After three years the appeals had run out, but so had the life of William Hayes. He died of unknown causes in 1849 before ever setting foot in jail, a criminal to his family and a disgrace in his community, but a hero to those whom he helped escape from slavery.

SUGGESTED READING: Carol Pirtle, *Escape Betwixt Two Suns: A True Tale of the Underground Railroad in Illinois,* Southern Illinois University Press, 2000.

Henry, William "Jerry" (1813–1853). William "Jerry" Henry, a slave, ran away from Missouri in 1843 and settled in Syracuse, New York, in 1849. Born in North Carolina, he was the son of a slave mother and her owner William Henry, who educated and trained him as his servant. A short, light-skinned, powerfully built man, Henry also had carpentry skills, and quickly found work. He was making barrels for the local salt works cooper shop on October 1, 1851, when federal marshals came and arrested him for stealing.

Syracuse was one of the centers of abolition in the northeast and was becoming an increasingly active stop on the Underground Railroad during that time, its passengers coming mainly from Philadelphia, New York, and Albany. Following the passage of the second Fugitive Slave Law, community members formed a vigilance committee, as had residents in many other Northern cities, which openly vowed to resist the law and help any fugitive slave who sought aid. In June of 1851, U.S. Secretary of State Daniel Webster visited the city and threatened the abolitionists.

"Those persons in this city who mean to oppose the execution of the Fugitive Slave Law are traitors!" Webster declared. "This law ought to be obeyed, and it will be enforced—yes . . . in the city of Syracuse it shall be enforced, and . . . in the midst of the next anti-slavery Convention, if then there shall be any occasion to enforce it."

On the day of Henry's arrest, both a state agricultural fair and a Liberty Party convention were being held, so the city had an unusually large number of visitors, including abolitionists from around the state. During the Liberty Party session, Charles Wheaton, a local hardware dealer, interrupted with news that a fugitive slave had been arrested. En masse, the party members left for the city courthouse, which was attached to the police station, while church bells tolled throughout the city and people gathered in the square nearby.

Wheaton also enlisted the services of party members, **Leonard Gibbs** and **Gerrit Smith**, to represent the fugitive slave. They hurried along with a quickly gathering crowd of angry citizens and entered the office of Joseph Sabine, the local federal commissioner appointed to hear fugitive slave cases, who was listening to the claims of Rev. James Lear, the representative of Henry's alleged owner, John McReynolds. Henry had been sold to McReynolds two years after he had fled. It was Sabine's first case as commissioner. Gibbs, the more experienced lawyer, took charge and demanded that Henry's shackles be removed. A man is innocent until proven guilty, he insisted. Gibbs also demanded that the pistols Lear displayed be surrendered. Sabine said he didn't have the authority to have Henry's shackles removed but suggested it to U.S. Marshal Henry Allen, the arresting officer. However, Allen refused to comply.

The office was soon overflowing as people continued to squeeze in, so Sabine decided to adjourn to the courtroom next door in the Journal Building, its ground floor also the site of the police office, which was located behind the courtroom. As they filed out, the sympathetic crowd urged Henry to escape. On impulse, he hurled himself across a table, and with the help of the crowd, separated himself from the marshals. Despite his shackles, he dashed into the street and made a run for it. After a short time, he found a carriage waiting to take him to safety, but before he could enter, the marshals intercepted him. He resisted with all his power, but the marshals pummeled him until he stopped. They put him in a wagon and sat atop him until reaching the police station. Bleeding and with his clothes tattered from the beating, Henry was placed under guard in a back room.

Henry was extremely agitated now. Black abolitionist Samuel Ringgold Ward, who saw him, wrote that Henry was in a "frenzy, constantly pacing and demanding that he be set free." Abolitionist minister Samuel May was called in to calm him. He promised Henry that a rescue attempt was going to be made.

Meanwhile, during the adjournment of the hearing, which was scheduled to resume in a few hours, at 5:30, Gerrit Smith, May, and black activist **Jermaine Loguen**, along with about thirty others, planned the rescue at the office of Dr. Hiram Hoyt on Warren Street, just a few blocks away from the courthouse.

It was their belief that Sabine would in all likelihood release Henry, but Gerrit Smith advanced the idea that rescuing him would serve as an example to the federal government and for the nation that the citizens in Syracuse were not about to adhere to the Fugitive Slave Law and would do all in their power to oppose slavery. A plan was made to break into the police station, overwhelm the police with their numbers, put Henry into a buggy, and drive him around without leaving the city. They feared that all the roads leading out would be either blocked or closely watched, so they planned to leave Henry at the home of an unlikely sympathizer until they felt it safe to move him on toward Canada. Strict orders were given, if at all possible, to avoid injuring the police.

With the plan in place, the hearing resumed with Gibbs defending Henry. However, the large crowd outside was becoming impatient and increasingly unruly. Before the matter could be settled, a stone crashed through a window. It startled Sabine, who called for an adjournment until the next morning and hastily left the scene. Everything was now left in the hands of the local sheriffs and the four federal marshals who had been brought in to enforce the national law.

County Sheriff William Gardner knew that they would be in for a tough time. He had tried to call in the local militia, but its commander refused, saying he wouldn't allow his soldiers to help kidnappers. At once, they took Henry to the holding cell in the rear of the building and bolted the door to the police office in preparation for the rescue attempt. Both of Henry's original claimants, Rev. Lear and Marshal Allen, went into hiding: Lear finding an office in another part of the building, and Allen obscuring his appearance in an overcoat and disappearing into the crowd. Remaining inside the police station were abolitionists Ira H. Cobb and L. D. Mansfield, who had been there since the afternoon to ensure that the authorities didn't try to surreptitiously remove Henry.

Before long the rescuers joined the angry crowd. They were armed with clubs and axes. Nearby, outside Charles Wheaton's hardware store, iron rods were placed and some in the crowd picked them up. Then one of the rescuers cried, "Bring him out!"

The rescuers, along with the crowd, charged the police station, smashing the windows with their clubs and axes. They went into the courtroom and used a hemlock plank to dislodge the police office door.

"Open the way! Old Oswego is coming!" one of them shouted.

The rescuers rushed in. However, they knew the authorities were armed with weapons. In order to reduce their effectiveness, Cobb and Mansfield had turned off the gas that lit the building. In desperation, the authorities took a couple futile shots in the dark. The rescuers were not deterred, and according to plan, began their effort to enter the holding cell through a partition, making use of the battering ram. One of the marshals opened the door that barred them from Henry and attempted to fire a shot, but was hit in the arm with a blow by an iron rod, knocking the gun from his hand and breaking his arm.

As the partition gave way, the marshal with the broken arm jumped out of a window into the Erie Canal about ten feet below; the other marshals decided to give up and sent Henry, still shackled, out the door. Two black men, Peter Hollinbeck and William Gray, met him, and the rescuers exulted with a cheer.

The Fugitive Slave Law of 1850

On September 18, 1850, the second Fugitive Slave Law was passed. It was a provision of the Compromise of 1850, which outlawed the slave trade in Washington, D.C., and slavery in California, but extended slavery into the territories of Utah and New Mexico.

The new law put the handling of fugitive slave cases solely under federal jurisdiction. It included some of the same provisions as the earlier act, and increased the fine for its violation to $1,000—equal to $24,000 today—and six months in prison for each fugitive slave assisted. It also established a system in which individuals were appointed to act as commissioners or judges to hear cases involving the law. All that was required for the conviction of alleged fugitive slaves was their identification by two witnesses under oath that the individual was a fugitive from slavery.

The decisions of the commissioners were prejudiced by a stipulation that paid them $10 for every fugitive slave convicted and $5 for those set free. Adding force to the law was a $1,000 fine imposed on federal marshals who failed to follow an order and arrest a fugitive slave. These marshals also were liable for the value of any slave who escaped from them. Perhaps the most noxious clause of the new law was that it required citizens to assist in the rendition of a fugitive slave or face the same penalties as one who aided them. As many in the North were quick to recognize, this clause of the law turned every citizen in the North into a slavecatcher.

It was a starry night, and thousands outside saw the still-shackled Henry in his tattered shirt and shorts leave the police station. He was led on a procession by the rescuers, who put him on their shoulders and paraded him through a crowd that both cheered and wept. Flaunting their success, they brought him outside the Syracuse House hotel, where many important public officials attending the state fair were staying. The crowd had thickened, and the rescuers needed to bring Henry to a safe place. A cry of "fire" was used as a ruse to open the way for the carriage. He was taken on a circuitous route to a black man's house, where his shackles were cut off and he was dressed in women's clothing before he was taken to the home of Caleb Davis, the unlikely sympathizer who had changed his proslavery views after seeing Henry arrested. There Henry remained in hiding for five days while he recovered from his injuries and arrangements were made to forward him to Canada.

On the fifth night, a covered wagon took Henry from Syracuse to the home of Orson Ames in the rural village of Mexico, and later to Sidney Clarke's home in Oswego. He remained in hiding until Clarke found a British boatman who agreed to take him to Canada.

Twenty-six indictments were made against fourteen white and twelve black men in the Henry rescue. Gerrit Smith, Samuel May, and Charles Wheaton, three of the most prominent ringleaders were never indicted despite public declarations of their involvement.

Others such as Jermaine Loguen, fled temporarily to Canada. Only one, Enoch Reed, a black man, was actually convicted, but he died while his case was on appeal.

Thereafter, throughout the decade, the first day of October was commemorated with major celebrations in Syracuse as the city continued to defy the Fugitive Slave Law and help an additional 1,500 fugitive slaves obtain their freedom.

Sadly, Henry, the man whose freedom was valiantly defended, died only two years later in Kingston, Canada.

SUGGESTED READING: Fergus Bordewich, *Bound for Canaan*, New York: HarperCollins, 2005; Ralph Volney Harlow, *Gerrit Smith: Philanthropist and Reformer*, New York: Henry Holt & Co., 1938; J. W. Loguen, *The Rev. J. W. Loguen as a Slave and as a Freeman*, New York: Negro Universities Press, 1968, [1859]; Samuel J. May, *Some Recollections of Our Anti-Slavery Conflict*, Boston: Fields, Osgood & Co., 1869; Arch Merrill, *The Underground, Freedom's Road, and Other Upstate Tales*, New York: American Book-Stratford Press, 1963; Milton Sernett, "Narrative of Historic Context, Onondaga County Freedom Trail," 2001.

Hopper, Isaac Tatum (1771–1852). Isaac T. Hopper has been called the "father of the Underground Railroad." and with good reason, for Hopper was aiding fugitive slaves long before the concept of the Underground Railroad existed. A member of the Philadelphia Abolition Society, probably the first organization to help fugitive slaves, Hopper helped hundreds of slaves obtain their freedom, and accounts of his efforts are detailed in his biography by author, abolitionist, and women's rights advocate Lydia Maria Child.

Hopper was born in Deptford, New Jersey, a short distance across the river from Philadelphia. It was said that he bore a close resemblance to Napoleon Bonaparte, even by the emperor's own brother, who lived in Philadelphia for a time. Though renowned as a Quaker, Hopper did not become a Friend until he was an adult. His hatred of slavery, however, stemmed from the time he was nine years old and became acquainted with Mingo, an old slave who attended the cows of a local farmer. One day Mingo told him the story of how, when he was a boy, he was kidnapped in Africa and sold into slavery, never to see his family again. The trauma of the experience forever haunted Mingo, who broke into tears. The story touched young Hopper deeply.

When Hopper turned sixteen, he started to consider his prospects for the future. After failing to obtain a position at a store in Philadelphia, he decided to accept the offer to apprentice with his uncle William Tatem, who was a tailor there. Though he never wanted to become a tailor, he long had been interested in his uncle's shop because its customers included Benjamin Franklin and George Washington.

An amusing incident occurred when, as a small boy, Hopper secretly followed Washington out of the shop. After several blocks, Washington, who was aware of Hopper's scrutiny, turned and gazed at him, tipped his hat, and then playfully extended a respectful bow. Hopper froze in astonishment. It was something he would never forget. It also illustrated the mischievous though harmless nature of Hopper, which was characteristic of him throughout his life.

Not long after his apprenticeship had begun, a mariner named Captain Cox came to the shop with a young man named Joe, who was a slave from Bermuda. According to Cox, the man had come north while working on a boat, but had been mistakenly left behind. He asked Tatem if the man could stay with him until another boat was ready to return to Bermuda.

Quaker abolitionist Isaac T. Hopper. Library of Congress, from *Isaac T. Hopper: A True Life*, by Lydia Maria Child (1853).

One evening Hopper found Joe sitting in the kitchen looking quite sad. He thought of Mingo and asked what was troubling him. The young man hesitated before confiding that he was a fugitive slave and had made up the story about being left behind. It was true that his master had sent him to work on the boat, but when it docked at the port of New York, he ran to freedom. He was told to go to Philadelphia to get help, but then he encountered Cox, who knew his master.

Hopper told Joe he would try to help. He consulted a friend, who told him that a Quaker named John Stapler in Bucks County was known to help fugitive slaves. A letter of introduction was written for Joe. But in order not to arouse suspicion, Joe waited for the captain to return and deliver him to the boat going to Bermuda. While the boat was still in port, Joe made up an excuse that he left clothing at Tatem's house. Instead, he went to Stapler's home, where he was warmly received, and was to live the rest of his life in Bucks County as a free man.

At the age of twenty-two, Hopper joined the Society of Friends. He already had been in regular attendance at the Friends meetings, and had become a devoted follower of their teachings, which he would continue for the rest of his life: avoiding music and dancing; wearing the traditional Quaker buckled shoes, high stockings, knee-length trousers, and broad-brimmed hat; using the customary forms of address, "thee" and "thou"; and following his inner light, whose guiding principle was that within every man or woman resided a portion of God. In 1795 he married Sarah Tatem, a Quaker and his third cousin, with whom he had been close since childhood. They would have nine children.

The following year he became a member of the Quaker-dominated Pennsylvania Abolition Society, which had formed around the year 1775, and whose president for a time was Benjamin Franklin. A 1786 letter from George Washington that refers to the society is the first known mention of any organized group aiding fugitive slaves: "And if the practice of this Society . . . is not discountenanced, none of those whose misfortune it is to have slaves as attendants, will visit the city if they can possibly avoid it." Hopper's first assignment was an appointment to a committee that visited the homes of poor blacks to help them find jobs and arrange the education of their children. He also taught classes to black adults several evenings each week at a school for blacks founded by the Quaker Anthony Benezet.

In 1801 the society appointed him to represent blacks who claimed their liberty was being illegally denied. This was common in Philadelphia, a city with a large and relatively prosperous free black population, less than twenty miles north of the Mason-Dixon Line. As a result, not only were kidnappings of blacks claimed as slaves common, but so were kidnappings of free blacks. Hopper's appointment was likely an official recognition of activities that had involved him at least as early as 1797, when he assisted in obtaining the freedom of Charles Webster.

The coachman and waiter of a prosperous Virginia slaveholder, Webster had come to Philadelphia with his master for an extended stay. He asked Hopper if coming to Pennsylvania, a free state, would grant him his freedom. Hopper explained that the law required six months residence for that to occur, and advised him not to attempt to escape, but rather to be patient because his master was probably ignorant of the law and might extend his visit beyond that time.

Hopper advised working within the law when possible because those who fled were always subject to rendition by slavecatchers. This was especially important in Pennsylvania, where the judicial system was sympathetic to the rights of blacks. As one judge had told Hopper: when the evidence for and against freedom was evenly balanced, he would decide in favor of freedom.

In Webster's case, his master stayed beyond the six month time limit, and at that time he went back to see Hopper. The next morning he and Hopper went to see the attorney William Lewis, who assisted Hopper in such cases. Lewis provided Webster with a letter for his former master, stating that under Pennsylvania law, Webster was now free and that any attempt to forcibly detain him would liable him to charges of kidnapping. Lewis also requested that Hopper visit the master before Webster returned with the letter.

The slaveholder became angry when Hopper informed him that Webster was free. However, Hopper warned him that he and others were ready to protect Webster's rights.

"If thy son were a slave in Algiers, thou wouldst thank me for tampering with him to procure his liberty," Hopper said. "But in the present case, I am not obnoxious to the charge thou hast brought; for thy servant came of his own accord to consult me. I merely made him acquainted with his legal rights; and I intend to see that he is protected in them."

Webster returned to his master and delivered the letter. They parted ways, never to see each other again, and Webster married and lived a respectable life as a free man, raising a family of fourteen children.

Hopper soon gained a reputation as a defender of the rights of blacks. At one point, he declared: "I believe there were no colored persons in the city who would wish to secrete themselves from me. They all knew I was their friend."

A reflection of Hopper's activity can be surmised from the many incidents involving him and fugitive slaves that appear in his biography by Child, many of which were derived from a column Hopper wrote for the *National Anti-Slavery Standard* that began in 1840.

Another incident that was characteristic of the way Hopper used the law to win the freedom of slaves involved Ben Jackson, a slave born in Virginia. At the age of twenty-five, Jackson fled to Philadelphia, where he found employment as a seaman and undertook several oceangoing voyages. After five years, he married and was hired as a coachman by Benjamin Rush, one of the signers of the Declaration of Independence. He was employed by Rush for two years, after which time he received a paper from Rush certifying that he was a free man. In 1799, however, Jackson's owner came to Philadelphia and arrested him as his fugitive slave. When his master brought him before Judge Joseph Bird, Jackson showed him the certificate signed by Rush.

Fortunately for Jackson, Bird was an opponent of slavery, and while sending Jackson to jail until the matter could be satisfactorily resolved, he informed Hopper. After visiting Rush to ascertain the validity of Jackson's claim, Hopper went to see Jackson, who admitted that he was a fugitive slave. Hopper told him not to worry, that he would do all in his power to set him free. Good fortune continued to smile on Jackson, for not only did the judge sympathize with his case, but so did the constable who arrested him. Hopper advised him to bring Jackson to the courthouse prior to his hearing. Hopper arrived early as well.

When it came time for the hearing, as luck would have it, Jackson's master had not yet arrived. Hopper hurried into the courtroom and pushed the proceedings forward. He told the judge that he had spoken with Rush, who confirmed that he had signed the certificate attesting to Jackson's freedom, and that since no evidence had been provided to prove that Jackson was a slave, the judge should release him. Judge Bird concurred.

Jackson left the courthouse immediately, and actually saw his master on his way out. He sped down the street and found refuge at a friend's house. However, he later fled to Hopper's home and awaited his return.

Realizing the imminent danger of Jackson's situation, Hopper put him in hiding, but after a week, Jackson returned home to his wife. His residence was on an upper floor of the building where he lived, and he put a ladder under his window that was held by a rope and extended about six feet above a shed. A week later, he was surprised by the appearance of his master and a constable, who proceeded to break down the door. Jackson hurried down his escape ladder, and when his master and the constable attempted to follow, Jackson's wife cut the rope, causing her husband's pursuers to fall to the ground and enabling Jackson to get away.

Jackson was immediately sent out on a ship to sea, and in the intervening period, Hopper negotiated the purchase of his freedom for $150.

In another case from 1802, an attempt was made to kidnap a free black man, William Bachelor. When Hopper was informed, he took off on his horse in pursuit, and when he caught the slavecatchers, he protested that Bachelor was a free man. Joseph Ennells, who was joined in the kidnapping by James Frazier, pointed a pistol at Hopper and said, "We have had him before a magistrate, and proved to his satisfaction that the fellow is my slave. I have got his certificate, and that is all that is required to authorize me to take him home. I will blow your brains out if you say another word on the subject, or make any attempt to molest me."

Undeterred, Hopper answered, "If thou wert not a coward, thou wouldst not try to intimidate me with a pistol. I do not believe thou hast the least intention of using it in any other way; but thou art much agitated, and may fire it accidentally; therefore I request thee not to point it toward me, but to turn it the other way. It is in vain for thee to think of taking this old man to Maryland. If thou wilt not return to the city voluntarily, I will certainly have thee stopped at the bridge, where thou wilt be likely to be handled much more roughly than I am disposed to do."

Finally, Hopper was able to persuade Ennells to bring back Bachelor. This time when Bachelor was brought before the judge, numerous witnesses testified that he was a free man, and he was released. Because it was believed that Ennells knew that he was free, charges of kidnapping were brought against him. However, through the influence of Hopper, who was not vindictive, the charges were dismissed, and Ennells was allowed to return to Maryland.

A case that illustrated the brutality of some slaveholders involved a fugitive slave who had been imprisoned. When his master was summoned, the slave begged that he be sold to someone else. This stopped the jailer, who hesitated to release the slave until he was commanded by the slaveholder to do so. At last he unlocked the cell and ordered the slave to go, when suddenly the slave pulled out a knife and slit his own throat. The prison doctor was called and said the man likely would not survive. Nevertheless, the slaveholder demanded that the slave be delivered to him. The prison officials refused, however, on the advice of the doctor. The slaveholder insisted that they should comply with his wishes because he had a warrant from the mayor. As a result, prison officials conferred with the mayor, who, on further review, agreed that the slave should not be removed until either he succumbed or his life was out of danger.

A week passed without any further word on the slave's condition. The doctor, however, confided to Hopper that he believed the man was going to live. Knowing this, Hopper offered to purchase the slave's freedom for a price far below his value. His owner, thinking he was going to die and would get nothing in return, readily agreed.

Hopper was always ready to help those enslaved obtain their freedom, but after he gained notoriety for his efforts, he did not think it safe for fugitive slaves to remain long at his residence. Once, during a court case, he was asked if he would deliver a fugitive slave to his master.

"Indeed I would not!" he answered. "My conscience would not permit me to do it. It would be a great crime; because it would be disobedience to my own dearest convictions of right. I should never expect to enjoy an hour of peace afterward. I would do for a fugitive slave whatever I should like to have done for myself, under similar circumstances. If he asked my protection, I would extend it to him to the utmost of my power. If he was hungry, I would feed him. If he was naked, I would clothe him. If he needed advice, I would give him such as I thought would be most beneficial to him."

Among those whom Hopper could rely on to harbor fugitive slaves was his brother-in-law, John Tatem, who had a farm across the river in New Jersey. But experience had taught him to use whatever means available to enable fugitive slaves to escape. Sometimes it was merely the use of his own wits, as happened with a woman whose case he was monitoring for the abolition society in 1808.

Extremely light in complexion, she was able to pass for white and escaped from Virginia when she was sixteen. Settled in Philadelphia, she married and was raising two children when her master claimed her thirteen years later. A trial was held to determine the validity of his claim. Out of court, Hopper interceded, and with the help of the employer of her husband, they offered her master $400 for her manumission. However, the master refused to consider any offers.

The trial continued, and Hopper introduced the possibility that the slaveholder had mistakenly identified the woman as his slave, considering the lengthy passage of time. Then an idea flashed in his brain. Knowing that the judge had a reputation as someone who imbibed liberally in alcohol, and realizing that his faculties were somewhat dulled that afternoon, he proposed to have the case adjourned until the next day, and said that he and the woman's lawyer, Thomas Harrison, would be responsible to the United States for her appearance the next day. Both the judge and the slaveholder consented to this request.

It was then recorded on the court docket that Hopper and Harrison were bound to the United States for the sum of $1,000 to produce the woman in court the next morning. When the copy of the recognizance was signed by the judge, Hopper had completed his objective. He immediately put the woman in hiding.

The next day he and Harrison appeared in court without the woman. After waiting for her about an hour, the judge said, "Well gentlemen, if the woman does not make her appearance, I shall be obliged to forfeit your recognizance."

"A thousand dollars is a large sum to lose," Hopper said. "I suppose we must make up our minds to pay the United States all the claims they have upon us."

"The United States?" exclaimed the judge, who looked at his docket and realized that what Hopper said was correct. But the United States had no jurisdiction in the case. It was the slaveholder who was making the claim.

"If I have broken any law," Hopper said, "I stand ready to meet the consequences."

The slaveholder searched frantically for the woman. Finally, he gave up and agreed to sell her manumission, but Hopper forced him to sell her at the discounted price of $150.

As the *New York Times* wrote in his obituary, "[Hopper] battled courageously, not from ambition, but from an inborn love of truth. He circumvented as adroitly as the most practiced politician; but it was always to defeat the plans of those who oppressed God's poor; never to advance his own self-interest."

This was never better illustrated than in the case of a nine-year-old mulatto girl who was employed as an indenture and, as Hopper learned from neighbors, being beaten and abused. After visiting the home of her employer, M. Bouilla, and being rudely turned away, Hopper obtained a warrant and went with a constable to enter the residence.

When informed of the warrant, Bouilla, who was blind and lived on an upper floor, went and got a gun, and from his landing, threatened to shoot anyone who tried to enter his home. As the constable refused to proceed further, Hopper took off his shoes and tip-toed up the stairs. Just before Hopper was about to take the gun, Bouilla realized someone was close to him. There was a struggle between him and Hopper, and the gun went off. No one was injured, and Bouilla was disarmed.

Inside they found the girl, whose name was Amy, bruised and emaciated. The court entrusted her to Hopper, and he and his family cared for her until she was healthy and strong. Thereafter he found another family to raise her until she was eighteen.

Hopper was a busy man: an overseer of the Benezet School; a teacher who worked without pay educating black adults; an inspector of the prisons; a founder of a society devoted to finding employment for the poor; an advocate for blacks being denied their freedom. He also had a large family to support. His many obligations simply became too much for him, and in 1812, he went bankrupt. Many of his possessions were auctioned off to pay debts, and he and his family were forced to move into a house owned by his brother-in-law, where his wife, Sarah, opened a general store in the bottom floor.

But the greatest tragedy of Hopper's life occurred when his wife died in 1822, at the age of forty-seven. This loss was followed a year later by the death of his fifteen-year-old son, Isaac. Soon after this, Hopper took a trip south with his brother-in-law, David Tatem, to visit his two sisters who were living in Maryland. Along the way they stopped at an inn where a black girl brought in a pitcher of water. When he learned the girl was a slave, he exploded and protested loudly that it was against his principles to be waited upon by a slave. The mistress of the inn heard him and complained about her slaves.

"I had sixteen slaves," she said, "but ten of them have run away, and I expect the rest will soon go."

"I hope they will," Hopper said. "I am sure I would run away, if I were a slave."

Hopper, however, later apologized for offending her, and explained why he felt this way, and they left the inn on friendly terms. His brother-in-law later said in recalling the incident that "I never again will travel in a Southern state with brother Isaac, for I am sure it would be at the risk of my life."

Two years after the death of his wife, Hopper married Hannah Attmore, who had been a close friend of his wife. He was fifty-three and she, thirty-five. They would have four children, two of whom died in early childhood.

During this period, discord had been developing in the Quaker sect as a result of the teachings of Elias Hicks, who advocated an activist approach in opposing slavery and refraining from the use of products made from slave labor. The conflict became so bitter that a division occurred within the sect in 1827. The followers of Hicks became known as the Hicksites; those who disagreed were called Orthodox. Hopper was a strong supporter of Hicks, and this affected business at his tailor shop because many of his customers were Orthodox Quakers. With his business in Philadelphia declining, Hopper decided in 1829 to move to New York City, where he was asked to open a bookstore that specialized in Hicksite-related material.

His bookstore on Pearl Street became a meeting place for Hicksites, and his gregarious personality was a great attraction. He especially enjoyed recounting the many episodes of his life involving fugitive slaves. Not long after Hopper's move to New York, *The Liberator* ushered in the movement calling for immediate emancipation. Hopper was naturally among its supporters. But it grew slowly at first, and opposition was heated. In 1834 an anti-abolition riot occurred in New York in which the homes of blacks and prominent abolitionists were vandalized. Hopper was a target because he sold abolitionist newspapers and literature. However, when the mob approached his store, he walked out and stood on the steps and looked calmly and firmly at them, and instead of attacking him, the cry was to move on to Rose Street, the location of the home of Lewis Tappan, one of the city's most outspoken abolitionists.

The following year, a slave escaped from a Mississippi judge who was visiting New York. Because of his reputation, Hopper was accused of harboring the fugitive slave. A search warrant was obtained, but the authorities preferred to search the store in his absence, and waited until he left his son there alone. When Hopper's son made a sarcastic remark, one of the men assaulted him. Hopper returned soon after and went to look for the constable who had conducted the search. When Hopper found the man, he protested their intrusion upon his store and assault of his son, and traded insults with the constable and his men. It proved to be a mistake, for a few days later, Hopper's son was attacked and severely beaten.

The Fugitive Slave Law of 1793

Ironically, the Fugitive Slave Law of 1793 did not originate from a case involving a fugitive slave, but from one involving slavecatchers, or to be more accurate, kidnappers. In 1791 in Pennsylvania, a free black man was seized and taken to Virginia. When the governor of Pennsylvania demanded his return, Virginia's governor refused, citing that no law existed to compel him to do so. It prompted a congressional committee to prepare the 1793 law, which provided for the extradition of individuals from one state to another. Among those covered by the law were fugitive slaves who had fled from service.

It imposed a fine of $500—equal to $6,000 today—and up to one year in prison for those convicted of helping fugitive slaves. Testimony of a slaveowner or his representative before any legally appointed judge was enough to commit the alleged fugitive to slavery. However, because of the travel and time needed to apprehend slaves, slaveowners became dependent on slavecatchers. The provisions of the law also facilitated slavecatchers in kidnapping free blacks and selling them into slavery, a practice which was common even before its passage. Among its provisions was the suspension of alleged fugitive slaves' right to a jury trial or to testify on their own behalf.

In 1838 Hopper's abolitionist activities created problems for him again. Because the New York Monthly Meeting had looked with disfavor on joining societies outside the Friends community, New York Friends who were abolitionists, such as Hopper, did not join the American Anti-Slavery Society and its auxiliaries. As a result, Hopper, his son-in-law, James Gibbons, and Charles Marriott founded The New York Association of Friends for the Relief of Those Held in Slavery and the Improvement of the Free People of Color. Throughout this early period of the antislavery movement, abolitionists were attacked in the pulpit at Quaker meetings in New York, notably by George F. White. In fact, a majority of the leadership in the New York Meeting espoused an anti-abolitionist view. They were able to act upon their resentment of Hopper when he became embroiled in a scandalous incident that came close to destroying the sterling reputation he had developed in more than forty years of combat against slavery and work in the Underground Railroad.

At midnight during the autumn of 1838, two black men rang his doorbell. Hopper's son-in-law, James Gibbons, answered their call. They asked for Hopper's son, John. One of the men was a waiter at a local hotel, and the other, a fugitive slave named Thomas Hughes. Hopper was awakened, and he readily offered accommodations, something, as he later wrote, that wasn't unusual. However, his home wasn't the safest place for a fugitive slave, as already related, and Hughes was sent the next morning to the home of Margaret Shoemaker, another Quaker abolitionist.

The next day Hopper saw an advertisement in the newspaper offering a reward of $1,000 for the apprehension of a fugitive slave who had stolen $8,000. Hopper suspected it might be Hughes, and he went and asked if he had stolen the money. Hughes denied it, saying it was merely a strategy used by his owner, John Darg, to apprehend him. At first Hopper believed him.

But after consulting with another Quaker abolitionist, Barney Corse, New York Vigilance Committee secretary **David Ruggles**, the committee's lawyer, Horace Dresser, and the newspaper editor who published the advertisement, it appeared that Hughes did steal the money. Hopper's next objective was to recover the money for Darg, because he felt complicit as a result of harboring Hughes.

The first person Hopper spoke with was the waiter, Henry Clark, who had brought Hughes to Hopper's residence. After some prodding, Clark admitted that Hughes had stolen the money and that a large portion of it had been given to him for safekeeping, though he wasn't sure how much. When he checked the roll of bills, he found a sum of $5,800. He then revealed that another man, Bob Jackson, had received $1,025. When Jackson was located, they learned he had put the money in safekeeping with a man who lived in Albany, New York. Corse was then sent with Jackson to Albany, where they retrieved the money.

However, this still left them more than $1,000 short. Nevertheless, a meeting was set up between Hopper, Corse, and Darg for the return of the money thus far recovered. It was the intention of Hopper and Corse to obtain a signed agreement from Darg that he would drop all criminal charges, manumit Hughes, and pay the expenses of Corse in his efforts to recover Darg's money. However, their plans were frustrated by a sting concocted by New York City police in which they suddenly appeared just as Corse was about to hand over the money to Darg. Their intention was to convict the abolitionists as accessories to the theft of Darg's money

It was not long after this that Hughes turned himself in. While in jail an offer was made by the police to drop the charges against him if he would testify that Hopper and Corse had advised him to undertake the robbery of Darg. He agreed to this bargain, but the district attorney would not.

In the end Hughes was found guilty and sentenced to two years in Sing Sing Prison, and the charges against Corse and Hopper were dropped after Hopper made a compelling speech during the hearing in their defense and Corse agreed to pay Darg the missing $1,200.

Some weeks before the close of Hughes's prison sentence, Darg brought Hughes's wife to see him and promised to manumit him if he returned to the South to be with her. Hopper also visited him on the day before he was to leave prison and told him that he would legally be a free man on his release, and that the vigilance committee was ready to protect him if he remained in the North. However, Hughes chose to return to Darg, only to learn he had sold his wife and had no intention of manumitting him. As a result, Hughes once again fled north to gain his freedom.

The affair tarnished the reputation of Hopper and opened him to criticism from the New York Monthly Meeting. It was the opening for which the anti-abolitionist leadership was waiting. Falsehoods were trumpeted from the pulpit by White, which Hopper was not about to ignore. He publicly denounced White and exposed his lies. But when an article related to the feud appeared in the *National Anti-Slavery Standard*, it opened Hopper up to the possibility of disownment from the Meeting based on their rules of discipline that stated the following:

> Should any of our members print or publish any writing against the advice of the Meeting for Sufferings, or which tends to excite disunity and discord amongst us, they should be treated with; and if they cannot be convinced of the impropriety of their conduct, and condemn the same to the satisfaction of the Monthly Meeting, they should be disowned.

Hopper, along with his son-in-law, James Gibbon, and another abolitionist, Charles Marriott, who had flaunted the wishes of the Monthly Meeting in holding an executive position in the American Anti-Slavery Society, were disowned. What followed was a series of appeals that eventually reached the Yearly Meeting, with unsuccessful results, the process being subverted each step along the way by the Monthly Meeting, as Hopper would detail in his explanation and defense of his actions in an 1843 narrative. In resolving the affair, Hopper wrote the following:

> I cannot close, without embracing the present opportunity to declare my unqualified attachment to the Society of Friends. My admiration for its great leading principles . . . remain(s) wholly unabated and unshaken . . . . In taking a retrospect of my past life . . . my most cherished recollections . . . have bound me in close affection to that religious communion which was the choice of my early days, and the principles of which shall be the strength, support, and gladness of my latter years.

Hopper quickly moved on from this unfortunate incident, and at the age of sixty-nine, began an entirely new career in the field of journalism. Lydia Maria Child had been chosen to become the editor of the *National Anti-Slavery Standard*, the mouthpiece of the American Anti-Slavery Society. As she and her husband David, the new assistant editor, needed lodging, she turned to Hopper, who welcomed them into his household; as he was in need of a job, she hired him to be the newspaper's treasurer and book agent. Hopper also became a columnist, and on June 11, 1840, he penned his first "Tale of Oppression," which led to the creation of a bi-weekly column that began on October 22, 1840, and ran for more than three years, offering seventy-nine more tales.

In 1847, after the death of Rev. **Theodore Wright**, the president of the New York Committee of Vigilance, the committee was reorganized to reflect a more statewide organization. Hopper was chosen as its first president. During its first six months of operation, the committee assisted 166 fugitive slaves, a number that would increase dramatically after the passage of the second Fugitive Slave Law in 1850.

Much of Hopper's time during the last years of his life was spent in ministering to the needs of prisoners, something with which he had familiarity, having been an inspector of the prisons when he lived in Pennsylvania. He was assisted in this by his daughter, Abby Hopper Gibbons. A fitting description of Hopper was given when defending himself against the false charges made at his hearing in the Hughes case:

> I have no wish to evade the charge against me for being an abolitionist. I am an abolitionist. In that, I am charged truly. I have been an abolitionist from my early years, and I always expect to remain so. For this, I am prosecuted and persecuted. I most sincerely believe that slavery is the greatest sin the Lord Almighty ever suffered to exist upon this earth. As sure as God is good and just, he will put an end to it; and all opposition will be in vain. As

> regards myself, I can only say, that having lived three-score and nearly ten years, with a character that placed me above suspicion in such matters as have been urged against me, I cannot now forego the principles which have always influenced my conduct in relation to slavery. Neither force on the one hand, nor persuasion on the other, will ever alter my course of action.

SUGGESTED READING: Fergus Bordewich, *Bound for Canaan*, New York: HarperCollins, 2005; L. Maria Child, *Isaac T. Hopper: A True Life*, Boston: John P. Jewett and Company, 1853; Isaac Hopper, "Narrative of The Proceedings of The Monthly Meeting of New York, and Their Subsequent Confirmation by the Quarterly and Yearly Meeting, in the Case of Isaac T. Hopper," New York, 1843; Daniel Meaders, "Kidnapping Blacks in Philadelphia: Isaac Hopper's Tales of Oppression," *The Journal of Negro History*, Vol. 80, No. 2, Spring, 1995; William Still, *The Underground Railroad*, Philadelphia: Porter and Coates, 1872.

Hussey, Erastus (1800–1889). Erastus Hussey made a significant contribution to ending slavery not only on the public stage, but also behind the scenes. He was one of Michigan's foremost abolitionist politicians as well as one of its most important Underground Railroad conductors.

Born in Cayuga County, New York, Hussey was a follower of the Quaker faith. As a youth he learned the professions of farming and teaching. At the age of twenty, he went to western New York in search of land to farm. But finding none to his satisfaction, he moved in 1824 to Michigan, which was still a wilderness. Much of his journey he made on foot. He traveled to a section where there were few settlers, and searched until he found a parcel of land that met his expectations. After making the trek to Detroit to enter his claim on 160 acres in the town on Plymouth, he took a boat to Erie, Pennsylvania, and then walked ninety miles to Collins, New York, where he taught school during the winter. He returned to Michigan in the summer of 1826 to develop his land, and found settlements there were booming. Back in Cayuga County, New York, that winter, he married Sarah Eddy Bowen, and in the summer of 1827, they set out for Michigan to homestead his property.

True pioneers, they started out in a shack that Hussey had built the prior summer, cultivating wheat and other crops. He also bought a cow and began cutting logs for a more comfortable lodging. They moved into their finished log house on New Year's Day in 1828, and shortly after, Sarah gave birth to their first and only child, Susan. Improvements to their land continued with the planting of apple trees and the building of another house.

A series of misfortunes forced a return to Cayuga County, where he taught school to recover his finances. They returned to Michigan the following year, where he resumed farming and sometimes taught school during the winters. He also became involved in local government, which he continued throughout most of his life. In 1836 Hussey sold the farm and traveled with his family in his own carriage through Ohio, Pennsylvania, New York, and New England. In 1838 they moved to Battle Creek, where they settled for the remainder of his life.

He went into the business of boot and shoe manufacture, and opened a grocery. The next year he sold out to his partner and took up the dry-goods business. He also became involved in politics as a member of the Whig party, and after losing two elections, became town clerk on his third try. In 1840 he supported Harrison for president, believing he would work to weaken slavery, but the sudden death of Harrison ended those hopes, and he shifted his support to the emerging antislavery Liberty Party.

It was about this time that Rev. **John Cross** from Galesburg, Illinois, paid a visit. Hussey was away on business, and Cross told Sarah that he wanted to talk to her husband about an urgent and confidential matter. Some time afterward, Cross explained the reason for his visit in a letter. He was establishing a line of the Underground Railroad from Illinois to Detroit, and wanted Hussey to manage the station in Battlecreek. At the time, Hussey later wrote, there were only five antislavery men there in addition to himself: Silas Dodge, who later moved to Vineland, N.J; Abel Densmore, who died in Rochester; Henry Willis; Theron E. Chadwick; and Samuel Strauther. It was the first time, he said, that he had ever heard of the Underground Railroad.

The date when Hussey "accepted" his agency in the Underground, as he described it in an 1885 interview, is unclear. Some place it as early as 1840. Others suggest 1844, when **Levi Coffin** and **William Beard** visited him on their first trip to Canada to check on fugitive slaves whom they had assisted. The latter date seems more likely because Hussey said the first fugitive slaves he helped were still being hidden by him when Coffin and Beard paid their visit.

In any case, he said that at that time he was living in a two-story wood-frame house that he had repaired. He used the lower front as a store, and the second floor for his residence. The lower rear of the building was the first location he hid fugitive slaves. In 1847 he invested in a commercial development of brick buildings, which were used for stores; these were called the Union block. Thereafter he hid fugitive slaves in one of them.

Hussey received fugitive slaves not only from the Illinois line managed by Cross, but also from the Indiana line managed by Coffin. Both were well traveled, so it's apparent that both contributed to the more than 1,000 fugitive slaves Hussey claimed to have fed and transported.

The route through Michigan came by way of Cassopolis, whose leader was Zachariah Shugart. A Quaker settlement at Young's Prairie had sprung up there, and not far from it, Ramptown, a community of blacks, many of whom had fled from slavery. The station after that was in Schoolcraft, and the agent was Nathan Thomas. The route continued on through Battlecreek, Marshall, Jackson, Ann Arbor, and finally to Detroit. Other smaller connecting stations included Albion, Parma, Michigan Center, Leoni, Grass Lake, Francisco, Dexter, Scio, and Geddes.

Hussey said the pass phrase was, "Can you give shelter and protection to one or more persons?" Generally, he drove the fugitive slaves to the next station, which was the home of Jabez Finch in Marshall, a distance of about ten miles.

In 1847 the *Michigan Liberty Press* started publication as the organ of the state Liberty Party, and Hussey was made editor. In a short time, however, he assumed responsibility for its entire operation. At first, he encountered resistance from the postmaster, who was reluctant to deliver the *Liberty Press* to subscribers. This did not deter Hussey, and for a time, he traveled throughout the state to deliver it himself. In his absence, his wife Sarah filled in as editor. His efforts were rewarded, as the paper helped to shape public opinion in favor of abolition.

Around this time, slaveholders in the counties of Carroll, Boone, and Bourbon, Kentucky, who had absorbed heavy losses because of slaves who had fled through the Underground Railroad, had begun organizing and discussing how they might recover them. They had learned that a large number of their slaves were living in southern Michigan.

To learn their exact whereabouts, they sent spies. The first one, Francis Troutman, posed as a schoolteacher, and tracked down the location of the Crosswhite family, who had escaped from Troutman's uncle in Carroll County, Kentucky, in 1843. They had settled in Marshall. On the morning of January 26, 1847, Troutman and three other men broke into Crosswhite's house and attempted to abduct him and his family. However, neighbors were alerted, and dozens of armed men surrounded the house and prevented them from leaving.

Before long, several hundred citizens from Marshall had gathered, and the Kentuckians were forced to submit to the judicial process. During the next two days, hearings were held while locals forwarded the Crosswhites to Canada. Troutman ended up returning to Kentucky after paying a $100 fine for housebreaking.

A second spy, using the name Carpenter, was sent to Kalamazoo posing as a Massachusetts abolitionist. He learned that Quakers in Calhoun and Cass counties were assisting fugitive slaves. On visiting them, he learned the whereabouts of a number of former Kentucky slaves.

Not coincidentally, thirteen Kentuckians led by Boone County Sheriff John L. Graves arrived in Battle Creek in August 1847. They posed as salesmen offering a new type of washing machine. Hussey was alerted and somehow discovered their true design. He went to their hotel and asked that they meet him in the hotel tavern. He then told them that their ruse had been uncovered and that once it became known to the townspeople, their lives might be in danger. After some consideration, the slavecatchers agreed to leave.

However, they were not about to abandon their mission, and Hussey, anticipating this, sent letters of warning to Cass County. Also sending a warning by way of a courier on horseback was Levi Coffin in Newport, Indiana, who had learned through his sources of the slavecatchers' mission to abduct former slaves in Cass County. But the warnings came too late.

After returning south to Indiana for a brief period, Graves led the group of Kentuckians into Cass County on August 16. They had maps, apparently made by Carpenter, which pinpointed the houses of fugitive slaves. They split into three groups.

At nightfall, one group went to the farm of Quaker Josiah Osborn, where a family of five former slaves occupied a small house. The three men were seized, but the mother and daughter escaped by jumping from a window. They quickly alerted neighbors, who rushed to the scene. The slavecatchers' plan had been to wait for their associates, but with angry locals gathering, they decided to move on.

The second group had gone to the farm of Quaker William East, where they captured three men, a woman, and a two-year-old child. One of the slavecatchers, Rev. A. Stevens, a Baptist minister, claimed the child as his property.

The third group went to the neighborhood of Zachariah Shugart, who had leased land to a family of former slaves. The husband was seized, but his wife escaped and gave the alarm. Shugart rode to the house of Stephen Bogue, who lived about two miles west and had a very fast horse. Bogue then raced into Cassopolis and roused the residents.

Meanwhile the slavecatchers had moved on to the farm of Stephen Bogue, where a former slave put up a great resistance and was badly wounded with the butt end of a riding whip, which cut a gash through his ear and across the side of his head.

They turned south toward Odell's Mill, to rendezvous with their associates. When they met them, they noticed a group of locals watching. About the same time, a much larger group of men from Cassopolis arrived armed with guns, axes, and clubs. Their leaders were Moses Brown, a powerfully built blacksmith, and "Nigger Bill" Jones, a Quaker who had been to Kentucky and had helped slaves escape. They far outnumbered the slavecatchers. Nevertheless, a battle seemed imminent, but Jones managed to disarm one of the slavecatchers who had drawn his gun. Though it was obvious the slavecatchers would not win this battle, the Quakers advised settling it lawfully and peacefully at the local courthouse in Cassopolis.

It was about 9:00 a.m. when they arrived, followed by a crowd of angry locals that had grown to as many as 300 persons. A telegram was sent to Niles, Michigan, requesting two abolitionist lawyers, E. S. Smith and James Sullivan, to represent the former slaves, and to request that Berrien County commissioner Ebenezer McIlvain be brought in to hear the case, because the Cass County commissioner was unavailable. The Kentuckians were unaware that McIlvain was part of the local Underground Railroad.

Though, based on the law, the Kentuckians had every right to seize their property, it was an open-and-shut case for McIlvain. He ordered the release of the nine fugitives. Shortly after, Zachariah Shugart and nine guards escorted a party of forty-five blacks to Battlecreek. When charges against the slavecatchers were finally dropped, their slaves were out of reach, and they were forced to return to Kentucky empty-handed.

The Kentucky Slavecatchers' Raids into Michigan

During the 1840s, slaveholders in the counties of Carroll, Boone, and Bourbon, Kentucky learned that many of their slaves who had escaped via the Underground Railroad had settled among the Quaker settlements in southern Michigan. In an attempt to recover them, they planned a series of raids, during which they tried to trick and surprise the residents there.

In September of 1849, the last of three raids they made into southern Michigan occurred when they attempted to abduct the David Powell family in Cass County. This one was nearly successful, as the slavecatchers made it as far as South Bend, Indiana, before they were overtaken by a posse of Quakers, who forced them to return to South Bend and let the matter be decided by the courts. As in the two prior attempts, the Kentuckians were thwarted, and the judge freed the Powells, who were sent to Canada.

In all three Kentucky raids, the higher courts overturned the local decisions and awarded judgments to the slaveholders, some of which were paid. It was a small price to pay. Not only did the actions of local citizens deter further attempts by slaveholders to come to Michigan, it preserved the freedom of a large number of black Americans.

Richard Dillingham, the Ohio Quaker who would later become a noted martyr to the abolitionist cause, was sent on ahead to the house of Hussey to inform him that forty-five fugitive slaves would be arriving.

Hussey immediately called a meeting with Abel Densmore, Silas Dodge, and Samuel Strauther to plan how they would prepare to receive that large a number of fugitive slaves.

They were able to obtain the use of a vacant building, Dodge getting the potatoes, and Strauther, the pork. It was a moonlit night when they arrived in Battlecreek, and by the time they arrived, everyone knew they were coming, and every man, woman, and child was out on the street. Hussey said "it looked as if the circus was coming to town." Nine white men on horseback escorted the blacks, with Zach Shugart in the lead wearing a broad-brimmed white hat. He spoke with Hussey, and then commanded the group in a military manner, saying, "Right about face!" They followed his order and marched down to the vacant building. They cooked their own dinner with food provided, and the next morning, the majority of them left for Canada. However, a few stayed and settled, the most notable being William Casey, who joined the local Underground Railroad.

On another occasion, word came that thirty armed men were coming to Battle Creek. Hussey and another man had 500 handbills printed saying that the abolitionists were prepared to confront them and advising them to stay away. Hussey sent them with an individual on the railroad, who posted them in every station. At Niles he met the slavecatchers, who, after seeing the handbills, decided to turn back.

In 1848 the convention of the successor to the more radical Liberty Party, the more broadly based Free-Soil Party, met at Buffalo. Hussey was in attendance as a delegate from Michigan. It was there that he finally met his Underground Railroad recruiter Rev. John Cross.

The following year the building that housed the *Liberty Press* was destroyed by fire. Hussey moved the newspaper to Marshall and published a few issues, but soon after, he abandoned it and concentrated on working in the political arena. That year he was elected under the Free-Soil banner to the Michigan State legislature. He also was elected Calhoun County clerk in 1850, and to the Michigan State senate in 1854. Among the organizers of the Republican Party, he introduced Michigan's Personal Liberty Bill, which protected the state of Michigan from kidnappers and secured the rights of fugitive slaves. It passed both houses by a large majority.

After 1855, Hussey said, the Underground Railroad traffic through Battlecreek decreased, and more fugitive slaves escaped through Ohio via the Erie Lake ports, such as Sandusky. One of the reasons also could've been because fugitive slaves were able to take trains directly to those ports. In 1856 and 1860, he took an active role in campaigning for Republican candidates John C. Fremont and Abraham Lincoln for president, and in 1859, he hosted **John Brown** during his storied flight with fugitive slaves from Missouri. The last public office he held was as mayor of Battle Creek, a post to which he was elected in 1867.

When asked if he and his associates ever received any pay for their work in the Underground Railroad, he would say, "We were working for humanity." Though it was never easy, he stood up for what he believed and the truth of his beliefs prevailed because he persisted. "Rather stand up assured with conscious pride, alone," he wrote describing his philosophy of life in a short poem, "than err with millions on thy side."

SUGGESTED READING: David G. Charavoyne, "Michigan and the Fugitive Slave Acts," *The Court Legacy*, Vol. 12, No. 3, November 2004; Larry Massie, "The Husseys of Battle Creek," *Encore Magazine*, October 2007; "The Underground Railroad and The Kentucky Raid," *The History of Cass County, Michigan*, Chicago: Waterman, Watkins & Co.,1882; "Battlecreek as a Station on the Underground Railroad," Siebert Collection, 48-01-05, interview with Erastus Hussey by Charles E. Barnes, *Michigan Pioneer and Historical*, 1885.

Hyde, Udney (1808–?). Udney Hyde, by his own account, aided 517 fugitive slaves. His fearless activities led to his involvement in the **Addison White** affair, one of the most prominent abduction attempts by slavecatchers in the annals of the Underground Railroad.

Born in Vermont, Hyde settled in Mechanicsburg, Ohio, where he was a farmer, clock peddler, and blacksmith. His participation in the Underground Railroad began in 1851, some time after the establishment of the route through Mechanicsburg by Joseph Ware. He said he first realized the righteousness of the cause of aiding fugitive slaves one day while observing young lambs being separated from their mothers. He noticed that the black sheep mourned for their lambs as much as the white. This made him realize that aiding fugitive slaves would be "keeping the laws of God." So he agreed to forward fugitive slaves from Ware's "catacombs," the name given to the intricate cellar where Ware harbored fugitive slaves.

Mechanicsburg, Ohio, abolitionist Udney Hyde. Courtesy of the Ohio Historical Society.

Most of those slaves escaping through Mechanicsburg came from Kentucky by way of Ripley, Ohio. On Hyde's first mission, he assisted seven fugitive slaves, all of whom stayed the night at Hyde's residence. The next morning he loaded them in his wagon and covered them up with hay. Among the fugitive slaves was a free black man named Penny from Ripley, Ohio.

Penny wanted to marry a slave girl owned by a Baptist preacher in Kentucky. Penny had made a bargain to work for the preacher for a year to pay for her emancipation. However, at the year's end, the preacher reneged, gave Penny $40, and told him to leave his property. The following Saturday night, Penny returned and carried off not only his sweetheart but her sister, her brother-in-law, and another man. They vowed that they would become free or die, and that if anyone tried to turn back, Penny would shoot them. When they reached the banks of the Ohio River, they were confronted by slavecatchers. There was an exchange of shots that wounded one of the slavecatchers and one of the slaves. Nevertheless, they crossed the river, leaving the wounded man with friends in Ripley, and moved up through the Underground Railroad to Mechanicsburg.

Hyde was known for his boldness, which disarmed his adversaries. One time, he had retrieved a slave who was of very light complexion during a trip to Ripley to get castings for his blacksmith shop. The roads were under close surveillance by federal marshals, and he decided to move her on to the next destination by dressing her in his wife's clothing with a bonnet and veil. They mounted two horses and headed toward Delaware, Ohio, where William Cratty, among others, maintained a station. Everything went well until they approached Bellepointe, along the Scioto River, where he realized they were being followed. The girl looked back and thought it was her master. Fortunately, they were nearing their destination, the farm of a Quaker preacher. Hyde told her to keep jerking on the right rein to make the horse prance, so as to keep her back facing the approaching riders and gave her directions to the clearing that led to the Quaker's farm.

"No matter what happens," he said, "pay no attention, just keep sauntering on down the road."

As the slavecatchers closed in, Hyde called out to the fugitive slave, addressing her as if she were his wife. When they rounded a bend, she sped off the road through the clearing that led directly to the Quaker farm, with Hyde following. The slavecatchers continued their pursuit, and as the fugitive slave reached the farmhouse, Hyde turned and approached them. They came to a halt.

"Now if you fellows ever follow me and my wife again," Hyde said as the fugitive slave took shelter in the preacher's house, "I'll shoot you."

Another time while transporting a load of fugitive slaves concealed in his wagon, he was asked by a posse of slavecatchers what was under the hay. Hyde responded, "Niggers, God damn you!"

Startled, they let him proceed.

Hyde's guile and ability to disguise his emotions were what enabled him to successfully transport so many fugitive slaves without one ever being returned to slavery. For instance, a fugitive slave frantically knocked on his door seeking a shelter from slavecatchers who followed close behind. At once Hyde hid the fugitive slave in his false-bottom wagon and headed back in the direction the fugitive slave had come. After a time, they came upon the wagon of a slaveholder whom Hyde knew.

"Here comes a slave-holder I know," he said. "I'll have to talk to him."

The wagons drew alongside and conversation began. The slaveholder, seeing that Hyde was headed south instead of north, cracked, "Why aren't you helpin' niggers, Hyde?"

"Well, if I knew of any needin' help, I would be helpin' 'em," Hyde replied. Then they went on their way. Hyde continued south for some distance, then turned and followed a roundabout route back to his house, concealing the fugitive slave in his cellar that night. Nevertheless, the authorities remained suspicious and visited Hyde. To allay their suspicions, he asked them to sleep over. But they never discovered that the fugitive slave was sleeping right below them.

Another time Hyde barely escaped detection was when he was hauling some fugitive slaves and his wagon got stuck in the mud. While attempting to extricate the wagon, Hyde was approached by federal marshals. They wanted to help and suggested he unload the wagon.

"I'll kill the damned horses first!" he shouted.

Fortunately, he managed to get the wagon out of the mud and to the next station.

In Mechanicsburg, Hyde most often hid fugitive slaves in his cellar, and on one occasion, a woman gave birth there. He also hid them in a livery stable and in a well in which he had a platform installed on which the fugitive slaves could rest while awaiting transport.

During the spring of 1857, Hyde moved from the village of Mechanicsburg to a farm about two and a half miles away. It was here that the most memorable incident of his days as a conductor occurred. More than likely his role in the Underground Railroad would have been lost to history if it hadn't been for the notoriety of his involvement with the fugitive slave **Addison White**.

One morning late in August of 1856, James Hunt, who lived in Catawba, about five miles south of Mechanicsburg, awoke to find the large and powerfully built White sitting outside on a woodpile. After feeding him, Hunt took him to Hyde.

White explained to Hyde that he had come into conflict with his owner, who had hired an overseer to beat him, but that White was the one who gave the beating. This outraged his owner, and White left before any more trouble occurred. As Hyde recently had injured his foot, he suggested that White remain and help with his chores while Hyde recovered. After this, Hyde promised to transport him along the Underground Railroad if he desired. Unfortunately, prior to this, White's owner learned of his whereabouts through mail White had sent his wife in Kentucky that had been intercepted by the postmaster.

White's master came to town in April of 1857 in search of him, but without luck. Thereafter there were frequent visits from federal marshals. At daybreak on May 21, 1857, five Kentucky slavecatchers, accompanied by three federal marshals, entered Hyde's homestead. They had been spotted by White, who took a gun and climbed into the loft in Hyde's cabin, where he was able to hold them off until help arrived from Mechanicsburg.

Fearing arrest, Hyde left his home and went into hiding for the next eight months, moving between various places, including locations in Indiana. Authorities returned six days later and arrested his son, Russell, and three others for obstructing justice. The party was followed by citizens of Mechanicsburg, and when it appeared they were going to take them to Kentucky to possibly face more serious charges, a writ of habeas corpus was obtained and a posse assembled to head them off. A confrontation occurred, and the marshals were lodged in jail. A lengthy court case followed.

As for Addison White, he also was sent into hiding. In settling the controversy, the citizens of Mechanicsburg purchased his freedom for $950, and after serving in the Civil War, he remarried and settled in Mechanicsburg.

Life eventually went back to normal again for Udney Hyde. After his first wife died, he married a woman twenty-seven years his junior and raised a second family.

SUGGESTED READING: Benjamin F. Prince, "The Rescue Case of 1857," *Ohio History*, Vol. 16, No. 3, July 1907; Ralph M. Watts, "History Of The Underground Railroad In Mechanicsburg," *Ohio History*, Vol. 43, No. 3, July 1934.

J

Jackson, Francis (1789–1861). Francis Jackson was born into a prominent Boston family that held sacred the principles of freedom and equality, which his father fought to gain in the Revolutionary War. A local government official and judge, Jackson and his brother William were strong supporters of abolitionist editor William Lloyd Garrison, which led to their involvement in Boston's Underground Railroad.

A prosperous lawyer and veteran of the War of 1812, Jackson was a lifelong temperance advocate, and later an advocate for women's rights. But the cause of antislavery claimed his greatest devotion. His belief in Garrison's view that the Constitution was a proslavery document finally caused Jackson to resign his position as a justice of the peace in 1844. He could not in good conscience serve a government whose constitution contained "provisions calculated and intended to foster, cherish, uphold and perpetuate slavery."

His leadership skills pressed him into service as president of the Massachusetts Anti-Slavery Society, and in 1850 when the Boston Vigilance Committee organized for a second time, he was made its treasurer, not only administering its financial operations but avidly participating in aiding and harboring fugitive slaves. In 1853 Jackson purchased the property at 66 Southac Street (then numbered 8), which was the home of the committee's most active conductor, **Lewis Hayden**. Living in a house owned by such a respected member of Boston society like Jackson provided Hayden with some insulation from legal interference.

Jackson was forced to resign his position as treasurer of the committee in 1859 because of poor health. He stated in his letter that though he was resigning, he would continue to aid "fugitive slaves, who for the last twelve or fifteen years have had much of my time and assistance. I cannot deny them, while I have any strength left."

Jackson's greatest contribution was his work behind the scenes, helping to administer the operations of Boston's Underground Railroad. His Boston Vigilance Committee Treasurers Accounts book, which has been preserved for posterity, is one of the most remarkable documents of the Underground Railroad, providing the financial and logistical details related to more than 300 fugitive slaves helped by the committee.

In his will, Jackson bequeathed more than $17,000 to fund activities to aid fugitive slaves, to end slavery, and to procure women's rights. Another $5,000 went to individual abolitionists in appreciation of their efforts to end slavery.

SUGGESTED READING: In memoriam: Testimonials to the life and character of the late Francis Jackson, Boston: R. F. Wallcut, 1861; Wilbur H. Siebert, *The Underground Railroad in Massachusetts,* Worcester: American Antiquarian Society, 1936; Harold Parker Williams, "Brookline in the Anti-Slavery Movement," Brookline, MA: Brookline Historical Publication Society, Publication Number 18, 1899.

Jackson, William (1783–1859). A member of a prominent, patriotic Boston family, William Jackson served in the U.S. Congress. He became a supporter of abolitionist William Lloyd Garrison, and helped his brother Francis in the management of Boston's Underground Railroad.

Jackson served two terms in the U.S. Congress, from 1833 to 1837. He later joined the Liberty Party and was president of the American Missionary Society, organizations which had connections to Underground Railroad activities. His home in Newton, Massachusetts was frequently used as a part of the network that connected with Brookline and the safe house operated by **William Bowditch**. A sewing circle also met at the Jackson homestead to make clothes for the fugitive slaves.

Interestingly, the family's Underground Railroad connections were enlarged through marriage when Jackson's daughter married Lewis Tappan, one of the nation's leading abolitionists and a member of the New York Committee of Vigilance.

In 1894 Jackson's daughter Ellen recalled a typical incident involving the Underground Railroad at the Jackson homestead:

> One night, between twelve and one o'clock, I well remember, father was awakened by pebbles thrown against his window. He rose, asked what was wanted. Mr. Bowditch replied, it was he with a runaway slave whom he wished father to hide until morning, and then help him on his way to Canada, for his master was in Boston looking for him. Father took him in and next morning carried him fifteen miles to a Station where he could take a car for Canada. He could not have safely left by any Boston station.

William Lloyd Garrison: "I Will Be Heard!"

On January 1, 1831, abolitionist William Lloyd Garrison launched his weekly newspaper, *The Liberator*, with these resounding and prophetic words:

> I shall contend for the immediate enfranchisement of our slave population. I will be as harsh as truth and as uncompromising as justice on this subject. I do not wish to think, or speak, or write with moderation. I am in earnest. I will not equivocate. I will not retreat a single inch, and I will be heard!

It was the beginning of an enterprise that would continue for nearly thirty-five years in its denunciation of slavery.

Garrison began as a printer in his hometown, Newburyport, Massachusetts. He moved to the *Journal of the Times* in Bennington, Vermont, where he became interested in the issue of slavery, at that time supporting gradual emancipation. In Vermont he met the noted abolitionist journalist Benjamin Lundy, who asked him to work with him on his newspaper, *The Genius of Universal Emancipation.*

In Baltimore Garrison saw the evils of slavery firsthand. He also spent time in the black community and learned of their opposition to the colonization society and its idea to send free blacks back to Africa. He later articulated this position in an influential pamphlet, "Thoughts on African Colonization." While working for *The Genius*, Garrison wrote that a New England sea captain was participating in the illegal international slave trade. The captain prosecuted him for libel, and Garrison ended up in jail for seven weeks until the evangelical abolitionist Arthur Tappan paid his fine.

He returned to Boston and began to publish *The Liberator*, whose offices would later be used to harbor fugitive slaves and as a meeting place for the Boston Vigilance Committee.

Interestingly, a Jackson family member, Francis Merriam, was among the men who joined **John Brown** in the assault on Harpers Ferry, and one of the few who escaped with his life.

SUGGESTED READING: Wilbur H. Siebert, *The Underground Railroad in Massachusetts,* Worcester: American Antiquarian Society, 1936; Harold Parker Williams, "Brookline in the Anti-Slavery Movement," Brookline, MA: Brookline Historical Publication Society, Publication Number 18, 1899.

Jones, John W. (1817–1900). One of the most active Underground Railroad agents in New York State, John Jones supervised the burial of Confederate soldiers who died in the federal prison established in Elmira in 1864. His careful organization of their personal records provided comfort to many Southerners who lost relatives during the Civil War. It is perhaps ironic that a former slave, a man who escaped to gain his freedom, would provide this service of mercy to those who had enslaved him. But John W. Jones was a true humanitarian.

Born in Leesburg, Virginia, on a large plantation, Jones was the favorite servant of the mistress Sally Ellzey and grew up under the care of his mother and grandmother. However, he never knew his father, who was sold before he was born. His first thought of becoming free occurred as a boy when he saw a flock of wild geese. He asked his grandmother where they were going, and she replied, "Up north where there is no slavery."

As his mistress grew older, her health began to decline, and she stopped managing her plantation and began to hire out her slaves. Jones, who had always been well treated, worried that he would be passed on to a relative or some other slaveholder who would not treat him as well. The idea of going north now became more than just a boyhood dream, and he confided to his mother that he wished to flee with his two half-brothers, Charles and George. She agreed it was for the best.

"In the name of God," she said, "if you can get away clear with the boys, I will be happy as long as I live, for my time on earth is short."

On June 3, 1844, he said good-bye to his mother, whom he never saw again, and set out on foot for his freedom with his half-brothers and two other slaves. They took enough food to last four days and a change of clothing. They also armed themselves with pistols, and Jones added a carving knife from his mistress's kitchen.

After traveling eighteen miles the first night, they hid in a barn. They continued this way, traveling by night and hiding during the day until they reached Maryland, when they felt they could abandon their nighttime travel. This was a mistake because they were soon confronted by three slavecatchers, who quickly withdrew once they realized the fugitive slaves were armed. The next day, however, they encountered a man who pretended to have a problem with his horse and kept stopping ahead of them as if he were monitoring their progress. Their suspicions were confirmed when they were approached by a posse of twelve men. Jones and his companions raced up a nearby forested hillside, which prevented the men from pursuing them on horseback.

Finally, Jones and the others arrived safely in the free state of Pennsylvania. Though it didn't prevent slavecatchers from pursuing them, it did make them feel safer. After continuing their journey for another 150 miles, they came to a farm in New York, near Elmira, owned by Nathaniel and Sarah Smith. They snuck into the Smiths' barn, "more dead then alive," and sunk into a haymow to rest. Mrs. Smith discovered them, and fed and cared for them, helping to restore their health.

Elmira, New York, abolitionist John W. Jones. Courtesy of the Ohio Historical Society.

After staying at the Smith farm for about a week, they arrived in Elmira on July 5, 1844. The city had a small but growing black population of 215 persons according to the 1850 census, and a small but staunch core of abolitionists who were ready to aid fugitive slaves. Their leader was Jervis Langdon, a prosperous businessman and the future father-in-law of Samuel Clemens, better known as Mark Twain.

That very year Langdon, Ed Messer, and Augustus Holt assisted a band of thirty-nine fugitive slaves who were making their way toward Canada while being pursued by slavecatchers. According to an 1876 letter written by Holt, a black preacher and Messer were each leading a party of fugitive slaves moving toward each other from different directions. Both groups met Langdon and Holt, who came in a carriage filled with supplies at a prearranged destination about nine miles outside Elmira. They distributed food and clothing, and gave them each $5 to help them along their way. Before they departed, Langdon led them in a prayer, asking God for their protection. They traveled by night along the Underground Railroad until they reached Oswego, where a schooner was chartered that took them to Canada.

Langdon was instrumental in Jones's success. For a time, Jones resided with him, and on one occasion when slavecatchers were passing through, Langdon had to put him in hiding in another part of town. On another occasion, during the summer of 1845, Langdon was called into the office of a judge who asked that his name be kept secret. The judge, knowing of Langdon's work in the Underground, informed him that two slaveholders accompanied by Southern law-enforcement officers were on their way to Elmira with a warrant for twelve local fugitive slaves. In fact, there were at least seventeen fugitive slaves then residing there.

Some of the men were working on farms outside of town, and Langdon's business partner at the time, Sylvester Andrus, went on horseback to warn them. He arrived only fifteen minutes before the slaveowners, but it was enough time for the fugitives to go into hiding. When it was safe, they moved on to Canada, though some eventually returned and settled in Elmira.

It would be several years before Jones took a leadership role in the Underground Railroad. When he arrived he could not read or write, so he attempted to enroll in school. But both of Elmira's public schools refused to admit him. Judge Ariel E. Thurston was impressed with him, however, and proposed that Jones should come to live with his family. The judge offered Jones a job as a caretaker at his sister's school for girls. Coincidentally, another one of the judge's tenants was Hugh Riddle, who operated one of the schools that had refused to admit Jones. Finally, Riddle agreed to accept him. Nevertheless, Jones credited a fellow fourteen-year-old student named Loop as the one who taught him to read and write.

"I might say I went to school to him, for he was the real teacher who took pains and taught me to read and write."

A busy canal town and transportation center, Elmira offered work for Jones. In October, 1847, he was appointed sexton (caretaker) of the First Baptist Church, a position he would hold for forty-three years. He also became assistant caretaker of the church's cemetery, and shortly after, caretaker of the Second Street Cemetery. As Jones secured his livelihood, the city became increasingly abolitionized. A schism occurred in the First Presbyterian Church because of a proslavery sermon given by its pastor. Among its leaders who helped form a new antislavery Congregational Church were Langdon, Andrus, and John Selover. Jones was soon to find another line of work, one that he did on the side.

After the second Fugitive Slave Law was passed, Jones became secretary of a society of "the colored citizens of Elmira," formed "for the purpose of protecting ourselves against those persons, [slave-catchers] prowling through different parts of this and other states," and reported their formation to *The Liberator*. For the next eleven years or more, his other line of work required him to be on call day and night.

During this time Jones formed an association with **William Still**, of the Philadelphia Vigilance Committee, and by the middle of the 1850s, had become known to the many

Underground Railroad conductors in southern Pennsylvania who worked with Still. An arrangement also had been worked out with the Northern Central Railroad so that Jones could forward fugitive slaves in the baggage car of the 4:00 a.m. train that took passengers to Canandaigua, where they picked up the New York Central Railroad that went all the way to St. Catherine's, Canada West. In addition to his black associates who harbored fugitive slaves, Jones also was able to call on the daughter of one of Elmira's pioneer citizens, Mrs. John Culp, who was the first person to employ Jones when he arrived, and Riggs Watrous, a member of his church.

The son of Charles Manley of Alba, Pennsylvania, later wrote that Manley—who operated an Underground Railroad station twenty-five miles south of Elmira—forwarded many fugitive slaves directly to Watrous.

In 1854 Jones bought a house next to the Baptist church. Two years later he married Rachel Swails, with whom he had three sons—one who died at the age of three—and a daughter. The Jones household must have been lively during this time, full of children and playing host to as many as thirty fugitive slaves at one time.

It is unknown how many fugitive slaves Jones aided. One estimate claims 860. But Jones was the first to admit he could not have done it without help, and most significantly the help of Jervis Langdon. When asked what part Langdon played in the local Underground Railroad, Jones said, "He was all of it, giving me at one [time] his last dollar, when he did not know where another would come from." Of course, Jones needed Langdon's money and support, but it was Jones who coordinated the efforts, found places to harbor fugitive slaves, and moved them on to Canada.

In 1859, while still very active in his Underground Railroad activities, Jones was appointed caretaker of the newly developed Woodlawn Cemetery. It was this appointment that led to the second important service he fulfilled in his life, burying Confederate prisoners of war. During the Civil War, a prison was built in Elmira to house captured Confederate soldiers. Conditions were shockingly unsanitary, and many of the prisoners became ill and died. To accommodate their remains, a section of Woodlawn was leased.

"The first day that I was called in my capacity," Jones wrote, "I thought nothing of it. Directly there were more dead. One day I had seven to bury. After that they began to die very fast."

The unsanitary conditions, starvation, lack of medical care, and exposure to subzero temperatures made Elmira Prison a living hell, far worse than any Southern prisoner-of-war camp.

With as many as forty-three prisoners dying in a single day, Jones found that he had to hire several men to keep pace with the burials. It was a bittersweet occupation for him, for nearly 3,000 men died at the prison, each one netting him a fee of $2.50, which made him a rich man. But Jones was not a man to shirk his responsibilities or disrespect his fellow man. He took this work very seriously. It caused one Confederate to comment sarcastically that "the care of the dead [at the prison] was better than that bestowed on the living."

Jones carefully attached the name, rank, company and regiment, grave number, and date of death to the lid of each coffin, basically a pine box, and wrote the information on a piece of paper that was inserted in a bottle deposited with the remains. He also made careful records of the names of the individuals and their locations, and had wooden headboards erected on which was painted the information written on the coffin.

When the federal government took over the Confederate burial plot in 1877, they replaced the wooden markers installed by Jones with headstones. Because of the careful records he kept, the federal government was able to list the burial sites of all but seven of the men buried by him. This enabled many Southern families to visit the burial place of their family members and reconcile their grief.

Jones was a man of honor who never forgot those who touched him. When he saw the name John R. Rollins attached to one of the men he was to bury, he wondered if it could be the same man he had known as a little boy, whose mother had always been kind to him. He contacted the family in Virginia and found that their son had been missing in action. Jones arranged the transport of Rollins's remains back to his family. A few years after the war, he also made a visit to the Ellzey plantation, the place of his birth, where he was well received.

Jones continued as sexton of the Baptist church until 1890 and retired to his farm. He was a wealthy man. Until the day he died, he took care to keep a fresh supply of flowers on the grave site of Sarah Smith, the first person in Elmira who helped him and his brothers during their flight to freedom.

SUGGESTED READING: Michael P. Gray, "Elmira, A City on a Prison-Camp Contract." *Civil War History*, Vol. 45, No. 4, 1999; Tendai Mutunhu, "John W. Jones: Underground Railroad Station-Master," *Negro History Bulletin,* Mar–Apr, 1978; Barbara S. Ramsdell, "A History of John W. Jones: His escape from slavery in Virginia, becoming a Stationmaster on the Underground Railroad in Elmira, his association with area Abolitionists, and his connection with the First Baptist Church of Elmira," 2002; Abner C. Wright, "Underground Railroad Activities in Elmira," Chemung County Historian, 1945.

L

Lambert, William (1819–1890). William Lambert was the secretary of the Detroit Colored Vigilant Association and the leading figure in Detroit's Underground Railroad, which he claimed forwarded to Canada as many as 1,600 fugitive slaves in a single year during the late 1850s.

Born in Trenton, New Jersey, the son of a free black woman and of a father who had purchased his own freedom, Lambert was educated by Quakers. In 1832 he accompanied his teacher Abner Francis to Buffalo, where Lambert remained while Francis went to Toronto for a short time. When Francis returned, he found that Lambert had taken a position as a cabin boy on a Lake Erie boat. Lambert left his employment when the boat arrived in Detroit, where he spent a few weeks before returning to New Jersey. In 1838 he returned to Detroit, where he resided the remainder of his life, working as a tailor.

Almost from the start, he became involved in the city's Underground Railroad, which he said began operating in 1829. It is evident from an 1886 interview that he had been well informed and keenly interested in the antislavery movement long before his move to Detroit. Among his prized possessions, he noted, was his copy of David Walker's 1829 *Appeal*, a radical monograph calling for slaves to revolt. At the same interview, he also claimed the existence of a gang of thieves in the South also dating from 1829 called the McKinseyites, who also abducted slaves.

"These men would," he said, "with the permission of the slave himself, steal him away from the owner who had a title to him and then sell him. From this second bondage they would steal him again and deliver him to us on the line of the Ohio River. They got their profit out of the sale, although they had to commit two thefts to do it."

Lambert said that there was some hesitation at first about dealing with such criminals but that it was finally "concluded that the end justified the means. Indeed we went further than that before we got through our work and held that the effort to secure liberty justified any means to overcome obstacles that intervened to defeat it."

The relationship ended, however, as some of the gang members were caught and sent to prison with the remainder dispersing. There is some question as to the validity of this story, however, considering the dates indicated. Furthermore, he did not say when the relationship ended or if it was still ongoing when he came to Detroit. Also, because Lambert was given to exaggeration in his later years, possibly related to his growing mental illness, the story cannot be trusted, though it is an intriguing story and merits further scrutiny.

Militant Detroit abolitionist William Lambert. Courtesy of Burton Historical Collection, Detroit Public Library.

Lambert also became involved in local politics and civil rights issues, joining the Liberty Party, working for the admission of blacks into the Detroit public schools, and organizing black political conventions. He was the driving force behind the 1843 Black State Convention in Michigan, whose other leaders were William Munroe and Henry Bibb and whose major purpose was to organize support for black suffrage in Michigan. In an "Address to the Citizens of the State of Michigan" presented at the convention, Lambert exhorted: "Fellow Citizens, proscribe us no longer by holding us in a degraded light, on account of natural inferiority, but rather extend to us our free born right, the Elective Franchise, which invigorates the soul and expands the mental powers of a free and independent people."

In 1846 his involvement in the Underground Railroad grew when **George DeBaptiste**, a veteran Underground Railroad worker from Indiana, moved to Detroit. Lambert claimed that this work included going into the South to aid the escape of slaves:

> We traveled at night, or if in daytime, with peddling wagons. We had at one time more than sixty tin peddling wagons with false bottoms, large enough to hold three men, traveling through the south.
>
> We used to work up the Wabash River to Ft. Wayne and then cross into Washtenaw county, where Ann Arbor is, you know. There, we had lots of friends and help. Then if the hue and cry had been sharply raised, we would keep our people in concealment and get them over the ferry when we could. They used to lay in barns and all sorts of retreats and doubtless underwent many hardships, which at times caused them almost to regret their flight, but we got them through all right at last. Girls we often brought as boys, and women disguised as men and men as women were frequent arrivals. When railways began to be built, we used to pack them in boxes and send them by express. We got thirty or forty through in that way, but the danger to their lives by reason of lack of careful handling and fear of suffocation made that means dangerous.

His Underground activities escalated even further after the passage of the second Fugitive Slave Law in 1850. A devoted member of the Masonic Lodge, Lambert wrote that a fraternal order similar to the lodge with passwords and rituals was incorporated into the Detroit Underground Railroad. In fact, he referred to his Underground Railroad offices as the "lodge." One of the ritual methods used to identify a fellow Underground Railroad agent or runaway was to make a distinctive sign with one's fingers. The sign was made by pulling the knuckle of the right forefinger over the knuckle of the same finger on the left hand. The response was to reverse the fingers as described.

He said his operation was "always suspicious of the white man, and so those we admitted we put to severe tests, and we had one ritual for them alone." Fugitive slaves would come first to the lodge. After dark, they were taken to the house of **George J. Reynolds** on Eighth Street, where they were fed and given new clothing before crossing the river to Canada. Another location where they were hidden until crossing the river into Canada was Seymour Finney's barn.

Once a runaway arrived at their lodge, Lambert said, they were as good as free, for he claimed never to have lost a runaway once they were placed in his care. He estimated the amount of money spent helping fugitive slaves during his twenty years of Underground activity to be about $120,000, close to $3 million in today's money. In all, he claimed that more than 40,000 fugitive slaves escaped through Detroit from 1829 to 1862.

In 1858 Lambert attended **John Brown**'s Chatham Convention and was selected to serve as treasurer of Brown's insurgent government that he hoped to establish after the raid on the arsenal at Harpers Ferry. Lambert said he met Brown when he brought a party of fugitive slaves to Detroit. According to Lambert, Brown brought more than 200 fugitive slaves to Detroit. He was a great admirer of Brown and praised both his humility and his courage.

In later years Lambert became a supporter of emigration by American blacks to Haiti.

When questioned during an 1887 interview about the reliability of the number of fugitive slaves he claimed to have helped, he showed the reporter a book in which he said were recorded the names of every fugitive slave he assisted along with their point of origin and the date they came to Detroit. But because of his mental illness, some of his claims during his later years are questioned, and whether his accounts book still exists is unknown.

In 1890 Lambert committed suicide by hanging himself.

SUGGESTED READING: Katherine DuPre Lumpkin, "The General Plan Was Freedom: A Negro Secret Order on the Underground," *Phylon*, Vol. 28, No. 1, 1967, http://clarke.cmich.edu/undergroundrailroad/freedomsrailway.htm.

Latimer, George (1819–1896). The escape of slaves George Latimer and his wife, Rebecca, from Virginia to Boston, Massachusetts, in 1842 created a national stir and was one of the incidents that prompted the passing of the second Fugitive Slave Law of 1850.

Latimer, then twenty-one, and Rebecca, who was twenty and pregnant, stowed away in the prow of a ship out of Norfolk, Virginia. However, the day after their arrival in Boston, a former employee of his owner recognized him and contacted his owner, James Gray. An advertisement for his rendition was put in the papers, and three days later Gray arrived in Boston. He immediately went to the local authorities and had Latimer arrested. Meanwhile, Latimer's wife was hidden by members of Boston's black community, who also took steps to prevent his removal to Virginia. The day after his incarceration about 300 blacks assembled outside the jail, demanding a promise that Latimer would not be sent back to slavery without a fair hearing, to which Gray's lawyer obliged. Attorney Samuel Sewall, who had represented two female fugitive slaves who were forcibly taken from the courtroom before a legal resolution was made in an 1836 slave rescue case, and who would become a dedicated member of the Boston Vigilance Committee, was enlisted to represent Latimer.

Both legal and extralegal pressures were put on police authorities and the slaveowner. Among those interceding on Latimer's behalf were abolitionist editor William Lloyd Garrison and John W. Hutchinson of the famous Hutchinson Family Singers. On October 30 a huge rally was held at Faneuil Hall. Featured among the speakers was abolitionist orator Wendell Phillips. They resolved "to provide additional safeguards for the protection of those claimed as fugitives from other states, or as slaves." On November 11, 1842, three weeks after Latimer's arrest, **Henry Bowditch**, William Francis Channing, and Frederick Cabot, three leading white citizens of Boston, founded the *Latimer Journal and North Star*. Its purpose was "to meet the urgency of the first enslavement in Boston" and "to rescue a fugitive slave from the custody in which he was detained." However, violence was discouraged. These pressures and others compelled Latimer's owners to negotiate for his sale, and an agreement was finally made on November 18 for the sum of $400, which was paid by Bowditch.

The *Latimer Journal* did not stop publishing until May 16, 1843. During this period, it led a campaign to collect signatures for a petition to the state legislature for a law to prevent the rendition of fugitive slaves in Massachusetts. In all more than 65,000 signatures were collected, and this led to one of the notable Personal Liberty Laws passed in several Northern states that interfered with the prosecution of the federal government's first Fugitive Slave Law. Their legal authority was based on a loophole provided in the 1842 U.S. Supreme Court "Prigg Decision," which concluded that states did not have any authority in the prosecution of federal laws related to the rendition of runaway slaves. The Massachusetts law that took effect on March 24, 1843, carried that one step further and stated that "all judges, justices of the peace, and officers of the commonwealth [of Massachusetts], are forbidden, under heavy penalties, to aid, or act in any manner in the arrest, detention, or delivery of any person claimed as a fugitive slave."

After participating in the rallies and meetings that led up to the passage of the state's personal liberty law, Latimer settled with his wife in Lynn, Massachusetts, and set up business as a paperhanger, which he continued for forty-five years. His wife gave birth to the child she was carrying during their escape. His name was Lewis Latimer, and he became a prominent inventor and associate of Thomas Edison.

SUGGESTED READING: Asa J. Davis, "The Two Autobiographical Fragments of George W. Latimer," *Journal of Afro-American Historical and Genealogical Society*, No. 1, Summer, 1980; Marion Gleason McDougall, *Fugitive Slaves (1619–1865)*, Boston: Ginn & Co., 1891; Joseph Nogee, "The Prigg Case and Fugitive Slavery, 1842–1850: Part I," *The Journal of Negro History*, July, 1954.

Lewis, Graceanna (1821–1912). Graceanna Lewis was a member of a large family of Quaker conductors in Chester County, Pennsylvania, among the nation's most active regions of the Underground Railroad. She lived on the family farm called Sunnyside with her mother and sisters Mariann and Elizabeth during the antebellum period, and all worked together in their efforts to aid runaway slaves. They also were aided also by their sister Rebecca and her husband, Edwin Fussell, a physician, who lived for a time on an adjoining farm. An accomplished naturalist and teacher, she devoted herself to that profession after the Civil War following the deaths of her sisters.

Lewis was born to devoutly abolitionist Quaker parents, John Lewis and Esther Fussell Lewis. In 1824 John ministered to a black family that had been afflicted with typhus when no one else would help because of their disreputable character. As a result of his act of mercy, however, he contracted the disease. Having been brought up in Maryland, when there had been abolitionist societies agitating for gradual emancipation, he regretted on his deathbed not having joined one of them. This spirit carried over to his children, who were quick to join the movement of immediate emancipation when it took hold in Chester County.

The family customarily hired fugitive slaves to work for them. In 1827 two fugitive slaves had been hired by Esther's brother, Solomon, who had taken over the management of their farm following the death of John. At the time, a slavecatcher, Abel Richardson, lived in the neighborhood. He came one day to Sunnyside with the masters of the two men. The slavecatchers moved to take possession of the men, but one of them, Henry, picked up an ax to defend himself. But before he used it, he asked Solomon whether he should strike the slavecatchers with it. Being a nonresistant by faith, the Quaker reluctantly forbade it. Henry dropped the ax, and he and the other man were tied up with ropes and led away. Graceanna and her sisters witnessed this abomination, and Graceanna recalled that the agony on the face of Henry, who was a kind man and friend to the children, was something that stayed with her the rest of her life.

Esther reinforced her daughters' abolitionist education by providing them with books of antislavery stories and poems. They committed them to memory and would recite them in the evenings. One of these, "Zambo's Story," was purchased by Graceanna on her first visit to Philadelphia when she was nine years old.

Described as a remarkable woman, Esther Lewis became the leader not only of her family but also of her community. In her youth she had wanted to be a doctor, but there were no schools to accommodate women. It was because of her lack of opportunity that her brother **Bartholomew Fussell**, who also was from Chester County and aided 2,000 fugitive slaves according to one estimate, began to tutor women in the field of medicine and led a movement that resulted in the opening of the first medical school to educate female doctors.

Chester County abolitionist Graceanna Lewis. Chester County Historical Society, West Chester, Pennsylvania.

Fugitive slaves sometimes came to Sunnyside from **Thomas Garrett** in Wilmington, though often not directly, as their farm was about twenty-five miles north and there were numerous other stations in between. Fugitive slaves coming east from Adams and Lancaster counties also made their way through John Vickers, a potter from Lionville, who brought them hidden in his wagon under pottery, with small children sometimes hidden inside large jars. As to forwarding fugitive slaves, the Lewises had a variety of options, with numerous stations along the route north, one being Richard Moore of Quakertown, a distance of twenty-five miles.

Esther died in 1848 at the age of sixty-six. She left four daughters, all to whom she gave birth after the age of thirty-seven. The head of the household passed to Graceanna, though younger than her sisters Elizabeth and Mariann, the former being fragile in health and the latter fragile emotionally. It was the period approaching the passage of the second Fugitive Slave Law, and their Underground Railroad work was about to increase. During this period they became more closely connected to the Philadelphia Vigilance Committee, which was reorganized under the direction of **William Still**.

An arrangement was made with the vigilance committee in which they would be supplied with train fare to forward fugitive slaves north on the Reading Railroad. By the mid-1850s the railroad would connect all the way to Canada. This arrangement required them to provide and fashion new clothes for fugitive slaves. As travelers on the railroad, they would need to be dressed in their Sunday best in order to pass as free blacks, and the sisters were helped not only by a local sewing circle that met regularly at Sunnyside but also by contributions of used clothing that were sent to them, donations filling as many as three bushel bags.

One week forty fugitive slaves passed through Sunnyside. Among them was a group of eleven that included three young men, a husband and wife, and a woman with five children, who were being hotly pursued by slavecatchers. They had come from Thomas Garrett, who sent them to the Longwood Meeting, from where they were brought to Sunnyside. Once there, it was decided to split up the party, sending the husband and wife and the three young men to Elijah Pennypacker, three miles to the east in Phoenixville. They were supposed to remain there until a plan could be devised to elude the slavecatchers. Graceanna wrote Still a letter dated October 28, 1855, asking for advice as to "the best method of forwarding them . . . to Canada" and for financial assistance. The next day, however, she wrote Still again; she was upset that the three young men sent to Pennypacker had been forwarded to Norristown to a conductor whom Lewis thought was unreliable and asked that the vigilance committee look into the matter.

In the meantime, the first order of business was to prepare a complete new wardrobe for the fugitive slaves, as the plan was to send them by the railroad all the way to Canada in care of Hiram Wilson, then in St. Catherine's. At the time the noted abolitionist orator Charles C. Burleigh was visiting with his wife and children, and they and some neighbors were all put to work. Dresses, bonnets, and veils were prepared. It was soon decided to forward them as quickly as possible. As they were split up, they would board the train at different locations. One little boy was dressed as a girl with a bonnet and artificial flowers.

Among the fugitive slaves who were harbored at Sunnyside were William Parker, Abe Johnson, and Alex Pinckney, who were brought there by Graceanna's uncle, Bartholomew Fussell, the night following the Christiana Riot in 1851. A number of fugitive slaves stayed and worked there, one man remaining for several years and saving $500 before moving on to Canada. Another, named Johnson, was less fortunate. He did not remain to work but was forced to stay because of an injury to his foot sustained when he hopped off a train in Wilmington after seeing his master. He somehow got to Kennett Square, and Samuel Pennock forwarded him to Sunnyside. It was an extremely serious injury and it was four months before the man was able to leave. He was sent to William Still, who forwarded him to Boston, where he was finally forced to have part of his leg amputated and given a wooden limb. Johnson returned to Sunnyside and spent the winter there, doing household chores. His injury continued to trouble him, and in the spring he was sent to

John Greenleaf Whittier: The Abolitionist Poet

The Quaker John Greenleaf Whittier of Amesbury, Massachusetts has sometimes been referred to as "the abolitionist poet." He wrote hundreds of poems to mark abolitionist events, celebrate abolitionist individuals, and tell the stories of those in slavery. He was also one of the leading abolitionist journalists of his time and active in the many societies and conventions of the day. He also was ready to aid in harboring fugitive slaves or to assist in fund-raising to purchase their freedom.

Whittier's first poem was published by a young William Lloyd Garrison in the *Newburyport Free Press* in 1826. A founding member of the American Anti-Slavery Society, Whittier traveled widely as an abolitionist reporter and became editor of one of the nation's leading abolitionist newspapers, the *Pennsylvania Freeman*, whose offices were relocated to the newly built Pennsylvania Hall. Whittier was there the day the building was burned down by a mob in 1838.

A leading proponent in the movement to obtain trial by jury in cases involving fugitive slaves, Whittier split from the Garrisonians when he supported the Liberty Party. He later became the literary editor of Gamaliel Bailey's *National Era*, occupying that position while remaining in Amesbury.

A good example of Whittier's abolition poems was one that commented on the famous incident involving seaman Jonathan Walker, who was caught aiding fugitive slaves in Florida in 1845 and whose handed was branded with the initials *SS* for *slave stealer*.

> Then lift that manly right hand, bold ploughman of the wave
> Its branded palm shall prophecy "SALVATION TO THE SLAVE"
> Hold up its fire-wrought language, that whoso reads may feel
> His heart swell strong within him, his sinews change to steel
> Hold it up before our sunshine, up against our Northern air—
> Ho! Men of Massachusetts, for the love of God look there!
> Take it henceforth for your standard—like Bruce's heart of yore
> In the dark strife closing round ye, let that hand be seen before!

the Caribbean, hoping the warmer climate would have a beneficial effect. However, he died there shortly after.

Graceanna was among the founding members of the Longwood Meeting in Kennett Square in 1853 that included Thomas Garrett, **Hannah Cox**, and **Lucretia Mott**. There she took up the cause of women's rights. In 1862 the meeting sent six of its members to meet with President Lincoln to urge him to emancipate the slaves. The Civil War was a tough period for the Lewis sisters. The homes of the Chester County abolitionists were believed to be targeted by the Confederate army for destruction, and they felt vulnerable being so close to the Mason-Dixon Line. One local soldier was brought to Sunnyside for care. He had contracted some type of fever and it took him months to recover. Elizabeth also contracted it and shortly after died in 1863. She was followed three years later by Mariann.

Graceanna now was alone. Having an interest in the natural sciences, she took up the study of ornithology and botany in Philadelphia. In 1870 she was elected to the city's Academy of Natural Sciences and returned to the teaching profession, which she had undertaken for a short period from 1842 to 1844 at a boarding school operated by her uncle, Bartholomew Fussell. She taught at a number of preparatory schools, including the Foster School for Girls at Clifton Springs, New York, from 1883 to 1885. Thereafter, she retired to Media, Pennsylvania, where she spent her remaining years, studying botany and ornithology and rendering many drawings of plants and birds.

SUGGESTED READING: William C. Kashatus, *Just over the Line,* West Chester, PA: Chester County Historical Society, 2002; R. C. Smedley, *History of the Underground Railroad in Chester and Neighboring Counties of Pennsylvania*, Lancaster, PA, 1883; William Still, *The Underground Railroad,* Philadelphia: Porter and Coates, 1872.

Loguen, Jermaine (1813–1872). Rev. Jermaine Loguen was among the leading spokesmen for blacks in New York State. He openly admitted he was a fugitive slave and publicized his Underground Railroad activities despite the fact that it endangered his freedom. He claimed to have aided about 1,500 runaway slaves during the period from 1851 to 1859.

Loguen was born a slave on a plantation in Mansker's Tennessee. His mother, Cherry, was kidnapped as a child from Ohio into slavery, and his father, David Logue, was his original master. He passed his early childhood in contentment, never leaving his mother and being shown fatherly attention by Logue. But as time passed and the affection between Logue and his mother diminished, he became just another slave. Logue finally sold him and his mother to his brutal, alcoholic brother, Manasseth.

On one occasion when Loguen was fourteen, Manasseth beat him with the wooden handle of a hoe because it had broken while Loguen was using it. Manasseth wedged it in Loguen's mouth, causing an injury that affected Loguen's speech for the rest of his life. On another occasion during a drunken rage, Manasseth bludgeoned Loguen on the head repeatedly and probably would have killed Loguen had not his mother set fire to a barn to distract their master. Loguen also witnessed a younger brother and sister being sold to slavetraders and his mother beaten until she was covered in blood when she tried to stop them. Finally, after one of his sisters was whipped and he resisted an attempt by Manasseth to whip him, Loguen resolved to run away.

He made careful plans with two slaves on neighboring plantations, Henry Wilks and John Farney. An old white man named Ross forged passes for them, provided them with pistols, and advised them as to how to conduct their journey. For this they paid him

Syracuse Underground Railroad stationmaster Jermaine Loguen. Courtesy of the Onondaga Historical Association Museum and Research Center, Syracuse, New York.

$10 each, plus some bacon, flour, and other provisions they stole from their masters. They set out on Christmas Eve in 1834, but Wilks backed out at the last minute, feeling obligated to his master because he had once saved Wilks's life.

Loguen and Farney went on horseback and were well stocked with provisions. They successfully passed themselves off as free men and boldly stayed at public houses as Ross had advised. Nevertheless, on two occasions they had to fight off slavecatchers, using their fists rather than pistols, having agreed to use the guns only as a last resort. A week later they reached the Ohio River. After crossing the river into Indiana, they fired their pistols, believing that because they were in a free state they were safe. But a black man informed them this was not so, that slavecatchers lurked everywhere. He sent them to a black man in Corydon, west of Louisville, who sent them to James Overrals, a black man in Indianapolis.

It was about a 100-mile journey due north to Overrals, but it was through a wilderness, and they lost their way. When they finally found someone to ask directions, they learned they were heading in the wrong direction. Finally, they arrived at a black settlement near the Quaker community of New Farmington, and they rested for three weeks, before meeting with Overrals. He sent them to a Quaker community forty miles north.

They battled snowstorms but eventually arrived in Detroit destitute and hungry. Two days later, they crossed into Windsor, Canada, rejoicing and thanking God for their deliverance. Loguen ended up at first in Hamilton, where he got a job, then moved to St. Catharine's. But by 1837 he had moved to Rochester, where he got a job in a hotel as a porter. He had become interested in the talk excited by the abolitionists and the movement to end slavery and wanted to become involved. But he had almost no education. He had heard of a school that welcomed black men, the Oneida Institute near Utica operated by Beriah Green, and he enrolled there. Green was a leading activist in the abolition movement during its first decade and well connected in abolitionist circles. The Oneida Institute also had been in the practice of aiding fugitive slaves, so it was the perfect training ground for Loguen's entry into the world of the Underground Railroad.

While at the Institute, Loguen met Caroline Storum, the daughter of a prosperous black family in western New York. They were married in 1840, and also that year he opened a school for black children in Utica. There was a compelling need for such a school because very few public schools allowed black children at that time. It was a success and gave Loguen confidence that his decision to further his education was the correct one.

During this time, circumstances unforeseen by him led him into the ministry. As his biography states, "His religious state long before made such a connection desirable; but his disgust of the Churches at the South, and North also, on account of their pro-slavery attachments, were so great, that he rejected all church relations until he found the colored church at Utica." He received his license as a preacher in the African Methodist Episcopal (AME) Church and began preaching at the AME Church in Whitesboro, near the Oneida Institute.

In 1841 Loguen moved to Syracuse, though it is not clear if his wife permanently resided with him at this time, and possibly they may have seen each other intermittently

Reverend Luther Lee: Disobedience of the Fugitive Slave Law Is Obedience to God

"My ground was that slavery was wrong, and hence all laws which aided and supported it must be wrong. . . . and every citizen is bound to disobey all such laws, and take the consequences rather than to disobey God," wrote Methodist minister Luther Lee.

Lee was one of numerous ministers during the antebellum period whose moral convictions conflicted with the official positions of their churches. As a result, despite opposition from some fellow Methodist Episcopal ministers, Lee took a position as an antislavery lecturer with the American Anti-Slavery Society in 1838. For two years he toured the Adirondack region in upstate New York and helped to abolitionize that area. In 1843, when 151 Methodist Episcopal ministers met in Utica to form a new denomination—the Wesleyan Methodists—with antislavery principles, Lee was one of the new group's leaders, and the Adirondack region became the site of many of their churches.

In 1852 Rev. Lee moved to Syracuse to assume the pastorate of its Wesleyan Methodist church. It was a time that saw heavy trafficking of fugitive slaves. "My name, the name of my street, and the number of my residence, came to be known as far south as Baltimore, and I did a large business," Lee later wrote of his three years in Syracuse.

In a speech he made in 1855 during an anti-Fugitive Slave Law demonstration in Syracuse, Lee made a bold declaration. In addition to calling the Fugitive Slave law "treason against God and humanity," he said that he had assisted thirty slaves to escape to Canada during the previous month and challenged the United States authorities to come and arrest him at his home, 39 Onondaga Street, and take him to prison.

How many fugitive slaves Lee assisted while in Syracuse is unknown, but according to Charles Merrick, a Syracuse abolitionist, Lee assisted 365 during just one of the years he was in residence there.

Lee later moved to Ohio in 1857, serving a Wesleyan Methodist church for two years in Felicity, Clermont County, Ohio—near the Ohio River border, where fugitive slave traffic was active—but it is not known whether he aided fugitive slaves there.

while she remained with her parents. He was the pastor at several congregations during this period, for two years ministering in Bath, New York, along the state's southern tier, and at the St. James AME Church in Ithaca, from 1844 to 1846. It was in 1844 that he began to speak publicly for the antislavery movement. It occurred quite by accident.

At the time, he was in Cortland, New York, on a trip to raise funds for the completion of his church at Bath. It was late September and the elections were just ahead. He was approached by two Liberty Party members, who asked him to speak about his experiences in slavery and urge people to vote the Liberty Party ticket. Appointments were arranged for him at the Presbyterian and Baptist churches.

Loguen began his lecture with an emotional prayer for his mother and brother and sisters in slavery that riveted his audience. He then talked of his own trials as a slave and asked for donations for his church in Bath. He also made a plea to his listeners to vote for Liberty Party candidates. His efforts were quite successful, and a lecture tour in behalf of the Liberty Party was arranged for him throughout the county. This led to further engagements as an antislavery lecturer and an introduction to **Gerrit Smith**.

Loguen returned to Syracuse in 1846 and became pastor at its AME Church. His antislavery labors had now become his principal occupation. Around this time Loguen purchased a house in Syracuse, and it is believed that from this point forward his family remained permanently with him. By this time he and his wife had two children with another on the way, and in all they would raise six children. It was also the beginning of a period when Loguen would invest in properties and create income that would help support his antislavery activities.

Early in the spring of 1848 he undertook a mission for Smith to the Adirondack region in order to enlist local abolitionists to aid Smith's land grantees. After his trip, he wrote a report to black leader James McCune Smith in New York City, describing the land grants in Essex County as good for farming and those in Franklin County as valuable for timber. Referring to the latter, he noted the increased number of sawmills in the region. He also issued a warning about the con games played by some locals with blacks who had gone to claim their land. They were leading claimants to the wrong plots, which often were worthless parcels on some remote hilltop, and offering to buy them at a very cheap price. He advised recipients not to sell their land and that they could identify their plots by marks on the trees made by surveyors.

In order to protect themselves, Loguen suggested that recipients find trustworthy individuals to assist them. He mentioned the following: Jesse Gay and Alfred S. Spooner in Elizabethtown; Uriah Mihills in Keene; J. Tobey Jr. in Jay; Wendell Lansing in Wilmington; William M. Flack in Ausable Forks; the Merills in Merillville; and Rensselaer Bigelow in Malone. His report was published in several newspapers. The Adirondack region was an alternate byway of the Underground Railroad where many residents welcomed fugitive slaves. Listing those names provided readers with a guide to its Underground Railroad there, though this was probably not Loguen's intention. It was not the last time, however, that Loguen would publicize the efforts of the Underground Railroad.

In the spring of 1850 Loguen moved to Troy, New York, to take over a church there. However, after the passage of the second Fugitive Slave Law, he returned to Syracuse, fearing that an attempt might be made to return him to slavery and that he would be better able to resist such an attempt in Syracuse. On October 4, 1850, the people of Syracuse filled city hall to hear a discussion of the law. Chairing the meeting was the city's mayor, Alfred Hovey. The featured speakers were two fugitive slaves, Rev. Samuel Ringgold Ward and Loguen. Loguen urged his listeners to resist the law and to make Syracuse an "open city" for fugitive slaves:

> The time has come to change the tones of submission into tones of defiance, he said—and to tell Mr. Fillmore and Mr. Webster, if they propose to execute this measure upon us, to send on their bloodhounds. . . . Whatever may be your decision, my ground is taken. I have declared it everywhere. It is known over the state and out of the state—over the line in the North, and over the line in the South. I don't respect this law—I don't fear it—I won't obey it! It outlaws me, and I outlaw it, and the men who attempt to enforce it on me. I place the governmental officials on the ground that they place me. I will not live a slave, and if force is employed to re-enslave me, I shall make preparations to meet the crisis as becomes a man.

Mayor Hovey supported Loguen's remarks: "The colored man must be protected—he must be secure among us. Come what will of political organizations, and fall where I may, I am with you. I hope I may never be called to obey this law."

A resolution was passed to form a vigilance committee of thirteen, to see that "no person is deprived of his liberty without due process of law." Those appointed were Charles A. Wheaton, Lyman Clary, Vivus W. Smith, Charles B. Sedgwick, Hiram Putnam, E. W. Leavenworth, Abner Bates, George Barnes, Patrick H. Agan, John Wilkinson, Rev. R. R. Raymond, John Thomas, and Loguen. But as Rev. Samuel May later wrote, there was a much larger association of supporters.

The following June, Daniel Webster, then U.S. secretary of state, came to Syracuse and warned that the Fugitive Slave Law needed to be obeyed and that the federal government would enforce that obedience.

Four months later during a Liberty Party convention in Syracuse, **William Henry**, a black carpenter known to all as Jerry, was taken into custody by federal officials because he was a fugitive slave. The news traveled fast and abolitionists rushed to city hall.

"I know him," Loguen said as he hurried into the city court. "He is a short time from slavery, and has few acquaintances . . . . They had their mind on taking somebody, and have picked him. Why didn't they take me?"

He challenged his white colleagues on the vigilance committee: "Now is the time to try the spunk of white men. I want to see whether they have courage only to make speeches and resolutions when there is no danger. Let us be here at nightfall, and if white men won't fight, let fugitives and black men smite down . . . anybody who holds Jerry—and rescue him or perish."

But they rose to the challenge, and led by Gerrit Smith, May, and Loguen, they rescued Jerry from the courtroom and placed him in hiding until it was safe to move him to Canada. Loguen, who had previously dared authorities to arrest him and who some claimed assaulted a marshal during the rescue, had become a marked man. Reports filtered down that the federal government had decided to prosecute him, and his wife and friends urged him to seek asylum in Canada.

He stayed for a few days in Skaneateles at the home of Lydia Fuller, the wife of the noted abolitionist James Canning Fuller, who had died two years earlier. After making his final decision to leave, Sumner Fuller, Lydia's son, took Loguen by carriage to Rochester and the home of Samuel D. Porter, who put Loguen on a steamboat to Lewiston, New York, from where he walked across the Suspension Bridge to Queenston, Canada. He made his way to St. Catherines where he had once lived and was immediately employed to minister to its black community, many of whom were fugitive slaves like himself.

Loguen also wrote New York governor Washington Hunt on December 2, 1851. Although he admitted participating in the Jerry Rescue, he denied committing any violent acts. He pointed to the injustice of the Fugitive Slave Law and asked the governor to guarantee that he would not be prosecuted if he returned to the United States. But the governor ignored his request, and finally in the spring of 1852 he decided to return to Syracuse and face the consequences.

A warrant had been served for Loguen's arrest, but Harry Allen, the U.S. marshal in Syracuse, was hesitant to serve it. Allen first went to see Charles Sedgwick, a prominent attorney, who was a member of the vigilance committee and asked Sedgwick to accompany him when he served the warrant. Sedgwick relayed the message that Loguen would comply only if the warrant was not related to the enforcement of the Fugitive Slave Law.

Allen served the warrant, assuring Sedgwick that it was related to the rescue of Jerry and not for violating the Fugitive Slave Law. However, Loguen refused to accept others to be responsible for his bail bond, and the marshal had to secretly obtain it from Loguen's friends. In the end Loguen's indictment was dropped, and the one person convicted in the Jerry Rescue died while on appeal.

What followed next for Loguen was an intense period of seven years' work in the Underground Railroad, during which he harbored on average more than 200 fugitive slaves per year. He set up the basement in his house at East Genesee Street with beds and other comforts for their accommodation. He and his wife had many sleepless nights, as fugitive slaves would arrive at all hours.

In 1857 the Syracuse Fugitive Aid Society, the formal name of the vigilance committee, published an advertisement requesting "that all fugitives from slavery coming this way may be directed to the care of Rev. J.W. Loguen; also, that all moneys contributed or subscribed be paid directly to him as Underground Railroad conductor; and that all clothing or provisions contributed may be sent to his house, or such places as he may designate." It was signed by May, William Abbott, James Fuller (another son of James Canning Fuller), Lucius Ormsbee, Joseph Allen, and Horace Knight. It added that Loguen would report his activities, including money received and fugitive slaves aided, to *Frederick Douglass's Paper* and the *Syracuse Standard and Journal* and that his account book was open to public inspection.

That year, **Frederick Douglass** had occasion to stop in Syracuse. While disembarking from the train, he encountered a group of nine fugitives who wanted to know where Loguen resided. Douglass took them there and wrote that

> we had scarcely struck the door when the manly voice of Loguen reached our ear. He knew the meaning of the rap, and sung out "hold on." A light was struck in a moment, the door opened and the whole company, the writer included, were invited in. Candles were lighted in different parts of the house, fires kindled, and the whole company made perfectly at home.

The huge public support, which Loguen in part had personally attracted, had made Syracuse almost as safe for fugitive slaves as Canada in the years approaching the Civil War. The public reaction to the Jerry Rescue and to the threats to Loguen's freedom made the government reluctant to try another rendition there.

In 1861, with Loguen's duties for the African Methodist Episcopal Zion Church (AMEZ) increasing, he was given an assignment at the Berry Street Church in Montrose, Pennsylvania. He returned to Syracuse in 1864 and was elected a bishop of the AMEZ Church, a position he filled until his death. In 1869 Loguen's daughter Amelia married Lewis Douglass, the son of Frederick Douglass, but Loguen did not live to see his daughter Marinda, better known as Sarah, become the first black American woman to graduate from medical school in 1876.

It was fitting that Loguen, a man who had escaped from slavery, would become known in his lifetime as "the king of the Underground Railroad," a title conferred on him in 1860 by the weekly journal of the AMEZ Church.

SUGGESTED READING: Fergus Bordewich, *Bound for Canaan*, New York: HarperCollins, 2005; J. W. Loguen, *The Rev. J.W. Loguen as a Slave and as a Freeman*, New York: Negro Universities Press, 1968, originally published in 1859; Milton Sernett, "Narrative of Historic Context, Onondaga County Freedom Trail," 2001.

Lovejoy, Owen (1811–1864). Throughout his adult life, Owen Lovejoy was known as the brother of the martyr Elijah Parish Lovejoy, the fearless journalist who gave up his life in defense of freedom of the press. After his brother's murder at the hands of a mob, Lovejoy devoted his life to the abolition of slavery, becoming an important Underground Railroad conductor and later, as an abolitionist congressman, a friend and confidant of President Lincoln.

Lovejoy was born in Albion, Maine, son of Rev. Daniel and Elizabeth Patte Lovejoy, the former a Congregational minister and farmer. He attended Bowdoin College from 1830 to 1833 but left the college at the death of his father. For a time he taught school and studied law but finally decided to follow in the footsteps of his father and older brothers and study for the ministry. It was for that purpose he went to join Elijah in

Princeton, Illinois, abolitionist Owen Lovejoy. Photography Collection, Miriam and Ira D. Wallach Division of Art, Prints and Photographs, The New York Public Library, Astor, Lenox and Tilden Foundations.

Alton, Illinois, in 1836 along with his younger brother John, a printer, who went to work for Elijah's newspaper, the *Observer*.

Elijah had moved his newspaper from St. Louis to Alton because of hostilities that resulted from his condemnation of the murder of a black man by a mob. The experience had transformed him from a supporter of gradual emancipation into an advocate of immediate emancipation. The night Elijah was murdered defending his press from a mob, Owen was with him. As he knelt down next to his brother, having watched his brother's life expire before his eyes, Owen experienced an epiphany:

> While I was beside the prostrate body of my murdered brother, Elijah, with fresh blood oozing from his perforated breast, on my knees, alone with the dead, I vowed never to forsake the cause for which his blood was sprinkled.

In 1838 Owen and another of his older brothers, Rev. Joseph C. Lovejoy, received a commission from the American Anti-Slavery Society to publish a memorial volume of Elijah's work. They went to the society offices in New York City, where they composed the book under the direction of Theodore Weld. It related the story of Elijah's life and showed his dedication to his beliefs.

After the completion of the book, Owen had offers to become an agent in Illinois for the American Anti-Slavery Society. Instead he sought to be ordained by the Episcopal Church, but when he was asked to sign a pledge saying that he would not discuss abolition from the pulpit, he refused.

Instead he went to Jacksonville, Illinois, the home of Rev. Edward Beecher, a close friend of his brother Elijah, who had helped him organize the Illinois Anti-Slavery Society two weeks before his death. He helped Owen receive his ordination as a Congregational minister in October 1838 and recommended him to a congregation in Princeton, Illinois. Lovejoy became pastor at the Hampshire Colony Congregational Church for the salary of $600 a year, a position he would hold for the next seventeen years.

Princeton was then a tiny village of about 200 people, but it would soon become a center of abolition in the West as a result of Lovejoy. When he began his ministry there, he was giving an antislavery sermon and some of his congregation walked out. He shouted after them, "I shall preach this doctrine until you like it and then I will preach it because you like it!" The small community did not initially accept his "radical" doctrines, and Lovejoy received several threats of violence, but he refused to back down from the pledge he had made at his brother's death.

Lovejoy boarded with the Butler Denham family. The Denhams were abolitionists, and it is believed that they sheltered fugitive slaves before Lovejoy's arrival. After three years, Butler Denham died and Lovejoy married his widow, Eunice. In addition to her three children with Butler, the couple had six children of their own. Their farmhouse was large, with fifteen rooms and many narrow hallways. The Lovejoys fed, clothed, and sheltered fugitive slaves, hiding them in an area behind a dresser, in a large storage area above the stairway, in their cornfields, in the barn, or in the basement. Lovejoy sometimes conducted them to the next stop.

With the contacts he had made in the abolitionist network through his brother, Lovejoy organized an extensive Underground Railroad network through northern Illinois. In order to advance the cause of abolition, he entered politics. Along with Rev. **John Cross**, journalist Zebina Eastman, and attorney James H. Collins, he helped organize the state's Liberty Party at a convention in Chicago on May 27, 1842. At that convention, Eastman was appointed as editor of the party's newspaper, the *Western Citizen,* which began publication two months later. It began advertising the Underground Railroad in Illinois, whose operations were confined generally in western and northern Illinois, with a major line originating from Quincy, Illinois, to Galesburg, then to Princeton, and finally to Chicago.

Proslavery elements in Illinois aware of this line, which had been organized by Cross and Lovejoy, attempted to stymie it by bringing charges against Lovejoy, and in May 1843

Elijah Lovejoy: Martyr to Freedom

On April 28, 1836, a free black man, Francis McIntosh, was burned alive by a mob after killing a policeman during a fight. This caused Rev. Elijah Lovejoy to condemn the atrocity in his newspaper, the *St. Louis Observer*. In retaliation, ruffians broke into his office and destroyed his press. This and other conflicts forced him to move twenty miles north from the slave state of Missouri to the city of Alton in the free state of Illinois, where he resumed his publication.

Lovejoy continued to condemn mob violence, and this fueled the viciousness of his enemies. They went to Alton and twice more destroyed his press. He refused to capitulate. At a public meeting in Alton on November 3, 1837, he said, "If the civil authorities refuse to protect me, I must look to God; and if I die, I have determined to make my grave in Alton."

Lovejoy's fourth press arrived on the night of November 5. It was placed in a warehouse under armed guard. Two nights later a mob surrounded the building. They were warned they would be shot if they tried to enter. They launched a volley of stones followed by several shots. Lovejoy's supporters returned the fire and killed one of their adversaries. This led the mob to attempt to burn the building. As they began, Lovejoy's supporters stormed outside and fired shots, dispersing them. At that point Lovejoy stepped outside. One of the mob was hiding behind a pile of lumber with a shotgun. He riddled Lovejoy with fire, hitting him five times. Holding his chest, Lovejoy turned and went inside, crying out, "Oh, God, I have been shot," and then fell to the floor and died.

His death reverberated throughout the North and not only inspired abolitionists to fight ever more zealously to end slavery but gained many new adherents to their cause.

he was indicted by a grand jury to stand trial for harboring fugitive slaves. In response, Lovejoy published and signed a broadside in the *Citizen*, which stated: "Notice of the Canada Line of Stages. *Cheap! Cheap!* The subscriber would very respectfully inform the ladies and gentlemen of color of the South, who wish to travel North, for the benefit of their condition, or any excursion of pleasure to the Falls of Niagara, that the above line of stages will be in active and efficient operation during the summer."

The trial was held in October, and Lovejoy's lawyer was Collins, who successfully argued that because the owner had willingly brought the slaves into the free territory of Illinois, they were free based on the Northwest Ordinance of 1787 and the state constitution. The acquittal was a major boost to the Underground Railroad in Illinois, but it did not end efforts to stop it, as similar charges were brought against Cross the following year. Again, they failed to stick. In contrast to southern Illinois, which was strongly proslavery in character, northern Illinois was strongly antislavery.

By 1849 Lovejoy had established himself as an influential force in Illinois and had a national reputation in abolitionist circles. In 1844 he had run for Congress on the Liberty Party ticket and again in 1848 on the Free Soil Party ticket. That year one of the few documented incidents occurred of his Underground Railroad activities, which incidentally has several different versions.

Two slaveholders from Missouri came to Princeton and took possession of a black man named John who was working on a local farm. His hands were tied behind him, and the slaveholder led him at the end of a rope like a dog through the streets of the village. News of this spread like wildfire, and people ran here and there in their excitement. John was led to the barroom of a local hotel. Soon Lovejoy and others arrived on the scene and presented a warrant charging the men with kidnapping. The sheriff then marched them off to the local courthouse.

The courtroom was filled and buzzing. Some sympathized with the slave, others with his master. While the trial was progressing, someone cut the rope that bound the slave, and during the confusion he escaped, followed by the excited crowd. A horse was provided for John, and he was told to go to the Lovejoy residence. Soon Lovejoy's house was surrounded by supporters of both sides.

The slaveholders demanded to go inside, but Lovejoy demanded a warrant. They sent for one, and while waiting they saw a man mount a horse in the barn behind the house. A cry was raised, "There goes the Negro." The slave party put their horses at full speed in pursuit, but after catching up with him they discovered instead a local black man. However, when the warrant finally arrived, the actual runaway was nowhere to be found. He had been dispatched in a carriage disguised as a woman during their chase of the wrong man.

As was the case with most abolitionists, the passage of the second Fugitive Slave Law increased Lovejoy's militancy. His daughter Ida later recounted an incident in which a wagon of fugitive slaves armed with clubs came to their house. They asked if Lovejoy approved of their weapons, and the minister told them that if it was their only means to obtain their freedom, then they should use them.

In 1854 Lovejoy was elected to the Illinois House of Representatives and was a founding member of the Republican Party. It was during this time that he struck up a friendship with Abraham Lincoln, who despite his opposition to slavery did not believe that defying the law was the answer. Two years later Lovejoy was elected to the U.S. Congress on the Republican ticket. While in Congress, he constantly fought for an end to slavery and soon gained the reputation as being the most aggressive of the antislavery orators associated with the Radical Republicans in Congress.

In 1859 he made perhaps his most memorable speech about slavery and his defiance of the Fugitive Slave Law:

> [Regarding *Negro Stealing*] I suppose I have a right to speak on this subject, having been made the object of this allegation. . . . If the object is to ascertain whether I assist fugitive slaves who come to my door and ask it, the matter is easily disposed of. I march right up to the confessional and say, I do.
>
> I recollect the case of a young woman who came to my house, who had not a single trace of African descent either in feature or complexion. According to her own story, she was betrothed to a man of her race, though not of her color, and was, before her marriage, sold to a libertine from the South, she being in St. Louis. She escaped, and in her flight from a life of infamy and a fate worse than death, she came and implored aid. Was I to refuse it? Was I to betray the wanderer? Was I to detain her and give her up a prey to the incarnate fiend who had selected her as a victim?
>
> No human being, black or white, bond or free, native or foreign, infidel or Christian, ever came to my door and asked for food and shelter, in the name of a common humanity, or of a pitying Christ, who did not receive it. This I have done. This I mean to do as long as God lets me live.
>
> . . . Is it desired to call attention to this fact? Proclaim it then upon the house-tops. Write it on every leaf that trembles in the forest, make it blaze from the sun at high noon, and shine forth in the milder radiance of every star that bedecks the firmament of God. Let it echo through all the arches of heaven, and reverberate and bellow along all the deep gorges of hell, where slave catchers will be very likely to hear it; Owen Lovejoy lives at Princeton, Illinois, three-quarters of a mile east of the village, and he aids every fugitive that comes to his door and asks it. Thou invisible demon of Slavery, does thou think to cross my humble threshold, and forbid me to give bread to the hungry and shelter to the houseless? I BID YOU DEFIANCE IN THE NAME OF MY GOD!

Lovejoy was an eloquent speaker and had few superiors on the rostrum. What made him so compelling was his utter faith and passion in his beliefs. In the 1860 presidential election he campaigned vigorously for Abraham Lincoln. After the outbreak of the Civil War, he was appointed a colonel of the infantry and took a leave of absence from Congress, serving in Missouri. Because of his close friendship with Lincoln, Lovejoy was not as critical of him as other Radical Republicans. At one speech on June 12, 1862, he said of the president, "If he does not drive as fast as I would, he is on the right road, and it is only a question of time." Nevertheless, he continued to argue that the president should free the slaves. He also argued for the recruitment of black regiments.

When the ceremony for the signing of the Emancipation Proclamation was held, Lovejoy, who had become afflicted with a kidney disease, was one of the special invited guests. He died on March 25, 1864, in Brooklyn, New York, and was buried at Oakland Cemetery in Princeton, Illinois.

In a letter written after Lovejoy's death, Lincoln wrote:

> My acquaintance with him began about ten years ago, since which time it has been quite intimate, and every step in it has been one of increasing respect and esteem, ending with his life, in no less than affection on my part. Throughout my heavy and perplexing responsibilities here to the day of his death it would scarcely wrong any other to say he was my most generous friend.

SUGGESTED READING: Joseph C. and Owen Lovejoy, *Memoir of Rev. Elijah P. Lovejoy*, New York: John S. Taylor, 1838; Edward Magdol, *Abolitionist in Congress*, New Brunswick, NJ: Rutgers University Press, 1967; N. Matson, *Reminiscences of Bureau County (IL)*, Princeton, IL: Republican Book & Job Office, 1872; William and Jane Ann Moore, editors, *Owen Lovejoy: His Brother's Blood, Speeches and Writings, 1838–1864*, Champaign: University of Illinois Press, 2004; Owen Muelder, *The Underground Railroad in Western Illinois*, Jefferson, NC: McFarland and Company, 2008; Hans L. Trefousse, "Owen Lovejoy and Abraham Lincoln during the Civil War," *Journal of the Abraham Lincoln Association*, Winter, 2001.

M

McKim, J. Miller (1810–1874). James Miller McKim was a voice of moderation and prudence in the abolitionist movement for more than twenty years. His steadfast leadership as the executive director of the Pennsylvania Anti-Slavery Society in Philadelphia contributed to its development as one of the most well organized Underground Railroad terminals in the nation.

Known as Miller McKim, he was born on a farm near Carlisle, Pennsylvania, one of eight children of James and Catherine Miller McKim, and graduated from Dickinson College in 1828. While studying medicine at the University of Pennsylvania, he came under the spell of the evangelical movement and enrolled at Princeton Theological Seminary in 1831 and Andover Theological Seminary in Massachusetts in 1832. However, this was interrupted by the death in rapid succession of his parents and older brother. He completed his religious preparation with the Reverend George Duffield, pastor of the First Presbyterian church of Carlisle, Pennsylvania, who later became a leader in the New School Presbyterian noted for their strong antislavery position.

But it was McKim's barber, a black man named John Peck of Carlisle, who would change McKim's life. Peck was a subscriber to *The Liberator*, and McKim first read it there around 1832. At the time McKim supported colonization while Peck opposed it and gave him a copy of Garrison's "Thoughts on African Colonization." It was after reading this work, McKim said, that he became a supporter of immediate emancipation.

The following year when a call came for the organizational meeting of the American Anti-Slavery Society in Philadelphia, McKim was chosen by the local abolitionists to be their representative. At twenty-three, he was the youngest participant at the convention. Here he met many of the individuals with whom he would work during the next thirty years, including William Lloyd Garrison, **Lucretia and James Mott**, **Robert Purvis**, Lewis Tappan, John Greenleaf Whittier, and Samuel J. May.

A constitution was adopted that declared the society's objective as "the entire abolition of slavery in the United States," and that "the duty, safety, and best interests of all concerned, require its immediate abandonment, without expatriation."

In the fall of 1835 he accepted the pastorate of a Presbyterian church near Reading, Pennsylvania, but a conflict with his denomination's orthodox view on slavery caused him to resign the following year and become one of Theodore Weld's heralded "seventy" abolitionist lecturers.

Chosen by a committee headed by Arthur Tappan, president of the national society and Weld's patron, the lecturers reported their work and expenses monthly. Unmarried lecturers received $8 a week and traveling expenses. Their emphasis was the sin of slavery and the need for its abolition. When arriving in a community, their method was to locate the leading abolitionist, find a location for a public meeting, and generate enough interest to form a local society.

McKim lectured for several years in Pennsylvania, New Jersey, and Delaware. It was a rigorous schedule that often brought him before hostile audiences. Tomatoes, eggs, garbage, and stones were sometimes thrown at lecturers, and at times their lives were threatened. But they persisted and achieved great success. By 1838 there were more than 100 antislavery societies in Pennsylvania and nearly 2,000 nationwide and 100,000 abolitionists under the umbrella of the American Anti-Slavery Society.

That year he made a memorable visit to Washington, D.C., which he described in a letter to the *Colored American*. Among his observations of slavery there was a visit to the notorious slave pen of W. H. Williams, which was near the nation's capital on Seventh Street between Pennsylvania and Maryland Avenue.

McKim became publishing agent of the Pennsylvania Anti-Slavery Society in 1840 and was given an office at its headquarters at 31 North Fifth Street. He would remain there for the next twenty-two years, eventually becoming executive director and a leading member of the vigilance committee, which also operated out of that location. That year, he not only began the foremost years of his life's work but also married his wife, Sarah, with whom he would spend thirty-four years and raise a son and a daughter, the latter of whom would marry William Lloyd Garrison's son, Wendell Phillips Garrison.

When the American Anti-Slavery Society underwent its schism that year, the Pennsylvania Anti-Slavery Society sided with the old organization led by Garrison. It stood firmly behind the Garrisonian principles of moral suasion, noninvolvement in politics, and equal participation for women. The latter principle was especially important considering that several women had leadership roles in the state society. However, they were split on the issue of political action until 1844. By that time, Garrison's view had become more extreme and he was advocating the secession of the North from the South. This position was finally endorsed by the state society, and it ran an editorial in the *Freeman* suggesting that those who could not support that position should withdraw from the state society.

The society thereafter consisted mainly of Hicksite Quakers, averaging about 1,500 members and dominated by a small group of leaders that included **Lucretia Mott** and her husband, James, the society's president for fourteen years; editor and lecturer Charles C. Burleigh; important black leader and Underground Railroad conductor **Robert Purvis**; vigilance committee secretary and society office manager **William Still**; and McKim.

As executive director, McKim oversaw the work of the society that consisted of the coordination of meetings and conventions to discuss important topics and activities; the sponsoring of lectures; the maintenance of the antislavery bookstore and library; the weekly publication of the *Pennsylvania Freeman*, which for brief periods he served as editor; and a large volume of correspondence. Money for its operation came from the sale of its publication, contributions, and an annual bazaar run by the Philadelphia Female Anti-Slavery Society.

Behind the scenes, the society's leading members coordinated the Underground Railroad, establishing a formal vigilance committee under the leadership of Still,

Purvis, and McKim, who had operated in an unofficial capacity before that. It assisted about 100 fugitive slaves per year. One of McKim's most memorable experiences undoubtedly was opening the cover of the box that held **Henry "Box" Brown**, who had himself shipped in it from Richmond, Virginia, to Philadelphia, and which the society had delivered from the post office to their office early one morning in 1849. The committee also alerted the fugitive slaves in Christiana, Pennsylvania to the approach of slavecatchers. However, their warning did not prove beneficial, because it resulted in the notorious riot that caused the death of a slaveholder and the dislocation of many local residents who were fugitive slaves, forcing them to flee to Canada.

"As a helper and friend of the fleeing bondman in numberless instances," William Still wrote of his colleague, "he never failed . . . in the hour of need. Whether on the Underground Railroad bound for Canada, or before a United States commissioner trying a fugitive case, the slave found no truer friend."

In 1854 the *Pennsylvania Freeman* closed its editorial office and transferred its business operations to the *National Anti-Slavery Standard.* From this period on, McKim took on editorial duties as the society's chief correspondent to the *Standard.*

Perhaps the most difficult task of his career occurred following **John Brown**'s execution. Just prior to it, a plan was being conceived to rescue Brown from jail in Charlestown, Virginia, by Thomas Wentworth Higginson, one of Brown's influential backers, who have become known as the "Secret Six." Before the attempt was made, Higginson asked Brown's wife, Mary, to visit and get Brown's consent. McKim was asked to be her escort, but when they arrived in Baltimore, they received word that Brown did not want to see her. He also had continually stated that he did not desire any rescue attempt to be made, that he was more than willing to die for the cause of abolition. "Let them hang me," he wrote to one of his lawyers from his prison cell. "I am worth inconceivably more to hang than for any other purpose."

As a result, Mary Brown stayed with members of the Philadelphia Anti-Slavery Society, including McKim. About a week before the execution, John Brown relented and Mary was permitted by Virginia governor Wise not only to visit Brown the night before the execution but also to take custody of the body. It was a mournful reunion for both Browns on December 1, and John Brown is supposed to have broken down and cried uncontrollably after discussing the future of his family. They requested that Mary stay the night, but the request was refused and the military escorted her back to Harpers Ferry.

The execution at Charlestown took place on Friday, December 2, 1859. After Brown's body was examined and he was pronounced dead, the body was conveyed under military escort to Harpers Ferry and placed on a train bound for Philadelphia with Mary Brown, Miller and Sarah McKim, and Philadelphia attorney Hector Tyndale, who also was part of Mary Brown's escort party.

They arrived on Saturday, and a large crowd, mostly blacks, had gathered at the station. The mayor and the police arrived and sensed trouble. McKim wanted to keep the body in Philadelphia until Monday and have it embalmed. But the mayor believed it was not safe and that perhaps the crowd might try to steal the body. In the baggage car was a long box that looked like a coffin. This was hastily covered and placed on a wagon in full view of the crowd, which was informed that the body was going to be taken to the antislavery office to lie in state until Monday. The crowd

> **The Williams Slave Pen**
>
> Slave pens were holding cells for slaves waiting to be sold or transferred to a new owner. **J. Miller McKim** was given a tour of W. H. Williams's slave pen in Washington, D.C., in 1838 and wrote about it for the *Colored American*.
>
> In a square room of 25 feet were about 30 slaves of all ages, sizes, and complexions, including one about two years old.
>
> The very small children were gamboling about unconscious of their situation but those of more advanced age were the most melancholy looking beings. The wistful, inquiring, anxious looks they cast at me (presuming I suppose that I came as a purchaser) were hard to endure . . .
>
> "Do all of these persons sleep down in that cellar?" I asked.
>
> "Yes, sir—all the males:—they lie upon the floor—each one has got a couple of blankets."
>
> When McKim asked how they could put so many slaves in a room so small, the jailer gave the following response:
>
> "O Lord, yes, sir, three times as many! . . . Last year we had as many as 139 in these three rooms."
>
> The jailer brought McKim to the area where the slaves ate their meals. It was in the open air, and the jailer said they ate there in both summer and winter.
>
> "We give them plenty of substantial food—herring, coffee sweetened with molasses and corn bread," the jailer said, two times a day, at nine in the morning and three in the afternoon.

followed the decoy, and the station was cleared. The coffin with Brown's body was then immediately taken to the harbor and loaded onto a boat for New York City.

McKim went on ahead and was waiting when the boat arrived with the casket. There he and others saw that the body was taken to an undertaker and embalmed, and then a friend of Brown helped place the body in a Northern casket. Mary Brown, completely exhausted, remained in Philadelphia over Sunday with Tyndale. She came to New York by train the following day.

Mary Brown and McKim were joined by Boston abolitionist Wendell Phillips in New York and from there began the long funeral procession north by carriage, passing through villages as solemn drums beat, church bells tolled, and people gathered along the road. The entire journey took five days, and the funeral was held on the morning of December 8, 1859. Both McKim and Wendell Phillips spoke at the funeral. McKim called Brown and his men "all martyrs in a holy cause."

When South Carolina seceded, McKim was glad the North had rid itself of the taint of slavery. He also supported the war, saying, "A virtuous war is better than a corrupt peace." With the huge migration of slave refugees north, he became involved in Freedmen's relief work and resigned his position with the Anti-Slavery Society in 1862, becoming in March 1862 general secretary of the Philadelphia Port Royal Relief Association, the first of several freedmen's organizations he became involved with.

The enactment of the Emancipation Proclamation on January 1, 1863, was a time of great rejoicing for him, and he called it "the great event of the century on this continent." His thirty years of labor to end slavery had come to fruition.

During the remainder of the decade McKim became corresponding secretary of the American Freedmen's Union Commission, whose headquarters were in New York. When it disbanded in 1869, his public life came to an end. His health failing, he wrote that he was satisfied "at the end that his life had been on the whole what . . . he would wish to make it."

In the war of words and the theoretical battle of abolitionism with slavery, William Still wrote that McKim "occupied a position of influence, labor and usefulness, scarcely second to Mr. Garrison."

SUGGESTED READING: Ira Brown, "Miller McKim and Pennsylvania Abolitionism," *Pennsylvania History,* No. 30, January, 1963; Stephen B. Oates, *To Purge This Land with Blood: A Biography of John Brown,* New York: Harper & Row, 1970; Edward J. Renehan, *The Secret Six: The True Tale of the Men Who Conspired with John Brown*, New York: Crown, 1995; William Still, *The Underground Railroad,* Philadelphia: Porter and Coates, 1872.

Minkins, Shadrach (1812–1875). Born in Norfolk, Virginia, Shadrach Minkins, a.k.a. **Frederick Wilkins/Jenkins**, was the subject of one of the most celebrated fugitive slave rescues in 1851.

His first owner, Thomas Glenn, operated the Eagle Tavern, one of the best eateries in Norfolk, where Shadrach, then known as Sherwood, undoubtedly was employed. After Glenn died in 1832, and his wife Ann in 1836, Minkins was sold to Martha Hutchings, who operated a grocery. By the end of the 1840s Hutchings's business failed, and Minkins was sold at auction to John DeBree, who after a career in the U.S. Navy had settled into a job at the harbor. Minkins became a house servant, and during this time he changed his name from Sherwood to Shadrach.

Some time around May 4, 1850, Minkins began his journey to freedom. It is speculated that he took passage aboard one of a number of boats leaving Norfolk for northern ports.

Minkins eventually wound up in Boston, and shortly after his arrival, he encountered a man, William Parks, who once had worked at the Hutchings grocery. Before long, Minkins found work at the Cornhill Coffee House and Hotel, which was only a few doors down the street from the offices of *The Liberator.*

No one knows how DeBree learned of Minkins's whereabouts, but on February 12, 1851, the slavecatcher John Caphart arrived in Boston as DeBree's representative to claim Minkins. After the federal government's failure to apprehend William and Ellen Craft in October, it is believed that a renewed effort was made to enforce the new Fugitive Slave Law in Boston, with Boston native and secretary of state Daniel Webster playing a major role.

Without warning, Minkins was seized at work and brought to the federal courthouse. News of the arrest spread quickly to the black community, and six lawyers from the Boston Vigilance Committee were at the courthouse within an hour. A crowd of about 150 had also pushed its way in, the majority of them black. The vigilance committee lawyers, among the best Boston had to offer, were able to obtain a three-day postponement to prepare their case.

The arrest had been made around eleven, and the hearing began after twelve and lasted another hour. It was not until two that the courtroom had been cleared. At this time Minkins was alone in a room with a couple of his lawyers and a couple of deputies. Outside in the hallways and on the stairs, spilling out into the square around the courthouse were several hundred onlookers, many of them black. A group of twenty blacks led by **Lewis Hayden** entered the courthouse acting in a jovial manner, so say accounts, determined to rescue Minkins. Forcing their way into the room where Minkins was held, they overpowered the deputies and literally carried Shadrach down the stairs and out of the courtroom. They dashed through the streets, accompanied by a mob that numbered as many as 200 persons, and eventually led Minkins to the attic apartment of a black woman who lived near Hayden. Then they quickly dispersed and went about their business as if nothing had happened.

A plan had been devised, however, to get Shadrach out of Boston quickly. A young Irish cabman, Thomas Murray, had been hired to be the driver, though what he was driving for, or whom he transporting, was totally unknown to him. He had been given rather circuitous directions to prevent him from being followed. After picking up two black men armed with pistols, who were Hayden and Minkins, he deposited them in Cambridge and drove off. Hayden obtained a horse and buggy and drove to Watertown, about four miles west. After spending the afternoon there, they returned to Cambridge, and while leaving Minkins with Rev. Joseph Lovejoy, a brother of the abolitionist martyr Elijah Lovejoy, Hayden obtained a wagon and two horses and returned with black barber and fellow conductor John J. Smith.

It was a stormy night and they did not complete the fifteen-mile journey to Concord and the home of abolitionists Francis and Ann Bigelow until very late—some accounts say 3 a.m. The next day, it is believed, Shadrach was taken to Fitchburg and from there to North Ashburnham. On the way to that stop, which may have been where he got on the train that took him to Canada, the carriage was pulled by a horse, who thereafter was called Shadrach.

On Friday, February 21, Shadrach arrived in Montreal, Canada, escaping as a passenger on the aboveground railroad, a journey that took him four days.

Three days earlier, President Millard Fillmore called for the prosecution of those involved in the rescue. Hayden was among several who were prosecuted, but with the able assistance of the vigilance committee no convictions were made, though the cases dragged on for more than two years.

In Montreal Shadrach started out his new life as a barber and within two years was married. As a free man, he decided to go into business for himself and tried several ventures. He opened some small restaurants and a trading business, but none of them lasted. Finally, he went back to barbering. This time, owing to a good location, he was able to find stability. In all he had four children, the first two dying before the age of five. He died in Canada, so far as is known, never returning again to the United States.

SUGGESTED READING: The authoritative work is Gary L. Collison, *Shadrach Minkins: From Fugitive Slave to Citizen*, Boston: Harvard University Press, 1997; Wilbur H. Siebert, *The Underground Railroad in Massachusetts*, Worcester: American Antiquarian Society, 1936.

Mitchell, William M. (unknown). Rev. William M. Mitchell was a black minister who worked the Underground Railroad in southern Ohio. His book *The Under-Ground Railroad* was published in Canada a year before the start of the Civil War.

Mitchell was an orphan born in Guilford County, North Carolina. His mother was Native American and his father a free black. He was indentured for twelve years, after which he became his employer's overseer for five years. In the latter position, he was obligated to assist his employer in the slave trade. He later expressed regret and horror at the role he played in punishing slaves and separating them from their families. When he moved to Ross County, Ohio, in 1843, he atoned for it by dedicating his life to the Underground Railroad.

The first fugitive slave incident in which he participated involved a slave from Maryland who had settled in Ohio and had joined the local Methodist church. To the runaway's shock and dismay, his pastor reported him to claim the $100 reward. Three slavecatchers led the man away with a rope around his neck. They had gone about three miles from town when a posse of about 200 black men, among them Mitchell, surged up behind them. The slavecatchers, fearing for their lives, cut the rope and dashed away before they could be captured. The man, Mitchell said, was never bothered by slavecatchers again.

Slavecatchers were a common sight in southern Ohio, and Mitchell said that an association of them had formed in the Kentucky counties of Mason and Bracken that bordered the Ohio River.

Mitchell said his greatest period of activity in the Underground Railroad occurred after he moved to Washington Courthouse in Fayette County, Ohio. Here, one of the road's greatest conductors became a regular visitor to his home. John Mason had escaped to Canada and then took up the profession of slave rescuing. Mitchell said that Mason brought 265 runaways to his home during a nineteen-month period. Obviously, to undertake such hazardous and lengthy missions, Mason would have by necessity been getting compensated. In all, Mason claimed that he aided as many as 1,300 fugitive slaves. But it was only a matter of time before he was captured. In the process both his arms were broken. Mason was sold and taken to New Orleans. Eighteen months after his capture, however, Mitchell received a letter from Mason stating that he was back in Canada.

On one occasion, Mitchell related that his house was surrounded by slavecatchers. They were searching for the fugitive slave he was hiding and they demanded to be allowed to enter. Mitchell said that they needed to get a warrant. While they did, Mitchell's wife dressed up the fugitive slave in women's clothing and took him in their wagon to the nearest safe house before the slavecatchers returned.

On another occasion, three fugitive slaves came to his locality with slavecatchers trailing close behind. While the slavecatchers searched the area, a wooden box large enough to accommodate two of them was constructed. The local agents transported two of them in the box to a station eight miles away and when the box was returned, sent the third one in it.

In his book, Mitchell relates additional stories about the Underground Railroad in which he was not involved, including one of a husband and wife who were reunited in Canada after twelve years when the woman came to a church looking for information about her husband and discovered that he was the pastor. A story he tells that has variations among the lore of Lake Erie incidents concerns eight fugitive slaves who boarded a steamer in Cleveland. They were hidden in the freight area and planned to disembark at the first stop in Fort Malden, now known as Amherstburg, Ontario. However, their owners boarded the ship before it left. En route, they were discovered. Learning that the first stop was in Canada, the slaveholders offered the captain $300 to bypass it and go straight to Detroit. He complied but tricked the slaveholders by arranging for the fugitive slaves to slip off in a skiff before the boat docked. Foiled, the slaveholders demanded that the captain chase the fugitive slaves. He agreed but only for the price of another $75. They did catch up to the fugitive slaves but only after the fugitives had landed in Ontario as free men.

Mitchell left Ohio to work as a missionary in Canada for the American Baptist Free Mission Society in 1855. His book, *The Under-Ground Railroad*, was published in 1860, and he donated a portion of its profits to his mission house in Toronto. It is not known when or where he died.

SUGGESTED READING: Rev. William M. Mitchell, *The Underground Railroad*, London: William Tweedie, 1860.

Moore, Noadiah (1797–1859). The son of a judge and former slaveowner, Moore was a prosperous farmer and businessman from Champlain in Clinton County, New York, who became his region's most vocal advocate of the Underground Railroad. His farm was only seven miles from the Canadian border, an advantageous location for an Underground Railroad conductor. He was in the prime of life when the antislavery crusade began, and he took a leadership role in his locality, being installed as the first president of the Clinton County Anti-Slavery Society at its organization in 1837.

Moore also inspired the local operation of the Underground Railroad, as testified to by Quaker **Stephen Keese Smith** of the Union Meeting in Peru, New York, who lived twenty-five miles south of Moore and with whom he worked closely. According to Keese Smith, fugitive slaves were run up to Moore, who took them to Canada and helped them find jobs. It is likely that he found them employment at the foundry, lumber mill, wagon shop, or general store that he owned in La Colle, Quebec, five miles north of the Canadian border.

When the Liberty Party formed in 1840, Moore became a strong supporter and again took a leadership role in Clinton County. He also took a public stand in his church, the First Presbyterian of Champlain, against fellowship with slaveholders. It caused a great stir, and shortly afterward the church was burned to the ground, though there is no record that the two events were related. Nevertheless, he had the strong support of his wife, Caroline, who wrote in a letter that "I have no fellowship with slaveholders" and who refused to form friendships with those who did not agree.

Moore also became acquainted with Liberty Party leader **Gerrit Smith**, and in 1846 he wrote Smith a letter urging him not to leave the party when Smith had become disillusioned. The strength of Moore's leadership in the party is reflected in the county's overwhelming support of the Liberty Party initiative that year to gain voting rights for free blacks, when the county supported the referendum with the highest plurality in the state at 72.8 percent. Overall, however, the state initiative failed by a vote of nearly 3 to 1.

It is not known how many fugitive slaves Moore helped, but his father's biographer said it is likely he spent as much on them as Keese Smith, who claimed to have spent about $1,000 of his own money. In terms of antebellum dollars, this would likely put the number of slaves he aided at somewhere in the neighborhood of 200.

SUGGESTED READING: Allan Seymour Everest, *Pliny Moore, North Country Pioneer of Champlain, NY,* Plattsburgh: Clinton County Historical Association, 1990; Allan S. Everest, editor, *Recollections,* Plattsburgh: Clinton County Historical Association, 1964.

Mott, Lucretia (1793–1880). Lucretia Mott was a leader in the abolitionist movement during an era when women were limited primarily to domestic duties, and this qualifies her as among the most remarkable women of the antebellum era. She was not only a charismatic speaker but also an untiring worker for the cause of abolition and, later, women's rights. Her home in Philadelphia was always open to those in need of shelter along the Underground Railroad, and though there are no records of numbers, it was likely in the hundreds. Her husband, James Mott, was her co-agitator and faithful supporter in the cause.

Born in Nantucket, Massachusetts, Mott was descended from the Quaker family of the Coffins on her father's side and the Folgers on her mother's side, through whom she was a relative of Benjamin Franklin. She was brought up in a morally upright household whose influence shaped her life, and she later remarked, "I . . . always loved the good, in childhood desired to do the right, and had no faith in the generally received idea of human depravity."

Philadelphia abolitionists James and Lucretia Mott. Courtesy of the Massachusetts Historical Society.

Living in a community of seafarers where the men often were absent added responsibilities to the women, and she modeled herself after their self-reliance. Her family moved to Boston and she was sent to the Nine Partners boarding school, a Quaker institution of which the noted reformer Elias Hicks was a founder and where she met her husband, James Mott, a young teacher there. During her second year, she became an assistant teacher.

Her family moved to Philadelphia, and James Mott soon followed. They were married in 1811 and James went into the hardware business with her father. The next years were difficult ones. The death of her father in 1812 put the business in the hands of James, who was young and inexperienced, while Lucretia gave birth to six children, one of whom died at the age of three. Despite the responsibilities of motherhood, she resumed teaching to supplement the family income and began her long career as a Quaker preacher in 1818, officially being recognized as a minister by her faith in 1821.

James was a good businessman, but an obstacle to their livelihood came when in 1827 the Quaker denomination began to split, the one side taking the lead of Elias Hicks, who preached that Quakers should take an active role in the social movements of the day, and the conservative Orthodox Quakers who believed in a passive approach. The Hicksites, as they were called and whom the Motts followed, forbade the use of products made from slave labor. Among the products offered by James were cotton fabrics, which he was obligated to abandon. Owing to his resourcefulness as a businessman, however, he found other avenues for profit and maintained the comfortable lifestyle of the Mott family.

As a Hicksite Quaker, Lucretia began preaching publicly against slavery in 1829. In many ways, her beliefs were patterned after Hicks: following her inner light, which was generally listening to one's own conscience rather than dogma created by human authority. Although she was a strong believer in nonviolence, her style was anything but passive, which ran counter to the style of the Orthodox Quakers. She believed that the true Quaker role was to agitate and speak out when moral wrongs or violations of human rights occurred: "I have no idea, because I am a Non-Resistant, of submitting tamely to injustice inflicted either on me or on the slave," she said. "I will oppose it with all the moral powers with which I am endowed."

She and James met William Lloyd Garrison in 1830 before he launched *The Liberator* and were his faithful supporters thereafter, and Garrison sometimes stayed with them when he visited Philadelphia. At the organizational meeting of the American Anti-Slavery Society (AAS) led by Garrison in Philadelphia, Mott was the only woman to make a public address. As was her lifelong custom, Mott wore her trademark Quaker bonnet and engaged in knitting while listening attentively to the proceedings.

Shortly after the AAS meeting, Mott organized the Philadelphia Female Anti-Slavery Society, the first meeting at which her husband, James, presided because there were no women who had prior experience in such a role. The society established a school for black children, purchased multiple subscriptions to *The Liberator* and other antislavery publications, and petitioned Congress urging the abolition of slavery in the District in Columbia and in the territories of the United States. Mott saw the distribution of antislavery literature as one of the society's primary roles. But its most important contribution was its annual antislavery fair that continued up through the Civil War and brought greater public awareness to the abolitionist cause, in addition to generating funds and other support for fugitive slaves.

In 1837 the Pennsylvania Anti-Slavery Society was organized, and the Motts became leading members, with James serving for many years as its president. They also became established members of the society's executive committee, which worked closely with the Philadelphia Vigilance Committee, the city's Underground Railroad organization.

Mott became the acknowledged leader among women in the national antislavery movement and perhaps the foremost female orator. Commentators of the day ranked her as the greatest Quaker orator, man or woman. Her most persuasive quality was not the logic of her thought but her calm and dignified presence that commanded everyone's attention. One commentator, on seeing her at the podium for the first time, said she looked like a saint. Although she generally kept to the high road, arguing the merits of her case, she was not averse to slipping into biting sarcasm in confronting moral evil.

She made many tours, mostly to Quaker meetings in the role of a minister for which she never received payment, and by her own admission traveled thousands of miles to speak about slavery and women's rights. One lecture tour took her 2,400 miles. She generally traveled by stage and stayed in public taverns, and though she was a woman, it was not beneath the propriety of the proslavery element to mob her. She even dared to speak in the South, in Maysville, Kentucky, on one occasion where she was invited, and also in Delaware, Maryland, and Virginia. Her calm, dignified manner protected her from harm.

Her major concerns, which she believed were related to the overriding issue of immediate emancipation, were to refrain from using products made from slave labor and for abolitionists to refrain from purchasing slaves to gain their freedom. Her reasoning behind the latter was that it supported the slave system and that the money would be used by the seller to purchase more slaves. Aiding fugitive slaves, she believed, was not the primary aim of the abolition movement because those emigrating annually amounted to less than the number of babies born into slavery each year. Nevertheless, she and James became active participants in the Underground Railroad.

The Mott residence at 136 North Ninth Street was a heavily frequented station on the Underground Railroad. Their residence was a spacious building connected on the second floor to the residence next door at 138 North Ninth Street, which was occupied by the Motts' daughter, Maria, and her husband, Edward Davis, also a member of the executive committee of the Philadelphia Anti-Slavery Society and involved in the Underground Railroad. It was often the next stop in the line from John and **Hannah Cox** in Kennett Square, Pennsylvania, and they worked closely with **William Still** and **Miller McKim** at the antislavery office on 31 North Fifth Street. The Cox and Mott residences were connections between **Thomas Garrett** in Wilmington, Delaware, and **Isaac Hopper** in New York, whose son married the Motts' daughter, Anna.

The Mott family played an important role in perhaps the most daring and imaginative flight to freedom in Underground Railroad lore, that of **Henry "Box" Brown**. It was their son-in-law, Edward Davis, who arranged the logistics for the delivery of the box from the post office to the antislavery office. Following Brown's emergence and a bath and change of clothes at Miller McKim's residence, a reception was hurriedly organized at the Motts' residence. Gifts of clothing and other necessities were furnished to Brown, and the atmosphere was one of jubilation. Among the notable guests was Samuel May, there for one of his many visits. Brown was in an ecstatic mood, and James Mott gave Brown a broad-brimmed hat. Having been cramped so in his box, Brown proceeded to prance about in the Motts' yard.

The Motts also were supportive of **Harriet Tubman**, who generally stopped in Philadelphia during her slave rescue missions. It was likely through them that she became acquainted with William Seward in Auburn, who helped her purchase a home there. Lucretia's sister Martha lived in Auburn and her husband was Seward's law partner.

Another notable runaway who visited the Motts on the way to freedom was Jane Johnson. In 1855 William Still and Passmore Williamson of the vigilance committee led Johnson and her two young sons, slaves of John Wheeler, the U.S. ambassador to Nicaragua, off a steamship docked in Philadelphia harbor. They did so forcibly against the wishes of Wheeler. However, they were acting under the jurisdiction of a state law in Pennsylvania that prohibited slaveholders from bringing their slaves into the state and which automatically granted their emancipation.

The Johnsons were brought to the Motts for lodging until plans could be arranged for their departure along the Underground Railroad. After three days, Lucretia told Jane that her master had charged Williamson and others with assault, kidnapping, and rioting. She asked her if she would be willing to testify in court against him but warned her that although state law granted her freedom, she could be apprehended under the jurisdiction of the federal law. Nevertheless, Jane agreed to testify.

Four days later she went to court accompanied by Lucretia, Sarah McKim, Sarah Pugh, and Rebecca Plumly. On the witness stand, when asked if the accused men had kidnapped her against her wishes, Jane replied, "I went away of my own free will. Always wanted to be free. Planned to be free when I came north." She added that she would rather die than become Wheeler's slave again.

Jane returned to the Mott home for several more days until she and her sons were sent along the Underground Railroad to Canada. The jury found the accused men not guilty of the kidnapping, though two blacks were found guilty of assault and spent a week in jail. Williamson, however, spent three months in jail on the charge of contempt of court for filing a false report regarding the whereabouts of Jane following her rescue.

Another prominent runaway slave case involving the Mott family occurred in 1859. Daniel Dangerfield, a.k.a. Daniel Webster, a runaway working on a farm in Harrisburg, was seized in 1859 under the jurisdiction of the Fugitive Slave Law. The Motts' son-in-law Edward Hopper, the son of Isaac Hopper, was retained to defend him, and Mott set out to do whatever she could to assist him. Her fame preceded her when she entered the courtroom. Before the proceedings, she had words with the presiding judge, Commissioner J. Cooke Longstreth, a Quaker, whom she reminded of the tenets of their faith. "Remember," she said, "the traitor to humanity is the traitor most accursed."

The claimant's attorney also became intimidated by the Mott's gaze and even asked that her chair be moved because she made him uncomfortable. In the end, the judge acquitted Dangerfield on the technicality that the warrant showed him to be a different height than he was. Dangerfield was then placed on the Underground Railroad, first to the house of Morris L. Hallowell, eight miles from Philadelphia, and then on to Canada.

Reverend Samuel J. May: The Modern Incarnation of the Sermon on the Mount

Samuel J. May was born into an upper-class Boston family, but his strong convictions led him to devote his life to the antislavery cause and the Underground Railroad.

May began aiding fugitive slaves in 1834 when he was a minister in Brooklyn, Connecticut, forwarding fugitives to Effingham L. Capron, in Uxbridge, Massachusetts. May had become interested in the antislavery movement as early as 1822, during a trip to the South when he observed blacks in chains.

Like many early white abolitionists, May supported colonization but came under the influence of Garrison and changed his opinion. Working with Garrison, May was a founding member of the American Anti-Slavery Society. He also became embroiled in an 1833 incident involving the closing of Prudence Crandall's women's school in nearby Canterbury, Connecticut, because she allowed black students.

"I felt ashamed of Canterbury," May wrote, "ashamed of Connecticut, ashamed of my country, ashamed of my color."

In 1845 May moved to Syracuse, where he became most active in the operation of the Underground Railroad. He was responsible for the movement of hundreds of fugitive slaves there, being that city's stationmaster until that duty was turned over in 1851 to **Jermaine Loguen**.

"Fugitives came to me from Maryland, Virginia, Kentucky, Tennessee, and Louisiana," May wrote. "They came, too, at all hours of day and night."

May was also one of the leaders of the Jerry Rescue in Syracuse, which freed fugitive slave **Jerry Henry** from federal authorities in 1851.

In 1855 May joined with radical abolitionists who met in Syracuse and advocated more extreme measures—though stopping short of violent overthrow—to combat slavery. An avowed pacifist, it was with great reluctance that May finally supported the Civil War.

May had been in the trenches for forty years, fighting slavery and racial prejudice. He personally knew many of the major players like **Gerrit Smith**, William Lloyd Garrison, and the Tappan brothers. This made May uniquely qualified to write *Some Recollections of Our Anti-Slavery Conflict*, published in 1869.

At his funeral in 1871, his eulogist said that May's life was "the modern incarnation of the Sermon on the Mount."

Among the luminaries of the antislavery pantheon who were frequent guests of the Motts were Samuel May, William Lloyd Garrison, Theodore Parker, and **Frederick Douglass**. Lucretia extended an open invitation to visit when notables in the movement came to town. Others who dined with her and James were Benjamin Lundy, John Quincy Adams, and Ralph Waldo Emerson. Another notable guest who stayed with the Motts at their sprawling mansion, the "Roadside," on the York Road outside Philadelphia where they had moved in 1857, was **John Brown**'s wife, Mary. While there, she received a letter from John saying he was an admirer of the Motts and was pleased that she was staying with them.

Although Mott is also renowned for her efforts in the women's rights movement—being among the leaders at the Seneca Falls Convention (New York) in 1848, and continuing in the forefront of the women's movement until the end of her life—bringing an end to slavery and achieving the social and political elevation of blacks remained her foremost interest.

"Of all the women who served the anti-slavery cause in its darkest days," wrote **William Still**, "there is not one whose labors were more effective, whose character is nobler, and who is more universally respected and beloved, than Lucretia Mott."

Frederick Douglass also paid her tribute, writing about the first time he saw her and the effect she had whenever he heard her speak thereafter:

> The speaker was attired in the usual Quaker dress, free from startling colors, plain, rich, elegant, and without superfluity—the very sight of her a sermon. In a few moments after she began to speak, I saw before me no more a woman, but a glorified presence, bearing a message of light and love.
>
> . . . She was comparatively young [then]. I have often heard her since, sometimes in the solemn temple, and, sometimes under the open sky, but whenever and wherever I have listened to her, my heart was always made better, and my spirit raised by her words.

SUGGESTED READING: Otelia Cromwell, *Lucretia Mott*, Cambridge, MA: Harvard University Press, 1958; Frederick Douglass, *Life and Times of Frederick Douglass*, Hartford, CT: Park Publishing Co., 1881; Lloyd C. Hare, *The Greatest American Woman*, New York: Negro Universities Press, 1970, reprint 1937; John F. Hume, *The Abolitionists*, New York: G.P. Putnam's Sons, 1905; William Still, *The Underground Railroad*, Philadelphia: Porter and Coates, 1872.

Myers, Stephen (1803?–1870). One of the leading Underground Railroad conductors in New York State, Stephen Myers was called "the superintendent" of the Underground Railroad in Albany, New York, by **Frederick Douglass**. He also was the first black lobbyist for "Negro" rights in the New York State legislature, a leading spokesman for the temperance movement, and a publisher of at least three "Negro" newspapers.

Born a slave in the town of Hoosick in Rensselaer County, New York, in 1803 (some sources say 1800), Myers was emancipated from the family of Dr. Eights in 1818. Myers may have started in the Underground Railroad business as early as 1831, for he stated in his newspaper the *Northern Star and Freeman's Advocate* that organized efforts to help fugitive slaves in Albany began that year.

The *Northern Star* was his first journalistic endeavor and published from 1842 to 1843. It was introduced on January 20, 1842, shortly after the demise of the *Colored American*, whose final issue came out on Christmas Day in 1841. Published by "three colored persons," Stephen Myers, John Stewart, and Charles Morton, the *Northern Star* advocated

Albany, New York, Underground Railroad conductor Stephen Myers. From *The Autobiography of Dr. William Henry Johnson* (1900).

temperance, abolition, and the moral and educational improvement of blacks. Myers was the editor but had a lot of help from his wife, Harriet, who had a better command of spelling and grammar. It had a wide distribution, likely made through the contacts the publishers had made at the state and national Negro conventions, with agents stretching from Buffalo to Salem, Massachusetts, and Concord, New Hampshire, and from New York City to Saratoga.

In its December 8, 1842, issue, Myers wrote the following:

> I will say a few words in relation to slaves who have passed through this city. There was one sent to our office by Mr. Morrell of Newark. We put him on board of a canal boat, paid his passage to Oswego, and furnished him with money to go into Canada . . . . We assisted two slaves that were sent to our office by William Garner of Elizabethtown [N.J.]; we furnished them with money for Canada by way of Lake Champlain.

With the aboveground railroad not extending from New York City to Albany until 1851, the most likely means of travel for these fugitive slaves was by boat, as described by New York Committee of Vigilance member **Charles Ray**:

> When we had parties to forward from here, we would alternate in sending between Albany and Troy, and when we had a large party we would divide between the two cities. We had

> on one occasion, a party of twenty-eight persons of all ages . . . . We destined them for Canada. I secured passage for them in a barge, and Mr. Wright and myself spent the day in providing food, and personally saw them off on the barge.

Myers began working on steamboats at least as early as 1838, being the ship steward on the vessel *Diamond*. It is likely that he used steamboats to transport fugitive slaves. Adding to support to this is the occupation of his wife's father, Captain Abram, a member of his vigilance committee, who was employed as a "skipper." These steamboats regularly took travelers on day trips. The description of the Armenia in an 1848 article in the *Albany Patriot* is particularly incriminating. A "neat, swift, little day-boat from New York to Troy," it could make the tip from New York to Albany in nine hours, and "nothing on the river is likely to slip by her in any fair contest." The boat's design was marked by a novel "improvement" for such ships that made it more amenable for the passage of fugitive slaves: "the table is set on the first deck instead of below, as is usual . . . . A light, airy saloon, of a hot or a dark day, is altogether more comfortable than a close and dungeon-like place." And its steward was Myers, of whom it said, "He really does up the thing, with the support of his assistants, in just about the best style. Stephen has had a long experience in the culinary department, and can't be beat by white folks."

During the early 1840s Myers's Underground Railroad group may have been working in tandem rather than cooperatively with the Eastern New York Antislavery Society (ENYAS) of **Abel Brown** and **Charles Torrey** that so publicly revealed its efforts. However, Myers certainly knew them, as is apparent by noting their joint participation at various antislavery meetings and conventions, and a battle of words and ideas between them that was published in issues of the *Tocsin of Liberty* and the *Northern Star*. With the deaths of Torrey and Brown, and the demise of the ENYAS, the likelihood is that the two groups were brought together in the Underground work, with Myers coordinating these efforts.

Myers was quite the organizer. Among the influential individuals he could count on to fund his Underground Railroad organization were editors Thurlow Weed, of the *Albany Evening Journal*, and Horace Greeley, of the *New York Tribune*; New York governors William H. Seward, John Alsop King, and Edward D. Morgan; New York City merchants Moses Grinnell, Simeon Draper, and Robert B. Minturn; philanthropist James W. Beekman; Livingston County, New York, patrician General James Wadsworth, considered to be the richest man in the Union Army and who died in the Civil War; New York City contractor John P. Cummings; Albany stone manufacturer William Newton; and John Jay, of Westchester County, the grandson of the Founding Father.

Myers also made the rounds at the state and national Negro conventions and as a temperance lecturer. A colored temperance society in Lee, Massachusetts, with thirty-six members was named after him. His letters also show that he was lobbying the New York State legislature to remove the state's property qualification for blacks to vote and to defeat a bill there to provide funding to the African Colonization Society. His activities cast a wide network of contacts.

Among those in the Underground Railroad he worked with were **Francis Jackson**, secretary of the Boston Vigilance Committee, who forwarded fugitive slaves to him through Thomas Harley in Springfield, Massachusetts; Lewis Tappan, who forwarded fugitive slaves in New York City; and **Gerrit Smith**, who from his central New York residence was by 1848 overseeing the operations of the New York Committee of Vigilance.

It is likely that he also had close contact with **William Still** in Philadelphia, as a number of fugitive slaves came to him by way of Philadelphia, including Harriet Tubman. Other noteworthy contacts were **Sidney Howard Gay** and Judge **Erastus Culver** of Brooklyn, whom he likely met as early as 1838 at a regional antislavery convention in Albany. The father of Chester Arthur—who was a member of Culver's law firm and tried some important cases involving fugitive slaves—pastored a church near Myers's vigilance committee office. His New York City contacts likely were cemented through his regular trips there on his boat runs.

Several documents that have survived tell whom Myers was working with, how many fugitive slaves he was aiding, what he did to help them, and how he managed the business end of the Underground Railroad.

The first was an 1856 broadside he issued publicizing his operations. In it he revealed that during one nine-month period between September 12, 1855, and July 15, 1856, he coordinated the movement of 287 fugitive slaves and paid $542.36 for their passage and $76.60 for their board. He also lists the names of the members of his vigilance committee—in all, twelve men including himself. In a later circular from 1858, he states that 121 fugitive slaves were helped during a five-month period with $242 being paid for their passage to Syracuse. Myers also wrote in the circular that "hundreds of fugitives have fallen to my care during the last twelve years" and that he was in need of funds to continue his efforts. He added that his financial books and accounts were open for anyone to inspect if they were concerned about the use of their contributions. He also appealed for clothing to be donated and added that to save expenses many fugitive slaves were sent into the country to work on farms, which was considered to be safe.

In a letter to Francis Jackson, six weeks later, he wrote that sixty-seven more runaways had passed through and that he was accommodating "three different branches of the underground road."

In another letter later that year to John Jay, he identified a number of his benefactors and explained that he collected ten cents on every dollar received because he was devoting his entire livelihood to the Underground business, and that if it did not amount to $450 annually, then his benefactors would compensate him. He also contrasted the way he ran his Underground with that in New York and Philadelphia, explaining that he had to collect and manage every dollar himself while they raised their funds through antislavery societies and fairs. He mentioned nine fugitive slaves that Jay's father had sent him during the previous eight years before his death.

Besides his networking, politicking, writing, preaching, and conducting, Myers found time to publish, in addition to the *Northern Star*, two other newspapers, the *Elevator* circa 1843 and the *Telegraph* circa 1856. During the Civil War, he enlisted the first company of more than forty colored men from Albany. When Governor Morgan would not accept them, they joined the war effort as part of the Fifty-fourth Massachusetts Regiment.

Myers's life was a tireless effort to further the rights of blacks in America and to defend the freedom of fugitive slaves. The following appeal, which he wrote in the January 2, 1843, issue of the *Northern Star*, was echoed in many speeches by black and white leaders until slavery was abolished:

> Let the voice of forty thousand colored citizens be heard at the Capitol of the Empire state; yes, and at Washington, until the prayers of two millions and a half be heard that are now held in abject bondage, and that Congress may not turn their petitions away unheard as formerly; and let us see American slavery immediately abolished from our land.

SUGGESTED READING: Tom Calarco, *The Underground Railroad in the Adirondack Region*, Jefferson, NC: McFarland, 2004; William Henry Johnson, *Autobiography of Dr. William Henry Johnson*, Albany: Argus Company Printers, 1900; *Northern Star and Freeman's Advocate*, 1842–1843; C. Peter Ripley, editor, *The Black Abolitionist Papers*, Vol. 4, Chapel Hill: University of North Carolina Press, 1991.

N

Northup, Solomon (1808–unknown). On the night of January 20, 1853, Solomon Northup, a free black man, returned home to Sandy Hill in Washington County, New York, a free man again after twelve years as a slave. The story of his ordeal was published later that year in a narrative, *Twelve Years a Slave,* in which the words of Northup were written by author David Wilson.

Northup was born free in Minerva, Essex County, New York. He had resided most of his life in neighboring Washington County, but in 1841 he was staying in Saratoga Springs about twenty miles south. He was working various jobs, including gigs as a fiddle player while his wife and children remained home. He was approached by two white men, Alexander Merrill and Joseph Russell, who were using the aliases Merrill Brown and Abram Hamilton and who said they needed a musician to accompany performances during which they advertised their circus. After performing one night in Albany, they went to New York City, where they urged him to continue with them to Washington to join their circus. They promised more work and good wages. At their suggestion, they visited the customhouse and obtained the necessary papers which certified that Northup was free, an important precaution for a free black entering a slave state. It solidified Northup's trust.

In Washington they further ingratiated themselves when they paid him a generous sum for his employment. But the following day they took him to a saloon where they drugged him. When Northup awakened, he found himself in chains in the slave pen of James H. Birch, without his identification papers or money. Northup protested that he was a free man but was beaten until he stopped.

While en route farther south, Northup was chained to another slave, who like himself was a free man kidnapped into slavery. His predicament was similar to Northup's in that he had been hired on a job and taken south before being kidnapped into slavery. Such kidnappings were not uncommon during this time, especially in New York City, which as early as 1836 was said to be "infested with slavecatchers." Not only were slavecatchers on the prowl but they were organized under the leadership of Tobias Boudinot, the constable of the city's Third Ward, who worked in coordination with attorney F. H. Pettis. Sometimes, slavecatchers like the ones who abducted Northup were Northern residents. In fact, Northup's kidnappers were from a locality near Saratoga Springs hundreds of miles from the Mason-Dixon Line.

As Northup wrote after his release, "I doubt not hundreds have been as unfortunate as myself; that hundreds of free citizens have been kidnapped and sold into slavery, and are at this moment wearing out their lives on plantations in Texas and Louisiana."

Undoubtedly, the dangers such activities posed to free blacks resulted in the state's passage on May 6 and May 14, 1840, of two laws: the first, to extend trial by jury to fugitive slaves; the second, "to protect the free citizens of this state from being kidnapped or reduced to slavery." Though these laws were not enough to prevent Northup's kidnapping, it was under the jurisdiction of the second that his eventual release from slavery was obtained.

Northup's book is a fascinating and detailed picture not only of slavery, but also of the measures used by slaveholders to keep slaves from running away and the atrocities slaveholders inflicted on slaves if they were caught. On the plantations in the Deep South where conditions were much harsher, security measures also were more stringent. Northup spent ten of his eleven years in slavery on one of those plantations in Louisiana, called Bayou Boeuf, owned by Edwin Epps. The harsher conditions naturally increased the desire for escape, as he wrote:

> There was not a day throughout the ten years I belonged to Epps that I did not consult with myself upon the prospect of escape. I laid many plans, which at the time I considered excellent ones, but one after the other they were all abandoned. No man who has never been placed in such a situation, can comprehend the thousand obstacles thrown in the way of the flying slave. Every white man's hand is raised against him—the patrollers are watching for him—the hounds are ready to follow on his track, and the nature of the country is such as renders it impossible to pass through it with any safety.
>
> Notwithstanding the certainty of being captured, the woods and swamps are nevertheless, continually filled with fugitive slaves. Many of them, when sick, or so worn out as to be unable to perform their tasks, escape into the swamps, willing to suffer the punishment inflicted for such offences, in order to obtain a day or two of rest.

Northup did escape for a time from one of his earlier owners. But after he was sold to Epps, he found escaping far more intimidating and described one runaway who was nearly chewed to death by hounds and died shortly after.

Patty Cannon: The Most Nefarious Slavecatcher

Countless men and women sold their souls for pieces of silver as slavecatchers. There also were a number of slavecatching organizations and gangs. One was led by New York City constable Tobias Boudinot. Another existed up through central Ohio, according to President Rutherford B. Hayes, an attorney in Cincinnati during the antebellum period. Among the most notorious individuals were Wright Ray of Madison, Indiana; William Padgett of Lancaster County, Pennsylvania; and Bacon Tate from Tennessee. But perhaps the most nefarious of all was Patty Cannon.

She lived along the border between Maryland and Virginia and was the head of a gang whose ringleaders included her husband, Jesse; her son-in-law, Joe Johnson; and a black man, John Purnell. They commanded thirty members operating within an area between Philadelphia and Accomak, Virginia, along the eastern coast of Chesapeake Bay.

Both slaves and free blacks were targeted, especially families with children. Cannon was known to have killed at least two children herself, one of whom was a five-year-old whose face she held in a fire until death. Finally, in 1829, Cannon was prosecuted for murder. Before her case was decided, she confessed to a priest that she had murdered eleven persons, including her husband and an infant born to her, and had been an accessory to twelve others. She died shortly after, apparently committing suicide by taking poison.

In 1852 a letter was mailed for Northup to a friend in Saratoga by a sympathetic, non-slaveholding white carpenter named Bass who lived near Bayou Boeuf. The lawyer Henry B. Northup of Sandy Hill, a village near Saratoga, was the son of the man who had manumitted Solomon's father from slavery. He went on Solomon's behalf to Bayou Boeuf and reclaimed Solomon's freedom by virtue of the aforementioned 1840 New York State statute.

Following his return to freedom and the publication of his book, Northup was in demand as a speaker at abolition meetings. He also is said to have participated in the Underground Railroad with Methodist minister Rev. Lame John Smith of Hartland, Vermont. Of his speeches, an account of his February 27, 1854, talk at the courthouse in St. Albans, the *Vermont Tribune* stated: "He talked pretty well for 'a chattel,' 'a thing,' as our government regards him. His unaffected simplicity, directness, and gentlemanly bearing impressed far more than many fervid appeals to which we have listened."

The last known whereabouts of Northup was in Streetville, a community southeast of Toronto, Canada West, where a mob prevented him from giving a lecture in 1857. There is also speculation that he may have moved to Constantia in Oswego County, where he had a brother, but no reference to his death or trace of his burial site has been found.

SUGGESTED READING: Michelle Genz, "Solomon's Wisdom," *The Washington Post*, March 7, 1999; Solomon Northup, *Twelve Years a Slave,* edited by Sue Eakin and Joseph Logsdon, Baton Rouge: LSU Press, 1968, reissue of 1853.

P

Parker, John P. (1827–1900). John Parker was among the most daring conductors of the Underground Railroad, working as a foundry owner in Ripley, Ohio, by day, and risking his life to rescue others from slavery by night.

Parker was born a slave in Norfolk, Virginia, the son of a slave and her master. At the age of eight, he was sold and sent to Richmond. His bitterness at being separated from his mother grew into a deep hatred after he learned of the whipping death of an old slave who had been kind to him during the journey to Richmond. He became rebellious, and this caused his new owner to sell him to a slave trader.

Thereafter he began a 400-mile trek on foot in a coffle gang to Alabama. Parker was bought by a doctor from Mobile, who had two sons about Parker's age. They treated him almost like a third brother and taught him to read and to write. When the doctor sent his sons east to go to Yale, he decided to also send Parker, who was then sixteen, to be their servant. When they stayed in Philadelphia, Parker was approached by free blacks, but his inexperience and immaturity caused him to misinterpret their overtures as threats. Upset by this, he wrote his master, who realized the men were not threatening Parker but trying to entice him to claim his freedom, and he called him back to Alabama.

His master suggested that Parker learn a trade and apprenticed him to a cruel plasterer who beat him with a lathe that had a nail embedded in it. It necessitated that he be sent to a hospital for slaves. It was kept by a woman who beat her patients. This was too much for him to endure, and when he witnessed her beating a sick woman, he tried to stop her. When she turned the whip on him, he took it away from her and beat her into submission. At once Parker took flight and boarded a steamboat to New Orleans. He was not sure how or even if he wanted to escape to freedom.

While stowing away in a northbound riverboat and looking for food, he was discovered and captured. A local sheriff was summoned and took custody of Parker. What followed was a series of escapes and captures that make Huck Finn's adventures seem very tame: in one instance Parker nearly lost his life. Finally captured and about to be sold at auction, he used his cunning to escape one last time and returned to his master in Mobile.

To his surprise, his master did not punish him but instead placed him in another apprenticeship with a friend who owned a foundry. Parker found that he had a knack for the work and became so good that it created hard feelings between him and his co-workers. A fight erupted and his master sent him to a different foundry, but it was more of the same. His master was perplexed and thought he might be forced to send Parker into the cotton fields.

Desperate, Parker went to the home of a woman who had been a patient of his master and asked her to purchase him. She reluctantly agreed and allowed him to work and save up the money to purchase his freedom. It took eighteen months.

Now eighteen or nineteen years old, he moved to Cincinnati. He was free and contented and had found a job. About a year into his residence there, at the boarding house where he lived, he met a black barber from Maysville. The man had moved to Cincinnati because his activities aiding fugitive slaves had come under suspicion.

> The man confided in me that several nights before he was forced to get out of town [he] met two girls in the act of running away. Knowing they had a good home and a kindly mistress, besides being young, he persuaded the girls to go back home and stay there. Now that he had been treated so brutally [in Maysville], he had made up his mind to run the girls away and proposed I accompany him back to Maysville to aid in the enterprise.

The plan was to go to Ripley, about ten miles west of Maysville, which at that time was unknown to Parker. From there, they would look for a rowboat to take during the night to the house of a free colored man who lived along the Kentucky shore near Maysville; this man would alert the girls. The barber would wait on the Ohio shore, as he did not want to be discovered in Maysville.

However, they ran into a problem at Ripley. They could not find a boat to use. After three days, the barber became frustrated and returned to Cincinnati. But once Parker set out to do something, he was going to finish it, and because no one knew him in Maysville, he decided to go to the black man's house to which the barber had given him directions.

The man was not very cordial but did secure a boat for Parker and alerted the girls. There was one unforeseen problem. The girls were so big that Parker feared they would capsize the boat. What he did not realize was that the girls were wearing several dresses atop each other in addition to hoop skirts. They also had large bundles of possessions that he forced them to leave behind. Finally he was able to get them in the boat by positioning them on each end.

They had a ten-mile trip, but before they reached Ripley, Parker heard the sound of oars. They were being pursued, and he told the girls to take off their extra clothing because they were going to have to go ashore and run for it. In their panic one of them fell out of the boat. Parker quickly fished her out and rowed ashore. With some difficulty they stumbled out of the boat and up the riverbank. They continued through the fields until daylight and hid in the bushes and slept. Shortly after dark, they reached a black settlement near Ripley. A man there said that Ripley was being watched but that he would go into the village to see if he could find a friend to help them. The man returned about midnight and led them to the home of Eli Collins, one of Ripley's most experienced conductors. Parker turned the girls over to him. It was the last time he would see them but not the last time he would see Ripley.

Parker married two years later and moved to Ripley in 1849, where he opened his own foundry business. Although the village had a large number of abolitionists, whose core included some of the most dedicated abolitionists anywhere, and was a short distance from two black communities, the countryside was populated by many who were proslavery. As Parker said, "In fact, the country was so antagonistic to abolitionism at this time, we could only take fugitives out of town and through the country along definite and limited routes."

Parker continued his work assisting fugitive slaves. Judging by the stories he told about it, the adventure and the risks involved seemed to fortify his manly character. He had kept a diary with the names, dates, and circumstances of the people he had helped but destroyed it after the Fugitive Slave Law was passed because he feared of endangering the considerable property he had accumulated. He had lived in Ripley only two years by this time and said he already had helped 315 fugitive slaves.

One particularly exciting story, which Parker tells in dramatic detail, was the rescue of a husband and wife and their baby. One of the men who worked for Parker was from Kentucky, and his father was a slaveowner. People suspected that Parker was in the business of helping fugitive slaves, which he did after work at night, and his employee continually teased Parker about it and dared him to rescue one of his father's slaves. Parker, being a proud man and perhaps a bit foolhardy at times, decided to accept the challenge. He made several trips during the evening to the slaveholder's farm before the opportunity to entice a slave presented itself. The man, who had a wife and baby girl, readily agreed, and a plan was arranged. But during their meeting, a farmhand stumbled upon them. The slave quickly departed, and Parker had to fight his way free. He was afraid he might have been recognized, but it turned out that in the darkness of the night the man thought Parker was just another fugitive slave.

When the appointed night came, however, a major obstacle was put in their path. After Parker's encounter with the farmhand, the slaveholder became suspicious, so he required the slave to bring his baby to his house and have the baby sleep in the slaveholder's bedroom. Parker told the slave to go to the house and get his baby, but when he refused out of fear, Parker told him that he would get the baby and that the slave should get his wife and wait for him at the boat.

Cautiously they approached the slaveholder's house. Parker took off his shoes and gave them to the slave, who then went to get his wife. Parker crept inside and tiptoed up the stairs. He noticed a light coming from a room and assumed it was the bedroom. The door was closed, and he had to turn the knob ever so carefully. When it opened, he noticed in the candlelight a large pistol on the nightstand next to the slaveholder's bed but did not see the baby. He assumed it might be at the foot of the bed behind its high footboard. He also assumed it would be on the side of the woman. He crawled forward and saw a bundle where he had expected it. Carefully, he snatched it, and the candle went out. He dashed out of the room, rousing the sleeping slaveholder, who fumbled in the darkness. Parker was not about to wait and see what would happen next and merely ran out of the house as fast as he could. In the distance, he heard the fire of shots as he raced to the boat. He found the couple waiting, and Parker brought them to a safe house in Ripley. There was one problem: in the excitement, the slave had left Parker's shoes behind. But while the slaveholder did find the shoes, Parker went to the shoemaker from whom he had bought them and asked the shoemaker to cover for him. Although the slaveholder did check all the local shoemakers, no one blew Parker's cover. And his employee, the son of the slaveholder, never came back to work for him.

After that a reward went out for Parker's head, but he was undeterred. Nevertheless, he was careful. As he said, "I never thought of going uptown without a pistol in my pocket, a knife in my belt, and a blackjack handy. Day or night I dare not walk on the sidewalks for fear someone might leap out of a narrow alley at me." It was said that in all he helped as many as 1,000 slaves obtain their freedom. It is not clear how often Parker worked with the Rankins in the Underground Railroad, but there was one occasion in which he saved the life of one of the Rankin boys during an encounter with a slavecatcher. But most of his slave rescue stories refer to his collaboration with the Collins family, who were probably Rankin's most active associates in Ripley and who lived just a few doors down the street from Parker.

Parker did indeed live a double life and was a very successful businessman and inventor of machinery used in his line of work. He obtained several patents on his inventions, one being a "screw for tobacco Presses." At one point, he employed more than twenty-five men at his foundry.

Most of what is known about Parker is based on an interview with him during the 1880s conducted by a journalist who had grown up in Ripley; the journalist published the account as Parker's autobiography. His tale was not meant necessarily for publication or to gain fame but merely to reminisce about Ripley during "the days of passion and battle which turned father against son, and neighbor against neighbor." Of two versions that exist, the earlier account has since gained more acceptance as the more authentic.

SUGGESTED READING: Stuart Seely Sprague, editor, *His Promised Land*, New York: W.W. Norton and Co., 1996; Louis Weeks, "John P. Parker: Black Abolitionist Entrepreneur, 1827–1900," *Ohio History*, No. 80, 1971.

Parker, William (1824?–unknown). William Parker was a fugitive slave who was the central figure in the Christiana Riot, which many consider the first confrontation of the Civil War. Though the riot that occurred at his residence took place in 1851, it symbolized the conflict between the North and the South over the moral and political consequences of slavery.

Born as a slave on the extensive plantation of Major William Brogdon in Anne Arundel County, Maryland, fifty miles south of the Pennsylvania border, Parker never knew his father, who may have been white. He was very young when his mother was sold, and the only adult relative he knew was his grandmother, the cook on his master's plantation.

In his memoir of 1866, he described his experience as a child in a large pen with other children called "the Quarters," about 100 by 30 feet. It was here that he learned how to fight to survive. The most vivid memory of his childhood experience was the occasions when slave sales took place and separated family members and friends. He vowed never to let that happen to him, and at about the age of seventeen, after a confrontation with his master, he and his brother fled to Pennsylvania.

By this time, Parker had grown into a tall, muscular young man described as a dark mulatto. During the escape he fought off an armed slavecatcher with his bare hands. He and his brother also were able to evade their master, who had tracked down their escape route and unknowingly had passed by close enough for them to spot him. The personal courage and physical strength Parker demonstrated during his escape would serve him well in the events for which he is remembered.

The young men soon found jobs in Lancaster County, Pennsylvania, where there were a large number of farmers sympathetic to blacks, which had resulted in a large number of blacks settling in the region, including many fugitive slaves.

However, the county also had a significant number of proslavery citizens who were open to conspiring with slavecatchers to assist the rendition and kidnapping of blacks,

Blacks fire upon slavecatchers at William Parker's house in Christiana, Pennsylvania. Courtesy of the William Still Foundation, Inc.

both free and unemancipated. It became common practice for whites to forcibly enter the homes of blacks in search of fugitive slaves. From this practice, the Gap gang, a group of vicious and brutal thugs, was formed. It was Parker who organized blacks to defend themselves against the gang and who on a number of occasions rescued blacks who had been kidnapped by them, in one incident beating a kidnapper to death.

"I thought of my fellow servants left behind, bound in the chains of slavery, and I was free!" Parker wrote as to his motivation. "I thought that if I had the power, they should soon be as free as I was; and I formed a resolution that I would assist in liberating every one within my reach at the risk of my life, and that I would devise some plan for their entire liberation."

Over a period of nearly ten years, Parker's reputation grew, and Sadsbury Underground Railroad conductor Lindley Coates described him as "bold as a lion, the kindest of men, and the most steadfast of friends." Parker certainly was the one man that blacks in the region could most depend on if they got into trouble.

After the passage of the Fugitive Slave Law of 1850, slavecatchers were emboldened, and the number of incursions by them over the state border increased. Several brutal renditions took place without due process of the law, one involving the death of John Williams, a fugitive slave who had settled in Lancaster County, and it was not surprising that a confrontation occurred with Parker at its center.

The confrontation, however, did not involve the illicit activities of the Gap gang but a legally sanctioned rendition by Maryland slaveholder Edward Gorsuch. Four of his slaves—Nelson Ford, Noah Buley, and Josh and George Hammond—had escaped in 1849 after Gorsuch had noticed that quantities of wheat were missing from his grain bin. He had been informed by a local resident that Abe Johnson, a free black, was selling wheat that he could not have cultivated. Johnson left the area, however, before Gorsuch could have him arrested. Though Gorsuch suspected that his slaves were involved, his intent was to get "his property" back and forgive them if he did. Gorsuch considered himself a benevolent master and had arranged for his slaves' emancipation when they turned twenty-eight. A devout Methodist and "class leader" in his church, he felt that he was acting in their best interests as their caretaker.

Gorsuch had received reports of the whereabouts of his former slaves and went to Philadelphia to obtain warrants for the rendition. Accompanying him were his son, Dickinson; his nephew, Thomas Pearce; his cousin, Joshua Gorsuch; and two slaveholders, who were his neighbors, Nicholas Hutchins and Nathan Nelson. They met with federal marshal Henry Kline to serve the warrants. They also were supposed to be assisted by two other law enforcement officers, who had come to Lancaster County from Philadelphia but at the last minute changed their minds.

Gorsuch's plans were discovered by the Philadelphia Vigilance Committee, likely through a contact at the courthouse, and one of their agents, Samuel Williams, was sent to learn the whereabouts of the Gorsuch posse and warn those in Lancaster County, who were identified in the warrants. The day before the posse arrived, the black community in Christiana had been made fully aware of the impending rendition through a handbill that had been circulated.

The night before their arrival, two of Gorsuch's slaves, Nelson Ford and Josh Hammond, spent the night at the home of William Parker along with Abe Johnson, the man who had stolen Gorsuch's wheat, and Parker's brother-in-law, Alex Pinckney. Both Eliza Parker and Hannah Pinckney, the wives of William and Alexander, also were there. They were expecting the Gorsuch posse, and some speculate that William Padgett, who was Gorsuch's guide, may have intentionally led them there to entrap them. However, Padgett was a notorious slavecatcher himself and a member of the Gap gang, so it seems more likely that he simply knew that Gorsuch's former slaves customarily visited Parker on Sundays and had no malicious intentions.

Before daybreak on September 11, the slavecatchers approached William Parker's house, a two-story stone structure. Apparently Nelson Ford, known now in Christiana as Josh Kite, was outside. Parker wrote in his description of the event that Kite was returning to his home at Levi Pownal's where he worked as a farmhand about a mile or so away when he spotted the posse. Some have thought though that he was actually on sentry duty. In any event, he rushed into the house to warn Parker and the others just before Kline, followed by Gorsuch, started up the stairs.

Parker met Kline on the stairs. It made no difference to Parker when Kline said he was a federal marshal; Parker warned Kline not to proceed farther.

Then began a parley in which threats were traded back and forth. Kline read the warrants, and Pinckney became apprehensive and questioned whether they should resist. But Parker vowed that he would fight to the death.

"You have my property," Gorsuch called to Parker.

"Go in the room down there," Parker answered, "and see if there is anything there belonging to you. There are beds and a bureau, chairs, and other things. Then go out to the barn; there you will find a cow and some hogs. See if any of them are yours."

Kline suggested that they begin to burn the house down. By this time it had become daylight, and Parker's wife blew the horn they used to signal their neighbors that there was trouble. When she began, some of the posse members began shooting at the window from which she stood, apparently at Kline's direction. Nevertheless, she continued the alarm out of their sight on her knees.

More shooting followed, from both sides now, but then there was a cease-fire and more quibbling back and forth, this time with Parker and the elder Gorsuch invoking scripture to justify and deny the morality of slavery.

Parker finally warned Gorsuch that if he did not withdraw, his life would be in danger. But Gorsuch would not listen.

"You had better give up," Gorsuch said, starting up the stairs, only to be stopped by Dickinson Gorsuch, who was standing on an oven and able to see inside the house.

"They have guns, swords, all kinds of weapons!" he shouted. "They'll kill you!"

Young Gorsuch wanted to retreat and asked Kline to get as many men as he needed to take the men, that money was no object. In response, Kline told Parker that he was going to send for more men, as many as 100, to assist them.

Nevertheless, Parker was unfazed and said that they could bring 500 men but they still would not be able to take him. Aside from Pinckney, whose wife reprimanded him for his lack of resolve, those inside stood behind Parker. About the time of Kline's decision to send for reinforcements, another one of Gorsuch's slaves approached the scene, and those in the house called out warnings to stay clear. He was followed by two Quaker neighbors, Elijah Lewis on foot and Castner Hanway on horseback. Kline asked for their assistance, but both declined and advised Kline to leave or be at risk for their lives. It was at this point that as many as 100 black men were seen approaching in the distance, coming with guns, corn cutters, and sickles, responding to the call of the horn.

While Kline was occupied with the Quakers, Parker and the others, emboldened by the support of their neighbors, came out and stood by the doorway. Edward Gorsuch called out that they were going to get away. Parker taunted the slavecatchers.

"You said you could and would take us. Now you have the chance."

One of the Gorsuchs then pulled out revolvers. It is not clear whether this was Edward or his son Dickinson, as accounts differ. In any case, Parker boldly walked up to Edward and put his hand on his shoulder. He told Gorsuch, who was shaking, that he had faced guns before and was not afraid. Kline, who had retreated at the suggestion of the Quakers, called to Gorsuch to get back.

"No," he said. "I will have my property, or go to hell."

Parker then said he was ready to fight. Kline answered that he would withdraw if Parker called off his men.

"You would not withdraw when you had the chance," Parker said. "You shall not now."

At this point Dickinson Gorsuch and Parker traded insults, and then the younger Gorsuch fired two shots at Parker, barely grazing his head but failing to break the skin. Parker ran up to him and knocked the gun out of his hand, and the younger Gorsuch turned and ran. Pinckney, who was nearby with a shotgun, fired and hit him in the side. Gorsuch got up and Pinckney shot him again. Gorsuch continued to retreat, finally falling and rolling into a corner of an adjacent field about 100 yards distant, blood pouring from his side and arm and oozing from his mouth.

During the shooting of the younger Gorsuch, Samuel Thompson, the Gorsuch slave formerly known as Joshua Hammond, had begun arguing with the elder Gorsuch. Thompson grabbed Pinckney's gun and hit Gorsuch with it, knocking him down. Kline

Reverend William King: Founder of Buxton

Although living in Canada was certainly better than living in slavery, it was in many respects anything but the Promised Land. There blacks faced discrimination and segregation, and in some places they simply were not wanted. When Rev. William King, an expatriate Irish minister, came to Chatham, Ontario with an idea to form a settlement for fugitive slaves in 1849, he faced such opposition.

King had moved to the United States with his family to a farm in Delta, Ohio, in 1834. His family was composed of abolitionists, and their home became a station on the Underground Railroad. However, he moved to Louisiana and taught school, and he met and married a woman who owned slaves. After ten years, he decided to study for the ministry and they went to Scotland. But during this time, a series of tragedies claimed the lives of his wife and two children. After completing his studies, he was sent to Canada by the Presbyterian Church as a missionary for fugitive slaves. There he conceived his idea for starting the settlement, only to be faced with the reality that he was a slaveowner. His father-in-law had died and he had inherited fourteen slaves. Given leave by the church, he brought his slaves to Ohio and emancipated them. He then asked for their help in Canada, and they agreed.

His idea was to provide both education and land to fugitive slaves so that they would have the skills and resources necessary to make their new life a success. He called it Buxton, after a noted British abolitionist. Supported by the Presbyterian Church of Canada, he never faltered despite local opposition; with his fifteen original settlers (another added en route) providing a good example, Buxton grew quickly and prospered. It became the most successful black settlement in Canada and continued until 1880. Today many descendants of the original settlement live in the Chatham area.

and the others in the Gorsuch party began retreating and began shooting in self-defense as the mob of armed black men moved in on them. Thompson pummeled and then shot Gorsuch in the chest.

Accounts differ as to exactly what happened during this time and thereafter. One thing is certain: the riot was under way, and the remaining five members of the slavecatching posse were running for their lives. All but Edward Gorsuch survived, even his son Dickinson, who was brought to the house of Levi Pownal, barely clinging to life for several days. He spent the next three weeks there recovering until he was well enough to return home. The elder Gorsuch was shot multiple times, and legends suggest that he also was mutilated with corn cutters by the wives of Parker and Pinckney; however, this has never been proven.

One death, however, was enough retribution. There is no doubt that if the blacks at Christiana had wanted to kill the rest of the slavecatchers, they could have. But they did not. In fact, it was Parker who saw to it that the younger Gorsuch be taken to Pownal's for the care that saved his life.

Meanwhile, local blacks scattered. Parker, Pinckney, and Johnson left that night. Their first thought was to head for Philadelphia, where abolitionists were well organized to protect them. Along the way, they passed through Christiana, where they reencountered Marshal Kline, who followed them with some others a short distance before giving up his pursuit. They went through Downington and stopped to rest at the home of a friend another six miles farther. The next day they headed toward Philadelphia but met a man along the way who advised them to get away as fast as possible because the incident had caused a great commotion and they were at great risk of being apprehended. Instead, he sent them to Norristown, where they received assistance. One account claims they stopped briefly at the home of **Graceanna Lewis**, about ten miles west of Norristown, having been brought there by her uncle, **Bartholomew Fussell**.

Their journey from this point became much like one fugitive slaves might take along the Underground Railroad, though more dangerous because the authorities were highly aware of their flight and were actively disseminating their description.

They proceeded to Quakertown, where they received a ride to an inn. After leaving the inn, they hired a private coach to Windgap and then another to Tannersville, where they took a train to Homerville. From there they took a stagecoach to Big Eddy, where they boarded a train that passed through Jefferson, New York (now Watkins Glen). It brought them to Rochester on the morning of September 21 and to their last stop before Canada, the home of **Frederick Douglass**.

How they managed to connect with Douglass neither Parker nor Douglass explained, but Douglass and Parker had known each other when both were slaves as young men in Maryland. In his autobiography, Douglass writes of this reunion and the harrowing hours before putting them on a boat to Canada.

> The work of getting these men safely into Canada was a delicate one. They were not only fugitives from slavery but charged with murder, and officers were in pursuit of them. There was no time for delay. I could not look upon them as murderers. To me, they were heroic defenders of the just rights of man against manstealers and murderers. So I fed them, and sheltered them in my house. Had they been pursued then and there, my home would have been stained with blood, for these men who had already tasted blood were well armed and prepared to sell their lives at any expense to the lives and limbs of their probable assailants. What they had already done at Christiana and the cool determination which showed very plainly especially in Parker . . . left no doubt on my mind that their courage was genuine and that their deeds would equal their words. . . . The telegraph had that day announced their deeds at Christiana, their escape, and that the mountains of Pennsylvania were being searched for the murderers. These men had reached me simultaneously with this news in the New York papers. Immediately after the occurrence at Christiana, they, instead of going into the mountains, were placed on a train which brought them to Rochester.

That night they took passage on a steamer for Kingston, Canada. Douglass saw them off, and as a token of his gratitude, Parker gave Douglass the gun alleged to have been taken from Gorsuch when he died, though it may have been one used by his son, as some accounts insist Gorsuch was not carrying a gun.

When they arrived in Canada, they found that the news of the incident had preceded them and that Governor Johnston of Pennsylvania had called for Parker's extradition. As a result, two days later they took a boat to Toronto, where Parker met with the governor of Canada, who promised that the Canadian government would not send him back to the United States. However, while Parker may have escaped prosecution, he had no prospects and needed to find work. He also worried about his wife. He had good cause to worry: she had been arrested.

Two months later, however, both the wives of Parker and Pinckney arrived safely in Canada. Shortly after, they took plots at the Buxton settlement. Parker and Johnson settled there and became farmers, while Pinckney served in the Fifty-fourth Massachusetts Black Regiment during the Civil War and, after the war, settled in Grand Rapids, Michigan.

Parker eventually left Buxton after splitting with his wife. Census information indicates he may have remarried and moved to Essex County, Ontario, where he started a new family.

SUGGESTED READING: Census of Canada, Ottawa, Canada: Library and Archives Canada, 1901; Ella Forbes, "'By My Own Right Arm': Redemptive Violence and the 1851 Christiana, Pennsylvania

Resistance," *The Journal of Negro History*, No. 83, Summer, 1998; W. U. Hensel, *The Christiana Riot and the Treason Trials of 1851*, Lancaster, PA: The New Era Printing Co., 1911; Roderick Nash, "William Parker and the Christiana Riot," *The Journal of Negro History*, No. 46, January, 1961; William Parker, "The Freedman's Story," *The Atlantic Monthly*, Feb.–March, 1866; Thomas B. Slaughter, *Bloody Dawn: The Christiana Riot and Racial Violence in the Antebellum North*, New York: Oxford University Press, 1991; R. C. Smedley, *History of the Underground Railroad in Chester and Neighboring Counties of Pennsylvania*, Lancaster, PA: 1883; William Still, *The Underground Railroad*, Philadelphia: Porter and Coates, 1872.

Pettit, Eber M. (1802–1885). Eber Pettit was an important conductor in western New York, whose Underground Railroad connections reached throughout the state. He wrote an interesting and revealing book, *Sketches in the History of the Underground Railroad*, which was published in 1879. Pettit was born in Hamilton, Madison County, New York to a devout Baptist family. Little is known of his childhood, but he became a member of the Delphi Baptist Church in Pompey, Onondaga County, New York, and married one of its members, Euretta Sweet, in 1823.

His father, James Pettit, was a doctor who dabbled in herbal medicine, though there is no record of where he studied. It is believed that he was a surgeon in the U.S. Army during the War of 1812. His specialty was as an eye doctor, and he created an eye salve that he began to sell. In 1835 he moved to Cordova, today part of Fredonia, Chautauqua County, as did Eber and his wife and three children. The Pettits became active members of the Fredonia Baptist Church. They also became involved in antislavery activities, area Baptists already having been abolitionized during the wave of evangelism that had burned through the area during the late 1820s and several years after. It is believed at this early date that both father and son began their involvement in the Underground Railroad.

James Pettit's house was at the corner of Chestnut and Matteson Streets in Fredonia, near the present-day state college, and had a wagon shed that stood on the road a short distance from the house. Both buildings were surrounded by a high picket fence to prevent intruders from noticing the presence of fugtive slaves. By 1839 James Pettit headed a local organization called the Society for the Abolition of Slavery, and throughout the 1840s both Eber and his father were active in promoting the Liberty Party and collaborating in the Underground Railroad.

Chautauqua County abolitionist Eber M. Pettit. Courtesy of Wendy J. W. Straight and the Fredonia First Baptist Church.

In 1837 Eber had moved to Versailles, a small community along Cattaraugus Creek near the Cattaraugus Indian reservation of the Seneca tribe, about fifteen miles from Fredonia. The Cattaraugus Creek, which even today is still a substantial body of water, was during that period of even greater volume and emptied into Lake Erie less than ten miles from Versailles, making it a convenient thoroughfare for escaping slaves. However, there was no harbor in that vicinity, and slaves moving toward Canada were sometimes sent to Pettit's father in Cordova until his death in 1849 or more frequently, based on accounts in his book, to a "Friend Andrew" who lived six miles from Pettit.

Generally, fugitive slaves coming to this region were piloted to Black Rock, a community south of Buffalo along the Niagara River and now a suburb of Buffalo near the Peace Bridge, about forty miles from Versailles, which was an easy trip by small boat.

Eber functioned as an agent for his father's herbal medicine company, which became very successful. This sent him west to Ohio and also south of the Mason-Dixon Line. It afforded opportunities for seeing slavery firsthand and learning about Underground Railroad incidents in the South. His book describes not only incidents in which he was personally involved but also those that he may have read about or been told about by other Underground Railroad conductors.

When his father died, Eber moved the business to Versailles, and his son-in-law Darwin Barker took over his role as agent of the company, which also offered a number of other remedies in addition to the eye salve, some of the formulas derived from remedies used by the Indians on the neighboring Cattaraugus Reservation. Throughout this period he continued his Underground Railroad activities.

Pettit's book has a fanciful flavor, and his preface is interesting for its metaphorical qualities that were adopted as part of the legend of the Underground Railroad. In part, he wrote the following:

> No institution has ever existed in this country, whose business was transacted with more perfect fidelity, more profound secrecy, more harmony in the working of its complicated machinery and yet with such tremendous results . . . It had, like all, other rail roads [*sic*], its offices and stations, engineers and conductors, ticket agents and train dispatchers, hotels and eating houses . . . open day and night, and well supplied with the best food the country afforded . . . The managers availed themselves of all manner of facilities for traveling; rail roads [*sic*] and steam boats [*sic*], canal boats and ferry boats, stage coaches, gentlemen's carriages and lumber wagons were pressed into active duty when needed.

Pettit admitted writing from memory, and though his dates of the events more than thirty years later are not precise, many of the details fit closely with descriptions of accounts elsewhere.

> [The] first well established line of the U.G.R.R. had its southern terminus in Washington, D.C. and extended in a pretty direct route to Albany, N.Y. . . . . The General Superintendent resided in Albany. [And] I knew him well. He was once an active member of one of the churches in Fredonia [**Abel Brown** lived in Fredonia for a time]. Mr. T [**Charles Torrey**], his agent in Washington city, was a very active and efficient man; the Superintendent at Albany was in daily communication by mail with him and other subordinate agents at all points along the line.

Pettit's first recollection of the term *Underground Railroad* was in a Washington, D.C., newspaper. It referred to fugitive slaves who ended up in Albany and told of a young black boy who said that "the railroad went underground all the way to Boston." The article contained an anecdote about a slaveowner who had a tobacco plantation near Washington and had lost five slaves. He learned of their whereabouts when he received a newspaper in the mail from Albany, according to Pettit, called the *Liberty Press* [the *Liberty Press* was published in Utica], which reported that his slaves escaped via the Underground Railroad. Pettit apparently confused the Utica paper with the *Tocsin of Liberty*, which did exactly that.

The itinerary of the fugitive slaves took them on foot to stops at the farms of Quakers on the way to Philadelphia, according to Pettit. From there, they took a boat along the Delaware River to Bordentown, New Jersey, where they took a train to New York City. Then they were moved on to Albany. A surprising detail about their mode of escape was that it was coordinated with the "liberty" newspaper. But the publication of the fugitive slaves' successful flight was actually a ruse. In reality, they were hiding not far from their point of departure. While they waited for the signal to move on, a newspaper article was published telling of the fugitive slaves' successful escape to Canada and was sent to their masters. This threw the slave hunters off their tracks and enabled them to make a safer getaway.

In one particular case that involved Albany operatives, a runaway named Jo Norton was sent to Pettit. Norton stayed on as a farmhand. Though he had gained his freedom, it was at the cost of leaving behind his wife, Mary. When Pettit later learned that "General" Chaplin had taken up residence in Washington, D.C., he suggested they contact Chaplin to inquire about the whereabouts of Mary. Chaplin located her and negotiated a price for her freedom with her master. The thankful Jo raised the money by giving speeches about his daring escape. The family was personally reunited by Chaplin in Utica, and for the first time Jo saw his child, who had been born after his flight.

Jo, whose true name was James Baker, settled in Syracuse and participated in the Jerry Rescue. Pettit was well acquainted with Underground Railroad operatives there. **Jermaine Loguen**, about whom he has a chapter in his book, came to western New York not only to give abolition lectures but also because his wife, Caroline Storum, was from a family involved in the Underground Railroad in Busti, New York, a western New York community about forty miles south of Versailles.

Pettit returned to Fredonia in 1863. He began his sketches about the Underground Railroad for the Fredonia newspaper, the *Censor*, in 1868 as a serial at the request of its owner, Willard McKinstry. President of the Fredonia Historical Society, McKinstry collected them and published them as Pettit's book. It was dedicated to **Frederick Douglass**, who said of Pettit that he "was one who stood by me and aided me in the publication of my paper in Rochester thirty years ago."

Pettit continued to manufacture medicines in Fredonia until 1876 when he sold his company. He was a wealthy man and retired to a life of leisure, spending his time fishing and cooking, and founding a Native American orphan asylum that he administered until his death.

SUGGESTED READING: William S. Bailey, "The Underground Railroad in Southern Chautauqua County," *New York History*, New York Historical Society, 1935; Eber Pettit, *Sketches in the History of the Underground Railroad*, Fredonia, NY: W. McKinstry & Son, 1879, reprint Westfield: Chautauqua Region Press, 1999; Helene C. Phelan, *And Why Not Everyman? An Account of Slavery, the Underground Railroad, and the Road to Freedom in New York's Southern Tier*, Interlaken, NY: Heart of the Lakes Publishing, 1987.

Posey, John W. (1801–1884). John Wesley Posey, one of the most active members of the Anti-Slavery League in Indiana, was born in Beaufort, South Carolina. In 1804 his parents, Richard and Frances Posey, came to Indiana where they freed their slaves. The family settled in Knox County, about ten miles north of Vincennes. Richard Posey organized a Methodist class in his home, where he also taught school.

In the area near Bruceville, Maria Creek, and Emison's Mill in Knox County lived neighbors who opposed slavery. Such views were uncommon in the heavily proslavery region of southwest Indiana. This small pocket of antislavery sentiment, as well as several manumissions, led to a black rural settlement developing nearby known as Cherry Grove. Ultimately Cherry Grove, like most free black settlements, provided refuge to fugitive slaves en route to freedom. In March 1851 **Seth Concklin** led Vina Still, the wife

Anti-Slavery League Underground Railroad conductor John W. Posey. From Cockrum's *History of the Underground Railroad* (1915).

of **Peter Still**, and her three children to either Cherry Grove or a free black settlement in southwest Sullivan County, where they were captured. The man requesting that they be jailed in Vincennes was James Emison.

About 1817 the Poseys moved a short distance north to Sullivan County, where in 1837 John W. Posey married Sarah Blackburn. They soon removed to nearby Pike County, where they purchased a farm abutting the White River. The farm contained coal fields that backed up to the river. Posey practiced medicine near Petersburg and aided fugitive slaves. Large groups could be secreted in the caves and coal shafts among Posey's coal banks for long periods. According to **William M. Cockrum**, Posey and his family helped at least 1,000 fugitives escape slavery. Posey was aided by John Stuckey, who piloted fugitives across the White River and to a safe place in Daviess, Greene, or Knox County.

Posey served on the Executive Committee of the Indiana Anti-Slavery League and was known as a fearless advocate of freedom. In the early 1850s he and Eldridge Hopkins, a Baptist minister and attorney, rescued two free blacks from kidnappers. The kidnapped men had been working on the Wabash Erie Canal but lived near Rockport, Indiana, along the Ohio River. Hopkins removed a linchpin from the abductor's wagon, knowing this would cause the wheel to slowly unseat, creating a crash. The scene unfolded as planned, giving Hopkins, Posey, and their helpers a chance to catch up with the thieves. An unofficial court-martial was held near the crash.

This unusual scene of frontier justice resulted in the flogging of the kidnappers by their victims, who were given hickory switches. The victims also received the wagon owned by their kidnappers.

SUGGESTED READING: Bruceville Christian Church, *A History of Bruceville*, 1954; William Cockrum, *History of the Underground Railroad*, 1915; Esarey, *History of Indiana*, 1924; Kate E. R. Pickard, *The Kidnapped and the Ransomed*, 1856; *Vincennes Sun*, Oct. 25, 1911.

Jennifer Harrison, Indiana

Powell, William P. (dates unknown). William Powell had been a fighter for the rights of black Americans since the early 1830s when he was a seaman living in New Bedford, Massachusetts, and was an original member of the American Anti-Slavery Society that formed in 1833. He was born in New York City, but little else is known about his early life aside from his being the son of a slave father, and his marriage to Mercy Haskins in New Bedford in 1832.

From 1836 to 1839 Powell ran a boarding house for sailors on 94 N. Water Street in New Bedford, after which he moved back to New York City and opened a similar boarding house affiliated with the American Seamen's Friend Society. The site, which moved its location several times, included a site at 330 Pearl Street that accommodated seventy seamen; today it is an apartment building. Powell admitted to housing fugitive slaves in New York and likely did so in New Bedford, a city that openly aided fugitive slaves.

More than 1,500 citizens filled the Zion African Methodist Episcopal Church in New York City to hear Powell denounce the second Fugitive Slave Law the week following its enactment.

"Shall we resist oppression? Shall we defend our liberties? Shall we be freemen or slaves?" he asked.

Powell was one of many that day who vowed to fight to the death to remain free. A call was made for members to join a secret committee to prevent the rendition of fugitive slaves under the supervision of Powell—a committee of thirteen—and the meeting concluded with the announcement that funds had been raised to purchase the freedom of James Hamlet, a New York City black, who had been the first fugitive slave arrested under the jurisdiction of the new law.

Powell also was the founder in 1840 of the Manhattan Anti-Slavery Society, which immediately enrolled 100 members and of which he said were "the real lapwater abolitionists of New York City" with "a platform broad enough to admit all without respect to sex or color." Powell also served as a member of the executive committee of the Garrison-led American Anti-Slavery Society from 1841 to 1844.

Representing seamen was an obvious link to the Underground Railroad, with many seamen being former slaves themselves and the sea being the thoroughfare through which many escaped to freedom. With perhaps as many as 50 percent of seamen in the United States at that time being black, it offered many opportunities and sympathetic abettors.

Because of this, black seamen became targets in Southern ports like Charleston, Savannah, Mobile, and New Orleans, where enforcement of the Negro Seamen's Acts prevented black seamen from disembarking from their vessels or, in some cases, caused them to be incarcerated until their ships left. In the latter case, the seamen or their employers were forced to pay the expenses incurred during their lockup. Powell campaigned vigorously against these discriminatory laws, which sometimes led to the seamen being sold into slavery when unable to pay for the lockup fees, and which Powell pointed out were unconstitutional.

The year following the passage of the second Fugitive Slave Law in 1851, Powell decided to move to England. He explained that his purpose was to raise and educate his children in a nation whose laws and prejudices did not hamper them. Powell worked in Liverpool as a clerk for ten years, and while there he continued to aid fugitive slaves from America, seeking a new life in a less prejudiced country.

When Powell returned to the United States in 1861, he reopened his boarding house at 2 Dover Street in New York City. He also formed the American Seamen's Protective Union Association on December 31, 1862, devoted to improving the conditions of seamen of all colors. Powell eventually moved to San Francisco. The last mention of him in the historical record is his participation in a William Lloyd Garrison Memorial Meeting there in 1879, shortly after Garrison's death.

SUGGESTED READING: R. J. M. Blackett, *Building an Anti-slavery Wall*, Baton Rouge: Louisiana State University Press, 1983; Philip S. Foner, "William Powell: Militant Champion of Black Seamen," *Essays in Afro-American History*, Philadelphia: Temple University Press, 1978; Kathryn Grover, *Fugitive Slave Traffic and the Maritime World of New Bedford*, New Bedford: New Bedford Whaling and National Historic Park, 1998.

Purvis, Robert (1810–1898). Robert Purvis was a leading figure in the antislavery movement and an active Underground Railroad conductor in Philadelphia.

Born in Charleston, South Carolina, he was of mixed racial descent, and though of fair complexion, he considered himself black through the line of his maternal grandmother, who was a Moor. He received his education as a child in Philadelphia and graduated from Amherst College in Massachusetts. His interest in abolition stemmed from childhood and reading books like Jesse Torrey's *Portraiture of Slavery*, which was given to him by his father. It was the beginning of his lifelong commitment to antislavery and the advancement of blacks in America.

This early acquaintance with the issue of slavery resulted in his first public address on slavery at the age of seventeen. He also became acquainted with Benjamin Lundy during the early years and was one of the founding members of the American Anti-Slavery Society. In 1837 Purvis was among the organizers of the Vigilant Association of Philadelphia. He was appointed president in 1839, and by the end of 1841 the association was aiding on average more than three fugitive slaves per week. During this time, Purvis's home on Ninth and Lombard streets had a secret room entered only by a trapdoor in which he hid fugitive slaves.

Fortifying Purvis's commitment to the antislavery cause was his marriage to Harriet Forten, the daughter of James Forten, the wealthy sail maker, who was among the earliest black abolitionists. When Purvis became president of the Philadelphia Vigilant Association in 1839, it immediately forged a close association with the Philadelphia Female Anti-Slavery Society, of which his wife and her mother and two sisters were members. The antislavery bazaars held by the female society raised $32,000 between 1840 and 1860, much of which went to a fund used to aid fugitive slaves. The society also collected used clothing for them.

However, during this period of abolitionist ferment, a series of race riots occurred in Philadelphia beginning in 1829 and culminating in one in 1842. The Vigilant Association apparently cut back on its operations after this last riot and Purvis moved out of the city. The Pennsylvania Anti-Slavery Society, which continued to function, assumed the role of the city's Underground Railroad organization. Purvis, an officer in both groups, continued to offer his assistance, for he wrote that "his horses and carriages, and his personal attendants were ever at the service of the travelers upon that road." After the passage of the Fugitive Slave Law of 1850, he threatened to shed the blood of "any pale-faced spectre who entered his dwelling to execute this law on me or mine."

In 1852, when the increase in fugitive slave traffic necessitated the formation of a new separate vigilance committee, Purvis was made chairman. The committee, which aided about 1,000 fugitive slaves from that time until the beginning of the Civil War, played a key role in coordinating Underground Railroad efforts throughout the Northeast and Canada.

William Still, his colleague on the vigilant committee, described Purvis as "fervent in soul, eloquent in speech, most gracious in manner, high-toned in moral nature" [and] "keenly sensitive in all matters pertaining to justice and integrity."

In addition to his membership in the American Anti-Slavery Society, in which he was active throughout its existence, Purvis also participated in the Negro Convention movement and was active in the Republican Party.

SUGGESTED READING: Nilgun Okur, "Underground Railroad in Philadelphia, 1830–1860," *Journal of Black Studies*, No. 25, May, 1995; William Still, *The Underground Railroad,* Philadelphia: Porter and Coates, 1872; Janice Sumler-Lewis, "The Forten-Purvis Women of Philadelphia and the American Anti-slavery Crusade," *The Journal of Negro History*, No. 66, Winter, 1981–1982.

R

Rachel, Aunt (unknown). Aunt Rachel was a slave from Lexington, Kentucky, whose story is known because it was told in the *Reminiscences* of **Levi Coffin**, who is often called the "president" of the Underground Railroad.

Like many other slaves, the most tragic events in Aunt Rachel's life occurred when her family was separated after being sold to other masters. Her life had been one of relative contentment despite her station. Her master and mistress were benevolent, she had a responsible position as their chief house servant, and she had a loving husband with whom she had a number of children, although he lived on a neighboring plantation.

Aunt Rachel's troubles began when her husband was sold down South. It was a terrible blow, for she never saw him again. But she had her children, and that gave her some consolation. Two years later misfortune struck again when both Rachel's master and mistress died. She and her children were put on the auction block. Her children were purchased by Lexington residents, but she was sold to a slave trader. He took her to Mississippi and sold her to a cotton plantation owner.

Rachel was not used to such hard physical labor, having been a house servant all her life. Because of her inability to keep up with the other slaves in the field, she was punished and her food allowance was reduced. Her strength was failing. She did not think she could survive long under such conditions. Her only option was to run away.

It was summer, and Rachel snuck off during the night. During the day she hid in the sugar cane fields. The next day she came to a plantation and got help from slaves there. Her object was to go back to Lexington, where she could hide with friends and see her children. It was a journey of more than 500 miles, but somehow her determination and will carried her through.

Once in Lexington, Rachel's friends tried to find someone to purchase her, but they had no luck. It was unsafe for her to remain there long, so her friends began making preparations to put her on the Underground Railroad. Before this could be done, Rachel's master showed up, knowing that her origin had been Lexington. He had posted a reward for Rachel's capture, and before long the police dragged her off to jail.

Rachel's master was furious. He beat her and promised further retribution when they returned to Mississippi. Along with other slaves the master had purchased for his plantation, Aunt Rachel was shackled with a ball and chain, and placed in a wagon. Their destination was Louisville, where they would take a boat to Mississippi. However, her capture didn't deter Rachel's resolve to be free.

One night while her master went into an inn to make arrangements for the night, Rachel crawled out of the wagon and hid in a nearby ditch. In the pitch black of the countryside, it was hard to find her. Finally, her master and his helpers gave up the search, and Aunt Rachel hurried into the woods, not stopping, despite the impediments of her shackles, until she had gone several miles. There she found a log under which to sleep until the next day.

In the daylight, Rachel came to a stream with large stones. It occurred to her that she could use them to break her chains. She was able to free herself of the ball but was unable to remove the manacles around her hands and the band around her ankle to which the ball had been attached. She came to a home of slaves who removed the manacles around her hands. The man of the house then took two of his master's horses and led her on horseback for several miles in the direction of Madison, Indiana, just across the Ohio River.

The next night a free black family helped Rachel, the husband removing the band around her ankle and the wife feeding and caring for her injuries. This man brought her to the house of a slave near the river, whose master allowed him the use of a boat to go to Madison to do business for him. The slave took Rachel across the river and directed her to a settlement of free blacks, where she stayed through the winter. It was good that she found a resting place, because she was no longer in any condition to travel. However, the capture of another fugitive slave in the vicinity convinced the members of this community to send Rachel to Levi Coffin in Newport, Indiana, eighty miles northeast of Madison.

Aunt Rachel stayed with the Coffins for six months. She wanted to remain there as long as possible in hopes of hearing from her children. The Coffins were glad to have her; Levi said that she was one of the best cooks and housekeepers his family ever had. However, Kentucky slavecatchers came to Newport looking for fugitive slaves, and it was thought best that Rachel be moved to Canada. Fortunately, a group of Quakers from the Young's Prairie, Michigan, settlement were attending the New Garden Quarterly. They were glad to help Aunt Rachel.

The Coffins provided Rachel with a trunk of clothing and other necessities, and dressed her in the typical clothes of a Quaker woman. From Young's Prairie, she was sent to Detroit, where the Underground Railroad brought her across the river to Canada in 1836.

In 1844 Coffin took a trip to Canada with **William Beard** to check on the conditions of fugitive slaves whom they had aided. They stopped in Detroit on the way, and by chance the men hitched their horses to a gate not far from Aunt Rachel's house. She had since married a prosperous black man in Detroit. She was in her yard picking up some kindling when, to the surprise of both of them, she spotted Coffin. She cried out with joy and ushered Coffin and Beard into her home to meet her husband. She said she still suffered pain from the chain that had been placed on her ankle.

What happened thereafter to Aunt Rachel and whether or not she ever saw her children again is unknown.

SUGGESTED READING: Levi Coffin, *Reminiscences of Levi Coffin*, Cincinnati, OH: Western Tract and Supply Co., 1876.

Rankin, John (1793–1886). Rev. John Rankin of Ripley, Ohio has been called the father of abolitionism and was arguably the most influential abolitionist of the antebellum period. He also was among the most active conductors of the Underground

Reverend John Rankin. From *The Soldier, the Battle, and the Victory*, by Andrew Ritche (1868).

Railroad, and his home atop a high hill overlooking the Ohio River was a beacon of liberty for fugitive slaves for thirty-five years.

Born into a family of Presbyterian ministers and Revolutionary War veterans, he was one of eleven boys reared in Jefferson County, Tennessee, when the area was still a virtual wilderness, the closest church being seven miles away and the countryside still populated by Native Americans. He had little formal schooling as a child and his main source of reading was the Bible. His family was greatly influenced by a wave of evangelism then sweeping through that section of the country, and from an early age he obsessed about religious matters.

Rankin grew into a handsome, impeccably dressed young man with an intellectual bent and a genial nature. At the age of seventeen he began his studies for the ministry under the Reverend James Henderson of Dandridge, Tennessee, and then entered Washington College at Jonesborough. While at the college, his brother David was killed in the War of 1812, at the Battle of Horseshoe Bend in 1814, and his father used the compensation from the government to help pay for Rankin's education. He would ever after acknowledge the sacrifice of his brother.

In 1814 Rankin married Jean Lowry, the granddaughter of the college president, a union that lasted sixty-three years. He also joined the Tennessee Manumission Society, which was organized by the noted pioneer abolitionist Charles Osborn and the first organization to advocate immediate emancipation, a position that Rankin publicly affirmed in 1815. He received his ministerial license in 1816 and took a position at the local church. But in 1817, after being censured for a sermon discussing the evils of slavery, he decided to move to Ohio.

He set out in a small carriage with his wife and infant son, Adam Lowry. It was a difficult journey through the Cumberland Mountains, and at one point their carriage broke down, forcing him to go on foot to seek help. About 200 miles from the point of their departure, they finally reached Lexington, Kentucky, where Rankin preached in a Presbyterian church. Moving on to Paris, Kentucky, they met the Reverend John Lyle, who offered Rankin a pastorate in Concord, Kentucky.

Rankin ended up staying in the area for the next four years as he found the residents disposed to his abolitionist views. He founded antislavery societies in Concord and Carlisle, both of them becoming auxiliaries of the state society, which had been founded in 1807.

"I preached against slavery in some of the most prominent parts of the state," he later wrote, "and was known as an abolitionist as far as I was known, and I spoke against slavery in families of wealthy slaveholders, and I never had an insult offered."

He also wrote articles against slavery, and in October 1821 he was a founder of the *Abolition Intelligencer and Missionary Magazine*. However, with the passage of the Missouri Compromise in 1820, the issue of slavery had become hotly contested in Kentucky and support for its maintenance grew there. One day at the Sabbath school where he taught slaves (with their masters' permission), he was confronted by a mob that drove the slaves out and beat some of them as they departed. This convinced him to leave for Ohio. Other abolitionists in his congregation also left, including Samuel Donnell who had become a close friend of Rankin's and who moved to Indiana. His son **Luther Donnell** later became a noted Underground Railroad conductor in Decatur County, Indiana.

In 1822 Rankin became pastor of the First Presbyterian Church in Ripley, where he served for forty-four years. A temperance advocate, he initially found Ripley "exceedingly immoral" with infidelity and heavy drinking commonplace. However, he also found it actively involved in the Underground Railroad.

His first house in Ripley was a two-story building with three doors that set on Front Street along the banks of the Ohio. It provided easy access to fugitive slaves crossing the river, who had been coming through Ripley on a regular basis since at least as early as 1815. Among locals who had been helping them were Nathaniel Collins, the first mayor of Ripley, who lived a few doors east of Rankin on Front Street; Alexander Campbell, Ripley's first physician, who also lived on Front Street, a little farther east; and the Reverend James Gilliland, who was the pastor of the Red Oak Presbyterian Church, five miles north of Ripley.

On December 2, 1823, Rankin received a letter from his brother Thomas, who lived in Virginia, telling him that he had purchased a slave. This information compelled him to write a series of twenty-one letters to his brother, but instead of mailing them, Rankin had them published in the local newspaper, the *Castigator*. They were then collected and put into a booklet, *Letters on American Slavery*, which was widely circulated in Ohio and

Kentucky. Among points covered by the letters were that the existence of slavery was opposed to the fundamental principle in the Declaration of Independence that "all men are created equal"; that prejudice against blacks was based solely on color; that to believe people of color did not have the same feelings as whites was wrong; that slavery corrupted the slaveholder; and that the Bible did not justify the practice of slavery.

The many antislavery societies founded in southwestern Ohio in the late 1820s were undoubtedly influenced by the *Letters*. The *Letters* also found their way east, and William Lloyd Garrison became acquainted with them in 1830, serializing them in *The Liberator* in 1832. A Quaker press also published them, and that edition was used in 1833 by the American Anti-Slavery Society to publish the first of their eighteen editions of the *Letters*. They gave Rankin a national reputation in abolitionist circles.

In 1833 Rankin attended the organizational meeting of the American Anti-Slavery Society in Philadelphia, and in 1835 he attended the organizational meeting of the Ohio Anti-Slavery Society in Putnam, Ohio, which was harassed by a mob. The latter was held largely due to the influence of Theodore Weld, who had become a prominent figure in the abolitionist movement as a result of the Lane Seminary debates, which Rankin attended, and who had been organizing antislavery societies throughout the state. It was Rankin's first experience with a mob, but it would not be his last.

The following year he was enlisted as an antislavery lecturer by Weld for the American Anti-Slavery Society, and he toured Ohio organizing antislavery societies. It was a grueling and stressful experience. A smaller-than-average man, he faced down more than twenty mobs by his own count and was attacked on several occasions. These confrontations evoked the comment from him that after all his arguments to show that all men ought to be free, perhaps there were some men of his own race who were not "fit to be free." The experience was harmful to his health and he was forced to resign after six months. Nevertheless, he had many successes and organized numerous antislavery societies.

Rankin returned to the pulpit and found that he could accomplish more by preaching than by lecturing. A sermon with the sanction of scripture was paid greater respect and posed less danger from mobs. His sermon against slavery usually began by evoking the opening words of the Declaration of Independence and showing their basis in scripture. All men, he emphasized, were created of one blood and possessed the same rights, regardless of color. His plan for immediate emancipation was to have the federal government buy all the slaves after their value had been fairly determined by a commission, and emancipate them upon purchase.

Some years later, Rankin received an invitation to lecture from a minister also named John Rankin (of no relation), who lived in Chester County, Pennsylvania—like Ripley, a major center of the Underground Railroad. Rankin accepted and delivered more than forty lectures in churches, halls, schoolhouses, and once in a barn.

Rankin also helped organize the Liberty Party in Ohio and worked with the Presbyterian Church to urge it to use its influence to end slavery. Though a general condemnation of slavery had been made by the denomination as early as 1818, it had been ignored in the South and even by many churches in the North. In 1837 this came to a head when there was a split between the New School, which supported abolitionism, and the Old School, which refused to censure its slaveholding brethren. But when the New School made a further decision to allow individual synods and sessions to decide how to deal with the issue of slavery, Rankin rose in opposition. This caused a division within his church at Ripley, and in 1845 a new church was built by the seceders. Rankin served both churches. Two years later Rankin led the formation of a come-outer synod called The Free

Presbyterian Church of America. It excluded all slaveholders from membership and eventually comprised seventy-two churches, ranging from eastern Pennsylvania to Iowa, and continued to operate as a separate synod until after the Civil War.

Education was another important interest of Rankin, and his work in the field not only advanced the cause of abolition but also aided in the education of people of color. In 1828 he founded Ripley College with the support of some of the leading citizens of Ripley, many of whom were his collaborators in the Underground Railroad. The objective of the college was to present students with a course of study "designed make practical men as well as theoretical scholars."

By 1831 the school was prospering with more than 100 students. One of these students, Benjamin Franklin Templeton, was a former slave from South Carolina, whose family had been freed and moved to Ohio. Suddenly a Ripley resident began to harass Templeton and finally confronted and beat him. The man was arrested and fined, and soon after moved to Kentucky. But this incident became a cause of concern among the college's trustees. To resolve the situation, Rankin offered to personally instruct the student at his home. Thereafter, Rankin customarily instructed black students at his home. Templeton later enrolled at Lane Seminary with Rankin's son, Adam, and went on to pastor churches in Pittsburgh and Philadelphia. Although the college prospered for only a short period, it was transformed into an academy in 1846 and was always open to enrolling blacks. Rankin also briefly opened a school for females on his farm, but this experiment was short-lived.

Another means through which Rankin educated the public was through the American Reform Tract and Book Society, behind which he was the driving force, and which published more than 200 books and tracts dealing mainly with the issue of slavery, many written by Rankin, from 1851 through the early 1860s.

Rankin's public efforts in spreading the message of abolition were acknowledged universally among abolitionists. But his efforts to help unfortunate fugitive slaves fleeing from slavery were no less significant. It was a personal endeavor for him. On one occasion when he learned of a fugitive slave who had been returned to slavery, he "was seized with such anguish of spirit that it seemed as if there were nothing in creation that could cheer me." The business of aiding fugitive slaves consequently became an essential part of his life, and he marshaled his entire family in this effort.

Rankin's wife, Jean, was responsible for keeping a fire in the hearth lit in the evening in case of unexpected guests, feeding the fugitive slaves, and providing them with dry clothing. His sons, once they reached the teenage years, were relied on to be the conductors, often being awakened in the middle of the night and leading the fugitive slaves on foot to the homes of conductors like Rev. Gilliland in Red Oak.

As Underground traffic increased, so did the intrusions of slavecatchers. Rankin decided to build a house atop the high hill behind the village, where he moved in 1829 and which gave him a bird's-eye view of the river and anyone who might approach his house. This would provide some warning of the approach of slavecatchers. He also began to light a lantern each night in his window facing the river, which became an unmistakable sign of his hospitality.

More than 2,000 fugitive slaves were estimated to have been aided by the Rankin family from 1830 until the end of the Civil War. And by the end of the 1830s, as many as 200 residents in the village could be called on to help. They acted out of a sense of humanity and justice, according to Rankin, and there never were any breaches of trust or betrayals during that period. Fugitive slaves were hidden in houses, barns, or other nearby buildings until they could be sent farther north. In the earlier period of Rankin's

Underground work, the homes of John Mahan and black conductor John Hudson in Sardinia, about twenty miles north, were the favored destinations. But in later periods, Red Oak, only five miles distant, became more common. This may have in part been caused by the prosecution and imprisonment of Mahan in 1838, but it also may have been the result of the maturing of Rankin's sons, who by the mid-1830s had reached their teenage years and were able to lead the fugitive slaves to Red Oak on foot.

Rankin hid as many as twelve fugitive slaves at one time and would hide them either in his house or his barn in the back, which had a hidden room under the floor. In 1838 a reward of $2,500 was offered in Kentucky for the assassination or abduction of Rankin and Alexander Campbell of Ripley, and Mahan and Isaac Beck of Sardinia. That year Mahan was arrested and taken to Mason County, Kentucky, on charges of aiding the slave of William Greathouse of Mason County. After spending more than ten weeks in jail, he was found innocent of the criminal charges, but later he was found guilty in civil court and forced to pay damages of $1,600. The trial exposed to a small degree the Underground Railroad activities in Ripley because Mahan's case involved a fugitive slave whom the Rankins had taken to him.

In February of that year, one of the Underground Railroad's most famous fugitive slaves crossed the river and was led to the Rankin house for a temporary respite. She had crossed during the winter with an infant, barely making it to the other side by hopping on the melting ice cakes. She was later immortalized as Eliza Harris by Harriet Beecher Stowe in *Uncle Tom's Cabin*. The story was told to Stowe by Rankin in 1839 when he was visiting his son Lowry, who was a student at Lane Seminary in Cincinnati, where Stowe's father was president and her husband a professor.

Separate accounts concerning Eliza by Rankin, his sons, and **Levi Coffin** differ as to the exact details, and there is a question whether her husband already had escaped to Canada and whether the infant with her was her daughter or granddaughter.

They all agree, however, that Eliza was a slave in Dover, Kentucky, less than two miles from the Ohio River bank opposite Ripley, and that one wintry night she fled with an infant, whom her master intended to sell. She was hoping to walk across the frozen river to Ripley, where she had heard there lived a man who helped slaves escape to freedom. Near the Kentucky side of the river, she was given temporary shelter by a man, who fed her and warned her that the ice had begun to thaw and that she would be risking both her life and that of her baby.

Nevertheless, Eliza was determined and he pulled out a rail from his fence that he thought she could use to help push her away across the floating cakes of ice. When she reached the shore, she heard the sound of barking dogs and realized the slavecatchers were closing in. She had to make a split-second decision and leaped onto the thawing ice, hearing it crack as she gingerly scurried across. Several times her feet plunged into the icy water, and on one occasion she nearly went under and had to toss the baby onto an ice cake ahead. But the rail helped her from going under and she managed to make it ashore, collapsing with exhaustion.

In the dark, a hand reached out to her. It was the hand of a local slavecatcher and town misfit named Chancey Shaw, who lived on the Ripley side of the river. He often patrolled the riverbank, watching for slaves that he might catch to claim the rewards. This time, though, the desperation of the woman and the helpless baby had softened his hardened heart.

"Any woman who crossed that river carrying her baby has won her freedom," he later said and took her to the path that led to the Rankins' home.

It was the custom of the Rankins to leave their door open and a fire in the hearth in case fugitive slaves might appear. On hearing the woman enter, Jean and John were roused from their bed, and food and a change of clothes were given to Eliza. Then he called his sons Calvin and John to lead the woman that night to Rev. Gilliland in Red Oak. They knew the slavecatchers would be coming, and it was urgent that she be moved before morning. It had become a common ritual for the boys, who were seventeen and twelve at that time.

From Rev. Gilliland's home, Eliza was taken to Decatur and then Sardinia. Because the slavecatchers had come the next day and found a piece of the baby's clothing on the Ohio side of the river, they continued their pursuit. As a result, instead of sending her due north as was the standard procedure, she was sent in a northwesterly direction to the home of Levi Coffin in Indiana.

Three years later in July of 1841, Eliza surprised the Rankins with a return visit. She came with a French Canadian man, whose name was never recorded and whom she was paying to help bring her daughter and seven grandchildren out of slavery. Their owner was Thomas Davis, who owned a farm near Dover. Rankin warned her not to go, that more than likely she would be caught and returned to slavery. But she had a plan and the Canadian was going to help her. Rankin agreed to do whatever he could to help her free her family, short of going to Kentucky.

It was his strict policy not to go into a slave state to rescue slaves, because he thought it would jeopardize his Underground activities. As a result he also was leery of individuals he did not know who sought his help in aiding fugitive slaves. An example of this was when he turned down **Calvin Fairbank**'s request for assistance in the rescue of **Lewis Hayden** that led to Fairbank's incarceration.

The plan was to have the Canadian hire himself out to Davis and spend his free time at taverns to learn what he could about the slave patrols along the river. He also would contact Eliza's daughter so she could prepare for the escape. While he was in Kentucky, Eliza was sent to work for Anthony Hopkins in Red Oak. She would wait there until he had arranged everything. The Canadian was very thorough, even noting locations where barking dogs might alert people, and accomplished everything they had planned. On the first Friday in August all the arrangements had been made.

That night Samuel and John Rankin, Jr., rode out to the Hopkins house, bringing with them an extra horse. Eliza was dressed as a man, and they went to the river where the Canadian and Tom Collins were waiting with a skiff. Collins and the Rankin boys then rowed them across and tied up the skiff behind the Collins house in preparation for their retrieval.

On Saturday night Eliza, her daughter, and six of the grandchildren fled. Because the oldest girl was a house servant, however, they were unable to bring her out. The Canadian wanted to return to Ripley that night, but he had not counted on all the possessions of Eliza's daughter. It was a three-and-a-half-mile trek through the woods, and the baggage slowed their progress. They were not able to make it to the river before daylight, so the Canadian devised an alternate plan. While Eliza and her family hid in a wooded section of a farmer's property that was located directly across from Ripley, he went to the shore and borrowed a skiff and rowed across the river, tying it up in full view from the Kentucky side. He figured that the slavecatchers would see the missing skiff and assume it was used by the fugitive slaves.

The plan worked to perfection. The next day the slavecatchers saw the skiff and went into Ripley with a large posse of men and scoured the village in search of the fugitive slaves while Eliza and her family hid in the woods. Unable to find them, the slavecatchers settled into a tavern and got drunk, and by midnight they went back to their homes in Kentucky. At 3 a.m. the Canadian took the Collinses' skiff over to the Kentucky side while Tom Collins and Robert Patton waited for him in a secluded place along the shore. Two hours later he returned with Eliza, her daughter, and six grandchildren and immediately left Ripley.

Collins and Patton helped the family over to the house of Thomas McCague, the richest man in Ripley. He owned a large flour mill and a large pork-packing warehouse that fueled the prosperity of the village, but no one but his closest intimates knew of the participation of him and his wife, Kitty, in the Underground Railroad. Both were from Kentucky, had friends and relatives who owned slaves, and were well connected politically. If their involvement had become known, it could have damaged not only their social status but also McCague's business interests.

The Lane Debates

Organized by the charismatic abolitionist orator Theodore Weld, the Lane debates were a public discussion of slavery held in 1834 at the Lane Theological Institute in Cincinnati. The sessions combined lecture, prayer, public confession, and strong appeals. They were held for eighteen nights, the first nine devoted to the wisdom of immediate emancipation and the next nine devoted to a consideration of African colonization. What added drama was the strong opposition taken by the students to the school's administrators, including its president Lyman Beecher, the father of **Harriet Beecher Stowe**, then an unknown writer whose husband, Calvin Stowe, was a teacher at Lane.

The Lane rebels did more than voice their opinions. Led by Weld, then thirty-one years old, they reached out to Cincinnati's black community, who were mainly former slaves. They opened a school teaching reading, writing, arithmetic, and geography, along with Sunday school and Bible classes. They also participated in the Underground Railroad.

When the rebels, who numbered fifty-one students, were expelled for their refusal to obey the board's ban of their abolitionist activities, they moved temporarily to a school funded by Arthur Tappan in Cumminsville. Many matriculated to Oberlin College while others joined Weld's band of seventy antislavery lecturers who abolitionized the North during the next several years.

Early Monday morning McCague left his house for his office. He sent one of his trusted assistants to the Rankins to tell them that everything was ready to move Eliza and her family. Originally the plan was to move them on Sunday, and a wagon had been procured to take them to the Hopkins farm. However, they had to return the wagon and now were forced to walk there. The only problem was that the youngest child still was not old enough to walk. As a result, Kitty McCague took the baby herself on horseback. The rest of the family was brought up to the Rankin house one at a time, so as not to invite suspicion. Once they all had arrived, they were led to Red Oak by John Rankin, Jr., and two of his schoolmates, Hugh Wiley and John Newton. From there, they were taken in a wagon to Hillsboro and on to Cleveland before heading to Canada.

On a number of occasions, Rankin's home was searched by slavecatchers, but no fugitive slaves were ever found there. Numerous threats also were lodged against him and his family, and following the Cincinnati race riot of 1841 he received a report that there was talk by some of going to Ripley and destroying his house. It was shortly after, on the evening of September 12, that his son Calvin noticed some strangers in town. Though the strangers' presence did not warrant any special precautions, Calvin was suspicious, and he and his cousin John P. Rankin, who was staying there at the time, heard a whistle at about 2:30 a.m. They woke up Lowry Rankin, the oldest Rankin son, and then the two boys armed themselves with pistols and slipped out the back door. Calvin went

The Lighthouse of Freedom

From **John Rankin**'s home on the hill in Ripley, Ohio, the lush panorama of the Ohio Valley spreads out. Across the river the sight of his lantern in his window must also have been magnificent during his time before the advent of electricity. But in the 1840s when he erected a thirty-foot pole and placed a lantern atop it, the night light must have been something magical. Arnold Gragston, a slave who lived on a Kentucky farm not far from Ripley and who rowed about 100 fugitive slaves across the river during the latter part of the antebellum period, said that the beacon could be seen for miles. He described it as a lighthouse and said that slaves knew it as the symbol of freedom.

around the front and encountered a man. When he demanded to know what he was doing there, the man fired a shot that barely missed him. At the rear of the house, another man took a shot at John but missed. When he began to run and exposed himself, John fired and hit him. The man got away but later died.

More shots followed, and Jean Rankin bolted the door inside. She and John figured the boys had been murdered, and they did not want any more family members to die. But Lowry and Sam were adamant and went out one of the windows. It was a good thing they did because the attackers had set fire to the barn. As Calvin, John, and Samuel engaged in a gun battle with the attackers, Lowry ran to the barn with a pail of water that he had retrieved at the cistern and put out the fire. At this point John Rankin allowed the rest of his boys out of the house, and the Rankin clan effectively warded off the attackers, who beat a hasty retreat as a mob of Ripley citizens stormed up the hill.

That week, Rankin published a warning in the *Ripley Bee*. Until now, he said he had prohibited his family from attacking strangers seen on their property. However, he announced, any strangers now found on his property after bedtime came at their own risk. The warning put an end to intruders, and the Rankins continued their work on the Underground Railroad up through the Civil War, never losing a passenger.

In 1866 Rankin retired as minister of the First Presbyterian Church in Ripley. Three of his sons followed him in the ministry: the Reverend Samuel W. Rankin, who for many years was a pastor in Hartford, Connecticut; the Reverend Arthur T. Rankin, who pastored a church in Greenburgh, Indiana; and the Reverend Adam Lowry Rankin, who served the ministry in California.

John Rankin later preached for a short time in Central Illinois and Linden, Kansas. In 1880, at the age of eighty-seven, he returned to Ripley, where he delivered a farewell sermon to the now reunited congregation of the First Presbyterian Church. He died in Ironton, Ohio.

SUGGESTED READING: Fergus Bordewich, *Bound for Canaan*, New York: HarperCollins, 2005; Paul Grim, "The Rev. John Rankin, Early Abolitionist," *Ohio History,* No. 46, 1937; Ann Hagedorn, *Beyond the River,* New York: Simon & Schuster, 2002; Andrew Ritchie, *The Soldier, the Battle, and the Victory: Being a Brief Account of the Work of Rev. John Rankin in the Anti-slavery Cause*, Cincinnati: Western Tract and Book Society, 1868.

Ray, Charles B. (1807–1886). Charles Ray started his career as a shoemaker and ended up as one of New York City's most esteemed black citizens. He likely had a hand in aiding more fugitive slaves than **William Still** but did not maintain records to write a book about his experiences. Based on numbers reported by various sources, during Ray's years as secretary of New York Vigilance from 1840 to 1853 from which there are reports, more than 1,700 fugitive slaves were assisted. How many more were assisted thereafter with his help is unknown.

Ray was born in Falmouth, Massachusetts, the son of a fugitive slave mother and a free black father. His mother was a slave with a family that was visiting Massachusetts and was hidden by locals just before her master's ship was set to sail back to the South. Her master was forced to leave without her, and she moved in with local families until she met Ray's father and married.

After learning the shoemaker's trade, Ray went on to study for the ministry. In 1832, with his religious education completed, he moved to New York City, where he resumed his work as a shoemaker. He became involved in the antislavery movement at the outset of the formation of the American Anti-Slavery Society in 1833. He became the agent in 1837 for *The Colored American*, a newspaper that was associated with the Tappan brothers, and the only black newspaper of national consequence that was publishing at this time. It advocated the "moral, social, and political elevation and improvement of the free colored people; and the peaceful emancipation of the enslaved," and "all lawful as well as moral measures to accomplish those objects."

Ray traveled extensively while in this position. The newspaper's name, Ray explained, was a reflection of its views on colonization:

> If the Colored Americans are citizens of this country, it follows, of course, that, in the broadest sense, this country is our home. . . .
>
> If we cannot be an elevated people here, in a country the resort of almost all nations to improve their condition; a country of which we are native, constituent members; our native home . . . and where there are more means available to bring the people into power and influence, and more territory to extend to them than in any other country . . . if we can not be raised up in this country, we are at great loss to know where, all things considered, we can be.

In June 1839 Samuel Cornish stepped down as editor of the newspaper, and Ray took over. During this period, in an effort to increase his subscribers, he made a noteworthy journey down the Ohio River from Pittsburgh to Cincinnati that summer. It was the first time he had seen slaves in their actual element enduring the hardships of the peculiar institution. He also witnessed the operations of the Underground Railroad along the front lines of the Ohio River, making the following observation about the frequency with which slaves escaped in the area of Wheeling, Virginia (now West Virginia):

> This species of property, they cannot keep here; as soon as they are sufficiently old, to be of any service to their masters . . . they are off to provide for themselves . . . The best of all was that none have recently been overtaken who have exercised this inalienable right. Our informant told us, he had known slaves to be missing, and in fifteen minutes a strict search set on foot, to no possible purpose, and they [were] never heard of unless by intelligence from Canada.

Following the departure of **David Ruggles** in January 1839 under a cloud of censure, Ray took over as secretary of the New York Committee of Vigilance. Of this period, he wrote the following:

> My principles and nature at once led me . . . especially in those measures for the aid and protection of fugitive slaves whose arrival during those times was almost of daily occurrence; and many a midnight hour have I, with others, walked the streets, their leader and guide; and my home was an almost daily receptacle for numbers of them at a time.

A typical situation, told later by family members, occurred one summer morning when a loud rap with the knocker was made at the front door. When the door was opened, the caller asked, "Does the Reverend Mr. Ray live here?"

Receiving an affirmative answer, the caller whistled as a signal to his comrades. "Come on, boys!" he called and fourteen men appeared and entered the Ray household. The nature of his Underground work was described as follows:

> This road had its regular lines all the way from Washington between Washington and Baltimore a kind of branch. It had its depots in Philadelphia, New York, Albany, Troy, Utica, Syracuse, Oswego and Niagara Falls. New York was a kind of receiving depot, whence we forwarded to Albany, Troy, sometimes to New Bedford and Boston, and occasionally . . . Long Island. . . . When we had parties to forward from here, we would alternate in sending between Albany and Troy, and when we had a large party we would divide between the two cities. We had on one occasion, a party of twenty-eight persons of all ages. . . . We destined them for Canada. I secured passage for them in a barge, and Mr. Wright and myself spent the day in providing food, and personally saw them off on the barge. I then took the regular passenger boat. . . . Arriving in the morning, I reported to the Committee at Albany, and then returned to Troy and gave Brother Garnet notice, and he and I spent the day in visiting friends of the cause there, to raise money to help the party through to Toronto, Canada, via Oswego. We succeeded . . . to send them all the way from here with safety.

During his first year as secretary, Ray wrote that the committee aided more than 178 fugitive slaves. He worked closely with such conductors as Rev. **Abel Brown**, the radical abolitionist from upstate New York; Ray officiated at Brown's second marriage to his wife, Catherine. A letter written by her revealed their collaboration:

> An extremely interesting case occurred, concerning a fugitive forwarded by Mr. Ray to Albany, care of Mr. Abel Brown. He arrived one morning during the absence of Mr. Brown, and was sheltered and cared for by his companion in labors three days, constantly in dread of being taken by his pursuers! The account of himself as a slave and of his journey on his way to a land of freedom was so peculiar that Mrs. B. wished to retain him. Mr. Brown, in the meantime, had found a place near Lake Champlain for this class of human beings, to which the fugitive was immediately conveyed.

In 1845 Ray achieved his lifelong dream and was made pastor of the Bethesda Congregational Church in New York City. He served in that capacity for twenty-two years.

The following year he became involved in **Gerrit Smith's** land donation plan to blacks and distributed a circular signed by himself, James McCune Smith, and **Theodore Wright** urging black men to consider Smith's generous offer of forty acres in upstate New York and become self-sufficient farmers.

The untimely death in 1847 of Theodore Wright, president of the New York Committee of Vigilance, led to a reorganization of the committee with **Isaac T. Hopper** as interim president. It also was renamed the New York State Committee of Vigilance, as its activities had expanded statewide. The following year it was further reorganized with Gerrit Smith becoming president. Through these changes, Ray remained as secretary.

In an excerpt from a letter Ray wrote to supporters about the committee's activities in 1849, he stated that "more than four hundred" runaway slaves had been assisted by the committee in New York City and that "as the principles of freedom are agitated in this land in one form and another, the slaves will be prompted to flee from their prison house and they are coming to us in rapidly augmenting numbers. Every month, every week, is bringing new labors and responsibilities on their account."

Among those in the New York City area on whom he could rely to assist him was the famed preacher Rev. Henry Ward Beecher, who became the pastor of the Plymouth Congregational Church in Brooklyn in 1847 and who harbored fugitive slaves at the church.

One of the more well known cases in which Ray was involved, and which shows the high level of organization that had developed in the Underground Railroad, was that of the Weems family. John Weems was free but his wife, five sons, and two daughters were slaves. The wife and sons were in Washington, D.C., waiting to be sold by slave traders. The slave traders agreed to delay their departure to allow Weems to go north and try to raise the money to purchase them but gave him a deadline.

Ellwood Harvey: The Mysterious "Dr. H."

For many years historians were uncertain of the identity of "Dr. H," who rendezvoused with the fugitive slave Ann Maria Weems near the White House. It has recently been confirmed that the mystery man was a Chester, Pennsylvania, physician, Dr. Ellwood Harvey, a member of the Longwood Meeting and close associate of abolitionist **Dr. Bartholomew Fussell.**

In the 1850s Harvey taught at the Female Medical College of Philadelphia, the world's first college for female doctors. A $300 reward from wealthy merchant and abolitionist Lewis Tappan for rescuing Weems was used by Harvey to buy a dissection mannequin for the women's college. Harvey also hid runaway slaves in his stable loft in Chester.

Weems came to see Ray in 1852 to ask for help in raising the money. Ray advised that there was not enough time to raise the sum requested and that the man should return to Washington and ask for more time. In the meantime, Ray wrote Henry Garnet, then in England, of the situation and asked him to try to raise the money there. The English abolitionists were very generous in such matters, and Garnet was able to secure $5,000.

Ray contacted Jacob Bigelow, a lawyer, who was part of the Underground Railroad in Washington, D.C., and whose role was to negotiate the sale of the slaves. Before they could make an offer, the wife and five sons had been sent to Montgomery, Alabama, but they were able to secure the sale of the eldest daughter, Catherine.

An effort to locate the mother and the boys was made, and an offer was circulated in Southern newspapers. Before long, contact was made and a price was negotiated for the sale of the mother and the two youngest sons, and they were brought to Washington. The younger daughter, Ann Maria, was another matter. The plan to rescue her through the Underground Railroad was finally accomplished in 1855. This was a cooperative effort between Bigelow, **William Still** of the Philadelphia Committee, and Ray and Lewis Tappan. After finally being taken to the house of Tappan, Ann Maria was successfully forwarded to Canada, where she became a resident at the Elgin Fugitive Slave settlement in Buxton.

Charles Ray's life was full. In addition to his work in the abolition movement and pastorate at the Bethesda Congregational Church, he was a member of the New York African Society for Mutual Relief for forty years, eight as president. He is best remembered, however, for helping hundreds of his oppressed brethren become free.

SUGGESTED READING: "Falmouth Man of Color," *Falmouth Enterprise,* Vol. 17, May, 1963; Florence T. Ray, *Sketch of the Life of Rev. Charles B. Ray*, New York: Press of J. J. Little & Co., 1887; C. Peter Ripley, editor, *The Black Abolitionist Papers,* Vol. 3 and 4, Chapel Hill: University of North Carolina Press, 1991; Munroe N. Work, "The Life of Rev. Charles B. Ray," *Journal of Negro History*, October, 1919.

Reynolds, George J. (dates unknown). George J. Reynolds was a radical black abolitionist and Underground Railroad conductor who operated out of Detroit, Michigan, and Sandusky, Ohio.

A blacksmith by trade, Reynolds worked closely with black abolition leaders George DeBaptiste and William Lambert during the late 1840s through 1860. **Levi Coffin**, a regional leader of the Underground Railroad, sent Reynolds to **George DeBaptiste** in Detroit about 1847. At this time Reynolds was known as J. C. Reynolds. Changes in identity were commonly used to protect fugitives, but aliases were sometimes adopted by agents of the Underground also. DeBaptiste and Coffin became friends when DeBaptiste lived in Madison, Indiana and sent many fugitives north from the Ohio River. DeBaptiste removed to Detroit in 1846 after a race riot in Madison threatened the safety of his young family.

William Lambert stated in an interview that Reynolds was employed by the Michigan Central Railroad then being connected from Detroit to Chicago. Reynolds's Detroit home on Eighth Street, near the grain elevator, housed numerous fugitive slaves. Pilots first took fugitives to Detroit's Prince Hall Masonic lodge. They were quickly moved to one of several hideaways. For a time, Reynolds's home was the most popular.

"We would fetch the fugitives there," said Lambert, "shipping them into the house by dark one by one. There they found food and warmth, and when, as frequently happened, they were ragged and thinly clad, we gave them clothing." The group concealed skiffs "under the docks, and before daylight we would have everyone over." A short trip across the Detroit River landed fugitives on Canadian soil, where they were free. "We never lost a man by capture at this point, so careful were we, and we took over as high as 1,600 in one year," added Lambert.When Reynolds's home was being watched, other resting spots were used including Seymour Finney's barn, near his hotel, as well as properties owned by Luther Beecher, Farmer Underwood, and another man named McChubb.

Reynolds's Detroit home must have come under increasing scrutiny by slavecatchers because by 1850 he was living in Sandusky, Ohio, a busy port city on Lake Erie. There he was known as George J. Reynolds and continued to be employed by the Detroit Underground Railroad. Reynolds's dwelling in Sandusky provided frequent quarters for fugitive slaves waiting for transport by water either to Detroit or across the lake to Canada West (now Ontario).

Henry Paden, a mayor of Clyde, Ohio, described Reynolds in an 1887 speech as an Indian Negro who lived in a "two-story brick house on Madison Street." Prior to the Civil War, Paden worked on the Sandusky, Mansfield & Newark Railroad and was involved in the Underground Railroad. Early in 1860 Paden took a group of nine fugitives to Reynolds's home in Sandusky.

Of the nine men , Paden wrote: "Five had left wives and children in the South; two of the others had a sweetheart, whom their masters wanted them to marry, but rather than do this under the conditions imposed by slavery they had chosen to run away." A few days later, Reynolds took the party to Canada by sled. This ice passage was "a mighty bridge, thirty miles across, treacherous withal, liable to be swept by furious winds and cruel blinding storms of snow. . . . with a pocket compass for their sole guide," according to Paden. Yet the group placed their lives "with trustful confidence in a God of freedom."

In May 1858, Reynolds attended abolitionist **John Brown**'s Chatham Convention. Brown called the meeting to develop a constitution for a black nation in North America. The thinking by the group was that blacks had been displaced from their homelands and not treated well in the United States. They did not expect better treatment following the 1857 Dred Scott United States Supreme Court decision. Like Native Americans, they desired their own government on land belonging to them, or a nation within a nation.

Reynolds attended the meeting in the company of James H. Harris and Osborne P. Anderson. The three men have been described by contemporaries as members of a secret, black paramilitary group. All three signed the constitution produced by the convention, although Reynolds signed "J. G. Reynolds." This minor subterfuge illustrates Reynolds's inclination to protect himself with small changes of identity. Of the three men, only Osborne P. Anderson followed John Brown to Harpers Ferry. Anderson was one of five men who escaped during the raid and survived.

Following the Civil War, Reynolds appears to have lived in London, Ontario. John P. Reynolds, a physician in Vincennes, Indiana, mentioned that his brother, G. J. Reynolds, lived there in 1869. John P. Reynolds was a leader of the black community in Vincennes and had recruited soldiers for the Massachusetts Fifty-fourth United States Colored Troops.

SUGGESTED READING: Reminiscences of Levi Coffin, New York: A.M. Kelly, 1968; "Freedom's Railway," *The Detroit Tribune*, Jan. 17, 1886; H. F. Paden, "Underground Railroad Reminiscences," *The Firelands Pioneer*, Vol. V, July 1888; Norwalk, OH: Firelands Historical Society; Wilbur Siebert's Papers, Ohio Historical Society; Benjamin Quarles, *Allies for Freedom*, New York:Oxford University Press, 1974; Edward J. Renehan, Jr., *The Secret Six*, New York: Crown Publishers, 1995; *Vincennes Weekly Western Sun*, Jan. 16, 1869.

Jennifer Harrison, Indiana

Richardson, Susan (1812–unknown). Susan Richardson, or Aunt Sukey as she was better known, was born in Georgia and brought in 1817 to the "free" territory of Illinois, where she was registered as an indentured servant. Though the Northwest Ordinance of 1787 prohibited slavery north of the Ohio River, the historical precedent set by the French permitting slavery in the region had made slavery customary. As a result, enforcement of the ordinance was lenient in that regard and the state established Black Codes in 1819 that allowed indentured servitude, a condition of virtual slavery, for men until the age of thirty-five and women until the age of thirty-two.

Sukey's master, Andrew Borders, was sometimes harsh in his treatment of his "servants." However, it is believed that he was the father of the oldest of her three children, which may have explained his refusal to beat her during the incident that led to her escape on the night of August 31, 1842. A fight between Sukey's oldest son, twelve-year-old Jarrot, and one of Borders's children caused him to be beaten by Borders's wife, Martha. She also demanded that her husband give Sukey a beating. He refused but as a compromise agreed that he would hold Sukey down while Martha beat her.

Learning of this persuaded Sukey to run away. Heading directly to the home of the nearest abolitionist, **William Hayes**, indicates she may have considered fleeing for some time. Accompanying Sukey and her three sons was a nineteen-year-old servant, Hannah, whose mother had fled four months earlier after a severe beating by Borders.

During the night, they set out on foot through a stony creek bed with steep banks and thick vegetation—not an easy trek in the darkness with two toddlers. But by morning they arrived at the farmhouse of Hayes, a devout member of the Covenanters, a religious sect that abhorred slavery and governmental influence in the lives of citizens. Hayes had moved to Illinois from upstate New York with his wife, four children, and two sisters-in-law in search of new opportunities.

On September 1 Hayes took them by wagon to Chester Landing and accompanied them aboard a steamboat on the Mississippi River. They disembarked at St. Louis and took a packet boat up the Illinois River, finally disembarking at the mouth of Copperas

Creek in the Tall Grass Prairie region of Fulton County. They reached Farmington on September 5, from where Eli Wilson and his son forwarded them to the home of Rev. **John Cross** in Knox County.

They were spotted by a justice of the peace, Jacob Kightlinger, to whom Cross had boldly announced that he had set up an Underground Railroad depot and dared anyone to catch him. On the Wilsons' return trip, Kightlinger and an armed posse of vigilantes stopped and asked where they had taken their passengers. They refused to cooperate, but Kightlinger suspected Cross, and the posse went to Cross's residence. They found the women and children resting in his cornfields while Mrs. Cross was preparing dinner for them. Cross, however, was away on a trip to meet another party of fugitive slaves. Kightlinger took custody of the women and children and had them lodged in the Knoxville jail.

A series of legal motions were made by the abolitionists of Knox County in their behalf while an advertisement was circulated seeking claimants. Borders learned of their whereabouts two weeks after the escape and went with his son to Knoxville to claim them. He claimed Sukey but admitted that Hannah had served out her indenture and was free to go where she pleased. However, he did not bring Sukey's indenture papers and the judge refused to release them. In an effort to rid himself of this legal entanglement, Borders attempted to sell his servants in exchange for a horse. That failing, Borders and his son left town.

With no legal claim established, Sukey and her children were set free the first week in October for six weeks. At that time, they were to be returned to the jail, where they were to be hired out to pay for their jail fees. The sale, which was held on November 10, was a failure. Most of those attending did not think it was right to pay the county for unfairly confining women and children.

For a time, their future looked bright. Hannah apparently found work in a neighboring town and Sukey rented a house in Knoxville, doing laundry for various families. Jarrot, the oldest boy, worked in the fields near town, and Sukey left the younger boys at a local hotel while she worked. But their optimism was short-lived. On November 24 Borders arrived with the indenture papers and went directly to Sheriff Frans to claim his property. Frans helped him take custody of all three boys, and they were placed back in the Knox County Jail. When Sukey learned of this, she became frantic. Local abolitionist Charles W. Gilbert persuaded her not to go to her boys and instead flee to Galesburg, where she would be protected from being captured.

Though local abolitionists filed suit against Borders for false imprisonment in taking the boys, the case was not scheduled until the following June. He paid bail and left town with the children apparently released to him by Sheriff Frans, an action that was illegal. Meanwhile Sukey remained near despair in Galesburg, where indictments had been brought against Rev. John Cross, George Washington Gale, Nehemiah West, and Charles Gilbert for harboring Borders's servants. Eventually, however, after some legal wrangling the suits were dropped, and Borders brought a successful civil suit against William Hayes. It broke Hayes financially, and he died at the age of fifty-four in 1849 while awaiting the results of an appeal for a criminal indictment against him in another case involving his aid to fugitive slaves.

Though Sukey never again saw her sons—Jarrot was killed in 1844, and the others were lost in slavery—she did receive her certificate of freedom on May 1, 1845, in the Randolph County Court, with the claims of Borders on her being dismissed. She settled in Galesburg and became a respectable citizen, marrying and changing her name to Susan Richardson and having more children. She also participated in the Underground Railroad, one notable documented incident that involved a runaway named Bill Casey. In the 1878 History of Knox County, she was described as "a very intelligent, fine-looking, and active old Negro lady." Hannah, the girl who joined her in escaping from Andrew Borders, eventually moved to New York City.

SUGGESTED READING: Charles Chapman, *History of Knox County, Illinois*, 1878; Carol Pirtle, *Escape betwixt Two Suns: A True Tale of the Underground Railroad in Illinois*, Carbondale, IL: Southern Illinois University Press, 2000.

Robinson, Rowland T. (1796–1879). Rowland T. Robinson was one of the leading abolitionists in Vermont. His remote farm Rokeby, near Lake Champlain in northeastern Vermont, is the best-documented Underground Railroad stop in the state.

Born in Ferrisburgh, Vermont, to Quaker parents, Robinson lived at the family farm his entire life. He attended the Nine Partners Quaker boarding school in Dutchess County, New York, a school known for its strong abolitionist views and its association with such noted abolitionists as Elias Hicks and **Lucretia Mott**. Robinson's wife, Rachel, also was a Quaker who shared Robinson's abolitionist views.

The first report of Robinson's abolitionist activities comes from the organization in 1834 of the Vermont Anti-Slavery Society, which William Lloyd Garrison noted was the first statewide antislavery organization in the country. Garrison had been an editor in Bennington, Vermont, from 1828 to early 1829 and likely had fomented some support for abolitionism, though at that time he had not yet unequivocally supported immediate emancipation.

Numerous antislavery organizations were formed throughout the state during the early period of Garrisonian abolitionism. Though they encountered a strong and vocal opposition in the beginning, more than 47,000 residents out of an approximately 290,000 had joined one of the state's eighty-nine antislavery societies by 1837. This illustrates how widely abolitionized the state already had become in a period when, nationwide, abolitionists were a very small minority. It also indicates that the state was well fertilized for Underground Railroad activities.

According to one statewide study in 1998, there were twenty-nine cases documenting aid to fugitive slaves in the state, accounting for forty-seven individuals in all. Many more were likely undocumented. However, it is impossible to determine at this time how many were assisted, and considering that Vermont was an off-the-beaten track thoroughfare, the numbers likely were not substantial.

Rokeby was in a remote, sparsely populated area bordered by mountains to the east and Lake Champlain on the west, and it was a good location to harbor fugitive slaves without concealment for an extended period. The first documented case of aid to a fugitive slave involving Robinson was reported in a January 27, 1837, letter from Oliver Johnson on behalf of a runaway named Simon. He had "intended going to Canada in the spring, but says he would prefer to stay in the US if he could be safe. . . . I could not help thinking he would be a good man for you to hire. . . . he is very trustworthy, of a kind disposition, and knows how to do almost all kinds of farm work."

Johnson was writing from Jenner Township in western Pennsylvania, where he was on a lecture tour for the American Anti-Slavery Society. A fellow Quaker, who was among the organizers of the Vermont Anti-Slavery Society, Johnson worked with Garrison in Bennington and later at *The Liberator*. He would move to New York and

Philadelphia, where he worked for abolitionist publications and was a member of the executive committee of the Pennsylvania Anti-Slavery Society, which worked in tandem with the Philadelphia Vigilance Committee during the 1850s.

On April 3, Johnson wrote back that he'd given Simon directions to Philadelphia, "where he will put himself under the direction of our friends, who will give him all needful information concerning the route to New York, at which place he will be befriended by the Committee of Vigilance [the New York committee]."

Robinson already had a runaway slave working for him at that time. His name was Jesse, and he had escaped from Perquimans County, North Carolina slaveowner, Ephram Elliott. Robinson wrote Elliott a letter negotiating for the price of Jesse's emancipation but later letters indicate that an agreement as to the price had not occurred.

Johnson had written to Robinson about fugitive slaves as early as 1835 when he was still in Vermont, relating an attempt to get the help of Chancy L. Knapp, a prominent state official, in situating a young fugitive slave named William in Montpelier. In 1838, Knapp picked up another fugitive slave, Charles, from Rokeby, and returned with him over the mountains to Montpelier. Knapp later wrote to a Saratoga, New York agent, Mason Anthony, who had taken Charles to Rokeby, that Knapp was seeking a good Montpelier family to board him as well as providing for his education and religious instruction.

Another letter to Robinson in 1842 from Charles Marriot, a Hudson, New York Quaker inquired about the possibility of Robinson hiring a slave couple, John and Martha Williams, then boarding at his residence. He said that John was "a good chopper and farmer" and that Martha was "useful and well conducted in the house." Marriott thought their prospects would be better in Vermont because of the overcrowding of fugitive slaves that was occurring in Canada.

Further letters testify to the Robinsons' aid to fugitive slaves in 1844 and 1851. Other references to activity in Vermont show regular traffic from the Albany-Troy area during the early 1840s when the Eastern New York Vigilance Committee, of which **Charles Torrey** and **Abel Brown** were the leading members, was active. An 1840 letter from committee member **Fayette Shipherd** of Troy to Charles Hicks of Bennington states that because of the closing of the Champlain Canal that led to the southern shores of Lake Champlain, which incidentally was near the residence of Robinson, "I shall send my Southern friends along your road and patronize your house. We had a fine run of business during the season." Another letter from this period, dated June 9, 1842, from Brown also is addressed to Hicks and says in part, "Please receive the Bearer as a friend who needs your aid and direct him on his way if you cannot give him work." Farther north, an account from **Samuel Boyd** of Glens Falls, New York, says that his father, Rufus Boyd, sometimes drove fugitive slaves all the way north to Swanton, Vermont, during the period following the passage of the second Fugitive Slave Law.

Other references collected by historian Wilbur Siebert in letters from Robinson's son, Rowland E. Robinson, indicate that Robinson sometimes forwarded fugitive slaves to his brother-in-law Nathan C. Hoag in Charlotte. Other reports received by Siebert note that fugitive slaves were directed to New York on McNeil's Ferry, which connects at Charlotte, Vermont. Longtime New York conductor **Samuel Keese Smith** of Peru, Clinton County, New York, also a Quaker, referred to Robinson in an 1887 memoir, saying that he aided "scores of fugitive slaves."

Rowland and Rachel Robinson not only were active in the antislavery movement and in aiding and employing runaway slaves but also boycotted slave-made goods and operated an interracial school at their farm. Although it is likely that the Robinsons' Underground Railroad activities were only sporadic, oral tradition suggests a more extensive and active Underground Railroad in Vermont.

SUGGESTED READING: Fergus Bordewich, *Bound for Canaan*, New York: HarperCollins, 2005; Tom Calarco, *The Underground Railroad in the Adirondack Region*, Jefferson, NC: McFarland and Company, 2004; Wilbur H. Sieber, *Vermont's Anti-slavery and Underground Railroad Record, 1937*, New York: Negro Universities Press, 1969; Jane Williamson, "Telling Like It Was at Rokeby," *Passages to Freedom*, David W. Blight, editor, Washington, DC: Smithsonian Books, 2004; Raymond Paul Zirblis, *Friends of Freedom*, Montpelier, VT: Vermont Division of Historic Preservation, 1996.

Ruggles, David (1810–1849). Underground Railroad conductor David Ruggles was a leader during the early years of the Underground Railroad in New York City. He devoted his life to helping the oppressed, the destitute, and the sick, often sacrificing his own well-being and shortening his remarkable life. But aside from a junior high school in Bedford-Stuyvesant named the David Ruggles School, he is virtually forgotten.

Ruggles was born to free black parents in Norwich, Connecticut, a river port fifteen miles from its outlet to the Atlantic Ocean and a city with a tradition of tolerance for blacks. Many of its residents took part in the Revolutionary War, and they realized the contradiction between fighting for their own liberty and owning slaves. His father, David Sr., was a blacksmith; his mother, Nancy, a caterer and devoted Methodist. Educated in Sabbath and Manumission Society schools, Ruggles at a very early age took a job as a sailor. By the age of seventeen he had moved to New York City and before long opened his own grocery, at first selling alcohol.

Ruggles became a temperance advocate when he became involved in the movement for emancipation, and turned his grocery, located at 36 Lispenard Street, into a bookstore and reading room. In 1833 he became an agent for the *Emancipator*, the abolitionist newspaper sponsored by the Tappan brothers. He lectured on antislavery, sought subscribers to the paper, and became a contributor. His home at 67 Lispenard was where he harbored **Frederick Douglass** when the legendary black leader made his escape to freedom.

Ruggles quickly developed a reputation as a writer and dynamic speaker, one who did not mince his words. One of his earliest causes was the repudiation of colonization, and his 1834 pamphlet, *The "Extinguisher" Extinguished*, pointed out colonization's evils. He wrote hundreds of articles, published at least five pamphlets, and operated a printing press. His magazine, *Mirror of Liberty*, issued between 1838 and 1841, is regarded as the first periodical published by a black American.

His aggressiveness, however, created enemies and may have led to the fire that destroyed his bookstore in 1835. That year also saw the organization of the New York Committee of Vigilance, whose objective was "to effect the protection and relief of such inhabitants of this city and state who are liable to be illegally aggrieved, kidnapped, and reduced to slavery." A report that year in the *Emancipator* stated that 5,000 fugitive slaves were living in New York City and that an organization of slavecatchers had formed to round them up and send them back to slavery. With the domestic slave trade offering substantial amounts for laborers, they also had no scruples about kidnapping free blacks, who were not given the same legal protections as whites. Ruggles was named its corresponding secretary.

It was through his work with the committee that Ruggles established his legacy. Although it began as an organization defending the rights of resident New Yorkers, its work in the Underground Railroad soon took precedence. In its first year, it reported that it had "saved about three hundred persons . . . from being carried back into slavery." The committee did more than simply help maintain their freedom. It also provided food and shelter and helped them find work. Ruggles became notorious for his bold methods.

Knowing his way around the shipyards, he would force his way aboard ships that were likely places for abducted blacks or fugitive slaves being held for transport to the South or for ships illegally engaged in the international slave trade, which had been outlawed in 1808. On one occasion, using a writ of habeas corpus, he boarded a Portuguese ship holding Africans for sale and had the captain arrested for slave trading. This led to an attempt to kidnap him into slavery.

On the night of December 28, 1836, two slavecatchers showed up at Ruggles's door. One was New York law enforcement official Tobias Boudinot and the other, D. D. Nash, a Georgia native who was part of a slavecatching organization led by Boudinot. They asked if they could enter and discuss the matter of the slave-trading charges. When Ruggles refused, they broke down his door, but not before he escaped out the back entrance. A hearing was later held at the police station. Boudinot had a warrant to arrest Ruggles as a fugitive slave, but when the charge against Ruggles was clearly found to be false, the matter was dropped.

On another occasion a domestic named Charity went to the committee and asked for help. She had been held as a slave in Brooklyn by D. K. Dodge for four years, well beyond the nine-month legal limit to keep a slave in the state. Ruggles went to Dodge's house unannounced. Though Dodge was absent, his wife allowed Ruggles to enter. He confronted her about Charity and three other slaves maintained there. When Mrs. Dodge said that they intended to set them free, Charity contradicted her. An argument followed and it caused a neighbor to intercede. But Ruggles did not back down, and the neighbor, an elderly man, was not about to use force. Charity, however, was the only one to leave with Ruggles, though freedom was not kind to her, and she ended up as a prostitute, asking Dodge to take her back.

Ruggles's help to another former slave had much more favorable results. It was September 1838. The runaway, exhilarated by his taste of freedom, was afraid he might be caught and sent back to slavery. Loitering in the harbor area, he met a sailor who directed him to Ruggles. The runaway was Frederick Douglass, and he remained with Ruggles until he was joined by his betrothed, Anna Murray, a free black woman, who according to plan rendezvoused with him in New York. They were married and then shipped off by Ruggles to New Bedford, Massachusetts, with a letter of recommendation to Quakers there.

"Procuring the escape of a slave from bondage to liberty is a violation of no law of the land," Ruggles wrote. "I may, I must, suffer the laws of the government under which I live, but I must not obey them if they are contrary to the laws of God . . . I would show, clearly, by the example of Paul and other Apostles, that wicked and unjust laws must be resisted even unto death."

Breaking the law was not without consequence, and Ruggles was constantly in trouble with the law. On August 25, 1838, John P. Darg, a Virginia slaveholder, arrived in New York City with his slave Thomas Hughes. A few days later Hughes went to the house of **Isaac Hopper**, who forwarded him to a place of safety. Afterward it was learned that Hughes had stolen $8,000 from his master before leaving him. Barney Corse, another Underground agent, also became involved and the abolitionists negotiated with Darg, asking for the manumission of Hughes in return for the money. But complicating matters was that Hughes no longer had all the money. Hopper, Ruggles, and Corse were charged with complicity in the robbery, as well as for aiding a fugitive slave. The matter dragged on for more than a year, but in the end the charges against them were dropped. However, Hughes was convicted of grand larceny and sentenced to two years in jail.

In 1837 Ruggles had received a letter charging a black innkeeper, John Russell, with allowing kidnappers to keep their captives at his hotel before sending them South. The letter was provided to Samuel Cornish, who published it in *The Colored American*. Russell sued the newspaper for libel and won a judgment in 1838 that nearly bankrupted the struggling publication. This infuriated Cornish, who also was a member of the vigilance committee, and he charged Ruggles with improper use of committee funds. He demanded an accounting of every expenditure made by Ruggles regarding the vigilance committee. It revealed a shortage of $400.

By 1839 the stress of his work had taken its toll. Ruggles had become afflicted with a severe bowel disorder that also affected his eyesight. Embarrassed and in failing health, he resigned his post as secretary of the committee in 1840.

Abolitionists in New England came to his assistance. William Nell, who worked under William Lloyd Garrison and who operated an Underground Railroad station in the basement of *The Liberator*, organized a testimonial dinner. In 1842 Author Lydia Maria Child and her husband, David Lee Child, arranged for Ruggles to join the Northampton Association of Education and Industry, a commune in Florence, Massachusetts. Other members of the community were Sojourner Truth and Basil Dorsey, a fugitive slave aided by Ruggles and the first black to settle there.

At Florence, Ruggles was introduced to water cure therapy and found that it improved his health. In 1845 he opened his own water cure hospital, which became quite successful. He also resumed writing for abolitionist publications and speaking at abolitionist conventions. Though the traffic was much slower here, he resumed his work in the Underground Railroad. However, seven years after moving to Florence, he succumbed

Vigilance Committees

Vigilance committee was the term used for an organization involved in the Underground Railroad. They provided food, clothing, shelter, medical care, transportation, jobs, and legal assistance for fugitive slaves. Sometimes they alerted slaves brought into free states by their masters of their right to become free, as most Northern states had laws by the early 1840s that stipulated this.

These committees needed money to operate. Oftentimes conductors used money out of their own pockets when the need arose. Committees held fund-raisers or made appeals through advertisements, broadsides, or flyers. The Albany committee coordinated by **Stephen Myers** in Albany, New York, was able to call on a network of wealthy benefactors.

Another important role of the vigilance committee was to alert former slaves who were not legally free of the presence of slavecatchers. In Syracuse, for instance, when **Jerry Henry** was apprehended church bells in the city began tolling.

The best-known committees were those in Philadelphia, Boston, and New York. Evidence suggests that the major vigilance committees were closely connected. For example, Joshua Coffin, a founder of the New England Anti-Slavery Society, who was known to have harbored fugitive slaves in Newburyport, Massachusetts, went on a mission for the New York Committee of Vigilance in 1838 to Tennessee to bring slaves out. In 1842 we also find him writing a letter from Philadelphia to Boston abolitionists, asking for funds to help the Philadelphia Vigilance Committee. There was also collaboration between **William Still** in Philadelphia and **Charles Ray** in New York. Among other cities with important vigilance committees were Chicago, Cleveland, Cincinnati, New Haven, Syracuse, Rochester, and Troy, New York.

to a bowel infection on December 26. His water cure hospital was filled to capacity, and his life of devotion to those in need was complete.

In all, Ruggles admitted to helping more than 600 fugitive slaves during his time as secretary of the New York Committee of Vigilance.

SUGGESTED READING: Fergus Bordewich, *Bound for Canaan*, New York: HarperCollins, 2005; Graham Hodges, "David Ruggles: The Hazards of Anti-slavery Journalism," *Media Studies Journal*, Spring/Summer, 2000; Dorothy B. Porter, "David Ruggles, An Apostle for Human Rights," *Journal of Negro History*, January, 1943; "The First Annual Report of the New York Committee of Vigilance for the Year 1837," New York: Piercy & Reed, 1837.

S

Shipherd, Fayette (1797–1878). An evangelical Christian minister and follower of Charles Finney, Fayette Shipherd was a militant abolitionist and active participant in the Underground Railroad who devoted his ministry to the poor and needy.

Shipherd's roots in the Underground Railroad began when he helped organize a church for the boatmen of Troy, New York, in 1832. It became the Bethel Church, of which he became pastor in 1833. It was an important connection because he would later use the waterways as a primary thoroughfare for Underground Railroad activities. However, a conflict with one of its founders, Gurdon Grant, which apparently was related to Shipherd's wife, Elmina, caused him to sever his ties with the church in August 1834.

Shortly after, he moved to Walton, in Delaware County, New York, where he became pastor of the First Congregational Church. But tragedy soon struck when Elmina died after a brief illness. The following year he married his second wife, Catherine, a temperance lecturer, and joined the county antislavery society, becoming an agent for the American Anti-Slavery Society.

In 1838, despite their differences, Grant recalled Shipherd to Troy to resume his duties as pastor at the Bethel Church. During this period, Shipherd also assisted Rev. Nathan Sidney Beman in establishing the Liberty Street Presbyterian Church to serve the city's black population. That year also marked the period when the Underground Railroad stepped up efforts to organize in upstate New York. The state antislavery society secretary at the time, William L. Chaplin, issued a directive published in *Friend of Man* calling on upstate cities to organize vigilance committees and initiate a close correspondence with the Committee of Vigilance in New York City.

In a letter to Shipherd dated June 5, 1840, his brother John Jay Shipherd, the founder of Oberlin College, indicated in euphemistic terms that he agreed with Fayette's actions in aiding fugitive slaves. He wrote: "The ground you take in housing ministers is right—Bible ground. . . .We do receive calls from colonists hastening to the North Star—not a few—comfort them and bid them God speed."

However, a letter later that year, dated November 24, from Shipherd to Vermont conductor Charles Hicks of Bennington was much more explicit. Apparently, Shipherd did not think it wise to send the letter by mail and had it delivered personally by Garret Van Hoosen, who lived in Hoosick, New York, which was along the route to Bennington. In it, Shipherd wrote the following:

> As the canal has closed I shall send my Southern friends along your road & patronize your house. We had a fine run of business during the season. C.G. We had 22 in two weeks 13 in the city at one time. Some of them noble looking fellows I assure you. One female so near white & so beautiful that her master had been offered at different times $1,200–1,500 & 2,000 for foulest purposes. A Baltimore officer—a man hunter was seen in our city making his observations but left without giving us any trouble. Several slaves were in our city from Baltimore at the time. Our Laws are now a terror to evil doers who live by robbery.

Shipherd was referring in the last sentence to two laws passed in May 1840 by the New York State legislature. The first guaranteed a trial by jury to alleged fugitive slaves, and the second provided protection for free black citizens of New York State "from being kidnapped, or reduced to slavery." The latter law granted power to the governor to send a commissioned agent to restore the liberty of any free citizen of the state who the governor believed, based on the evidence, was wrongly being held in slavery.

Shipherd left Bethel again in 1841, but he remained in Troy and formed his own Free Congregational Church, with seventy-two members of the Bethel Church moving to his new congregation. In order to pay for the lot and construction of the church, he negotiated with contractors, borrowed money, and taught school on the side. The church was completed in 1844. He also joined the Liberty Party and became active in the Eastern New York Anti-Slavery Society (ENYASS) of **Abel Brown** and **Charles Torrey**, becoming a member of its executive committee, their euphemism for the Underground Railroad. The ENYASS soon became notorious in its efforts to aid fugitive slaves through its publication the *Tocsin of Liberty*.

When Abel Brown moved to Troy in 1844, Shipherd gave him support. It was at Shipherd's Congregational Church that a series of lectures by Brown caused a riot and provoked his attack by the mob on the streets of Troy from which he was lucky to escape alive. Brown died shortly after when he came down with meningitis during a trip to Rochester, and Torrey was imprisoned for aiding fugitive slaves in Baltimore. This was a blow to the ENYASS from which they could not recover, and it disbanded sometime after its annual meeting in May 1845.

How the dissolution of the society affected the ministry of Shipherd is uncertain, but he left his church in Troy in 1846 and was unemployed for several months until receiving an invitation from Stephentown, in eastern Rensselaer County not far from its border with Massachusetts. He remained there until May 1849 when he moved to a church in West Nassau just a short distance from Stephentown. This is an extremely rural and mountainous area through which local history recorded the occasional movement of fugitive slaves. Though there is no record or other evidence of Shipherd forwarding fugitive slaves at this time, it is possible that he continued his activities as a conductor there.

After 1851 Shipherd moved first to Jefferson and then to Oswego County, which was extremely active in the Underground Railroad with a variety of nearby Lake Ontario ports available to send fugitive slaves to Canada. Then in 1858 he moved to Oberlin, where his son Jacob, one of the infamous Oberlin-Wellington rescuers, attended college. Shipherd died in Sydney, New York.

Shipherd complained in his unpublished autobiography of the lack of monetary compensation he received for his ministerial efforts and provided an account of his life earnings, describing them as "paltry pittances" for forty-five years of hard labor. His obituary stated, "Few men of such remarkable talents have been content to forego deliberately every opportunity for personal preferment for the single privilege of preaching the Gospel to the poor in literal obedience to the Master's command."

SUGGESTED READING: Fayette Shipherd, "A Legacy for My Beloved Wife, Catherine Shipherd," unpublished memoir, Troy, 1846, and "My Legacy to My Beloved Wife and Children," unpublished memoir, 1870, Bragdon Family papers, Rush Rhees Library, University of Rochester, Rare Books & Special Collections; Letter from Fayette Shipherd to Charles Hicks, Rensselaer County, NY, Nov. 24, 1840.

Sims, Thomas (1834–unknown). In 1851 fugitive slave Thomas Sims stowed away aboard the brig *M. & H. Gilmore* in Savannah, Georgia. Its destination was Boston, and he escaped detection almost the entire journey. After being discovered, he was locked in a cabin with the intention of turning him over to the legal authorities. However, he managed to escape and take a small boat ashore to apparent freedom.

But his freedom was short-lived. While lodging in a seamen's boardinghouse, he telegraphed his alleged wife, also a slave, in Virginia for money. Her master learned of it and notified Sims's master, who immediately contacted authorities. The next day Sims was apprehended by police on a falsified charge of theft. His apprehension came only after a violent struggle during which he stabbed a policeman. Thereafter, Sims was taken to the federal courthouse, where he was imprisoned on the third floor.

Sims's arrest came less than two months after the rescue of **Shadrach Minkins**, and authorities took extra precautions. A ring of guards and a makeshift chain surrounded the courthouse. The Boston Vigilance Committee met at the office of *The Liberator* to develop a plan to prevent Sims's return to slavery. Handbills and posters were distributed throughout Boston, especially in the black community, warning of slavecatchers.

The vigilance committee could not come up with a plan for rescue, and it was noted by one of its black members, **Lewis Hayden**, who led the rescue of Shadrach, that the number of blacks available for a rescue had been diminished by recent emigrations to Canada. Nevertheless, a plan was hatched by Hayden, radical abolitionist Thomas Wentworth Higginson, and Leonard Grimes, pastor of the Twelfth Colored Baptist Church. Because clergy had access to prisoners in lockup, Grimes was sent to the courthouse to visit with Sims. While there, Grimes directed Sims to the location of an unbarred window on the third floor in the courthouse and told him that he should jump down to mattresses that would be provided below. Awaiting would be a buggy to take him to freedom. However, the plan had to be scrapped when workmen barred the window.

With a rescue no longer an option, the focus turned to legal measures. U.S. Senator Robert Rantoul, Jr., and attorneys Charles Loring and Samuel E. Sewall, who had represented George Latimer, were enlisted as Sims's counsel. They argued not only that the Fugitive Slave Law was unconstitutional but also that Sims was being illegally held because state authorities had acted in behalf of the law, which was a violation of the 1843 state law that forbade this. Nevertheless, the federal commissioner ruled against them, and during the wee hours of the morning of April 12, 1851, Sims was led out of his cell, escorted to the wharf by 200 policemen and another 100 volunteers. About 100 members of the Boston Vigilance Committee were on hand to witness the procession. They also rigged up an improvised coffin draped in black carried by, among others, Wendell Phillips, Theodore Parker, and Nathaniel Bowditch, which followed the military escort in protest.

While Sims, who was in tears, was put aboard the brig *Acorn* for return to Savannah, the Reverend Daniel Foster led the protestors in prayer in his support.

That day, at the request of the vigilance committee, church bells tolled in neighboring towns to note the rendition. On April 24 a poster that has been saved for posterity was placed throughout the Boston area. It warned "to avoid conversing with the watchmen and police officers . . . empowered to act as Kidnappers and Slave Catchers. . . . Therefore if you value your liberty and the Welfare of the Fugitives among you, shun them in every manner possible."

The rendition was costly. The actions called forth by Secretary of State Daniel Webster and President Millard Fillmore, who were behind the scenes directing it, required expenditures of more than $10,000 each by the federal government and the city of Boston. In addition, more than $2,000 was paid out by Sims's owner. But more costly was the increased antipathy in Boston toward the Fugitive Slave Law.

Sims was publicly flogged in Savannah, Georgia, and then put in jail and not allowed to see anyone, including his mother. He went back to his job as a bricklayer and remained in slavery until 1863, when he escaped again, this time with a wife and child, along with three other slaves. They armed themselves because they had to pass through territory occupied by the Confederate army. Upon reaching the safety of the Union army, they were given papers by General Ulysses S. Grant himself, authorizing their free passage north. In May 1863 they reached Boston, where a great celebration was held at the Tremont Temple.

Interestingly, U.S. Marshal Charles Devens, who had Sims arrested, later atoned for his actions when he became U.S. attorney general in 1877 and hired Sims to work for the Justice Department.

SUGGESTED READING: Austin Bearse, *Reminiscences of Fugitive Slave Days,* Boston: Warren Richardson, 1880; Gary L. Collison, *Shadrach Minkins: From Fugitive Slave to Citizen*, Cambridge, MA: Harvard University Press, 1997; Leonard W. Levy, "Sims' Case: The Fugitive Slave Law in Boston in 1851," *Journal of Negro History,* January, 1950.

Sloane, Rush R. (1828–1908). Rush Sloane was the most well-known Underground Railroad agent in Sandusky, Ohio, the location of which on Lake Erie made it a destination for fugitive slaves as early as 1820. After 1850 it became one of the most important terminals of the Underground Railroad.

A Sandusky native, Sloane was the son of a lawyer and a grandson of a Revolutionary War officer who had given his life for freedom. At the age of sixteen, Sloane apprenticed in the law offices of Francis D. Parish, the third lawyer to set up practice in Sandusky and a known abolitionist whose services were used by the local Underground Railroad to defend abolitionists and fugitive slaves. Ironically, in 1834 Parish had prosecuted a local black conductor for violating the Fugitive Slave Law but shortly after had a change of heart. In 1845, the year after Sloane joined his firm, Parish himself was prosecuted for harboring a woman and her four children by their Kentucky master and was fined for hindering and obstructing their arrest.

After five years at the law offices of Parish, Sloane received his license to practice in 1849. It was not long before he followed the example of his mentor. In 1852 two men, two women, and three children had been arrested and taken from a steamboat about to leave for Detroit. The fugitive slaves were brought before Mayor F. M. Follett by a man who claimed to be their owner, and Sloane was enlisted to represent them. Because no warrant was produced for their apprehension, Sloane suggested that there was no reason to detain them. At once, the crowd of mostly black men led by John Lott hurried the fugitive slaves out the door. Despite the protests of a man who shouted that he was the owner, the crowd brought them to a steamboat that transported them to Canada. The owner held Sloane responsible, and two court cases followed that resulted

Sandusky abolitionist Rush R. Sloane. Courtesy of the Ohio Historical Society.

in Sloane being found guilty because under the federal law, a slave's owner was not required to have a warrant to apprehend one of his slaves.

Sandusky's Underground Railroad started out as an enterprise operated solely by blacks but started to become integrated after 1837. Its activities were only sporadic until 1845. While the Fugitive Slave Law stimulated a rush to Canada by both free blacks and slaves, what pushed fugitive slaves to Sandusky was the development of the rail system that connected it with Cincinnati and Columbus just before the passage of the law. Before 1850 the common mode of travel for fugitive slaves to the Lake Erie ports was by wagon, fifteen miles at a time or sometimes more, by individual conductors. When the rail connection between Cincinnati and the Lake Erie ports was completed around 1850 with the extension of the Little Miami Railroad from the south and the Mad River Railroad from the north, the use of the aboveground railroad became common. Being one of two terminals of this railroad system, along with Cleveland, made Sandusky an obvious destination for fugitive slaves.

Sloane was active in the development of this rail system. He was a man who lived on both sides of the law and was involved in a number of questionable financial dealings. There is some evidence to suggest that he became rich in part because of illicit maneuverings in financing the railroads. In 1875, for example, he was charged with embezzling while president of the Cincinnati, Sandusky, and Cleveland railroad and forfeited bail of $46,000, an enormous sum in those days.

Salmon P. Chase: Attorney General for the Fugitive Slave

Salmon P. Chase was called "the attorney general for the fugitive slave," and he received his introduction to the antislavery movement at the Lane Debates in Cincinnati. He represented numerous fugitive slaves in court, as well as abolitionists like **John Van Zandt**, who was arrested in 1842 for aiding fugitive slaves. Chase's argument in the Van Zandt case before the Supreme Court in 1846 was one of the most persuasive arguments ever made in opposition of the fugitive slave law.

Among his colleagues in Cincinnati representing fugitive slaves was Rutherford B. Hayes, who said that for every fugitive slave case in which he publicly represented, there were ten not made public. Every vigilance committee had its legal consultant, and sometimes several. The New York Committee had Horace Dresser, Chester Arthur, and **Erastus Culver**, whose services as a judge sometimes proved helpful; the Boston Committee had Richard Henry Dana, Samuel Sewall, and Ellis Gray Loring; in Lancaster County, Pennsylvania, there was Thaddeus Stevens, an Underground Railroad agent and future leader of the Radical Republicans in Congress. Attorneys became the second line of defense when conductors were not able to outmaneuver slavecatchers, and they were used by the Underground Railroad far more than many realize. Noted upstate New York abolitionist attorney Alvan Stewart, who was a prominent exponent of the unconstitutionality of slavery, said that more than 4,000 fugitives were tried in New York State alone from 1840 to 1848.

Chase's work in behalf of fugitive slaves carried over into the political arena, as he became a leader in the Liberty Party. In 1849 he was elected to the Senate on the Free Soil Party ticket. When his term was up, he was elected governor of Ohio. A leading candidate for the Republican presidential nomination in 1860 before losing to Abraham Lincoln, he accepted Lincoln's appointment as secretary of the Treasury, and in 1864 he accepted Lincoln's appointment as chief justice of the Supreme Court.

At the same time, he was a community leader; he brought together the black and white communities in coordinating an extremely active Underground Railroad that sent fugitive slaves to Canada on one of the many steamboats visiting its port, and later in 1879 became Sandusky's mayor. For example, in recognition of his efforts in the Underground Railroad, he was presented with a silver-headed cane by members of the black community.

Among Sloane's cohorts in the black community was John Lott, a free black who had moved to Sandusky from Madison, Indiana, where he was a colleague on the front line of the Underground Railroad with **Elijah Anderson** and **George DeBaptiste.** Lott left Madison following a race riot there in 1846, the same time as Anderson and DeBaptiste, both of whom worked with Sandusky operatives thereafter: DeBaptiste was the owner of a steamboat that stopped in Sandusky, and Anderson used the rail system to take fugitive slaves to both Sandusky and Cleveland. Another important Sandusky agent was **George Reynolds**, a former slave and founding member of the Zion Baptist Church in 1849. Its founders included seven former slaves, and shortly after, it changed its name to the First Regular Anti-Slavery Baptist Church and became a haven for fugitive slaves. The church is still in existence today and is known as the Second Baptist Church.

Reynolds was identified by Alexander Milton Ross as a member of the Liberty League, an organization of "armed and drilled men" stationed along Lake Erie to help fugitive slaves along the final leg of their journey to freedom. He also participated in **John Brown**'s Chatham Convention and established a residence in Hamilton, Ontario, which suggests that he may have been piloting fugitive slaves to various destinations in Canada.

Easy access to steamers that traveled regularly to Canada also made Sandusky a coveted destination for fugitive slaves. Among notable fugitive slaves who made their escape through Sandusky were Josiah Henson, **Lewis Hayden**, and Lewis Clark, as well as the

Eliza on whom the character in **Harriet Beecher Stowe**'s famous novel *Uncle Tom's Cabin* was based. Among the ship captains known to transport fugitive slaves were Captain James Nugent, Captain Thomas McGee, Captain George Swiegel, Captain J. W. Keith, and a Captain Atwood, whose ship the *Arrow* was called the abolition boat. Other noted ships include DeBaptiste's *T. Whitney*, the *Bay City*, the *Mayflower*, and the *United States*, which was involved in an often told story of how its captain tricked slavecatchers into thinking he would take their fugitive slaves to Detroit instead of Canada, only to supply them with a skiff so they could sneak off the boat before docking and make their way to Canada.

In 1888, while vice president of the Firelands Historical Society, Sloane gave an address that detailed the operations of the Underground Railroad in Sandusky and identified many of the individuals involved. It was published in the society's journal. Having amassed a considerable fortune, he devoted his later years to civic and cultural affairs.

SUGGESTED READING: Blaine J. Hudson, *Fugitive Slaves and the Underground Railroad in the Kentucky Borderlands*, Jefferson, NC: McFarland, 2001; Wilbur Siebert, *The Mysteries of Ohio's Underground Railroads*, Columbus, OH: Long's College Book Company, 1951; Rush R. Sloane, "The Underground Railroad of the Firelands," *The Firelands Pioneer*, Norwalk, OH: The Historical Society, 1888; *Men of Northwestern Ohio: A Collection of Portraits and Biographies of Well Known Men in This Section of the Professional, Business and Commercial World*, Bowling Green and Toledo, OH: C. S. Van Tassel, publisher, 1898.

Smith, Gerrit (1797–1874). Gerrit Smith was a towering figure of the abolitionist movement. Being one of the richest men in America, he was bound to command attention, but it was his dignified nobility, highly developed intellect, and compassionate nature that drew respect and admiration. Smith felt an obligation to use his wealth for the benefit of those less fortunate and is reputed to officially have donated more than $8 million during his lifetime, a figure in the realm of $200 million today. That does not include thousands of acres of land that he bequeathed to blacks and poor whites, as well as untold dollars he gave to abolitionists constantly imposing on his benevolence.

As he said near the close of his life, "God gives me money to give away."

Smith openly admitted that his home in Peterboro, New York, welcomed runaway slaves. However, circumstantial evidence suggests that Smith was doing much more. As early as 1839, Smith was listening to advice urging the use of forceful means to end slavery. By the mid-1850s he was funding not only **John Brown**'s personal war against slavery but also missions by slave rescuers like Alexander Milton Ross to go into the South and entice slaves to take the Underground Railroad to freedom.

Although Smith did not personally assist nearly as many fugitive slaves as **John Rankin**, **Levi Coffin**, or **Thomas Garrett**, nor did he have the literary prominence of abolitionist editor **William Lloyd Garrison** or **Harriet Beecher Stowe**, or the dramatic flair of Brown, **Frederick Douglass**, and **Harriet Tubman**, he nevertheless may have been the most important individual in the abolitionist movement. He also may have been the point man in a more militant and aggressive type of Underground Railroad that was emerging after 1850, though based on current evidence this is only speculation. Although it cannot be said that he knew everyone in the abolitionist movement, there probably were not many abolitionists who did not know of him.

Smith was born in Utica, New York, to Dutch parents. His father, Peter, was a self-made multimillionaire who prospered as John Jacob Astor's partner in the fur-trading business. Peter Smith then used the profits to buy hundreds of thousands of acres of land in New York, Vermont, Virginia, and Michigan. Gerrit Smith claimed that his total

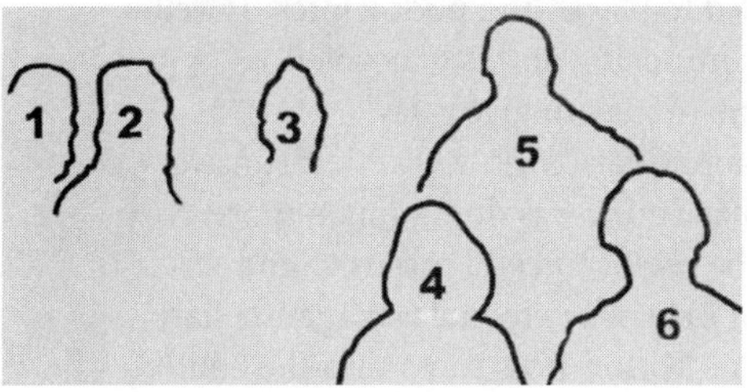

Anti-Fugitive Slave Law convention at Cazenovia, New York, August 22, 1850. Pictured, left to right: 1. Charles B. Ray, 2. Samuel J. May, 3. George W. Clark, 4. Theodosia Gilbert, 5. Gerrit Smith, 6. Frederick Douglass. From the Collection of the Madison County Historical Society, Oneida, New York.

landing holdings amounted to 750,000 acres, a land mass equivalent to all of the New England states. He was brought up in a devoutly Christian home and excelled as a student at Hamilton College. There he met and married the school president's daughter, but she died seven months later of meningitis. Around the same time his father, despondent after the death of Gerrit's mother the year before, began to prepare his son to manage the family fortune. Gerrit remarried in 1822 and remained in Madison County, where he lived the rest of his life, while his father retired to Schenectady in 1825, living the rest of his days in virtual seclusion.

Gerrit's second wife, Ann Carol Fitzhugh, had been born in Maryland to a wealthy slaveholding family (Peter Smith also owned slaves for a time). Called Nancy by everyone, she and Gerrit had eight children, only two of whom survived into adulthood. They were a close, loving couple, who wrote poetry to each other even in their later years. They shared a commitment to the reform movements of the day and a devout Christianity whose guide was the Golden Rule. Smith was a true evangelical Christian who had committed a large portion of the Bible to memory and would often quote scripture.

Smith's first cause was temperance, one that he would advocate throughout his life. He also was attracted by the colonization movement. Growing up with slaves on his father's farm, he became sympathetic to the condition of blacks at an early age and believed that their condition was unjust and that all they needed was the opportunity to prove their equality with whites. Initially, he accepted the benevolent premise of the colonization society: that it provided blacks with a better opportunity to realize their potential in an environment free of prejudice. But gradually he began to understand that its real motive was based on racial prejudice and a desire to remove free blacks from American society.

A defining moment in Smith's life came during the organizational meeting of the New York Anti-Slavery Society in Utica on October 21, 1835. An estimated 1,000 delegates arrived that day to organize a state society in order to coordinate the increasing number of antislavery societies in the state. When the delegates learned of plans to disrupt the meeting the night before, it was moved from the courthouse to a local church. Alvan Stewart, a renowned trial lawyer who had turned his talents to abolition and was president of the Utica Anti-Slavery Society, made an inspirational opening speech. Stewart recalled the legacy of the Founding Fathers and urged the delegates to remain steadfast in the face of opposition or see their liberties erode.

After Stewart's speech, a constitution was passed with the primary objectives of the society being the abolition of slavery in the United States and the elevation of its people of color. Lewis Tappan was reading a declaration of sentiments to the convention when a committee representing the proslavery mob that had gathered at the courthouse barged in and demanded to speak. Consent was given and their spokesperson, Judge Chester Hayden, read a series of statements that condemned the society and abolitionists in general. The protesters also demanded an apology from the abolitionists for disrupting their community. But it was not the abolitionists who were causing a disruption but drunken members of the mob who were intruding from the outside and disrupting the meeting.

Smith, who was not a member of an antislavery society at the time but had come by invitation, said that though he was not an abolitionist in the immediate sense of the word, he believed that Americans had the right to express their beliefs and was appalled by the actions of the mob. In order that the abolitionists be allowed to speak freely, he offered the use of his estate in Peterboro and suggested the meeting be reconvened at the Presbyterian Church in Peterboro. His offer was accepted and the convention adjourned until the following day.

As the delegates departed, the angry mob outside hurled obscenities. They did not physically attack the delegates, however, reserving their violence for the *Utica Standard and Democrat*. While its workers were at supper, the mob broke into the newspaper's office and threw the type into the street so that the journalists could not publish a report of the day's events.

In Peterboro the entire Smith household worked round the clock the next day, mixing bread, grinding coffee, making pies, baking rolls, and preparing the necessities of hospitality while Smith worked on his speech. It rained the next morning, but thirty guests arrived for breakfast. By afternoon the sun was shining on the 590 delegates who attended the convention at the church in Peterboro and signed their names to the convention roster.

The proceedings resumed and resolutions were discussed. Among them were recommendations that monthly concerts of prayer be held the last Monday of the month to pray for the slave, that ladies' antislavery societies be formed, and that citizens appeal to their congressmen for the abolition of slavery in the District of Columbia. A strong denunciation of the actions of the mob was approved, and pledges were accepted for $1,200 to be paid by the end of the year.

When these items were concluded, Smith addressed the delegates. His speech that day was among the most memorable in his prolific career. Foremost in his thoughts was the sacred right of free speech, which he observed was being threatened by those attempting to suppress the abolitionists throughout the nation:

> If God made me to be one of his instruments for carrying forward the salvation of the world, then is the right of free discussion among my inherent rights: then may I, must I, speak of sin, any sin, every sin, that comes in my way . . . which it is my duty to search out and to assail.

Though Smith had not yet committed himself to the abolitionist cause, his closing words left little doubt where he stood:

> True permanent peace can never be restored, until slavery, the occasion of the war, has ceased. The sword, which is now drawn, will never be returned to its scabbard, until victory, entire, decisive victory is ours or theirs.

The words were prophetic, for they signaled the beginning of his obsessive crusade to end slavery that continued until the Civil War. Letters, speeches, personal meetings, and money flowed ceaselessly from him to assist free blacks, aid fugitive slaves, support the efforts of abolitionists, and propagate his ideas on ending slavery. Smith quickly assumed a leadership role in the state antislavery society and devoted his energies to creative solutions to end slavery.

Among his early activities to aid the elevation of people of color were his attempts to provide educational opportunities. In 1834 he had opened a manual labor school for blacks at Peterboro and continued his support of advancing the status of blacks in society with his funding of the Oneida Institute, another manual labor school in central New York. He also contributed to the support of Oberlin College in Ohio, the first college to admit both blacks and women together with white men. In later years, he also gave liberally to the New York Central College at McGrawville, which employed the first black professors, among them **William G. Allen**.

He also began strenuous efforts to help fugitive slaves, either through purchasing their freedom or harboring them at his home. As early as 1836 central New York abolitionists were attending the meetings of the New York Committee of Vigilance, which had formed the previous year to assist runaway slaves, and Smith's close relationship with its members in succeeding years was indicative of his support and early collaboration with them. After the committee was reorganized in 1848 to represent a statewide collaboration, Smith became its president the following year.

Possibly the first instance of Smith purchasing the freedom of slaves occurred in 1836, when he paid John Thomson Mason of Hagerstown, Maryland, $1,000 to liberate his slaves. Five years later, he wrote, "I have bought so many slaves, that I have none of the common abolition squeamishness about buying them."

Smith was not shy about his illegal efforts to aid fugitive slaves. He wrote a letter to the editor of the Madison County newspaper, the *Union Herald*, in December 1838, detailing his interaction with two fugitive slaves who had enjoyed his hospitality. They had identified themselves as John Williams and John Williams Scott, but Smith found them to be less than credible. For instance, one of them claimed he had never been in a church and did not even know who Christ was; the other had not been in a church in fifteen years. At the same time, they were surprised at Smith's benevolence, not surprisingly as they both bore the scars of severe whippings. Despite their lack of candor, their scars reassured Smith that though he had broken the law, his actions were divinely sanctioned.

Smith could not act unless he believed his actions met with God's approval, and he could not imagine that God would sanction slavery. In 1839 he acted even more brazenly in a case involving a Mississippi slave named Harriet Powell, whose master, J. Davenport, was visiting Syracuse. This was before the enactment of the 1841 law that prohibited slaveholders from bringing slaves into the state, on the penalty that the slaves would automatically become free.

The Davenports were staying at the Syracuse House hotel, and Tom Leonard, a black waiter there, learned of Powell's desire for freedom. He informed William M. Clarke, deputy county clerk, and John Owen, a marble dealer, of her desire. The night before the Davenports were to return home, October 7, 1839, was set as the time for the escape. A farewell party for the Davenports was being held at the home of Major William Cook. Leonard enlisted the help of other black staff at the hotel. The plan was to bundle up Powell's clothes and throw them out the window to him. Another black man would wait at the rear of Cook's house and take Powell to a buggy driven by Abraham Nottingham. He would take Powell to the home of a man named Sheppard near Marcellus, about ten miles away.

When the hour to escape arrived, the party was in motion, and Harriet was upstairs with the Davenports' infant. She took the child downstairs and handed the baby to her mistress, saying she needed to step outside. The plan was then executed, and by the time the Davenports realized that Powell was missing, she was well on her way to Marcellus. The packet boats heading for Oswego were searched, and the port of Oswego and the homes of Smith and James Canning Fuller, a Quaker known to harbor fugitive slaves, were put under surveillance.

The next day, Davenport went to the authorities and secured warrants to search the premises of local abolitionists. He also had a handbill posted throughout the vicinity, and Leonard was arrested for stealing Powell's clothes. Meanwhile, Powell remained with Sheppard about a week until her whereabouts were discovered and she had to be moved. In the middle of the night, she was transferred to the house of Nottingham, the man who had driven her from Syracuse, three miles away. She stayed there briefly before being moved to Lebanon, New York, and the home of John Clarke, the uncle of William Clarke, where she stayed another three weeks. Thereafter, she was moved to the home of Gerrit Smith, where she remained until it was felt safe to send her to a ferry from a point opposite Kingston, Canada.

Smith's cousin, the noted feminist Elizabeth Cady Stanton, came for a visit just before Powell left Peterboro. Stanton wrote that Powell was dressed as a Quaker and sent in a carriage to Oswego. Eighteen hours later J. Davenport arrived with law enforcement officials. Smith was gracious and invited them to dine, and during the meal they carried on a cordial conversation about the problem of slavery. This was done intentionally to give Powell as much time as possible to make her escape.

When Smith finally received word that Powell was safe in Canada, he wrote an open letter in the *New York Tribune* informing Davenport that Harriet "was now a free woman, safe under the shadow of the British throne. I had the honor of entertaining her under my roof, sending her in my carriage to Lake Ontario, just eighteen hours before your arrival."

It is believed that hundreds of fugitive slaves were harbored in Peterboro. According to Smith's first biographer, Octavius Frothingham, Smith spent as much as $5,000 in one year for the aid of fugitive slaves. Those seeking his home on the Underground Railroad were treated not merely to food and shelter but also to his advice to refrain from alcohol and his counsel that they be industrious, frugal, and virtuous. Cady Stanton said that fugitive slaves were hidden in Smith's barn or merely slept in the kitchen. Apprehending a fugitive slave in Peterboro was no easy matter because of Smith's influence and connections. In an 1848 letter published in Frederick Douglass's *North Star*, **Henry Garnet** wrote that "there are yet two places where slaveholders cannot come, Heaven and Peterboro."

In 1852 Smith hosted a party of fifty fugitive slaves at one time. His only problem was to decide where to send them, as he had an inquiry from a central New York abolitionist that indicated he knew a number of individuals who would welcome them and give them jobs if they stayed in New York State.

In 1840 the Liberty Party, the first abolitionist political party, was formed. Its major tenet was that the Constitution was an antislavery document whose spirit was being violated by the legality of slavery, a view in direct opposition to the views of William Lloyd Garrison and his followers, who viewed the Constitution as supportive of slavery and counseled disunion. The party soon became synonymous with Smith, who was one of its formative influences and gave to it its name. As early as 1836 a close advisor, Jabez D. Hammond, a lawyer from Cherry Valley, New York, who also served in the U.S. Congress and New York State Senate, advocated political action as necessary to eliminate slavery. With the moral suasion strategy of Garrison antagonizing rather than converting the South, the move to form an abolitionist political party grew stronger. The party chose **James Birney**, who had become Smith's close friend and later his brother-in-law, as its presidential candidate. But it was Smith who was the driving force behind the party. Its national decline began in 1845, but it maintained a presence in central New York into the next decade under the leadership of Smith.

In 1846 a major initiative of the Liberty Party in New York State to bring full suffrage to black men was soundly defeated in a statewide referendum by a margin of nearly three to one. Disillusioned and frustrated by the slow process of politics, Smith thought of abandoning the party but instead decided to take matters into his own hands. He set aside 120,000 acres of his own land in the Adirondacks and other sections of northeastern and central New York to be parceled into forty-acre homesteads for needy, temperate black men between the ages of twenty-one and sixty. This would not only give them a new beginning but also qualify them to vote under the state property qualification. Assisting Smith in the process of selecting candidates were **Theodore Wright**, **Charles Ray**, and James McCune Smith, all of them black men intimately involved with the Underground Railroad in New York City.

At first this was viewed by some as a great opportunity for free black men. A meeting of the "colored people" in Troy, New York, at **Henry Garnet**'s Liberty Street Church in October 1846 to promote his land giveaway was attended by Smith. One of his first recipients, Robert Grooms, was there and presented potatoes, wheat, and corn that he had grown on the land given to him by Smith. Also speaking at the meeting was William Jones, a fugitive slave, who hoped to be accepted as a beneficiary.

"I will go to work for myself. I will cut down my own trees, build my own cabin, plant my own grain, eat the fruit of my own stall," he said to a round of applause. "God Bless, Mr. Gerrit Smith. . . .Come off from the steamboats and leave your barbershops. Leave the kitchen, where you have to live underground all day and climb up ten pair of stairs at night. Tomorrow morning I intend to leave for Essex County to see for myself."

However, the climate in the Adirondacks was harsh and the land ill-suited for farming. In one area, a group of Smith grantees had formed a colony called Timbucto in the town of North Elba, near the present-day site of Lake Placid. **John Brown** had heard about their struggles and took a trip to investigate. Thereafter, he wrote Smith, whom he had never met, offering his services to move to North Elba and help them.

Brown showed up at Smith's mansion after several days on horseback from Springfield. His farming knowledge and passion impressed Smith, and they agreed on an arrangement in which Smith would sell a parcel of land at a discount to Brown, who would move there to assist the black farmers.

Less than a month before Smith and Brown met, Rev. **Jermaine Loguen** of Syracuse, the former fugitive slave and Underground Railroad conductor, made a trip into the Adirondacks to report on the status of the land grantees. He noted that some of the land was good for farming and other sections were valuable for their timber. He advised recipients not to sell their land but to find trustworthy local individuals, some of whom he named, to assist them in making the best use of the land.

However, only a handful of black families remained in Timbucto after 1850, and even John Brown left for several years after 1851 for a business opportunity in Ohio. In the end, Smith's experiment was a failure, with only a small number of those given land actually attempting to homestead it. Nevertheless, the experiment turned out to be fateful, for it brought together Smith and Brown.

The passage of the Fugitive Slave Law in 1850 escalated the tensions between antislavery and proslavery forces. Smith called it "the greatest of all outrages upon religion and humanity" and urged resistance with every possible means. In a resolution at one of the public meetings protesting the law, he wrote, "It is our duty to peril life, liberty, and property in behalf of the fugitive slave to as great an extent as we would peril them in behalf of ourselves."

The enforcement of the law had put at peril a close associate and friend of Smith, William L. Chaplin, a leading New York abolitionist, lecturer, and journalist. He had been living in Washington, D.C., reporting events and conspiring with the Underground Railroad network that had been developed by his now deceased colleague, **Charles T. Torrey**. Chaplin, whose activities were being assisted with funding from Smith, was captured while attempting to aid the escape of two slaves owned by Robert Toombs and Alexander H. Stephens.

Chaplin was indicted on charges in both the District of Columbia and the state of Maryland for assisting fugitive slaves. Bail was set at $6,000 in the District of Columbia and $19,000 in Maryland. A major convention was organized in Cazenovia on August 21 and 22 to rally support for Chaplin and raise money for his bail. Presiding over it was Smith and **Frederick Douglass**, who had become his close associate since his move to Rochester in 1847. During the convention, Smith gave one of his most radical speeches in which he called on slaves "to plunder, burn, and kill, as you may have occasion to do to promote your escape."

Bail was raised for Chaplin, with Smith contributing $12,000 of the total. It was a foregone conclusion that Chaplin would jump bail, but his refusal to do a lecture tour to raise money to pay back his bail angered his benefactors and effectively ended his friendship with Smith.

The following year Smith's resolutions to openly resist the Fugitive Slave Law were put to the test when an attempt was made by federal authorities to enforce the law in Syracuse with the rendition of the runaway **Jerry Henry**. It was Smith who played a leading role in marshaling the forces that rescued Henry and sent him to freedom in Canada. In a meeting during which the rescue was planned, he exhorted the rescuers of the propriety of their actions: "A forcible rescue will demonstrate the strength of public opinion against the possible legality of slavery and this Fugitive Slave Law in particular. It will honor Syracuse and be a powerful example everywhere."

In 1852, prodded by supporters but against his better judgment, Smith was elected to the U.S. Congress as a representative of Madison and Oswego counties. The first session of his term began in December of 1853, and Smith moved his household to Washington, where he gave two dinner parties every week and open invitations to every member of Congress. However, those who attended were not allowed to drink or smoke. Nevertheless, the Smiths were among the most gracious of hosts, as his cousin Cady Stanton said of her visits to Peterboro: "To go anywhere else, after a visit there, was like coming down from the divine heights into the valley of humiliation."

Smith was an active member during his term in Congress and made a number of important speeches that he later had published. However, they made little impact because his views were far outside the mainstream. He was a radical and an idealist who did not know the meaning of compromise, and he could not abide with the slow mechanism of government. He resigned before finishing his full term in office, following the completion of his first session on August 7, 1854.

After resigning from Congress, Smith wrote Garrison that "I have acquired no new hope of the peaceful termination of slavery by coming to Washington." He also wrote Frederick Douglass expressing a similar sentiment, while also decrying the intemperance and godlessness of many in Congress. A radical reformer like Smith simply was not suited to be a politician. He needed the freedom to work in other areas of society where his money and influence were not bound by government's cumbersome procedures.

Not long after leaving Congress, Smith organized the Radical Abolitionist Party, which met for the first time in Syracuse in September of 1855. Among those in attendance were Frederick Douglass, Lewis Tappan, Jermaine Loguen, Samuel May, William Goodell, and John Brown. James McCune Smith, a longtime member of the New York Committee of Vigilance, was appointed as chairman. The party was generally an outgrowth of the Liberty Party, its central position being that the Constitution was an antislavery document and that slavery was unconstitutional. However, it moved beyond the Liberty Party in advocating the use of force if necessary to end slavery. It based their position on "holy ground," that the laws of nature and God forbid slavery.

At this meeting, Smith read letters from John Brown's sons in Kansas and the struggles of the abolitionists there against proslavery elements in the battle to establish the territory as a free or slave state. A collection was raised for Brown, who was on his way to Kansas to join his sons. At a private meeting, Smith supplied Brown with weapons.

When Smith first committed himself to a violent course of action to end slavery is difficult to say. His rhetoric was militant from the start in 1835 when he proclaimed that a battle had begun between the foes of slavery and slaveholders. As early as 1839 Jabez Hammond had counseled him that "the only way in which slavery at the South can be abolished is by force. It will never be done by peaceable means." And in 1845 he confessed that "I have not great confidence that American slavery will die a peaceful death. The strong probability is that this infatuated nation will go on its proslavery wickedness, until her slavery has come to a violent and bloody end." As the South became more intractable, and the federal government became more accommodating to the South's demands with the second Fugitive Slave Law in 1850 and the Kansas-Nebraska Act in

1854 that permitted newly formed states in the Northwest Territories to choose freedom or slavery, his increased militancy was inevitable. By 1855 he had joined hands with John Brown in a life-or-death battle over slavery, though at the time his vision had clouded the reality of the situation.

That year Smith also became acquainted with Alexander Milton Ross, a young idealist who longed to help those in slavery escape their bonds. Ross had lived in Washington during the winter of 1850 while a student and had made contact with abolitionist politicians like Joshua Giddings, who may have provided him with access to Smith. A plan was hatched between Smith and Ross to send the young man into the South, posing as an ornithologist, the study of birds being a field of study in which he later became an international authority. But the real purpose of Ross's mission was to direct slaves to freedom along the Underground Railroad. They went on a lengthy tour of the North from New England as far west as Indiana, during which they visited those involved in the Underground Railroad.

There are suggestions that Ross was not the first person Smith had sent into the South to bring slaves out. In 1841, for example, he sent Quaker abolitionist James Canning Fuller of Skaneateles, New York, to Kentucky to purchase the freedom of slaves. Even earlier, James Watkins Seward, a student at the Peterboro Manual Labor School, was involved in a bank robbery in St. Louis and was consorting with individuals who may have been aiding fugitive slaves along the Mississippi and Ohio rivers. Seward, who was executed for his part in the robbery that resulted in the murder of one of the bank's employees, was in touch with Smith during his incarceration. Smith also supplied aid to the slave rescuers **Charles Torrey** and Chaplin.

Smith's connections to multiple vigilance committees also suggests his possible involvement in funding slave rescuers. For example, in 1848 Smith was made president of the New York committee of **Charles Ray**, **Isaac Hopper**, and James McCune Smith. That committee was still very active during the 1850s. Smith also was in contact with **George DeBaptiste** of Detroit, which had the most active vigilance committee during the later years of the Underground Railroad, visiting with him during trips to Michigan in the mid-1850s. Smith also could have been one of the eastern abolitionists, whom William Cockrum claimed financed the Ohio River Valley's Anti-Slavery League.

These connections come full circle with the association that developed between Smith and John Brown. In an 1893 letter, Ross claimed to be a part of another group of radical abolitionists called the Liberty League, which included Smith and Lewis Tappan and which aided runaway slaves along the Lake Erie river ports. One of its members, **George Reynolds**, who attended Brown's Chatham convention, claimed to have been going into the South to organize militant groups of slaves in preparation for a revolt.

However, there is no concrete evidence that Smith was the man behind the scenes directing a strategy that would ignite a revolt of the slaves in the South. But that is exactly what Brown was planning and what Smith, his leading supporter, had come to believe was needed to end slavery. They were firmly united in their mission to end slavery and believed that their actions were sanctioned by God. From 1855 on, they maintained a regular correspondence and had numerous meetings through 1859.

In February 1858 Brown came to Peterboro and revealed his plan to capture Harpers Ferry to Smith and Boston abolitionist Franklin Sanborn, who were two of the "Secret Six" supporting Brown's activities; this group also included Thomas Wentworth Higginson of

Worcester, Massachusetts, and George Stearns, Samuel Gridley Howe, and Theodore Parker of Boston. The last meeting between Smith and Brown was a three-day visit to Peterboro by Brown following his successful rescue and escort of twelve fugitive slaves from Missouri to Canada. After a meeting in which Brown revealed his plans to prosecute his guerilla war against slavery, Smith was moved to tears and said, "If I were asked to point out—I will say it in his presence—to point out the man in all this world I think most truly a Christian, I would point out John Brown. I was once doubtful in my own mind as to Captain Brown's course. I now approve of it heartily, having given my mind to it more of late."

The close relationship between Smith and Brown can be inferred from what happened after Harpers Ferry, for immediately after Brown's capture at Harpers Ferry, Smith destroyed all his correspondence with Brown. He also sent his son-in-law to Boston to have all correspondence between him and Brown's other backers destroyed, as well as to the home of John Brown, Jr., in Ohio to destroy any other correspondence between them.

The astonishing mental collapse by Smith after the failure at Harpers Ferry serves as a reflection of how deeply affected he was by the failure of Brown's mission to end slavery. It was as if his own mission had failed. The catastrophic result of the raid and the deaths it caused were too much for Smith to bear. Despite his effort to destroy all evidence that incriminated him in connection with Brown, some papers survived and there was talk of Smith being extradited to Virginia to stand trial along with Brown. Even an upstate New York newspaper, the *Rochester Union and Advertiser*, charged Smith with treason. Some suggested that Smith should flee to Canada as had Sanborn, Howe, and Stearns.

A reporter from the *New York Herald* sent a reporter to Peterboro, to whom Smith remarked, "I am going to be indicted, sir, indicted! You must not talk to me about it. . . . If any man in the Union is taken, it will be me." The reporter also noted Smith's agitation, which betrayed the reaction of a guilty man. Another observer reported to an Albany newspaper that Smith displayed a wild-eyed appearance, was despondent, and was experiencing insomnia. Some in his family worried that he might attempt suicide. Finally, it was agreed after consulting with his physician to have him committed to the asylum in Utica.

Smith recovered from his collapse and six months later was once again speaking in public. During the Civil War he became a strong advocate and fund-raiser for Union causes. After the war, he called for reconciliation and was one of three prominent Americans, along with ten Richmond business owners, who signed the bail bond for Confederate leader Jefferson Davis.

Smith remained active in reform efforts, advocating for temperance and for the rights of blacks and women. Though he maintained his admiration for John Brown, he insisted until his dying day that he had no foreknowledge of Harpers Ferry, which was untrue. In fact, Smith was never the same after Harpers Ferry. His vision of the end of slavery did not anticipate a Civil War and the loss of so many lives, and he withdrew from many of his abolitionist friends, especially those who were black and with whom he had bonded so closely.

Smith died on December 28 at the home of his nephew, Gen. John Cochrane. Despite his withdrawal from society, Smith continued until the end of his life working for the causes of those less fortunate; the last of his published circulars, written just two weeks before he died, was titled "Will the American People Never Cease to Oppress and Torture the Helpless Poor?"

SUGGESTED READING: Donna D. Burdick and Norman K. Dann, "Heaven and Peterboro: The Current Relevance of 19th Century Peterboro to Human Rights Today," Peterboro, 2003; Tom Calarco, *The Underground Railroad in the Adirondack Region*, Jefferson, NC: McFarland, 2004; Octavius Brooks Frothingham, *Gerrit Smith: A Biography*, New York: G.P. Putnam's Sons, 1878; John R. McKivigan and Madeleine Leveille, "The 'Black Dream' of Gerrit Smith, New York Abolitionist," Syracuse University: *Library Associates Courier*, Vol. xx, No. 2, Fall, 1985; Edward J. Renehan, *The Secret Six: The True Tale of the Men Who Conspired with John Brown*, New York: Crown Publishers, 1995; Alexander Milton Ross, *Memoirs of a Reformer*, Toronto: Hunter, Rose, 1893; Elizabeth Cady Stanton, *Eighty Years and More: Reminiscences 1815–1897*, T. Fisher Unwin, 1898; Ralph Volney Harlow, *Gerrit Smith: Philanthropist and Reformer*, New York: Henry Holt & Co., 1938.

Smith, Stephen Keese (1806–1894). In 1887 Stephen Keese Smith gave an interview about his activities in the Underground Railroad, naming names, giving fascinating details, and providing a picture of how the Underground operated in his native Clinton County, New York, which borders Canada.

"Samuel Keese [Smith's uncle] was the head of the depot in Peru," Smith said. "His son, John Keese, myself, and Wendell Lansing at Keeseville were actors. I had large buildings and concealed the Negroes in them. I kept them, fed them, often gave them shoes and clothing. I presume I have spent a thousand dollars for them in one way and another."

Smith said the fugitive slaves came from Albany, Glens Falls, and Vermont. He also identified Rowland T. Robinson as an important conductor in Vermont, and at least one source indicated that Robinson forwarded some on McNeil's Ferry across Lake Champlain to Clinton County.

"Scores of slaves made their escape through him [Robinson]," Smith said.

Noadiah Moore coordinated activities in the northern part of the county, according to Smith, and brought the fugitive slaves to Canada and helped them find jobs.

Virginia Mason Burdick remembered her grandfather, Samuel Smith, the son of Stephen K. Smith, telling her, "The slaves come into the kitchen to be fed, how they were chattering with the cold, and how the firelight would light up their dark, startled, terrified faces."

Smith also provided details of the organization of the county antislavery society in 1837. By that time there were six societies, including three in Peru, the town where Smith lived, the earliest a female society. The abolitionists who came together for the first countywide meeting were mobbed, harassed, and ridiculed and were forced to change the location of their meeting, but they carried on and managed to forward fugitive slaves to Canada without any major mishap until the Civil War.

Smith's abolitionist convictions were born of his Quaker religion and his membership in the Union, the large Quaker community in Peru, New York. By the end of the American Revolution, nearly all American Quakers had manumitted their slaves. Those who had not were liable to disownment. This voluntary manumission was the result of a movement by Quakers to abolish slavery that began in 1688 at the meeting in Germantown, then a rural community near Philadelphia.

Peru was bestowed with such convictions when Huldah Hoag, a female Quaker minister from Vermont, founded its Union meeting. With her infant on her back, Huldah Hoag rode nine miles on horseback, crossed Lake Champlain during a thunderstorm, and then walked five miles to her final destination in Peru.

In 1803, Huldah's husband, Joseph, heard a voice speak to him from out of a dark patch of clouds, foretelling of a "dividing spirit" that would affect the nation and its churches because of the iniquity of slavery. This divisiveness, the voice foretold, would culminate "many days in the future" in a civil war and the end of slavery.

Relatives of the Hoags moved to Peru and before long the Union was a settlement. Though situated in a remote outpost of northern New York, these Friends did all they could to end slavery and aid any fugitive slaves that might come their way. Their history told them it was their destiny.

Clinton County's first antislavery society, the Peru Female Anti-Slavery Society, was organized by women in 1835. At their third annual meeting in 1838, they proclaimed the following:

> We deem it a privilege, thus peaceably to assemble and exercise the rights of free people, in expressing our thoughts on subject presented to this meeting, instead of sharing in the degradation and the calamity of our colored sisters, for whose special benefit the society first organized. An unalterable conviction, that liberty or despotism, must ere long gain the undisputed supremacy of this nation . . . Repent or perish, is the only alternative left for this Republic.

The report also stated that they had sent a petition with 600 names to Washington, protesting the gag rule then in place in Congress. It was signed by society president Hannah E. Keese, Stephen's aunt.

In a reference to their agitation and the petitions they were continuing to send to Washington, the female society's report in 1841 asked, "Shall we withhold this cup of cold water from the toil-worn slave and the panting fugitive . . . In the name of humanity, we answer NO!" It was signed by Mary Smith, president, and Eliza T. Smith, Stephen's daughters.

SUGGESTED READING: Allan S. Everest, editor, *Recollections*, Plattsburgh: Clinton County Historical Association, 1964; "Sixth Annual Report of the Female Anti-Slavery Society," *Clinton County Whig*, Jan. 23, 1841; Addie L. Shields, *The John Townsend Addoms Homestead: Including a Study of Slavery and the Underground Railroad as It Pertains to Clinton County, NY*, Plattsburgh, 1981.

Still, Peter (1801–1868). Separated from his family for more than forty years as a slave, Peter Still had a chance encounter with his brother, the famed Underground Railroad conductor **William Still**, that changed both their lives. Their meeting not only was personally important but also played a significant role in the preservation of the history of the Underground Railroad.

Peter's story begins when he was six years old, and his mother left him and his brother Levin, who was eight, with their grandmother. They were living in slavery along the Maryland eastern shore, and his mother had taken his two sisters to join their father, who had purchased his freedom and was living in New Jersey. It was her second attempt to escape from slavery. The first time, with all four of her children, she had been stopped by slavecatchers, but this time she succeeded.

Shortly after their mother left, the boys were sold to a slave trader, who sent them to Kentucky and the plantation of John Fisher in Lexington. His home was only a mile from the plantation of Henry Clay, where Peter became a playmate of Clay's sons. Peter and Levin spent twelve years in Kentucky, serving a second master, Nattie Gist. When Gist died, Peter was passed on to Gist's nephew who had a plantation in Alabama, where Levin had moved two years earlier.

Peter spent the next thirty-one years in Alabama. Both he and his brother married when they reached manhood. Peter's foremost concern became his wife, Vina, and their children. They had eight children, but only three survived into adulthood. Although Peter was not able to live with his family, their master's plantation was only a mile away from the Gist plantation, and Peter built them a cabin. He did his best to bring them all the material comforts he could. His master had tried to purchase them so that they could live together, but Vina's master refused to sell them.

In 1830 Peter's master died suddenly, and Peter's brother died in 1831 of an illness he contracted shortly after marrying his wife, who came from a plantation that operated a brothel. Nevertheless, Peter's life went on as before. He was a dutiful slave, and his mistress treated him well, but in 1833 she married a wealthy slaveholder. She moved in with her new husband, but her slaves were required to remain and to work at the Gist property. The overseer moved into their mistress's house, and Peter was made foreman. This conferred new responsibilities on him: in the morning, to wake his fellow slaves and see that they began their work; at night, to see that the tools were returned to their proper place and that everyone was in their cabin at bedtime; and at picking time, to weigh the cotton and report the quantity to the overseer. This continued until 1839 when it was decided to sell the plantation and hire out the slaves. At first, Peter was unhappy, fearing it would take him farther from his family, but it was this turn of events that enabled him to gain his freedom.

His first year he was hired out to a man named Threat, only four miles way, and the following year to his family's master, McKiernan. Despite being able to live with his family, he was not pleased by this. McKiernan was known to be cruel. During Peter's year there, McKiernan hired a brutal overseer, who took delight in whipping and torturing the slaves for the slightest offense. Things took a better turn in 1842 when Peter was hired out to James A. Stoddard in nearby Tuscumbia, Alabama. A teacher from New England and an elder in the Presbyterian Church, Stoddard fed and furnished Peter generously, and also allowed him to earn income from odd jobs. This enabled him to bring his family many comforts during his biweekly visits.

The next year, Stoddard recommended Peter's services to his pastor, Rev. Stedman. His duties were varied: he was the caretaker of the church; hauled wood and water for the family of the minister, as well as two other families; and filled in for the cook when needed. He did his work cheerfully because the minister and his family were kind and treated him with respect. Morning and evening the minister's slaves were called to pray with his family, and he asked the Lord's blessing on each one. The Stedmans also filled Peter's imagination with stories of the North and made him long to move there to be free.

Peter's next hire-out was John Pollock, also of Tuscumbia. He gained Pollock's trust, so that summer Peter asked if he could go to a political convention of Whigs in Nashville, Tennessee, where he had the opportunity to work as a cook. He had hidden motives. He thought that perhaps it might present him with the opportunity to flee to the North. He brought his life savings of $15, but the opportunity never presented itself.

In 1845 Peter entered the service of Michael Brady, a wealthy merchant in Tuscumbia, and worked in his store. Peter's freedom increased with his hire-out in 1846 to Allen Pollock, a bookseller in Tuscumbia, who proposed that Peter live with him and hire his own time. Because Peter had only minor tasks to do, he was able to get other work and save money. This arrangement was illegal, so it was kept secret. Consequently, Peter found work at a local hotel as a waiter and at a school where he worked as a janitor; he also worked at weddings, as a house painter, as a fill-in cook, as a gravedigger, and at other odd jobs. His reliability made him a busy man. At the end of the year he had saved $75, in addition to extra comforts for his family.

Tuscumbia storekeeper Joseph Friedman, the man who would eventually set Peter free, was the last man to hire him. In the past, Peter had done odd jobs for Friedman and his younger brother Isaac, and he sensed that they might be the right people to help him gain his freedom. Their agreement was that Peter would take care of his own necessities and keep whatever he earned above the cost of his hiring out. The Friedmans were generous, often giving him clothes from the store, which he in turn sometimes sold to other slaves for food that he would sell to hotels or give to his family. He continued doing odd jobs and obtained even more work at the school, which had changed hands and became the Tuscumbia Female Seminary. He now had saved a total of $210 to apply to his freedom.

After Friedman agreed to hire him for another year, Peter confessed that he wanted to be free. He asked Friedman if he would purchase him and set him free after Peter had saved enough money to pay off the purchase price. Friedman agreed, and Peter suggested that he offer his master $500. His master refused to sell, stating that Peter was worth more, and in any case the family did not wish to sell. The next year, Friedman agreed to the same arrangement, but this time Peter's master had a change of heart because he needed the extra money to buy young slaves that were being offered at an auction.

On January 15, 1849, Peter became the possession of Friedman, who offered new terms: "You may work, as you did before," he said to Peter, "but you may keep your earnings. When you get two hundred dollars more, I will give you free papers, and you shall go where you like. I do not want your work—get all you can for yourself." Fifteen months later, on April 16, 1850, Peter paid the final installment of his purchase. Despite the loss of a son, William, who had drowned accidentally during the previous year, it was a happy day.

Because Alabama law required emancipated slaves to leave the state within thirty days, Peter had to keep his freedom secret. He continued working odd jobs in Tuscumbia, contemplating his next move. To his surprise, the Friedmans sold their business, with Joseph moving to California and Isaac departing for Cincinnati. Peter joined Isaac on the trip there. They stayed with another Friedman brother, and he related the tale of his life: how he was separated from his mother and brought to Kentucky with his brother, his memory of the Delaware River that passed by Philadelphia being close to her house, and his intention to go there to see if he could find his family.

From Cincinnati, Peter took a steamboat to Pittsburgh. He was closely watched by slavecatchers despite his status as a free man, and one man offered him money to get off the boat to avoid them, but he stuck to his plan and remained until he reached Pittsburgh. There he was taken by a black man who had been on the boat and put on a stagecoach that took him to a train that went all the way to Philadelphia. Referred to the boardinghouse of a James J. G. Bias, he found a black man who showed him the way. Bias, a black physician and clergyman, was a member of the Philadelphia Vigilance Committee who offered medical care to fugitive slaves and sometimes boarded them until they were ready to go to their next stop on the Underground Railroad.

The next day, after asking Mrs. Bias the way to the Delaware River, Peter went in search of his former home. But nothing was recognizable. He felt hopeless, and that night when he discussed this with Mrs. Bias, she suggested he go to the antislavery office the following day where they kept records of black people. If anyone could help, she thought they could. But he was apprehensive. Down South all he heard about the so-called abolitionists was that they were evil. He was worried that if he went to them, they might kidnap him and sell him back into slavery.

Mrs. Bias found a friend to escort Peter to the antislavery office. When they walked in, he saw a well-dressed black man sitting at a desk. He had never seen an educated black person like him. The man, **William Still**, stopped his work and asked them to sit down. Peter's escort explained that he had once lived in Philadelphia and was looking for his family. Still asked Peter to explain further. He said that he and his brother had been kidnapped from their mother more than forty years before, or so he thought. His mother's name was Sidney and his father Levin, and he remembered they said he had been born near the Delaware River.

The man did not say anything. He seemed puzzled. He asked Peter to wait while he finished his correspondence and told his escort that he could leave, that he would show Peter the way back to the boardinghouse. Peter was apprehensive. He did not trust abolitionists. He wanted to leave too, but his escort urged him to stay.

When the work was done, Still asked Peter some questions. Something was troubling him, Peter thought, as Still fell silent. Finally, Still looked him in the eye and said the most shocking words Peter had ever heard:

"Suppose I should tell you that I am your brother?"

Peter was shocked but dubious. Nevertheless, after further discussion, it seemed that Still was indeed his brother. He had even more shocking news for him. Peter's long-lost mother, whom he had long ago given up as dead, was still alive. When Still walked back with him to the boardinghouse, he asked Peter to come to his house to stay. Peter was reluctant, but Mrs. Bias urged him to go.

What followed in the next days were a series of tearful reunions with brothers and sisters, eight in all, and finally his mother. He could not believe that the biggest dream of his life had come true.

In spite of it all, Peter could not be truly happy while Vina and his three children remained in slavery. Somehow he had to get them out. Purchasing them was out of the question, so it was decided that his brother would try to find someone to rescue them.

Meanwhile, Peter left for Alabama to tell his family all that had happened and of his plans to free them from slavery. He went by way of Cincinnati to see the Friedmans. He needed them to write him a pass so he could return as if he were still a slave because free blacks were not permitted to immigrate into the state. He stayed in Tuscumbia for a couple months, working odd jobs as he had done in the past. Before he left, Vina gave him a gingham cape to give to her rescuer so that she could identify him. Peter also revealed the plan to William Handy, a minister and slave on the McKiernan plantation, who agreed to help. When Peter returned to Philadelphia, he found that someone had offered to undertake the dangerous rescue mission. The rescuer's only request was to be paid for his expenses. His name was **Seth Concklin**.

A soldier of fortune, the forty-nine-year-old Concklin was an experienced Underground Railroad conductor who worked independently. After obtaining all the necessary information about Florence, Alabama, and the McKiernan plantation from Peter, he set out to Cincinnati to confer with Levi Coffin. On January 28, 1851, he arrived in Florence to meet Peter's family and plan the escape. He left as soon as he had finished meeting with Peter's family, and returned in March. On March 16 they set out in a six-oared rowboat down the Tennessee River with Peter and Levin, Peter's twenty-two- and twenty-year-old sons, supplying most of the muscle. After seven days they had rowed about 370 miles and arrived at their destination in New Harmony, Indiana. They met their first two appointments on the Underground Railroad and were more than ninety miles north of the Ohio River when they were stopped by slavecatchers.

On the way back to Alabama on the steamboat *Paul Anderson*, the manacled Concklin somehow fell into the river and drowned; there were strong suspicions that he was murdered, for when his body was retrieved, his skull was smashed. When Peter learned of the failure of the mission and the return to slavery of his family, he decided to inquire about purchasing their freedom. He had his brother write a letter to L. B. Thornton, an attorney in Tuscumbia, and ask McKiernan the price for Peter's family. In August 1851 McKiernan replied that he wanted $5,000.

This was out of the question, for the time being. But in 1852 Peter decided to go on a fund-raising tour. It began in November of that year. He traveled from city to city with letters of introduction to leading businessmen, abolitionists, and ministers. He spoke at churches, at antislavery meetings, and to benevolent associations. His appeal was simple: he described his experience as a slave, his struggle for freedom, and his effort to bring his family out of slavery. He never gave up, and after twenty-three months he had raised the $5,000.

With John Simpson (a Florence merchant) handling the transaction, Peter's family was placed on a boat in Florence during the Christmas season. Early in January they held a joyful reunion in Philadelphia. Peter and Vina were remarried in a church according to the laws of Pennsylvania. His daughter, age thirteen, began school, and his sons found jobs as free men. Peter bought ten acres of land near Burlington, New Jersey, and operated a vegetable farm until his death. And it was his fortuitous meeting with his brother, William, that had made it possible. Not only that, but William Still later said that it was his meeting with Peter that had motivated him to begin keeping the detailed records of the fugitive slaves he assisted, which later were used to write his important book about the Underground Railroad.

SUGGESTED READING: Kenneth R. Johnson, "Peter Still, the Colbert County, Alabama, Slave Who Bought His Freedom: A Slave Family's Struggle for Freedom," *The Journal of Muscle Shoals History*, Tennessee Valley Historical Society, Vol. 6, 1978; Kate E. R. Pickard, *The Kidnapped and the Ransomed: Being the Personal Recollections of Peter Still and His Wife "Vina," after Forty Years of Slavery*, New York: Miller, Orton and Mulligan, 1856; William Still, *The Underground Railroad: A Record of Facts, Authentic Narratives, Letters, Narrating the Hardships, Hair-Breadth Escapes and Death Struggle of the Slaves in Their Efforts for Freedom by Themselves and Others, or Witnessed by the Author Together with Sketches of Some of the Largest Stockholders and Most Liberal Aiders and Advisers of the Road,* Philadelphia: Porter and Coates, 1872.

Still, William (1821–1902). William Still was unique in Underground Railroad history not only because of the careful records he kept of the fugitive slaves he helped but also because he was among the few who preserved these records. In all, he recorded the accounts of nearly 900 fugitive slaves. He later used them to write the most authentic and detailed history of the Underground Railroad on record.

He was born near Medford, in Burlington County, New Jersey. Both his parents were former slaves. His father, Levin Steel, had purchased his freedom, but his mother, whose slave name was Sidney, escaped to gain hers. His father changed the family surname to Still, and his mother changed her name to Charity in an effort to conceal her from slavecatchers.

As a boy, Still worked on his father's farm and had little formal education. At the age of twenty he left home and worked as a farmhand and in 1844 moved to Philadelphia, where he worked as a handyman.

In 1847 he learned that they needed help at the Pennsylvania Anti-Slavery Society office. The starting salary was only $14 per month, but he saw it as meaningful work and

Philadelphia Underground Railroad stationmaster William Still. Courtesy of the William Still Foundation, Inc.

said, "I go for liberty and improvement." He started out doing janitorial work, sorting mail, and assisting **J. Miller McKim**, the society's executive director. A journalist who met him at the time described him as "tall, neat, gentlemanly [with] a smiling face." He was not only congenial but also quite able, and his duties and salary quickly increased.

That year Still also met and married Letitia George, a dressmaker, who supplemented their income by taking in boarders. Before long many of these boarders were getting free room and board, as the Still house became a frequent shelter for fugitive slaves he met through his work.

During his early years, before greater responsibilities were entrusted to him, Still was present when William and Ellen Craft were assisted at the antislavery society office and when **Henry "Box" Brown** made his resurrection from his box. Brown spent his first two nights of freedom at the Still residence.

In 1852, when a more formalized committee was organized, Still was named corresponding secretary and chairman of the acting committee, which supervised the day-to-day operations of the local Underground Railroad. He already had begun to maintain careful records of the fugitive slaves that the committee assisted, a practice he would continue throughout his tenure.

Still recorded some of the most amazing stories in Underground Railroad lore. But none may be more amazing than the one in which he was personally involved.

It was August 1850, a month before the second dreaded Fugitive Slave Law was passed. Still was in the antislavery office tending to his duties, much of which was correspondence, when a middle-aged black man, who called himself Peter Friedman, entered his office. The stranger had been brought there by a friend of the landlady at the boardinghouse where he was staying. The landlady was the wife of Dr. James J. G. Bias, an original member of the Philadelphia Vigilance Committee when it was founded by Robert Purvis in 1837. The men sat down in Still's office, and Peter said that he was looking for his long-lost family. He believed he had lived in Philadelphia more than forty years earlier and had been kidnapped with his brother Levin when he was about six years old. He remembered that his mother's name was Sidney and his father's name was Levin and that he had two younger sisters.

Peter was visibly apprehensive and wanted to leave as quickly as possible. Still had become speechless. The story of his lost brothers was one of the great tragedies of his family, which now included five sisters and two brothers. His mother, Charity, whose slave name was Sidney, was now eighty, but his father, whose name was Levin, and eight other siblings had gone to their reward. Still asked Peter to remain while he finished preparing the daily mail for the post office and suggested that his guide leave because he wished to show Peter back to the boardinghouse himself. Peter balked at first, but the guide urged him to trust Still and left.

When he finished his mail duties, Still asked a few questions and then looked Peter in the eye and said, "Suppose I should tell you I'm your brother?"

It was only the beginning of an incredible family reunion. What actually had happened, the family explained, was not that Peter and Levin had been kidnapped but that Charity reluctantly had left him and his brother with their grandmother while she attempted to escape with his sisters. Angered by her departure, their master sold the boys to a slave trader.

After rejoicing with the Still family, Peter revealed that he had a wife and three children in slavery. He told them that he was going to try to bring them out and hoped that he could find someone to help rescue them. Despite his mother's pleas, Peter returned to the South to tell his family of his plans.

During Peter's absence, at McKim's request, Still wrote about his brother's return from slavery and the joyous reunion experienced by his family for the *Pennsylvania Freeman*. He explained that Peter's greatest wish was to find someone to help his family out of slavery. Reading that article was a fearless veteran of the Underground Railroad named **Seth Concklin**. He offered his services and the following spring made a heroic but unsuccessful attempt to rescue them that cost him his life. Not to be denied, Peter raised $5,000 during a two-year tour of Northern cities to pay for their emancipation. They were freed during the Christmas season of 1854.

This experience was momentous not only in Still's personal life but also in his professional life, for it led him to carefully preserve the records of fugitive slaves that he helped in the event that these records could help others reconnect with missing family members. These records included correspondence between Still, Underground Railroad conductors, and fugitive slaves, as well as information he collected from interviews with fugitive slaves, during which he recorded their name (including aliases), age, height, color, the name of their master, where they had lived, family information, and personal history. He also recorded their experiences under slavery, their reasons for fleeing, and the details of their escape.

In 1855 Still journeyed to Canada to monitor the progress of those he had aided. Among the many noteworthy Underground Railroad agents he worked with was **Harriet Tubman**, who came and stayed at the Vigilance Committee office on a number of occasions. He also worked with numerous other significant Underground Railroad conductors and had a particularly close association with **Thomas Garrett** in Wilmington, Delaware. In 1859, following **John Brown**'s capture at Harpers Ferry, Brown's wife, Mary, stayed at his home.

Safeguarding the Personal Liberty of Fugitive Slaves and the Prigg Decision

On March 1, 1842, the Prigg Decision of the Supreme Court decreed that states had no right to interfere with the recovery of slaves by their owner. In effect, it overruled state laws that protected the rights of fugitive slaves, which had hampered prosecution of the federal government's Fugitive Slave Law.

However, the Supreme Court had left a loophole when they stated that such reclamations could be made only through the use of federal authorities. As a result, Massachusetts, Vermont, Pennsylvania, and Rhode Island passed Personal Liberty Laws that forbade the use of state officers and jails in cases involving fugitive slaves.

Following the passage of the Fugitive Slave Law of 1850, additional Personal Liberty Laws were passed by a number of Northern states. Their purpose was to obstruct the 1850 law and provide legal safeguards. For example, in some Northern states, the identity of the person claimed needed to be proved by two witnesses. If not, the alleged fugitive slave was allowed the right to a writ of habeas corpus, which gave the slave the opportunity to a trial by jury. The right to a public defender was also granted, and penalties were levied for false testimony. Any violation of these clauses by state officers was punished by penalties varying from a $500 fine and six months in jail, as in Pennsylvania, to the maximum punishment in Vermont, of a $2,000 fine and ten years in prison.

Still's work expanded to other areas of social improvement for blacks. In 1859 he protested against the racial discrimination on the Philadelphia railroad cars in a letter to a local newspaper. It was the beginning of an eight-year campaign that led to a state law prohibiting this. After the Civil War he served on the Freedman's Aid Commission, helped organized a YMCA for black youths, and was involved in the management of homes for destitute children and the aged.

In business, Still was no less successful. During the period of his antislavery work, Still began investing in real estate, and when he left his position with the Vigilance Committee in 1861, he opened a store selling new and used stoves. He later went into the coal business, which made him quite wealthy.

But his work on the Underground Railroad, chronicled in his book, *The Underground Railroad: A Record of Facts, Authentic Narratives, Letters, Narrating the Hardships, Hairbreadth Escapes and Death Struggles of the Slaves in Their Efforts for Freedom as Related by Themselves and Others, or Witnessed by the Author; Together with Sketches of Some of the Largest Stockholders, and Most Liberal Aiders and Advisers of the Road,* was his most important achievement in terms of his place in history. In addition to the records of the fugitive slaves and Underground Railroad correspondence he preserved, he included excerpts from newspapers, legal documents, and biographical sketches, both white and black. The purpose of the book was to "encourage the race in efforts of self elevation" and "serve as additional testimony to the intellectual capacity of his race."

When Still died, it was estimated that his personal fortune was nearly $1 million.

SUGGESTED READING: Kate E. R. Pickard, *The Kidnapped and the Ransomed: Being the Personal Recollections of Peter Still and His Wife "Vina," after Forty Years of Slavery*, New York and Auburn: Miller, Orton and Mulligan, 1856; William Still, *The Underground Railroad: A Record of Facts, Authentic Narratives, Letters, Narrating the Hardships, Hair-breadth Escapes and Death Struggle of the Slaves in Their Efforts for Freedom by Themselves and Others, or Witnessed by the Author Together with Sketches of Some of the Largest Stockholders and Most Liberal Aiders and Advisers of the Road*, Philadelphia: Porter and Coates, 1872; "From Slavery to a Fortune," *Atlanta Constitution*, July 15, 1902; William Still Foundation, http://www.undergroundrr.com/.

Stowe, Harriet Beecher (1811–1896). Harriet Beecher Stowe's book *Uncle Tom's Cabin* was a poignant and melodramatic, though realistic, picture of slavery and the conditions that led slaves to seek their freedom. It also portrayed the Underground Railroad in action, as Stowe observed it during the seventeen years she lived in Cincinnati, where fugitive slaves were continually passing through.

In 1832 Stowe moved with her family to Cincinnati, Ohio, a prosperous town of steamboat building and pork production, settled by German and Irish immigrants. It also was a cauldron of racial tension, in part because it sat along the Ohio River, the borderline between slavery and freedom. In 1829 a race riot had occurred when unjust Black Codes were enforced on the city's free black population, who refused to comply. Mobs of whites went on a rampage, and more than 1,000 blacks fled the city. Many headed for Canada, where a plot of land had been obtained to start the first of many such black colonies. It also was only the first of more race riots to follow.

Here slaveowners, fugitive slaves, and slavecatchers were part of the city's fabric, a perfect place for Harriet to learn about slavery and the Underground Railroad. In 1833, at a plantation in Washington, Kentucky, sixty miles southeast of Cincinnati, she witnessed a slave auction and saw the worst horror slaves faced: the separation from their families.

Mary Dutton, who accompanied Stowe on the Kentucky trip, recalled the visit:

> Harriet did not seem to notice anything in particular that happened, but sat much of the time as though abstracted in thought . . . I recognized scene after scene of that visit portrayed with the most minute fidelity, and knew at once where the material for that portion of the story had been gathered.

A major event that certainly influenced Stowe was the debates on slavery organized by student Theodore Weld in 1834 at the Lane Theological Institute, of which her father was president and her husband a faculty member. In addition to strongly arguing their opposition to slavery and the colonization society, the Lane students reached out to Cincinnati's black community, many of whom were former slaves who had purchased their freedom. The students started a school teaching reading, writing, arithmetic, and geography and a Sunday school with Bible classes. They also participated in the Underground Railroad.

That may have been Stowe's first exposure to what was a wide-ranging Underground network in the Ohio Valley. That fall she also accompanied her father for a visit to the home of Rev. **John Rankin** during a meeting of the Cincinnati Synod of the Presbyterian Church in Ripley. It was from Rankin that she learned of the story of the fugitive slave who in 1838 crossed the frozen Ohio River with her baby, and whom Stowe immortalized as Eliza in her novel *Uncle Tom's Cabin.* In 1836 Rankin's son Adam Lowry enrolled at Lane. During his years there, he aided more than 300 fugitive slaves and once enlisted the help of Harriet's husband, Calvin. The Stowes were well

Author of *Uncle Tom's Cabin*, Harriet Beecher Stowe. Library of Congress.

aware of Adam Rankin's activities, and in later years Stowe admitted in a letter that "time would fail me to tell you all that I learnt incidentally of the working of the slave system, in the history of various slaves, who came into my family and of the underground railroad, which I may say ran through our barn."

Many of the servants hired by the Stowes were blacks who lived in a small community near their residence. One turned out to be a fugitive slave.

"In the year 1839," Stowe wrote, "the writer received into her family, as a servant, a girl from Kentucky. She had been the slave of one of the lowest and most brutal families, with whom she had been brought up, in a log-cabin, in a state of half-barbarism."

By the laws of Ohio, the woman was entitled to her freedom, but when it was learned that her master had come to Cincinnati to look for her, the Stowes were advised by a local judge to move her along the Underground Railroad because of the possibility that she would not get a fair hearing. Consequently Stowe's husband and one of her brothers drove her in the middle of the night to the house of **John Van Zandt**, whom Stowe used as the model for her character Von Tromp in *Uncle Tom's Cabin*.

Josiah Henson: The Real Uncle Tom

Josiah Henson was among the most well-known and respected black figures of the antebellum period. His life is an incredible story of patience and perseverance: patience in trusting the master who later betrayed him; and perseverance in making a new life in Canada after escaping to freedom.

While Henson was a slave, he was uncommonly trustworthy. He had frequent opportunities to escape; however, he felt that an escape would violate the trust placed in him by his master. After a time, he entered into an arrangement whereby he would purchase his freedom and a price was agreed upon. When it appeared that his master was reneging on the agreement, Henson arranged for his family's escape in 1830 when he was forty-one.

In Canada, Henson not only was a founder of the fugitive slave community, Dawn, and assisted Hiram Wilson in establishing the British and American Institute, but also undertook missions into the South to bring out slaves through the Underground Railroad. In all, by his own account, they numbered 118.

Henson, who published the first version of his autobiography in 1849, claimed to have been the model for **Harriet Beecher Stowe's** character Uncle Tom and claimed to have met her before she wrote *Uncle Tom's Cabin*. Although Stowe admits that Henson was among the models for Uncle Tom, she did not meet him until after the book was published.

Though the 1833 account of her visit to Kentucky is the only documented instance of her venturing into the South, there are claims that she crossed the Mason-Dixon Line on a number of occasions.

One strong claim is made in Garrard County in central Kentucky, near the village of Berea. According to oral tradition, Harriet visited the rural community of Paint Lick in 1840 with Mary Dutton, the same friend who had accompanied her to Washington, Kentucky. They allegedly stayed at the Stillman residence and went to the Kennedy plantation, where more than 100 slaves resided. These local stories claim that Harriet used the plantation as the model for the Shelby plantation at which the story of *Uncle Tom's Cabin* opens. In fact, today a plaque marks the area where the plantation once existed, making that claim. Local legend also claims that Harriet visited Centre College in nearby Danville with her father.

There are suggestions that some of these visits might have occurred. For example, there was a slave on the Kennedy plantation at the time of Harriet's alleged visit, whom she later acknowledged that she knew and whom she said served as one of the models for her partly white slave character, George Harris, in *Uncle Tom's Cabin*.

Lewis Clark, who escaped from the Kennedy plantation in 1841 and wrote a narrative about his experiences that was published in 1846, actually lived with Harriet's sister-in-law, Mary Safford, in Boston for seven years beginning in 1843. During a return visit to Paint Lick in 1881, he was interviewed by a Louisville *Courier Journal* reporter and talked about his personal acquaintance with Harriet while still a slave in Kentucky and made the claim that he was indeed the real George Harris in the book.

Also, in a biography of Harriet written by her son Charles and grandson Lyman, they state that she "frequently visited Kentucky slave plantations, where she saw Negro slavery in that mild and patriarchal form in which she pictures it in the opening chapters of *Uncle Tom's Cabin*." Harriet herself wrote that "while the writer was traveling in Kentucky, many years ago, she attended church in a small country town." It is unclear whether this was a reference to the Washington, Kentucky, visit or some other one.

Harriet had many opportunities to gather information in Cincinnati. In one letter, she told of witnessing a sale of slaves aboard a steamboat on the Ohio River that resulted in the separation of a mother and child. She later used this experience for a scene in *Uncle Tom's Cabin*.

Written at the instigation of her sister-in-law, Isabella, who sent Harriet a letter urging her to write something about the injustice of the second Fugitive Slave Law, *Uncle Tom's Cabin* was published in 1852 and became the best-selling book of the nineteenth century.

SUGGESTED READING: Joan D. Hedrick, *The Oxford Harriet Beecher Stowe Reader,* New York: Oxford University Press, 1999; Bruce Kirkham, *The Building of Uncle Tom's Cabin*, Knoxville, TN: University of Tennessee Press, 1977; Charles Beecher Stowe and Lyman Beecher Stowe, *How Uncle Tom's Cabin Was Built,* Boston: Houghton-Mifflin, 1911; Harriet Beecher Stowe, *The Key to Uncle Tom's Cabin*, London: Clarke, Beeton, and Co., 1853.

T

Tibbets, John Henry (1818–1907). John Henry Tibbets was among a cadre of abolitionists involved in the Underground Railroad in the small rural community of Lancaster, Indiana.

Tibbetts grew up in Clermont County, Ohio, where his father, Samuel, had moved the family from Maine in 1810. Sometime afterward, his father became associated with **Rev. John Rankin** of Ripley, and Tibbetts had his first experience aiding fugitive slaves in 1838. In his "Reminiscences," Tibbets wrote that he was with a friend, Thomas Coombs, a teenager like himself, when they encountered a fugitive slave. Unsure what to do, they waited until dark and brought him to a man they knew would help. Two years later another incident involved a man who came to his father for help in aiding fugitive slaves. Tibbets agreed to participate and drive the man to a Deacon Barwood in Cincinnati, which was twenty-two miles to the west. His greatest obstacle, he said, was passing through three tollgates, because the men operating them could not be trusted.

Tibbets participated in the Underground Railroad next in 1845 after he had moved to Lancaster, in Jefferson County, Indiana, a small rural community about ten miles north of Madison, Indiana, founded by evangelical Christians from New England. The first family to put down stakes there was the Nelsons. Brothers James and Daniel, veterans of the War of 1812, came from Vermont in 1820. They were followed in 1834 by Lyman Hoyt, also from Vermont and whose wife, Lucy, was the sister of James's wife.

It was in these households that the Neil's Creek Anti-Slavery Society was born in 1839, with Lyman Hoyt emerging as their leader.

An 1883 history of Southern Indiana by William Wesley Woollen testifies to the society's activities: "The abolition sentiment in Lancaster was considered a plague-spot on the body politic. The Hoyts, the Nelsons and the Tibbetses of that neighborhood, although honorable and peaceable men, were tabooed because they believed in the equality of all men before the law."

Tibbets married James Nelson's daughter, Sarah, and given his prior experience, he resumed his participation in the Underground Railroad in Indiana. His first opportunity there came when word had been sent to Lancaster from **George DeBaptiste** of Madison that ten fugitive slaves were ready to be forwarded and that he needed them to be transported. A free black barber, DeBaptiste had moved to Indiana from Virginia and for a short time had been the valet of President William Henry Harrison until Harrison's untimely death in 1841. Tibbets wrote the following:

> About five o'clock in the evening my wife and myself got into my big covered wagon and started for my wife's uncle, Lyman Hoyt. He lived about three miles from where we lived on the road to Madison. After dark I drove to the place agreed upon to meet in a piece of woods one mile from the town of Wirt (a short distance from Lancaster). I had been at the appointed place but a very short time when Mr. DeBaptist[e] sang out.

The fugitive slaves were loaded in the wagon and they rendezvoused with his wife's brother James Nelson, Tibbets's nephew, and another friend, Leonidas Cushman. Those three young conductors drove throughout the rest of the night, at daybreak reaching the home of Albert Allie, where they took breakfast. After resting during the day, they resumed their journey the next night to the home of James Hamilton, seven miles from Greensburgh, Indiana, about forty miles from Lancaster.

Tibbets's memoir reveals a number of additional incidents that outline a network of Underground Railroad conductors who worked together from Madison to Greensburg, Indiana. Notable among them were the Hicklin brothers, who were Methodist ministers. Another important conductor mentioned in three separate incidents by Tibbets was **Elijah Anderson**, an important black leader in Madison, who made trips into Kentucky to aid the escape of slaves and later coordinated Underground Railroad activities in western Ohio after a riot in Madison by a proslavery mob persuaded him to leave town.

More than thirty conductors have been documented in Jefferson County, Indiana. Tibbets was only one of many, but his memoir testifies to the Underground Railroad's widespread operation in the county's rural sections.

SUGGESTED READING: J. Blaine Hudson, *Fugitive Slaves and the Underground Railroad in the Kentucky Borderlands*, Jefferson, NC: McFarland, 2001; John Henry Tibbets, "Reminiscences of Slavery Times," unpublished memoir written in 1888.

Todd, John (1818–1894). Rev. John Todd was a Congregational minister and graduate of Oberlin College who founded the settlement of Tabor, Iowa, and was among that state's pioneers in the Underground Railroad.

Todd was born in West Hanover, Dauphin County, Pennsylvania, to James and Sally Ainsworth Todd. His father was a captain in the infantry during the War of 1812 and an early advocate of temperance and abolition, and for this reason he sent John to Oberlin College. Todd's time there coincided with the school's opening and its experiment in coeducation and radical abolitionism. His life also was touched by the legendary evangelical preacher Charles Finney, under whom Todd studied after he received a bachelor's degree and entered the school's theological seminary.

After graduation in 1844 he became pastor of the Congregational Church at Clarksfield, Ohio, about fifteen miles from Oberlin, and married Martha Atkins, a classmate at Oberlin. He became acquainted with George B. Gaston, a young farmer who for four years had been a missionary among the Pawnee Indians with his sister Elvira Gaston Platt, a classmate of Todd's, and her husband, Lester Ward Platt, on what is now the Missouri River border between Nebraska and Iowa. In 1848 Gaston proposed that Todd join him on a trip to the Midwest to survey prospects for a homestead. Gaston was excited by the prospect of starting a new settlement in that part of the Northwest

Iowa abolitionist Reverend John Todd. Courtesy of the Ohio Historical Society.

Territory and establishing a college there modeled on Oberlin with strict abolitionist principles and open to all regardless of race or gender.

After identifying an area near the Missouri River that they deemed as a desirable location, they returned to Ohio with plans to move. In 1850 they transported their families and endured the privations of pioneer life. The nearest store was twenty miles away, the nearest grist mill farther. Hulled corn was the main diet, wheat bread was a rare treat, and they lived in crude temporary huts built without shingles, boards, or nails. But they endured as Todd offered ministerial services for two years at the communities of Civil Bend, Florence, Traders Point, Honey Creek, Cutlers Camp, and High Creek. Their intended location at Civil Bend, near the Missouri River, was found to be unsuitable because of flooding and the susceptibility to malaria. So, they moved farther from the river on higher ground to a plateau. They called their settlement Tabor, after Mt. Tabor, the mountain of biblical renown near Nazareth in ancient Palestine.

In 1853 they incorporated the Tabor Literary Institute, but it would be seven years before the college would open. In the meantime, they began putting their abolitionist principles into practice. Todd recalled in his autobiography that it was appropriately on July 4, 1854, that the Underground Railroad began in Tabor.

A Mormon family stopped in Tabor with three covered wagons and a carriage, as well as six slaves. The slaves were two men, one of whom had a wife and two children, and another woman. They camped along the Main Street, and a couple of the slaves went to fetch some water at a local well. It was there that they revealed their predicament: they wanted someone to help them become free. The only problem was that the second woman wanted to stay with their master. At once the word was passed, and with many being natives of Ohio and familiar with the procedures of the Underground Railroad, which had been in operation throughout that state for more than thirty years, they quickly made arrangements.

Four men, S. H. Adams, John Hallam, Jas. K. Gaston and Irish Henry, were to be conductors while Gaston visited C. W. Tolles on Silver Creek to make arrangements for the fugitive slaves to be hidden.

When their Mormon master awoke the next morning, the slaves had already been put into hiding. Nevertheless, the master was able to find proslavery sympathizers in a neighborhood to help him conduct a search. But one of the abolitionists posed as a proslavery sympathizer and volunteered to help with the search. He suggested that he be sent to the area where the fugitive slaves had been hidden, to ensure that the search party would not discover them.

Once the search was called off, Cephas Case and William L. Clark took the fugitive slaves to a Quaker settlement near the Des Moines River. This may have been Salem, Iowa, a distance of about 200 miles, where Quakers from Wayne County, Indiana, had settled in the 1840s and had a well-established Underground Railroad station. On the way they encountered a man on horseback, but feeling apprehensive, they led him to believe that they were going in a different direction. It was a wise decision, for when the man reached Tabor, he reported that he had seen the likely party and that he knew where they were headed. Eventually, Todd wrote, the fugitive slaves successfully reached Canada.

Todd also mentioned a fellow Oberlin alum, John H. Byrd, who was the pastor of a Congregational church in Atchison, Kansas, who sent him a runaway slave in 1857. Todd dressed her in a cloak and veil and piloted her in his wagon to the village of Lewis, a distance of forty miles, where Rev. George B. Hitchcock was the agent and which was the next stop of the western Iowa Underground Railroad.

In 1856, with the Kansas war heating up, the citizens of Tabor organized the Republican Association "to co-operate with all true Republicans in all parts of the country to rescue the government from the control of the slave holding oligarchy." R. B. Foster was named president; Todd, vice president; and Jonas Jones, secretary. It also organized its own military company with Gaston as captain; Mortimer P. Clark, first lieutenant; and E. S. Hill, second lieutenant. Being only a few miles from the Nebraska border and the nearest point to Kansas in sympathy with the Free State movement, Tabor became a way station for abolitionist emigrants and soldiers. Among them were Free State military leader Jim Lane; two members of John Brown's "Secret Six," Samuel Gridley Howe and Thomas W. Higginson; and **John Brown** himself.

Brown first came to Tabor sometime after the Battle of Black Jack seeking care for his wounded men, including son-in-law Henry Thompson and sons Salmon and Owen.

Also in company with them were his sons Oliver and Frederick. Todd described the scene in Tabor during this time:

> That summer and autumn our houses, before too full, were much overfilled and our comforts shared with those passing to and from Kansas to secure it to Freedom. When houses would hold no more, woodsheds were temporized for bedrooms, where the sick and dying were cared for. Barns also were fixed for sleeping rooms. Every place where a bed could be put or a blanket thrown down was at once so occupied. There were comers and goers all times of day or night—meals at all hours—many free hotels, perhaps entertaining angels unawares. After battles they were here for rest—before for preparation.

Following the burning of his homestead at Osawatomie, Brown made his way north and stopped again in Tabor. Here he rested, and decided that he would make Tabor the site of a training ground for his future army. It was the beginning of the period when he would prepare for his eventual assault at Harpers Ferry. Brown left his sons in Tabor while he went to Chicago to raise funds and to discuss his plans with the Kansas National Committee. They agreed to have a shipment of 200 Sharps rifles and thousands of rounds of ammunition sent to Tabor; the guns and ammunition were stored in Todd's cellar. Brown then returned to Tabor to rejoin his sons, and they then returned to the East; there he would meet the men who would become his "Secret Six," who would supply the financial support for his planned war to liberate the slaves.

In August 1857 Brown returned to Tabor and was joined by his son Owen and a man named Hugh Forbes, whom Brown had hired to train his army and provide military expertise. They remained several months, Brown boarding with Jonas Jones. In early November Forbes returned to the East, and the Browns went to Kansas. There he began to recruit his army. These men would gather in Tabor at the end of the month and leave two weeks later, during which time they took with them the rifles, ammunition, and other military supplies stored at Todd's.

In December 1858 a particularly unsettling incident occurred involving fugitive slaves. A peddler named John Williamson brought three or four slaves of Nebraska City merchant Stephen F. Nuckolls across the river into Iowa and the home of Ira D. Blanchard of Civil Bend, one of Tabor's primary Underground collaborators. Blanchard brought them to Tabor, where they were hidden at the home of B. F. Ladd and where they remained until nightfall. Meanwhile, as soon as Nuckolls realized that the slaves were missing, he set out in pursuit and organized a search party with relatives who lived in the vicinity. Their destination was a bridge on Silver Creek about twenty miles northwest of Tabor. However, their search proved unsuccessful.

Nuckolls then returned to Nebraska City and gathered a posse of vigilantes and stormed into the area surrounding Percival and Civil Bend, where he believed the fugitive slaves might still be hiding. The members of the posse forced their way into people's homes and searched their premises without a warrant. When Reuben Williams resisted, he was bludgeoned on the head. The injury permanently damaged his hearing, and a trial that later took place awarded Williams several thousand dollars in damages. But as Todd recounts, some years later, during a visit to the area by Nuckolls, Williams's barn caught fire and the fire nearly spread to his house. Locals suspected but never could prove that the fire had been started by Nuckolls.

February 1859 saw the return of John Brown and his men. They were in flight following the renowned Missouri Raid that took place on the night of December 19, 1858, and the governor of Missouri had offered a $3,000 reward for their capture.

Brown's raid had disappointed the settlers in Tabor. Brown's men had killed a slaveowner and had abducted twelve slaves. Some would say that Brown's men had rescued the slaves, but although those in Tabor would do all in their power to assist fugitive slaves who were fleeing of their own volition, they were opposed to using force to free slaves and could not in good conscience condone the murder of the slaveowner. As Todd wrote, "While [we] were not accustomed to entice or coax slaves to leave their masters, yet when they had sense enough to want freedom, and grit enough to strike out, and attempt to get it, [we] always stood ready to help the slave, rather than the master."

Brown and his men received a lukewarm reception when they arrived in Tabor on February 5. Nevertheless, an old cookstove was set up in the schoolhouse, bedding and cooking utensils were loaned, and the fugitive slaves and Brown's men were made as comfortable as possible. The following day was the Sabbath, and Brown attended Todd's services. Prior to the service, Brown gave him a note:

> John Brown respectfully requests the church at Tabor to offer public thanksgiving to Almighty God in behalf of himself, and company: and of their rescued captives, in particular for his gracious preservation of their lives, and health; and his signal deliverance of all out of the hand of the wicked, hitherto, "Oh give thanks unto the Lord for He is good: for His mercy endureth forever."

Todd conferred with his associate Rev. H. D. King for advice in the matter. It was decided that a public thanksgiving was not in agreement with the views of the church. During the service Todd suggested that those wishing to bless the efforts of Brown could do it privately. Todd did not wish to totally repudiate Brown, however, so a public meeting was called to give Brown a chance to defend his actions.

When Brown began to address the meeting that night at the church, a slaveowner from Missouri in Tabor on business entered. Brown apparently knew he was a slaveowner and asked him to leave. But a Tabor resident countered that whatever Brown said should be heard by all. Brown refused to accept this and left. One of Brown's men, Aaron Stevens, then rose and declared that "so help him God he never would sit in council with one who bought and sold human flesh."

The end result was that the following resolution was passed by the citizens of Tabor:

> RESOLVED: That while we sympathize with the oppressed, and will do all that we conscientiously can to help them in their efforts for freedom, nevertheless, we have no Sympathy with those who go to Slave States, to entice away Slaves, and take property or life when necessary to attain that end.

Brown was hurt by this loss of support. Even so, on September 1, 1859, he returned to Tabor to see Jonas Jones. "Goodbye," he said on leaving. "I don't say where I am going, but you'll hear from me. There has been enough said about 'bleeding Kansas.' I intend to make a bloody spot at another point and carry the war into Africa."

Todd recounts two other incidents involving fugitive slaves, one in which slavecatchers overtook a wagon of local conductors, who were brought to trial. However, they were found innocent, and the fugitive slaves were once again forwarded on the Underground Railroad. Another case involved two fugitive slaves who were caught and placed in Linden, Nebraska, and provided with the means for their escape. During their flight, they were separated during a blizzard. One arrived in Tabor and stayed with Gaston, hopeful that his friend would appear. After about a week, his prayers were answered, and the men were forwarded on the Underground Railroad.

The Oberlin-Wellington Rescue

By 1858 Oberlin, Ohio, had developed a national reputation as a center of abolitionism and the Underground Railroad. Its college was the nation's first to permit blacks, women, and white men to be educated in the same classroom in 1835. More than thirty fugitive slaves lived there during the 1850s, so when fugitive slave John Price settled in Oberlin in 1856, he felt perfectly safe.

He was not suspicious when a thirteen-year-old boy driving a buggy stopped and asked if he wanted a job that afternoon digging up potatoes. He got in, but after they had gone about a mile, another carriage overtook them. Three men with guns ordered Price to get in their carriage. One of them was U.S. Marshal Jacob Lowe, who had a warrant for his arrest under the jurisdiction of the Fugitive Slave Law.

On the way to their hotel in Wellington about nine miles south, they passed a couple of young men and Price cried out. One of the young men, Ansel Lyman, had fought in the war in Kansas and was a militant abolitionist. As soon as he arrived in Oberlin he aroused the residents.

As many as 300 students, professors, and citizens were part of a caravan of horses and wagons that sped to Wellington that afternoon. In all more than 500 people, many of them armed, surrounded the Wadsworth Hotel. A local judge read aloud the federal warrant that had been issued for Price's arrest, but this did not deter the mob. They rushed the room where Price was being held and took him by force back to Oberlin, where he stayed several days at the home of the college's president, James Fairchild, before being forwarded to Canada.

Thirty-seven individuals were indicted in the rescue, while countercharges of kidnapping were brought against Lowe and three others who assisted him. The defendants refused bail en masse and spent nearly three months in jail together before the charges were dropped.

In a third account, Todd relates the story of the kidnapping of two free blacks who were brought to St. Louis to a slave pen to be sold. Learning of this, Blanchard and Gaston undertook a search along the Missouri River to trace their whereabouts. When they learned they had been taken to St. Louis to be sold as slaves, Blanchard made the 350-mile journey to St. Louis to provide proof that they were free and obtain their release.

During the Civil War, Todd spent 100 days as chaplain of the Forty-sixth Infantry in 1864. The remainder of his life was spent as pastor of the Congregational church in Tabor, where he would finally step down in 1883, and serving in various capacities as teacher and administrator at Tabor College, which opened its doors in 1860 and which continued to offer a Christian education to scholars until 1927.

Rev. Todd was a man who, as his son wrote, "believed in practicing what he preached, and expected all others to do the same," and who, as one of the soldiers under him during the Civil War wrote, "was earnest, constant in season and out of season, doing his duty no matter where it was."

SUGGESTED READING: Glenn Noble, *John Brown and the Jim Lane Trail*, Broken Bow, NE: Purcells, 1977; Charles Edward Smith, "The Underground Railroad in Iowa," master's thesis, Northeast Missouri State College, August 1971; John Todd, *Early Settlement and Growth of Western Iowa or Reminiscences*, Des Moines: Iowa Historical Department, 1906; J. E. Todd, *Biographical Sketch of Rev. John Todd, of Tabor Iowa.*

Torrey, Charles T. (1813–1846). Charles Turner Torrey was one of the most celebrated abolitionists and daring Underground Railroad conductors of the antebellum period. Short, slight, and boyishly handsome, he surprised his foes with his aggressive and unyielding manner. The cause to end slavery became his overwhelming obsession, and like **John Brown** after him he willingly sacrificed his life to that end.

Born in Scituate, Massachusetts, along the south shore of Boston, Torrey was orphaned at the age of four and raised by his maternal grandparents. His grandfather had achieved some prominence, having served in the Revolution under George Washington and having been a member of Congress. His upbringing was strongly influenced by the evangelical movement that had blazed through New York and New England during that period, and he was provided with an excellent education, attending Phillips Exeter Academy and Yale University. He thereafter studied for the ministry at Andover Seminary, where he founded a student antislavery society in 1833. Poor health forced him to withdraw from Andover, but he completed his studies with Rev. Jacob Ide in West Medway, Massachusetts, and was ordained in 1837. That year he married Ide's daughter, Mary, and they had two children, Charles born in 1838 and Mary in 1840.

He had brief pastorates in Providence, Rhode Island, and Salem, Massachusetts, but in both instances withdrew because of his preoccupation with the cause of abolition. Considering that he had a family to support, this was no small matter, and his growing obsession with abolition soon took precedence over all else.

Early on Torrey saw that the most important point of abolition was not the legal removal of slavery but the social improvement of blacks. By 1838 he had become engaged in a public quarrel with abolitionist editor William Lloyd Garrison over the use of political action as a tactic for ending slavery that led to the formation of the Massachusetts Abolition Society in 1839. He began to focus his energies on lecturing and on writing for abolition publications, and the following year he took a leadership role in the organization of the Liberty Party.

In the spring of 1841 he organized the earliest incarnation of the Boston Vigilance Committee. Among his efforts in this capacity occurred in June of that year when he had the captain and mate of the schooner *Wellington* arrested for kidnapping the fugitive slave John Torrance, who had stowed away aboard their ship and who had been confined against his will after arriving in Boston Harbor. His work with this committee prepared him for his later work on the Underground Railroad.

By December of that year, Torrey had moved to Washington, D.C., to work as a correspondent for newspapers in Boston and New York. There he mingled with congressional leaders who were disposed to abolition like Seth Gates of western New York and Joshua Giddings of Ohio. He also formed a friendship with abolitionist editor Joshua Leavitt. All three men lived at that time in the same boardinghouse run by Ann Spriggs that included abolitionist orator and writer Theodore Weld. It was through these abolitionist contacts that he would begin to develop a network of the Underground Railroad that led from Washington, D.C. to New York. He also immersed himself in the black community of Washington and made a decision to confine his worship to black churches. Though this decision facilitated his work in the Underground Railroad, it was not done for this purpose. As Torrey himself explained it in a letter to his wife, it satisfied his spiritual needs:

> In the afternoon, I went to a colored church, one of the Wesleyan, so called, a denomination of Methodists, who have separated entirely from white slaveholding churches; they are all colored. There was no sermon, only a class-meeting; but I have not enjoyed the communion of saints, so much, for a long time, as when mingling with that little band of despised colored people, partly slaves; and, when one of the poor women, nearly white, spoke of the persecution she endured, with sobs, I felt my heart filled with new energy to make war upon that hateful institution that so crushes the disciples of the Lord to the earth. I have determined to commune only with the colored churches, while I stay here; I will strive to be pure from the blood of the poor. I have had much more communion with God, since I came here, than for months before.

At the urging of his abolitionist associates, Torrey went to Annapolis, Maryland, as a reporter to cover a slaveholders' convention that began on January 12, 1842. The purpose of the convention was to discuss how to combat the growing support for abolition in the state. Among proposals to be considered were the expulsion from the state of free blacks, the promotion of the domestic slave trade, the reduction of slave escapes, and the prohibition of abolitionist newspapers. For an abolitionist like Torrey who made little secret of his views, it was like entering a hornet's nest.

Well-known Baltimore abolitionist John Needles also made an appearance. But it was Torrey who caused the havoc. It all began when the president of the convention asked that all nonmembers of the convention retire to the lobbies. Torrey noticed, however, that other reporters remained, and when he moved to the gallery and continued taking notes, the doorman asked him to leave. This led to a dispute that stirred up the entire convention. Finally, Torrey was expelled from the convention.

Sympathizers suggested that it might be prudent for him to leave town. After he returned to the tavern where he was staying, a mob showed up, searched his property, forced him to check out, and took possession of him, debating whether they should hang or tar and feather him. A local magistrate interceded and issued a warrant to send him to the local jail. A mob of more than 200 men and boys followed him there, Torrey wrote, "with screams, yells, and curses that [would give] one a lively idea of pandemonium broke loose."

Torrey sent for abolitionist lawyer Thomas Alexander to represent him. In the meantime, he was placed in a cell with a family of thirteen slaves, who were waiting for a court to rule whether they would be free. Their deceased master had set them free in his will, but it was being contested by his heirs. They were, however, expecting the worst and realized that if their master's heirs won the case, they would be sold to a slave trader, which likely meant the breakup of their family. Their tale of woe moved Torrey deeply, and he later wrote that he "could not help weeping as I looked at the two little infants . . . in their mothers' arms, mewling in sweet unconsciousness of the bitter doom their parents were anticipating, a sale to the trader." Torrey then made "a solemn consecration of myself to the work of freeing the slaves, until no slaves shall be found in the land. May God help me to be faithful to that pledge." It was a pledge that he would do his heartfelt best to keep.

Torrey faced charges of mutiny, distributing incendiary matter, and exciting discontent among the colored people. In addition to Alexander, two other attorneys assisted in his defense, Joseph Palmer of Frederick, Maryland, and David A. Simmons of Boston, who had been obtained with the help of his friends in Washington. In the end, the charges were dismissed, but the notoriety he gained as a result would come back to haunt him.

When Torrey returned from Maryland, he met Thomas Smallwood, a free black man who had read about his arrest in Maryland. Smallwood had asked his wife, who did laundry for the boardinghouse where Torrey stayed, to arrange a meeting. They found that they were kindred spirits, and Torrey informed him of a plan to rescue a family of slaves owned by Secretary of the Navy George Badger, who was planning to sell them into the dreaded Deep South. But the family was saved by purchase of abolitionists in the North, and an alternate rescue was found. This involved fifteen men, women, and children, one of whom was a cook at Spriggs's boardinghouse. Congressman Giddings hinted in a letter to his son that he knew about it.

But pulling off the rescue was no easy task. The plan was to send the fugitive slaves in a wagon all the way to Troy, New York, where they would then be shipped off to

Canada via canal. In fact a route by way of the Champlain Canal, which began in Troy, led to Lake Champlain, where steamers made regular runs to Canada. When no one could be found to drive the team, Torrey assumed the responsibility. He successfully drove them the entire 350 miles, breaking down only once, and sent them to Canada by way of the canal. The breakdown was a fortuitous mishap, for it forced them to leave the road and deceived the pursuing slavecatchers into thinking they had fled by a water route.

Shortly after, Torrey moved with his wife and children, who had remained in Massachusetts while he was in Washington, to Albany. There he was hired to work as an editor of an abolitionist newspaper, the *Tocsin of Liberty*. It was a recently launched publication, and its publisher, **Rev. Abel Brown**, had been regularly aiding fugitive slaves at least as early as 1838. He was as zealous as Torrey, and shortly after Torrey's arrival, they organized the Eastern New York Anti-Slavery Society, among whose foremost occupations was to aid fugitive slaves. Not only did they not conceal their Underground activities, but they published them in the *Tocsin*.

Brown's biography states the following:

> It was then the *Tocsin* rung with the joyful intelligence of the arrival of fugitive slaves from the land of chains—and often too, sounded the note of alarm, to the *watchmen* on freedom's walls, who neither slumbered nor slept in their untiring vigilance, to *protect* these "outcasts" of humanity from farther invasion of southern man-hunters, and legalized robbers.

This left Smallwood in charge of Underground Railroad operations in Washington. He reported his activities in letters to Torrey, under the name Samivel Weller Jr., which were published in the *Tocsin* and the *Albany Patriot*, the *Tocsin's* later name.

During 1842 the Albany Vigilance Committee reported assisting 350 runaway slaves, and a price of $1,500 was put on the heads of Torrey, Brown, and their cohort, Edwin W. Goodwin, who succeeded Torrey as editor of the *Patriot*. Many came from the Washington, D.C., area and were aided by Smallwood. In one of his Weller letters that November, he had reported aiding 150 fugitive slaves worth $75,000 during the preceding six months. Assisting Smallwood in his operations was Torrey's former landlady, a Mrs. Padgett, and his wife. Other contacts Torrey had made during his earlier stay, like Giddings and Gates, also were complicit. For example, Smallwood brought a party of eighteen on foot to a spot just north of Philadelphia, where he put them on a train to Albany. Among those fugitive slaves was John Douglass, a slave who worked as a waiter at Mrs. Spriggs's boardinghouse. It was through Gates that Torrey and Smallwood learned of the readiness of those slaves to escape.

Their general mode of operation was to assemble at a secret meeting place, which was continually changed with each escape. "Places of deposit" also were established along the way if concealment from slavecatchers was necessary. One agent known to have harbored Torrey during his journeys with fugitive slaves was Samuel Mifflin, the nephew of noted conductor **William Wright**, who lived just south of Wrightsville, Pennsylvania, on the west side of the Susquehanna River. Passengers generally were slave families facing separation or slaves who could assist with funding their escape. Escapees often were harbored at Smallwood's home or Padgett's boardinghouse prior to departure. They generally traveled at night by carriage to Pennsylvania, where they would then take the train to New York City. Travel to upstate New York at this time was made by boat, by carriage, or on foot.

In December 1842 Torrey purchased the *Tocsin* along with Linnaeus P. Noble, a Syracuse canal boat owner, who later moved to Washington to become publisher of the *National Era*. Through the summer of 1843 Torrey continued to operate the *Patriot*, whose pages included advertisements that identified fugitive slaves that he and his associates had helped, and their masters. Written in a mocking tone, they were in turn mailed to the very slaveholders identified. Weller's letters also boasted of Torrey's complicity. But it became increasingly more difficult for Smallwood to move fugitive slaves out of Washington, and he complained about the increased vigilance of Washington's Auxiliary Guard, who enforced the city's 10 p.m. curfew for blacks.

Smallwood also made some poor choices in selecting men to help him move fugitive slaves out of the city. More than one betrayed him for monetary gain. What had especially discouraged him was that the men were black. Armed with details of his operations, the authorities closed in on him, and he found it necessary in October of 1843 to leave with his family for Canada, a move fraught with great difficulty.

After being in Canada a few weeks, Smallwood was approached by four men, whom he had helped to get to Canada. They wanted him to make an attempt to free their families still in Washington. Smallwood reluctantly agreed. He wrote Torrey in Albany. Struggling financially, Torrey was ready to leave Albany. He was not about to give up his crusade, however, and he sent his family back to Massachusetts to live with his in-laws.

Smallwood joined Torrey in Albany on what would be his last mission with him on the Underground Railroad. Torrey's idea was to obtain a large wagon with a team of horses and drive into Washington and take out as many slaves as they could hold. Among those he hoped to rescue were the wife and child of James Baker, a runaway who had become a lecturer for the Eastern New York Anti-Slavery Society.

Having obtained their wagon and horses with the help of abolitionists at Kennett Square, Pennsylvania, they spent the night at the home of **Thomas Garrett** in Wilmington, Delaware, before heading to Baltimore. There, Smallwood met two of the four designated families at the steamboat landing, the other two deciding not to come, and arrangements were made to send them to Philadelphia. Then Torrey and Smallwood set out to Washington, where arrangements had been made with John Bush for the rescue of fourteen additional fugitive slaves.

They arrived at Bush's home on November 24, 1843, but while preparing the wagon for departure, they were confronted by the police, who apparently had tracked them down. Torrey and Smallwood left at once, barely escaping, and leaving the unfortunate fugitive slaves in the wagon to be apprehended by the police. They quickly separated and met in Baltimore several days later. Smallwood had been identified, and his name had been published in the newspaper, so he had to be sent by way of the Underground Railroad back to Canada. Along the way, he met with the two families he had assisted in Baltimore, and together they made the trip, arriving in Toronto on December 23, 1843.

Thereafter Smallwood remained in Toronto, becoming a leader in the city's black community. Torrey meanwhile expanded his Underground Railroad activities and became a regular participant at the meetings of the Philadelphia Vigilant Association, whose leading members at the time included **Robert Purvis** and James J. G. Bias. Though he was warned of a plot to apprehend him by friends like Rev. Daniel Payne, the noted African Methodist Episcopal minister then in Washington, Torrey would not listen. As Payne wrote, "The warnings were unheeded. The idea of liberty consumed him."

Using Bias's home as his base of operations, Torrey undertook a series of rescues in Virginia and Maryland. In December he traveled by carriage south through Gettysburg and Harpers Ferry to Winchester, Virginia, to rendezvous with John Webb, who was bringing himself and five of his children out of slavery. Barely escaping capture in Chambersburg, Pennsylvania, Torrey took them to Philadelphia, where he put them on a train to New York.

Torrey also was becoming bolder and more aggressive in his attacks on slaveholders and their informants in the pages of the *Patriot*, for whom he continued to write, threatening the lives of blacks who served as informers and that of a Gettysburg policeman. It was claimed by some that he also had begun arming himself with pistols.

In March 1844 Torrey addressed a special meeting of the Philadelphia Vigilant Association asking for support of a scheme to rescue slaves that would reach into the Carolinas and eventually as far south as Louisiana. In June he helped three slaves escape from William Heckrotte of Baltimore and once again barely eluded capture. But it was his attempt to negotiate the release of Big Ben, a free black man kidnapped in Bucks County, Pennsylvania, from Slatter's slave pen in Baltimore that put an end to Torrey's rescue efforts. Slatter recognized Torrey, whose part in the rescue of the Webb family in December had been reported in the local newspapers, and he contacted Bushrod Taylor, who obtained a warrant for Torrey's arrest.

On June 25, 1844, Torrey was arrested at Baltimore, Maryland, for aiding the Webb family, and shortly after was charged in the escape of the Heckrotte slaves.

In a letter Torrey wrote while in the Baltimore jail, he said he had hoped to have his case tried in a federal court to test the constitutionality of the fugitive slave laws:

> In this, as well as in the other case, where I am charged with aiding a mother with her son and daughter to flee from this city, another and broader general issue will be taken, both before the State and United States courts. It is this: That by the laws of God and nature, by the common law, by the Constitutions of the United States, of Maryland, and of Virginia even, it is no crime for a slave to escape if he can, and therefore it can be no crime to help him. The local statute laws, consequently, which undertake to convert acts of humanity and mercy into felonies are null and void, not less so in law, than in morality.

Prosecutors gave the Heckrotte case priority to avoid extradition to Virginia and prevent Torrey from seeking a writ of habeas corpus so that he could have his case tried in a federal court.

While in jail, Torrey maintained his defiant stance. He wrote **Gerrit Smith**, "The question of my prudence, I must adjourn to Judgement day. I have done, many things in the South, that prudent men dared not do. . . . I am bold and decided. God made me so. He did not make me cautious."

He also planned a jailbreak and had a saw and chisels brought to him. He contemplated the escape for several weeks without telling anyone, but when the attempt was made he was joined by other inmates. However, they were betrayed by another prisoner.

Finally on November 29, 1844, his case was tried. He was found guilty on testimony that was obviously perjured but that had strong circumstantial facts to buttress it, and he was sentenced to six years in the penitentiary.

His attorneys had given him hope that a pardon from the governor might be possible, and committees were formed in the North to assist the funding of his legal needs. Such a pardon, however, was conditioned on Torrey expressing his regret and asking forgiveness for aiding the 400 slaves, whom by his own admission he had helped. His family pleaded with him to accept the concessions, but his reply was that "it is better to die in prison with the peace of God in our hearts, than live in freedom with a polluted conscience." As time passed and the likelihood of a pardon decreased, Torrey became despondent and his health worsened. He became resigned to his fate, and on May 9, 1846, he died of consumption at age thirty-three.

Torrey's body was brought home to Boston, where it was denied a burial by the Congregational Church, where he had been a minister. The funeral was moved to the Tremont Temple, whose pastor was **Nathaniel Colver**. The body was visited by thousands. Those giving eulogies included William C. Nell and the Wesleyan-Methodist minister Lucius Matlack. When services ended, a violent rainstorm began, delaying the procession to the cemetery. Because of this and the large number of carriages, Tremont Street was blocked for more than half an hour. Finally the body was carried to Mt. Auburn Cemetery in Cambridge.

Blacks especially expressed grief and anger at Torrey's passing. In Oberlin they offered sympathy to his wife and children and condemned the governor of Maryland for not allowing him to go home after the state of his health had become hopeless. In Boston, blacks voted to erect a monument to him. It was placed at his grave in 1847 despite opposition from some abolitionists like William Lloyd Garrison, and became a site of veneration throughout the remainder of the antebellum period.

Many abolitionists who supported Torrey's goals did not approve of his methods. Some were reticent to work with him because of his recklessness. Many of the agents in southeastern Pennsylvania, which was an important part of Torrey's Underground network, were afraid that he would get them all in trouble. Others, however, like a Maryland abolitionist, wrote that more abolitionists should be like Torrey rather than "sneaking cowards.... May God in mercy multiply the Torreyites a thousand-fold per annum, and speed the operations of the Patent Railroad to freedom! Amen." They would grow in numbers as the conflict grew between freedom and slavery, especially after the passage of the second Fugitive Slave Law in 1850.

William L. Chaplin: Torrey's Able Replacement

William L. Chaplin was a close colleague of abolitionist **Charles T. Torrey** and admired his courage, but did not think he could ever measure up to such boldness. "As I am a living man, I believe that one hundred men like Charles T. Torrey, in courage and devotion to his object, would do more to deliver the slave speedily, than all our paper resolutions, windy speeches, presses and votes into the bargain," he wrote to the *Albany Patriot*.

Chaplin was the third member of the indefatigable trinity of zealous Underground Railroad workers based in Albany, New York, that included Torrey and **Abel Brown**. He had been lecturing up and down the state of New York since the early 1830s, and as early as 1838, as secretary of the state antislavery society, he publicly called for the organization of the Underground Railroad throughout the state.

In 1844 he had moved to Washington as a correspondent for the *Patriot* and after Torrey's death began following in his footsteps, aiding fugitive slaves and assisting in their purchase through the generous purse of **Gerrit Smith**. He was the undisputed mastermind of the unsuccessful *Pearl* rescue of 1848, during which seventy-seven fugitive slaves were placed aboard a boat that was apprehended by the authorities en route to the North. But in August of 1850 he was caught in the act while aiding two fugitive slaves attempting to flee with him in a carriage and was imprisoned. An earnest campaign in the North to raise funds for his bail of $25,000 was successful.

It was hoped that Chaplin would return to the lecture circuit and raise funds to repay his bail. However, after a few appearances, Chaplin retired from the abolitionist wars and married Theodosia Gilbert, a young nurse, who opened the Glen Haven Water Cure facility in partnership with Chaplin's longtime abolitionist colleague, James C. Jackson. The couple had two children, but Gilbert died in 1855 during the birth of the second, leaving Chaplin, who was approaching his sixtieth birthday, to care for two children still in their infancy.

SUGGESTED READING: Vincent Bowditch, *Life and Correspondence of Henry Ingersoll Bowditch*, Boston: Houghton, Mifflin and Company, 1902; Catherine S. Brown, *Abel Brown, Abolitionist*, edited by Tom Calarco, Jefferson, NC: McFarland, 2006, reprint of 1849 edition; Stanley Harrold, *Subversives: Antislavery Community in Washington, D.C., 1828–1865*, Baton Rouge: LSU Press, 2003; J. C. Lovejoy, *Memoir of Rev. Charles T. Torrey, Who Died in the Penitentiary of Maryland, Where He Was Confined for Showing Mercy to the Poor*, Boston: John P. Jewett & Co., 1847; Thomas Smallwood, *A Narrative of Thomas Smallwood, Giving an Account of His Birth—The Period He Was Held in Slavery—His Release—And Removal to Canada, Etc. Together with an Account of the Underground Railroad*, Toronto: 1851; R. C. Smedley, *History of the Underground Railroad in Chester and Neighboring Counties of Pennsylvania*, Lancaster, PA, 1883.

Tubman, Harriet (1822–1913). Harriet Tubman was one of the most successful Underground Railroad agents during the 1850s. Her struggle to secure freedom, equality, justice and self-determination for herself and others places her among our nation's most remarkable heroes.

Tubman was born Araminta, or "Minty," Ross on the plantation of Anthony Thompson, south of Madison and Woolford in Dorchester County, Maryland. She was the fifth of nine children of Ben and Rit Green Ross, both slaves. Her father, Ben, enslaved by Thompson, supervised the cutting of timber on Thompson's large plantation, while her mother, Rit, probably worked in Thompson's house or in the fields. Harriet, her brothers and sisters, and her mother belonged to Thompson's stepson, Edward Brodess. When Tubman was a small child, she was taken by Brodess from the Thompson plantation to his own small farm about ten miles away in Bucktown, Maryland. Separated from Ben and the large free and enslaved black community that lived on and near Thompson's property, Harriet and her family experienced intense hardship and loneliness.

Brodess had too many slaves to work on his small farm, so he hired some of them out to other farmers. From the young age of six, Harriet rarely lived on the Brodess farm but was hired out to a series of cruel and neglectful masters, who physically and emotionally abused her. She bore the marks of whippings that she received from them until the day she died. Brodess also sold some of his slaves to traders from the Deep South, including Harriet's sisters, Linah, Soph, and Mariah Ritty, permanently tearing her family apart.

During the early 1800s, agriculture on the Eastern Shore of Maryland changed from tobacco growing to grain and timber production. The planting and harvesting of wheat, corn, and oats required a smaller labor force, and therefore many Eastern Shore slaveholders discovered that they no longer needed so many slaves. Some set their enslaved people free, while others chose to profit from their ownership of human beings. In 1808 the international trade in enslaved African peoples was banned, leaving North American slaveholders looking for new sources of slave labor. Cotton production, which required a very large labor force, was expanding rapidly in the Deep South, so many slaveholders, like Edward Brodess in Maryland, decided to sell their slaves to work on plantations in Georgia, South Carolina, Alabama, Mississippi, Louisiana, and Texas. Many black families in Maryland consisted of both free and enslaved members, and they lived with the constant threat of painful, permanent separations.

While working as a field hand on a neighboring plantation near Bucktown when she was about thirteen years old, Tubman was nearly killed by a blow to her head from an iron weight, thrown by a local overseer. It occurred during late autumn, and she had been breaking flax in the field when she was called by the plantation cook to accompany

Slave rescuer Harriet Tubman. Courtesy of the Ohio Historical Society.

her to the nearby dry goods store. When Tubman and the cook arrived at the store, they came upon an overseer chasing a young enslaved man who had abandoned his work in the fields. The young man and the overseer ran into the store; moments later, the enslaved man tried to run out of the store, but the overseer called to Harriet to stop him. She refused and allowed the young man to get away. As she stepped into the doorway of the store, the overseer threw an iron weight from the store counter, hoping to hit the young man and stop him from escaping. But the weight struck Harriet in the head instead, and the blow fractured her skull. It took months for her mother to nurse her back to health. The severe injury left Tubman suffering from headaches, seizures, and sleeping spells—possibly temporal lobe epilepsy—that affected her for the rest of her life.

After Tubman recovered, however, Brodess hired her out to John T. Stewart, a Madison merchant and shipbuilder. This was an important turn of events for Tubman; it brought her back to the black community of free and enslaved people where her father, Ben, lived and where she had been born. Harriet worked for Stewart in a variety of capacities: as a domestic worker, field hand, dock worker, and, finally, timber cutter.

It was during this time that Tubman learned valuable survival skills that would contribute to her success on the Underground Railroad and during the Civil War. She was exposed to the ways of the forests with her father, and she learned important information about freedom in the North from black sailors who came on boats of all sizes to Stewart's wharves. These mariners may have told her of safe places in Baltimore, Philadelphia, New York, and New England. She may also have learned about the hidden communication networks that were supported by black watermen, shipyard workers, and dockworkers, who were perfectly positioned to carry messages back and forth between family and friends in different communities throughout the Chesapeake Bay and along the Atlantic seaboard. The networks would prove crucial to Tubman's future success on the Underground Railroad.

About 1844, when she was twenty-two years old, Harriet married a local freeman named John Tubman. It was at this time that she may have shed her childhood name Minty in favor of Harriet. Brodess allowed her to hire herself out after paying him $60 per year. Everything she earned above that amount she could keep for herself. This enabled her to buy a pair of oxen, which in turn helped increase her earnings by plowing fields and hauling timber. Perhaps she was hoping to buy her freedom from Brodess.

On March 7, 1849, Edward Brodess died on his farm in Bucktown at the age of forty-seven, leaving behind eight children, a widow, and considerable debts. This put Tubman and the rest of her family at risk of being sold to settle Brodess's financial obligations. Tubman could not risk being sold to the Deep South, so in the late fall of 1849, after an unsuccessful attempt to flee with her brothers Ben and Henry, she ran away on her own and tapped into an Underground Railroad that was already operating secretly on the Eastern Shore of Maryland. Traveling by night and using the North Star and instructions from white and black helpers stationed along the way, she reached Philadelphia. There, she began working as a housekeeper, launderer, and cook, saving as much money as possible to help the rest of her family escape.

In December 1850 Tubman conducted her first rescue mission. Her niece, Kessiah, and Kessiah's two children were set to be auctioned to the highest bidder at the courthouse in Cambridge, Maryland. By way of secret communication with Harriet in Philadelphia, Kessiah's free husband, John Bowley, devised a plan to rescue Kessiah and the children. On the day of the auction, John bid on his wife and children, even though he did not have the money to pay for them. Before the auctioneer knew what was happening, John whisked his family away and sailed them all the way to Baltimore's busy waterfront. There the Bowleys were met by Tubman and other family members and friends who worked as seamen, stevedores, ship carpenters, and caulkers on the wharves in Fells Point. They were hidden safely among family and friends living in homes near the docks until Tubman could safely bring them on to Philadelphia.

Her dangerous missions continued throughout the 1850s, as she sought to bring away her sister Rachel, her brothers Robert, Ben, Henry, and Moses, her parents, and other friends and family members. In all, Tubman conducted approximately thirteen escape missions, personally bringing away about seventy individuals, while also giving instructions to about seventy more who found their way to freedom on their own. Tubman used a variety of routes to move back and forth between Maryland and the North; some traversed Dorchester and Caroline counties on the Eastern Shore of Maryland into Delaware, while other routes included water passage through the Chesapeake Bay to Baltimore and then Philadelphia and beyond.

The Underground network that Tubman relied upon was dominated by free and enslaved blacks, like Jacob Jackson and Samuel Green in Dorchester County, Maryland; Tom Tubman and others in Baltimore; William Brinkley and brothers Nat and Abraham Gibbs in Camden, Delaware; and **William Still** of Philadelphia. These people risked their lives to help fugitive slaves reach safety in the North. This network was also supported by white abolitionists, including Quakers Jonah Kelley and Jacob Leverton from the Eastern Shore; **Thomas Garrett** of Wilmington, Delaware; and **Lucretia Mott**, among others, in Philadelphia and neighboring Chester and Lancaster counties and across the Delaware River in New Jersey. After leaving Philadelphia, Tubman sought help from Jacob Gibbs and others in New York City, who would send Tubman along to Albany, where **Stephen Myers**, a black abolitionist and the leader of the local Vigilance Committee, sheltered them. In many of the places Tubman traveled, she could depend on the support of friends and relatives who were also Maryland fugitive slaves, some of whom had fled years before Tubman had done so. Harriet also depended on the help of the **Reverend Jermaine Loguen** in Syracuse and **Frederick Douglass** in Rochester, who sent her along to the Suspension Bridge at Niagara Falls for the last leg of the journey to freedom in Canada.

Tubman to the Rescue: The Charles Nalle Incident

Shortly before the outbreak of the Civil War, fugitive slave Charles Nalle of Virginia was the object of one of America's most dramatic rescues. He had run away from his master (and half-brother), Blucher W. Hansbrough of Culpeper County, Virginia, in mid-October 1858. Accompanied by another local slave, Jim Banks, he traveled to Washington, D.C., using a valid pass, then fled via the Georgetown waterfront, assisted by Minot Crosby and other members of the Underground Railroad, to Philadelphia. **William Still** helped arrange his passage farther north.

In early 1860 while in Sand Lake, New York, Nalle was learning to read when a scoundrel uncovered his true identity. Meanwhile, Nalle moved to nearby Troy to take a job as coachman for one of the region's wealthiest industrialists, and the betrayer contacted Nalle's master for the reward. On April 27, 1860, a Virginia slavecatcher and a deputy U.S. marshal nabbed Nalle in Troy and quickly adjudicated him under the Fugitive Slave Law. But before Nalle could be sent home, a mob numbering several hundred persons, both blacks and whites, surrounded the U.S. commissioner's office. **Harriet Tubman** (in town visiting relatives) and others wrestled with police and finally freed Nalle.

Despite escaping across the Hudson River, Nalle was recaptured in West Troy. Several hundred enraged citizens stormed the stronghold, braving police gunfire, and Nalle was liberated again. Weeks later, locals purchased his freedom for $650, enabling Nalle to reunite with his already freed wife and children, making him the only slave whom the Underground Railroad freed four times—once by stealth from Georgetown, twice by force, and the final time by purchase.

Scott Christianson

Tubman used various strategies to fool pursuing slavecatchers: acting as an old woman, dressing like a man, or traveling south to throw hunters off her tracks. She used songs, like "Go Down Moses" and "Bound for the Promised Land," to signal to her charges that it was safe to come out of their hiding places. She also carried a pistol not only for protection from dangerous, roving slavecatchers but also to encourage weary and hesitant fugitive slaves who wanted to turn back.

The Fugitive Slave Act of 1850 left most refugee slaves vulnerable to recapture in Northern cities and towns, and many fled to the safety of Canada. Tubman brought many of her charges to St. Catharines, Ontario, where they settled into a growing community of self-liberators who sought to re-create a community of mutual support and assistance. She successfully rescued her brother Moses in 1851, and three years later on Christmas Day 1854, she brought away her three other brothers, Robert, Ben, and Henry. When Tubman brought them to William Still's office in Philadelphia, where they were provided food, warm clothing, and transportation, the three brothers changed their names to John, James, and William Henry Stewart. In the spring of 1857 Tubman's father came under suspicion for being an Underground Railroad agent. Having aided in the escape of several fugitive slaves throughout the 1850s, he was now at risk of being thrown in jail. Tubman came to their aid and brought her parents, Ben and Rit, to Canada, where they joined their sons, who had established homes in St. Catharines.

Tubman's dangerous missions won the admiration of black and white abolitionists throughout the North who provided her with funds to continue her activities. In 1858 Tubman met the legendary freedom fighter **John Brown** in her North Street home in St. Catharines. Impressed by his passion for ending slavery, she committed herself to helping him recruit former slaves to join his planned raid at Harpers Ferry, Virginia. Though she hoped to be at his side when the raid took place in October 1859, illness may have prevented her from joining him.

In 1859 William Henry Seward, Lincoln's future secretary of state, sold Tubman a home on the outskirts of Auburn, New York, in the town of Fleming, where she eventually settled her aged parents and other family members. On her way to Boston in April 1860, Tubman became the heroine of the day when she helped rescue a fugitive slave, **Charles Nalle**, from the custody of U.S. marshals charged with returning him to his Virginia master. In November 1860 Tubman made a last attempt to rescue her sister Rachel and Rachel's two children, Ben and Angerine. Rachel died before she could be rescued, and Tubman was unable to pay a $30 bribe to have her orphaned nieces brought to her. However, she did bring away another young family: Stephen and Maria Ennals and their three little children. This was her last rescue mission.

In early 1862 Tubman joined Northern abolitionists in support of Union activities at Port Royal, South Carolina. Throughout the Civil War she provided badly needed nursing care to black soldiers and hundreds of newly liberated slaves who crowded Union camps. Tubman's military service expanded to include spying and scouting behind Confederate lines. In early June 1863 she became the first woman to command an armed military raid when she guided Col. James Montgomery and his Second South Carolina Black Regiment up the Combahee River, routing Confederate forces, destroying stockpiles of cotton, food, and weapons, and liberating over 750 slaves. She witnessed the famed battle of Fort Wagner in Charleston Harbor, where the Massachusetts Fifty-fourth Regiment fought so valiantly and demonstrated the courage and military skills of black troops. Tubman worked as a spy, cook, launderer, and teacher during the war, slipping in and out of her various roles as wartime needs demanded.

After the war, Tubman rejoined family and friends who had returned to the United States from Canada and settled in Auburn. She began another career as a community activist, humanitarian, and suffragist. In 1869 Sarah Bradford published a short biography of Tubman called *Scenes in the Life of Harriet Tubman,* bringing brief fame and financial relief to Tubman and her family. Tubman married Nelson Davis, a veteran, that same year, her husband John Tubman having been killed in 1867 in Dorchester County, Maryland. Though she and Davis ran a brick-making business and sold crops grown on their small farm, she struggled financially the rest of her life. Denied a military pension, she eventually received a widow's pension as the wife of Nelson Davis and, later, a Civil War nurse's pension.

Active in the woman's suffrage movement, Tubman appeared at local and national suffrage conventions until the early 1900s. Throughout the last decades of the nineteenth century, Tubman welcomed scores of sick, disabled, homeless, orphaned, and destitute people into her home in Fleming, New York. Her humanitarian work triumphed with the opening of the Harriet Tubman Home for the Aged, located on land abutting her own property in Auburn, which she successfully purchased by mortgage and then transferred to the African Methodist Episcopal Zion Church in 1903. She died of pneumonia at the age of ninety-one on March 10, 1913, and was buried at Fort Hill cemetery in Auburn, New York.

SUGGESTED READING: Catherine Clinton, *The Road to Freedom*, Boston: Little, Brown and Company, 2004; Jean McMahon Humez, *Harriet Tubman: The Life and the Life Stories*, Madison: University of Wisconsin Press, 2003; Kate Clifford Larson, *Bound for the Promised Land: Portrait of an American Hero*, New York: Ballantine Books, 2004.

Kate Clifford Larson

Turner, Nat (1800–1831). Nat Turner led the bloodiest and most influential slave revolt in U.S. history. Slavery in the Southern states and living conditions for free blacks in America were never quite the same thereafter during the antebellum period. The revolt induced more oppressive conditions that compelled an increasing number of slaves to seek their freedom, which in turn increased the need for the Underground Railroad.

Born a slave in Southampton County, Virginia, to pious parents, Turner was taught from the age of three by his mother, grandmother, and preacher father that he was destined to be a prophet and a "Moses" for his people. He also found that he had uncommon gifts and was able to read without being taught. His prodigious displays of learning at an early age resulted in special treatment from other slaves, and he began to believe in his destiny. Because of this, he was very serious as a child and often kept to himself.

Thomas Gray, who interviewed Turner for his *Confessions*, recorded the day before his execution, wrote the following about him:

> He . . . possesses all uncommon share of intelligence, with a mind capable of attaining anything, but warped and perverted by the influence of early impressions. He is below the ordinary stature, though strong and active, having the true Negro face, every feature of which is strongly marked. . . . The calm, deliberate composure with which he spoke of his late deeds and intentions, the expression of his fiend-like face when excited by enthusiasm, still bearing the stains of the blood of helpless innocence about him . . . yet daring to raise his manacled hands to heaven, with a spirit soaring above the attributes of man; I looked on him and my blood curdled in my veins.

About the age of twenty-five, Turner sensed the approaching fulfillment of his destiny and ran away for thirty days. He was criticized for returning by fellow slaves, who said that a man of his abilities should not serve any master. At this time he withdrew from his social relationships and engaged in prayer and fasting. Over the course of several years, a series of visions communicated his purpose: to bring about that time "when the first should be last and the last should be first," when he "should arise and slay [his] enemies with their own weapons." A total eclipse of the sun on February 12, 1831, was the sign that his preparations should begin.

Another celestial event on August 13 signaled to him "that the great day of judgment was at hand." On August 22, the Sabbath day, he joined six comrades for dinner. They included Hark Travers, his friend Jack, Samuel Edwards, Henry Porter, Nelson Williams, and a slave known only as Will, whose master had treated him with great cruelty and had sold his wife to slave traders.

Later that night, armed with guns, swords, and axes, they began to massacre every white person, regardless of sex or age, in their path. The first to suffer their wrath was the family of Turner's master, Joseph Travis, whom Turner described in his *Confessions* "as a kind master" and of whom he "had no cause to complain." They continued on to the next plantation and went from house to house, killing white people in their beds. Will, armed with a large ax, was particularly brutal. As they proceeded, they were joined by many of the slaves freed during the rampage, and his band at one point numbered fifty or more.

However, word of the massacre spread, and the band came to a farm where they met armed resistance, in which not only the whites but also slaves fought them. The militia soon joined the fighting, and some of Turner's men were killed and wounded. They eventually were subdued by greater numbers.

In all, they succeeded in reaching nine plantations and killing more than fifty persons. Turner, being separated from his men, went back to his master's plantation. He gathered provisions and dug a hole under a pile of fence rails, where he concealed himself for six weeks. After that he began to sneak out, trying to learn information that might help him escape. But he was afraid to speak to anyone. This went on for about two weeks when a dog alerted his presence to two blacks, who on learning his identity ran away. From that point on, Turner was a hunted man. Finally, after two weeks of evasion, he was discovered by Benjamin Phipps. Turner had a sword, but Phipps had a gun and was about to shoot Turner until Turner dropped his sword and surrendered. On November 11, 1831, Turner was hung in Jerusalem, Virginia, after which his body was skinned.

The massacre had terrified the South, and during the period that Turner was at large, atrocities were carried out against blacks in Virginia and the neighboring Southern states in which their properties were invaded and ransacked, and many innocent blacks were whipped, attacked, or even lynched. One particularly cruel practice that occurred was half hanging in which attackers suspended blacks from a tree with a rope about their necks, adjusted so as to not quite strangle them and allow them to be the targets of men and boys who pelted them with rotten eggs.

The climate of fear that was created is aptly described in this excerpt from James McDowell's address in 1832 at the Virginia House of Delegates:

> We are in peril of our lives—[the Turner affair has] erected a peaceful and confiding portion of the State into a military camp . . . outlawed from pity the unfortunate beings whose brothers had offended . . . barred every door, penetrated every bosom with fear or suspicion . . . banished every sense of security from every man's dwelling. . . . Was it the fear of Nat. Turner . . . which produced such effects? . . . No, sir, it was the suspicion eternally attached to the slave himself; the suspicion that a Nat Turner might be in every family—that the same bloody deed might be acted over at any time, and in any place—that the materials for it were spread through the land, and were always ready for a like explosion.

More repressive laws regarding slaves were passed in Virginia and other Southern states, and these laws became the legacy of Nat Turner. A significant measure adopted widely was a legal restriction on black preachers, like Turner, who had the ear of the slaves. In many areas of the South, religious services by blacks without the presence of a white person were prohibited. In some cases, blacks were not even permitted to have their own churches and were required to go to white churches, where they were placed in segregated pews. Laws to restrict the meeting of groups of black persons were also put in effect as well as greater restrictions on their freedom of movement. Other laws prevented the sale of guns or liquor to free blacks and banished free blacks who could not get a character reference from a white person. Societies supporting the abolition of slavery in the South virtually ceased to exist after Nat Turner, and arguments using the Bible to justify slavery grew in popularity. Nightly slave patrols increased, and gradually the South turned into an increasingly repressive police state.

Even in the North, blacks were forced to organize self-help groups because of Black Codes and rigid laws that limited their freedom, laws made partly because of the fear created by the Nat Turner insurrection.

SUGGESTED READING: Herbert Aptheker, *American Negro Slave Revolts*, 1943; Henry Brown, *Narrative of Henry Box Brown, Who Escaped from Slavery Enclosed in a Box Three Feet Long, Two Wide, and Two and a Half High*, Boston: Brown & Stearns, 1849; Joshua Coffin, *An Account of Some of the Principal Slave Insurrections, and Others, Which Have Occurred, or Been Attempted in the United States and Elsewhere, during the Last Two Centuries*, New York: The American Anti-Slavery Society, 1860; Thomas Gray, *The Confessions of Nat Turner*, 1831; Harriet Jacobs, *Incidents in the Life of a Slave Girl*, Boston, 1861; Leila Amos Pendleton, *A Narrative of the Negro*, Washington DC: Press of R. L. Pendleton, 1912.

V

Van Zandt, John (1791–1847). John Van Zandt is best known as the model for the character of John Van Tromp in **Harriet Beecher Stowe**'s 1852 novel *Uncle Tom's Cabin.* He was a highly moral man who sacrificed his well-being so that others could be free.

Born in Fleming County, Kentucky, John Van Zandt inherited a large plantation with slaves. A devout Methodist strongly grounded in the teachings of John Wesley, he concluded that slavery was a sin. In one account it is said he was influenced by a dream in which God spoke to him. It compelled Van Zandt to sell his farm and move north to Ohio. He soon purchased land near the town of Sharon on Mt. Pierpont, using bricks from a demolished Presbyterian church to build his hilltop home.

Van Zandt's new home became an Underground Railroad station and was the stop before the Spread Eagle Tavern, an inn and stagecoach stop near Sharonville about four miles away. Harriet Beecher Stowe's use of Van Zandt as a model for her character John Van Tromp was based on an actual experience of her family. One of her servants was being pursued by her former owner, and it was advised by legal counsel to put her in hiding. One rainy night, Stowe's husband secreted the servant with Van Zandt. In Stowe's book, Van Tromp is described as a tall, muscular man, much like Van Zandt.

According to a letter written by his son N. L. Van Zandt in 1892, Van Zandt rendezvoused with fugitive slaves in Cincinnati and took them in his covered wagon as far north as Wilmington, a distance of forty miles. His son also forwarded fugitive slaves to the Spread Eagle Tavern on occasion, using a sleigh or carriage.

However, the night of May 23, 1842, proved to be Van Zandt's undoing. Nine slaves had escaped from the farm of Wharton Jones in Boone County, Kentucky. They ranged in age from forty-five to a toddler aged two: six men and three women that included a family of five. They crossed the Ohio River and were directed by a man named Alley to Lane Seminary. There they were told to get into a covered wagon and wait. They waited until three o'clock the next morning when Van Zandt arrived. He told Andrew, one of the fugitive slaves, to take the reins and head toward Springboro.

As they sped forward, the wagon was noticed by two men, Hargrave and Hefferman, who knew Van Zandt and became suspicious because someone else was driving his wagon. Aware of Van Zandt's activities and hoping for a reward, they signaled the wagon to stop. The two were armed, and riding up to the wagon, Hargrave demanded that Andrew come to a halt while Hefferman brought his horse around to the front. When Andrew pulled to a halt, Van Zandt inside the wagon ordered Andrew not to stop and to run over the men. Andrew cracked the whip and knocked Heffernan off his mount. But Hefferman was able to seize the reins from Andrew and stop the wagon. Andrew jumped off, and Van Zandt came from inside and took the reins, but Hefferman held the horses fast. Another slave, a boy of thirteen named Jackson, also ran off.

At this point, others approached the wagon. A man named Bates who knew Van Zandt asked, "Have you a load of fugitive slaves?" to which Van Zandt replied, "They are, by nature, as free as you or I."

The remaining seven slaves were carted off and lodged in the jail at Covington, Kentucky until their return to Wharton Jones. Van Zandt also was arrested and put in jail.

Jones had suffered a considerable loss. Not only was he required to pay Hargrave and Hefferman a mandatory reward of $450, as required by Kentucky law, along with $150 for their expenses, but he also had lost the services of Andrew, valued at $600 (the boy Jackson did return, however). He intended to recoup his loss through litigation. He brought two civil actions against Van Zandt in federal court. The first was for $1,200, to recover the costs of Andrew and the reward to Hefferman and Hargrave. The other was for the $500 owed to him under the provisions of the Fugitive Slave Law. Van Zandt enlisted the legal services of Salmon P. Chase, then a young and promising lawyer, who was making a reputation for himself defending fugitive slaves and abolitionists.

The first trial was held before U.S. Supreme Court Judge John McLean (before 1869, Supreme Court justices were required to act as judges in the various circuit courts). Chase claimed that Van Zandt had no foreknowledge of the slaves' arrival at his wagon and believed that they were free persons. But the facts and the witnesses did not corroborate this, and the judge cautioned the jury against feeling sympathy for him. Under such guidelines, the question of his guilt was undeniable.

Chase filed a countermotion and appealed for a new trial to the Supreme Court, alleging procedural errors and appealing to a higher law that transcended human law. Although the judge granted his appeal, he took issue with Chase's position on the higher law. The judge said that decisions must be based only on the law as it is and not on whether they believed that law to be just. If they believed it to be unjust, then they must change it. Arbitrary decisions about whether to obey a law based on one's beliefs, he said, would be tantamount to anarchy.

Despite losing his case, Van Zandt resumed his agency with the Underground Railroad. During the summer of 1843 William Cornell, a farmer who knew Van Zandt, recalled picking up two young blacks. They were silent until they reached Mt. Pierpont, the site of his farm, when one of them exclaimed, "There it is!" Cornell then took them to the road leading to Van Zandt's house, where they got off.

The case would impair not only Van Zandt's finances but also his reputation. His church enacted sanctions against him, barring him from church privileges, and his friends avoided him. After the 1847 Supreme Court decision that rejected Chase's appeal by a vote of 9–0, Van Zandt was nearing death and sold his properties to pay the judgment. Chase asked him during a visit to his office if he had any regrets.

Van Zandt's eyes lit up, and then, Chase wrote, he replied, "No. If a single word could restore the man who escaped and save me from all sacrifice, I would not utter it. And such I believe is the universal spirit of those who have aided the oppressed in regaining their freedom."

On May 25, 1847, Van Zandt died. His gravestone, which stood near Mt. Pierpont, was repeatedly vandalized and eventually moved to Wesleyan Cemetery in Cincinnati. Its inscription reads as follows:

> In him Christianity had a living witness. He saw God as his father, and received every man as his brother, the cause of the poor, the orphan and the oppressed was his cause. He fed clothed sheltered and guarded them. He was eyes to the blind, and feet to the lame. He was a tender father, a devoted husband, and a friend to all. He is what is here described, because he was a Christian Philanthropist who practiced what he believed and he thus lived practicing his faith.

SUGGESTED READING: Wilbur Siebert, *The Mysteries of Ohio's Underground Railroads*, Columbus, OH: Long's College Book Company, 1951; Mark S. Weiner, *Black Trials*, "Silent Witness," ch. 6, New York: Knopf, 2004.

W

Webster, Delia (1817–1904). Delia Webster was one of the boldest individuals to have aided slaves as a conductor along the Underground Railroad. She charmed angry mobs, law enforcement officials, and slavecatchers alike. So skillful was she at handling her adversaries that abolitionists sometimes wondered if she had betrayed the cause. But despite her notoriety, the evidence suggests that she aided only a handful of runaway slaves.

Born in Vergennes, Vermont, a tiny and remote rural community within walking distance of **Rowland T. Robinson**'s Underground Railroad station in Ferrisburgh, Webster was a teacher's aide by the age of twelve at the Vergennes Classical Institute. By 1835 she was teaching full-time in a neighboring town. Her parents were farmers who supported abolitionism, as did most of their neighbors, with the Ferrisburgh Anti-Slavery Society boasting 205 members in 1837. Her health began to decline in 1839, and with local doctors unable to find a remedy, she was sent to Saratoga, New York, where an older sister lived, in the hope that the healing properties of its spa would restore her. It proved beneficial, and her life took on a peripatetic existence until she enrolled at Oberlin College in 1842.

At Oberlin, she met a couple named Spencer and joined them on a trip to Kentucky, where they conducted art classes in Georgetown, Cynthiana, and Fleming County, locations just north of Lexington. The Spencers started the Lexington Academy for young ladies, but both became ill and decided to leave Kentucky. They turned over the school to Webster. She quickly made it a success, and at the time of her arrest, her school had an enrollment approaching 100 students.

In early September of 1844, **Calvin Fairbank**, a minister and student at Oberlin College, came to Lexington and moved into the boardinghouse where Webster lived. His purpose was to rescue the wife and children of Gilson Berry, a slave who had escaped to Oberlin with the help of Webster. Fairbank had written her a letter explaining his intentions. However, the plan to aid Berry's family went awry. Fairbank was unable to obtain the funds for a conveyance, and Berry's wife was unable to meet with him. Webster then introduced **Lewis Hayden**, a slave with a wife and child, who desperately wanted to obtain his freedom and who had saved up enough money to pay for the necessary carriage and horses.

On the night of September 28, Fairbank and Webster rendezvoused with the Hayden family near the home of Cassius Clay. They were employing a slave named Israel to drive a two-horse carriage, which they rented from Parker Craig. A couple of weeks earlier, Fairbank had organized the seventy-five-mile itinerary to Maysville and across the state border to Red Oak, Ohio. But a fateful delay occurred when one of their horses became too sick to continue, and they were forced to stop in Millersburg, about twenty-five miles from Lexington. They stopped at a tavern, where they obtained a fresh horse from Holloway, the proprietor. After crossing the Ohio River on a ferry, Webster was dropped off at the home of Eli Collins in Ripley, eight miles from the ferry crossing, while Fairbank took the Haydens to Red Oak, another five miles, and the home of Gordon Hopkins.

Their problems began on the return trip when they stopped to retrieve the sick horse and found that it had died. Rather than use Holloway's horse, they hitched up a stray horse that had been following them for their rest of their return trip, thinking that it might belong to someone in Lexington. While returning, they met Craig along the road near Paris. He had heard about his horse and was on his way to Millersburg, but now that he learned that the story was true, he held Fairbank responsible and said that he would need to pay for it. Fairbank balked at the sum demanded and said that Israel had noticed that the horse was ill when they started. He said he would agree to arbitration and pay whatever sum was decided. Craig would not yield and near Lexington took over the reins of the carriage and parked it in front of the Megowan Hotel. Craig then demanded payment, but Fairbank countered that he was not carrying the requested amount and that he would pay only what was decided after arbitration. This infuriated Craig, who demanded that Fairbank get out of the carriage. Fairbank responded that he needed to return Webster to her home. By this time a crowd had begun to gather. Craig's fury and boldness increased, and he seized Fairbank by the collar and cried out to the crowd, "Bring a rope. Bring a rope quick. I've got the man that killed my horse."

Webster, who until this time had suffered in silence, came to Fairbank's defense. She suggested that they go to the boardinghouse and discuss the matter in a reasonable manner and that if all else failed, she would lend Fairbank the money or even pay for the horse herself. Craig suggested that Webster return to her boardinghouse while he and Fairbank discussed the matter and ordered her driver to proceed. However, as they pulled away, the mob seized Fairbank, who cried out not to tie him up, and she ordered the driver to stop. Moments later her carriage was surrounded by a huge mob, and James Megowan, the hotel's proprietor, came to her assistance and agreed to accompany her to the boardinghouse.

When Webster returned, she found that some things in her room had been moved around and that her window, which she had locked shut before leaving, was open. Her landlady denied that she or anyone else had entered, but Webster knew better.

At midnight a banging at the front door awakened them. Men had come for Webster. They took her to back to Megowan's and locked her in the debtor's room, a large, comfortable apartment. What Webster would learn was that Megowan's not only was a hotel that accommodated up to 100 guests but also served as the city jail and that her commodious room sat just above the dungeon where the jail's cells were located.

What Webster also did not know at the time was that incriminating evidence of her role in aiding slaves had been found in her room: a letter from John Mifflin Brown, a black Oberlin minister, who had recruited Fairbank for the Berry rescue. In the letter, he relayed Berry's thanks to Webster for helping him to escape. Also, a letter was found on Fairbank that he had not as yet delivered that incriminated both of them. It was dated September 24 and signed "Frater." In it, Fairbank had written the following:

> You well know . . . that . . . before I left, expressed some doubt as to his [Berry's] honesty . . . I have spent my money searching for his children and his wife. . . . I am now living upon the money of one Lewis, whom, in consequence of this failure, I intend to fetch with me, likewise his wife and child—a very active man, worth ten of Berry.
>
> . . . . Miss W. will not come away, but will come across the river with us; then I shall have to put these on the underground line and send them on, till I go back with Miss W. I must go back with her, because the people will suppose us to have gone riding, or rather to spend the Sabbath in another place, and it would create suspicion if I were not to return with her.

The next morning the full weight of her predicament thrust itself on Webster. First, there was the hammering of the shackles upon Fairbank and his cries of pain, which she witnessed from her window. But worse to come were the fifty lashes upon the back of the old slave, Israel, the driver on their mission, who begged for mercy as he protested his innocence.

Indictments were handed down, with three charges against Fairbank and four against Webster. They were to be tried separately, which worked out in her favor. In the meantime, she steadfastly maintained her innocence, and it was decided to try her on only one of the charges. As she awaited her trial, her health broke down and she was bedridden for a month. But as the days leading up to her trial approached, her health improved and her father, Benajah Webster, made the long trip from Vermont to Kentucky to fortify her spirits and be with her during her trial.

Despite Webster's refusal to admit to her obvious guilt, and contradictions in her statements that suggested she was lying, she made a favorable impression on the jury. Although they found her guilty and sentenced her to two years in the penitentiary, they presented her with a letter, signed by all twelve jurors and addressed to Kentucky governor William Owsley, requesting an immediate pardon.

Webster wanted a retrial, and she continued to protest her innocence. But at the insistence of her father and her lawyer, she agreed to write to Owsley and ask for a pardon. She included not only the letter from the jury but also many other letters supporting her character, including letters from Henry Clay and William Slade, the governor of Vermont.

The move from the Megowan Hotel to the penitentiary in Frankfort turned out much more favorably than she expected. The prison warden, Newton Craig, was the brother-in-law of Parker Craig, the man whose carriage Fairbank had rented. He was a man who had been brought up in the Southern tradition of treating ladies with deference and promised Webster that he would not allow anyone to abuse or treat her unkindly.

As a special consideration to her gender, a small house was built for her. It was described by Webster as "well furnished, and sufficiently large and commodious to answer the purposes of workshop, study, lodging, dining-room and parlor." Here she was free to open her windows, step outside at any time, dress as she pleased, and read any number of books, a large number of which were at her disposal. Craig's wife, Lucy, developed a friendship with her and "took care that [Webster's] food was of the best and most delicious quality." She was not without company either. Most if not all of the state's legislators paid a visit, according to Webster, and Lucy sometimes took her on trips into Frankfort. The only work required was some occasional sewing. "I was treated more like a daughter than a prisoner," Webster wrote.

She had been there only a few days when Owsley contacted her about the pardon. He said he would grant it only on the condition of her promise never to return to Kentucky. But Webster would not accept this. So, the matter was left unfinished, for the time.

Meanwhile, Fairbank had successfully petitioned the legislature for a change of venue for his trial. All that was needed was the okay from Owsley. However, the governor made it known that he would not pardon Webster until after Fairbank's trial. Because the change of venue involved a long delay, Fairbank abandoned his request. He also decided to change his plea to guilty and beg the mercy of the court. These events worked in the favor of Webster, whom Fairbank continually claimed was totally innocent. These statements by Fairbank, and the favor she cultivated during the visits by the governor and the members of the state legislature, improved the public's opinion of her and made her pardon more palatable.

Fairbank was found guilty and sentenced to fifteen years in the penitentiary. Six days after he entered the prison walls, Webster was granted her pardon and the following day began her journey home to Vermont with her father.

What followed continues to baffle historians. Webster wrote a pamphlet proclaiming her innocence while at the same time championing her persecutors. Called *Kentucky Jurisprudence*, it includes a little biography, a recounting of the events that led to her incarceration, a narration of her time at the Megowan Hotel, a recap of her trial, and a description of her six weeks at the Frankfort Penitentiary. Although she admits to abhorring slavery, she wrote the following:

> It is true I denied being an Abolitionist in the sense of Kentucky construction, and I still deny it; for I am, and ever have been, as bitterly opposed to what is termed "Negro Stealing;" as Kentuckians themselves. . . . Nor do I approve of any thing which has a tendency to sow discord or to create feelings of animosity between the North and South. I am decidedly opposed to a dissolution of the Union. For I consider the North as deeply implicated in the guilt of slavery as the South.

These words need to be considered in light of damaging evidence that clearly indicated that Webster had indeed been involved in "Negro Stealing" as she termed it.

After the publication of her pamphlet, Webster attended a major antislavery convention in Boston in October of 1845 to promote its sale. Accompanying her was Rev. Norris Day, a resident of Ferrisburgh and an evangelical minister and abolitionist lecturer of considerable accomplishment. Day acted as her spokesperson, but what he would say was quite puzzling. Webster did aid fugitive slaves, he claimed, and not only in the case in which she was charged but on other occasions. However, she was not guilty of the charges, which stated that she "seduced" and "enticed" slaves to run away, and in the eyes of Southerners, this was much different from merely aiding them.

These statements caused an uproar among some abolitionists who charged Webster with duplicity, notably Amos Phelps, editor of the *Anti-Slavery Reporter*, who noted that in her letter requesting a pardon from Governor Owsley, which was included in *Jurisprudence*, she stated that she did not "aid" fugitive slaves. Furthermore, as to her claim that Southerners viewed seducing and enticing as entirely different from aiding fugitive slaves, a remonstrance against her pardon sent by 120 citizens of Fayette County, where Lexington is located, opposed the pardon because she "aided" fugitive slaves. Also troubling was her praise of Southern slaveholders and her apologetic tone toward them.

In several letters to editors, however, Webster made it perfectly clear that she strongly believed that it was proper to influence slaves to seek their freedom. She even repudiated an affidavit made by Calvin Fairbank included in her *Jurisprudence*, in which Fairbank disavowed her role in aiding Hayden, saying that she was coerced into including it by her father. Hayden, who had a reunion with Webster at the Boston convention and who knew the truth about her, wrote in a letter shortly after that she was "a lady whom I shall ever revere notwithstanding all that has been said against her."

Webster's duplicity may be explained by her continuing relationship with Newton and Lucy Craig. Webster's comment that she was treated like a daughter was fitting. In fact, during the fall of 1846, Webster returned to Frankfort as the guest of the Craigs for a duration of "many" months. At this time, it is believed, she became romantically involved with Newton Craig. An article published in the *Louisville Democrat* in 1854 stated that "she entered the habitation of the Keeper himself. . . . Not content merely to take this open and convicted abolitionist. . . . under his own roof. . . . he gallanted her in the streets of Frankfort, and flaunted with her in his carriage from place to place."

Craig was a man of means as result of his position as warden of the prison, which was run as a business, using the labor of his 150 or so inmates in occupations at the prison and in raising crops at his nearby farm in Georgetown. He even opened up opportunities for Webster family members, and one of Webster's sisters and her husband moved to Frankfort in 1847; her brother and his family followed in 1848. Although Webster concealed her relationship with the Craigs from the public, saying later that she remained in the East during this period, she did admit to being "constantly beset with entreaties and the most urgent solicitations to return to Kentucky" to either start a new school or be provided with a farm from which she could derive a comfortable living. According to her, during this time she was teaching in Vermont, and then she moved to New York City to teach for a year. However, she claimed that poor health led her to return to the South again in 1849, where she took up residence in Madison, Indiana.

The choice of Madison was calculated. Craig Newton had business dealings there, and he moved his children there, where they came under the tutelage of Webster. It is not clear how many of the six Craig children were her pupils, but apparently all but the youngest were at one time or another being instructed by her. Letters that Craig wrote to her also suggest an ongoing long-distance relationship. In one from 1849, he included the following endearment: "I LOVE you most dearly, and can never prosper in your absence."

Also, during the summers of 1849 and 1850, Craig traveled to Vermont to accompany Webster to the Midwest after her visits to see her parents. In January 1851 Webster's father died. At the time she was in Madison teaching Craig's children, and in May 1851 she took them along when she went back to Vermont to console her grieving mother. She remained there until November 1851. At this point, the relationship between Webster and Craig had become strained. Nevertheless Craig, who had become friends with Webster's brother Warren, had set him up with a good job in Kentucky. In a letter to another family member during this time, Warren suggested that the relationship between Delia and Craig was souring.

Whatever happened, it opened the way for Rev. Norris Day to return into Webster's life, if indeed he had ever left, and he moved in with Webster in Madison. Apparently, he and Craig had clashed during the latter's visit to Vermont in 1849. In November of 1852 he, Webster, and two others purchased a 600-acre plot of land on the Kentucky side of the Ohio River in Trimble County just south of Madison. Her hope was to establish a school on the plan of Oberlin, a dream she envisioned in 1849 when passing through that section. But establishing such a school in Kentucky prior to the Civil War was asking for trouble. Rev. John Fee nearly lost his life after he founded Berea College, the first college to admit blacks in Kentucky, in 1855.

Taking possession of the land during the summer of 1853, they moved into separate residences on adjoining plots of land. As soon as they moved, it seemed that local slaves began disappearing. According to the *Louisville Democrat*, strange steamboats were stopping at night along the shore near Webster's property, and an estimated $25,000 to $30,000 worth of slaves had disappeared in the short period since their move.

On November 29, 1853, Day was brought to trial for aiding two fugitive slaves. However, a hung jury forced the judge to dismiss the case. In February 1854 indictments were brought against both Day and Webster, charging them with suspicion of aiding about twenty fugitive slaves in Trimble County, the number who had vanished since they had moved into the county. These indictments were primarily speculative, however.

A posse surrounded Day's house one night late in January. They banged on his door and demanded entry. But when no one would let them in, they sent one of their members to get a warrant while they watched the house to prevent Day from leaving. At the time, Day's nephew was living with him. He was about the same size and build, and he put on his uncle's coat and hat and ran from the house. This led the posse astray long enough for Day to sneak out and hurry down to the riverbank and take a boat across the river to Madison. The next day he went to see his lawyer, but before he could take the necessary legal action, the governor of Indiana, responding to the Kentucky indictment, issued a warrant for Day's arrest, which occurred on February 1.

Day's hearing began on February 7, but the judge recessed for two days in order to consider his decision. The result was a dismissal because the prosecution did not present the proper documents. As soon as the hearing ended, a horse was waiting for Day, and he was accompanied by a friend who led him on the road out of town, never to return.

Meanwhile Webster, who had spent much of the week visiting Day in jail, faced a similar predicament. The same day that Day initially went to court for his hearing, a mob of about fifty angry men surrounded her house. She invited them inside, and her friendliness at once disarmed them. After about forty-five minutes, they finally brought up the subject of their visit. They were concerned about her "running off slaves" and demanded that she leave the state. Webster was outnumbered but not intimidated. First, she said that their demand was illegal, and second, she described the method of its delivery as cowardly. She said she would not allow anyone to force her to leave her home. The men left and Webster sent a note to the court expressing these same views.

However, a month later, a smaller committee came out to her house. Although their appearance was not nearly so menacing, their message was as follows:

> Unless you consent forthwith to sell us your plantation, and speedily leave the State, no more to return, you will be mobbed at a dead hour of the night. And . . . your fences will be burned, your fine orchard ruined, your valuable timber destroyed, you cattle and horses slain before your eyes, your barns and outhouses burned, you dwelling houses blown up, and yourself assassinated at the midnight hour.

Webster told them to go right ahead, that she would be home waiting for them, that she was a law-abiding citizen who paid her taxes and was not about to give up her home and would sacrifice her life in defense of it.

Six days later a posse of armed men surrounded her house while she was away. The next day after she returned, the sheriff took her into custody, put her in jail, and refused to allow her to contact a lawyer. There was a cold spell that spring, and the temperature dropped to twenty-nine degrees one night before the jailer finally consented to light the jail cell's stove. However, there was no vent, and so though there was heat, there also was smoke. The conditions were very uncomfortable; fortunately, Webster was rescued by the goodwill of a wealthy slaveholder's wife, who brought clothing and other necessities, and contacted her lawyer, who obtained a writ of habeas corpus to have Webster released.

Attempts at eviction were not Webster's only legal problems. Nearly a year before, Newton Craig had filed a suit against her for money she apparently owed him. It was the beginning of a bitter battle between the former lovers. The position of state prison warden was an elected one, and Craig was running for reelection. Webster sent five personal letters that he had written to her from 1846 to 1851, including the one in which he professed his love, to a Louisville newspaper. The publication of these letters brought on a scandal and led to his defeat. Craig responded by having the three charges on which Webster was not tried in 1844 reactivated. He then set out with a posse of men to serve the warrant himself and get his revenge. Webster was warned in time and able to flee to Madison. She hid there until a requisition for her arrest on the Kentucky warrant was issued. Upon finding her one night, the Madison sheriff attempted to take her back to Kentucky but was unable to locate a boat to cross the river and locked her up in Madison. In the morning, before the sheriff could return her to Kentucky, Webster's lawyer obtained a writ of habeas corpus, which mandated that the trial be held in Madison.

Public opinion was strongly in her favor. Nevertheless, Craig came to town with a posse of his own men, and though he did not attend the trial, he awaited the results, hoping to have her back under his control again at the prison, as he still had another year left to serve as warden. In the end, Webster was vindicated, and the charges were thrown out by the judge.

On leaving, Craig and his men were surrounded by a mob, and Craig was shot in the back and critically wounded. He asked to see Webster one last time. However, his wife Lucy, who had come to be by his side, would not allow it, and he managed to pull through.

Following Webster's trial in July of 1854, she journeyed to Vermont to visit her mother. While she was there, her Kentucky property was ruthlessly plundered: her house was robbed, her clothes were taken, her farming equipment was stolen, and her livestock was driven off. For the next fifteen years her Kentucky property would burden her life. She tried various schemes to get rid of it: offering the land to be used for a college; bringing thirty families from Massachusetts to live there and open a shoe factory; and offering it as a site for a memorial to Abraham Lincoln after the assassination. As late as 1866 it was vandalized again, and as late as 1869 she was still trying to hang on to it despite court orders that relinquished her possession.

By 1874 Webster had moved to Iowa. She lived at several residences there over the next thirty years and also owned a house for a time in Wisconsin. When she died in 1904, she was living with her niece, Alice Goodrich, the first female graduate of the medical school at the University of Iowa.

SUGGESTED READING: Frances K. Eisan, *Saint of Demon? The Legendary Delia Webster Opposing Slavery,* New York: Pace University Press, 1998; Randolph Paul Runyon, *Delia Webster and the Underground Railroad*, Lexington: University of Kentucky Press, 1996; Delia Webster, *Kentucky Jurisprudence*, Vergennes, VT: E.W. Blaisdell, 1845.

Whipper, William (1804–1876). William Whipper was among the most important black leaders of the antebellum period. His residence in Columbia, Pennsylvania, along the Susquehanna River, and his personal wealth and influence contributed to make his home an important stop along the Underground Railroad. By his own estimation, he aided hundreds of fugitive slaves.

His obituary incorrectly lists him as having been born in Little Britain, Lancaster County, Pennsylvania, near the Maryland border, but he and his two brothers and sister actually were born in North Carolina. His mother being the slave of his father made for an inhospitable situation, and they moved to Pennsylvania, where his father purchased a lumber business in Columbia.

Whipper was already well educated when he moved to Philadelphia sometime in the mid- to late 1820s. In 1828 he organized a Reading Room Society for Men of Color. His interest in the abolition of slavery was already evident in a letter he sent to a local newspaper in opposition to the American Colonization Society. As early as 1831 he joined with **Robert Purvis** in organizing a meeting to gather support for *The Liberator*. He also became involved in the Negro Convention movement that sought to elevate the status of blacks in American society and was a prominent presence at the first six conventions.

While involved in the social movements of the day, he also worked his way from being a steam cleaner in 1830 to opening his own free labor and temperance store in 1834.

He was known not as a gifted speaker but as a very thorough thinker and intellectual. A strong proponent of integration, he believed during his earlier years that prejudice against blacks was due not to color but to condition. The way to eliminate prejudice and attain equal status, he believed, was through moral improvement, which would not require blacks to leave the country.

At the 1835 National Negro Convention, Whipper organized the National Moral Reform Society, which was open to anyone who pledged to support reform in education, temperance, economy, and universal liberty. It called on the black churches for support, advocated the avoidance of products made from slave labor, and urged nonviolence in the struggle for the elevation of people of color. It urged blacks to integrate into white society and to stop using terms like *colored* or *Negro* to distinguish themselves. This idea, Whipper admitted, took its roots from abolitionist editor William Lloyd Garrison's motto, "My country is the world—my countrymen are all mankind." However, the society never gained widespread support, despite the publishing of a periodical by Whipper, the *National Reformer*, which promoted its principles. Twelve issues of the periodical were published between September 1838 and December 1839, reporting on public affairs, presenting essays of moral improvement, condemning colonization, and praising nonviolence.

"We must," Whipper wrote, "learn on all occasions to rebuke the spirit of violence, both in sentiment and in practice."

Nevertheless, Whipper's views on the reasons behind the slow progress of black elevation in American society were changing. He began to see that it had little to do with morality and everything to do with race.

By 1854 the evolution of his views had brought him to the following conclusion about racial prejudice, which he articulated in a letter to *Frederick Douglass' Paper*:

> Its foundation is in man's selfish nature, pride and ambition, which rule and govern his worst passions. It grows spontaneous, inflates the instincts of the ignorant, and directs the minds of the learned. It has a home at the fireside and the altar. It follows men to the loftiest heights of ambition, and down to the deepest grave.

In 1835, while still absorbed in the intellectual fever of the day regarding the condition of blacks in America, Whipper moved back to Columbia. He took up his father's lumber business, which he had inherited, and on March 10, 1836, he married Harriet Smith of Columbia. He also initiated a business partnership with her brother Stephen Smith.

A former slave, Smith had been purchased in 1804 by the Revolutionary War general Thomas Boude and emancipated. Smith's mother, who was still enslaved, ran away to be with him and was the object of the first attempted rendition of a runaway slave in Lancaster County. Historians mark this incident as the roots of the region's Underground Railroad.

With the suspension of the *National Reformer* in 1839 and the breakup of the National Reform Society in 1841, Whipper devoted himself to his business, which not only proved financially lucrative but also contributed to his own moral improvement by aiding fugitive slaves.

In a memoir written for **William Still**'s book on the Underground Railroad, Whipper wrote that the Underground route through Columbia became more widely traveled after 1840 as a result of the hazards involved in crossing the Susquehanna at the bridge in Le Havre de Grace, Pennsylvania, and the Prigg Decision in 1842 that ironically made enforcement of the Fugitive Slave Law of 1793 more difficult.

As a result, the bridge over the Susquehanna to Columbia became a major landmark for fugitive slaves because once they crossed it, their chances of being captured were greatly reduced. Whipper, who had enlarged his business interests to include the Columbia Railroad, shipped both lumber and fugitive slaves in his railroad cars to Philadelphia. He wrote the following:

> My house was at the end of the bridge, and as I kept the station, I was frequently called up in the night to take charge of the passengers. On their arrival they were generally hungry and penniless. I have received hundreds in this condition; fed and sheltered from one to seventeen at a time in a single night. At this point the road forked; some I sent west by boats, to Pittsburgh, and others . . . in our cars to Philadelphia.

Of this period, he wrote that as much as "I loved anti-slavery meetings, I did not feel that I could afford to attend them, as my immediate duty was to the flying fugitive." From 1847 until the end of the Civil War, he said he contributed more than $1,000 annually to aid fugitive slaves.

Before the passage of the second Fugitive Slave Law in 1850, Whipper said that it was thought to be secure for fugitive slaves to remain in Columbia and either settle there or work to save money for their move to Canada. However, he advised against it, and the new law forced many blacks who were living in Columbia to flee.

Although it was relatively safe for blacks to stay in the area before the passage of the law, slavecatchers were common because of Columbia's close proximity to the slave state of Maryland. However, after the passage of the law, the slavecatchers became emboldened, and a slavecatching ring, the Gap Gang, stepped up its activities. A group that had formed to protect blacks in that area against the gang became involved in the famed confrontation known as the Christiana Riot, which many attribute to have been the result of these kidnapping activities.

Whipper did not refer to Christiana but mentioned other incidents that were unsettling to blacks in Columbia. One of them involved a runaway, William Smith, who was murdered by a slavecatcher in his lumberyard. Even worse was that the murderer escaped and was never prosecuted. Whipper confessed that during this period he also worried about his own welfare and said his lumberyard had been set on fire twice. The Fugitive Slave Law had made life perilous for blacks in Columbia, and the black population there declined from 943 in 1850 to 487 in 1855.

Whipper's sister Mary Ann and his brother Alfred, who had moved to Dresden, Canada, urged him to join them. Mary Ann had married James Hollinsworth, a lumber dealer, and they were aiding fugitive slaves. Alfred, who would later be a supporter of **John Brown** at the Chatham Convention, was working as an agent for the *Provincial Freeman.*

His family ties persuaded him to visit. During the summer of 1853, Whipper and his partner, Stephen Smith, purchased property in Dresden and constructed a warehouse and other buildings to engage in the lumber business. He was preparing to move to Canada when the start of the Civil War changed his plans.

Whipper's involvement in the Underground Railroad caused him to take a different view on the emigration of American blacks. He also had come to the conclusion that for some colonization was a viable option, writing: "[I] deny the moral right of any man, or body of men, to dictate to me, and say in what place I shall reside or what country shall be my home."

Following the Civil War, Whipper moved to Philadelphia, next door to Stephen Smith, who had amassed a huge fortune. He continued to play a role in the social movements of his race, and his eminent reputation brought him invitations to speak at various occasions. For four years he lived in New Jersey, but he returned to his Philadelphia residence at 919 Lombard Street, where he lived the last five years of his life. Though his views about the status of blacks in American society changed during his life, he never wavered from the motto that "my countrymen are all mankind."

SUGGESTED READING: Richard P. McCormick, "William Whipper: Moral Reformer," *Pennsylvania History*, January, 1976; R. C. Smedley, *History of the Underground Railroad in Chester and Neighboring Counties of Pennsylvania*, Lancaster, PA, 1883; William Still, *The Underground Railroad*, Philadelphia: Porter and Coates, 1872; The Whipper Family, http://www.ckblackhistoricalsociety.org/ck-history/profilearchive/whipperfamily/whipperfamily.html.

White, Addison (dates unknown). Addison White was the subject of one of the most celebrated attempted slave renditions of the antebellum period.

Owned by Daniel White of Flemingsburg, Kentucky, Addison was a large, powerfully built man. When a problem occurred between the two, Daniel White hired an overseer to beat Addison. However, the only beating that occurred was the one Addison administered to the overseer. This outraged his owner, and Addison fled in fear. Proceeding through Ripley, Ohio, he ended up on the farm of James Hunt in Catawba, Ohio, who took him to Mechanicsburg conductor Udney Hyde.

Laid up with an injured foot, Hyde welcomed White into his home and offered him a job on his farm. Hyde promised to forward him along the Underground Railroad once he recovered from his injury, if White wished. However, White's master learned of his whereabouts through letters to his wife, a free woman in Kentucky, which had been intercepted by the postmaster in Springfield and passed on to federal authorities. To confirm this, a spy was sent to Hyde asking for work and remained on his farm for two weeks, then suddenly disappeared the day before federal marshals arrived.

At daybreak on May 21, 1857, eight months after White's escape, three federal marshals accompanied by five Kentucky representatives of Daniel White entered Hyde's homestead. They were first noticed by Addison, who took refuge in Hyde's cabin. Arming himself with a gun, he secured himself in the cabin's small loft. The marshals entered the cabin and noticed movement above in the loft. Assuming it was Addison, one of them fired a shot. This awakened Hyde and his family. One of the marshals then mounted the ladder to the loft with a double-barreled shotgun, but as he emerged through the opening, White shot at him. The bullet glanced off the marshal's gun, nipping the marshal's cheek and ear, and caused him to fall back off the ladder.

By this time one of Hyde's sons had been seized, and Hyde was instructing his fourteen-year-old daughter to go to the house of her brother, Russell, who lived next door. As she went outside, one of the marshals told her to stop, threatening to shoot, but she kept running and was able to get to her brother's house, about 100 yards away. Russell hurried into town to rouse the citizens.

The slavecatchers hesitated. They were not about to risk their lives going up into the loft. While they discussed their options, a mob of people were seen coming in the distance. They were armed with various makeshift weapons, including pitchforks, clubs, and carpet beaters. Making one last effort to scare White into coming out, the marshals fired a volley of shots up through the ceiling into the loft but without effect. By this time, the citizens from Mechanicsburg had descended on the Hyde property. There were men and women of all ages. After a brief dialogue, the leader of the citizens pulled out his watch and said that the slavecatchers had five minutes to leave. The slavecatchers decided to comply and got into their carriages and drove off.

Both Addison and Hyde then went into hiding. Six days later, ten federal marshals returned with a warrant for Hyde's arrest and in the process got into a scrape with Udney's son Russell and three other men. The four were arrested and taken into custody. Before the marshals left, the locals made it understood that they were prepared to prevent the marshals from leaving, but Russell Hyde and the others called them off. Nevertheless, the locals were suspicious and followed the party. When the marshals turned south from Urbana, where they stated they were going to book the men, the locals became alarmed and feared that the marshals were going to take the prisoners to Kentucky to face much more serious charges. But the actual reason they changed course was that they feared the hostility that they might encounter in a large, abolitionist community like Urbana. They also decided to shackle the prisoners, so that in case of attack, they could not escape. Marshal Benjamin P. Churchill, who was in charge, was expecting trouble and had vowed that nothing would stop him but a superior show of force. The men from Mechanicsburg applied for a writ of habeas corpus and formed a posse led by local law enforcement officials, to stop them.

By this time every horse and vehicle that could be secured in Urbana and Mechanicsburg were put into use to overtake the federal marshals, who were heading toward South Charleston to take the train on the Little Miami Railroad to Cincinnati. Others from Springfield also joined the chase. At South Charleston the marshals were headed off by one of the posses. When one of the local sheriffs attempted to serve the writ, he was pummeled by Churchill with his revolver. Shots were fired but no one was hit, and as a second posse arrived, the marshals quickly fled.

The horses of the posses chasing the marshals were in no condition to pursue. After a respite during which fresh horses were obtained, the pursuit resumed. All night long the posses chased the marshals, passing through Green County and entering Clinton County. At sunrise, at the village of Lumberton, they overtook the marshals and the prisoners. The marshals scattered in every direction, but most of them were apprehended and returned to South Charleston, where they were arraigned on various charges and put in jail.

In the end, charges and countercharges were made, but all were dropped when the citizens of Mechanicsburg agreed to pay $950 to Addison White's master for his emancipation. This also allowed Udney Hyde, who had been in hiding for eight months, to return home.

White later served with Company E, Fifty-fourth Massachusetts Infantry, during the Civil War. With his first wife in Kentucky refusing to come north, he married again and settled in Mechanicsburg, where he became a fixture in the town, driving the water wagon. He had a daughter and eight grandchildren.

SUGGESTED READING: Benjamin F. Prince, "The Rescue Case of 1857," *Ohio History*, Vol. 16, No. 3, July, 1907.

Wilbur, Esther (1791–1859). Esther and Job Wilbur were a devout Quaker couple in the Quaker farming community of Easton in Washington County, New York, who opened their home to fugitive slaves. A frail and sickly woman, Esther had a vigorous spirit and a compassionate soul, and she led those in her community to open the doors of their North Meeting House to antislavery meetings after initial resistance. Their activities were revealed in the memoirs of Esther's grandson Oren.

One incident involved a fugitive slave who was tracked to the Wilbur farmhouse during the early 1850s:

> [The fugitive slave] was in the house but a short time, when they heard the pursuers coming down the lane. The poor fugitive was hustled up into the garret by means of a ladder and trap door. On the way through the dining room, the slave saw on the table a long carving knife which he grabbed as he went along, but his hosts, being Friends, and in favor of nonviolence objected; but the colored man insisted that he was not going to be taken alive.

Two men came to their door and demanded that the slave be turned over. The Wilburs insisted they knew of no such person. But possessing a warrant under the authority of the Fugitive Slave Act, they entered and searched the house. They noticed a ladder leading up to the home's garret, and one of the men climbed up and stuck his head through the trapdoor. The runaway gazed at the slavecatcher defiantly, brandishing the knife and threatening to use it. This deterred the slavecatcher, who retreated, and the men left the Wilbur residence to secure more help.

When they felt certain that it was safe, Esther dressed the man in her clothes, including a thick veil inside her Quaker bonnet, and Job took him in his wagon to the home of **Hiram Corliss** in Union Village, a distance of about five miles, where he was more secure.

Oren Wilbur also related a story of a fugitive slave named Frank, who arrived at the Wilbur home suffering from pneumonia:

> At another time . . . a slave arrived at this home in a great state of exhaustion, having contracted a severe cold from exposure during the flight from his pursuers. This developed into an attack of pneumonia and later into consumption. His pursuers had evidently lost his trail, for they never came after him, and he remained at the Wilbur home and was taken care for one or two years until he died. He had with him a strong cane with the head of a deer horn with deadly prongs. He said he had used it twice on his flight to kill bloodhounds which had been sent to track him down . . . His name was Frank and when someone suggested he ought to have a last name, he said he would call himself, Frank Quaintance. Asked why, he replied, "it was through the quaintance of this good Wilbur family that I am still alive and comfortable."

After Esther managed to persuade the more conservative Quakers at the North Easton Meeting House to open it to antislavery meetings, it became a regular meeting place for local abolitionists. In 1851, the Old Saratoga Anti-Slavery Society was established. Its members comprised mainly Easton Quakers and the Quaker Springs Meeting, many of whom were known to harbor fugitive slaves, and whose officers included Esther's husband Job, her nephew Joseph Peckham, and other members of the Wilbur family.

The North Easton meeting house also became a center of women's abolitionism, where such notable speakers as Sojourner Truth and **Lucretia Mott** came to speak. Other notable abolitionists who spoke there were Charles C. Burleigh and Aaron Powell. It is also likely that **Frederick Douglass** spoke there when he toured Washington County in 1854.

A long illness led up to Esther's death in 1859, but she continued during her last days to work for the cause of antislavery, being involved in the Personal Liberty Law movement. At a meeting of the Old Saratoga Anti-Slavery Society, it was resolved thirteen days after her death on June 5, 1859, that "the anti-slavery cause has lost one of its most clear-sighted, radical, and intrepid supporters."

She was, as her eulogist wrote, "the friend of all—the widow, the fatherless, the destitute and the trembling fugitive, [a woman whose] heart always beat in sympathy with their necessities, and an open hand to render all the aid in her power."

SUGGESTED READING: Joseph Peckham, "Obituary," *National Antislavery Standard,* June 11, 1859; Oren B. Wilbur, unpublished papers, Easton, NY: Wilbur Family.

Wing, Asa Sylvester (1815–1854). Asa Wing was a simple farmer and devoutly religious man who dedicated his life to ending slavery. He was best remembered as an outstanding speaker whose eloquence drew praise and whose home was a refuge for fugitive slaves for nearly twenty years.

Born in Sangerfield, New York, he moved with his parents to Oswego County in central New York as a boy. As a young man he joined the Baptist Church and was aiding fugitive slaves at least as early as 1837, according to a story reported in the *Emancipator* that year. In it, Wing was described as sending a runaway to Hiram Gilbert, who in turn sent the runaway to Samuel Cuyler in Pultneyville, where the boats of Captain Horatio Throop and others were available for passage across Lake Ontario. According to the story, Wing was then living in Onondaga County. By the time he married Caroline Mitchell in 1843, however, he had moved to a farm outside the village of Mexico in Oswego County where he settled.

A tiny "Burned-Over District" community, fired up by the evangelical fervor of the early decades of the nineteenth century, Mexico had a clique of abolitionists who were available to the Underground Railroad. In addition to Wing, there was Starr Clark, a tinsmith, who lived in the village; James C. Jackson, who became a nationally prominent abolitionist journalist; and the Ames brothers, Harlow, Leonard, and Orson. The noted runaway **William "Jerry" Henry** stayed overnight with Orson after being secretly moved from Syracuse on the fifth night after the rescue.

A large network of conductors had developed in Oswego County by 1850, and many fugitive slaves were shipped to freedom from the port of Oswego along Lake Ontario. Among the conductors were the Clarke brothers; Sidney, to whom "Jerry" Henry was sent by Ames; and Edwin, a local attorney. **Gerrit Smith** played a prominent role in the Underground Railroad in the county because of his business concerns there. Smith's business agent, John B. Edwards, maintained an office in the city of Oswego, and Smith owned the Oswego Hydraulic Canal and the Pier and Dock Company along the canal that empties into Lake Ontario. This provided access to the lake and the many boats in the port that could transport fugitive slaves to Canada. Evidence suggests that Edwards often arranged for such passage. A good friend of the Wings, Smith wrote Asa a personal letter of concern shortly before his death.

The Wings had two children, and their home was modest and rather small. Nevertheless, fugitive slaves stayed for days at a time and were hidden in the cellar, which was accessed through a trapdoor concealed by a rug. An early supporter of the Liberty Party, Asa probably met Gerrit Smith through his work for the party. It is believed that Smith sometimes forwarded fugitive slaves to Wing. Another agent who collaborated with Wing was George Bragdon in Richland.

Wing was ardent in his abolitionism and began giving talks and sermons at churches, meetinghouses, and private homes. He spoke throughout central New York and in parts of Connecticut on an abolitionist tour in 1846 and visited the Adirondack region in 1848. His lecture tours were sponsored by local abolitionists. In his speeches, Wing attacked slavery by the application of the Ten Commandments. He often quoted scripture verbatim from memory. Among the titles of his lectures were "On the Sinfulness of Slavery" and "On the Design of God in Authorizing Government."

Following the passage of the second Fugitive Slave Law, Wing's abolitionist efforts increased. His diary notes that in October 1850 he and Caroline attended the National Liberty Party convention held in Oswego. The highlight of the convention was the nomination of Gerrit Smith for president and the black minister, Samuel Ringgold Ward, for vice president. A friend of the Wings, Ward had been a guest at their home.

On October 25, 1850, Wing attended a meeting in Fayetteville to protest the new Fugitive Slave Law, and during this period he went to the trial of the boatmen accused of abusing William and Catherine Harris and their three-year-old daughter, fugitives from slavery. The result of the abuse caused William to cut his throat and Catherine to jump off the boat and into the canal with their daughter, causing the child to drown.

On Tuesday, December 24, 1850, Wing noted in his diary that "today a colored man, his wife and five small girls came to my house on their way to Canada." The family name was Thompson, and they were being pursued by slavecatchers and stayed several days. They apparently had difficulty finding passage across Lake Ontario and attempted to cross in a sleigh, but Wing never learned whether they reached Canada alive.

About this time, Wing was actively involved in raising funds for the bail of William L. Chaplin, a journalist who had moved to central New York during the early period of the antislavery ferment and who had been imprisoned for aiding fugitive slaves in Maryland. On January 7, 1851, Wing was part of a group from Mexico who attended a Liberty Party convention in Syracuse to celebrate Chaplin's release from prison.

Wing's health slackened. A serious throat ailment developed, and he ignored warnings of physicians to curtail his lecturing. The disease progressed to the point where he could utter only a whisper, and he was diagnosed with tuberculosis.

His last days were very peaceful and happy, his wife wrote in answering Gerrit Smith's last letter. "He felt that he had a 'conscious void of offence towards man,' that he had done what he could."

On March 8 Wing died. **Frederick Douglass**, another of his friends, delivered the eulogy at his funeral:

> He poured out his life for the perishing slave, pleading for him with an eloquence and earnestness which could scarcely have been more direct, pathetic and touching, had his own wife and children been on the auction block.

On September 11, 1855, more than 3,000 people attended a ceremony dedicating a monument erected in Wing's memory. Among noted abolitionists participating were the Wesleyan-Methodist minister and Underground Railroad conductor Luther Lee, who gave the invocation; the Liberty singer George W. Clark, who sang several songs; and Frederick Douglass, who gave the celebratory address. The inscription on his monument, which still stands today in a remote Mexico, New York, cemetery, reads, "He trusted in God and Loved his Neighbor."

SUGGESTED READING: Tom Calarco, *The Underground Railroad in the Adirondack Region,* McFarland, 2004; Arch Merrill, *The Underground: Freedom's Road, and Other Upstate Tales,* New York: American Book-Stratford Press, 1963; Judith Wellman, "Asa Wing," discussion from application to National Register of Historic Places of Asa and Caroline Wing property, Mexico, Oswego County, New York, 2000.

Wright, Theodore Sedgwick (1797–1847). The first black graduate of Princeton and a leader in civil rights and educational improvement, whose highest priority was the poor and needy, Rev. Wright was a man who worked quietly behind the scenes and turned the other cheek. He also was a leader in New York City's Underground Railroad.

Born in Providence, Rhode Island, he was the son of Richard P. G. Wright, a free black barber who took an early interest in civil rights and educational improvement. In 1817, after having moved from New England to Schenectady, New York, sometime before 1810, Wright's father took a trip to Philadelphia to participate in the first great civil rights meeting in America concerning the American Colonization Society. His father was one of 3,000 participants who voiced overwhelming opposition to its plan of sending free blacks back to Africa.

Theodore enrolled in the African Free School in New York City, where he came under the guidance of Samuel Cornish, who became a lifetime mentor and associate. Through the likely sponsorship of the Presbyterian Education Society, which was patronized by the wealthy New York abolitionists Arthur and Lewis Tappan, Wright was accepted as Princeton's first black student at its Theological Institute. While there, he became an agent for Cornish's weekly newspaper, *Freedom's Journal*, the nation's first black newspaper, whose first issue was published on March 16, 1827. It stressed black self-improvement, called for immediate emancipation, and condemned colonization. This latter position was opposed by many of his school's supporters and administrators. As a result, the newspaper was banned at Princeton, and the Theological Institute's distinguished professor of church history and government, Rev. Samuel Miller, threatened to have any teacher or student who violated this rule dismissed. Nevertheless, Wright publicly admitted his views and was incarcerated. Thanks to the efforts of the Tappans, his fine was paid and he managed to graduate the following year.

That year he was called to be pastor of the Shiloh Presbyterian Church in New York City, a position vacated by Cornish, who had been its founder in 1821. Under Wright's leadership, the church's popularity grew and moved in 1831 from a room in a school to a full-sized church. It was in 1833 that **Henry Highland Garnet**, then eighteen, joined its Sunday school.

Garnet, who had escaped from slavery as a boy with his parents, was permanently injured during the journey and partially crippled as a result. But he showed an amazing aptitude as a student that was immediately recognized by Wright, and they began a lifelong relationship, of which one abolitionist later wrote, "They were one in life."

During this time, Wright became a member of the American Anti-Slavery Society and was one of four blacks named to its executive committee. He also made memorable speeches at the New York State Anti-Slavery Society's annual meetings in 1836 and 1837, during which he attacked the American Colonization Society and racial prejudice. During the 1837 meeting, he spoke of the exclusion of "colored" children from public schools, the refusal of service in most restaurants, the denial of apprenticeships through which to learn trades, and the prohibition of blacks indoors on boat rides. The last was especially poignant to Wright because his wife, whom he had married the previous year, had died from complications of an illness worsened by a night on the open deck of a steamboat.

Life could be particularly difficult for blacks, free or not, in the North during this period. Just the year before, while attending a service at the annual meeting of the Princeton Theological Institute, Wright was assaulted and physically thrown out of the chapel by a disgruntled former student of the school, who was the son of a slaveholder and who did not think that blacks should be permitted to attend such services. Wright did not offer resistance, and fortunately others interceded to prevent further abuse. To make matters worse, some falsely accused Wright of precipitating the incident, which caused him further pain and prompted him to write a letter in defense of his innocence to his former advisor at the college.

Though Wright was not one to resort to physical resistance, he did not shirk his duties to battle unjust laws. In 1835, when the New York Committee of Vigilance formed to help free blacks, who were being kidnapped into slavery, and to help fugitive slaves, Wright became part of the leadership. An estimated 5,000 fugitive slaves were living in New York City at that time.

Charles B. Ray, another committee member, described their work on the Underground Railroad: "We destined them for Canada. I secured passage for them in a barge, and Mr. Wright and myself spent the day in providing food, and personally saw them off on the barge."

Arthur and Lewis Tappan: Brothers Working Behind the Lines to End Slavery

There were certainly thousands of foot soldiers in the war to end slavery. But as in any conflict, there also were a few generals who helped direct them. Among them were Arthur and Lewis Tappan, wealthy merchants from New York City, whose roots extended to the Boston area.

The brothers came to antislavery by way of the evangelical movement that swept through the northeast during the early part of the nineteenth century. Being quite successful as merchants, especially Arthur, they opened their purses like **Gerrit Smith** to a large number of humanitarian causes, including the antislavery movement, which became their foremost cause. Among the brothers' actions in support of their beliefs were the establishment of Lane Seminary and the interracial Oberlin College, and the sponsorship of Theodore Weld's speaking tours and the tours of Weld's antislavery agents through the North.

The Tappan brothers strongly supported the New York Committee of Vigilance—the initially black organization in New York City that became a model for later Underground Railroad organizations—and Lewis became a regular participant at their meetings. The brothers also were instrumental in bringing about the formation of the Liberty Party, in their advocacy of using political action to end slavery. Their influence and monetary contributions also assisted the establishment of abolitionist newspapers such as the New York *Emancipator*, *The Colored American*, the *Anti-Slavery Bugle*, and the *National Era*.

Another organization that the Tappan brothers helped to establish was the American Missionary Association, a number of whose employees were involved in the Underground Railroad. And slave rescuers like Alexander Milton Ross credited the Tappans' assistance.

But their work was not always done from a distance. One incident involving Ann Maria Weems, the fugitive slave whose freedom was arranged with assistance from both **William Still** and **Charles Ray**, saw Weems spending several days in hiding at the home of Lewis Tappan.

Wright also was one of the founding members of the Phoenix Literary Society, which provided public debates and intellectual stimulation to the black community, and the Phoenix High School for black youths of both sexes. His efforts led to greater positions of responsibility as he became a traveling agent of the American Anti-Slavery Society, a leader in the United Anti-Slavery Society that sought to unite the efforts of black organizations throughout the city, and a member of the executive committee of the American Missionary Society.

Along with the majority of the black leadership in New York City, Wright broke with the Garrisonian abolitionists and sided with the evangelicals led by the Tappans in the formation of the American and Foreign Anti-Slavery Society. This split was partly related to the evangelicals' support of the use of political action to combat slavery, in opposition to the Garrisonians. As a result Wright became a supporter of the Liberty Party.

In a report of the Eastern New York Anti-Slavery Society, an arm of the Liberty Party, Wright's father was identified as one who forwarded fugitive slaves. In fact, his father also was a member of the New York Committee of Vigilance, whose meetings the elder Wright occasionally attended and of which Theodore had by around 1840 become president. It is also believed that Theodore harbored fugitive slaves at the Shiloh Church.

Wright and his father also had become active in the black convention movement and helped organize the state's first black convention in 1840. However, at the 1843 national convention, while at first supporting the speech of his "adopted son," Henry Highland Garnet, who advocated a violent revolt by slaves, Wright was persuaded to change his vote. The vote hinged on this decision, with the resolution to support Garnet being defeated by one vote. Wright's opposition was based on the view that a revolt was unlikely to succeed and would result only in a great deal of bloodshed.

Wright stood behind his principles of nonviolence while fighting to end slavery and injustice against blacks until his untimely death at the age of fifty. He was known even to ask for prayers for slaveholders at his services, and one slaveholder who attended a service exclaimed that the experience had converted him to abolition. As the *New York Evangelist* wrote in its obituary, "Few men have been more generally esteemed and few indeed have left behind them records of a life so pure and benevolent." Blacks lined the streets during his funeral procession, and Henry Garnet delivered the funeral sermon.

SUGGESTED READING: Bella Gross, "Life and Times of Theodore S. Wright, 1797–1847, *The Negro History Bulletin*, June, 1940; Document 15, "Theodore S. Wright and Racial Prejudice" from *The Black Abolitionist Papers. The United States*, Vol. 3, 1830–1846, edited by C. Peter Ripley, Chapel Hill: University of North Carolina Press, 1991; Carter G. Woodson, *Negro Orators and Their Orations*, Washington, DC: The Associated Publishers, 1925.

Wright, William (1788–1865). William Wright was among the earliest Underground Railroad conductors, his home near the borderline between Maryland and eastern Pennsylvania, putting him in a strategic location.

He was born into the Quaker faith in Adams County, Pennsylvania, and settled in York Springs. In 1726 his ancestor John Wright founded the town of Wright's Ferry, where he operated a ferry across the Susquehanna River on the present location of Columbia, Pennsylvania. A later ancestor, Samuel Wright, laid out an expanded settlement in 1787, when they renamed it Columbia. As a result, Wright has sometimes been thought to be two persons, one William Wright who lived in Adams County and another who lived in Columbia in Lancaster County.

Wright actually lived thirty miles west of Columbia, but the association between Wright and Columbia in regard to the Underground Railroad is understandable, as Columbia was one of the earliest locations where organized assistance was given to fugitive slaves. This assistance was rooted in an 1804 incident in which an attempted rendition of a fugitive slave was stopped by Revolutionary War general Thomas Boude, who purchased and freed the slave.

Wright first put his beliefs into practice in 1810 when Charles Sewell, a Maryland slaveholder, moved to York County with nine slaves. Wright sued in court for their freedom and won. After the trial, Sewell chased Wright on horseback and caught him and began whipping him with rawhide, but Wright managed to get away and get home safely. Wright's opportunities to aid those fleeing slavery grew in part because of two major migrations of emancipated slaves from Virginia to Columbia, one of fifty-six slaves from Virginia in 1819 and another of about 100 slaves the following year. As a result, Columbia, which rested on the eastern side of the Susquehanna, became a destination for fugitive slaves.

A bridge was built across the river as early as 1812, followed by another in 1834. The latter one became a landmark for fugitive slaves, and in one account from 1842 a group of twenty-six fugitive slaves from Maryland thought that on crossing the bridge, they had arrived in Canada. By the 1840s Columbia had become a major Underground Railroad terminal, and contributing even further to this notion was that the aboveground railroad, which by then connected York County with Philadelphia, was owned in this region by agents of the Underground Railroad. Nevertheless, boats were still used to bring fugitive slaves across, probably because of the increased security required in later years, especially after the passage of the second Fugitive Slave Law.

Wright sometimes brought fugitive slaves to the home of Daniel Gibbons, whose wife was the sister of Wright's wife, Phebe. He also worked with his sister, Susannah; her husband, Jonathan Mifflin; and later his nephew Samuel. They lived on the east side of the river from Columbia. Samuel recounted an incident when he came home to find thirteen fugitive slaves waiting for him in his house. They had been found wandering nearby and were brought to him. After staying with him for two days, the fugitive slaves were ferried across the river. Mifflin also was host to the noted slave rescuer **Charles T. Torrey** before his ill-fated rescue attempt that sent him to prison in 1843.

An 1851 incident that has been passed down involving four fugitive slaves shows the cunning behavior of conductors like Wright.

The fugitive slaves came shoeless in tattered clothing, apparently having been exposed to the elements for quite some time. They needed to rest and recuperate, and two were sent to a neighboring farm while two stayed with Wright. Some days later, some slaveholders rode into the Wright homestead and spotted their slaves working in the field. The slaveholders' arrival happened so fast that no resistance was offered. Instead, the slaves asked if they could get the coats that the Quakers had given them.

While the slaves went into the barn, Wright asked the slaveholders to come inside his home for refreshment. They proceeded at a leisurely pace and were brought into the dining area. They sat around the dining table, and Wright nodded to his daughter to prepare the offerings. Small talk continued, and Wright did his best to stall them. Finally his daughter brought them some fresh cherries and water. The men were relaxed and the atmosphere congenial.

Suddenly, Phebe asked one of the slaveholders if he believed in the Bible. The man assured her of his faith and added that he was an elder in the Baptist Church. Phebe left

John Vickers: The Potter Who Hid Fugitive Slaves

John Vickers, of Chester County, Pennsylvania, was well-known in the pottery business: he had taken up the family trade where his father, Thomas Vickers, had left off. But this was not the only business the two men shared. Both were staunch abolitionists who were always ready to aid fugitive slaves.

In fact, Thomas Vickers was one of the original members of the Pennsylvania Abolition Society, founded in 1777 in Philadelphia, which is believed to be the first organization dedicated to aiding fugitive slaves. Son John became an even more active Underground Railroad conductor than his father, and his home in Lionville—today a restaurant—became almost as notorious for such activity as the home of **Thomas Garrett** in Wilmington, Delaware. Indeed, Garrett often forwarded fugitive slaves to Vickers or to the potter's associates.

Vickers not only hid fugitive slaves at his home in a cellar that was accessed through a closet off a dining room, but also was known to hide small children in large pottery jars when he transported fugitive slaves in his wagon. In addition to Garrett, he worked with such notable conductors as **Bartholomew Fussell, Graceanna Lewis, J. Miller McKim**, James and **Lucretia Mott**, and **Isaac Hopper**.

Vickers was one of 132 known Underground Railroad agents in Chester County. This number included 82 Quakers and 31 blacks, representing probably the best-documented network of conductors anywhere.

On a number of occasions, fugitive slaves remained at the Vickers homestead for extended periods to work and get situated for their new lives as free men and women. However, after the passage of the second Fugitive Slave Law in 1850, Vickers no longer kept fugitive slaves at his household; instead he forwarded them to neighboring black agents. In doing so, he would write a letter of introduction for the fugitive slave, signing it "Thy friend, Pot."

---

the table and fetched her Bible. She turned to a passage that showed slaveholding to be a sin. She asked the man how he could profess to follow the teachings of the Bible and yet remain a slaveholder. The man was speechless. One of the others interrupted. He thought it was time to return to business, take their slaves, and be on their way. But the slaves were nowhere in sight, and he asked Wright to get them.

Wright was not about to get them. Of course, he also was not going to conceal them or prevent the slaveholders from taking their property: that was against the law. Although he was not going to help them find the slaves, he said they were welcome to search his house and his property.

Wright's offer to allow the slaveholders to search his premises gave the fleeing slaves even more time than the half-hour that had elapsed, and the slaveholders, without thinking, had been conned into accepting this. They searched every nook and cranny, and Wright even pointed out places they had forgotten. But their efforts were in vain, and they left feeling not only unhappy but also a little guilty.

The slaves had made use of the time to find good hiding places, and almost all of them were forwarded to Canada. However, one of the slaves, who had been sent to a neighboring farm, was spotted by the slaveholders and was returned to slavery.

William Wright not only worked in the Underground Railroad but also was a leader in the formation of both the Liberty and Free Soil parties in southern Pennsylvania. He lived just long enough to see his work come to fruition with the end of the Civil War.

SUGGESTED READING: Robert C. Smedley, *History of the Underground Railroad in Chester and Neighboring Counties of Pennsylvania*, Lancaster, PA, 1883; "The Underground Railroad: Reminiscences of Slavery," *Titusville Morning Herald*, May 16, 1870.

Selected Bibliography

General

Contemporary

Blockson, Charles L. *The Underground Railroad: First Person Narratives of Escapes from Slavery.* New York: Prentice Hall, 1987.
Bordewich, Fergus. *Bound for Canaan.* New York: HarperCollins, 2005.
Calarco, Tom. *The Underground Railroad in the Adirondack Region.* Jefferson, NC: McFarland, 2004.
Gara, Larry. *The Liberty Line: The Legend of the Underground Railroad.* Lexington, KY: University of Kentucky Press, 1967.
Griffler, Keith P. *Front Line of Freedom: African Americans and the Forging of the Underground Railroad in the Ohio Valley.* Lexington: University Press of Kentucky, 2004.
Grover, Kathryn. *The Fugitive's Gibraltar.* Amherst: University of Massachusetts Press, 2001.
Hagedorn, Ann. *Beyond the River.* New York: Simon & Schuster, 2002.
Harrold, Stanley. *Subversives: Antislavery Community in Washington, D.C.* Baton Rouge: Louisiana State University Press, 2003.
Hudson, J. Blaine. *Fugitive Slaves and the Underground Railroad in the Kentucky Borderlands.* Jefferson, NC: McFarland, 2001.
Hunter, Carol M. *To Set the Captives Free: Reverend Jermain Wesley Loguen and the Struggle for Freedom in Central New York, 1835–1872.* New York: Garland, 1993.
Kashatus, William C. *Just over the Line.* West Chester, PA: Chester County Historical Society, 2002.
Merrill, Arch. *The Underground, Freedom's Road, and Other Upstate Tales.* New York: American Book-Stratford Press, 1963.
Muelder, Owen. *The Underground Railroad in Western Illinois.* Jefferson, NC: McFarland and Company, Inc., 2007.
Noble, Glenn. *John Brown and the Jim Lane Trail.* Broken Bow, NE: Purcells, 1977.
Peters, Pamela. *The Underground Railroad in Floyd County.* Jefferson, NC: McFarland, 2001.
Phelan, Helene C. *And Why Not Everyman? An Account of Slavery, the Underground Railroad, and the Road to Freedom in New York's Southern Tier.* Interlaken, NY: Heart of the Lakes Publishing, 1987.

Pirtle, Carol. *Escape betwixt Two Suns: A True Tale of the Underground Railroad in Illinois*. Carbondale, IL: Southern Illinois University Press, 2000.
Prince, Bryan. *I Came as a Stranger*. Toronto: Tundra Books, 2004.
Quarles, Benjamin. *Black Abolitionists*. New York: Oxford University Press, 1969.
Ricks, Mary Kay. *Escape on the Pearl*. New York: William Morrow, 2007.
Sernett, Milton. *North Star Country*. Syracuse: Syracuse University Press, 2002.
Siebert, Wilbur. *The Mysteries of Ohio's Underground Railroads*. Columbus, OH: Long's College Book Company, 1951.
———. *The Underground Railroad in Massachusetts*. Worcester: American Antiquarian Society, 1936.
———. *The Underground Railroad from Slavery to Freedom*. New York: Macmillan, 1898.
———. *Vermont's Anti-Slavery and Underground Railroad Record. 1937*. New York: Negro Universities Press, 1969.
Strother, Horatio. *The Underground Railroad in Connecticut*. Middletown, CT: Wesleyan University Press, 1962.
Switala, William J. *The Underground Railroad in Delaware, Maryland and West Virginia*. Mechanicsburg, PA: Stackpole Books, 2004.
———. *The Underground Railroad in New Jersey and New York*. Mechanicsburg, PA: Stackpole Books, 2006.
———. *The Underground Railroad in Pennsylvania*. Mechanicsburg, PA: Stackpole Books, 2001.

Historical

Cockrum, William M. *History of the Underground Railroad: As It Was Conducted by the Anti-Slavery League*. Oakland City, IN: J.M. Cockrum Press, 1915.
Johnson, H. U. *From Dixie to Canada: Romance and Realities in the Underground Railroad*. Buffalo: Charles Wells Moulton, 1894.
Mitchell, Rev. William M. *The Underground Railroad*. London: William Tweedie, 1860.
Northup, Solomon. *Twelve Years a Slave*. Edited by Sue Eakin and Joseph Logsdon. Baton Rouge: LSU Press, 1968 (1853).
Pettit, Eber. *Sketches in the History of the Underground Railroad*. Fredonia, NY: W. McKinstry & Son, 1879.
Smedley, R. C. *History of the Underground Railroad in Chester and Neighboring Counties of Pennsylvania*. Lancaster, PA, 1883.
Still, William. *The Underground Railroad*. Philadelphia: Porter & Coates, 1872.
Stowe, Harriet Beecher. *The Key to Uncle Tom's Cabin*. London: Clarke, Beeton, and Co., 1853.

Biographies

Contemporary

Danforth, Mildred E. *A Quaker Pioneer*. New York: Exposition Press, 1961.
Hamilton, Virginia. *Anthony Burns: The Defeat and Triumph of a Fugitive Slave*. New York: Random House, 1988.
Harlow, Ralph Volney. *Gerrit Smith: Philanthropist and Reformer*. New York: Henry Holt & Co., 1938.

McGowan, James A. *Station Master on the Underground Railroad: The Life and Letters of Thomas Garrett*. Rev. ed. Jefferson, NC: McFarland, 2004.
Pasternak, Martin B. *Rise Now and Fly to Arms: The Life of Henry Highland Garnet*. New York: Garland Publishers, 1995.
Ripley, C. Peter, ed. *The Black Abolitionist Papers*. 4 vols. Chapel Hill: University of North Carolina Press, 1991.
Runyon, Randolph Paul. *Delia Webster and the Underground Railroad*. University Press of Kentucky, 1996.
Slaughter, Thomas B. *Bloody Dawn: The Christiana Riot and Racial Violence in the Antebellum North*. New York: Oxford University Press, 1991.
Stauffer, John. *The Black Hearts of Men*. Cambridge, MA: Harvard University Press, 2002.

Historical

Benedict, A. L. *Memoir of Richard Dillingham*. Philadelphia: Merrihew & Thompson, 1852.
Birney, William. *James G. Birney and His Times*. New York: D. Appleton and Company, 1890.
Bowditch, Vincent Y. *Life and Correspondence of Henry Ingersoll Bowditch*. Boston: Houghton, Mifflin & Company, 1902.
Brown, C. S. *Abel Brown Abolitionist*. Edited by Tom Calarco. Jefferson, NC: McFarland, 2006 (1849).
Child, L. Maria. *Isaac T. Hopper: A True Life*. Boston: John P. Jewett and Company, 1853.
Coffin, Levi. *Reminiscences of Levi Coffin*. Cincinnati, OH: Western Tract and Supply Co., 1876.
Douglass, Frederick Douglass. *Life and Times of Frederick Douglass*. Hartford, CT: Park Publishing Co., 1881.
———. *My Bondage and My Freedom*. New York: Miller, Orton, & Mulligan, 1855.
Fairbank, Calvin. *Rev. Calvin Fairbank during Slavery Times*. Chicago: Patriotic Publishing Co., 1890.
Frothingham, Octavius Brooks. *Gerrit Smith: A Biography*. New York: G.P. Putnam's Sons, 1878.
Haviland, Laura. *A Woman's Life-Work: Labors and Experiences of Laura S. Haviland*. Walden & Stowe, 1882.
Hensel, W. U. *The Christiana Riot and the Treason Trials of 1851*. Lancaster, PA: The New Era Printing Co., 1911.
Lee, Luther. *Autobiography of Luther Lee*. New York: Phillips & Hunt, 1882.
Lovejoy, J. C. *Memoir of Rev. Charles T. Torrey, Who Died in the Penitentiary of Maryland, Where He Was Confined for Showing Mercy to the Poor*. Boston: John P. Jewett & Co., 1847.
May, Samuel J. *Some Recollections of Our Anti-slavery Conflict*. Boston: Fields, Osgood & Co., 1869.
Ray, Florence T. *Sketch of the Life of Rev. Charles B. Ray*. New York: Press of J. J. Little & Co., 1887.
Ritchie, Andrew. *The Soldier, the Battle, and the Victory: Being a Brief Account of the Work of Rev. John Rankin in the Anti-slavery Cause*. Cincinnati: Western Tract and Book Society, 1868.

Ross, Alexander Milton. *Memoirs of a Reformer.* Toronto: Hunter, Rose, 1893.
Sprague, Stuart Seely, ed. *His Promised Land: The Autobiography of John Parker.* New York: W.W. Norton and Co., 1996 (1880).
Todd, John. *Early Settlement and Growth of Western Iowa or Reminiscences.* Des Moines: Iowa Historical Department, 1906.

Fugitive Slaves

Contemporary

Brode, Patrick. *The Odyssey of John Anderson.* Toronto: Toronto University Press, 1989.
Collison, Gary L. *Shadrach Minkins: From Fugitive Slave to Citizen.* Cambridge, MA: Harvard University Press, 1997.
Hill, Daniel. *The Freedom Seekers.* Toronto: Stoddardt Publishing, 1981.
Ruggles, Jeffrey. *The Unboxing of Henry Brown.* Richmond: Library of Virginia, 2003.
Weisenburger, Steven. *Modern Medea.* New York: Hill and Wang, 1998.
Winks, Robin W. *The Blacks in Canada.* Montreal: McGill-Queen's University Press, 1971.

Historical

Drew, Benjamin. *A North-Side View of Slavery. The Refugee: Or the Narratives of Fugitive Slaves in Canada. Related by Themselves, with an Account of the History and Condition of the Colored Population of Upper Canada.* Boston: John P. Jewett And Company, 1856.
Howe, Samuel G. "The Refugees from Slavery in Canada West: Report to the Freedmen's Inquiry Commission." Boston: Wright & Potter, 1864.
May, Samuel J. *The Fugitive Slave Law and Its Victims.* New York: American Anti-Slavery Society, 1861.
McDougall, Marion Gleason. *Fugitive Slaves (1619–1865).* Boston: Ginn & Co., 1891.
Pickard, Kate E. R. *The Kidnapped and the Ransomed: Being the Personal Recollections of Peter Still and His Wife "Vina," after Forty Years of Slavery.* New York and Auburn: Miller, Orton and Mulligan, 1856.
Stevens, Charles Emery. *Anthony Burns: A History.* Boston: John P. Jewett & Company, 1856.

Slave Narratives

Documenting the South, University of North Carolina, http://docsouth.unc.edu/browse/author/. This website includes all of the following narratives plus many more—all of which can be downloaded for viewing.
Anderson, William. *Life and Narrative of William J. Anderson, Twenty-Four Years a Slave; Sold Eight Times! In Jail Sixty Times!! Whipped Three Hundred Times!!! Or the Dark Deeds of American Slavery Revealed . . .* Chicago: Daily Tribune Book and Job Printing Office, 1857.
Bibb, Henry. *Narrative of the Life and Adventures of Henry Bibb, an American Slave.* New York, 1850.
Brown, Henry. *Narrative of Henry Box Brown, Who Escaped from Slavery Enclosed in a Box Three Feet Long, Two Wide, and Two and a Half High.* Boston: Brown & Stearns, 1849.

———. *Narrative of the Life of Henry Box Brown.* Manchester, England: Lee and Glynn, 1851.
Brown, William Wells. *Narrative of William W. Brown, an American Slave.* London: Charles Gilpin, 1849.
Craft, William. *Running a Thousand Miles for Freedom; or, the Escape of William and Ellen Craft from Slavery.* London: William Tweedie, 1860.
Henson, Josiah. *An Autobiography of the Rev. Josiah Henson ("Uncle Tom"). From 1789 to 1881.* London, Ontario: Schuyler, Smith, & Co., 1881.
Jacobs, Harriet. *Incidents in the Life of a Slave Girl.* Boston, Mineola, New York: Dover Publications, Inc., 2001 (1861).
Loguen, J. W. *The Rev. J. W. Loguen as a Slave and as a Freeman.* New York: Negro Universities Press, 1968 (1859).
Smallwood, Thomas. *A Narrative of Thomas Smallwood, Giving an Account of His Birth—The Period He Was Held in Slavery—His Release—And Removal to Canada, etc. Together with an Account of the Underground Railroad.* Toronto: James Stephens, printer, 1851.
Steward, Austin. *Twenty-Two Years a Slave, and Forty Years a Freeman; Embracing a Correspondence of Several Years, while President of Wilberforce Colony, London, Canada West.* Rochester, NY: William Alling, 1857.
Twelvetrees, Harper, ed. *Story of the Life of John Anderson, the Fugitive Slave.* London: William Tweedie, 1863.
Ward, Samuel Ringgold. *Autobiography of a Fugitive Negro: His Anti-slavery Labours in the United States, Canada, and England.* London: John Snow, 1855.

Slavecatchers

Campbell, Stanley W. *The Slave Catchers 1850–1860.* Chapel Hill: University of North Carolina Press, 1970.
Wilson, Carol. *Freedom at Risk: The Kidnapping of Free Blacks in America—1780–1865.* Lexington: University of Kentucky Press, 1994.

John Brown

Carton, Evan. *Patriotic Treason: John Brown and the Soul of America.* New York: Simon and Schuster, 2006.
DeCaro, Louis A. *"Fire from the Midst of You": A Religious Life of John Brown.* New York: New York University Press, 2002.
Hearn, Chester G. *Companions in Conspiracy.* Gettysburg, PA: Thomas Publications, 1996.
Hinton, Richard J. *John Brown and His Men with Some Account of the Roads They Traveled to Reach Harper's Ferry.* New York: Funk & Wagnalls, 1894.
Oates, Stephen B. *To Purge This Land with Blood: A Biography of John Brown.* New York: Harper & Row, 1970.
Redpath, James. *The Public Life of Capt. John Brown.* Boston: Thayer and Eldridge, 1860.
Renehan, Edward J. *The Secret Six: The True Tale of the Men Who Conspired with John Brown.* New York: Crown Publishers, 1995.
Reynolds, David S. *John Brown, Abolitionist: The Man Who Killed Slavery, Sparked the Civil War.* New York: Random House, 2005.
Sanborn, F. B. *The Life and Letters of John Brown; Liberator of Kansas, and Martyr of Virginia.* Concord, MA: F. B. Sanborn, 1885.

Stavis, Barrie. *John Brown: The Sword and the Word.* New York: A.S. Barnes and Company, 1970.
Villard, Oswald Garrison. *John Brown, 1800–1859: A Biography Fifty Years.* Boston: Houghton Mifflin, 1910.

Harriet Tubman

Clinton, Catherine. *The Road to Freedom.* Boston: Little, Brown, 2004.
Humez, Jean McMahon. *Harriet Tubman: The Life and the Life Stories.* Madison: University of Wisconsin Press, 2003.
Larson, Kate Clifford. *Bound for the Promised Land: Portrait of an American Hero.* New York: Ballantine Books, 2004.

Articles

Bailey, William S. "The Underground Railroad in Southern Chautauqua County." *New York History*, New York Historical Society (1935).
Cecelski, David. "The Shores of Freedom: The Maritime Underground Railroad in North Carolina, 1800–1861." *North Carolina Historical Review* 1, no. 2 (April 1994).
Lumpkin, Katherine DuPre, "The General Plan Was Freedom: A Negro Secret Order on the Underground." *Phylon* 28, no. 1 (1967).
Meaders, Daniel. "Kidnapping Blacks in Philadelphia: Isaac Hopper's Tales of Oppression." *The Journal of Negro History* 80, no. 2 (Spring 1995).
Ohio History Index. "Abolition Movement" and "Underground Railroad." http://publications.ohiohistory.org/ohstemplate.cfm?action=index.
Okur, Nilgun. "Underground Railroad in Philadelphia, 1830–1860." *Journal of Black Studies* 25 (May 1995).
Pritchard, James M. "Into the Fiery Furnace: Anti-slavery Prisoners in the Kentucky State Penitentiary 1844–1870." http://www.ket.org/underground/research/prichard.htm.

Monographs

Contemporary

Coon, Diane Perrine. *Southeastern Indiana's Underground Railroad Routes and Operations.* A Project of the State of Indiana, Dept. of Natural Resources, Division of Historic Preservation and Archaeology and the U.S. Dept. of the Interior, NPS, April 2001.
Crenshaw, Gwendolyn. *Bury Me in a Free Land: The Abolitionist Movement in Indiana.* Indianapolis: Indiana Historical Bureau, 1993.
Grover, Kathryn, and Janine da Silva. *Historic Resource Study: Boston African American National Historic Site.* National Parks Service, 2002.
Zirblis, Raymond Paul. *Friends of Freedom.* Montpelier, VT: Vermont Division of Historic Preservation, 1996.

Historical

Bearse, Austin. *Reminiscences of Fugitive Slave Days in Boston.* Boston: Warren Richarson, 1880.
Parker, William. "The Freedman's Story." *The Atlantic Monthly*, Feb.–March 1866.

Sloane, Rush R. "The Underground Railroad of the Firelands." *The Firelands Pioneer.* Norwalk, OH: The Historical Society, 1888.

Tibberts, John Henry. "Reminiscences of Slavery Times." Unpublished memoir written in 1888.

Williams, Harold Parker. *Brookline in the Anti-slavery Movement.* Brookline, MA: Brookline Historical Publication Society, Publication Number 18, 1899.

Indexes

Blassingame, John W., and Mae G. Henderson, eds. *Antislavery Newspapers and Periodicals.* 5 vols. Boston: G.K. Hall, 1980–1984.

Archives

American Antiquarian Society, Worcester, MA.

Boston Public Library, Boston, MA.

Gerrit Smith Papers, Syracuse University, Syracuse, NY.

New York Public Library, Schomburg Center for Research in Black Culture, 515 Malcolm X Boulevard, New York, NY.

Pennsylvania Abolition Society papers, 1748–1979, Historical Society of Pennsylvania Archives (includes William Still papers, 1852–1902), Philadelphia.

Wilbur Henry Siebert Collection, Ohio Historical Society, Columbus.

Wilbur H. Siebert Collection. Houghton Library: Harvard College, Cambridge, MA.

Websites

The African American Mosaic, http://www.loc.gov/exhibits/african/intro.html

The African American Pamphlet Collection, Library of Congress, http://lcweb2.loc.gov/ammem/aapchtml/aapchome.html

http://www.blackpast.org/—exhaustive site

World Wide Web Virtual Library, http://vlib.iue.it/history/USA/african-american.html

Gerrit Smith Virtual Museum, http://library.syr.edu/digital/exhibits/g/GerritSmith/

Cornell University / *Friend of Man*, New York State Anti-Slavery Society weekly, http://newspapers.library.cornell.edu/collect/FOM/index.php

Cornell University, the Samuel J. May Collection, http://dlxs.library.cornell.edu/m/mayantislavery/

The Liberator Files, http://www.theliberatorfiles.com/

American Abolitionism, http://americanabolitionist.liberalarts.iupui.edu/index.htm

National Parks Service Network to Freedom, http://www.nps.gov/history/ugrr/

National Parks Service Underground Railroad sites, http://www.nps.gov/history/nr/travel/underground/states.htm

http://www.academicinfo.net/africanamslavery.htm

INDEX BY STATE OF PEOPLE WHO AIDED FUGITIVE SLAVES

Note: This is by no means a comprehensive list; it covers only people referenced in the text who aided a fugitive slave. Page numbers in **bold** refer to main entries in the encyclopedia. Sidebars also appear in **boldface** type.

Index to Places That Aided Fugitive Slaves

Note: This is by no means a comprehensive list of places where slaves found help, but only of places referenced in the text as aiding fugitive slaves. Sidebars appear in **boldface** type.

Index

Note: Page numbers in **bold** refer to main entries in the encyclopedia. Sidebars also appear in **boldface** type. Subentries are organized chronologically.

About the Author and Contributors

Tom Calarco is an independent researcher whose travels have taken him across the country and through Ontario, Canada, in search of the history of the Underground Railroad. He is also the author of *The Underground Railroad in the Adirondack Region* (2004) and editor of the reprint *Abel Brown, Abolitionist* (2006).

Scott Christianson is the author of the seminal work on the history of prisons in America, *With Liberty for Some* (1998). His book *Freeing Charles*, the story of the life and rescue of the fugitive slave Charles Nalle in Troy, New York, in 1860, will be published in 2009.

Jennifer Harrison is an independent researcher and expert on the Underground Railroad in Indiana and Illinois.

Kate Clifford Larson is a lecturer in the History Department at Simmons College in Boston and the author of *Bound for the Promised Land: Harriet Tubman, Portrait of an American Hero* (2004), and *The Assassin's Accomplice* (2008).

Don Papson is president of the North Country Underground Railroad Association in New York State. He is an expert on black history in the Adirondack Region and Vermont.